The International Handbook *of*

Children, Media *and* Culture

The International Handbook *of*

Children, Media *and* Culture

Edited by

Kirsten Drotner

and

Sonia Livingstone

Los Angeles • London • New Delhi • Singapore

First published 2008

SAGE Publications Ltd
1 Oliver's Yard
55 City Road
London EC1Y 1SP

SAGE Publications Inc.
2455 Teller Road
Thousand Oaks, California 91320

SAGE Publications India Pvt Ltd
B 1/I 1 Mohan Cooperative Industrial Area
Mathura Road
New Delhi 110 044

SAGE Publications Asia-Pacific Pte Ltd
33 Pekin Street #02-01
Far East Square
Singapore 048763

Library of Congress Control Number: **2007927909**

British Library Cataloguing in Publication data

A catalogue record for this book is available from the British Library

ISBN 978-1-4129-2832-8

Typeset by CEPHA Imaging Pvt. Ltd., Bangalore, India
Printed in Great Britain by Cromwell Press
Printed on paper from sustainable resources

Contents

Acknowledgements

As editors, we would first like to thank our contributors for their enthusiasm and commitment in participating in this project. We are also most grateful to our International Advisory Board for suggesting possible contributors and, especially, reading draft chapters and offering constructive comments to the authors. Shenja van der Graaf has played an invaluable role in ensuring the whole project stays on track by chasing up contributors, reviewers and, indeed, us as editors. We thank Julia Hall, Gurdeep Mattu and their colleagues at Sage for supporting this project so positively, believing in our ambitions and being patient with our delays. Last, we thank our partners and children for their loving support and encouragement throughout the preparation and writing of this volume.

International Advisory Board

[†]Deceased.

Figures

Tables

The Editors

Kirsten Drotner is a professor in the Department of Literature, Culture and Media Studies at the University of Southern Denmark and founding director of DREAM: Danish Research Centre on Education and Advanced Media Materials. Author or editor of 15 books, her research interests include media history, qualitative methodologies, and young people's media uses. Her most recent work focuses on media globalization as developed in out-of-school contexts.

Sonia Livingstone is a professor in the Department of Media and Communications at the London School of Economics and Political Science. Author or editor of nine books, she specializes in the field of media audiences, examining the domestic contexts and public consequences of media use. Her recent work explores the experiences of children and young people in relation to new information and communication technologies. She currently directs EU Kids Online, a comparative European network on children's online use, risk and safety issues.

The Contributors

Amita Bhide is an Associate Professor, School of Social Work, Tata Institute of Social Sciences, Mumbai. She is engaged in both research and practice experience. Her recent work has focused on issues of community participation in a globalizing context. Her doctoral work brings together these twin interests in community and the media institutions. Recent publications include articles on civil society and participation in Social Development Initiatives, Microcredit as an instrument of mobilization in *Indian Social Science Review* and community participation in Slum Sanitation in the *Economic and Political Weekly*.

Priscilla Boshoff lectures in the Department of Journalism and Media Studies at Rhodes University, South Africa. Her Master's research looked at the meanings that South African Indian youth at Rhodes University make of Bollywood movies.

David Buckingham is Professor of Education at the Institute of Education, London University, where he directs the Centre for the Study of Children, Youth and Media (www.childrenyouthandmediacentre.co.uk). He has directed several major research projects on media education, and on children's and young people's interactions with electronic media. His books include *Children Talking Television*, *Moving Images*, *The Making of Citizens*, *After the Death of Childhood*, *Media Education* and, most recently, *Beyond Technology: Children's Learning in the Age of Digital Culture*.

Elizabeth Bullen lectures in the School of Communication and Creative Arts at Deakin University's Melbourne campus. Specializing in children's literature, her current research project focuses on representations of social class in recent children's print and screen texts and the implications for citizenship. She is a co-author of *Haunting the Knowledge Economy* (Routledge 2006) and *Consuming Children: Education, Entertainment, Advertising* (Open University Press 2001).

André H. Caron is the Bell Chair in the Communication Department at Université de Montréal. He is Founding Director of the Centre for Youth and Media Studies and the Centre for Interdisciplinary Research on Emerging Technologies (CITÉ). His research interests include broadcasting policy, political and cultural appropriations of media and new technologies and mobile culture. Author of a number of publications in French, English, Italian, Spanish and Japanese, he is co-author of *Moving Cultures: Mobile Communication in Everyday Life* (McGill-Queen's University Press 2007)

Letitizia Caronia is Professor of Media Education in the Department of Education at the University of Bologna (Italy). She is a visiting scholar at the Centre for Interdisciplinary

Research on Emerging Technologies (CITÉ, Department of Communication, University of Montreal, Canada). Her research focuses on the use of the media as a situated activity and on the role of language, interaction and culture in people's making sense of the media. She has published a number of books, articles and essays on the relationship between everyday language and media socialization. Her most recent publications are *Growing up Wireless: 'Being a Parent' and 'Being a Child' in the Age of Mobile Communication* (2008) and *Moving Cultures: Mobile Communication in Everyday Life* (McGill-Queen's University Press 2007) with André H. Caron.

Lynn Schofield Clark is Assistant Professor and Director of the Estlow International Center for Journalism and New Media at the University of Denver. She is author of *From Angels to Aliens: Teenagers, the Media, and the Supernatural* (Oxford 2003), co-author of *Media, Home, and Family* (Routledge 2004), and editor of *Religion, Media, and the Marketplace* (Rutgers 2007). She is currently writing a book on shifting relations of authority in the digital media environment based on interviews and observations with young people and the authority figures in their lives.

Chas Critcher is Visiting Professor in Media and Communications at Swansea University and Emeritus Professor of Communications at Sheffield Hallam University. He originally co-authored *Policing the Crisis* (Macmillan 1979), a study of social reaction to mugging. His most recent publications include for the Open University Press *Moral Panics and the Media* (2003) and an edited collection *Critical Readings in Moral Panics and the Media* (2006). His current research interests include a range perceived threats to children, from the mass media to mass inoculation.

Peter Dahlgren is Professor of Media and Communication at Lund University, Sweden. His research focuses on democracy, the evolution of the media and contemporary socio-cultural processes. At present he heads the Swedish participation in a seven-nation comparative EU-funded project on young citizens, new media technologies and democracy (CIVICWEB). He has published on journalism, television, the public sphere and civic culture. He recently published an edited collection, *Young Citizens and the New Media*; his *Media and Civic Engagement* is forthcoming in 2008.

Máire Messenger Davies is Professor of Media Studies and Director of the Centre for Media Research in the School of Media, Film and Journalism at the University of Ulster, Coleraine. She is the author of a number of books on media audiences, including *Television is Good for Your Kids* (1989, 2001), *Fake, Fact and Fantasy: Children's Interpretation of Television Reality* (1997) and *'Dear BBC': Children, Television Storytelling and the Public Sphere* (2001). Her most recent book is *Practical Research Methods for Media and Cultural Studies: Making People Count* (2006) with Nick Mosdell.

Stephanie Hemelryk Donald is Director and Professor of International Studies at the Institute for International Studies, UTS, Sydney. She is the author of *Little Friends: Children's Film Culture in China*, *The State of China Atlas*, *Branding Cities on the West Pacific Rim: Tourism, Film and Urban Identity* and *Public Secrets, Public Spaces*. She is currently writing on middle-class taste structures in contemporary China, with a focus on education and media. She is also working on the project 'Mobile Me' a study of young people's use of mobile technology in Sydney.

Dan Fleming is Professor and Chair of Department in Screen and Media Studies at the University of Waikato in New Zealand. His published work ranges widely across media literacy, new technologies, critical pedagogy, film and children's culture. He is the author of several unsold screenplays, the designer of several unproduced toy lines, the writer of several unpublished hypertext fictions and the initiator of several unfinished schemes to improve how media studies is taught. Dan is also an alpaca farmer.

James Paul Gee, formerly the Tashia Morgridge Professor of Reading at the University of Wisconsin–Madison, is now the Mary Lou Fulton Presidential Professor of Literacy Studies at Arizona State University. He received his PhD in linguistics in 1975 from Stanford University and has published widely in linguistics and education. His books include, among others: *Sociolinguistics and Literacies* (1990); *An Introduction to Discourse Analysis* (1999); *What Video Games Have to Teach Us About Learning and Literacy* (2003); and *Situated Language and Learning* (2004).

Leslie Haddon is a part-time lecturer and a researcher at the London School of Economics. He has written numerous articles and authored, co-authored and edited three books about the production and consumption of information and communication technologies, including computers, the Internet, telephony, the mobile phone, cable TV and intelligent homes. He is currently working on the EU Kids Online project.

Cees J. Hamelink studied philosophy and psychology in Amsterdam. He is Professor Emeritus of International Communication at the University of Amsterdam, Athena Professor of Globalization, Human Rights and Public Health at the Vrije Universiteit in Amsterdam and Honorary Professor at the University of Queensland in Brisbane, Australia. He is the editor-in-chief of the *International Communication Gazette*. His current work includes projects on intercultural communication among children in EU countries (United Kids of Europe) and on broadcast programmes produced by children.

Maria Heller is a sociologist and linguist. She is the Director of the Institute of Sociology of the Faculty of Social Sciences at Eötvös Loránd University, Budapest. Her fields of research encompass communications theory, media-sociology and sociolinguistics. Her recent work focuses on the theory of the public sphere and discursive norms and strategies. She has explored problems of the European public sphere and has done discourse analysis on public debates, advertisements and games.

Renee Hobbs is a Professor at Temple University School of Communications and Theater in Philadelphia, Pennsylvania, where she directs the Media Education Lab. She has worked closely with K-12 educators to integrate media literacy into the classroom and created print, video and online curriculum materials. She also conducts research on the effects of media literacy education on adolescents' academic performance. Currently, she is exploring the impact of copyright regulations on the instructional practices of educators who use digital media and popular culture texts in the classroom.

Patricia Holland is a writer and researcher, and currently is a senior lecturer at Bournemouth University. She has published widely in the fields of television, popular media and visual culture, and is especially interested in the imagery of childhood and family photography. She is co-editor with Jo Spence of *Family Snaps* (Virago 1991) and author of *Picturing Childhood: The Myth of the Child in Popular Imagery* (I.B. Tauris 2004). Her most recent book is *The Angry Buzz: 'This Week' and Current Affairs Television* (I.B. Tauris 2006).

Stewart M. Hoover is Professor of Media Studies in the School of Journalism and Mass Communication at the University of Colorado at Boulder. The author or editor of nine books, his research centres on media audience and reception studies rooted in cultural studies, anthropology and interpretive sociology. Within this, he has concentrated on studies of media and religion, media in domestic spaces, media and civic engagement, and research methods.

Mizuko (Mimi) Ito is a cultural anthropologist of technology use, focusing on children and youth's changing relationships to media and communications. She has been conducting ongoing research on kids' technoculture in Japan and the USA, and is co-editor of *Personal, Portable, Pedestrian: Mobile Phones in Japanese Life*. She is a research scientist at the Annenberg Center for Communication and a visiting associate professor at Keio University in Japan. http://www.itofisher.com/mito.

Anne Jerslev is a senior lecturer at the Section of Film and Media Studies at the Department of Media, Cognition, and Communication, University of Copenhagen. Anne Jerslev has published books on youth and media, on cult films, and on media and intimacy. She has edited and co-edited anthologies in Danish and English, and she has contributed to journals and anthologies with articles on youth and media, reality television and documentary. She is currently working on a project about makeover television.

Jane Kenway (Professor, Education Faculty, Monash University, Australia). Her research expertise is in socio-cultural studies of education in the context of wider social and cultural change. Her most recent jointly written books are *Masculinity Beyond the Metropolis* (Palgrave 2006), *Haunting the Knowledge Economy* (Routledge 2006) and *Consuming Children: Education – Advertising – Entertainment* (Open University Press 2001). Her latest jointly edited books are *Innovation and Tradition: The Arts and Humanities in the Knowledge Economy* (2004) and *Globalising Education: Policies, Pedagogies and Politics* (2005).

Joe F. Khalil is a PhD student at Southern Illinois University in Carbondale. He has more than 12 years of professional television experience as director, executive producer and consultant with CNBC Arabiya, MBC, MTV and Orbit. For 7 years, he was an instructor at the Lebanese American University where his teaching and research focused on transnational broadcasting, programming and production. He has consulted for various academic and professional organizations on issues pertaining to media in the Middle East. His dissertation is about youth-produced media in Lebanon and Saudi Arabia.

Marwan M. Kraidy is Associate Professor of Communication at the Annenberg School for Communication at the University of Pennsylvania. He is a scholar of global communication and an expert on Arab media. Previously a Scholar-in-Residence at the Annenberg School, a fellow at the Woodrow Wilson International Center for Scholars, and Director of the Arab Media and Public Life (AMPLE) project at American

University, Kraidy has published two books, *Global Media Studies: Ethnographic Perspectives* (Routledge 2003) and *Hybridity, or, The Cultural Logic of Globalization* (Temple University Press 2005), and more than 40 articles and essays. Current projects include a book about reality TV and Arab politics, a reference work on the Arab television industries (under contract, British Film Institute) and a text on global media studies (under contract, Polity).

Dafna Lemish (PhD, The Ohio State University, 1982), from the Department of Communication, Tel Aviv University, Israel, is editor of the *Journal of Children and Media*. Her research and teaching interests include children and media and gender representations and consumption. She has published extensively in academic journals and books. Her most recent books are *Children and Television: A Global Perspective* (2007); *Media and the Make-Believe Worlds of Children* (co-authored, 2005), and *Children and Media at times of Conflict and War* (co-edited, 2007).

Rich Ling is a sociologist at Telenor's research institute and he has an adjunct position at the University of Michigan. He is the author of *The Mobile Connection* and *New Tech, New Ties: How Mobile Communication is Reshaping Social Cohesion* (due early 2008). He has a PhD in sociology from the University of Colorado. He is an associate editor for *The Information Society* and *Norsk Mediatidskrift*. He is interested in the social consequences of mobile communication.

Usha S. Nayar is Deputy Director and Professor, Tata Institute of Social Sciences, Mumbai, India. Recipient of awards like Fellow, International Beliefs and Values, James Madison University, USA, Vidya Ratna, Dayanand Anglo Vedic Society, India, and designated by the World Health Organization as an Expert on Mental Health and Social Change. Her publications are in the field of marginalization, exclusion, globalization, media, information and communication technology, digital divide, child participation, inequity and bridging the gaps between research and policy for child and youth.

Tobias Olsson is a senior lecturer in Media and Communication Studies at Växjö University, and a researcher at Lund University. His research focuses on political dimensions of new media, and he has published a number of journal articles and book chapters in the area. From 2003 to 2006 he was a researcher in the Swedish project 'Young people, ICTs and Learning' (the Swedish Knowledge Foundation), and his most recent research appointment is within the EU-funded project 'Young People, The Internet and Civic Participation' (CIVICWEB).

David Oswell is a senior lecturer in the Department of Sociology, Goldsmiths, University of London. He is the author of *Television, Childhood and the Home: A History of the Making of the Child Television Audience in Britain* (OUP), *Culture and Society* (Sage) and *The Sociology of Childhood* (CUP). He specializes in cultural theory, social theories of technology, and media and communications history and regulation, with particular reference to children and childhood. His current research focuses on the national and transnational regulatory cultures concerning child protection, internet and mobile ubiquitous media.

Dominique Pasquier is a sociologist and researcher at the National Centre for Scientific Research in France. She is also a professor at the EHESS (School for High

Studies in Social Sciences) in Paris. Author or editor of seven books, she has been studying television professionals and media reception by young people. Her recent work examines the transformation of cultural practices and the articulation between social networks and cultural universes.

Alan Prout is Director of the Institute of Education and Professor of Sociology and Childhood Studies at the University of Warwick. He was Director of the ESRC Research Programme 'Children 5–16'. His publications include: *Constructing and Reconstructing Childhood* (FalmerRoutledge 1990/1997); *Theorizing Childhood* (Polity 1998); *The Body, Childhood and Society* (Macmillan 2000); *Hearing the Voices of Children* (FalmerRoutledge 2003) and *The Future of Childhood* (FalmerRoutledge 2005).

Jette Rygaard is an Associate Professor and head of the department in the Department of Language, Literature and Media at Ilisimatusarfik, University of Greenland. She is author of several articles on youth culture, media and globalization in Greenland and editor – or on the editorial board on – *Cultural and Social Research in Greenland/Ilisimatusarfik*. Her recent work deals with transgressive methods and visual representation of children and youth executed in collaboration with Birgit Kleist Pedersen.

Larry Strelitz is a Professor in the Department of Journalism and Media Studies at Rhodes University in Grahamstown, South Africa. His most current research has been in the field of media audience studies and his recently published book examined how a cross-section of South African youth responded to media texts which were produced internationally but broadcast locally.

Toshie Takahashi is an Associate Professor in the Department of Communication and Media Studies at the Rikkyo University, Tokyo, Japan. She has an MA in Sociology from the University of Tokyo and a PhD in Media and Communications from the London School of Economics and Political Science. She is a media ethnographer and her recent research explores how, in their various ways of engaging with media and ICT in everyday life, Japanese audiences reflexively 'create' and 'recreate' their sense of self and the social groups to which they belong in the context of social changes and globalization.

Jacqueline Reid-Walsh is a specialist in historical and contemporary children's literature, culture, and media and fascinated by girls' culture. In these areas she has published on topics ranging from early moveable books and Jane Austen's juvenilia to Nancy Drew mysteries and girls' websites. She is co-author of Researching Children's Popular Culture (Routledge 2002), co-editor of Seven Going on Seventeen (Peter Lang 2005), and of Girl Culture: an encyclopedia (Greenwood in press) with Claudia Mitchell. She is a beginning a new book project comparing historical and contemporary media for children and youth with Peter Lang. She teaches at Université Laval and Bishop's University, both in Quebec.

Janet Wasko is the Knight Chair for Communication Research at the University of Oregon (USA). She is the author of *How Hollywood Works*, *Understanding Disney: The Manufacture of Fantasy* and *Hollywood in the Information Age: Beyond the Silver*

Screen, editor of *A Companion to Television* and *Dazzled by Disney? The Global Disney Audience Project*, as well as other volumes on the political economy of communication and democratic media.

Bu Wei is a Professor in the Institute of Journalism and Communication (IJC) at the Chinese Academy of Social Sciences (CASS), director in the Research Center for Children and Media, based in the IJC of CASS, author or editor of six books. She does mainly research on children's/youth's use of media and ICTs, feminist media studies, and empowering vulnerable (margining) groups through communication. Her recent work explores the communication campaigns from below by youth – to improve public health, reduce domestic violence, deliver social welfare and so on. She currently directs media strategy programmes on violence against children, children and HIV/AIDS campaigns in China as consultant for UNICEF China.

Norbert Wildermuth is an Associate Professor in the Department of Media Studies at the University of Southern Denmark. He has worked and published on issues of media globalization, including a PhD on transnational satellite television in India. His recent work includes field studies in Zambia, Vietnam and Brazil with a focus on young people and their media uses, as part of 'Youth and the City', an interdisciplinary and comparative research project funded by DANIDA (Danish State Agency for Development Aid).

Editors' Introduction

Sonia Livingstone and Kirsten Drotner

QUESTIONING CHILDHOOD, MEDIA AND CULTURE

In many parts of the world, and for many decades, children have been early and avid adopters of new media. Indeed, they often challenge normative socio-cultural practices through the ways in which they use media. Yet, at the same time, many parents, educationalists and marketers consider that media permeate, even control, children's lives to a degree that was unknown just a generation ago. Is it, then, the case that children's media practices differ in both scale and scope from what today's adults knew from their own childhoods? It seems undeniable that the global reach of many recent media technologies, such as satellite television, the internet and mobile devices, has been instrumental in recontextualising children's media practices, not merely for the prolific young blogger or texting enthusiast, but equally for children for whom these activities are beyond practical reach – nearly all youngsters around the world know of transnational television series, of mobile conversations and internet chats, of the top music stars and, of course, the global brands of Nike, Coca Cola, McDonalds and many more. More profoundly, it also seems that few are unaffected by the shifting priorities in education, identity, politics and commercial marketing strategies that the changing media and information environment ushers in for today's youth.

The combined developments of globalised communication networks and new media technologies have catapulted children's media culture to the centre of public attention. In many parts of the world, debates are rife over the regulation of children's media fare, for this is often more personalised, more globalised and certainly more volatile and versatile than is, for example, the more familiar print media. When poor children in India with little or no schooling get the opportunity to take up computing, access the internet and enter game worlds, questions begin to be asked about these children's position in public life, the material and symbolic resources which grant them a voice and a new visibility, and the institutional consequences of such 'digital inclusion'. When highly profitable transborder flows of marketing and media products push the boundaries between local and global forms of representation, questions arise regarding children's identity development and sense of belonging to a community. Arguably, globalising media processes favour new forms of cosmopolitanism by providing opportunities for children to encounter and engage with greater cultural and social diversity. On the other hand, possibly the commercial basis of these media downplays such diversities in order to cater to audiences across spatial boundaries? Questions such as these are asked with varying inflections around the world, but the local answers offered rarely embrace the global phenomenon of having to answer in the first place.

While debates over children's media uses have repeatedly resurfaced since the advent of modern mass media in the nineteenth century, their ramifications and implications are, in many ways, different today. This is partly because of transformations in childhood, as formally expressed in both Article 12 of the UN Convention of Human Rights, which stresses the need to respect and listen to children, to act in the child's best interests and not to discriminate against children, as well as by the UN Convention on the Rights of the Child. It is also because debates over children's media are shaped by the pervasive global discourses on 'the information society', 'the knowledge society' and 'the network society'. Irrespective of the terminology chosen, these discourses focus on how information and communication technologies both enable and enforce 'new economies' characterised by increased global competition and by a rise in immaterial forms of production known, for example, as 'experience economies' (such as tourism, film, design and life styles) and 'service economies' (such as online call centres, banking and health care). Since the mid-1990s, interest in information and communication technologies has been magnified by the technological potential to digitise all text, images and sound and, hence, to facilitate convergence across hitherto distinct media platforms and services. While this in no way makes all media output look the same, or makes all media appropriations resemble each other, it does mean increasing overlap among the often hotly contested public debates on young people, media and information technologies.

A pressing question arising from these changes in the global economy is how to ensure people are qualified in terms of the resources and competencies required to handle these transformations. In this context, children's literacies assume a new urgency: should they be media literate, computer literate, multimedia literate, information literate or something completely different? Perhaps, simply, it is critical literacy that is ever more urgent in a complex media environment. If 'the ability to access, adapt, and create new knowledge using new information and communication technology is critical to social inclusion in today's era' (Warschauer, 2003: 9), then young people's uses of new communication technologies has far greater significance than their traditional relation to audiovisual technologies, generally (though arguably inappropriately) relegated to the domains of entertainment and leisure. Indeed, this concern echoes the importance long accorded to print media, though this latter is now neglected as a field of study (except within the field of education), despite its crucial and continued importance for policies of social inclusion both within nations and cross-nationally. Analysis of young people's emerging literacies in this fast-changing information and communication environment is only now moving from speculative hype to grounded empirical investigation, with a plethora of concepts being advanced, with too little agreement on their substance or use, and with many still wedded to a highly optimistic view of the transformative potential of media technologies for children's life chances.

This optimism contrasts strongly with another equally long-standing and persistent debate regarding children and media, namely that concerned with the perceived threats or risk of harm to children of particular forms of media representations or appropriations. As with literacy debates more recently, the moral or media panics associated with these latter risks have also been catalysts in bringing children's media uses into the public eye, thus providing the major motivation for conducting and, certainly, funding research on children and media over decades. As has long been the case (Drotner, 1992), questions of media harm become drawn into urgent debates over the regulation and governance of both media and childhood, with the laudable desire to protect children from harm uneasily balanced against both adult freedom of expression and, less noticed but equally important, children's own rights to expression, exploration and, even, risk-taking (Millwood Hargrave and Livingstone, 2006). It is the pessimism inherent in these moral panics, uneasily combined with society's idealistic optimism regarding the new, which has informed the dominant (and highly ambivalent) frameworks for researching children's media. However, both the moral panics over potentially harmful media and the excitement over potentially empowering media are not really, or not simply, debates over media, but rather more profoundly are debates over the cultural values that society should promulgate to its children. They concern, in short, the potential and actual meaning-making processes of communication and social interaction, and these are precisely the defining features of the cultural dimension of life.

While the media harm argument is little supported by commerce, this powerful lobby preferring to align with campaigners for freedom of expression, it does echo more enthusiastically the optimism of public bodies regarding the prospects of the changing media environment to benefit children This construes children today as empowered not only in terms of disposable income, but also, more significantly, in terms of personal choice and agency. Such discourses challenge established definitions of childhood as vulnerable, instead positioning children as in the vanguard compared with 'their elders and betters'. Thus, these commercial discourses support a liberal or rights-based critique of traditional hierarchies of generational power in Western societies, recognising that consumerism (and a pioneering approach to new technologies) is now a defining element of youthful leisure practices especially, supporting claims for the further individualisation of society (Beck and Beck-Gernsheim, 2002), with childhood and youth increasingly focused on horizontal, peer networks rather than traditional hierarchies of authority and value. As the historian Gadlin (1978: 253) observes, 'the most important characteristic of contemporary child rearing is the continued diminution of parental authority and responsibility', a claim one might extend to adult authority more generally (including teachers, politicians, community leaders, etc.). To many it seems that new forms of interactive and individualised media especially further the emergence of a reverse generation gap by which children are now teaching their parents, transforming normative expectations regarding socialisation. However, critics have countered that these often celebratory discourses of children's generational power serve to downplay and underestimate the persistence of very real divisions in terms of social class, ethnicity, gender and region. These differences of perspective highlight the ways in which debates over children and media throw into relief our basic understandings of childhood and, additionally, of media.

A MULTIDISCIPLINARY FIELD OF RESEARCH

Since the societal position of media has changed, and because the societal position of children is also changing in many societies, children's media cultures have come to assume a central position in many public debates regarding cultural values, social norms and expectations for the future. The same cannot be said for research. This lack of prominence given to research partly reflects the traditionally low level of public interest in academic research, with only paediatricians and psychologists really capturing the public agenda on matters concerning children – consider the widespread attention devoted to the American Academy of Pediatrics' claim that children should not be allowed to watch more than two hours of television per day (American Academy of Pediatrics: Committee on Public Education, 2001). The result is often that little attention is paid to the often more subtle and contextualised insights of educationalists, let alone sociologists, cultural theorists, media scholars and others with expertise in children's lifeworlds. We must also acknowledge the relative paucity of research on children's media cultures in many countries and within many disciplines. This was a point that occasioned us some difficulties in commissioning chapters for this volume, as well as for our contributors from many parts of the world in their attempts to survey the available literature. And last, the lack of prominence accorded to this field also reflects the fact that the empirical complexity of children's media practices is not, in the main, matched by an equally complex or sophisticated body of theory and methodology, though in this respect – as we hope to show within this volume – things are progressing rapidly, resulting in some exciting prospects for the field. One welcome marker of these developments is the recent launch of a new journal, *Journal of Children and Media*, by Routledge.

The present volume grew out of our interest in and a long-term engagement with capturing and conceptualising these complex problematics. Our editorial work has highlighted the considerable mismatch between an acute perception around the world of the importance of children's media cultures in society and the dispersal (or even neglect) of these concerns among the intellectual developments within diverse academic fields. The main aim of putting this Handbook together has been to map out the diversities and the commonalities in children's media cultures around the world as they are positioned in relation to particular sites, at particular times and within particular social relations. The potent combination of children, media and culture is, simply, hard to grasp from the scattering of articles published without extensive searching across very different literatures, libraries and sources. A second aim, important to securing future developments in research on children, media and culture across the range of contributing disciplines, has been to bring together contributors expert in a range of fields in order to scope the interdisciplinary domain of research on children, media and culture, and to demonstrate its collective strengths as well as highlighting the current gaps in knowledge. Consequently, rather than nurturing a specific theoretical position, we have sought to identify the major research themes and issues that apply to the diversity of children's media cultures as these are played out under the broader and shifting conditions of globalisation, commercialisation and media convergence.

Thus, our purposefully multi- and interdisciplinary approach brings together a number of discrete analytic discourses in the hope that their multiple voices will help strengthen the depth of contextualisation within studies of media and of childhood both in theoretical and empirical terms. Within this, media studies and childhood studies are the two principal traditions of research on which this volume builds. For those working at the intersection, it often seems that these two traditions take the other as an assumed, but unacknowledged, context of explanation. In media studies, economic structures, textual articulations and historical trajectories take centre stage, and so children are routinely relegated to the contextual margins of interest, a specialist topic of interest only to the few, and not a very high-status topic at that. In childhood studies, children (and youth) as social agents, psychological subjects or cultural producers are positioned as key areas of interest, but here the media are accorded only a minimal role, being defined as a narrow and compartmentalised theme, a target for the application of ideas rather than a substantive area in its own right for either theory development or, indeed, a substantial dimension of children's lives (Livingstone, 1998). So, although each approach has much to offer, in terms of lessons from past research, cumulative findings from empirical investigation, and conceptual insights and frameworks, each also tends to be defined by, or even restricted by, its object of study (children, media) and by the particular disciplines that support it. In consequence, studies on children and media tend to follow rather than form the trends in their more mainstream parent disciplines.

Additionally, both media studies and childhood studies draw more broadly on the social and human sciences, for the study of children's media cultures intersects with the study of family, adolescence, school, literacy, sexuality, civic participation and much more. Yet the contribution, actual and potential, of other disciplines regarding issues that intersect with childhood, media, technology and culture often remains tangential, with too few really productive connections either linking across the fields of education, anthropology, literature, political science, history and so forth or, indeed, between these fields and the core fields of childhood and media studies. This tendency to work in parallel means that research misses out on the connections between, for example, social science studies on television narrative as a structuring element in children's everyday lives and humanities-based accounts of story-telling in children's literature. Moreover, synchronic and diachronic perspectives rarely inform one another, so that obvious structural commonalities remain unexplored: for example, particular tensions and oppositions mapped out in historical studies on childhood in Europe and North America may be found in sociological studies on contemporary childhood in non-Western countries – children's work versus schooling or conceptions of 'proper' public versus private childhood spaces. Although exploration of the relations between past and present tensions, let alone explanation of these relations, remains fairly thin on the ground, our contributors have worked hard to give recognition to those that they have identified. Further, we hope that the present volume stimulates the development of just such productive connections, occasioning conversations across fields and so enabling new insights, research projects and integrative conclusions to illuminate a multidimensional understanding of children, media and culture.

EVERYDAY CULTURE MATTERS

How shall we identify, analyse and understand children's media cultures around the world? The American anthropologist Clifford Geertz cogently defines culture as 'a system of inherited conceptions expressed in symbolic forms by means of which people communicate, perpetuate, and develop their knowledge about and attitudes toward life' (Geertz, 1973: 89). The 'symbolic forms' noted by Geertz can be words, images, written text or numbers (that is, a range of semiotic sign repertoires), and this process of sense-making, or signification, is increasingly mediated by global media, such as satellite television, the internet and mobile communication. This foregrounding of the cultural dimension is encapsulated by American Roland Robertson, who argues that cultural globalisation serves to accelerate everybody's notion of living in 'a single place' whose properties cannot simply be written off as extraneous to oneself, but whose handling is still informed by different positions and priorities. Accelerated interdependence goes together with confrontations among different, even clashing, world views. So, globalisation involves 'comparative interaction of different forms of life' (Robertson, 1992: 6, 27). It is the increasing mediation, or mediatisation (Thompson, 1995), of these interactions that operates as a primary reason for our interest in the cultural dimensions of children's interactions with media. As Roger Silverstone put it, 'mediation ... describes the fundamentally, but fundamentally uneven, dialectical process in which institutionalised media are involved in the general circulation of symbols in social life' (Silverstone, 2006: 109). If we understand these diverse interpretative practices, we will also gain a solid knowledge base for more applied forms of action in this area – for example, in order to advance children's interests in relation to education, health provision, political citizenship or marketing. For these are all areas, along with many others, that are now shaped, in part at least, by the rich media and information environment that touches, indeed that mediates, all children's lives in one way or another.

The importance of contextualising children's media culture within a multidimensional account of societal change cannot be overestimated, for only thus can we avoid technological determinism (Smith and Marx, 1994) in evaluating the social, cultural and personal consequences of media and information technologies. We are committed, in short, to contextualising specific research questions within a broad account of the complex and changing cultural environment within which children live. This means analysing children's media culture as it is positioned in relation to the dimensions of space, time and social relations – as John Thompson does in his account of media and modernity, but as is so rarely extended to include children; however, see Meyrowitz (1984). It also means recognising that these dimensions are themselves culturally and historically contingent. To take a simple example: rather than ask about the impact of television on children, we urge the importance of asking when and why different children use different aspects of television (form, content, technology) and how these practices may be directly and indirectly shaped by the media, family circumstances, educational expectations, broadcasting traditions, economic pressures and cultural values.

However, a contextual approach is no mean feat in practice, even though in principle it is hard to gainsay. Like many, we have been influenced by Raymond Williams' stress on capturing 'the whole way of life' (Williams, 1961), developed in the field of media and communications by the ethnographic turn (Drotner, 1994) and in childhood studies by the new sociology of childhood (James *et al.*, 1998). The synergies here are stimulating. For example, Janice Radway's (1988: 366) call for 'radical contextualism' in audience studies, namely the analytic displacement of the moment of audience response to media by ethnographic studies of the everyday, in order to capture what she describes as 'the kaleidoscope of daily life' seems especially appropriate for analysing children's activities, for, in their everyday lives, children and young people weave together practices involving a wide range of media and cultural forms and technologies, generating a rich symbolic tapestry in a manner that is in some ways deliberate or agentic but which is in other ways accidental, part of the sheer serendipity of childhood (Corsaro, 1997). Since the links and connections among play, toys and media are also, increasingly, managed and marketed, as part of the regulation and the commercialisation of children's culture, a critical perspective is vital if we are to judge how far children's culture is being transformed into promotional culture as modern marketing directs flows of popular culture, identity is refashioned through consumption and the citizen (or viewer) is transformed into the consumer (Kenway and Bullen, 2001). Only a critical perspective can judge, further, the question of inequalities: the degree to which some children gain access to certain kinds of meanings and practices, along with certain kinds of opportunities or dangers, while others lack such opportunities, restricted by certain social arrangements of time, space and cultural norms and values, as well as personal preferences and lifestyles.

Analysis of these micro-practices of childhood – what de Certeau (1984) called 'the tactics' of everyday life – must, then, be balanced with an analysis of the structures of family, school, community and society that encompass them in multiple circles of influence and constraint (Bronfenbrenner, 1980). Lest the reader becomes anxious at the sheer scale of the task, we would acknowledge the methodological difficulty of knowing where context ends, when analysis may legitimately stop. Indeed, following research questions through multiple layers of context can quickly exhaust a researcher's expertise, for media researchers may lack knowledge of family dynamics, educationalists may not know what children do at home, gender specialists may know little about ethnicity and so on. Hence, it is reassuring to know, as several of chapters included here illustrate, that often it is the detailed case study that offers the most illuminating account of a particular practice in context, thereby revealing the historical and cultural specificities of children's media experiences within a broader sketch of the underlying dimensions that structure and contextualise that experience. We have, therefore, invited our contributors to adopt a double focus, combining a close-up exploration of selected practices of media culture with a long-distance gaze on the shifting contours of the landscape within which these practices are situated. To clarify at least some of these contours from the outset, and in order to situate our own approach to the international study of children, media and culture, we now map out the scientific terrain on which much research draws, namely childhood studies and media studies, in order to examine their intersection for our field of study.

THE VIEW FROM CHILDHOOD STUDIES

Since the 1990s, the term childhood studies has been closely associated with the so-called 'new sociology of childhood' (Qvortrup, 1994; James *et al.*, 1998), which has positioned itself against the social psychological and cognitive developmental studies of childhood that was until then the mainstream approach within the social sciences. But studies of children and childhood have also been conducted in several other disciplines, including anthropology, history, education, literary studies and gender studies. Drawing on both the social sciences and humanities, these disciplines also inform studies of the intersection between media and children.

Within the social sciences, Swiss Jean Piaget's developmental psychology has provided the dominant research paradigm for many decades, with the focus on the individual child's cognitive development in 'ages and stages' that are defined in universalising terms with little attention being paid to socio-cultural divergences. Although the child is, it is stressed, conceptualised as an active participant in the development process, this role is more cognitive than social, with the child's curiosity driving an engagement with the environment that stimulates learning. Insofar as the family is regarded as central to socialisation, it is interpersonal forms of interaction and play that are seen as formative to children's development, and less attention is paid to social practices, values and norms (Piaget and Inhelder, 1969). Followers of Piaget studying children and media pay particular attention to the ways in which media facilitate the child's cognitive development as they advance from one stage of understanding to the next. They have also examined children's developing understanding of the 'reality claims' of television, proposing stages of progression towards a mature adult understanding (Dorr, 1986) and exploring the confusions about modality that, productively, stimulate the move to the next stage (Hodge and Tripp, 1986) and, ultimately, to adulthood. The social and cultural importance of learning was developed by Piaget's contemporary, Vygotsky, who stressed how child development is mediated by social interactions with others, so that the child gains not only cognitive sophistication, but also the shared symbolic knowledge of its culture and, thus, of his or herself (Vygotsky, [1934] 1986). Though this approach would seem more in tune with a contemporary analysis of media and communications in the life of the child, curiously this remains underdeveloped; instead, research has taken two largely incommensurate directions: one, focused on media literacy and media effects on 'the child', follows Piaget; the other rejects this approach, instead turning to sociology for a more cultural and social account of 'children', plural.

The new sociology of childhood emerged in the 1990s largely as a reaction to the dominance of Piagetian psychological individualism and universalism (Qvortrup, 1994; Chisholm *et al.*, 1995; Corsaro, 1997; James *et al.*, 1998). As noted by one of its proponents, Alan Prout, in this volume, the sociological approach defines the modern, Western notion of childhood as a socio-cultural construction which conceives of children as active agents in shaping, sharing and transforming their own lives, rather than as adults-to-be, valued for their future potential rather than their present actuality. Critical of these assumptions, the focus is instead on children in their own right, identifying children's own practices as these are exercised in their everyday lives, be it in self-styled peer networks or in more formal organisational settings such as school. For example, drawing on Goffman's (1961) notion of secondary adjustments, Corsaro shows how, through daily actions often invisible to adult eyes, children contribute to the construction and reconstruction of social structures which have consequences for both children and adults. Applying this to the analysis of childhood, Buchner (1990: 77–78) argues that:

> every child is increasingly expected to behave in an "individualised way" … children must somehow orient themselves to an *anticipated* life course. The more childhood in the family is eclipsed by influences and orientation patterns from outside the family (…) the more independent the opportunity (and drive) to making up one's own mind, making one's own choice … described here as the *biographization* of the life course.

In supporting this identity work, the domestic environment affords access to certain kinds of activities and interconnections among activities, depending on social arrangements of time, space, cultural norms and values and personal preferences and lifestyle. Given these arrangements, children use media both to construct their own local contexts and to transcend their locality, forging wider connections through both mediated communication and through imagination. In accounting for these practices, sociologists of childhood rarely draw on historical studies, despite obvious similarities in the questions raised and the kinds of oppositions located in the social positioning of children – for example, the changing definition of children from being based on social position to one being based on age, or changing discourses on childhood depending on demographic shifts in children's relative proportion of the population. The sociological opposition to developmental psychology is apparent in the efforts being expended accounting for the social constructedness of childhood and the diversities in children practising 'childhood' within particular temporally and spatially situated contexts. As an unacknowledged commonality with developmental psychology, the sociological strand of research also focuses on interpersonal practices and forms of communication, and few media studies have been conducted from a sociology of childhood perspective – but see Baacke *et al.* (1990a,b).

Anthropologists have a long tradition of studying childhood across cultures, and their contemporary approaches share important theoretical perspectives with sociological accounts, with the premium being placed on interpersonal networks such as family and peers and on the diversities of children's everyday practices, but with the anthropologists adding important dimensions of socio-cultural difference across boundaries of space. In addition, anthropology has been formative in methodological terms – participant observation, case-based or idiographic designs and open, in-depth interviews have influenced many fields, including media studies (Schrøder *et al.*, 2003), just as has the anthropological tradition of employing categories that are meaningful to the informants, the so-called emic perspective (Pike, 1967). Perhaps because Westernised media differ so visibly from the local cultures often studied by anthropologists, a number of anthropological studies on children include media uses (e.g. Davis and Davis, 1989; Fuglesang, 1994), and arguments have been made that new technology, such as the internet, is a formative influence not only on children's lives, but also equally on received definitions of childhood and adolescence (for example, the expectation that development pivots around identity crises; Larson, 2002).

Within the humanities, studies of childhood are mainly found within history, linguistics and studies of play culture, and, as is the case with social-science approaches, interest in media and mediatized cultures remain fairly thin on the ground. The most notable historian of childhood is French Philippe Ariès (1914–1984), whose *Centuries of Childhood* (1962) precedes sociological accounts in its focus on childhood as a modern construct born out of Western conceptions of modernity and its gradual increasing differentiation of social spheres over *la longue durée*. Later studies have focused on the history of youth (Gillis, 1974; Mitterauer, 1992) including accounts on the gendering of this history (Steedman, 1995; Nielsen and Rudberg, 2000). However, despite the considerable diversity of research that has taken place in this area since the 1970s, few scholars pay sustained attention to the ways in which books and magazines, film, radio and television play into the cultural articulations of the young. In that sense, historians mirror sociologists in the valorisation of self-styled youth cultures and the downgrading of mediatised practices.

Linguists share the widespread focus on interpersonal, rather than mediatised, forms of communication. Naturally, scholars studying language development have focused on children and they often adopt a developmental view drawing on Piagetian psychology. Linguistic investigations of children's media uses are, therefore, often conducted with a view to the ways in which, for example, television viewing influences children's socialisation in general and linguistic proficiency in particular (see overview in Close (2004)). While these studies are divided in terms of positive correlations between the acquisition of language skills and media use, their theoretical prioritisation of face-to-face, localized communication easily slides into normative, empirical oppositions between interpersonal and mediatised forms of communication in which the latter is found wanting. Similar oppositions are found in studies of play. These studies need not necessarily focus on children, as the Dutch historian Johan Huizinga (1872–1945) has demonstrated in his classic *Homo ludens* (1938), which charts the changing role of play in Western culture since the Middle Ages. But other researchers have picked up on play as a defining feature of modern childhood (Opie and Opie, 1959, 1969; Sutton-Smith, 1997), with a particular interest in the position of play in relation to children's agency and inventiveness within self-styled cultural practices. Play is sometimes defined in relation to games which are rule-based, structured and often collective activities, and these definitions feed into computer games design and research (see Gee, this volume). Other scholars draw on play theories in studying children's toys that are objects appropriated for play but not necessarily manufactured as such. With digitisation, toys and media are increasingly interlaced into the so-called 'smart toys', as described by Dan Fleming in this volume (see also Goldstein *et al.*, 2004).

THE VIEW FROM MEDIA STUDIES

Together, the main strands of childhood studies within the human and social sciences illuminate two pervasive discourses on childhood that also inform media studies, namely the discourse of the vulnerable child and the discourse of the competent child. These discourses hark back to the respective Western notions of the sinful child in need of adult supervision, guidance and protection and the romantic notion, encapsulated by French philosopher Jean-Jacques Rousseau, and, conversely, of the perfect child endowed with all necessary faculties and in little need of external socialising agents. They continue today to operate through a binary logic that frames academic as well as applied studies on childhood (Cleverley and Phillips, 1986). That these dual discourses retain their potency results less from their apposite insights into childhood than their speaking to deep-seated tensions in adults' relations to both their offspring and to their own childhoods. On both a personal and a societal level, adults are in a position of power *vis-à-vis* (young) children for obvious reasons of care; but at the same time adults are wholly dependent upon children to secure the continuation of life, whether in an economic, biological, social or cultural sense. This makes children's 'proper' conditions of life an issue of continual adult concern, with a persistent focus on the opposition of dependence/independence, as well as that of continuity/change.

These basic concerns go a long way towards explaining why most theories of childhood, including those from media studies, assume a normative dimension even when their parent disciplines typically critique and seek to deconstruct normative assumptions in other domains. Indeed, in both childhood studies and media studies of children, the normative assumptions are too often left unacknowledged, for when adults investigate children and childhood they are offered an opportunity to revisit their own past with a view to framing the future; and this trajectory seems to undermine the distance required to position oneself as researcher in relation to the object of research. This tacit normativity equally offers an explanatory framework for another set of key oppositions that may be identified in studies on childhood, namely the opposition between interpersonal and mediatised practices. The first is often more tangible to adults, since they may partake in conversations and face-to-face interactions with children, whereas children's interactions with media seem more dispersed and less transparent to the adult eye. And what one does not know or understand tends to be neglected or forgotten. Herein lies a challenge to both social sciences and humanities as they seek to understand the importance of media in childhood, a challenge that many contributors to the present volume seek to meet.

Studies on children's relation to media are almost as old as media themselves, and normative approaches dominate from the outset. When children and young people in Europe and North America became avid readers of the so-called 'penny dreadfuls' or dime novels in the late 1800s, studies warned against their perceived ill-effects (Salmon, 1888; Denning, 1987; Drotner, 1988), and later investigations on comics continued this approach (Barker, 1989; Barker and Petley, 2001). The advent of film equally spurred pioneer research on children's and young people's film-going, such as the 13 reports from the USA known as the Payne Fund Studies (1929–1932) and an earlier German study by Emilie Altenloh (1914).

The professionalisation of many academic fields during the twentieth century includes literary studies, film studies and media studies, all of which conduct research focused on children. Still, these traditions rarely interact; so, for example, the fairly comprehensive research on children's books follows an 'arts' tradition in literary studies that is at odds with the formative tradition within media studies 'proper'. Throughout the twentieth century, particularly the second half, the interdisciplinary field of media studies, or communication, has developed diverse strands of theory, method and focus. Yet, when we turn to the work on children in particular, it seems that most has followed one main approach, namely an investigation into the effects – mainly harmful, though also some positive – of the media, mainly television. In consequence, the particular intersection of media and children has become ensnared in the hotly contested debates not only over the effects of the media, but also over this very emphasis on media influences on individuals and its often tacit dependence on particular agendas of public concern, research funding and regulatory policy. Perhaps in consequence, for many in media studies, a focus on children seems narrow, uncritical, empiricist or conservative. It also seems to address an irresolvable problem; as UK researcher Denis McQuail (1987: 251) observes, 'the entire study of mass communication is based on the premise that there are effects from the media, yet it seems to be the issue on which there is least certainty and least agreement'. Partly, the problem lies outside the field, with the kinds of questions that are asked of it. Parents, school and peers are all readily acknowledged as major influences on children's development, though the theories and methods designed to investigate them are complex, diverse and contested. However, in relation to media influence, these complexities seem to frustrate, for it seems that straightforward answers are expected and, yet, not forthcoming (Barker and Petley, 2001; Kline, 2003). Indeed, more recent research argues that instead of asking what the effect of the media is on a particular and usually problematic aspect of childhood, research should instead identify the range of factors that directly, and indirectly, through interactions with each other, combine to explain particular social phenomena – for any particular social problem (e.g. aggression, prejudice, obesity, bullying, etc.) is associated with a distinct and complex array of putative causes of which one may be media content or use (Millwood Hargrave and Livingstone, 2006). In other words, instead of asking whether the media harm children, one should instead ask: 'Of the many causes of particular social ills, what role do the media play?' This invites a recognition of the wider context within which media are located, thus avoiding a media-centric approach.

Additionally, there are many other ways that media studies does and can research the relation between media and children, though these undoubtedly receive less attention from the research community, policy makers and the public. Audience studies, particularly approaches stressing an active and interpretative audience, have been productively applied to children in the context of television in the family and home (Hodge and Tripp, 1986; Palmer, 1986; Buckingham, 1993), and later to computers and the internet at home and at school, in the community, among peers and so on (e.g. Buckingham and Willett, 2006). While media theory has always been committed in principle to the integrated analysis of production, texts and audiences, empirical research on audiences was somehow marginalised by comparison with texts especially. Reception studies rectified this tendency by foregrounding the cultural contexts within which meanings are both encoded and decoded and acknowledging the importance of the socially shared (or diversified) aspects of those contexts. Hence, empirical reception studies have variously explored the relationships between media texts (film, soap opera, news, etc.) and their audiences. Audience interpretations or decodings have been found to diverge depending on viewers' socio-economic position, gender, ethnicity, and so forth, while the possibilities for critical or oppositional readings are anticipated, enabled or restricted by the degree of closure semiotically encoded into the text and by audiences' variable access to symbolic resources. The point is not that audiences are 'wrong' but that they construct their interpretations according to diverse discursive contexts which are themselves socially determined.

As a result of this now considerable body of work, audiences are no longer thought of according to the popular image which always threatens to recur, as homogeneous, passive and uncritical or vulnerable to the direct influence of meanings transmitted by, and perhaps manipulated by, the mass media. Extending this approach to children and young people, one early example of this approach was Patricia Palmer's study of 'the lively audience', which showed how the symbolic and identity relations between children and television change as children develop intellectually: 'with the development of an understanding of narratives, of story and character, older children make more complex demands on their favourite TV shows' (Palmer, 1986: 121). Another was David Buckingham's exploration of how teenagers interpreted the popular British soap opera, *EastEnders*, following an encoding/decoding approach to show how different groups of young people draw on distinct cultural resources to interpret the programmes divergently, as guided by the deliberate openness structured into the genre (Buckingham, 1987). Possibly the most creative study in this tradition was Bob Hodge and David Tripp's re-examination of children's responses to cartoons, which explicitly critiqued the tradition of media effects in its assumption that children are uncritical and, indeed, vulnerable to persuasion when faced with violent cartoon imagery. They combined a semiotic and Piagetian approach to reveal the subtleties with which children negotiate the reality claims of cartoons, responding to the invitation to engage creatively with the fantasies portrayed (Hodge and Tripp, 1986).

More recently, these interpretative approaches to children's television have been extended to other screen-based media, especially computers, games and the internet. Possibly because computer-based media incorporate print as well as audiovisual forms, the emphasis on interpretation has been reframed in terms of literacy, so that the interpretative resources and capabilities that children evince in response to these screen media are revealed to draw partly on the long tradition of print literacy as well as on more recent challenges posed by alternative, multimedia literacies – whether termed computer literacy, visual literacy, internet literacy, etc. (Kress, 2003; Snyder and Beavis, 2004). As noted earlier, children's skills in using, interpreting and critiquing such media become more urgent, as these are valuable not only for entertainment purposes, but also transfer across, in ways still little understood, to the realms of education, work and participation. The continuities with reception studies remain important, even in this fast-changing media and information environment, with key questions including the ways in which children diversely interpret media contents, the cultural and social resources they draw upon in so doing, and the value of the skills and literacies they develop in consequence (Livingstone, 2004, Drotner, 2005).

These approaches, however, are more focused on media content and its interpretation than on media as material goods, part of the cycles of consumption in everyday life. An alternative strand of research, now known as domestication research, examines how the practices and routines of daily life serve to incorporate new media goods (the television set, the computer, the personal radio, the mobile phone and so forth), rendering them meaningful within particular local contexts in ways not necessarily anticipated by their manufacturers and marketers. In this literature, children play a fairly central role because, as diffusion statistics repeatedly show, it is often families with children who lead in the adoption of new media goods and, when interviewed, parents point to children's demands or parental perceptions of children's needs as a major driver of new purchases. Hence, there is a growing body of research examining how children and families appropriate computers, games, the internet, the mobile phone (e.g. Lohr and Meyer, 1999; Facer *et al.*, 2003; Holloway and Valentine, 2003; Ling, 2004).

As in the interpretative approach outlined above, the stress in domestication research is also on people as agents, co-constructing the meaning of goods rather than passively receiving the meanings as given by powerful media producers. This seems particularly apt for children, for their creative appropriations of media goods can be not only significant for them (as in their colourful arrangements of media goods, images and paraphernalia in their bedrooms, for example), but also significant for the market as a whole – consider young people's active role in the 'discovery' of text messaging, or the music and fashion industries' repackaging of street style and habits. As this last point highlights, the political economic dimensions of children and young people's everyday activities in relation to media are far from negligible. One emerging tradition, still too little practised because, perhaps, of its considerable methodological demands, combines the analysis of political economy and cultural appropriations. Examples of research in this tradition include Janet Wasko *et al.*'s (2001) analysis of the global phenomenon of Disney, the work of David Buckingham (2000) on the 'edutainment' market for children, and the recent work by Sara Grimes and Leslie Shade on Neopets (Grimes and Shade, 2005). Often triangulating an account of production, text and audience or user response, these studies portray children's relation to media in the round, tracing the consequences of particular forms of engagement in economic and cultural terms, but also, more critically, revealing how children's opportunities and practices are subtly shaped and constrained by the wider political economy of the child and youth markets.

OUR APPROACH IN THIS VOLUME

In this volume, we adopt a holistic approach to children's media culture by integrating a media and a child perspective and by drawing on both the humanities and social sciences as theoretical and empirical tools of analysis and explanation. We are aware that this approach is fairly inclusive and ambitious, and naturally different contributors introduce different inflections in defining and developing their disciplinary specialisms and crossovers. Indeed, in selecting contributors, our aim was to encompass a broad range of perspectives and interests, and part of our excitement about the volume derives from the often unexpected, as well as the anticipated, parallels and interconnections that have emerged and which can be traced across different combinations of chapters. In particular, and by contrast with many studies in this field, this volume does not treat the North American experience as primary, but instead seeks to address the cultural diversity (and, of course, commonalities) of children's mediated culture around the world. For we concur with Curran and Park (2000: 3) that, although 'it has become routine for universalistic observations about the media to be advanced in English-language books on the basis of evidence derived from a tiny handful of countries', the field must now 'de-Westernise', recognising the importance of globalisation as a grand narrative and prioritising comparative analysis in terms of method.

Thus, in this volume, we situate American culture, and the dominance in English language circles of the North American research tradition, within multidisciplinary and multilingual debates about globalisation, for the American experience is as particular and, to many, as 'other', as is that of the rest of the world. It offers, indeed, an interesting point of contrast, too little analysed as such, in relation to the cultures of childhood and media on the other four continents. We explicitly tasked our contributors with representing research conducted in diverse countries, often published in languages other than English, so as to permit a wider lens on existing research and to invite a broader recognition of emerging research trends. For some, this means an exploration of how a North American tradition has been applied to, and perhaps modified for, a particular region of the world, while for others it means introducing a distinct research tradition, grounded in a different locale, within an English-language volume. For the reader, a comparative focus is clearly invited, not only to learn about 'other' cultures, but also to question one's own from the perspective of elsewhere (Alasuutari, 1995; Livingstone, 2003).

Not only did we urge upon our contributors the importance of multiple cultural and national standpoints from which to survey the field, we further stretched them by inviting a historical gaze. As John Thompson (1995: 46) observes:

> if we focus ... on symbolic forms and their modes of production and circulation in the social world, then we shall see that, with the advent of modern societies in the later mediaeval and early modern periods, a systematic cultural transformation began to take hold".

Yet, there is something about the combustible combination of children, media and social change that makes for a field that too readily falls foul of the twin problems of a heartfelt nostalgia for 'the past' and a fascination with the potential of 'the future'. Beyond encouraging researchers to eschew these pitfalls, both of which mar the quality of much public debate, the intellectual challenge remains to understand the present. This, we contend, requires researchers to balance a recognition of historical continuities where these exist (and so refusing easy but unsubstantiated claims for 'the new') with the careful identification not only of (the rather rare instances of) genuine transformation, but also of the subtle processes that serve to integrate change within the context of the familiar – processes of social shaping and of remediation or reconfiguration, for instance, by which media innovations are rendered meaningful by the cultural practices within which they are appropriated, these in turn serving to refashion or reposition pre-existing practices (Bolter and Grusin, 1999; Berker *et al.*, 2006). On a grander canvas, we must recognise the ways in which both childhood and media are caught up with the longer history of modernity and late modernity, for it is the slower but profound processes of globalisation, individualisation, commercialisation and privatisation of culture that set the conditions for both children's lives and for media practices, albeit inflected in different ways in different times and places, according to path dependencies shaped by the structures and conditions of everyday life.

As will be evident from the contributors' brief biographies, we have invited specialists in children's media culture from the fields of sociology, education, anthropology, history, literature and so forth, as well as media, communications and cultural studies, making for a fertile mix that will surely stimulate productive comparisons of approaches and findings in the mind of the curious reader, comparisons across chapters, topics, methodologies, disciplines and subfields, and countries and regions of the world. In reflecting on the process of selecting contributors, we must acknowledge our own limitations in soliciting contributions especially from certain parts of the world, despite disseminating calls for contributions across diverse networks of contacts. We implemented a rigorous review process, for which we extend profuse thanks to our International Advisory Board for their constructive reviews, as well as to our authors for their willingness to revise and improve chapters as requested. But not all contributions made it through this inevitably culturally shaped process of review, and not all of those contacted were willing or able to write in English, this being another impediment commonly placed in the way of international collaboration (for, unlike the world of commerce, the academy has little budget for translation costs and so relies, serendipitously, on the variable linguistic skills of its members). Last, we reluctantly reached the view that, to the best of our knowledge, not all of the countries or regions we wished to represent between these covers sustain a critical mass of scholarship in this particular area, this again impeding the range and scope of our international ambitions.

Nonetheless, we hope it is not immodest to observe that we still see no competition for a volume of such breadth and scope on the shelves of bookshops and libraries, for none encompasses so many experiences, cultures and diversity, and so none so explicitly counters universalistic (or even imperialistic) assumptions about 'childhood' or 'media' as homogeneous phenomena. Thus, we hope that this volume will represent, and act to promote, the international and comparative study of children, media and culture, mapping an agenda for future research that shares insights from one location or perspective to another, so that, in future years, other volumes can be (even) more inclusive in their coverage.

REFERENCES

Alasuutari, P. (1995) *Researching Culture: Qualitative Methods and Cultural Studies*. London: Sage.

Altenloh, E. (1914) *Zur Soziologie des Kino: Die Kino-Unternehmung und die sozialen Schichten ihrer Besucher*. Leipzig: Der Spamerschen Buchdruckerei.

American Academy of Pediatrics: Committee on Public Education (2001) 'Children, adolescents and television'. *Pediatrics*, 107(2): 423–426.

Baacke, D., Sander, U. and Vollbrecht, R. (eds) (1990a) *Lebenswelten sind Medienwelten: Medienwelten Jugendlicher*, vol. I. Leverkusen: Leske & Budrich.

Baacke, D., Sander, U. and Vollbrecht, R. (eds) (1990b) *Lebensgeschichten sind Mediengeschichten: Medienwelten Jugendlicher*, vol. II. Leverkusen: Leske & Budrich.

Barker, M. (1989) *Comics: Ideology, Power and the Critics*. Manchester: Manchester University Press.

Barker, M. and Petley, J. (2001) *Ill Effects: The Media/Violence Debate* (2nd edition). New York City, NY: Routledge.

Beck, U. and Beck-Gernsheim, E. (2002) *Individualization*. London: Sage.

Berker, T., Hartmann, M., Punie, Y. and Ward, K.J. (eds) (2006) *The Domestication of Media and Technology*. Maidenhead: Open University Press.

Bolter, J.D. and Grusin, R. (1999) *Remediation: Understanding New Media*. Cambridge, MA: MIT Press.

Bronfenbrenner, U. (1980) 'Ecology of childhood'. *The Social Psychology Review*, 9(4): 294–297.

Buchner, P. (1990) 'Growing up in the eighties: changes in the social biography of childhood in the FRG'. In L. Chisholm, P. Buchner, H.H. Kruger and P. Brown (eds) *Childhood, Youth and Social Change: A Comparative Perspective*. London: Falmer Press.

Buckingham, D. (1987) *Public Secrets: EastEnders and its Audience*. London: British Film Institute.

Buckingham, D. (1993) *Children Talking Television: The Making of Television Literacy*. London: Falmer Press.

Buckingham, D. (2000) *After the Death of Childhood: Growing Up in the Age of Electronic Media*. Cambridge: Polity Press.

Buckingham, D. and Willett, R. (eds) (2006) *Digital Generations*. Mahwah, NJ: Lawrence Erlbaum Associates.

Chisholm, L, Buchner, P., Kruger, H.-H. and Du Bois-Reymond, M. (eds) (1995) *Growing Up in Europe: Contemporary Horizons in Childhood and Youth Studies*. Berlin: Walter du Gruyter.

Cleverley, J. and Phillips, D.C. (1986) *Visions of Childhood: Influential Models from Locke to Spock*. New York: Teachers College Press (revised edition, original 1976).

Close, R. (2004) *Television and Language Development in the Early Years: A Review of the Literature*. London: National Literary Trust.

Corsaro, W.A. (1997) *The Sociology of Childhood*. Thousand Oaks, CA: Pine Forge Press.

Curran, J. and Park, M. (eds) (2000) *Dewesternising Media Studies*. London: Routledge.

Davis, S.S. and Davis, D.A. (1989) *Adolescence in a Moroccan Town: Making Social Sense*. New Brunswick, NJ: Rutgers University Press.

De Certeau, M. (1984) *The Practices of Everyday Life*. Los Angeles: University of California Press.

Denning, M. (1987) *Mechanic Accents: Dime Novels and Working-Class Culture in America*. London: Verso.

Dorr, A. (1986) *Television and Children: A Special Medium for a Special Audience*. Beverley Hills, CA: Sage.

Drotner, K. (1988) *English Children and Their Magazines, 1751–1945*. New Haven, CT: Yale University Press (original 1985).

Drotner, K. (1992) 'Modernity and media panics'. In M. Skovmand and K.C. Schroeder (eds) *Media Cultures: Reappraising Transnational Media*. London: Routledge; 42–62.

Drotner, K. (1994) 'Ethnographic enigmas: "the everyday" in recent media studies'. *Cultural Studies*, 8(2): 341–357.

Drotner, K. (2005) 'Mediatized childhoods: discourses, dilemmas and directions'. In J. Qvortrup (ed.) *Studies in Modern Childhood: Society, Agency and Culture*. London: Palgrave Macmillan; 39–58.

Facer, K., Furlong, J., Furlong, R. and Sutherland, R. (2003) *ScreenPlay: Children and Computing in the Home*. London: RoutledgeFalmer.

Fuglesang, M. (1994) *Veils and videos: female youth culture on the Kenyan coast*. Dissertation. Stockholm Studies in Social Anthropology 32, Department of Social Anthropology, Stockholm University.

Gadlin, H. (1978) 'Child discipline and the pursuit of self: an historical interpretation'. In H.W. Reese and L.P. Lipsitt (eds) *Advances in Child Development and Behavior*, vol. 12. New York: Academic Press; 231–261.

Geertz, C. (1973) *The Interpretation of Cultures: Selected Essays*. New York: Basic Books.

Gillis, J. (1974) *Youth and History: Tradition and Change in European Age Relations, 1770–Present*. New York: Academic Press.

Goffman, E. (1961) *Asylums: Essays on the Social Situation of Mental Patients and Other Inmates*. Harmondsworth: Penguin.

Goldstein, J., Buckingham, D. and Brougere, G. (eds) (2004) *Toys, Games and Media*. Mahwah, NJ: Lawrence Erlbaum.

Grimes, S.M. and Shade, L.R. (2005) 'Neopian economics of play: children's cyberpets and online communities as immersive advertising in NeoPets.com'. *International Journal of Media and Cultural Politics*, 1(2): 181–198.

Hodge, B. and Tripp, D. (1986) *Children and Television: a Semiotic Approach*. Cambridge: Polity.

Holloway, S.L. and Valentine, G. (2003) *Cyberkids: Children in the Information Age*. London: RoutledgeFalmer.

James, A., Jenks, C. and Prout, A. (1998) *Theorizing Childhood*. Cambridge: Cambridge University Press.

Kenway, J. and Bullen, E. (2001) *Consuming Children: Education–Entertainment–Advertising*. Buckingham: Open University Press.

Kline, S. (2003) 'Media effects: redux or reductive?' *Particip@tions*, 1(1).

Kress, G. (2003) *Literacy in the New Media Age*. London: Routledge.

Larson, R.W. (2002) 'Globalization, societal change, and new technologies: what they mean for the future of adolescence'. *Journal of Research on Adolescence*, 12(1): 1–30.

Ling, R. (2004) *The Mobile Connection: The Cell Phone's Impact on Society*. San Francisco: Elsevier.

Livingstone, S. (1998). 'Mediated childhoods: a comparative approach to young people's changing media environment in Europe'. *European Journal of Communication*, 13(4): 435–456.

Livingstone, S. (2003) 'On the challenges of cross-national comparative media research'. *European Journal of Communication*, 18(4): 477–500.

Livingstone, S. (2004) 'The challenge of changing audiences: or, what is the audience researcher to do in the internet age?' *European Journal of Communication*, 19(1): 75–86.

Lohr, P. and Meyer, M. (1999) *Children, Television and the New Media*. Luton: University of Luton Press.

McQuail, D. (1987) *Mass Communication Theory: An Introduction* (2nd edition). London: Sage.

Meyrowitz, J. (1984) 'The adultlike child and the childlike adult: Socialization in an electronic world'. *Daedalus,* 113(3): 19–48.

Millwood Hargrave, A. and Livingstone, S. (2006) *Harm and Offence in Media Content: A Review of the Evidence.* Bristol: Intellect.

Mitterauer, M. (1992) *A History of Youth.* Oxford: Blackwell (original 1986).

Nielsen, H.B. and Rudberg, M. (2000) 'Gender, love and education in three generations'. *European Journal of Women's Studies,* 7(4): 423–453.

Opie, I. and Opie, P. (1959) *Children's Games in Street and Playground: Chasing, Catching, Seeking, Hunting, Racing, Duelling, Exerting, Daring, Guessing, Acting, Pretending.* Oxford: Clarendon Press.

Opie, I. and Opie, P. (1969) *The Lore and Language of Schoolchildren.* Oxford: Oxford University Press.

Palmer, P. (1986) *The Lively Audience: A Study of Children around the TV Set.* London: Allen & Unwin.

Piaget, J. and Inhelder, B. (1969) *The Psychology of the Child.* London: Routledge and Paul Kegan Ltd.

Pike, K. (1967) *Language in Relation to a Unified Theory of the Structure of Human Behavior.* The Hague: Mouton (original 1954).

Qvortrup, J. (1994) *Childhood Matters: Social Theory, Practice and Politics.* Avebury: Aldershot.

Radway, J. (1988) 'Reception study: ethnography and the problems of dispersed audiences and nomadic subjects'. *Cultural Studies,* 2(3): 359–376.

Robertson, R. (1992) *Globalization: Social Theory and Global Culture.* London: Sage.

Salmon, E. (1888) *Juvenile Literature As It Is.* London: Drane.

Schrøder, K.S., Drotner, K., Kline, S. and Murray, C. (2003) *Researching Audiences.* London: Arnold.

Silverstone, R. (2006) *Media and Morality: On the Rise of the Mediapolis.* Cambridge: Polity.

Smith, M.R. and Marx, L. (eds) (1994) *Does Technology Drive History? The Dilemma of Technological Determinism.* Cambridge, MA: MIT Press.

Snyder, I. and Beavis, C. (eds) (2004) *Doing Literacy Online: Teaching, learning and Playing in an Electronic World.* Cresskill, NJ: Hampton Press.

Steedman, C. (1995) *Strange Dislocations: Childhood and the Idea of Human Inferiority, 1780–1930.* London: Virago Press.

Sutton-Smith, B. (1997) *The Ambiguity of Play.* Harvard, MA: Harvard University Press.

Thompson, J.B. (1995) *The Media and Modernity: A Social Theory of the Media.* Cambridge: Polity.

Vygotsky, L.S. ([1934] 1986) *Thought and Language.* Cambridge: MIT Press.

Warschauer, M. (2003) *Technology and Social Inclusion: Rethinking the Digital Divide.* Cambridge, MA: MIT Press.

Wasko, J., Phillips, M. and Meehan, E.R. (eds) (2001) *Dazzled by Disney? The Global Disney Audiences Project.* London: Leicester University Press.

Williams, R. (1961) *Culture and Society.* London: Fontana.

PART 1

Continuities and Change

Children are often thought of in terms of change, representing the future. Indeed, this is one of the stable features of modern discourses on childhood. In a similar manner, since the early days of print, media have been defined and debated in terms of innovation. These continual mappings of change are themselves indications of the dilemmas and challenges which are taken up and analysed in this first part of the *Handbook*. The contributors set children's media culture within a historical perspective in order to trace the continuities and possible changes in the ways in which these cultures have been positioned by adults and practised by children. In so doing, they stress that historical analysis is a necessary antidote to any simple accounts of the relations between children and media, balancing the often grand claims made regarding the beneficial or detrimental implications for children. In pursuing this main argument, the authors range widely across theoretical conceptions, from a mainly deconstructionist focus on discourses on childhood (Prout) to a mainly socio-cultural focus on practices of appropriation (Fleming). These four chapters were selected in order to display some of these key conceptual approaches and to represent some of the main fields pursuing historical studies of the relations between childhood and media culture (sociology, visual culture, literary criticism, film studies). In their differing accounts, the authors take up a number of key questions and debates of significance for anyone wishing to engage with children's media culture from a time-based perspective. This introduction maps out some of the questions and debates that underpin most historical studies of children's media culture in order to clarify the theoretical and empirical landscape and draw out some of the main implications for future research.

The first argument concerns the very notion of historical enquiry itself. A popular claim is that we need systematic studies of the past in order to understand the present better, and even be in a position to predict the future. Historical studies are based on an underlying understanding of research in which comparisons across time appear valid, and so a salient issue is on what grounds such comparisons may be made. Most prevalent through much of the past two centuries has been a teleological view of history whereby historical development is understood as new events adding to existing states of affairs like pearls on a string. Such a view frames standard histories of childhood (Aries, 1973; Walvin, 1982) as well as most media histories (Briggs and Burke, 2002). Inspired by philosophers such as Nietzsche and Foucault, historical scholarship from the 1980s onwards began to argue for the adoption of an archaeological view of history. Here, the focus is on deconstruction rather than construction, on detecting possible sediments of practices and excavating conflicting claims to power, with the present operating as the starting and end point of enquiry. This change of focus is part of a wider scholarly reorientation in the history of science towards shifting ramifications of power and claims-making, and it surfaces, for example, in new histories of women (Offen *et al.*, 1991), children (Stearns, 2006) and ethnic minorities (Gilroy, 1993). In media studies, the clearest examples of this more deconstructionist approach appear in histories of technology and new media (Marvin, 1988; Winston, 1998).

The archaeological approach to history has served to undermine a determinist view of both childhood and media, and it has offered a welcome reflexive component to historical scholarship by insisting that analytical complexity is no less when studying the past than in understanding the present. In so doing, histories of childhood, for example, have gained in analytical insight by tracing commonalities across generations and by highlighting shifting definitions. For example, the pre-modern definition of youth according to social status may be resurfacing in late-modern societies permeated by discourses of youthfulness to a degree that it becomes less relevant to define youth in terms of age, as has been common in modern, industrialized societies.

The archaeological approach to history tends to offer fairly abstract, macro-level forms of analysis. Its popularity over the past two decades has meant that academic attention has moved away from studying children's media and their social uses in a historical context towards critiquing discursive constructions of childhood and media culture. This shifting focus brings into view another key question in historical scholarship. Is it at all possible to make distinctions between historical discourses and practices, or, as Swedish ethnologist Orvar Löfgren terms it, Sunday culture and everyday culture (Löfgren, 2001)? The authors in this part of the *Handbook* offer differing answers, ranging from Prout's meta-discursive stand in deconstructing historical notions of childhood as varying inflections of a dichotomous discourse of modernity to Reid-Walsh's incisive and eye-opening empirical study of analogies of interactivity in children's media since the advent of moveable books in the eighteenth century.

If it is, indeed, possible to conduct historical studies of children's media and their social uses, then we may begin to ask more pragmatic questions about what it is we may learn about today's media (and even tomorrow's) by investigating media in the past. How have media operated in children's everyday lives in the past, and may we identify similar functions today? Which aspects of children's relation to media have changed and for what reasons? Comparing media cultures across time is to begin asking questions about the grounds on which we may study empirical continuities and changes. The possible correlations between continuity and change remain among the most vexed debates in historiography; this is perhaps the historians' equivalent of social science debates about structure and agency. As Prout (this volume) cogently states, these very oppositions are not neutral conceptualizations, but are modern constructions. He links the discussion of continuity and change to a wider epistemological debate on universalism and particularism in which universalism is linked to biological laws and particularism is linked to socio-cultural factors; and he argues for an inclusive understanding of childhood as 'a heterogeneous biological-discursive-social-technological ensemble'.

This inclusiveness is productive, in that it stresses the value of conceptual complexity in understanding childhood. Still, in terms of empirical analysis, it leaves the problematic of development, or formative change, unresolved; or, rather, it transports it into a discussion of universalism and particularism which may be helpful in framing research questions but which is less felicitous in seeking to unpack more mundane dimensions of empirical analysis. So, the question of continuity and change raises fundamental epistemological issues about the knowledge claims made within different scientific paradigms (Danermark *et al.*, 2002;

Schrøder *et al.*, 2003); and it points to the necessity of defining which dimensions of analysis are appropriate for conducting particular types of research. The contributions to this part of the *Handbook* represent forms of analysis ranging from macro-level (Prout, Holland) to meso-level (Fleming) and micro-level (Reid-Walsh).

All contributors to this part of the *Handbook* endorse the formative role played by media in children's lives both today and in the past. Prout emphasizes the conceptual importance played by Vygotsky's notion of material and symbolic technologies, including language, text and images, mediating between inner and outer realities through joint practices. Fleming and Reid-Walsh both note how technologies of play, such as toys, help constitute modern, Westernized definitions of childhood as an age-bound phase of life defined by the removal from economic production, yet preparing for its gendered realities; and they both offer insightful examples of the conflation of toys as objects of play and media as symbolic resources for play. The insistence on (mediatized) play as a defining feature of modern childhood is specifically linked by Holland to the visual representation of children as playful innocents set in the midst of nature, supposedly untainted by civilization and its perceived discontents. Speaking about 'the marketing of sentiment', she notes how this imagery has been reappropriated by media corporations for posters, press footage, and film, offering contemporary audiences a mental map against which other images may be set: of the deviant, the rebellious, the promiscuous, the victim.

When conducting empirical historical studies, the opposition between continuity and change quickly transforms into a more mundane question of defining and understanding the relations between differences and commonalities. Moveable books of the early eighteenth century display 'strange' characters such as Clown and Columbine; dolls dating from the 1920s seem oddly lifeless to an untrained eye; while images of teenagers from the 1950s look exotic with 'strange' postures and hair style. Historical scholarship immediately prompts discussions, not only of empirical contextualization and its limits, but of analytical contextualization and its possibilities. How much does the researcher need to know about which contextual aspects in order to make a valid analysis of, for example, children's film of the 1920s? Knowing very little, one detects only difference; knowing too much, one may recognize only commonalities. There is room for reflection on these demarcations in the following chapters, since they illuminate various historical moments in children's culture and offer analytical insights about childhood across a wide temporal and spatial spectrum.

The authors in this first part of the *Handbook* make a claim for the usefulness of historical studies in understanding the complexity of children's mediatized cultures of today. In doing so, they also illustrate important debates for future study. First, all the accounts are by adults and are framed by adult eyes and experiences, while children's own voices are absent. Attempts have been made by oral historians and others to collect interviews with children, their diaries and autobiographies (Stickland, 1973; Burnett, 1982) and this material, though piecemeal and partial, may operate as a contextual frame for more child-centred histories of children's culture, including irreverent or subversive uses of official cultural forms handed down to the young. When it comes to historical takes on children's media cultures, children's own accounts are even sparser, and historical audience studies focusing on children are few and far between (Drotner, 1988).

The bias of sources may become even more difficult to tackle in future. For while many children around the world produce an abundance of mediatized communication today, just how many text messages or chat strings are stored, and by which criteria? How will we know about the significance young people pay to being offline or online, if studying their social uses is decoupled from their textual practices? The current focus in internet and mobile research on political and economic implications of new media and on the more spectacular cultural practices may easily result in a research perspective where children's own voices figure just as partially as in research on children's cultures of the past.

The chapters in this first part of the *Handbook* attempt to convey a holistic research perspective in studying children's media cultures. Such an ideal prompts discussions over social context and its limits, as we have noted. It equally prompts discussions on textual boundaries. While it is widely recognized that today's complex empirical media landscape requires equally complex theoretical approaches (Drotner, 2002), it is less debated what this entails for studies of children's media cultures in the past. Can we speak about a simpler media landscape in, for example, the 1920s than the 1960s; and, if so, does this make it more valid to select a single medium or genre when studying the 1920s? Questions such as these beg us to reflect on the interlocking and transmuting processes of mediatized meaning-making, on the ways in which textual practices have been interlaced also in the past (Bolter and Grusin, 1999; Peters, 1999). Evidently, the challenges are no less when studying children's media practices. As Fleming notes, reflecting on his own reminiscences of a favourite toy, to articulate the child's perspective at the time would not be accessible to any research technique in the methodological toolkit.

In this introduction we have mapped out some of the main challenges that are involved when approaching the relations between children and media from a historical perspective. A number of these issues tread on ground familiar to media studies and historiography in general. Others are more specifically linked to the particular socio-cultural position of children in modern, Westernized societies. This demonstrates that the research agenda that the authors of this first part draw up has much to offer major research traditions, just as it feeds on their conceptual advances. Children's media culture, now, as in the past, cannot feasibly be understood in splendid isolation from other scholarly insights and interventions.

REFERENCES

Aries, P. (1973) *Centuries of Childhood.* Harmondsworth: Penguin. (Orig. 1960.)

Bolter, J.D. and Grusin, R. (1999) *Remediation: Understanding New Media.* Cambridge, MA: MIT Press.

Briggs, A. and Burke, P. (2002) *A Social History of the Media: From Gutenberg to the Internet* Cambridge: Polity.

Burnett, J. (ed.) (1982) *Destiny Obscure: Autobiographies of Childhood, Education and Family from the 1820s to the 1920s.* London: Allen Lane.

Danermark, B., Ekstrom, M., Jokobsen, L. and Karlsson, J.C. (2002). *Explaining Society: Critical Realism in the Social Sciences.* London: Routledge.

Drotner, K. (1988) *English Children and Their Magazines, 1751–1945.* New Haven, CT: Yale University Press. (Orig. 1985.)

Drotner, K. (2002) 'New media, new options, new communities? Towards a convergent media and ICT research'. *Nordicom*, 24(2–3): 11–22 (rpt. in *Nordicom Review*, 23(1–2) (2002): 11–22).

Gilroy, P. (1993) *The Black Atlantic: Modernity and Double Consciousness.* Cambridge, MA: Harvard University Press.

Löfgren, O. (2001) 'The nation as home or motel? Metaphors and media of belonging'. *Yearbook of Sociology*, 2001: 1–34.

Marvin, C. (1988) *When Old Technologies Were New: Thinking About Electronic Communication in the Late Nineteenth Century* Oxford: Oxford University Press.

Offen, K., Roach Pierson, R. and Rendall, J. (eds) (1991) *Writing Women's History: International Perspectives.* Basingstoke: Macmillan.

Peters, J.D. (1999) *Speaking into the Air: A History of the Idea of Communication.* Chicago, IL: University of Chicago Press.

Schrøder, K.C., Drotner, K., Kline, S. and Murray, C. (2003) *Researching Audiences.* London: Edward Arnold.

Stearns, P.N. (2006) *Childhood in World History.* New York: Routledge.

Stickland, I. (1982). *The Voices of Children, 1700–1914.* Oxford: Blackwell.

Walvin, J. (1982). *A Child's World: A Social History of English Childhood, 1800–1914.* Harmondsworth: Penguin.

Winston, B. (1998) *Media, Technology and Society: a History. From the Telegraph to the Internet* London: Routledge.

1

Culture–Nature and the Construction of Childhood

Alan Prout

... simultaneously real, like nature, narrated, like discourse and collective, like society (Latour, 1993: 6).

INTRODUCTION

How childhood has been constructed and understood, both contemporaneously and in the past, is a key concern for scholars of children and the mass media. Changing childhood and changing media, and the shifting and reciprocal relationships between them, is the context for many of the different strands of study discussed in this volume. In this chapter I will focus on one side of that relationship: the constitution of childhood as a phenomenon and the problem of studying its complexity, heterogeneity and ambiguity. The purpose of this, however, is to sketch out the theoretical grounds for an enhanced dialogue between childhood and media studies.

Although there were antecedents, the study of childhood in its modern form is often understood as beginning with Darwin's efforts to understand child development, an effort about what today would be referred to as evolutionary biology. The heyday of Child Study, as the movement inspired by Darwin came to be known, lasted from the 1880s through to the second decade of the twentieth century, though its influence lasted much longer than this. During the intervening period, childhood has continued to exert a fascination over scholars from a wide range of disciplines, a range so wide in fact that it encompasses the natural and social sciences as well as the humanities. Over this time, the leading discipline (in the sense that it imparted a new vigour to the effort) has changed, with the baton being taken up at various times by medicine, psychology and sociology. Along the way, important, indeed crucial, insights have come from anthropology and history, whilst many other disciplines (for example, geography and literary studies) have made significant contributions. Today, childhood studies is emerging as a distinct multi- or inter-disciplinary field of study in its own right. Its ambition and promise, difficult though it is to accomplish, is to draw on these different disciplinary perspectives, holding them together in a more or less coherent whole.

One way to understand the emergence of contemporary childhood studies as an inter- or multi-disciplinary field is to trace its historical development through the nineteenth and twentieth centuries. In the chapter, therefore, I will sketch its different moments and phases. In particular, I will examine three key strands of thinking: the Darwin-inspired Child Study movement and the later re-emergence of an evolutionary biology of childhood; the creation of paediatric medicine, its relationship with child psychology and its extension into concerns with the social conditions of children's lives; and, finally, the development of social constructionist accounts of childhood at the end of the twentieth century.

At each phase of its emergence, the perspective, with both its strengths and limitations, of whatever discipline happened to be dominant at a particular time shaped how children have been studied. Nevertheless, despite the waxing and waning of disciplinary contributions, the process of forming childhood studies took place in a framework characteristically modernist in its mode of thinking. According to Bauman (1991), the basic project of modernity was the search for order, purity and the drive to exclude ambivalence. As a consequence Bauman (1991: 14) writes:

> The horror of mixing reflects the obsession with separating... The central frame of both modern intellect and modern practice is opposition – more precisely, dichotomy.

Modernist thinking is marked by the proliferation of such dichotomies. The division between childhood and adulthood, and their association with various qualities (such as rationality, dependency and competence), is an example of this. It is also well illustrated by modernist social theory (see Jenks (1998)), which proceeds by dividing the social world into discrete aspects, each set in relation to its opposite: structure versus agency; local versus global; identity versus difference; continuity versus change; ... and so on. A particular dualism, that of nature and culture, is, however, not only a very important axis of modernist thinking, but also has, I want to suggest, a particular salience to the trajectory taken by childhood studies during the modern period. This has, in its different phases, tended to zigzag between the poles of culture and nature. It is, I suggest, by breaking out of the conceptual limitation of this culture–nature opposition that childhood studies can traverse and project itself across a wide range of disciplines. However, the means that allow thinking of childhood in a complex way, as a biological–discursive–social–technological ensemble, have taken almost the whole of the twentieth century to appear, assembling and accreting along a circuitous route.

Why should such a theoretical reconfiguration be of concern to those interested in children and the media? The answer to this question lies in the relationship between childhood and media studies. A number of media studies scholars (for example, see Hengst (2000) and Livingstone (1998)) have been critical of contemporary childhood studies for its neglect of the media in children's lives. In this vein, for example, Buckingham (2000: 118) writes:

> ... it has paid very little attention to culture, to the media, or even children's use of commercially produced artefacts more generally... In the process, it has effectively neglected the mediated nature of contemporary childhood.

True, this criticism is aimed specifically at that relatively recent strand of childhood studies that has been shaped by the sociological tradition. Nevertheless, the point is well made. For, if contemporary studies of children have neglected mediatization and the artefacts associated with it, this is, I contend, part of a more general tendency in childhood studies to eclipse the role of material entities (such as bodies, technologies, artefacts) in constituting childhood. In line with much sociological thinking, emphasis is placed more on the linguistic and symbolic aspects of social construction than on the material aspects, especially technological aspects. Unlocking that conundrum, one deeply entangled with modernity's tendency to hold nature and culture in opposition is, I suggest, in the interests of both childhood and media studies.

Such a move is currently being made within childhood studies. Prout (2000, 2005) and Lee (2001), for example, draw on ideas such as 'actor networks' (Latour, 1993) or 'assemblages' (Deleuze and Guattari, 1988) to explore the potential for understanding childhood as a complex, *heterogeneously* constructed phenomenon. Such concepts break down the boundaries that separate the material and the discursive, the biological and the cultural, the technological and the social, and open up the possibility of merging these different perspectives and their disciplinary correlates. My suggestion is that both childhood and the mass media will benefit from such an approach and that it could form a set of shared conceptual resources that will deepen their dialogue.

CHILDHOOD AND MODERNITY

Before enquiring into the trajectory that childhood studies has taken, it is necessary to note that its emergence took place during a historical period when childhood, or at least the modern form of it, was itself under construction. The ground-breaking research of the French historian Aries (1962) is generally credited with first recognizing the historical specificities of childhood. Later work (Archard, 1993; Cunningham, 1991; Hendrick, 1997; Heywood, 2001) has questioned some of his assumptions, methods and conclusions. Nevertheless, the idea that between the seventeenth and twentieth centuries there took place the construction of a distinctively modern conception of childhood remains a powerful one. This modern form of childhood was characterized by its heightened separation from adulthood, a state of affairs accomplished through a labour of division carried out in many different spheres. One very important arena of this was the prolonged process by which children, first in Europe and the USA and then increasingly but very unevenly across the globe, were excluded from full-time paid employment but included in compulsory schooling (Cunningham, 1991; Lavalette, 1994; Cunningham and Viazzo, 1996; Hendrick, 1997; Heywood, 2003). This process, which took most of the nineteenth century and some of the twentieth century to achieve even in the then industrializing societies, was a continuation of the course of events described by Aries. By the end of the nineteenth century, conceptions of children as innocent, ignorant, dependent, vulnerable, incompetent and in need of protection and discipline were widespread. In general terms, by the start of the twentieth century these ideas had been diffused through most of the different social classes and groupings within industrial societies. They supported and were, in turn, reinforced by the effort to construct the school and the family as the 'proper place' for children. This emerged as an intended and unintended effect of many different strategies and practices, including the struggles of the early labour movement (Montanari, 2000), attempts at social reform and efforts at 'child saving' (Platt, 1977; Pearson, 1983). The overall effect of these practices was the establishment of the idea that children do not properly belong in the public space but should be located in the private domestic space of home or in the specialized and age-segregated institution of the school and related institutions. This idea of childhood, as an ideal if not a reality, has been propogated globally. As Cunningham (1991: 7) comments:

> ... between the late seventeenth and mid-twentieth centuries there occurred a major and irreversible shift in the representations of childhood, to the point where all children throughout the world were thought to be entitled to certain common elements and rights of childhood.

DARWINISM AND THE CHILD STUDY MOVEMENT

Childhood studies, then, emerged alongside the modern idea of childhood. As noted above, its beginnings are often located in Darwin's work, produced at a time when the mass of children did not in fact experience childhood as a distinct, protected and extended period of 'growing up'. This kind of childhood was confined primarily to aristocratic children and those of the emerging middle classes. Nevertheless, childhood as an idea and as an ideal against which the lives of poor children were measured exercised an animating influence. Darwin seems to have been caught by its fascination. Based on observations of his son, he published two books, *The Expression of Emotions in Man and Animals* (1872) and *Biographical Sketch of an Infant* (1877). These triggered a wave of interest in child development in the form of the Child Study movement. In large measure, this Darwinian legacy tied childhood studies in its earliest phase to a largely biological view of childhood. Hendrick (1997: 48) sums up the situation thus:

> In effect, Child Study helped to spread the techniques of natural history to the study of children, showing them to be 'natural creatures'; through its lectures, literature and the practice of its influential members, it popularized the view that the child's conception differed from that of adults, that there were marked stages in normal mental development; and that there were similarities between the mental worlds of children and primitives....

The Child Study movement *per se* was in decline by the first decade of the twentieth century. Its legacy was its emphasis on the biological roots of behaviour and its preference for an (albeit nineteenth century) idea of scientific knowledge – themes that continued, primarily through polarized discussions about 'nature' and 'nurture', to swirl around childhood studies until the present day. However, it was not until the end of the twentieth century that a more completely realized evolutionary biological account of childhood started to be expounded. Like Darwinist Child Study, this has its starting point in the idea that humans are a species with an evolutionary history, but it adds elements from contemporary mathematics (especially games theory, see Maynard Smith (1982) and Axelrod (1984)), primatology (Pereira, 2002) and physical anthropology (especially work on the co-emergence of human language, sociality and tool use – see Ingold (1993)).

Through this combination it is suggested that the observation that some species have a juvenile stage in which individuals are no longer dependent on parental care for survival but are not sexually mature is an important evolutionary puzzle in search of a solution. At first blush such a phenomenon would seem contrary to evolutionary theory, because the main direction of evolutionary pressures would seem to be towards reproducing as much and as quickly as possible – a pattern that is, indeed, seen in many species. However, as Pereira insists, the emergence of a juvenile stage of development can also be understood as an evolutionary strategy (Pereira, 2002: 26):

> The general function of animal juvenility is modulation of growth and the onset of reproduction. In many cases it functions to maximize the rate and/or extend the duration of growth, therefore allowing it to escape the period during which small size renders it particularly vulnerable to predation and virtually ineligible to compete for reproductive opportunity .... Conversely, when small size entails little cost or when large size is penalised by the environment, juvenility often is abbreviated or does not occur in a life history. Juvenility is also diminished when adult size can be attained by or soon after the exhaustion of parental provision, as in many birds and mammals, or when early reproductive effort does not compromise further growth.

In this sense, an extended period of juvenility in humans, longer than that found even in other primates, is a key feature of the evolution of the human species and is associated with other species characteristics, such as the development of sophisticated linguistic communication and the use of tools. This human evolutionary strategy can be understood as resulting in a long life, a long period of immaturity, few offspring but high levels of care, survival, mental agility and culture. The distinctive human pattern of growth and development over life course has some specific features that make it different from even close relatives such as chimps. In particular, Bogin (1998) argues that, compared with other primates, human evolution has involved the creation of a new phase, which he terms 'childhood', in the ontogenic pattern. For example, the human child uses an enormous proportion of metabolic effort on brain development, greater even than chimps, and this continues rapidly after birth. Human children, therefore, display a pattern involving very extended juvenility, the intense acquisition of skills and a prolonged period of socialization and developmental plasticity. As a reproductive strategy this allows mothers to share care of young with other competent members of the social group (fathers, grandmothers, other young), freeing them to give birth to other young. Developmental plasticity allows a long period of interaction between the individual and the environment, leading to greater adaptedness and greater survival rates.

CHILDREN, BIOPOLITICS AND THE NATION STATE

At the end of the twentieth century, this reappearance of an evolutionary biological account of childhood, together with new ideas about the role of language, technology and material artefacts in human life (see also below), created the possibility of thinking of childhood as a heterogeneous biological–discursive–social–technological ensemble. However, this possibility took almost the whole of the twentieth century to appear, unevenly accreting along a complex and circuitous route. So, at the *start* of the twentieth century the proximal effect of the Child Study movement was paradoxical, for, despite its roots in a biological conception of the child, it helped to create an intellectual climate in which childhood was no longer seen to occur naturally. It did this by promoting the idea that childhood needed the attention and intervention of experts. The opening of this space accounts for many of the developments in the study of children in the decades up to and beyond the Second World War. What started as an essentially biological project, locating childhood as a natural phenomenon, was marked by a growing awareness of the social and cultural ramifications of childhood. Childhood studies thus described an uneven trajectory during which it gradually accreted such elements.

However, at the time, viewing children as natural primitives played into nineteenth and twentieth century concerns with Empire and race. The child became an instance of the 'Other', a homologue for all such 'primitives' and a demonstration of the gulf that divided the 'civilized' from the 'uncivilized' (see Christensen (1994)). This divide was applied both to internal social divisions, such as the abiding concern of nineteenth and twentieth century social policy with how to handle the 'troublesome classes', and to external 'Others', like the subjects of imperial rule, deemed racially inferior. However, alongside its ideological kinship with such ideas, the Child Study movement can also be seen as part of another key development of the nineteenth century: the construction of children as a concern of the Nation. The advent of compulsory schooling in the industrializing societies of Europe and North America gave children as a social group an unprecedented visibility. Much 'biopolitical' concern, to use Foucault's term, was generated through research and discussion about the physical and mental state of what came to be seen as a national resource for international military and economic competition. Children became a target for investment and were seen as the 'children of the nation' (Hendrick, 1997: 49).

Armstrong's (1983) work suggests that this trajectory can be seen particularly in the development of paediatric medicine from the late-nineteenth to mid-twentieth century. A crucial step in it was the migration of child surveillance from the clinic to the community setting, a move that created an enormous new terrain for panoptical practices. This, he writes:

> … further refined this (medical) gaze, these techniques of analysis, to fix them, not on individual bodies so much as the interstices of society; (it) was a mechanism of power which imposed on the spatial arrangements of bodies the social configuration of their relationship … a device, above all else, for making visible to constant surveillance the interaction between people, normal and abnormal, and thereby transforming the physical space between bodies into social space traversed by power. At the beginning of the

> twentieth century the 'social' was born as an autonomous realm. (Armstrong, 1983: 9–10)

Armstrong is, of course, not the first to borrow this account of the emergence of disciplinary society from Foucault. Donzelot (1979) makes essentially the same point in relation to the surveillance of the family in France. As he points out, children were the points of access for the surveillance of the French family, the great moral cause that sanctioned the breaching of its privacy. In the USA too, child saving was an influential and important social movement (Platt, 1977) that opened up the family to inspection.

In addition to health and the family, children were also enmeshed in another set of panoptical powers, exercised through mass schooling. Indeed, all the areas of surveillance overlapped. The understanding of childhood disease as a specific and separate branch of medicine emerged alongside the extension of the modern ideal of childhood to greater and greater numbers of children from a wider and wider range of social classes. Through the intersection of educational and medical regimes childhood became one of the main targets for new practices of preventive medicine, applied, for instance in surveillance practices such as health visiting, school health inspections, clinics for mothers and children and so on. By the first quarter of the twentieth century, then, mechanisms were in place in the UK, and with parallels in other countries, through which the health of children could become a topic in its own right and be monitored, studied and measured in systematic ways.

However, it was not until the Second World War that a panoptical device was created through which the social aspect of childhood was brought to a high level of refinement. This device was the child development survey. In the UK, the survey technique can be traced back to the nineteenth century, where the work of Rowntree and Booth springs immediately to mind, and in the medical sphere was developed in the inter-war period. Studies of child development had been carried out in the USA by Gesell during the 1920s, although these were still relatively small samples and often carried out in special observation domes rather than in the settings and communities in which the children lived. However, the surveying of children in the family and community found its clearest expression internationally in the post-1945 era with the institution of the longitudinal survey. For example, in England, four main studies have been started, in 1946, 1958, 1970 and 2000. These continue to track cohorts of children and their descendants. The 1958 study, for example, is currently tracking the grandchildren of those born at the start of the study. These longitudinal studies had their counterparts in countries around the world and were added to by many cross-sectional studies looking at different aspects of child growth, development and rearing. During the second half of the twentieth century, then, a vast amount of data on many of the key physical, behavioural and emotional patterns of growth were established, especially for children growing up in the industrialized countries. Normal development and growth, the product of hundreds of thousands of individual measurements, was used as the template against which the abnormal could be identified.

In such studies the development and growth of nationally representative samples of children could be tracked over time. Through this the object that was constructed was not the pathology of the individual child, as had proliferated in the pre-war period, but a picture of the 'normal child'. It was this emphasis on the normal, together with the developmental perspective, that gave paediatrics its distinction as a medical specialism. Even more crucially, through this it was possible to draw together a range of disciplinary inputs under the umbrella of paediatrics:

> ... such diverse aspects of growth as the bio-chemical and immunological, the intellectual, the emotional and the social. (Apley, cited in Armstrong (1983: 59))

This broad multidimensional perspective could be and was readily endorsed by social scientists. Indeed, such a statement describes the arc from the biological to the social, which paediatrics had described over the previous period.

Interwoven in the growth and extension of medical studies of children was the emergence of psychology, the discipline that perhaps most directly took on the mantle of the Child Study movement. The history of child psychology in the twentieth century is a highly complex matter, which it is here possible merely to gesture towards. In the UK, as well as other industrial societies of the time, its growth overlaps substantially with the developments in paediatrics described above. In 1944, for example, the British Paediatric Association created a Child Psychology Sub-Committee concerned to challenge too firm a line between physical and psychological disabilities. Illingworth's (1986) landmark paediatric text, *The Normal Child*, was as concerned with psychological development as it was with the physical, and these concerns were both rolled up into the wave of surveys that aimed to establish patterns of growth and their correlates.

Whilst child psychology has developed a large number of different theoretical schools and strands (Freudianism, Skinnerian behaviourism, Piagetian developmentalism, Vygotskian activity theory and so on), its concern with the individual child won an almost hegemonic position among the emerging social sciences of the early twentieth century. As Rose (1989) has suggested, its wide range of topics and approaches to children, which he terms the 'psy complex', became closely entwined with the emergence of health and welfare policies and practices around children. These too were, according to Rose, a form of biopolitics through which the state and other organizations sought to define and regulate normality. Like paediatricians, psychologists set about examining and testing children in order to define the 'normal' range of functioning and behaviour. In the process, they constituted what was abnormal, pathological and in need of intervention. These processes straddled the main locales of children's lives, but they were especially concentrated in nurseries and schools. Their object of intervention was often the family, and, as many have noted, the child became the entry point for the state and other agencies into the family. From the 1920s onwards, and up to the present day, there was a proliferation of professions concerned with identifying children's abnormality and attending in some way to it: Child Guidance Clinics, educational psychology services, school attendance officers and so on. These practices have, in turn, demonstrated a huge appetite for childhood studies, represented in the libraries of books and papers, and the hundreds of professional associations and research institutes that are its inheritance.

However, towards the end of the twentieth century there was growing academic criticism of how psychology handled childhood. This came from both within and outside psychology as a discipline. Rather than seeing childhood as a universal constant, whether biological or cultural, in the post-Aries intellectual landscape it became possible to think of childhood as a variable and changing entity. This insight was greatly strengthened by the findings of social and cultural anthropology, which reinforced this possibility. These arguments marked psychology in many ways, such that by the 1970s a critical psychology began to emerge that was much more sensitive to the social context of individual behaviour. Significant and influential statements of this new thinking in psychology were, for example, found in volumes edited by Richards (1974) and Richards and Light (1986). In the second collection, Richards and Light (1986: 3) commented:

> A central theme in the earlier volume was the criticism of a psychology based on universal laws that were supposed to hold good across all societies and at all historical times. It was argued that terms such as "the mother" and "the child" not only conveyed a meaningless generality but misrepresented the relationship between individuals and social worlds and portrayed social arrangements as if they were fixed laws of nature.

Another statement of this approach came from Bronfenbrenner (1979) in the so-called 'ecological model' of child development, which envisions child development at the centre of a set of social contexts, including local ones such as the family, household and neighbourhood, and more distant ones such as social structure and policy. Another, perhaps more radical, has emerged from Vygotsky's (1962, 1978) concern to develop a psychology that could encompass social and biological concerns, and which assigns crucial importance to the mediating role of artefacts and technologies. According to Vygotsky, society provides the symbolic tools, both material and linguistic, which shape the development of thinking. Cognition can, thus, not be separated from the conditions and practices of life with which a child grows up. Indeed, thinking is not seen as located in the head of an individual, but in the interaction, including the material practices, taking place between the individual and the collectively constituted and historically situated culture created through joint activity (for example, see Engeström (2001)).

SOCIAL CONSTRUCTIONISM AND THE SOCIOLOGY OF CHILDHOOD

By the 1980s it was clear that childhood studies, through its engagement with children as biological and psychological entities, had brought itself, in both paediatrics and psychology, and the practices of biopolitical surveillance associated with them, to a position where the importance of society and culture was clearly recognized. This is not to say, however, that the way in which the social was incorporated into thinking was necessarily adequate. Social life was usually imported into medical and psychological thinking under the rubric of a shared scientific method, which claimed the production of objective and value-free facts in relation to social, psychological and biological phenomena. Although the outer reaches of these disciplines may have started to question the universal applicability of science, in general terms social life was admitted to knowledge only on the same terms as nature. Furthermore, the accretion of the social to thinking about childhood did not happen uniformly. The process was more akin to a genealogy in which certain branches or practitioners of the disciplines concerned were able to create new, more socially aware versions of their craft whilst leaving other streams of thinking more or less untouched.

The picture was one in which the addition of the social to the biological and psychological formed a blurred and fragmented mosaic. Perhaps the underlying reason for this was that, in general (and apart from pioneers such as Vygotsky, who was only just becoming recognized in Western thinking), the methodology was generally additive. In a characteristically modernist mode of thought, nature and culture were thought of as two more or less equivalent but opposite principles. The key questions were about 'how much' of each could be seen as constituting the mix. The implicit dualism of such an additive method is well captured by Cole's (1998) discussion of the three models of nature and culture that he sees as dominating theory about children's psychological development in the twentieth century. Each sees an interaction between 'biology' and 'culture', but gives a different weighting to them. The first is represented by Gessell, who recognizes both biology and culture as important but who places most weight on endogenous processes of biological growth. In this view, whilst the social environment can affect the intensity and timing of development it cannot influence its basic direction, because this is determined by inherent, maturational mechanisms. The basic picture is the same in the second stream of psychological thought, behaviourism, except that in this case the estimate of quantity is reversed. The biological material is likened to an inert lump of clay, which is shaped and sculpted by the action of operant conditioning, whose source is the social environment. The third, represented by Piaget, is a somewhat more sophisticated but still dualistic account. Here, equal weight is given to biological and social environmental factors, which are pictured as interacting together, with individuals also an active factor in shaping their developmental pathway as they adapt to their environments.

Inadequate though these dualistic formulations may be, they each had the merit of viewing the child as heterogeneous, as somehow both biological and social. This additive approach to culture and nature was, however, to be radically disturbed in the final decades of the twentieth century through the appearance of an influential set of ideas that came to be known as 'social constructionism'. In its most general sense this term refers to what is almost axiomatic in the sociological tradition: that reality is made in specific social circumstances, varies across both history and culture, and is open to change, both intended and unintended. Building on the historical insights of Aries (1962), social constructionism in childhood studies stressed the variable, culturally relative and plural character of childhood. It did this, as Wyness (2006: 20) notes, by '... separat(ing) the cultural and biological aspects of childhood, with the former taking precedence over the latter... (a)ccentuating ideas, sentiments and meaning rather than the material elements ...'.

Although social constructionism was widely influential across the social sciences, it played an especially important role in the creation of the sociology of childhood (Jenks, 1990; Prout and James, 1990/1997; Stainton Rogers and Stainton Rogers, 1992; Thorne, 1993; Mayall, 1994; Frones, 1995; Corsaro, 1997; James *et al.*, 1998; Christensen and James, 2000; Lee, 2001; Wyness, 2006). This body of ideas, emerging in the 1980s and 1990s, was critical of two concepts that had dominated academic discussion of children in the previous period. The first, socialization, was criticized primarily for rendering children as passive; it was argued that children should be seen as active participants in social life and as actors with the potential for agency. In addition, because socialization focuses attention on its outcome in adulthood, it marginalizes the process of growing up and sidelines children's own actions, meanings and cultures. For this reason it was suggested that children should be seen as 'beings' rather than 'becomings'.[1] The emphasis on children as social actors has given rise to a rich variety of empirical studies that re-examine familiar settings of children's lives with greater sensitivity to children's active participation in them, often finding evidence for their agency and co-constructive capacities, as well as exploring the limits of them.

The second approach to be critiqued by social constructionists was the developmentalism dominant within psychological discourses of childhood. It was argued that developmentalism tends to set up adulthood as the standard of rationality against which children are judged deficient, that it renders putative stages of growth as natural, and assumes a universality to childhood which historical, social and cultural studies suggest that it does not have.

These critiques were informed by a number of theoretical resources deployed to highlight the social character of childhood. The sociology of childhood drew heavily on the interactionist sociology, developed primarily in the USA during the 1970s, which had problematized the concept of socialization as rendering children too passive (for example, see Dreitzel (1973)). Another strand of thinking applied the basic sociological notion of social structure to childhood by arguing that it should be seen as a permanent feature of society (Qvortrup *et al.*, 1994). Writers such as Mayall (1994) combined this with the influence of feminist ideas in order to portray children as a minority group, subject to oppression by adults.

Prout and James (1990/1997) synthesized a number of different critical elements in a programmatic statement for the 'new paradigm in the sociology of childhood'. I will quote its six points in their entirety:

1 Childhood is understood as a social construction. As such it provides an interpretive frame for contextualizing the early years of human life. Childhood, as distinct from biological immaturity, is neither a natural nor universal feature of human groups but appears as a specific structural and cultural component of many societies.
2 Childhood is a variable of social analysis. It can never be divorced from other variables such as

class, gender or ethnicity. Comparative and cross-cultural analysis reveals a variety of childhoods rather than a single and universal phenomenon.
3 Children's social relationships are worthy of study in their own right, independent of the perspective and concerns of adults.
4 Children must be seen as active in the construction and determination of their own social lives, the lives of those around them and of the societies in which they live. Children are not just passive subjects of social structures and processes.
5 Ethnography is a particularly useful methodology for the study of childhood. It allows children a more direct voice and participation in the production of sociological data than is usually possible through experimental or survey styles of research.
6 Childhood is a phenomenon in relation to which the double hermeneutic of the social sciences is acutely present (see Giddens, 1976). That is to say to proclaim a new paradigm of childhood sociology is also to engage in and respond to the process of reconstructing childhood in society. (Prout and James, 1990: 8)

In addition to creating a new emphasis on children as social actors and highlighting children's agency, social contructionism's benefit was that it problematized and destabilized taken-for-granted concepts of childhood. It insisted on the historical and temporal specificity of childhoods and focused on their construction through discourse (for example, see Jenks (1982, 1990)). However, whilst this energized an important new wave of social studies of childhood, it unwittingly entrenched the culture–nature dualism through which childhood studies had zizzagged throughout the twentieth century. Through it, the separation between nature and culture was heightened in an overreaching work of purification. The mediation that goes on between culture and nature, which the additive approach of paediatrics and psychology had at least recognized, was occluded. A strong statement of this perspective came from Rex and Wendy Stainton Rogers (Stainton Rogers and Stainton Rogers, 1992: 6–7). For them, the childhood is created through narrative practices. They write, for example, that:

> The basic thesis … is very simple. We live in a world that is produced through stories – stories that we are told, stories that we recount and stories that we create.

The implication of this statement for a social constructionist view of childhood is clearly spelt out: 'we regard "childhood" as constructed through its telling … there can *only be* stories and storytellers of childhood' (Stainton Rogers and Stainton Rogers, 1992: 12, my emphasis). This position entails a double move: culture is made dominant, whilst nature is excluded (except perhaps as stories about nature); at the same time, culture is itself reduced to narrative practices.

Of course, the insight that childhood is discursively constructed is very important. Showing how socially situated discursive practices apprehend and construct different aspects of childhood is illuminating. Nevertheless, it stands in danger of becoming merely a reverse discourse, declaring 'culture' (reduced to language or even narrative) where previously had been written 'nature'. Equally important, because the world is divided into the natural and the social/cultural, the character of the world in which children actually grow up is misapprehended. Consider, for example, the following statements (Maybin and Woodhead, 2003):

> Childhood is a social phenomenon … Childhood contexts and social practices are socially constructed. There is not much 'natural' about the environments in which children grow-up in and spend their time: for children in Western societies mainly centred around home, classroom, and playground, as well as in cars, buses and other forms of transport, in shopping malls and discos. These are human creations that regulate children's lives.

Although these statements usefully draw attention to the population of children's lives by artefacts of one sort or another (like the ones listed above), by gathering them up under the category of the 'social' it misrepresents what an artefact is. In fact, such a statement only makes sense if one wishes to separate out nature and culture, forcing all entities to belong to either one or the other. In reality, there is much (but not everything) about technological artefacts that is 'natural', just as there is much (but not everything) that is 'social'. In them, natural materials and processes are ordered (more or less successfully) around human purposes, interests and meanings. As such, they have an ambiguous quality, neither purely natural nor purely cultural; they are exactly hybrids of culture and nature.

CULTURE AND NATURE RECONFIGURED

This point has obvious relevance to the mass media, which depend upon and operate through material artefacts – be they based on 'old' technologies like print or the 'new' ones like electronic and digital devices. As the proliferation of technologies and artefacts proceeded through the twentieth century, social scientists began to ask new questions about the role of technology in social life. Their answers have produced new ways of thinking, not just about artefacts and technological devices, but through this also about the relationship between culture and nature. These new formulations challenge the assumption that the world can be divided into these two mutually exclusive kinds of entity. A number of different thinkers have addressed this possibility, but Latour (1993), in his book *We Have Never Been Modern*, makes a comprehensive case for reconfiguring the relationship. The essence of his argument is that what has been called modernity consists of a double set of practices. On the one hand, there is the work of *purification*, through which the spheres of nature and culture have been kept separate, with nature assigned to 'science', thought of as a culture-free, socially neutral practice that produces truth. Modernist discourse is constructed as a set of extremely powerful interlocking but paradoxical concepts, which until recently have proved difficult to crack open. Nature is simultaneously treated as both transcendent of society and immanent in the practices of science, a human activity that promises unlimited possibilities. Society is similarly both immanent (with humans free to construct it as they wish) and transcendent (with humans unable to act against its laws). Seen in these terms, modernist thinking seems to block all the escape routes and cover all possibilities.

Critically, however, Latour suggests that this credo has eventually been undermined by another great but unacknowledged work of modernity – that of *mediation* – for, whilst modernity separated Nature and Culture in its conceptual schema, it simultaneously proliferated actual, real, material hybrids of them. Every device, machine, technology is neither pure nature nor pure culture, but a networked set of natural and social associations. Modernity's submerged, unacknowledged but crucial work is the proliferation of such hybrid culture–nature entities, which Latour terms hybrid socio-technical networks. The scale of their proliferation has now become so great that the modernist edifice of Nature–Culture opposition has become insupportable.

In making this general point Latour is not alone. For example, Haraway (1991) urges the importance of the 'cyborg image' for understanding feminist politics in an age when the human and the technical are conspicuously merging. We cannot, she suggests, understand modern societies except by understanding the ways in which we, as humans, are produced within and are inseparable from socio-technical and biological networks. Similarly, in Deleuze and Guattari's (1988) writing, the world, including its human and social parts, is seen as a set of *assemblages* constituted from heterogeneous elements. Their vision is a very broad one, taking in wide sweeps of human and pre-human history, encompassing a Darwinian view of human life in which human existence is seen in the context of the evolution of life. The Enlightenment belief in the uniqueness and separateness of humans is no longer regarded as tenable, and human life has to be seen in terms of its emergence from, connections with and dependence on the heterogeneous materials that make up the world. Deluze and Guattari decentre the human world, seeing it in the context of broader physical and biological processes. Their discussion pays a great deal of attention to characteristics of the human species, such as technology and language. Indeed, they see the emergence of the human species as involving the modification of the function of the hand and the mouth in a way that makes possible the use of tools and language. This led to the creation of what they term a 'social technological machine' (an ensemble of 'man–tool–animal–thing') and a 'semiotic machine' (or 'regime of signs'). These assemble heterogeneous materials – humans, animals, plants, minerals – in entities that mediate nature and culture and which produce new capacities to act and new fields of power. Technologies, artefacts and devices of various kinds, including those associated with the media, play a central role in this process. What it is to be human is thus decentred. Rather than seeing humans as isolated from the world, human capacities and powers derive from their connection with it. Human history is the process of borrowing from the non-human world and thus creating new combinations and new extensions of the human body and the mind.

Bringing these insights to the study of childhood, Lee (2001: 115) has noted that:

> ... humans find themselves in an open-ended swirl of extensions and supplementations, changing their powers and characteristics as they pass through different assemblages .... Looking through Deleuze and Guattari's ... eyes we do not see a single incomplete natural order waiting to be finished by human beings, we see many incomplete orderings that remain open to change...a picture of human life, whether adult or child, as an involvement in multiple becomings .... Deleuze and Guattari have given us a framework within which to compare (...) various childhoods.... Whether children are in or out of place, or whether new places are being made for them, we can ask what assemblages they are involved in and what extensions they are living through.

This perspective (see also Prout (2005)) has a number of implications for the relationship between childhood studies and media studies. First, it opens the way for a more coherent (but not necessarily more unified) multidisciplinary practice of childhood studies. Through a reconceptualization of childhood's ontology, it could move towards seeing children as neither 'natural' nor 'cultural', but rather as a multiplicity of 'nature–cultures'; that is, as a variety of complex hybrids constituted from heterogeneous materials (biological, social, individual, historical, technological, spatial, material, discursive, ...) and emergent through time. In this approach, childhood is not seen as a unitary phenomenon, but as a multiple set of constructions emergent from the connection and disconnection, fusion and separation of these heterogeneous materials. Each particular construction, and these come in scales running from the individual child to historically constituted forms of childhood, has a non-linear history, a being in becoming that is open-ended and non-teleological.

Second, such a perspective could link childhood and media studies across these different scales of social research and enquiry. At the relatively large scale, information and communication technologies play a crucial role in the changing (material and symbolic) construction of contemporary childhoods. During the early and mid-twentieth century, children were wrapped up in layers of protection, including family, home, school and welfare institutions. However, towards the end of the twentieth century this set of arrangements began to unravel. The strong boundary around the family home, which constituted it as a private sphere, began to weaken. The growing entry of women into the labour market significantly affected the division between the public, secular world of work, which had previously been monopolized by men, and the private sphere of the family. The home increasingly became the locus for the consumption of all sorts of new technologies. 'Labour saving' technologies, such as the refrigerator and the washing machine, responded to, but also helped to make possible, the emergence of a new division of labour between men and women. This created the possibility of further and broader forms of consumption; and with this, ideas about choice, rights and decision-making arose. The media played an important role in this, conveying into the 'private' sphere of the home ideas about consumer choice, as well as information and values about a multitude of other topics. So it was that the split between the public and the private, one of the oppositional dichotomies through which modern childhood was represented and constructed, began to weaken. As Lee (2001a: 156–7) notes:

> The form of patriarchy practised in the family home was dependent on the sustainability of men's position as exclusive interface between the family and the world of production. As long as productive work belonged to men, and as long as men could rely on finding employment, the family home could remain a place of 'innocence' and all within it could remain trivial. The private, secret space of the family home involved an infantalisation of children as much as it did an infantalisation of women.

The outcome of the encounter between childhood and the information and communication technologies is uncertain and still emergent. However, it is clear that, whatever direction it takes in the future, it has, for the moment, begun to create shifts in children's position and the character of childhood. Through their associations with media and communications technologies the reach of their experience is extended and the range of the images, facts and values that they encounter is multiplied. This occurs within the context of their existing everyday lives and not as a disjuncture from it, suggesting that it can be played out in many different ways. It is clear, however, that new socio-technical assemblages can extend children's reach into worlds of ideas and information previously unavailable to them, giving them the potential power to multiply these beyond those contained within the physical and temporal boundaries of their everyday locales (Prout, 2005).

In the smaller-scale settings of children's lives, the perspective offers a way of understanding how children enrol and are enrolled by a large range of artefacts. This point is emphasized by Ogilvie-Whyte (2003) in her ethnography of a Scottish school, where she comments:

> In the micro setting of the Hillend playground it becomes more than apparent that the majority of social relations are held together in the interaction of humans and non-humans. A cursory glance shows that the landscape of the playground is characterized by small groups of children – each group bound together by an object or objects of sorts. The types of objects are diverse indeed – footballs, beyblades, beyblade stadiums, skateboards, inline skates, wrestling figures and wrestling rings, Barbie dolls, Gameboys and so on ....

Media-related artefacts are just a part of this heterogeneously populated world. But, as she shows, whatever their specific affordances, they are not merely props for social interaction; rather, they are embedded in and are part of social processes as much as the human actors are. Throughout her ethnography she explores how the field of possibilities from which children can draw such supplements and extensions is limited. Some people and things are available to some children but not to others, and it is often, she argues, these limitations that shape the outcome of interactions, especially the struggles that children engage in with each other and with adults. Ogilvie-Whyte (2003) shows how the agency of children is, in part, an effect of their relationship with such artefacts, commenting that

> ... in their discussions of such issues (whether it be football boots, trainers or any other things) children have an implicit recognition that they can extend their agency as collective in some senses. At times they recognize that they can extend their agency through assemblages with some actants but also that, likewise, some assemblages – some actants – may impair their agentic powers.

In drawing attention to this, her analysis maintains the focus on children as social actors, retaining this valuable and energizing contribution of social constructionism to the study of childhood. However, by showing how children's agency is produced through both linguistic practices and their relationships with material artefacts, she overcomes and renders unnecessary its tendency to one-sidedly emphasize the role of language in social relations.

CONCLUSION

In this chapter I have sought ways in which to merge the concerns of childhood studies with those of researchers in the field of children and the mass media. To do this I have retraced the steps of childhood studies, uncovering its history of multidisciplinarity and panopticism, mapping its zigzag route through the relationship between culture and nature. Underlying this is a modernist practice of discursively separating or purifying culture and nature, while in the same moment carrying out an unacknowledged but intense mediation of them. Technology is formed from, and in turn intermingles with, nature and culture. The intellectual resources for understanding and, at least partially, unpicking, this imbroglio have only recently become available. From the perspective of childhood studies, this is beginning to allow childhood to be understood in terms of assemblages of heterogeneous materials. In order to understand this it is important to move away from the idea of a determinant process in which one entity, natural, social or technological, drives this process. Whilst the properties of nature and culture are not infinitely malleable, they are overdetermined, in the sense that they are complex, emergent and open to contingency. In fact, the entities that we call 'biological', 'technological' and 'social' are already networked together. The effects that are created by their interweaving create new assemblages, possibilities and problems in an unfolding but non-teleological process. Such shifting networks of heterogeneous elements span the life course in combinations that are empirically varied but do not, in principle, demand different kinds of analysis. There is no need in this respect to separate children from adults arbitrarily, as if they were some different species of being. Rather, the task is to see how different versions of child or adult emerge from the complex interplay, networking and orchestration of different natural, discursive, collective, hybrid and (especially) technological materials. It is in this task that childhood and media researchers can find common ground and shared interests.

NOTES

1 However, the being–becoming opposition, although useful in refocusing on children in the present, is perhaps another questionable dualism – see Christensen (1994), Lee (2001) and Prout (2005).

REFERENCES

Archard, D. (1993) *Children: Rights and Childhood.* London: Routledge.

Aries, P. (1962) *Centuries of Childhood: A Social History of Family Life.* London: Jonathan Cape.

Armstrong, D. (1983) *Political Anatomy of the Body: Medical Knowledge in Britain in the Twentieth Century.* Cambridge: Cambridge University Press.

Axelrod, R. (1984) *The Evolution of Cooperation.* New York: Basic Books.

Bauman, Z. (1991) *Modernity and ambivalence.* Cambridge: Polity Press.

Bogin, B. (1998) 'Evolutionary and Biological Aspects of Childhood'. In Panther-Brick, C. (ed) (1998) *Biosocial Perspectives on Children.* Cambridge: Cambridge University Press.

Bronfenbrenner, E. (1979) *The Ecology of Human Development: Experiments by Nature and Design.* Cambridge, MA: Harvard University Press.

Buckingham, D. (2000) *After the Death of Childhood: Growing Up in the Age of the Electronic Media.* Cambridge: Polity Press.

Christensen, P. (1994) 'Children as the cultural other', *KEA: Zeischrift fur Kulturwissenschaften, TEMA: Kinderwelten,* 6: 1–16.

Christensen, P. and James, A. (eds) (2000) *Research with Children: Perspectives and Practices.* London: Falmer Press.

Cole, M. (1998) 'Culture in development'. In M. Woodhead, D. Faulkner and K. Littleton (eds) *Cultural Worlds of Early Childhood.* London: Routledge.

Corsaro, W.A. (1997) *The Sociology of Childhood.* Thousand Oaks, CA: Pine Forge Press.

Cunningham, H. (1991) *The Children of the Poor: Representations of Childhood since the Seventeenth Century.* Oxford: Blackwell.

Cunningham, H. and Viazzo, P.P. (1996) *Child Labour in Historical Perspective 1800–1995.* Florence: UNICEF.

Deleuze, G. and Guattari, F. (1988) *A Thousand Plateaus: Capitalism and Schizophrenia II.* London: Athlone.

Donzelot, J. (1979) *The Policing of Families.* London: Hutchinson.

Dreitzel, H.P. (ed.) (1973) *Childhood and Socialization.* San Francisco: Jossey-Bass.

Engeström, Y. (2001) 'Expansive learning at work: toward an activity theoretical reconceptualization'. *Journal of Education and Work,* 14(1): 133–156.

Frones, I. (1995) *Among Peers: On the Meaning of Peers in the Process of Socialisation.* Oslo: Scandinavian University Press.

Giddens, A. (1976) *The New Rules of Sociological Method.* London: Hutchinson.

Haraway, D. (1991) 'A cyborg manifesto: science, technology and socialist-feminism in the twentieth century'. In *Simians, Cyborgs and Women: The Reinvention of Nature.* New York: Routledge.

Hendrick, H. (1997) *Children, Childhood and English Society 1880–1990.* Cambridge: Cambridge University Press.

Hengst, H. (2000) *Reconquering urban spots and spaces? Children's public(ness) and the script of media industry.* Working Paper 18. Child and Youth Culture. Odense University: Department of Contemporary Cultural Studies.

Heywood, C. (2001) *A History of Childhood.* Cambridge: Polity Press.

Illingworth, R. (1986) *The Normal Child: Some Problems of the Early Years and their Treatment* (9th edition). Edinburgh: Churchill Livingstone.

Ingold, T. (1993) 'Tool use, sociality and intelligence'. In K.R. Gibson and T. Ingold (eds) *Tools, Language and Cognition in Human Evolution.* Cambridge: Cambridge University Press.

James, A., Jenks, C. and Prout, A. (1998) *Theorising Childhood.* Cambridge: Polity Press.

Jenks, C. (ed.) (1982) *The Sociology of Childhood – Essential Readings.* London: Batsford.

Jenks, C. (1990) *Childhood.* London: Routledge.

Jenks, C. (ed.) (1998) *Core Sociological Dichotomies.* London: Sage.

Latour, B. (1993) *We Have Never Been Modern.* Hemel Hempstead: Harvester/Wheatsheaf.

Lavalette, M. (1994) *Child Employment in the Capitalist Labour Market.* Aldershot: Avebury.

Lee, N. (2001) *Childhood and Society: Growing Up in an Age of Uncertainty*, Buckingham: Open University Press.

Lee, N. (2001a) 'The Extensions of Childhood: Technologies, children and independence'. In Hutchby, I. and Moran-Ellis, J. (eds) *Children, Technology and Culture: the Impacts of Technologies in Children's Everyday Lives.* London: RoutledgeFalmer.

Livingstone, S. (1998) 'Mediated childhoods: a comparative approach to young people's changing media environment in Europe'. *European Journal of Communication*, 13(4): 435–456.

Mayall, B. (ed.) (1994) *Children's Childhoods: Observed and Experienced.* London: Falmer.

Maybin, J. and Woodhead, M. (eds) (2003) *Childhood in Context.* Chichester: Wiley/Open University Press.

Maynard-Smith, J. (1982) *Evolution and the Theory of Games.* Cambridge: Cambridge University Press.

Montanari I. (2000) 'From family wage to marriage subsidy and child benefits: controversy and consensus in the development of family support'. *Journal of European Social Policy*, 10(4): 307–333.

Ogilvie-Whyte, S. (2003) Paper to the Childhood and Youth Seminar Group, University of Stirling, May, 2003.

Pearson, G. (1983) *Hooligan: A History of Respectable Fears.* London: Macmillan.

Pereira, M.E. (2002) 'Juvenility in animals'. In M.E. Pereira and L.A. Fairbanks (eds) *Juvenile Primates: Life History, Development and Behaviour.* Chicago: Chicago University Press.

Platt, A.M. (1977) *The Child Savers: The Invention of Delinquency.* Chicago: Chicago University Press.

Prout, A. (2000) 'Childhood bodies, construction, agency and hybridity'. In A. Prout (ed.) *The Body, Childhood and Society.* London: Macmillan.

Prout, A. (2005) *The Future of Childhood: Towards the Interdisciplinary Study of Children.* London: RoutledgeFalmer.

Prout, A. and James, A. (1990/1997) 'A new paradigm for the sociology of childhood? Provenance, promise and problems'. In A. James and A. Prout (eds) *Constructing and Reconstructing Childhood: Contemporary Issues in the Sociological Study of Childhood.* Basingstoke: Falmer Press (second revised edition, London: Falmer Press).

Qvortrup, J., Bardy, M. and Wintersberger, H. (eds) (1994) *Childhood Matters: Social Theory, Practice and Politics.* Aldershot: Avebury.

Richards, M.P.M. (ed.) (1974) *The Integration of a Child into a Social World.* Cambridge: Cambridge University Press.

Richards, M.P.M. and Light, P. (eds) (1986) *Children of Social Worlds: Development in a Social Context.* Cambridge: Polity Press.

Rose, N. (1989) *Governing the Soul.* London: Routledge.

Stainton Rogers, R. and Stainton Rogers, W. (1992) *Stories of Childhood: Shifting Agendas of Child Concern.* London: Harvester/Wheatsheaf.

Thorne, B. (1993) *Gender Play: Boys and Girls in School.* New Brunswick, NJ: Rutgers University Press.

Vygotsky, L.S. (1962) *Thought and Language.* Cambridge, MA: MIT Press.

Vygotsky, L.S. (1978) *Mind in Society.* Cambridge, MA: MIT Press.

Wyness, M. (2006) *An Introduction to the Sociology of Childhood.* Basingstoke: Palgrave Macmillan.

2

The Child in the Picture

Patricia Holland

This article draws on material from my book *Picturing Childhood: the Myth of the Child in Popular Imagery* published by I.B. Tauris, 2004.

POPULAR IMAGERY

The child in the picture

The London *Evening Standard* greeted the New Year of 2005 with a picture of a weeping child and a huge headline 'Horror plight of a million children'. This was the aftermath of the appalling tsunami that struck coastlines around the Indian Ocean on 26 December, 2004. As in many other disasters, the *Evening Standard* focused on the plight of the children: the most vulnerable of those affected, the least able to help themselves, the epitome of dependence. As the sort of image familiar from many reports of natural disasters and charity appeals, the photograph came from a familiar repertoire. It was part of a cultural image bank of instantly recognized pictures, and it moved the newspaper's presentation beyond a literal illustration of this single event. The picture was laden with half-articulated political implications, standing as a metaphor for the vulnerability of childhood and the childlike qualities of helplessness and dependency. And it implied (not necessarily intentionally) that child victims with a brown skin, like this one, are not only dependent on adults (parents and family) but on charity, the charity of rich nations giving to child-like developing ones. The purpose of the picture was partly an appeal to philanthropy, which was urgent and necessary. But, at the same time, it could not avoid confirming a relationship, which is all too easily taken for granted, between the poorer nations and those metropolitan societies that can stand in the quasi-parental position of giving and protecting.

The picture was an appeal to childhood as a universal value, as a quality that every child should enjoy, even if it remains a remote aspiration for many. At the same time, it recycled a reassuring image of childhood dependence, of childhood as an *attribute* – standing in stark contrast to competent adulthood and in no way challenging adult power.

Public imagery

In Western metropolitan societies, pictures of children are part of the texture of

UN charity warns of huge starvation threat

HORROR PLIGHT OF A MILLION CHILDREN

Figure 2.1 ***Evening Standard,*** **30 December 2004. Courtesy** ***Evening Standard,*** **Picture Getty Images**

everyday life. They carry powerful ideas and attitudes about the nature of childhood and, by the same token, are part of the lives of the children within those cultures. My research has involved a close study of this imagery, especially as it developed over the last quarter of the twentieth century and into the twenty-first century (Holland, 1992a, 2004).

I am especially concerned with *popular* imagery and *public* imagery, by which I mean imagery that is easily available, designed for indiscriminate public consumption and widely circulated within the media and public spaces. This includes news imagery which aims to inform; posters, advertisements, catalogues, consumer magazines and innumerable materials designed to promote and sell; the entertainment imagery of film, television and the internet; as well as post cards, greetings cards, museum kitsch, packaging and ephemera of all sorts – in other words, the incidental and the trivial, as well as the powerful and significant. Along with other authors (Baudrillard, 1985; de Zengotita, 2005) I argue that a discussion of such imagery only in terms of the accuracy or otherwise of its representation is not adequate, since images are themselves a powerful contributor to the public discourse and to cultural expectations. This wealth of interlocking images is embedded in social practice in many different ways and plays an active part in the mapping of social, political and emotional worlds. The imagery of childhood contributes to public narratives about children and their relation to adult society, as it deals with topics such as family relationships, sexuality, nature, schooling, education, violence, the move from childhood to adulthood and the limits of humanity itself.

This popular imagery of childhood is part of adult culture, not children's culture. Since it contributes to a general cultural competence, children share in it – but it is not addressed to them. It is *about* them, not *for* them. In some ways, real flesh-and-blood children seem incidental, a mere by-product, as adult society reflects on the meanings of childhood, the values which attach to it, the social obligations it entails and the pleasures it can give. Children see their image refracted through adult ideas and attitudes. However, despite this second-hand relationship, the imagery of childhood can have a real impact on children's lives, partly as it contributes to their consciousness of who they are and the ways in which they deal with everyday experiences, but even more importantly as it contributes to political and cultural judgements which bring real social changes, both in provision for children and in adults' treatment of them.

So, rather than studying children's responses to media (Buckingham, 1996) or the practical ways in which children make use of media (Livingstone, 2002), I am exploring the cultural environment which contributes to children's competence, their expectations and their social experience. And, except when it overlaps with adult media, I have not considered imagery specifically created *for* children, which, of course, has a rich and prolific history, whether in books, films, television programmes, comics, magazines or the newer media (e.g. Skirrow, 1986; Messenger Davies, 1989; Warner 1994, 1998; Bazalgette and Buckingham, 1995; Staples, 1997; Buckingham *et al*., 1999).

My research was carried out in the context of two newish academic disciplines: the 'new' sociology of childhood, which considers childhood as a social phenomenon freed from the value-laden, instrumental preoccupations of developmental and educational approaches (classically stated by James and Prout (1990) and James *et al.* (1998)), and the burgeoning literature on visual culture, which detaches a study of the visual from its art historical roots and explores the proliferation of popular visual forms and the nature of imagery itself (Mitchell, 1986; Barthes [1957] 1993; Mirzoeff, 1999: especially chapter 1 'What is an image?'). Images bring particular qualities to the discourse, partly because their implications are slippery and easy to appropriate and reinterpret, and partly because they have the ability to condense many meanings within themselves, very often underpinned by a powerful emotional charge. In considering the imagery of childhood it is essential to take into account what Roland Barthes called the 'pleasure of the text' (Barthes, 1976). Through their familiarity and intertextuality, some images have gained a particular resonance as 'desired' images – often in unexpected and contradictory ways, as I indicated with the picture of a weeping child. An image may display pleasure in precisely that which it condemns.

This approach to popular imagery means that my discussion is not about real flesh-and-blood children, but about child*hood,* as a social, cultural and political concept. I hope it helps to illuminate the complexity of that concept and the ways in which it can hold together different and contradictory expectations.

It is important to note that, until very recently, this all-pervasive popular imagery was a Western phenomenon, which means that its views of childhood are inevitably from a Western perspective. We would probably have very different insights if studying other visual traditions.

Childhood and visual culture

In recent years a new interest in the public imagery of childhood has taken several forms: at issue is who constructs the image and in what context.

1 *An intense discourse of outrage in the popular press prompted by images of children, particularly young girls, which are judged inappropriate.*

A critique of such images has accompanied debates about childhood which, on the one hand, stress children's weakness and vulnerability to exploitation and, on the other hand, deplore children's unacceptable behaviour. A key complaint is that the boundaries between childhood and adulthood are breaking down and children's childhood is being lost. Many authors have identified a *crisis* of childhood at the end of the twentieth century (Scraton, 1997).

The theme of sexual abuse has become a major concern, especially as the new medium of the internet has facilitated the circulation of pornographic images. It is illegal to own child pornography (whether in printed form or downloaded onto a computer hard disc) and also to access and view it. Such pictures are the more powerful because they are forbidden, and reports of their distressing nature play a compelling role in the public debate. Even *looking* at a picture of a child has become, at times, a suspect activity.

2 *The expansion of consumer culture and the increase of advertising, promotional and consumer imagery.*

Increasingly, promotional materials have constructed their own rich imagery of childhood, to the extent that it can appear to be the only source of images and popular meanings (Kenway and Bullen, 2001; Schor, 2004). In the early days of advertising, a picture of a child tended to be used as a sales prop, persuading adults to buy (Kline, 1994); then, as the twentieth century developed and prosperity became more widespread in Western metropolitan societies, advertisers first constructed 'youth' as a market segment, then targeted children themselves – both on the strength of their pocket money and on their 'pester power', their influence on their parents. The move from an image of sweetly appealing youngsters to assertive brats has been seen in this context. The trend is most highly developed in the USA, where cultural critic Henry Giroux argues that 'childhood [has been] transformed into a market strategy and a fashion aesthetic … the only type of citizenship that adult society offers to children is that of consumerism' (Giroux, 2000: 18–19).

3 *Studies of specific aspects of childhood and youth, in which imagery plays an important role.*

Many authors have discussed representations of children while exploring aspects of childhood and children's culture. Feminist writers, including Angela McRobbie and Valerie Walkerdine, have studied the social construction of *girlhood*, partly in the light of the feminist critique of images of women (e.g. Walkerdine, 1990; McRobbie, [1978] 2000). Dick Hebdige (1979, 1988) looked at the development of 'youth' as a set of vibrant subcultures and visual 'styles'. Considering the earliest years, Sandra Matthews and Laura Wexler dissected the popular imagery of pregnancy, childbirth and babyhood (Matthews and Wexler, 2000; see also Holland (2000b)), while Christina Hardyment (1993) reviewed the literature on babycare with its implied images of babyhood. Historians, including Anna Davin and Denise Riley, have looked at the transformations in the image of young children in relation to the 'Save the Babies' campaign of the First World War (Davin, 1978) and the provision of nurseries in the Second World War (Riley, 1983). In these studies of nurseries, clinics and state intervention in children's lives, it becomes clear that the *institutions* of childhood have generated a powerful set of definitions and images – which are often at odds with those produced by consumer culture.

4 *Institutional imagery.*

The increasingly specialized institutions set up for children have established a set of overlapping but socially workable definitions of childhood, and the 'desired' images which accompany them. Of these, the school is clearly the most important, but there are also nurseries, clinics, hospitals and medical institutions, disciplinary institutions and others. The more formal and enclosed the institution, the more rigid and regimented the desired image of the child within it (Goffman, 1961). Although such institutional imagery is heavy with ideological meanings, it tends to be low key and unexciting and has been overlooked by many commentators (but see Phillipe Aries ([1960] 1973: Part 2); Valerie Walkerdine (1984, 1990) on schools; Carolyn Steedman (1990) on the establishment of nursery provision, Andy West (1999) on children and young people in care).

The obverse of the institutionalized child is the child who is beyond such social controls. The twin images of 'waif' and 'hooligan' – the wild children of the streets – have long had a powerful presence in the imagery (Cunningham, 1991).

5 *'Other' children.*

'An association is constantly made between white children who have a correct childhood and black children who have none' wrote anthropologist Judith Ennew (1986: 22). And the tendency for *children from non-Western cultures* to appear in Western media either as the victims of disasters or as 'tourist' imagery – an exotic enhancement of a travel location – has been changing very slowly, despite the present era of multiculturalism and globalization (Urry, 1990; Save the Children, 1991; Benthall, 1993; Cohen, 2001). A study of children in Bangladesh reports the opposite. The imagery of children on Bangladeshi television showed 'the lives of children … as too well protected and too well taken care of', leaving 'many children and youth unacknowledged' (Blanchet, 1996).

Baroque imagery, the uncanny, *the gothic tradition*, is a different example of children's supposed 'otherness' which has had a strong visual presence in the media (Cavallaro, 2002). It reflects an underlying sense that all children are potentially alien, strange and impossible to understand, together with a fascination with the 'evil' which may be the obverse of a too innocent surface. Is children's attractiveness merely a 'mask of seemliness' in the words of Maria Montessori (1936: 189)? The gothic sensibility has been revisited in films such as *The Exorcist* (USA: 1973), and *Damien, The Omen* (USA:1976) (Petley, 1999). In recent years it has resurfaced as 'extreme' images, such as the advertisements for the Barnardo's children's charity, which envisage a destroyed future by showing a baby as a heroin addict.

It is an imagery that comes disturbingly close to a vision of abuse, and is linked to what has been described as 'neo-kitsch' which 'capitalises on an acquired taste for tackiness ... popularisation of camp sensibility ... refined decadence ... ironic enjoyment from a position of enlightened superiority' (Henning, 2000: 237).

6 *Historical studies and a re-evaluation of imagery from the past.*

The twentieth century concern with imagery as a carrier of social meanings has led to a renewed interest in the imagery of the past. The works of painters, photographers and other representations of childhood have been revisited with a new, reflexive awareness, which frequently draws on a psychoanalytic as well as a historical analysis (e.g. Mavor, 1996; Smith, 1998; Wullschlager, 2001; Brown, 2002). At issue in such debates are the pleasures offered by the image: whose are those pleasures and what is their legitimacy?

But above all, from the mid-twentieth century, an awareness of the imagery of the past has gained a powerful hold on accounts of children's history, and has focused attention on child*hood* as a dynamic historical concept, with ever-changing social and cultural implications (Coveney, 1967; Aries, [1960] 1973; Cunningham, 1991). It has given rise to persuasive narratives which locate the birth of the concept of childhood at specific moments in Western culture. My rapid review of these debates will not be a historical account, but will aim to highlight twentieth and twenty-first century rediscoveries, reinterpretations and re-appropriations, which have tended to focus on three historical, visual moments.

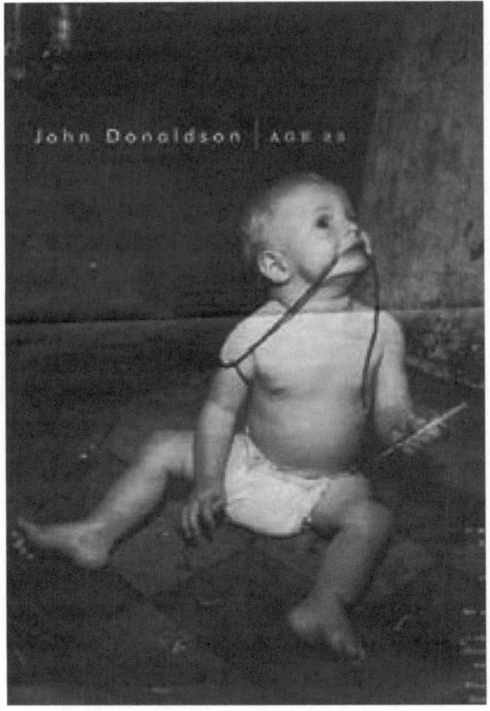

Figure 2.2 Advertisement for the Barnardo's children's charity 2000. Courtesy Barnardo's and BBH

THE 'BIRTH' OF CHILDHOOD

Discovering the birth of childhood: Three visual moments

Possibly the book with the greatest influence on debates around the nature of childhood in the second half of the twentieth century was written not by an academic sociologist or psychologist, but by a French cultural historian. In his 1960 study, translated as *Centuries of Childhood*, the representation of children as miniature adults in mediaeval paintings led Phillipe Aries ([1960] 1973: 125) to the much-quoted conclusion that 'in mediaeval society the idea of childhood did not exist'. Many strongly held preconceptions and convictions about the naturalness and universality of childhood were thrown into question by his observation, and the exciting prospect that 'childhood' itself was 'invented' – a mere social construct – was enthusiastically adopted by cultural commentators, if not by historians (see Cunningham (1991: 2)).

Aries's approach chimed with other key texts from France and the USA. Roland Barthes's ([1957] 1993) influential *Mythologies* revealed the workings of popular imagery (from toys to wrestling matches), and destabilized commentary on literary texts by developing a semiotic analysis that paid attention to structure and form rather than to content and portrayal; sociology was reinvented, as social constructionism was applied to diverse areas of study (Berger and Luckman, [1966] 1984); Michel Foucault (1972, 1977) argued that history should be read not as established fact, but as 'regimes of truth', embedded in institutional practices, to be excavated through an archaeology of knowledge. In the UK, Raymond Williams's (1958) *Culture and Society* reassessed the history and meaning of 'culture' itself. Scepticism and irreverence were in the air. In the following decade a radical student movement evolved which spilt over into schools, and was taken up by a short-lived, but vocal, Children's Liberation Movement – which created an impudent imagery of its own. For a brief moment, the voices of children were heard in the public debate (Wagg, 1996; Holland, 2004: chapter 4).

Traditional forms of schooling were questioned by many writers – often from poorer societies, such as Paolo Freire (1972) from Brazil and Ivan Illich (1971) from Mexico, whose work struck a campaigning note and

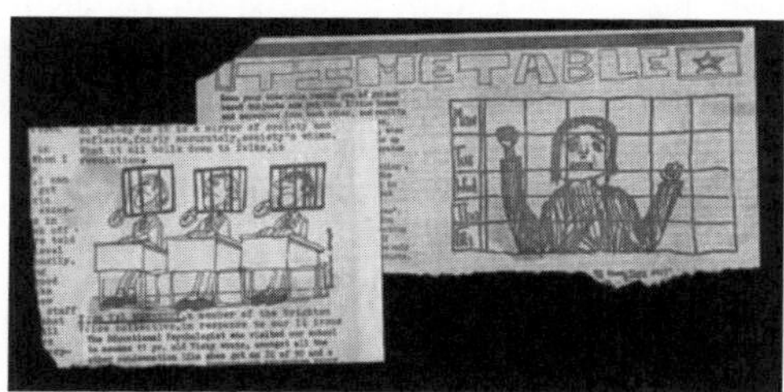

Figure 2.3 'Schools as prisons' from 'School Kids' magazines, early 1970s

straddled the academic and the popular. Accepted forms of discipline were challenged and the notion of 'childishness' was itself seen as oppressive (see *Escape from Childhood* by John Holt (1975)).

The study of childhood imagery was launched within a context, which saw 'taken-for-granted' attitudes as themselves an object of study, and refused to accept stereotypes and established meanings (Hoyles, 1979). Attention was focused on the social *concept* of childhood, as much as the actual facts of children's lives. It was a striking shift in perception.

Romanticism and enlightenment values

For the literary historian Peter Coveney, writing in Britain in the 1950s, images of childhood were reflected in poetry and fiction. (His study was originally published as *Poor Monkey* in 1957 and re-titled *The Image of Childhood* in 1967). If Aries placed the invention of childhood in the late Middle Ages, Coveney emphasized a second moment of its birth. Childhood was central to the 18th century cult of sensibility, which culminated in the Romantic movement which swept across the arts. Coveney (1967: 31) wrote:

> The child could be seen as the symbol of the artist's dissatisfaction with the society which was in the process of harsh development about him. In a world given increasingly to utilitarian values and the machine, a child could become the symbol of Imagination and Sensibility, a symbol of Nature set against the forces abroad in society actively de-naturing humanity.

'Innocence' was key. Anne Higgonnet, who called her detailed exploration of pictures of children from the late eighteenth century onwards *Pictures of Innocence*, identified five ways in which the innocence of the child was proclaimed, all 'concentrating on the body in order to diminish its corporeality': they were children in special costumes; children with pets; naked children, babies, angels, cupids; babies with a mother attached; children unconsciously pre-figuring adult gender roles (Higgonnet, 1998: 33).

e evocation of a childhood as a state was also a move towards a alism in the recognition of children's ırt of an Enlightenment discourse on humanity, rationality and rights (Porter, 2000: chapter 15). Practical advice on avoiding the corruptions of rigid education and forced learning was offered by the philosopher Jean-Jaques Rousseau, who insisted 'a child must be a child before he is a man'. His book *Emile* (1762) 'admitted floods of light and air into the tightly closed nurseries and schoolrooms .... It was the charter of youthful deliverance' wrote a contemporary commentator (Coveney, 1967: 43).

Emile was highly influential; the British artist Sir Joshua Reynolds painted his sister, the mother of five children, reading it (Postle, 2005: 20). Portraitists such as Thomas Gainsborough (1727–1788) and Thomas Lawrence (1769–1830) reflected the new mood. Their children are dressed in looser, more comfortable clothes, instead of the smaller versions of adult dress of earlier decades; they are portrayed at play, chasing a butterfly or climbing a tree, rather than posing stiffly alongside their family; and more attention is paid to a realistic portrayal of children's bodies – with different proportions from those of adults (Postle, 2005).

But for Higgonnet, Sir Joshua Reynolds's *The Age of Innocence* (*c*. 1788), which shows a girl of about four, sitting under a tree in a loose white dress, looking dreamily into the distance, was a pivotal moment in the construction of the archetypal Romantic image.

It was pivotal in other ways, too, as it became, in the words of art historian Martin Postle, 'the commercial face of childhood'. As well as commissioned portraits, painters of the time produced 'fancy pictures' – a popular genre of images that could be reproduced for sale by engravers and copiers. The evocative title of *The Age of Innocence* was given not by Reynolds himself, but added after his death by the print maker who marketed engravings of the picture. It went on to be 'replicated in prints, postcards and countless ephemera on both sides of the Atlantic' (Postle, 2005: 7–8).

Figure 2.4 Sir Joshua Reynolds's *The Age of Innocence, c.* 1788. Courtesy Tate London

Victorian commerce and the marketing of sentiment

As important for present-day visions of childhood was a third possible moment of its birth: the late nineteenth century. The image of the child was embedded in the new technologies which astounded the 1890s: moving pictures; the mass circulation press, soon to be with photographs; display advertising and posters; the lightweight easy-to-use Kodak camera, which enabled families to create their own archive of personal images (Holland, 2000a; West, 2000). The imagery of childhood could now take several different, but interrelated, forms: personal, entertaining, informational and, above all, promotional.

In many ways, photography was the key. From the 1840s it brought the ability to record the surrounding world with an apparently unmediated accuracy. For art historian Carol Mavor, 'Childhood as we now understand it, innocent and pure ... was perfected side by side with the development of photography' (Mavor, 2002: 27). The claims made by the photographic image to innocence, authenticity and simplicity paralleled the establishment of innocence as a quality of childhood (Holland, 1992b). But photography had many different facets. It could also be part of a rational approach to childhood, helping to understand infancy as a phenomenon and to record children's development with unprecedented accuracy. A continuing strand in the imagery of childhood has been the high level of scrutiny and observation to which children have been subjected, whether in the name of science and understanding (child development, child psychology) or simply greater control.

But photography was also part of a Victorian 'cult of the child' – an idealization of childhood reflected in different ways in the pictures of artists such as Julia Margaret Cameron and Lewis Carroll. Recent writers have revisited such imagery with the newer awareness of the sexual potential in relations between adults and children (Mavor, 1996; Smith, 1998; Wullschlager, 2001; Brown, 2002). More controversially, James Kincaid (1992) has argued that the open eroticism of a more explicit strand of Victorian imagery (including the hidden undergrowth of pornography) is an inevitable part of relations between adults and children.

Photography, with all its attractions and multiple meanings, could also be mass-produced to gratify popular taste. In the mid-nineteenth century, photographic cards were collected in special albums: royalty and celebrities were favourites, including the Princess of Wales giving her daughter a piggy-back (Linkman, 1993: 68). Picture postcards, with a repertoire of views, quaint characters, jokes and appealing children, gained huge popularity from the 1890s (Willoughby, 1992). The romantic view of childhood rapidly became popular kitsch.

Kitsch combined brash vulgarity with what some saw as the embarrassing pretentiousness of the aspirant classes (Calinescu, 1987: 230). Kitsch art, including popular pictures of children, evolved as a form of visual pleasure which could easily slide into a working class front parlour – becoming part of the widening cult of domesticity which put children at its centre. And the image of childhood was already part of an evolving consumer culture (Kline, 1994). One of the most famous pictures of a child, a little boy with curly hair and a lacy collar, gazing up at some floating iridescent bubbles, was sold by its creator, John Everett Millais, to the Pears Company in 1886 for £2,200 for use as an advertisement. Pears added a bar of soap at the bottom of the picture (McLintock, 1995).

(Several writers have reflected on the linking of soap with early twentieth century childhood. Soap stood for cleanliness, the medicalization of childhood as well as the increasing prosperity of the working class (Cunningham, 1995: 153); cleanliness was linked to moral purity and innocence. It figured in the increasing overlap between

Figure 2.5 Bubbles as an advertisement for Pears Soap. John Everett Millais 1886. Postcard 1910

child development studies, advice literature and the promotion of useful products (Kline, 1994: 53). And, in the age of high colonialism, soap also signified 'whiteness'. For Anne McLintock the overall Pears promotion represented 'commodity racism'. One advertisement shows a black child in a bath, being scrubbed white (McLintock, 1995: 213).)

But a shift of perspective reveals a different archaeology of images. In his study of representations of children since the seventeenth century, historian Hugh Cunningham illustrates a dual concept of childhood, 'on the one hand, properly happy and free while protected and dependent; on the other hand the children of the poor ... represented as both exploited and independent, slaves and savages' (Cunningham, 1991: 6–7). He argues that the conventional history of childhood is a 'story' which locates the universal values of 'childhood' – the need for protection from abuse and inappropriate sexuality; the separation from the adult world and from economic activity; its location at the heart of a consuming, well provided for home – in middle-class nineteenth century practices. In contrast, the children of the poor were portrayed as street children who caused nothing but trouble, or as poor chimney sweepers, or pathetic 'waifs and strays' who must be 'rescued'. Cunningham (1991: 6, 233) notes how 'the representations constituted frames within which the detail of state and philanthropic action were formulated. They were a crucial ingredient in the formulation of state policy and in the establishment and functioning of voluntary organisations'.

A separation between adults and children, defined as two mutually exclusive groups, was at the basis of both the romantic and the rational concepts of childhood. And Aries ([1960] 1973: 301) argued that separation by social class went along with separation by age. Separate provision for children would improve their objective conditions, get them out of workplaces which exploited them, off the public streets, and ensure that a 'childhood' was available to them. And the popular imagery displayed the desired qualities of such a childhood.

Traces

The great cultural theorist Raymond Williams (1981: 204) noted that at any point in time there exist 'residual' cultural forms which linger from a previous age and are concurrent with the dominant forms of the day and with newly emerging forms. It is not possible to make sense of the contemporary imagery of childhood without observing such traces from the past and the ways in which they have been re-appropriated. Many contemporary attitudes and expectations refer back to that lingering nineteenth-century moment when the cult of childhood blossomed in literature and the visual media. Images from the period remain part of the present-day cultural repertoire: John Tenniel's illustrations for Lewis Carroll's *Alice in Wonderland*; Millais's *Cherry Ripe*, the most reproduced painting of the nineteenth century; Little Lord Fauntleroy in his velvet suit and lacy collar; Julia Margaret Cameron's misty photographs of cherubic infants; Kate Greenaway's playful drawings. They still appear across the media (from book illustrations, posters and greeting cards to television programmes and internet imagery), and they continue to carry a powerful visual reference to the quintessence of childhood.

And traces remain in the continued evocation of innocence and its loss. A cynical twentieth century consciousness set out to debunk the sentimentality of the inherited image, yet the association of childhood with nature, freedom and spontaneity has continued to be part of twenty-first century attitudes. It is surprising how often that contemporary writers deplore changes in the condition of childhood not as an attack on the *concept* of innocence, but as an attack on 'innocence' itself (Giroux, 2000).

MODERNITY AND AFTER

Institutions: School

By the mid-twentieth century, the separation of childhood from adulthood was well established in the dominant ideology. Children had been gradually expelled from the public spaces of Western cities and became confined to locations designed especially for them. Schools, nurseries and adventure playgrounds had been created, their layout and equipment designed to suit the codes of behaviour and bodily disposition deemed suitable. Each institution indicates a *conceptual* as well as an actual space and suggests a particular set of possibilities for childish lives, constructed with the values and interests of the institution in mind (James *et al.*, 1998: chapter 3, 'Childhood in social space'; Foucault, 1977; Prout, 2000). While an important part of the public imagery of childhood (and many of its most 'desired' images) became institution based, the image of a child or group of children unattended in the public streets became a matter of serious public concern.

As an illustration of the prolific imagery generated by institutions – and of its contribution to political and ideological debates- I shall take two examples from the powerful institution of the school. The first concerns children of primary school age (5–11) when the markers of childhood are possibly at their most expressive; the second from secondary school (11–18), when the visible qualities of childhood are modified by the requirements of schooling.

At the end of the 1960s, echoing Rousseau, the Plowden Report *Children and Their Primary Schools* (Central Advisory Council for Education (England), 1967) recommended a primary education that would be 'in harmony with the nature of the child', in which the distinction between playing and learning would be minimized (but see Walkerdine (1990)). The report was illustrated with photographs of children making models, dancing, painting, working with tools – engrossed in their activities, with teachers hardly visible.

But the Plowden-style child-centred classroom became an object of scorn for an unsympathetic press, for whom a confusion between learning and playing was symptomatic of disorder and political subversion – and their criticisms centred on the image:

> Gone are the two-by-two rows of desks. Pupils sit haphazardly grouped at work tables ... one half of the class were sitting with their backs to the blackboard. (*London Evening News* 9.5.1978).

The campaign was on to change the image, to get the teacher back at the front of the class and the desks in orderly lines. The preferred image of a 'traditional' classroom associated itself with educational 'standards', implying they must be imposed on children rather than drawn out of them.

When state-funded secondary education was hesitantly established at the beginning of the twentieth century, Robert Morant, the civil servant in charge of implementing the 1902 Education Act, wrote that 'uniforms, badges and latin mottoes' were the essential characteristics of a true secondary school. At the beginning of the twenty-first century, despite the new glass-clad city academies and the possibility of commercially run 'trust schools', the visible signs of the 'best' education still include the teacher's gown, the monastic cloister and the gothic arch. Wilfred Carr and Anthony Hartnett write: 'To come into contact with the formal academic curriculum, English working class children have to pass through another "symbolic universe" of uniforms, honours boards, prize days ... etc. ...' (Carr and Hartnett, 1996: 120). This 'invention of tradition' is also discussed by Bell and Grant (1974) and Hobsbawm and Ranger ([1983] 1992).

Youth: Bad behaviour – 'evil' children

Anxieties about children who remain outside the established institutions have returned regularly to the popular media. In the UK, the mid-1990s saw an event which would define childhood for the decade. This was the murder of 2-year-old James Bulger by two 11-year-old boys. James was abducted in a shopping mall in a suburb of Liverpool, and a low-resolution frame from a surveillance camera became an iconic image which signified

Figure 2.6 Enhanced frame from a security camera showing the abduction of James Bulger 1993. Courtesy Mercury Press, Liverpool

both the vulnerability of children and their potential for uncontrolled viciousness. The image (enhanced on behalf of the Liverpool police by a local photographic agency and reproduced in many different formats and layouts across the media) shows the boys leading the 2-year-old away – ironically under a shop sign, Mothercare. The image became a near compulsory reference in academic texts on visual culture (Kember, 1995; Mirzoeff, 1999: 2) as well as childhood. The crime provoked an outpouring of soul searching on the nature of children and childhood, as well as an intense debate on child criminality and the age of responsibility. How was it, it was asked, that children were capable of such 'evil'? The blame was put on a video (which, it turned out, the boys had not seen) significantly entitled *Child's Play 3*, and the image of Chucky (a demonic doll which 'played' by terrorizing children), scowling from the front pages of the tabloid press became the evil face of contemporary childhood (Franklin and Petley, 1996; Holland, 1997).

Several writers have traced the recurring discourse of young males as a 'problem' as they assert their presence in the public streets. Their activities are reflected in a series of 'moral panics' and an apocalyptic imagery of threat and disorder (Pearson, 1983; Hendrick, 1990). The phrase was coined by Stanley Cohen (1973) to describe the reporting of some highly visible confrontations between the 'folk devils' of the 1960s – the rival youth cults, 'mods' and 'rockers', who fought running battles on Brighton beach. As the cultural phenomenon of 'youth' developed over the second half of the twentieth century, many young people began to challenge their public reputation. They simultaneously engaged with and rejected consumer culture by constructing themselves as a variety of eye-catching images, based on musical taste and styles of dress.

It was an entertaining, if sometimes threatening, youth spectacle, perceptively described by Dick Hebdige (1988) as 'hiding in the light'. (At the time of writing the 'folk devils' of popular mythology have become the 'hoodies'. No longer choosing the light, these young people *literally* hide, shielding their faces from the all-pervading gaze of the surveillance cameras under the hoods of their jackets. It is an image which has, recalling the words of Hugh Cunningham, provided a 'frame', 'a crucial ingredient in the formulation of state policy' towards disorderly young people, outside institutional

Figure 2.7 In the Gutter, published by Quartet 1978

control, defined as potential delinquents (Cunningham, 1991: 6, 233).)

Girls and sexuality

The press outrage over wild and uncontrollable children (mostly boys) has been paralleled by a different sort of outrage over an image of childhood which is all about sexuality – mostly girls. As advertisements, fashion pages and teen magazines began to circulate a newly sexualized image of young girls, a prolific commentary on that image has ranged from a salacious interest to expressions of horror at the apparent violation of childhood itself. Valerie Walkerdine quotes the reaction in the *Sunday Times* to Channel Four's 1983 television series *Minipops*, which featured child singers and dancers

> lasciviously courting the camera ... [with] lashings of make up on mini-mouths and rippling leather wrappings around embryo biceps .... In the twinkling of an eye the childhood of these children seems to have been stolen from them (Walkerdine, 1997: 161).

The 'Minipops' were amateurs, but profitable industries have been built around 'professional' child models and other performers.

Henry Giroux describes the American 'pageant' industry in which pre-teens compete in beauty shows. Images like that of JonBenet Ramsey, the 6-year-old beauty queen who was murdered in mysterious circumstances, are supported by an army of coaches, stylists, make-up artists and others, whose trade magazines are filled with pictures of similarly posing children (Giroux, 2000: 51).

The history of girlhood has long involved a need to come to terms with the implications of the image and the attractions of youth itself ('you'd better grow a little younger – go back to your last birthday but one' Lewis Carroll wrote to one of his child models (Smith, 1998: 101)). But the public image of the young girl has long been required to repress or redefine sexuality. In the 1970s and 1980s feminist writers highlighted an ideology of romance in girls' picture-comics, which created a fairy-tale world in which a princess with flowing golden hair innocently dreams of her prince (Walkerdine, [1985] 1990; McRobbie, [1978] 2000). By the 1990s romance had given way to a much more assertive image, and what Anne Higonnet (1998: 193) describes as a 'knowing' childhood.

Figure 2.8 JonBenet Ramsey. Courtesy Rex Features

For writers such as Henry Giroux, such imagery is pure exploitation. However, both Valerie Walkerdine and Angela McRobbie, who have tracked the changes over the decades, point to its ambiguities, and the importance of the girls' own contribution. Walkerdine compares the 'minipops' to the young girls she has studied, who would love to be on television, and she remembers her own childish pleasure in dressing up and posing for pictures (Walkerdine, 1997). Both writers are clear about the political implications and power relations which underlie the image. For Walkerdine the key is social class. It is the little *working-class* girl who 'presents an image which threatens the safety of the discourse of the innocent and natural child'. For working class girls, sexuality and display can represent upward mobility, while the discourse of protection has a long history as part of bourgeois mores. 'The little seductress is a complex phenomenon' and the protection of childhood 'innocence' is an 'adult defence' (Walkerdine, 1997: 182).

Concern about sexualized imagery became linked to the public outrage over paedophilia and pornographic pictures which gripped the UK media from the mid-1990s. This escalated in the 2000s with the exposure of international pornography 'clubs' whose members circulate shocking images via the internet. The moral outrage generated led to an uncertainty as to which images are, in fact, acceptable. Children's nakedness itself became suspect, even when pictured by their parents. In London in 2001 the police threatened to shut down an art exhibition because of Tierney Gearon's oversized, brightly coloured images of her naked children; in 2004, another London gallery withdrew the work of American artist Betsy Schneider, who had photographed her 8-year-old daughter every day since her birth. The gallery became anxious when a visitor was seen taking photographs of the work. Significantly, in both cases the press took the opportunity to recycle the pictures on the pretext of a debate about pornography.

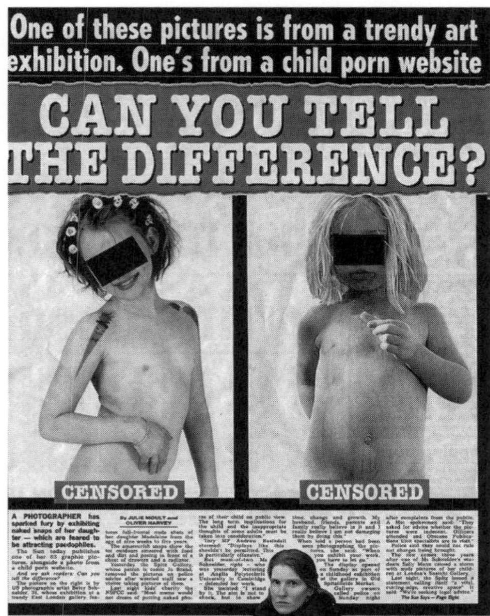

One of these pictures is from a trendy art exhibition. One's from a child porn website

CAN YOU TELL THE DIFFERENCE?

CENSORED

CENSORED

Figure 2.9 *The Sun*, 9 March 2004. *The Sun* published Betsy Schneider's photograph of her daughter, on the right, alongside a picture from a pornographic website, without her permission Courtesy News International. Photograph courtesy Betsy Schneider

The death of childhood: Total media and consumer culture

Premature sexuality, violent and uncontrollable behaviour and an increase in abuse and vulnerability: it is not really surprising that the discovery of the 'birth' of childhood was rapidly followed by a proclamation of its 'death'. In some ways such an announcement was an unsurprising consequence of the recognition of child*hood* as an abstraction and an observation of its contingent nature. Indeed, Peter Coveney (1967: 291) had placed the collapse of the concept at the beginning of the twentieth century, with the work of Freud and his revelation of infantile sexuality and the tumultuous life of the unconscious. In that sense it was a useful death, and arguably in the interests of children themselves.

But for Neil Postman, the disappearance of childhood (which he proclaimed in 1983) was brought about by the electronic media, which caused a breakdown of the all-important separation from adulthood. Television was a 'total disclosure medium', indiscriminately available in all its vulgarity and mass appeal (Postman, 1983: 142). For others, the death of childhood was due to the permeation of Western societies by commercial values to the exclusion of all others. The media are just part of an all-pervading consumer culture which is 'assaulting childhood' (Goulart, 1970) and 'stealing innocence' (Giroux, 2000). Advertisers, promoters and marketers are, it is argued, prepared to exploit both the image of childhood and children themselves.

The removal of children from the work place and the separation of their needs from those of adults had changed their economic role from producers to consumers. At the same time, the extension of a protected childhood across the social spectrum created marketing opportunities for consumer goods designed especially for them (Zelizer, 1985). By the early twentieth century the technologies of mass production brought an ever-widening range of toys and many other branded products (Kline, 1994: 18–19). Advertising and promoting those goods generated a rich imagery of happy children and pleasurable consumption. The smile said it all.

By the beginning of the twenty-first century, powerful marketing industries had developed increasingly subtle forms of differentiation, creating products carefully tailored for different groups of children. New categories, and with them new images, were constructed – such as the 'tweens', assertive youngsters who do not see themselves as 'children' but are not yet teenagers (Schor, 2004). With ever more sophisticated goods, children are 'getting older younger' (the title of a BBC television documentary that explored the tactics of the Saatchi agency (1999)). In the UK, the late 1990s saw a spate of television programmes following consuming children, particularly little girls who long for adult fashions (*Mini-me: Kids who have it all*, Channel 5, 2002; *What kids want and how they get it*, BBC, 2001). (Interestingly, by allowing children to discuss their carefully planned tactics for persuading their parents to buy, such programmes do much to assert their individuality and agency.)

Figure 2.10 Party Pieces 2007 catalogue. Courtesy Party Pieces. Photograph Millie Pillaington

However, at the same time as targeting children as individuals at the expense of their social and institutional roles, the imagery of advertising has also tended to reassert a public image of 'the family'. The home was the first centre of consumption, and goods have continued to be promoted as creating family cohesion (see Davidoff and Hall (1987)). Whether for cars, washing powder, fast foods or package holidays, consumer goods are portrayed as sustaining pleasurable links between parents and children. (In her survey of advertisements in six long-running American magazines, Victoria Alexander (1994: 757) demonstrated that the portrayal of children as the centre of family life fluctuated over the years with 'fertility and child nurture cycles'.) The happy families of the advertisements may well be fantasy families, but, as the historian John Gillis (1997: xv) has demonstrated in his account of myth and ritual in family life, mythologies can create a sense of solidarity, whatever the real experience. So, advertising creates the perfect Christmas, the moment of togetherness over the Sunday roast and a positive feeling about family relationships. Childish values are seen as part of a family structure.

AFTER CHILDHOOD

After childhood?

'We are entering another stage in the construction of the young as the demarcations between education, entertainment and advertising collapse, and as the lines between the generations both blur and harden' write Jane Kenway and Elizabeth Bullen, surveying the Australian experience (Kenway and Bullen, 2001: 3). Much contemporary imagery of adults echoes that of children, for consumerism itself requires the childish qualities of self-indulgence, impulsiveness and playfulness. Marsha Kinder writes of a 'trans-generational address' with infantilized adults and precocious children, and several writers have noted the phenomenon of 'cross-over media' (Kinder, 1995: 77; Holland, 1996). John Hartley (1987) described what he called a 'paedocratic regime' on US television, in which broadcasters 'appeal to the playful, imaginative, fantasy, irresponsible aspects of adult behaviour'.

For Kenway and Bullen (2001: 8), this 'consumer–media culture' has 'transformed the lives of children, the institutions of the family and the school, and ultimately the nature of childhood', and there has been much speculation about what is happening to children in the totally mediated environment. An image of a child bathed in an other-worldly glow and gazing beyond adult horizons has long represented the unknown future, and since the 1990s that future has been seen as an electronic one. Nervous press reports suggest that children's facility with the newer media of mobile phones, texting, Ipods, high-speed internet connections and the rest have already taken them to realms incomprehensible to their elders. They 'will bring about "a generational explosion" a "social awakening" that will overthrow traditional hierarchies of knowledge and power' (see Buckingham (2000: chapter 3)). A new form of 'childhood' is born, transformed by digital technology, leading the adult world into a future based in cyberspace (for a more grounded account, see Holloway and Valentine (2003)).

A second image of an imagined future sees a social realignment of girlhood. For Anita Harris (2005: 1), girls 'are being constructed as the vanguard of a new subjectivity' (see also McRobbie (2000: 200)). An image is created which presents girls in their teens as liberated by consumer values from the constraints of traditional relationships. Girls can inhabit an apparently classless middle ground – and they are now 'heard from' as well as 'looked at'. In *Future Girl*, Harris quotes the Australian advertisement for Bonne Belle lip gloss: 'I know I will succeed: I have a brain, I have lip gloss, I have a plan, I have a choice, I can change my mind, I am a girl', inscribed over a wide eyed, apparently pre-teen face (Harris, 2005: 21). In this vision, the inappropriate lipstick of the minipops has become a sign of 'empowerment' (to use a voguish word) within the safe parameters of consumer culture.

Images of girlpower (originally stated as grrrlpower, beginning with a growl of anger) straddle popular music and television: the Spice Girls, Tank Girl and Buffy the Vampire Slayer (said to be a 'hero' rather than a 'heroine'), in which the image of the fictional or performance characters overlap with styles that girls can appropriate for themselves. 'Media visibility, public recognition and notoriety' are part of the aspiration. However, Harris recognizes the class difference which persists between media constructions of young women. Those who 'can do' must be careful not to collapse into the category of those who are 'at risk' (Harris, 2005: 10).

A closer look at UK television reveals another view, as a range of new genres feature children in very practical situations and leave much less space for a mythologized image. In the mid-1990s, a set of children's 'video diaries' gave an illuminating insight as children from many different backgrounds used camcorders to record their experiences (BBC Community Programmes Unit, 1996). In the new millennium, children's everyday lives have been publicly worked over, explored and examined more than even before. *Child of our Time* follows children born in the year 2000, in regular programmes which feature psychological tests, interviews, observational filming and a great deal of collaboration from the diverse families involved (BBC, 2000). And in numerous series with titles like *Teaching the unteachables*; *Bratcamp*, *Honey we're killing the kids*, and *I didn't divorce my kids*, advice on how to deal with 'difficult' children as often as not turns on the adults' own behaviour, attitudes and misunderstandings. In this brash new 'reality' genre, a somewhat paternalist mixture of child observation and 'expert' advice is moderated by the device of a social experiment, the participation of the children themselves, an element of competition and, perhaps surprisingly, by entertainment values. They have created a dynamic and participatory image of childhood, firmly rooted within real social relationships

Final note

Over history, children have been the objects of imagery, very rarely its makers. Their voices have had only limited access to the channels that produce public meanings, and even then the tools that are available to them have been inevitably honed by adults. Until very recently they have been defined as incapable of meaningful expression.

In recent years children have made a greater contribution to the public discourse, but the terms on which they are present have been both resented and hotly disputed – especially as their new visibility and economic power have been largely constructed by the demands of a consumer society, and challenge the nostalgic view of childhood as outside commerce and monetary values. But, at the same time, the discourse of children's rights has become more powerful. Children have been listened to more seriously and have participated more widely, and this, too, has contributed to their changing image (see Franklin (2002)).

Figure 2.11 From Focus on Images 1991. Courtesy Save the Children Fund

When Channel Four television ran a series called *Look Who's Talking* (1994), narrated and controlled by children, the biggest problem faced by the child presenters was being taken seriously as they sought to interview those in positions of power. For the viewer, it was possible to observe the *burden* of childishness, the weight of adult fantasies about childhood as they are borne by actual children as they enter the public sphere. It is only when children's voices are effective that adults' definitions can become less rigid

REFERENCES

Alexander, V. (1994) 'The image of children in magazine advertisements from 1905–1990'. *Communication Research*, 21(6): 742–765.

Aries, P. ([1960] 1973) *Centuries of Childhood: A Social History of Family Life*, R. Baldock (transl.). Harmondsworth: Penguin. (Original: *L'Enfant et la Vie Familiale sous l'Ancien Régime*. Paris: Libraire Plon.)

Barthes, R. (1976) *The Pleasure of the Text*, R. Miller (transl.), London: Jonathan Cape.

Barthes, R. ([1957] 1993) *Mythologies*, A. Lavers (transl.). London: Vintage. (Original: *Mythologies*. Paris: Editions du Seuil.)

Baudrillard, J. (1985) 'The ecstasy of communication'. In H. Foster (ed.) *Postmodern Culture*. London: Pluto.

Bazalgette, C. and Buckingham, D. (eds) (1995) *In Front of the Children: Screen Entertainment and Young Audiences*. London: BFI.

Bell, R. and Grant, N. (1974) *A Mythology of British Education*. St Albans: Panther.

Benthall, J. (1993) *Disasters, Relief and the Media*. London: I.B. Tauris.

Berger, P. and Luckman, T. ([1966] 1984) *The Social Construction of Reality: a Treatise on the Sociology of Knowledge*. Harmondsworth: Penguin.

Blanchet, T. (1996) *Lost Innocence, Stolen Childhood*. Dhaka: The University Press.

Brown, M.R. (ed.) (2002) *Picturing Children: Constructions of Childhood Between Rousseau and Freud*. Aldershot: Ashgate.

Buckingham, D. (1996) *Moving Images: Understanding Children's Emotional Responses to Television*. Manchester: Manchester University Press.

Buckingham, D. (2000) *After the Death of Childhood: Growing Up in the Age of Electronic Media*. Cambridge: Polity.

Buckingham, D., Davies, H., Jones, K. and Kelley, P. (1999) *Children's Television in Britain: History, Discourse and Policy*. London: BFI.

Calinescu, M. (1987) *Five Faces of Modernity*. Durham, NC: Duke University Press.

Carr, W. and Hartnett, A. (1996) *Education and the Struggle for Democracy: the Politics of Educational Ideas*. Buckingham: OU Press.

Cavallaro, D. (2002) *The Gothic Vision: Three Centuries of Horror, Terror and Fear*. London: Continuum.

Central Advisory Council for Education (England) (1967) *The Plowden Report: Children and Their Primary Schools*. London: HMSO.

Cohen, S. (1973) *Folk Devils and Moral Panics*. St Albans: Paladin.

Cohen, S. (2001) *States of Denial: Knowing About Atrocities and Suffering*. Cambridge: Polity.

Coveney, P. (1967) *The Image of Childhood*. Harmondsworth: Peregrine.

Cunningham, H. (1991) *Children of the Poor*. Oxford: Blackwell.

Cunningham, H. (1995) *Children and Childhood in Western Society since 1500*. London: Longman.

Davidoff, L. and Hall, C. (1987) *Family Fortunes: Men and Women of the English Middle Class 1780 to 1850*. London: Hutchinson.

Davin, A. (1978) 'Imperialism and motherhood'. *History Workshop Journal*, 5: 9–65.

De Zengotita, A. (2005) *Mediated: How the Media Shape Your World*. London: Bloomsbury.

Ennew, J. (1986) *The Sexual Exploitation of Children*. London: Polity.

Foucault, M. (1972) *The Archaeology of Knowledge*. London: Allen Lane.

Foucault, M. (1977) *Discipline and Punish*. London: Allen Lane.

Franklin, B. (ed.) (2002) *The New Handbook of Children's Rights: Comparative Policy and Practice*. London: Routledge.

Franklin, B. and Petley, J. (1996) 'Killing the age of innocence: newspaper reporting of the death of James Bulger'. In J. Pilcher and S. Wagg (eds) *Thatcher's Children: Politics, Childhood and Society in the 1980s and 1990s*. London: Falmer.

Freire, P. (1972) *The Pedagogy of the Oppressed*. Harmondsworth: Penguin.

Gillis, J. (1997) *A World of Their Own Making: A History of Myth and Ritual in Family Life*. Oxford: Oxford University Press.

Giroux, H.A. (2000) *Stealing Innocence: Corporate Culture's War on Children*. New York: Palgrave.

Goffman, G. (1961) *Asylums: Essays on the Social Situation of Mental Patients and Other Inmates*. New York: Anchor.

Goulart, R. (1970) *The Assault on Childhood*. London: Gollancz.

Hardyment, C. (1993) *Dream Babies: Childcare from Locke to Spock*. London: Jonathan Cape.

Harris, A. (2005) *Future Girl*. London: Routledge.

Hartley, J. (1987) 'Invisible fictions, television audiences, paedocracy, pleasure'. *Textual Practice*, 1(2): 121–138.

Hebdige, D. (1979) *Subculture: the Meaning of Style*. London: Methuen.

Hebdige, D. (1988) *Hiding in the Light*. London: Routledge.

Hendrick, H. (1990) *Images of Youth*. Oxford: Clarendon.

Henning, M. (2000) 'The subject as object: photography and the human body'. In L. Wells (ed.) *Photography: a Critical Introduction*. London: Routledge.

Higonnet, A. (1998) *Pictures of Innocence: The History and Crisis of Ideal Childhood*. London: Thames and Hudson.

Hobsbawm, E. and Ranger, T. (eds) ([1983] 1992) *The Invention of Tradition*. Cambridge: Canto.

Holland, P. (1992a) *What is a Child? Popular Images of Childhood*. London: Virago.

Holland, P. (1992b) 'Childhood and the uses of photography'. In P. Holland and A. Dewdney (eds) *The Child: Seen But Not Heard? Childhood and the Photographic Image*. Bristol: Watershed Media Centre.

Holland, P. (1996) 'I've just seen a hole in the reality barrier! Children, childishness and the media in the ruins of the twentieth century'. In J. Pilcher and S. Wagg (eds) *Thatcher's Children? Politics, Childhood and Society in the 1980s and 1990s*. London: Falmer Press.

Holland, P. (1997) 'Living for libido or childs play 4: the imagery of childhood and the call for censorship'. In M. Barker and J. Petley (eds) *Ill Effects, the Media/Violence Debate*. London: Routledge.

Holland, P. (2000a) "'Sweet it is to scan...": personal photographs and popular photography'. In L. Wells (ed.) *Photography: A Critical Introduction*. London: Routledge.

Holland, P. (2000b) 'Looking at babies: pleasures and taboos'. In J. Fletcher and K. Newton (eds) *I Spy*. London: I.B. Tauris.

Holland, P. (2004) *Picturing Childhood: The Myth of the Child in Popular Imagery*. London: I.B. Tauris.

Holloway, S. and Valentine, G. (2003) *Cyberkids: Children in the Information Age*. London: Routledge-Falmer.

Holt, J. (1975) *Escape from Childhood: The Needs and Rights of Children*. Harmondsworth: Penguin.

Hoyles M. (ed.) (1979) *Changing Childhood*. London: Writers and Readers (including Peter Fuller's pictorial essay 'Uncovering childhood').

Illich, I. (1971) *Deschooling Society.* London: Calder and Boyars.

James, A. and Prout, A. (eds) (1990) *Constructing and Reconstructing Childhood: Contemporary Issues in the Sociological Study of Childhood.* London: Falmer.

James, A., Jenks, C. and Prout, A. (1998) *Theorising Childhood.* Cambridge: Polity.

Kember, S. (1995) 'Surveillance, technology and crime: the James Bulger case'. In M. Lister (ed.) *The Photographic Image in Digital Culture.* London: Routledge.

Kenway, J. and Bullen, B. (2001) *Consuming Children: Education–Entertainment–Advertsing.* Buckingham: Open University Press.

Kincaid, J. (1992) *Childloving: the Erotic Child and Victorian Culture.* London: Routledge.

Kinder, M. (1995) 'Home alone in the nineties: generational war and transgenerational address in American movies, television and presidential politics'. In C. Bazalgette and D. Buckingham (eds) *In Front of the Children: Screen Entertainment and Young Audiences.* London: BFI.

Kline, S. (1994) *Out of the Garden.* London: Verso.

Linkman, A. (1993) *The Victorians: Photographic Portraits.* London: Tauris Parke Books.

Livingstone, S. (2002) *Young People and New Media.* London: Sage.

Matthews, S. and Wexler, S. (2000) *Pregnant Pictures.* New York: Routledge.

Mavor, C. (1996) *Pleasures Taken: Performances of Sexuality and Loss in Victorian Photographs.* London: I.B. Tauris.

Mavor, C. (2002) 'Introduction: the unmaking of childhood'. In M.R. Brown (ed.) *Picturing Children: Constructions of Childhood between Rousseau and Freud.* Aldershot: Ashgate.

McLintock, A. (1995) *Imperial Leather: Race, Gender and Sexuality in the Colonial Conquest.* London: Routledge.

McRobbie, A. ([1978] 2000) *Feminism and Youth Culture: from 'Jackie' to 'Just Seventeen'.* London: Macmillan.

Messenger Davies, M. (1989) *Television is Good for your Kids.* London: Hilary Shipman.

Mirzoeff, N. (1999) *An Introduction to Visual Culture.* London: Routledge.

Mitchell, W.J.T. (1986) *Iconology: Image, Text, Ideology.* Chicago: University of Chicago Press.

Montessori, M. (1936) *The Secret of Childhood.* London: Longman.

Pearson, G. (1983) *Hooligan: A History of Respectable Fears.* London: Macmillan.

Petley, J. (1999) 'The monstrous child'. In M. Aaron (ed.) *The Body of Perilous Pleasures.* Edinburgh: Edinburgh University Press.

Porter, R. (2000) *Enlightenment.* London: Penguin.

Postle, M. (2005) "'The Age of Innocence": child portraiture in Georgian art and society'. In *Pictures of innocence: portraits of children from Hogarth to Lawrence.* Catalogue of exhibition curated by Amina Wright at the Holburne Museum of Art, Bath.

Postman, N. (1983) *The Disappearance of Childhood.* London: Vintage.

Prout, A. (ed.) (2000) *The Body, Childhood and Society.* London: Macmillan.

Riley, D. (1983) *War in the Nursery: Theories of the Child and Mother.* London: Virago.

Save the Children (1991) *Focus on Images.* London: STC.

Schor, J.B. (2004) *Born to Buy.* New York: Scribner.

Scraton, P. (ed.) (1997) *'Childhood' in 'Crisis'.* London: UCL Press.

Skirrow, G. (1986) 'Hellivision: an analysis of video games'. In C. MacCabe (ed.) *High Theory/Low Culture: Analysis Popular Television and Film.* Manchester: Manchester University Press.

Smith, S. (1998) *The Politics of Focus: Women, Children and Nineteenth Century Photography.* Manchester: Manchester University Press.

Staples, T. (1997) *All Pals Together: The Story of Children's Cinema.* Edinburgh: Edinburgh University Press.

Steedman, C. (1990) *Childhood, Culture and Class in Britain: Margaret Macmillan: 1860–1931.* London: Virago.

Urry, J. (1990) *The Tourist Gaze: Leisure and Travel in Contemporary Societies.* London: Sage.

Wagg, S. (1996) 'Don't try to understand them: politics, childhood and the new education market'. In J. Pilcher and S. Wagg (eds) *Thatcher's Children: Politics, Childhood and Society in the 1980s and 1990s.* London: Falmer.

Walkerdine, V. (1984) 'Developmental psychology and the child centred pedagogy: the insertion of Piaget into early education'. In J. Henriques, W. Holloway, C. Urwin, C. Venn and V. Walkerdine (eds) *Changing the Subject: Psychology, Social Regulation, Subjectivity.* London: Methuen.

Walkerdine, V. (1990) *Schoolgirl Fictions.* London: Verso (including 'Progressive pedagogy and political struggle').

Walkerdine, V. (1997) *Daddy's Girl.* London: Macmillan.

Warner, M. (1994) *From the Beast to the Blonde.* London: Chatto and Windus.

Warner, M. (1998) *No Go the Bogeyman: Scaring, Lulling and Making Mock.* London: Chatto and Windus.

West, A. (1999) 'They make us out to be monsters: images of children and young people in care'.

In B. Franklin (ed.) *Social Policy, the Media and Misrepresentation*. London: Routledge.

West, N.M. (2000) *Kodak and the Lens of Nostalgia*. Charlottsville and London: University of Virginia Press.

Williams, R. (1958) *Culture and Society: 1780–1950*. London: Chatto and Windus.

Williams, R. (1981) *Culture*. London: Fontana.

Willoughby, M. (1992) *A History of Postcards*. London: Studio Editions.

Wullschlager, J. (2001) *Inventing Wonderland: The Lives of Lewis Carroll, Edward Lear, J.M. Barrie, Kenneth Grahame and A.A. Milne*. London: Methuen.

Zelizer, V. (1985) *Pricing the Priceless Child*. New York: Basic Books.

3

Managing Monsters: Videogames and the 'Mediatization' of the Toy

Dan Fleming

INTRODUCTION

A major online retailer of toys routinely asks its adult customers a monthly question about their toy-buying experiences and analyses the responses, obtaining a higher response rate and an evolving picture of trends, attitudes and explanations that is more revealing than any fixed 'snapshot' obtained by more conventional pieces of market research. Thus, February 2005 Question: What influences your purchase decision most? Answers: Children's requests 54%, Brand 34%, Price 12% (3084 respondents). April 2004 Question: How do your children find out about toys? Answers: TV 71%, Visiting shops 12%, Retail catalogues 10%, Playground talk 3%, Magazines/internet 3%, Don't know 1% (4139 respondents). June 2003 Question: Do you mind so many toys being linked to TV and movie characters? Answers: No 73%, Yes 13%, No opinion 14% (1678 respondents). May 2003 Question: Do you think that military toys are a bad influence on children? Answers: No 59%, Yes 28%, No opinion 13% (2223 respondents). January 2004 Question: On average, how long do your kids play with their Christmas toys after December 25th? Answers: One year 47%, One month 40%, One week 13% (3498 respondents). August 2005 Question: Are your kids getting older, younger? Yes 85%, No 15% (2824 responses). (Unpublished data, courtesy of Mail Order Express in association with *Toy News* magazine.)

What picture emerges from this small sample of questions and responses? It reveals that acquiring toys is a process driven largely by what children say they want, that what they want is predominantly influenced by television, that brands loom large in that process, that parents are by and large comfortable with the TV and movie tie-ins that feature so strongly on the toy shelves these days, and that fewer than a quarter of them have concerns about military toys, that as many toys are quickly abandoned after the Christmas buying season as survive beyond a year in the typical child's affections, and that a large majority of parents share Neil Postman's prediction that childhood is contracting fast (Postman, 1982). Is the invasion of the supposedly once more innocent world of toys by things from the adult world a significant part of that perceived contraction? The central argument of this chapter is that, culturally, this may be a necessary process. In order to develop this argument, the approach taken is more in keeping with Sutton-Smith (1986) and Kline (1993), in the sense of focusing on toys, culture and industry more than on child development and psychology, for which Garvey (1991) and Goldstein (1994) are better guides to the traditional research literature; also see Fleming (1996, 1999, 2003). In order to develop the argument here, two major questions are deferred until the end: those of gender and race in relation to toys and computer games, for the first of which Miedzian (1992, especially chapter 15) makes the 'worried' case, while Carr (2006) is rather more balanced.

TODAY'S TOY INDUSTRY

A few major global brands (Bandai, Hasbro, Mattel, etc.) dominate a toy market that is now inextricably linked to the media, and they rely on manipulating a cycle of demand peaks for specific, heavily marketed toys. Meanwhile, children keep up the pressure on toy-buying adults. Most of the latter (at least on the evidence quoted above) are not uncomfortable with the sorts of toy on offer, even if a traditional notion of the child might be disappearing fast under the onslaught. More than anything else, it is the very routinization (the normalizing) of this situation that makes toys worth examining today, though we may need to bring together a variety of perspectives in order to make sense of what the toys mean. While there are other ways of thinking about computer games, considering them as toys helps the comprehensiveness of the argument and, along the way, will reveal in return some interesting things about toys as more conventionally conceived.

'Exercise is very important. It keeps their weight down and makes them strong and active. Also, don't be afraid to scold them if they're making a fuss for no real reason. No one likes a brat that throws temper tantrums. So discipline is a must'. This is not some off-the-cuff piece of stern child-rearing advice for novice parents, but strictures from Lori Moreno, Tamagotchi brand manager at Bandai (interviewed in *Animefringe* (2004) magazine) for owners of Tamagotchi Connexion, the UK's best-selling toy in 2005 with retail sales of £12 million. The Tamagotchi Connexion range ('Connection' in the USA, 'Plus' in Japan) revived the 1997 Tamagotchi phenomenon after Japanese manufacturer Bandai's market research revealed, 7 years on, an almost 100% name recognition among consumers in key markets. Indeed, there is something almost insistently symbolic of the contemporary about the untranslatable coinage 'Tamagotchi' ('cute egg friend' comes closest), carrying as it does connotations of digital plaything, mobile communications, pet and 'mediatized' toy all at the same time. The little egg-shaped key-chained personal digital companions – the chips behind their miniature screens housing tiny, electronically represented creatures that grow, need attention and even die – seem very much characteristic of the times, even more so perhaps than Furby (interactive robot pet cum cuddly toy) which also got revitalized with new features and re-entered the 'top 10' lists in the Christmas buying season of 2005. These things capture a contemporary fascination with the seeming 'intelligence' of digital devices and channel it into the intimate relationships that children can have with their most treasured possessions. The infrared communication features of the new Tamagotchi devices allow their owners to communicate with each other, to play collaborative Tamagotchi-rearing games, exchange gifts and store information about each other's cyber pets. Truly a plaything for the mobile phone generation.

We can use the ugly but useful coinage 'mediatization' to mean the embedding of such objects in a media-constructed popular culture, with meanings circulating through object and culture in mutually reinforcing ways. This often involves spin-off toys from TV series, movies or comics (or vice versa, if the toys have come first); but not always: the Tamagotchi, for instance, is not a direct spin-off from TV or movies, nor has it migrated to those media. (It was an invention of then 30-year-old Bandai employee Aki Maita, based partly on interviews about their interests that she conducted with schoolgirls in Tokyo shopping malls.) But always there is a dense network of multiple media channels criss-crossing the space occupied by such toys and amplifying their significance. For the Tamagotchi this not only includes comics and computer games directly related to the toy, but also the broader influence of (the transnational intermingling that is rooted in) the Japanese comics and animation (manga and anime) that have had such a striking impact on mainstream children's culture in the West, at least since the Mighty Morphin' Power Rangers in the mid-1990s, and more recently represented by Yu-Gi-Oh! (a whole 'system' of trading cards and collectables supported by mixed-media variants). This mediatization also encourages and sustains a space for intense consumer marketing that can include everything from McDonalds 'happy meal' giveaways to children's clothing.

This space, moreover, offers encouragement to a range of participatory (sometimes virtually tribal) fan activities, especially in recent years for those mediated by the internet. These frequently embrace elements of self-consciousness and pastiche, not least for those who have just outgrown yesterday's fan obsession. Thus, a simple but hugely popular free online game was called 'Godzilla vs. Tamagotchi', in which, on a simulated Tamagotchi screen, a giant Godzilla foot is made to flatten scuttling Tamagotchi, with accompanying sound effects and blood. The game had to be taken offline after 1.6 million downloads became too much for the server:

> You are Godzilla [Japanese cinema's answer to the original King Kong]. Tokyo has hired you to wipe out the tamagotchi menace. You must squoosh three tamagotchi per level. For each tamagotchi you allow to escape, you will get in more trouble with the Tokyo city council. Get in trouble twelve times, and they'll replace you with King Kong (game instructions by its designer Kristen Brennan).

Roboraptor, another of the top selling toys of 2005, drew on a long fascination with toy robots and dinosaurs to offer a hybrid beast and machine, programmable to run and snap or to be let loose in 'free roam' mode, and looking part Star Wars machine, part prehistoric denizen of King Kong's Skull Island.

It is important to place these and other 'mediatized' toys in the context of the global toy industry more generally ('global' in the sense of American and Japanese concepts made in China and globally distributed). It is now an industry that tends to organize itself around three categories of toy: the big hits, like Tamagotchi, Roboraptor or Furby; the staple 'mediatized' toy ranges, typically those closely interdependent with TV, movie and comic versions, such as Transformers, Teenage Mutant Ninja Turtles or Spiderman; and the pre-school toys that seldom, if ever, share fully in these processes of mediatization, such as the highly successful and reassuringly 'timeless' Playmobil range of stylized plastic pirates in their island playset. There is clearly a permeable boundary between the first two categories, with some crossovers.

Although both industries feed the human need for play, the computer game industry has tended to operate largely independently of the toy industry (at least in terms of institutional and labour infrastructures, given the very different production processes involved) but is being drawn into the 'mediatized' networks of popular culture no less inexorably, with the recent King Kong movie, toy range and computer game among the most striking examples to date. The Playmobil toys, with a lineage that connects them right back to the birth of modern toy-making (in the post-Reformation diversification of the German wood-carving industry, when religious figurines were in reduced demand), are the stuff of traditional psychological understandings of the plaything. To understand the more insistently contemporary mediatized toy we need the conceptual toolkits of media and cultural studies as well, and a historical perspective.

TOYING WITH THE BEAST-MACHINE

Descartes saw the non-human world as made up of what he called 'beast-machines' (Gaukroger, 1995). Unintentionally, though not perhaps coincidentally, he gave us in that vivid turn of phrase one of the best formulations for thinking about the world as it often presents itself to the mind of the child – the world of which the child seeks meaningful representations, not least through toys. Children's culture is now (and has been for a long time) full of beast-machines, variously represented according to the techniques of the day in print, wood, fabric, metal, plastic, film or video, and digital bits. What is particularly useful about applying Descartes' term to these things is that it blurs the distinction between animal and machine. The beast-machine may be the steam engine or battleship represented in tinplate in the late nineteenth century, the diecast metal rocket of the Cold War era, the dinosaur as unthinking killing machine and nature's revenge done in plastic in the late twentieth century, or the digital King Kong of the early twenty-first century computer game. But even better, the term 'beast-machines' captures something of the child's likely puzzlement over the kind of life that these things appear to have: the paradox of the energy apparent in the merely mechanical; the paradox, too, of the machine-like power of nature's most fearsome creations, real or imagined. These must all be monsters (whether animal or machine) to the child, all distillations of what is at best perplexing, at worst threatening, while at the same time oddly enthralling, out there beyond the bedroom curtains, beyond the front door, beyond the television screen.

The King Kong of 2005–06 (movie, computer game, toy range, etc.) is a good example of the old beast-machine deployed in a distinctly contemporary way in the imaginative lives of child and adult. Like some of the other most successful instances of recent years (Roboraptor, say), King Kong's appeal is not just to the child. The adult who sees the movies, who buys toys for the child, who witnesses or intervenes in their use, who listens to the child talk about these things, may also need to experience, however subliminally, a frisson of recognition and significance when regarding the toy if it is really to work. Many of today's successful toys do not 'work' in the sense of doing something (chugging round an oval of rail or whatever), but they do work as objects of popular culture. Older adults are often not a little perplexed by this: the grandmother who takes a contemporary toy in her hand, registers that look betraying a complete failure of recognition and says 'But what does it do?' Their playability as objects is twofold, therefore. There is their playability as physical artefact – their manipulability as things in the hand. There is also their playability as symbolic artefact – their manipulability as things in the mind. Oddly enough, child psychology for a long time was relatively pedestrian in telling us much about the latter, tending to focus instead on theories of child development in which the toy in the hand finds a significant place in the fine-tuning of specific skills and competencies (Millar, 1968). This still carries over into the often silly things that people say about computer games as a training in manual dexterity and hand–eye coordination, as if the young player might just as well take up juggling to obtain the same satisfactions – or wants to be a juggler when they grow up and needs the practice. In fact, the latest game controllers seek, through better ergonomic design, to minimize the purely manual dexterity involved, so that being ham-fisted does not get in the way too much of enjoying the game. Older adults trying out computer games to see what all the fuss is about tend to find the required hand–eye coordination so initially challenging, even debilitating, that they cannot see beyond it to how today's computer games really work – to their manipulability as things in the mind.

'Peter Jackson's King Kong: the Official Game of the Movie' (2005) represents one of several recent moments of transition for computer games from 'closed' to 'open' play environments. Game design and related programming techniques that have been evolving for some time, and have certainly been present in a number of other games, converge especially powerfully in the King Kong game, thanks largely to the work of game designer Michel Ancel. These techniques are concerned with the relationship between scripted events, or the programming that drives the game action, and the in-game engine, the programming that generates an audio-visual world of settings, objects and characters. Until very recently the in-game engine only provided the environment, the container, within which the scripted action played out its options. The container may have become increasingly 'realistic', in the sense of being vividly rendered with a wealth of detail, and the scripted action may have become increasingly diverse, in the sense of permitting more extensively branching options; but until relatively recently these two components did not interact except in the most superficial of senses. So an action could impact on the environment and vice versa (a game character being played could knock a coconut out of a tree or be hit on the head by a falling coconut), but there was no place for the player to be except at the point of convergence of these interactions, locked into seeing and doing what the script permitted, step by branching step, each 'branch' of action strictly dependent on the outcome of the previous step.

This tension, between structure and agency, typifies the relationship that the playing child must inevitably have with toys that are spin-offs from movies, TV programmes or comics, which embrace most popular toys today. To what extent will playing with the objects simply follow a 'script' familiar from the screen or comic-book version? The whole point of playing with toys, of course, is that such apparent limitations are not limitations at all, so a Teenage Mutant Ninja Turtle can find itself face to face on the bedroom floor with a giant robot from Transformers. But the computer game has tended to dramatize the most determinist version of the structure/agency problem – allowing frenzied action, but only on the head of a pin, moment by vivid moment, with nowhere else to go. Some of the latest games have found the beginnings of a way beyond these closed systems. The King Kong game uses this freedom to include a 'perspective switch' for the player between the human protagonist's point of view (small, threatened, often overwhelmed) and Kong's (powerful, confident, empowering). This creates an emotional subtlety, especially as tables turn and Kong comes under threat, which is still quite unusual for a computer game. The game also uses the coupling of in-game engine and scripted action to generate a still unusual sense of agency: the player as protagonist can, in effect, turn and walk away from the scripted action. It is in this sense, in particular, that the objects in the King Kong game (human 'action figures', dinosaurs, Kong) have become toys, not mere illustrations of a script.

This allows us now to broaden the category of toy to include the digital versions in the computer game world, where up to now the computer game may be considered to have been technologically 'progressive' but very largely in this respect a regressive form, captivating but not liberating, overly dependent on closing rather than opening, to evoke Klapp's (1978) use of these terms to identify the embedding of the structure/agency tension in the very dynamics of information systems. More important, however, drawing something like 'Peter Jackson's King Kong: the Official Game of the Movie' into the orbit of our consideration of toys has another effect. It highlights something that may have been deeply characteristic of toys all along, but that only clearly came into view with these new digital incarnations: that the structure/agency problem intersects with the beast-machine fascination to map out a whole semiotic terrain on which toys have been 'working' for some time. The 2005–06 King Kong, in all his forms across the various media, is in this sense one of the clearest manifestations of the beast-machine.

COGNITIVE MAPPING: A PERSONAL EXAMPLE

I vividly recall a little plastic toy I had as a child, one that I had relatively meagre interest in initially, but which was to come magically alive for me. It was a green plastic soldier: an American parachutist, tiny Stars 'n' Stripes on one shoulder, some eight inches or so in height, clutching a moulded plastic rifle to his chest, with a hollow backpack into which could be folded a big plastic parachute and its lines of thin green cord. I threw him out of an upstairs bedroom window a few times and he plummeted to the ground, his chute popping out only long enough to break his fall onto the gravel at the last moment. He got consigned to a cupboard after that, until taken on impulse to a sports field one windy day and launched off the balcony of a pavilion overlooking the field. He soared into the sky, his parachute popping open and catching the wind. Up he went until just a speck high above; then the wind dropped and he floated gracefully down, landing out on the grass several hundred yards away. His journey probably only took 2 or 3 minutes but, nearly 40 years later, I still vividly recall the heady mixture of trepidation that I was going to lose him and utter excitement at his public adventure. Retrieved, he then spent several months taking pride of place on a shelf next to my bed. When I glanced at him I felt every time a rush of admiration for what he had done. But there was something else too. This was August 1968. I was 12 years old. The Prague Spring, a period of liberal reform in Czechoslovakia, had just ended in the Soviet invasion of that country. For several days I listened to live reports about the invasion from the transistor radio on that same shelf beside my bed. My parents, with a better sense of the geopolitics of the day, were relatively unconcerned, but my 12-year-old thinking had been formed by the Cold War and I simply believed that the Soviet army was on its way from Czechoslovakia to our backyard in Ireland. My little green plastic US paratrooper, symbolically brought to life by his having taken to the sky, was a deeply reassuring object. I became utterly convinced that an army just like him would descend to stop the Soviets from reaching me. Looking back, I remain astonished by the ideological potency of that toy with its tiny but vivid US flag imprinted on otherwise uniformly green plastic.

Several things are going on simultaneously in this example, and I take it to be typical of many interactions among toy, child and times, although there is no research to my knowledge on adults' memories of toys and so this must remain a hypothesis. As a 12-year-old I would not have been able to articulate any of this of course; it would not at the time have been accessible to any research technique in our methodological toolkit, so there is an important point to be made about how we might come to understand toys better from this kind of perspective.

The 'beast-machine' here was the whole apparatus of the Cold War – the inhuman military behemoths, ranged in opposition to each other, and the promise of ultimate destruction they represented, even (or perhaps especially) to the mind of a child. The toy paratrooper in 1968 was the manageable symbol of those behemoths, made meaningful by his soaring, magical power to transcend his own mere plasticity, to excite and to reassure. The events on the radio had all the seeming inexorability of a scripted action – this was what the Cold War was supposed to be about – but the parachuting toy soldier could take off unexpectedly into the air with an unpredictable agency of his own and quite possibly save the day. In fact he didn't in the end. Later that year I took him down from the shelf and orchestrated a 'nuclear' conflagration in the garden that reduced him to a broiling lump of molten plastic.

Cue a series of snapshots of other children with other toys at other times: the Transformer toy of the late twentieth century was a part familiar object, part beast-machine, saying something to the child about an era of unbelievably powerful machinery that seems to verge on being alive; the Meccano or Erector Set construction toys of the early twentieth century were all gears and girders, saying something to the child about the 'second' industrial revolution of rising productivity and building booms that made the modern world; the Star Wars neo-anthropological collection of action figures of the 1970s, with manufacturer Kenner selling over 26 million of their 90-odd little plastic aliens in 1978 alone, saying something to the child about cultural identities at a moment when that term, part product of globalization, had barely entered the public lexicon, or even the now forgotten Verminous Skumm toy, half man, half giant sewer rat, from the Captain Planet toy range in the early 1990s, spin-offs from an eponymous TV animation series, saying something to the child about a new world of global environmental hazards and mutating organisms. What these toys, and all the others like them, have to 'say' to children is not encoded in any adult-intended message per se. Rather, the toys, and the popular culture that produces and sustains them, encode something of the times in much the same manner as adroitly explained by Fredric Jameson in his numerous analyses of how the most resonant fictional forms relate to historical moments (Jameson, 1992, 2005.)

When it happens, this potent matching, or mapping, of toy, times and child tells us a good deal about the vagaries of the toy market. It is not easy to design deliberately for such powerful correspondences (or, therefore, to make a new toy that sells reliably), but some such serendipitous cultural process quite clearly underpins the success of these toys and so many others: from the late-nineteenth century tinplate trains and ships of Marklin in Germany (a shiny industrialized world in motion in new and ambitious ways) to the late-twentieth century Teenage Mutant Ninja Turtles in the USA (managing to be at home in a neon-lit post-industrial world of frightened cities and social disintegration). So, taking one or two examples and looking at them in more detail should help us to see what is going on in these other instances. It is also important, though, to note another set of processes that criss-cross those evoked in the examples already given. These are the processes through which the adult world imagines the child and reflects that imagining in what it makes (and buys) for the child – processes that often harbour an insistent imposition of gender categories.

THE ADULT CONSTRUCTION OF THE CHILD

This adult imagining of the child through toys operates on two levels. There is the level of the 'perennial favourites' on the toy shelves, the toys that adults tend to believe children want, perhaps even need. These are not, by and large, the sorts of toy already mentioned. Rather, they are the 'learning toys' that have the fringe benefit of helping adults to feel good about spending their money on toys and also the toys that evoke, to the adult mind, a simpler world, perhaps ostensibly the one of their own childhoods (such as Playmobil). Such distinctions are very age dependent, and there is some overlap here: a toy range such as the Lego construction sets even manages to be both things and, through its clever updating with digital components, to claim a contemporaneity of its own. There is seldom, however, anything uneasy or unsettling about such toys, which tends to betray their relative innocence in relation to the cultural processes being described here. This does not prevent them from selling well and consistently over time, where the other toys (the 'junk' from this perspective) tend to have their brief moments of intense marketing-driven mass popularity and then to fade. So the best-selling toy in the United States in 2001–02 was the LeapPad, a hand-held educational videogame console cum talking book, and in 2003 the device itself was only outsold by its own content cartridges. LeapFrog, the company that designed and makes the LeapPad, was propelled into being the fastest-growing toy maker ever. Undeniably good at what it does, and pleasurably useful to its young owners, the LeapPad still looks like something of an adult backlash against the popular 'junk' toys, such as the Teenage Mutant Ninja Turtles, that have driven buying frenzies in recent years. In those terms, it epitomizes perhaps an adult imagining of a child who does not want stuff like the Turtles, the Power Rangers (the latter the must-have objects of desire of the Christmas 1994 and 1995 toy-buying seasons) or the violence-oriented King Kong toys. There is something in the processes described here as operating around and through such 'junk' toys that many adults seem to like less and less. It may be no coincidence, therefore, that the conservative, entirely worthy and morally unambiguous LeapPad was the toy of choice in the United States immediately after the September 11th attack on the World Trade Centre.

The second level on which the adult's imagining of the child operates through toys is that of the child-like toy object itself, the doll. Nineteenth-century European manufacturing innovations led to materials and techniques capable of replacing previously stylized dolls' faces with a sort of mirror image for the child. The old styles of wooden, rag or 'pincushion' dolls, often homemade, then saw a rapid divergence into the 'plush' or soft toy on the one hand and, on the other hand, the papier mâché, wax, unglazed china (bisque) and eventually plastic-faced doll with its increasingly realistic appearance. By 1889 the French doll-making firm Jumeau claimed to be selling 300,000 baby-like dolls a week. Jumeau's approach, based on manufacturing an endearingly realistic face that played well with increasing bourgeois sentimentalization of the child, influenced Californian art teacher Grace Storey Putnam when she designed the 'By-Lo Baby' head for doll manufacturer George Borgfeldt and saw it sell so well from the 1920s that it came to be known as the 'Million Dollar Baby'. Some of the descendants of these dolls in the last decade or so, representing little girls and often collected by adults rather than played with by children, have a provocative verisimilitude that can be not a little unsettling, recalling the anecdote about Descartes' 'daughter': a lifelike doll called Francine, with mechanical parts, that he reportedly kept by his bedside, until a seriously spooked captain of a ship on which the philosopher was sailing threw her overboard.

The ambiguities, then, in the adult's imagining of the child – as good, as willing to learn, but also as controllable object – are worth exploring in detail. But only one aspect needs to be highlighted at this point, and that is the glaring mismatch between such conceptions of the child and the different image of the child that is refracted through the mass-marketed, media-interlinked toys we have been describing. These latter seem, if anything, so much more suited to the amusement of rogue psychoanalyst Alice Miller's bad, ugly, angry, jealous, lazy, dirty, smelly, opportunistic, inconsiderate, domineering, sadistic little other, on whom the culturally constructed label of 'child' sits uneasily (Miller, 1987, 1992). Miller's key argument – that dealing with the mismatch between 'good' child as cultural invention and actual child can be emotionally crippling for both parents and children – is not something that can be directly pursued here. But the resulting 'drama' of which she writes so eloquently is a persuasively described context in which the 'beast-machines' of the toy world do seem very much at home as facilitators of an unruly imagination and tools for young minds needing to come to terms with a world that is not nice.

That these tools are mass-produced consumerist objects, marketed with all the manipulative techniques in the sellers' arsenal, is only one version of a larger truth about popular culture: that things are complicated. A stronger version of Miller's insight – Lyotard's (1991) proposal that the child is inhuman until 'humanized' – allows that the child itself is one of Descartes' beast-machines until the adult world makes it over in its own image, and so the child might discover itself to be one of the 'monsters' it has now to make sense of, especially if the mismatch between adult expectations and how it feels itself to be is especially troubling and/or self-evident.

THE LESSONS OF TOY HISTORY

Putting on hold this possible insight into how the imagining of the beast-machine by the child may not enshrine a clear-cut separation of self and other, we can step back and seek to finish our very selective historical consideration of toys through two contrasting examples. One is the evocatively English range of toys produced by Britains (especially farm toys), the other will be the 2005–06 King Kong toys. The first is revealing because it demonstrates, in the form of a failure to become 'mediatized', something of the general shifts in toys' cultural constructions that we are concerned to grasp here. The second, with its tight interlinking of movie, toys and computer game, perfectly explicates that process of mediatization. In particular, we will suggest that the 'perspective shift' between the human and the inhuman in the King Kong computer game neatly encodes something of the process of identification that characterizes these kinds of toy more generally – especially the unruly 'junk' toys.

But first, to the bustling streets of the English industrial city in the 1890s, where the new industrialising energies were almost palpable in the very atmosphere. Victorian inventor William Britain founded his toy-making business, which would become England's oldest, in part to counter Germany's dominance of the toy industry up to that point. The solid lead German toy soldier in particular had been enjoying international success as an archetypal toy – although we need to bear in mind that the word 'toy' was itself still evolving, from labelling miniature representations of real objects for adult amusement to the more modern notion of a child's plaything. (The child with its need for play was also a relatively recent invention, it can be argued; see deMause (1976).) In 1893 William Britain devised a hollow-casting technique that permitted faster, cheaper manufacturing of lighter toy figures and Britains rapidly emerged as something of a national icon, representing not just a successful challenge to Germany on the battlefield of toy armies, but also a stereotypical image of the English inventor at the centre of a family business – the homely face of an otherwise increasingly impersonal market capitalism. Britains' product ranges nicely reinforced this iconic quality. Dennis Britain, grandson of the founder, oversaw the firm's successful expansion from the 1930s to the 1970s by complementing its toy soldiers with a hugely successful collection of little plastic farm animals and implements (having shifted into plastic in the 1950s), as well as other similar products (e.g. a distinctly English garden collection of plastic plantable flowerbeds and tiny flowers, and a 'Zoo' range, later renamed the 'Nature' range for a greener sensibility). All were deliberately aimed at a pocket-money culture centred around regularly acquiring another relatively inexpensive item to add to the growing whole.

It was the farm toys that developed a particular aura for this 'whole', launched during the First World War as the 'Home Farm' range, with all the connotations of something worth defending, and then developing over the years into a timeless rural English idyll of miniature portly farmers, long-haired buxom milkmaids, neat stone walls and wooden fences, healthy-looking free-range animals, small-scale husbandry practices and pristine farm implements, all representing a symbolic counterbalance to the increasing industrialization and globalization of agri-business. With the range still looking superficially confident in its own continuing success, a more stylized collection for younger children in the early 1990s finally distilled the imagery of the Britains farm into its most symbolically revealing. New flat-fronted plastic farm buildings with big open windows, set amidst animals and people now simplified to the point of being more caricature than realistic representation, looked uncannily like a summer 1846 picture in *The Northern Star*, newspaper of the radical Chartist movement in England. Reacting against the worsening conditions of the labouring poor, as industrialization got under way, the Chartists proposed a vision – a Charter – for reform, based on rediscovering a more harmonious relationship between man (sic) and nature. But their vision was already nostalgic, evoking an idealized farmed landscape as 'characteristically' England in a way that Britains would still be able to tap into so effectively some 70 years later. Ironically, no sooner had this late, even purer manifestation of its underpinning nostalgic impulse appeared in the 1990s than Britains ran into trouble. Despite launching a videotape called 'The Farm Year', for sale particularly in rural outlets where its farm toys still sold in loose form, rather than in the sealed bubble-plastic units suited to toy supermarkets, Britains could not enter the then rapidly emerging era of the fully mediatized toy. Meanwhile, the company's fortunes as a business enterprise mirrored the larger cultural changes.

In the 1980s, national toy firms were consolidating or selling up as the only apparent ways to compete with the big corporations that had begun to dominate an internationalizing marketplace. The Britains brand was combined with Petite, manufacturer of things such as toy typewriters, when the parent companies of both were acquired by Dobson Park Industries, an aspiring multinational with a fashionably diverse portfolio of holdings across various sectors, including mining equipment. Interestingly, Petite's original owners, Byron International (previously Byron Business Machines), had once made real typewriters, rooting this aspect of Britains' new corporate stablemate in the commercial realities of industrialization that the Britains farm had symbolically countered. Dobson Park then determinedly shifted the emphasis of their Britains Petite toy division towards global mall culture by releasing toys such as a Pizza Hut 'activity centre', a large chunky plastic carrying case that unfolded to form pizza oven, tables, cash desk, phone for takeaway orders, etc. With the Britains side of the new brand now badly mismatched with what the company as a whole was doing, and Dobson Park itself soon acquired by US mining industry heavyweight Harnischfeger as part of the latter's own attempted expansion through diversification, Britains Petite was sold off to US toy-maker Ertl. This had been another family business originally, this one founded in rural Iowa by Fred Ertl just after the Second World War. Ertl had had a successful range of farm toys of its own and wanted the traditional brand connotations of Britains. But this attempt to turn back the clock proved ill founded. Ertl (despite having licensed tie-in characters such as Bugs Bunny for its diecast metal toy vehicle range) was also having trouble coming fully to terms with the new kinds of media-interlinked toy that had been gradually reshaping the industry since the late 1970s, when Star Wars and LucasArts Licensing first demonstrated what could be achieved. In 2000 Ertl was absorbed by Racing Champions Ltd, which wanted the former's toy automobile range (meanwhile Harnischfeger had filed for bankruptcy, so Britains had had a timely escape). Having been embraced and then abandoned by ill-fated players in the new arena of industrial globalization, Britains was on its way to finding a very narrowly defined market niche for itself, one that tells us in its own way something interesting about the toy business in these new times.

In 2005 Britains was sold again, this time to a specialist US company called First Gear, and what they will concentrate on is traditional metal toy soldiers just like the ones that William Britain launched his manufacturing business with in the 1890s. In fact, the brand name has now been changed to William Britain. But these will no longer be toys in any meaningful sense: they will be aimed at adult collectors who will be buying the 'tradition' and the Englishness of the Britains name, now condensed down into small totemic objects deliberately designed to reconnect with the brand's earliest days in Victorian Britain, days when its brightly painted metal soldiers carried distinct connotations of Empire. This remilitarization of Britains and the distillation to cultural essence, in a sense, of a long history of representing England, reveal both a failure to 'mediatize' (and, therefore, to survive as toys) and, at the same time, the logic of the cultural processes that now encase toys in these systems of signification.

Where toys once reflected the material realities of the manufacturing processes that underpinned their own physical making (tinplate toys matching the Fordist production lines, plastic ones the emergence of flexible production), they now also reflect the symbolic realities of the cultural processes that underpin their semiotic making. Britains is uniquely revealing of this, because it survived against the odds by coming to reflect in the end only the symbolic reality of its own origin, having once successfully signified in its seemingly innocent little farm toys a whole national identity at a historical moment when such comprehensiveness appeared to be just about possible. This uncouples the toy's physical nature (as once again metal toy soldier) from the contemporary and also renders it nostalgic. And yet does the new William Britain's imperial little soldier, no longer serving a pocket-money culture, instead now for adult collectors willing to pay the price, still have lingering about him some vestige of that cultural function, except that his hollow-cast body now resonates only with an echo, with some trace of the empty symbolism still central to a newly militaristic world order? No matter, children's attention is most certainly elsewhere.

The story of Britains passes through two key moments during which the contemporary mediatized toy invented itself. The 2005–06 King Kong movie, toys and, especially, computer game may rather definitively mark the end of the second of these moments, as does perhaps Tamagotchi Connexion. In the first moment, LucasAts Licensing, based (appropriately) in California, invented the fully mediatized toy as we now know it, embedded in a new form of total marketing. The 1960s had seen a massive expansion of TV-related toys, direct spin-offs from popular TV series, from Gunsmoke playsets of plastic cowboys and Indians to the now iconic diecast James Bond Aston Martin with working ejector seat. But LucasArts Licensing took this principle and pushed it to its extreme, capturing the interest triggered by the Star Wars movies and channelling it into just about every corner of consumer culture and manufacturing industry. Food packaging all over the world had Star Wars scenes printed on it; you could walk on Star Wars sneakers and sleep under Star Wars sheets. And for at least a decade, between 1977 and the late 1980s, a wildly successful proliferation of Star Wars toys sat at the centre of all this, teaching the toy industry some entirely new principles.

What was absolutely timely about the Star Wars toys was that they were able to extract and develop a key theme of the movies: the opening up of a world in which proliferating human, alien and machine 'identities' jostled, intermingled, formed into shifting alliances and antagonisms. The *mise en scène* for this, the places in the movies and in the imagination where it was staged, the bars and cantinas, the public places (and there was even a top-selling Cantina Playset from manufacturer Kenner) prefigured something like Babylon 5, in the eponymous TV series of the 1990s, a galactic transport hub of a sort, characterized by an endless through-traffic of beings and machines of every conceivable kind. This putting into play of identity questions, so characteristic of science fiction's exploration of utopian impulses in representations of otherness and other communities, took plastic form in the Star Wars toys, mostly figures representing the imagined universe's alien and machine life forms, twenty-six million of which escaped into the world the year after the release of the first film.

We are now in a position to look back at the 1990s to see that the distinctive toys of that decade by and large just continued this process, expanding the imagined universe to include transforming robot life forms, mutated human-sized intelligent amphibians, various damaged superheroes distinguished by being not quite human, and a variety of toy beings that look now as though they were the products of environmental pollution, nuclear war, scientific experiments gone wrong or space expeditions that encountered more than they bargained for (Thundercats, Toxic Crusaders, Terminator, Power Rangers, Ninja Turtles, Alien, Transformers, X-Men and so on); even My Little Pony, in retrospect, seems to fit better than we might have thought at the time, the dayglow talking ponies every bit as much a mutated life form as any of the others. One apparent exception, the revived GI Joe in both a new large soldier doll incarnation, that reprised the Vietnam War era original, and a Star Wars influenced range of plastic action figures, also fits this second phase on closer examination. GI Joe came back from the first Persian Gulf War, in desert fatigues, accompanied by a very strange shadow called Snake Eyes, a character in both large 'doll' version and plastic action figure, whose scimitar-wielding, hooded appearance now looks uncannily prescient in relation to the video imagery of Islamic kidnappers hovering above hostages in internet-distributed videos; at which point the second phase of the mediatized toy, with all its sustaining manifestations in other media, makes an uneasy jump from culture to reality and crackles disturbingly like a short-circuit.

These toys, sold to children through the super-efficient control mechanisms of the new total marketing and, at the same time, carrying for the period in question these encodings of multiplicity, fit right into Jameson's description of a globalization that 'can indeed pass effortlessly from a dystopian vision of world control to the celebration of world multiculturalism with the mere changing of a valence' (Jameson, 2005: 215). The surcharge of proliferating identities in all of this, veering towards a sort of semiotic breakdown or schizophrenia in something like GI Joe's 'other', Snake Eyes, is not unrelated to something that Jameson finds in science fiction and the 'art literature' cross-fertilized by it, with particular reference here to Samuel R. Delany and Thomas Pynchon: utopian multiplicities that 'will assuredly be Delanyian ones, a Bakhtinian polyphony run wild, as with that hyperactive DJ husband of Oedipa Maas of whom his friends say that, when he comes through a door, "the room is suddenly full of people" (Jameson, 2005: 214); except that for children, inhabiting a Babylon-world with these toys, they are not really people at all.

And that is, more or less, the main point here. What gave the original story of King Kong its lasting appeal was the possibility of sympathy for (even fleeting identification with) the monster. So, too, surely with the little monsters and misfits of this particular toy world, at this point in time offering a possibility of sympathy or identification that is simultaneously at moments merely Disneyfied (crying for the anthropomorphized cartoon animal) and yet fleetingly something more, an opening of the imaginative reach to include things that are more intransigently inhuman, even horrible. (Heinrich Hoffmann, in his Struwwelpeter picture-book of 1845, sensed an imminent sea-change towards more sanitized conceptions of the child's imagination and got in there with one last dose of the horrible that went unmatched until more recent times.) This is where the well-intentioned adult pursuit of the 'good' toy, like the 'good' child (the one that develops learning and sociability), though not inherently unhelpful, can none the less stumble badly. The 'bad' toys may be opening onto something meaningful for children that has nothing to do with proper child development as conventionally understood and researched, and may be doing so not as a result of design (what is 'designed' is more the controlling apparatus of total marketing around the toy), but of cultural processes that are always working through and reworking possible formal solutions to the ongoing problem of making sense of things that are more and more anxiously challenging to sense-making.

PLAYING IN THE (CULTURAL) FLOW CHANNEL

I want to introduce some closure to this chapter, first by depicting these cultural processes involving toys in the following way (see Figure 3.1). This is an adaptation of Mihaly Csikszentmihalyi's (1992) notion of the 'flow channel' that characterizes our happiest activities, one that I have presented and discussed in more detail elsewhere. Where Csikszentmihalyi posits slipping out of the channel into zones of dissatisfaction that he calls boredom and anxiety, I have replaced these terms for the present purpose with the notions of 'imaginative apathy' and 'cultural anxiety'. Otherwise the basic dynamic is the same: give people something that involves too much challenge for their skills and they become anxious, give them too little and they become bored. (Tennis is a good example of playing something that loses its satisfaction very quickly, especially for children, if one cannot stay in the flow channel.) By cultural anxiety I mean a failure to find cultural resources that offer those formal solutions to the ongoing problem of making sense of things (if all we had to play with today were Britains farm toys I'd suggest this lack would ratchet up our 'cultural anxiety' considerably), but this remains more a label of convenience than a comprehensive explanatory term. In this expanded and adapted version of Csikszentmihalyi's original, the challenge may now be as much to do with the social world (with reality and its small- and large-scale perplexities) and skills may be as much cultural as practical, including skills in 'reading' popular cultural texts and objects. But what is especially interesting about the computer game is that it retains much of the original sense of Csikszentmihalyi's terms, even as it simultaneously engages with a sense of challenge in the world 'out there' and with the cultural skills needed to make sense of the proffered representational solutions.

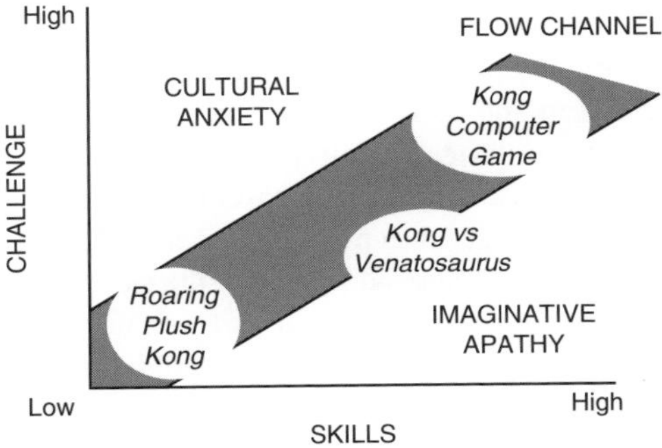

Figure 3.1 An adaptation of Csikszentmihalyi's flow channel to position some of the 2005–06 movie tie-ins for *King Kong* (2005, dir. Peter Jackson)

The contemporary King Kong rehearses in its toy range much of the history that has threaded its way through the discussion above. A beautifully made large 'Roaring Plush' Kong anchors everything, sitting comfortably in the long tradition of soft toys and dolls, even if its jaws gape angrily and (with a press of its chest) it roars with a not-too-frightening degree of menace. The success of this toy for younger fans, engaging as it does only a low degree of challenge and skills on both practical and conceptual levels, depended entirely on how long the marketing momentum derived from the film managed to last. It hasn't been long. Then there has been a proliferation of 1990s-style figures, creatures and playsets ('Battling Game', 'Skull Island Playset'), of which I have selected just one example: Kong versus Venatosaurus. Plastic Kong here has button-activated 'power slam arms' and Venatosaurus has a 'sweet-spot-activated collapsing action'; in other words, pit them manually against each other and Kong can knock its adversary into a state of near disarticulation, from which it has to be 'reset' by winding a knob. Other similar toys in the range reflect the movie production company's invention of a whole off-screen world on Skull Island, much of which only briefly or never appears on screen in the film version. The problem with these toys is, in a way, their familiarity as merely versions of those we have described above as populating a post-Star Wars toy world over the last three decades. Their comparative lack of semiotic complexity, of cultural resonance – their failure to approach closely enough to the sources of contemporary cultural anxiety, when compared, say, with Teenage Mutant Ninja Turtles in their time – would suggest that they were in danger of being met by an imaginative apathy, once the movie's hype died down. Indeed, their moment has evidently passed. The notorious Ninja Turtles, like sponges able to absorb all sorts of themes from the culture at large, are in fact still there on the shelves, more than 15 years after their first appearance, probably because the source, a thoughtful 1980s comic book about alienation by Kevin Eastman and Peter Laird, tapped into more that is still going on now than Kong's 1933 prototype can.

So it is instead in the computer game that King Kong comes rather triumphantly into its own. Indeed, in the longer term, one wonders if toys and possibly movie might not begin to look like adjuncts to (even advertisements for) the still-selling computer game. We can take the features described earlier in this chapter – the perspective switch between human and beast, the unusually open gameworld in which the player-protagonist can roam freely – and suggest that they dramatize in the very fact of being a computer game the things that the plastic toys cannot now get much of a grip on. In short, the new version of the 'beast-machine', a way of handling the structure–agency problem that seems better suited to how it is working out there in the real world these days. Digital Kong is about the apparent life in the new kind of machine, the energy that animates the string of digital code. Embedding this code behind the face of an old monster produces a plaything with which to imagine a new world. And in the consequent adult imagining of the young person as a player matched to that world (and as still residing within oneself, for the game's adult users), there is a *promise* of an opening onto a space of freedom. It remains just that of course: merely a promise.

SUBSTITUTIONAL TRUST AND DOMINANT READINGS

That might have been an effective note on which to end this chapter, were it not for what we have been largely deferring throughout: the questions of gender and race. Varney (1994, 1995a,b, 1996, 1999, 2002a–c) and du Cille (1994) are among those critics of contemporary toys who have insisted, against what they see as the sloppy generosity of claims such as mine for toys' semiotic openness, that certain 'readings' are always being 'privileged' (a respectable line long familiar from film theory) and that, especially where gender and race are concerned, it is, therefore, simply inexcusable to excuse what so many of today's toys are doing in this regard – the dirty work of patriarchy and racism – even while recognizing that children may not always 'read' toys unquestioningly. (For instance, du Cille (1994: 31) refers dismissively to the 'ethnic' Barbies as Mattel's 'dye jobs'.)

Varney (2002a: paragraphs 9–14) draws attention to the phenomenon of *substitutional love* through toys, whereby access to love that may have been worn thin by increasingly busy parents, by pressures on the traditional nuclear family and by growing cultural distrust of adult–child relationships, is regained by turning to, for example, a cuddly bear whose poignantly bleak marketing slogan is 'When there's no one else to trust' and whose substitutional efficacy well-intentioned but preoccupied parents (of the unworried kind in the survey quoted at the beginning of this chapter?) are all too willing to buy into. (See also Jacob *et al*., (1987).) My final proposition here is that *substitutional trust* is ultimately a more powerful explanatory notion than substitutional love in identifying the core relationship that may be at work between children and their things. Children trust their favourite things to deliver – to deliver sense and a sense of security, to deliver meaning and a defence from meaninglessness. That an aggressive white male vision of the world (and its projection of gendered and racial others) tends to determine the 'preferred' subject positions is both awful and yet secondary. Optimism here does not depend on children having some kind of innate capacity to come up with supposedly deviant readings, to interpret against the grain, to fail to internalize the dominant meanings of things. They may achieve all of this on occasion, but it is a bit much to expect it of them routinely in order to assuage our anxieties. Rather, optimism resides in the position-switching potential that play always already allows children: to switch empathy from white male 'action figure', say, to the enemy, the monster, the non-male, the non-white; not because the child has some unexpectedly clever capacity to resist dominant meanings, but precisely because the child is always already one of these others itself before becoming fully socialized (or positioned by hegemonic articulation, in another vocabulary) into forgetting, repressing or unlearning its own otherness.

Put more straightforwardly, will not the child automatically put its substitutional trust in a Kong toy, not in Jack Driscoll or Ann Darrow, who, given cinematic bodies, may be the gendered, racially determined objects of adult identification but who are ineffective as little plastic playthings? (See Rosen (1975) on race and gender in the original *King Kong* movie.) For older players then, the digital version of Kong, in the contemporary computer game, momentarily revives this more primitive engagement, cutting through the secondary elaborations of filmic and, one might say, social narrative to re-engage with play's basic position-switching potential. At the same time, of course, computer games of this kind function as 'mediatized' symbolic objects in ways that are in the process of replacing traditional toy objects, especially for boys. In that 'especially' resides the beginning of the rapid slippage back again into gendered and racial narratives that themselves function as mechanisms for managing a monster – this monster being the child that is itself momentarily other.

REFERENCES

Animefringe (2004), no. 10, October, unnumbered pages.

Carr, D. (2006) 'Games and gender'. In D. Carr, D. Buckingham, A. Burn and G. Schott (eds) *Computer Games: Text, Narrative and Play*. Cambridge: Polity, pp. 162–178.

Csikszentmihalyi, M. (1992) *Flow: the Psychology of Happiness*. London: Random.

DeMause, L. (1976) *The History of Childhood*. London: Souvenir Press.

Du Cille, A. (1994) 'Dyes and dolls: multicultural Barbie and the merchandising of difference'. *Differences*, 6(1): 46–68.

Fleming, D. (1996) *Powerplay: Toys as Popular Culture*. Manchester: Manchester University Press.

Fleming, D. (1999) 'Toys and games'. In R. Gottesman (ed.) *Violence in America: an Encyclopedia* vol. 3. New York: Scribner's, pp. 336–343.

Fleming, D. (2003) 'From Tamagotchi to Robokoneko – playing with artifical life'. In A. Nelson, L.-E. Berg and K. Svensson (eds) *Toys as Communication: Toy Research in the Late Twentieth Century*. Stockholm: SITREC, pp. 365–377.

Garvey, C. (1991) *Play*, 2nd edn. London: Fontana.

Gaukroger, S. (1995) *Descartes: an Intellectual Biography*. Oxford: Clarendon.

Goldstein, J.H. (ed.) (1994) *Toys, Play and Child Development*. Cambridge: Cambridge University Press.

Jacob, J.E., Rodenhauser, P. and Markert, R.J. (1987) 'The benign exploitation of human emotions: adult women and the marketing of Cabbage Patch Kids'. *Journal of American Culture*, 10(Fall): 61–71.

Jameson, F. (1992) *Signatures of the Visible*. New York: Routledge.

Jameson, F. (2005) *Archaeologies of the Future*. London: Verso.

Klapp, O.E. (1978) *Opening and Closing: Strategies of Information Adaptation in Society*. Cambridge: Cambridge University Press.

Kline, S. (1993) *Out of the Garden: Toys, TV, and Children's Culture in the Age of Marketing*. London: Verso.

Lyotard, J.-F. (1991) *The Inhuman*. Oxford: Polity.

Miedzian, M. (1992) *Boys will be Boys*. London: Virago.

Millar, S. (1968) *The Psychology of Play*. Harmondsworth: Penguin.

Miller, A. (1987) *The Drama of Being a Child*. London: Virago.

Miller, A. (1992) *Breaking Down the Wall of Silence (to Join the Waiting Child)*. London: Virago.

Postman, N. (1982) *The Disappearance of Childhood*. New York: Dell Publishing.

Rosen, D.N. (1975) 'King Kong: race, sex, and rebellion'. *Jump Cut*, (6): 7–10.

Sutton-Smith, B. (1986) *Toys as Culture*. New York: Gardner Press.

Varney, W. (1994) 'The playful sell: marketing through toys'. In S. Frith and B. Biggins (eds) *Children and Advertising: A Fair Game?* Sydney: New College Institute for Values Research, pp. 57–61.

Varney, W. (1995a) The social shaping of children's manufactured toys. PhD thesis, University of Wollongong, Australia (unpublished).

Varney, W. (1995b) 'Playing into corporate hands: the hyper-commercialisation of children's toys'. In S. Frith, B. Biggins and T. Newlands (eds) *Marketing Toys: It's Child's Play*. Sydney: Institute for Values Research, pp. 57–65.

Varney, W. (1996) 'The briar around the strawberry patch: toys, women and food'. *Women's Studies International Forum*, 19(3): 267–276.

Varney, W. (1999) 'Toys, play and participation', with commentaries by L. Bartholomew and S. Khanna. In B. Martin (ed.) *Technology and Public Participation*. Wollongong, Australia: Science and Technology Studies, University of Wollongong, pp. 15–36.

Varney, W. (2002a) 'Love in toyland'. *M/C: A Journal of Media and Culture*, 5(6). http://www.media-culture.org.au/0211/loveintotytown.html [April 2006].

Varney, W. (2002b) 'Bang bang! Ka-ching! War profits from the toy box'. *Social Alternatives*, 21(2): 41–45.

Varney, W. (2002c) 'Of men and machines: images of masculinity in boys' toys'. *Feminist Studies*, 28(1): 153–174.

4

Harlequin Meets *The SIMS*: A History of Interactive Narrative Media for Children and Youth from Early Flap Books to Contemporary Multimedia

Jacqueline Reid-Walsh

INTRODUCTION

Interactivity is an overused term. When applied to media for children and youth we tend to think of digital environments such as websites or CD ROMs that are 'tie-ins' to popular toys, games, and books such as *Barbie*, *Pokemon* and *Harry Potter* or to computer games such as *Paper Mario* for little children and *The SIMS* for teens. Yet interactive texts on paper platforms, such as moveable books, predate the invention of printing, and board games and puzzles have been produced since the earliest period of publication for children. This chapter presents a comparative cultural history of interactive narrative media for children produced in two periods of intense production: the late 18th century–early 19th century, when the commercial children's market first took shape in England (Plumb, 1982), and the late 20th–early 21st century, when, similarly, digital production is targeting the young computer user (Buckingham, 2000).

This chapter has three sections: the first section provides a historical overview of some different ideas of interactivity. The second section discusses examples of late

18th–early 19th century moveable books as interactive media: the flap book, paper doll book, paignion (paper dollhouse play set) and toy theatre, artefacts accessible in rare books repositories. The third section analyses two popular digital environments: the Mattel *Barbie* website and *The SIMS* CD ROM computer games as formal and ideological reworkings of contemporary and historical toys, including early moveable books. The approach to these narrative texts combines textual analysis of the interactive design and depiction of motion with a discussion of the role of the interactive implied reader/viewer/user (from Iser (1974)). The analysis is contextualized by a consideration of the social, economic and ideological aspects of production and consumption of these texts.

INTERACTIVITY IN A HISTORICAL CONTEXT

In the late 17th century, educational reformers like Thomas Sprat and John Locke expressed the belief that education (of young elite males) was not a passive endeavour composed of rote memory work but should be an active process appealing to the senses. Considering play a natural activity, they advocated that children should be encouraged to play into learning: 'I have always had a fancy that learning might be made a play and recreation to children' (Locke, 1693: section 148). Locke even proposed prototypes of literacy games drawing on the prevalence of gaming in the period such as pasting the letters of the alphabet on the different sides of an ivory ball (Locke, 1693: section 150).

Usually removing devices associated with gambling, the earliest English commercial publishers and printmakers for children produced educational games and toys. These innovators were extending active education to include the rising 'middling' classes. Some of these educational materials are still popular today. Examples include John Spilsbury's invention of 'dissected maps' to teach geography, educational cards such as a *Set of Squares* (1743) to teach reading, produced by Newbery and B. Collins, and board games that are precursors to *Scrabble* (Shefrin, 1999). Newbery describes a literacy game in his famous *The History of Little Goody Two Shoes* (1765) where the heroine carves letters on small pieces of wood in order to teach children to read. By making his hero a young girl, and the daughter of a destitute farmer, he is extending the educational message to girls and to the lower classes who sought to raise their status through literacy. Newbery was also an innovator in cross-marketing. He created 'tie-ins' for his first book *A Little Pretty Pocket Book* (1744) that depicted many children's diversions by selling gendered accessories for an extra twopence: a ball for boys and a pincushion for girls (Plumb, 1982: 272–273). By the turn of the 19th century, educational reformers Richard and Maria Edgeworth had developed a wide programme of active learning. *Practical Education* (1798) begins with a discussion of dissected maps, board games and other toys with educational applications such as blocks, dolls and unfurnished 'baby-houses'.

During the same period a few publishers started to develop moveable books, initially for didactic purposes and then for pleasure. Moveable books are texts in codex form designed so the illustrations and/or words are presented in the form of a device such as a flap, wheel, slot or pop-up. In order to make meaning the reader not only has to look at the words and gaze at the pictures, as in a picture book, but also to engage physically with the book by manipulating parts of the text, as in a puzzle, game or toy (Hurst, 1995; Laws, 2002). The history of moveable books is ancient: there are moveable parts in manuscript books from the 13th century and in printed books from the 15th century. Volvelles, or revolving discs, were used to illustrate scientific works, especially astrology and astronomy, projections were used to illustrate Euclid and flaps were used by the mid 14th century to illustrate anatomy texts.

The earliest commercial moveable books were simple, inexpensive flap books that appealed to a broad readership; later, more complex ones were marketed to affluent children. The moveable book reached a high point of complexity in the late Victorian period that has been matched today by the work of paper engineers such as Robert Saluba. In both periods these elaborate constructions are fragile, labour intensive to produce, costly to purchase and their production rests on exploited workers. In the earlier periods, moveable books (as all illustrated books) were hand coloured by children too poor to buy them; today they are assembled by women in developing countries (Montanaro, 2001).

The idea of interactivity has multiple and shifting meanings. Margaret Morse notes that in the late 18th century the term 'interactive' was used to describe theatrical entertainment that occurred between the acts of a play and that by the early Victorian period the term also included the ideas of reciprocity and influence between two forces. By contrast, the term is now used almost exclusively to identify a mode of engagement between people and machines, with the exception of its use in reception theory to refer to the cognitive interaction of book reader, theatre and film spectator with a text by filling in the gaps (Morse, 2003: 18, 32 n. 7). Regarding new media applications, Sally McMillan (2002) classifies different models of interactivity in terms of their respective emphasis on user-to-user, user-to-documents or user-to-system.

In her influential *Hamlet on the Holodeck*, Janet Murray (1997) explores ideas of interactivity in terms of user control and participation (McMillan, 2002: 164, 173). Murray considers the essential properties of digital environments to be that they are procedural, participatory, spatial and encyclopaedic, the first two properties composing what is usually understood by the term interactive and the last two comprising what is meant by immersive. She notes that procedural environments are appealing not only because they display rule-generated behaviour, but also because the user can induce the behaviour. She states '...the primary representational property of the computer is the codified rendering of responsive behaviours. This is what is most often meant when we say that computers are interactive' (Murray, 1997: 71–74). Murray goes on to adapt the term 'interactor' to describe the relation of the user to a narrative in computer games, for by choosing a set of alternatives from a fixed menu the user believes he or she is collaborating in the invention (Murray, 1997: 78–79). She distinguishes between playing a creative role in an authored environment, such as in a simulation game, and being author of the environment itself. The pleasure the interactor feels is not that of authorship but of agency (Murray, 1997: 152–153). To demonstrate the difference between agency and activity, Murray provides examples from different media. For activity she cites board games where the user throws dice, turns a dial or moves counters or in a digital environment clicks a mouse or moves a joystick. In both cases the player's actions achieve an effect, but these actions are not chosen by the player nor are they related to the player's intentions. By contrast, agency occurs in a game such as chess when the player's actions are autonomous, selected from a wide range of choices and determine the course of events. Agency goes beyond participation and activity to be an aesthetic pleasure, and she believes that a successful digital storytelling environment needs to possess this quality (Murray, 1997: 128–129). In the following sections I apply these remarks about interactivity to an analysis of different types of storytelling media on paper and digital platforms intended for the entertainment of children and youth.

PAPER PLATFORMS: EARLY MOVEABLE BOOKS AS INTERACTIVE MEDIA

Harlequinade flap books: crossover texts from the stage to page

Flap books are narrow octavo (word and picture) books consisting of a single engraved sheet of paper, folded perpendicularly into four sections. A second sheet is cut in half and hinged at the top and bottom edges of the first so that each flap can be lifted separately. When the flap is turned the viewer sees that half of the new picture fits onto the half of the unraised flap, which creates a 'surprise' unfolding of the simple story (Muir, 1954: 204, 209). Initially concerning biblical and moral instruction, around 1770 the topics became mainly secular. The sections of the pantomime featuring harlequin were especially popular; hence, these books came to be known as harlequinades (Speaight 1991: 70–71). These books were inexpensive commodities, since the two main publishers, Robert Sayer and the Tringham family, priced their texts at '6d plain, 1s coloured'. These two prices corresponded to the price of an evening's entertainment, the admission to most pleasure gardens and to the cheapest theatre seats being one shilling which was cut after the second act to sixpence. This half-price admission was roughly equivalent to the price of two quarts of ale, so would be within the limits of an artisan earning between £40 and £60 a year (Brewer, 1997: 92–93, 351).

The anonymous harlequinade books must be contextualized within the appeal of the popular theatre. In 18th century England, attending the theatre was a widespread practice that cut across boundaries of age, gender and class. Although the Licensing Act of 1737 had restricted spoken drama to two official London theatres, Covent Garden and Drury Lane (Mayer, 1969: 5), people not only attended official theatres to see spoken drama, but also flocked to other venues to see different types of performances and spectacles ranging from equestrian acts to water extravaganzas, to puppet shows and to different types of combination of musical, sung and danced entertainments, such as the opera, burletta and especially pantomime. These spectacular multimedia productions featured elaborate scenery, tricks and illusions, and often contained topical satire embedded within the plots. The core of the pantomime was the harlequinade loosely based on the Italian *commedia dell'arte* form featuring the characters of Harlequin, Columbine, Clown and Pantaloon and often performed in 'dumb show'. As with most popular theatrical performances, many pantomimes did not have published scripts, nor were they conventionally authored. Mounting a pantomime was a collaborative effort, and designers' and actors' names were usually included on the theatre bills and programmes while the playwright's was usually omitted. Attending the theatre was a participatory event, for throughout the evening the members of the audience socialized with one another and commented loudly and on occasion violently to all aspects of the performance. Attending the theatre was considered to be a right of a free individual and the mixed composition of the audience considered to reflect the constitution of British society. The right of the poorest to attend was entrenched in the mind of the public, for when in 1763 David Garrick tried to remove this concession a riot ensued (Brewer, 1997: 351).

Because the plot of a harlequinade is conventional, both theatre spectator and book reader know the outcome. Accordingly, in each mode the focus is not on the 'what' but on the 'how', and the narratives are propelled along by visual spectacles of antic transformation (Mayer, 1969). I consider the flap books as texts of performance in terms of the book design and in the role of the reader. In their appearance, harlequinade books suggest an adaptation of stage design and theatrical methods, including a representation of the characters as performers on stage, analogies between the flap and scene change, and the representation of the mechanics of stage tricks. For instance, in *Mother Shipton* (Tringham *et al.*, 1771), when the narrative states the characters are sinking to the underworld through the mouth of a coal pit, lifting the flap reveals a stage 'grave' trap to be in use. In *Harlequin Skeleton* (Sayer, 1772) the illustrations on the flaps not only relay the high points of the action, but the act of unfolding also recreates in miniature the impact of attending a performance. A key comic sequence begins with Clown alone in the old anatomist's study with stuffed animals and skeletons, including a human one in the closet. When the upper flap is raised (Harlequin) Skeleton becomes alive and seems to step forward. The humour lies mainly in observing the facial expressions and bodily attitudes of Clown.

The flaps are also a space for suggesting motion. One technique is by the careful overlaying of images in relation to the break created by the flap; see Figures 4.1–4.3. The focus on the reaction of Clown is broken down into stages so that when the flaps are lifted his body becomes animated part by part. Because the figure of Harlequin is restricted to the upper flap his animation seems to be achieved by placing slightly different poses one over the other, so when the reader lifts the flap up the skeleton apparently pops out of the closet. As both characters appear to move downstage towards the reader/viewer, an uninitiated reader may be surprised by the effect of their sudden movements. Since the depiction of movement recalls that of early comic strip narratives or two flicks of pages in a flick book, I consider this to be

Figure 4.1 Clown in the study

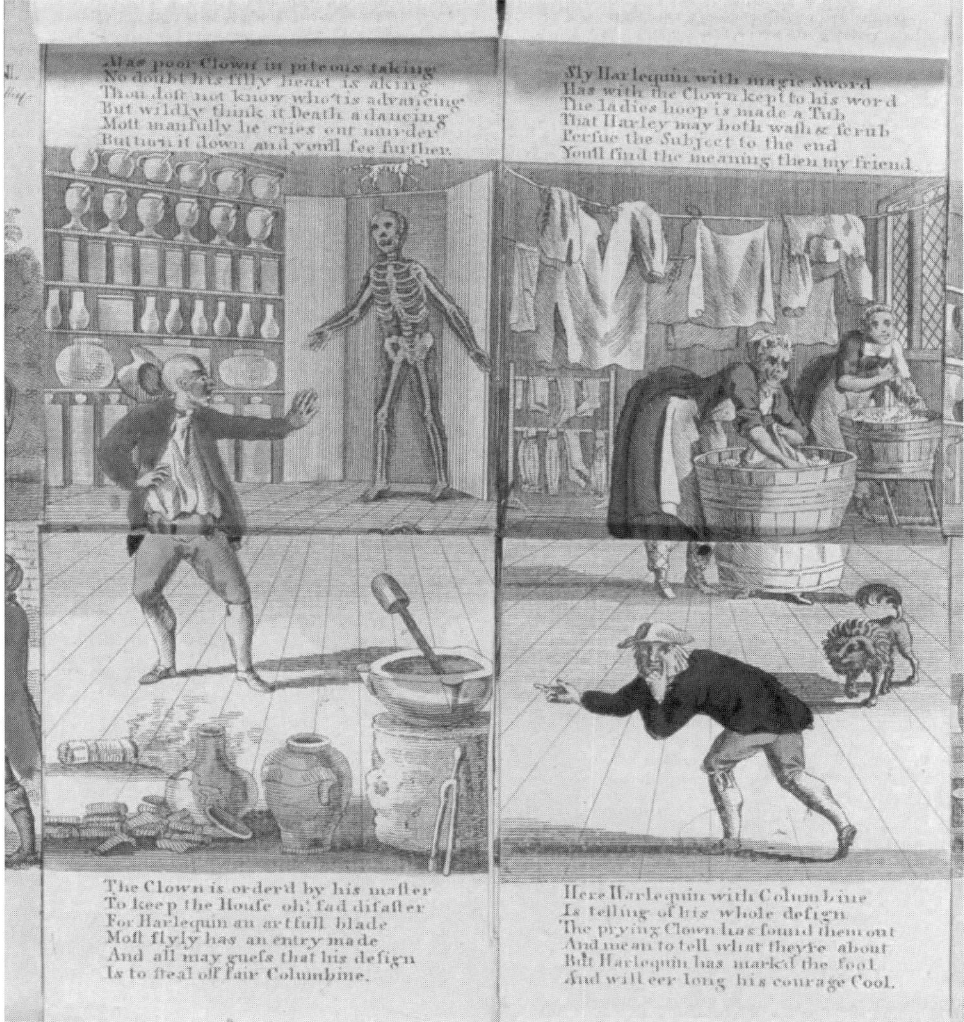

Figure 4.2 Harlequin Skeleton walks out of closet

an instance of early animation or pre-cinema effect (Reid-Walsh, in press).

The harlequinade books also draw the reader/viewer in as an active participant in the performance both as an enabler and critical onlooker. In terms of Murray's distinction between activity and agency in interactive texts, the harlequinade seems to emphasize the first, for while the reader/viewer lifts the flaps in order to move the action of the plot along, he or she does not determine the outcome. Rather, the active viewer seems to be an interactor who is a collaborator in the construction of the plot. Indeed, the reader is often addressed by the narrator in this capacity. Instructions to turn the flap may be integrated into the plot, or the reader may be invited to aid Harlequin in his attempts to win Columbine. At the same time, the reader possesses critical agency. Analogous to the 18th century theatre spectator who is a participatory critical viewer and who not only has the power to critique but also to end the performance, the narrator urges the reader to keep turning the flaps, thereby keeping the miniature production going, and invites

Figure 4.3 Clown runs away

critical comments on the effect of the tricks depicted on the miniature stage.

Paper doll books: gendered activities for elite children

In contrast to the harlequinades that had an inclusive readership, by 1810–1811 moveable books such as paper doll books, the paignion and toy theatres were being produced that were directed towards specific genders and ages of middle-class children. Paper doll books were invented by S. Fuller and J. Fuller in London (1810–1816), sellers of art instruction for ladies (McGrath, 2002: 14). Consisting of seven to nine coloured cutouts, mostly clothes or accessories, a head with neck, and a storybook all in a case, the books told brief stories centred on the character represented by the paper doll. As the story progressed, the child reader was intended to dress the doll in the appropriate attire. Most of the paper doll books feature child protagonists, with the exceptions of *Lucinda* (1812) and *Cinderella* (1814), who are teenage heroines, and *St. Julien* (Wallis 1812), a male youth.

Selling from five to eight shillings each, the books would have been marketed towards the affluent; and, as inscriptions indicate, they were probably intended as gifts.[1]

Paper doll books are a hybrid form, tapping into the popularity of paper dolls, the children's story and gendered play patterns that were emerging (Speaight, 1969:89–90). Around 1790, paper dolls began to be produced in England modelled on the shapely form of the expensive three-dimensional fashion doll. About eight inches high, they initially cost three shillings, but due to large production runs they were soon reduced to a few pence. Since they were inexpensive commodities, they appealed to all classes and ages of girls and women (Mitchell and Reid-Walsh, 2002: 176–177). The design of the paper doll books is different from that of the fashion paper doll, for they tend to show a child's undeveloped form. They are also constructed differently, for they do not consist of a body that is dressed but are of one head and neck that has multiple dressed bodies. The neck serves as a tab that slides into slots in the backs of the elaborate outfits.

The narratives are usually didactic; many are retellings of the prodigal son plot (Immel, 2006), but this is strongly inflected by gender and genre. Narratives featuring girls tend to be miniature conduct book narratives, a popular female genre featuring heroines who must learn to behave properly due to a censorious public eye that interprets their actions, demeanour and dress as transparent indicators of their moral nature. There are two types of heroine: the naïve 'reformable' heroine who is shown learning from her mistakes, as in the early novels of Frances Burney and Jane Austen, and the 'exemplary' heroine, who models correct behaviour, as in the novels of Maria Edgeworth and later Burney (Spencer, 1986). Paper doll books about young girls, such as *Fanny* or *Ellen*, are of the first type, whereas books featuring older heroines, such as *Cinderella* or *Lucinda*, are of the second type. On the economic level, the narratives are about middle-class girls and the tenuousness of their status, which is dependent on their conventional behaviour. On the ideological level, the lesson is about the dangers of female vanity, frivolity and fashion. By contrast, the narratives featuring boys tend to have little didacticism and concern real or imagined adventures. *Little Henry* is an exemplary figure who suffers through no fault of his own, for he is lost by his nursery maid. His adventures and successful rise could be seen as a miniature precursor of the boy's adventure story later popularized by Robert Louis Stevenson. *St. Julien* is an exception. Published by a map and puzzle maker, it teaches geography.

Some of the paper doll books featuring boys establish a link between play as activity and play as theatre. Legitimate theatre of tragedy and serious drama is represented by *Young Albert, the Roscius, exhibited in a series of characters from Shakespeare and other authors* (Fuller, 1811), based on an actor who was a child prodigy. The text consists mainly of key dramatic monologues and the costumes include those for Othello, Hamlet, Falstaff and Douglas. At the other end of the theatrical and class spectrum, *Frank Feignwell's Attempts to Amuse his Friends* (Fuller, 1811) concerns an affluent Regency boy engaging in amateur theatricals by dressing up in different costumes to entertain his house party. Roles include a King, 'Rolla' a Peruvian hero, a barber and Harlequin.

The intended manner of engagement for the child player of the paper doll books is a set of interrelated activities: cutting out the figures, matching the costumes to the narrative by inserting the head into the appropriate figure and arranging them while reading the story. There is no emphasis on performance play. The dolls are not called characters, and the only instructions concern costumes. Even the theatrically based books do not have casts of characters or play scripts. There is no sense of movement in the design or intended play with the figures, and most need to be laid flat on a table (Speaight, 1969: 87). An exception is *Lucinda*, which is a truncated paper fashion doll ending at the hips, similar to a dressmaker's manikin, and whose clothes are slipped onto her as with a fashion doll. She is provided with a stand so that she can be placed upright.

In terms of Murray's distinction between activity and agency in interactive texts, the role of implied child reader of the paper doll books is different than with the harlequinade flap books. With the latter, by turning the flaps and making the transformations possible the reader/viewer plays two roles. One is that of a collaborator in the flapbook 'production' of the harlequinade, analogous to a stagehand, perhaps, and the other is that of participatory spectator who critiques the narrative and the special effects, including the depiction of motion, a role with agency. By contrast, with paper doll books the emphasis is solely on activity and there is no sense of collaboration on the part of the child player. Nor is there a sense of critical agency, for when the narrator addresses the child reader it is within a didactic framework. As suggested by the term 'figure' to refer to the paper dolls, the role of the implied child player is analogous to that of a book illustrator. The only agency would exist in play that extends or subverts the texts. For example, one copy of *Frank Feignwell* has a seventh figure, a midshipman, drawn in by hand along with a new verse section, both by the book's owners. This figure might reflect the occupation of one of the owner's family members, an impression substantiated by the final line of verse, in which the sailor vows that he will 'ne'er bring disgrace on the clothes I now wear'.[2]

Paignion playsets and toy theatres: tranquil activities and melodramatic spectacles

Each type of moveable book has certain affordances on the part of the implied reader/player. A small child can manipulate the flaps of a harlequinade, a slightly older one could engage in more involved activities provided by paper doll books and a still older child would demand complex projects such as toy theatres (Speaight, 1969: 83–87). The paignion *circa* 1825–1830 is a hybrid text combining several types of domestic activity. An elaborate artefact, it was presumably expensive and given as a gift, as indicated by the inscriptions.[3] It consists of 65 'figures' which can be placed into any of the 12 'views' to produce a wide number of scenes. The publisher Westley described it as follows:

> This novel and interesting little work is intended to afford a fund of entertainment: it comprises all the charms of a Baby-house, and many other toys, in this compact form. As the figures are moveable, the children may arrange them in a variety of situations, to personate and illustrate any scene in domestic life that is familiar to them: *viz*, Taking a walk; shopping; going to the Bazaar, or Zoological Gardens; sitting down to Dinner; retiring to the Drawing-room or Theatre; going to Bed; and Sunday to Church. Or They may imagine it a number of families visiting each others houses and forming parties of pleasure, in short any child may form its own subject.

Unlike the fashion paper doll with a shapely female form or the paper doll books with mainly child figures, the paignion figures include male and female adults crossing classes and occupations, such as parents, servants, storekeeper, omnibus driver, and boys and girls of different ages from babyhood upwards. Considered as a paper dollhouse, the scenes expand the domestic world associated with girls and young children to include a range of carefully supervised activities outside the home. Since the slots occur throughout the sheets, the figures may be placed in different locations. Although the figures may be posed in an attitude of action, they are fixed temporarily in their places and are played with flat, similar to play sets today. As the language of the publisher suggests, similar to the paper doll books, the play analogy seems to be to art illustration not drama. There is no narrative text, but the set of figures and range of scenes suggest a progression through a week of an affluent family's life from the child's point of view. The type of play implied seems to be imitative, for there are no exciting adventures depicted.

In terms of Murray's distinctions about types of interactivity, the design of the paignion seems to emphasize activity, for the number of variations possible is vast. At the same time, since there is no constraining narrative text, just a set of slots into which any figure can be placed, there is high degree of narrative agency possible, since the player's actions are autonomous within the large range of choices provided (Murray, 1997: 128). Each scene implies a type of tranquil play set in the home or restricted public world, but, since the figures can be placed anywhere, there are possibilities for the child player to subvert established adult and child roles. Frances Armstrong (1996) has discussed how subversive dollhouse play creates a degree of individual autonomy and agency for the girl players. The design of the paignion affords similar subversive play within a paper dollhouse and a restricted public world, but, like paper doll books, includes boys and girls.

This interpretation is reinforced by two pieces of evidence. One artefact has two scenes where the figures are slotted in unexpected ways: in the church the pose of the young boy figure with arms flailing is inappropriate demeanour, and in the theatre the stage seems to be transformed into a social dance floor, and the arranger has put the mother playing a guitar looking away from the performance towards the audience. Although the bookplate states 'David Laing Philips' there is no other marginalia. If a boy has been the arranger, then the placement serves as a record of a frozen moment of play, similar to that recorded in a 18th century boy's scrapbook (Immell, 2005). In the paignion play the child is constructing a narrative counter to the direction implied by the scene.[4]

In contrast to the paignion, which was directed towards elite English children, toy theatres were popular across Europe for all classes, ages and genders of children, including some notable figures: Hans Christian Andersen played with homemade theatres and dolls as an impoverished child and as a successful author using cut-out figures in scrapbooks for the daughters of affluent Danish friends (Andersen and Drewsen,1984; Baldwin, 1992). In 19th century England, toy theatres were popular with middle-class youths who, freed from domestic needlework, required complex activities to fill their leisure time. The term encompasses the wooden model stage, the sheets of theatrical characters, stage scenery and wings, and the abbreviated play scripts. The sheets had their origins in late 18th century theatrical portraits and the harlequinade flap books and were published initially by theatrical publishers such as William West 1811–1831, his apprentice (*circa* 1808) J.K. Green 1832–1860, Martin Skelt and family from the 1840s to 1860s and Benjamin Pollock (1876–1937) (Reid-Walsh, 2006).

Toy theatres tapped into the popularity of the theatre in the education of middle-class boys (Speaight, 1969: 85–90). Theatre education ranged from learning elocution by declaiming standard passages from a set of canonical dramas (as seen in the paper doll book *Young Albert the Roscius*) to attending theatrical performances of many types both at legitimate theatres and at popular venues (as seen in the range of harlequinade topics) and engaging in private theatricals at home (as seen in the paper doll book *Frank Feignwell*). There is a strong link between the theatre of the period and its representation and modification in toy theatre plays, since it was a drama based on grand spectacle and/or violent action that appealed to boy audiences (Wilson, 1932: 79).The most popular scripts were melodramas, such as *The Miller and his Men*, horse spectacles, such as *The Battle of Waterloo*, and pantomimes such as *Sleeping Beauty in the Wood,* or *Harlequin and the Magic Horn.* Reading the scripts while looking at the scenes and characters indicates they are full of broad action with individual fight scenes, large battle scenes and the pace swiftly proceeds through a rapid rise in action to conclude with an explosion (*Miller and his Men*) or battle scene (*Battle of Waterloo*). The elaborate figures and scenery for the pantomimes include tricks such as turning carts into people and transformation scenes such as a cityscape changing into a drawing room.

To perform a full toy theatre play was an expensive undertaking, for publishers employed incremental marketing techniques. A boy could buy sheets piecemeal, the price per sheet in the height of popularity being usually 'A Penny Plain and Twopence Coloured' (Stevenson, 1884). To stage a play was complicated and time consuming, for the child was required to assemble the stage, cut out the pieces, colour them, mount the figures, sets and stage wings on cardboard, re-cut the models and then using the abbreviated play script complete with elaborate stage directions enact the dramas (Speaight, 1969: 101–102). Unlike paper doll books, which provided different costumes in different stances but only one head, toy theatre sheets provided different images of the same character in different poses and costumes for each scene of the two-act play. The characters were obviously intended to be mounted so that they could stand up. Significantly for the focus of this chapter on the representation of movement in interactive texts, the greatest challenge for the player was how to move the characters, which are presented in a narrow repertoire of set attitudes. The boy had to manage the contradiction between these attitudes and the constant motion required by the action of the plot. The detailed stage directions mostly concerned bringing people onstage and off, engaging in fight scenes and so on.

The structure of the toy theatre stage afforded certain types of movement. Vertical motion was enabled by some stages having miniature 'grave' traps to allow characters to rise and sink through the floor, and in Danish stages the use of wires held from above would enable characters to 'fly' (Baldwin, 1992). Horizontal motion was enabled by some stages having miniature grooves, but this restricted the characters to parallel motion. A more effective means was facilitated by long-handled metal pointers called slides with a raised tab on which to slot the figures.

In terms of the different kinds of interactivity inherent in the design of toy theatres, they promote complex types of preparation that could encourage collaboration between the boy as producer/director of the drama and other children. The detailed stage directions which dominate over the brief plot include multimedia effects such as the sound bugles, armies fighting and special ef of smoke and fire. While the latter effect called 'red fire' was available for extra cost, battle sounds could be easily produced by smashing the metal slides together (Speaight, 1969: 102–105). In terms of Janet Murray's discussion of narrative agency, her question about the relation of the interactor to author in an inactive story environment can be posed here. She states that the role of the interactor is always limited due to the constraints of the writing and programming. The interactor may be navigator, protagonist, explorer or builder, but never author (Murray, 1997: 153). In a similar way, the child director/producer is never the scriptwriter. Yet, most of the writing about toy theatre play is by men who became famous authors, such as Robert Louis Stevenson, G.K. Chesterton or Hans Christian Andersen, who suggest otherwise. They describe the near impossibility of successfully staging a toy theatre play and detail their creative failures or partial productions to suggest that non-traditional or subversive play created agency for the players. In particular, Stevenson described how he invented multimedia dramas based on the names of the characters and places, and that when he touched the individual sheets of the figures and scenes in the shop he was fantasizing about the 'raw stuff of story-books'. Yet he never performed a full play (Stevenson, 1884: 201–205).

DIGITAL TEXTS AS VIRTUAL REMEDIATIONS OF MATERIAL PLAY CULTURE: THE BARBIE WEBSITE AND THE SIMS CD ROMS

There are a plethora of digital play texts directed towards children on the web, on CD ROMs and as stand-alone computer games. Their design often evokes the binary, gendered world of children's popular culture play, a largely domestic, 'bedroom culture' for girls (McRobbie and Garber, 1991) and an outdoor world of exploration and adventure for boys (Cassell and Jenkins, 1998). While CD ROMs and stand-alone computer games have to be purchased, to access websites children may use a multiple-use family computer and internet connection. Commercial websites are often tie-ins to other products, targeting children as consumers (Kline *et al.*, 2003: 51–53), but since children accept the commercial imperative of the web as the norm they tend to see websites as places for information and 'free' online play. This section examines two popular digital texts, the Mattel *Barbie* website and *The SIMS* computer game CD ROMs, in terms of their interactive design, representation of movement and the implied active role of the child reader/viewer/user. I argue that they remediate contemporary toys and, by extension, historical toys, including paper dolls and moveable books. I employ the term remediation as defined by Jay David Bolter and Richard Grusin to be 'the formal logic by which new media refashion prior media forms' and in so doing reworking economic, social and political beliefs (Bolter and Grusin, 1999: 273, 77ff).

Ellen Seiter observes about the web play of small children that the computer seems to function as a transitional object moving them from playing games (such as collecting *Barbie* images) to perusing media-based fan activities (in Goldstein *et al.* (2004: 96)). The *Barbie* website at http://barbie.everythinggirl.com/ is a good example of this. As the domain name indicates, it is part of microworld of tie-ins to Mattel dolls, toys and related media. The sites range from the miniature houses and protected domestic and garden environments of *Polly Pocket* for young girls to *My Scene* dolls and accessories that evoke a trendy but bowdlerized tween world that includes pop music, celebrities and dancing. The *Barbie* site contains numerous activities around the theme of self and home decoration and uses the design metaphor of a 'celebrity'-style house and garden with adjacent mall. Since *Barbie* says 'hello' in eight European languages and two American dialects, the intended players are Eurocentric but global in spread.

The virtual doll dressing games emphasize the 'flow of play' between material and virtual spaces, for print options permit a user to have paper copies of the dolls and clothes. The dolls are situated in two locations: a room-size closet and a garden. In each, *Barbie* stands motionless. In the closet, *Barbie* addresses the girl viewer and directs her actions in 'dressing up' play. A sense of collaboration with the user is reinforced by captions like 'help *Barbie* and her friends try on clothes'. There are four virtual dolls, one white *Barbie* and three non-white friends, and they are posed as if they are walking in a range of fashionable but modest outfits. In the garden, Barbie plays the heroine in three 'fairy tales': *Rapunzel*, *Swan Lake* and the *Nutcracker*. Despite the action implied by the titles and the background music, the only action occurs when a user clicks the accessories and they appear on the doll.

Unlike buying *Barbie*, the virtual website dolls are 'free' to anyone with access to the technology. In this way they remediate the paper fashion doll of the 1790s which, due to a low price, similarly extended fashion play beyond the elite who could afford to buy three-dimensional dolls. Ironically, in terms of the history of *Barbie* (the authorized origin story states she is based on a 1950s paper fashion doll) and the early fashion doll, it is apparent that the virtual dolls only slightly adapt the shapely body, didactic fashion play and middle-class feminine ideology of previous centuries (Mitchell and Reid-Walsh, 2002: chapter 6).

In terms of Murray's distinction between activity and agency in interactive texts, the implied girl user is restricted to the former. Even this occurs within a narrow range, for despite being addressed as a collaborator with a set of choices, the virtual mechanism of 'dressing' the dolls is programmed in such a way that it forestalls subversive play.[5] In most locations the virtual doll is unable to move (except in links to *Barbie* videos), and despite being textually and aurally represented as an actor she is a manikin. The virtual dolls are formal and ideological remediations of the early 19th century fashion paper doll book and the paignion, although the shapely form is not a truncated figure, like *Lucinda.* Notably, the attendant conduct book dimension is present, whereby *Barbie*, like *Lucinda*, models the exemplary role for the girl viewer in terms of appropriate dress and behaviour. The concise aural narrative prescribes the circumscribed school and mall scenes as carefully as the paignion presents the limited range of domestic and public spaces deemed appropriate to middle-class children. *Barbie*, though, is accompanied by her multicultural friends, not a nanny.

The SIMS CD ROMs are a set of sophisticated simulation games that model human figures in their built environments, including houses, neighbourhoods and universities within a set of loose dramatic scenarios. *SIMS2* is rated as 'teen' according to the sexual content, but the avid usership includes younger children and adults, both male and female. According to their author Will Wright, the design contains different levels of metaphor. The initial comparison is to 'a dollhouse come to life'; but the less obvious ones depend on how the game is played: he states, 'for a lot of people, the mainstream game is more like juggling, or balancing plates' but for others who engage in storytelling 'eventually the metaphor becomes that of a director on a set. You're trying to coerce these actors into doing what you want them to do, but they're busy leading their own lives....' (cited in Pearce (2002)). These intentional remediations beg fascinating comparisons with earlier interactive paper texts that also remediate dollhouse and performance play, such as the paignion, toy theatre and harlequinade.

In *The SIMS* games, the design, the representation and facilitation of movement and the roles of the implied player/user are interconnected. In terms of Murray's discussion of interactivity versus agency, the design allows the player to assume a number of roles that combine both aspects, so he or she becomes a creative interactor in different ways, such as a 'builder' (Murray, 1997: 152). Indeed, the player builds houses and the non-anatomically constructed characters in the same way: either by modifying an existing pattern or by designing one from a wide range of components. There is a broad selection of houses to choose from in terms of price and design. The styles are cross-cultural, particularly when (as Wright intends) the input of 'fan' contributions is included, as in the house styles available at sims2.com exchange (Becker, 2004). To construct the cartoon-like characters similarly involves selecting from a wide range of variables, including race, ethnicity, age, gender and personality. Sexuality is represented as a lifestyle choice. The characters are complex virtual automatons that are individuated in their exterior construction and interior characteristics. They sit, lie down, stand, move in different directions, walk, run and dance with grace. Notably, they have their own language ('Simlish'). As Wright notes above, the 'actors' also possess individual will with their own needs, concerns and emotions.

The player as interactor assumes the agency of a stage or film director, since the game provides brief scenarios for clusters of characters and communities that can be developed in many ways due to the vast number of options. Thus, agency can become an aesthetic pleasure. Similar to toy theatre play, the player can return repeatedly and develop multiple long-running narratives for all his or her communities within the Simian life cycle of 28 Simian days. As a virtual builder, the player can also design aesthetically pleasing environments, thereby combining features of construction play and dollhouse play, associated with boys and girls respectively (Cassell and Jenkins, 1998).

The perspective of the player to the simulated environment is that of omniscience, which reinforces a sense of agency. In an interview on the launch of *SIMS2* Wright remarked that the visual perspective was enhanced due to a three-dimensional engine that allows the player to zoom in and out and feel that they are in the room with the characters (Becker, 2004: 1–2). This perspective is 'real' in the arena of the simulated world, since the user is the 'maker'. As Murray (1997: 153) notes, though, the creative 'interactor' is not the author Wright. In fact the player only possesses limited omniscience, for the perspective is limited at key moments when the characters are not seen clearly, such as taking a shower or engaging in sexual intercourse. By these means Wright grants the characters privacy and enhances the illusion of their separate existence.

The SIMS is an expensive product (about US$50) and is dependent on access to a recent computer with high-resolution screen and multimedia capabilities. In terms of cultural remediation, the ranges of house design and interior decoration are global, but the worldview is a Westernized world of commodities (Klein *et al.*, 2003: 271ff). In terms of social remediation, the games are inclusive, for the construction of characters is so complex that they achieve an intersectional identity where race, class, age and gender attributes can be combined in complex ways. Similarly, the game's appeal crosses boundaries of ages, genders, sexuality, race and geographic locations.

Significantly, the tone of the texts and gameplay is satiric at both the micro and macro levels: for example, the interior design options parody catalogue copy, while the act of purchasing something turns off the clock or 'life mode'. In addition to the cartoon-like style of the characters, this suggests that the tone of the implied play is satiric. This satiric aspect suggests that the games are not only a simulation of, but also a critique of, commodity culture. Henry Jenkins notes that the strict limits of the microworld of the game invites the player to examine their own lives (cited in Kline *et al.* (2003: 277)) To play the game in a self-consciousness way would raise questions about the attendant social, political and ideological remediations of the play, which in turn critiques Western society itself. Indeed, in 'From game-story to cyberdrama', Janet Murray (2004) states there are visionary possibilities inherent in *The SIMS*. She notes that the world view has an ambivalent vision of consumerism, that the logic of the characters' actions in their world have a kind of 'moral physics' with a lifespan and consequences, and that the game play is a kind of cyberdrama driven by a new kind of synthetic actor authored by Wright and collaborated with by the player (Murray, 2004: 4–5).

CONCLUSION: THE SIMS MEETS HARLEQUIN

The SIMS is a computer game of intentional multiple remediation, for it reworks prior interactive texts on material and paper platforms, the implied play patterns of the child users and different theories of interactivity. On the one hand, it promotes 'rational play', for it is a virtual refashioning of construction play and dollhouse play lauded by rational educationalists from the late 18th century onwards. Indeed, in *Practical Education* (1798) the influential Richard and Maria Edgeworth recommended building blocks and dollhouse construction play that required boys to engage in carpentry and girls in sewing in order to 'fit up' a house, but they disapproved of a furnished 'baby house' because there is nothing to do (Edgeworth and Edgeworth, 1974: chapter 1). As an ideological reworking of a consumer culture associated with the rise of middle-class children that has been developing since the late 18th century, the game is expensive and can be purchased only by latter day descendants of these children. Yet thoughtful play could encompass a re-examination of this commodity culture at the same time the player is participating in it. On the other hand, *The SIMS* encourages irrational play. It refashions some of the creative and subversive possibilities glimpsed in accounts of toy theatre play and hearkens back to its forerunner the harlequinade with the surprise unfolding of zany antics and possibility of irreverent critique due to it being a crossover text from the stage to the page. The appeal of the game is comparably wide, for it is attractive to a constituency that crosses boundaries of race, age and gender. The role of *The SIMS* player remediates that of the harlequinade theatrical spectator with a self-conscious and critical participatory practice. In all instances the reader/player/viewer is a collaborative 'interactor' participating with and critiquing texts that are microcosms of contemporary societies. In so doing the player is engaging in both rational application and irrational pleasure while exploring new directions afforded only by digital media.

NOTES

1 See Matthew Grenby's notes to Hockliffe collection copy of *Little Fanny* where the inscription reads 'Miss. Boys: given her by her Sister Sarah on her Birthday' http://www.cts.dmu.ac.uk/AnaServer?hockliffe+105540+imager.anv+single=true.

2 See Matthew Grenby notes to Hockliffe collection copy of *Frank Feignwell* about the additions by the child owner: http://www.cts.dmu.ac.uk/AnaServer?hockliffe+105271+hoccview.anv.

3 In the text seen at the Bodleian Library the inscription states 'given to Sarah Jane Sheila Dance<y>? By her aunt Matilda 1857'.

4 This is the layout of the text seen at the Cotsen Collection.

5 Pamela Ivenski makes a similar point about the now defunct *Barbie Designer* CD ROM (in Cassel and Jenkins (1998)).

ACKNOWLEDGEMENTS

I wish to thank Leslie McGrath (curator of the Osborne Collection), Andrea Immel (curator of the Cotsen Collection), Clive Hurst (Head of Rare Books & Printed Ephemera, Bodleian Library), Emma Laws (curator of the Victoria and Albert picture library) and Richard Virr (Acting Head and Curator of Manuscripts, Rare Books and Special Collections Division, McGill University Library). They not only generously allowed me to see and play with rare materials, but also talked with me about these texts as interactive media on paper platforms. I particularly want to thank Clive Hurst for showing me a harlequinade and asking 'Is this a book or a toy?'

REFERENCES

Andersen, H.C. and Drewsen, A. (1984) *Christine's Billedbog. Christine's Picture Book.* Introduction Erik Dal. London: Kingfisher. (Facsimile of 1859 volume.)

Armstrong, F. (1996) 'The dollhouse as ludic space, 1690–1920'. *Children's Literature*, 24: 23–54.

Baldwin, P. (1992) *Toy Theatres of the World.* London: Zwemmer.

Becker, D. (2004) 'Controlling the Sims', CNET com. http://news.com.com/Controlling+The+Sims/2008-1043_3-5366681.html [21 December 2005].

Bolter, J.D. and Grusin, R. (1999) *Remediation Understanding New Media.* Cambridge, MA: MIT Press.

Brewer, J. (1997) *The Pleasures of the Imagination: English Culture in the Eighteenth Century.* New York: Farrar, Straus, Giroux.

Buckingham, D. (2000) *After the Death of Childhood: Growing Up in the Age of the Electronic Media.* London: Taylor & Francis.

Cassell, J. and Jenkins, H. (eds) (1998) *From Barbie to Mortal Kombat: Gender and Computer Games.* Cambridge, MA: MIT Press.

Edgeworth, R. and Edgeworth, M. (1974) *Practical Education*, Vol. 1, G. Lurie (ed.). New York: Garland. (First published 1798.)

Goldstein, J., Buckingham, D. and Brougere, G. (eds) (2004) *Toys, Games, and Media.* Mahwah, NJ: Lawrence Erlbaum.

Hurst, C. (1995) *Early Children's Books in the Bodleian Library.* Exhibition Catalogue. Oxford: Bodleian Library.

Immel, A. (2005) 'Frederick Lock's scrapbook: patterns in the picture and writing in the margins'. *The Lion and the Unicorn*, 29: 56–86.

Immel, A. (2006) 'Fuller, S. & J'. In J. Zipes (ed.) *Oxford Encyclopedia of Children's Literature.* New York: Oxford University Press.

Iser, W. (1974) *The Implied Reader: Patterns of Communication in Prose Fiction from Bunyan to Beckett.* Baltimore: The John's Hopkins University Press.

Kline, S., Dyer-Witheford, N. and de Peuter, G. (2003) *Digital Play: The Interaction of Technology, Culture and Marketing.* Montreal: McGill Queen's University Press.

Laws, E. (2002) *Miniature Libraries from the Children's Books Collection.* Exhibition Catalogue. London: Victoria and Albert Museum.

Locke, J. (1693) *Some Thoughts Concerning Education.* London: A. & J. Churchill.

Mayer, D. (1969) *Harlequin in his Element: The English Pantomime, 1806–1836.* Cambridge: Harvard University Press.

McGrath, L. (2002) *This Magical Book Movable Books for Children, 1771–2001.* Exhibition Catalogue. Toronto: Toronto Public Library.

McRobbie, A. and Garber, J. (1991) 'Girls and subcultures' (1978). Rpt. in A. McRobbie *Feminism and Youth Culture: From Jackie to Just Seventeen.* Cambridge, MS: Unwin Hyman.

McMillan, S. (2002) 'Exploring models of interactivity from multiple research traditions, users, documents, and systems'. In L.A. Lievrouw and S. Livingstone (eds) *Handbook of New Media: Social Shaping and Consequences of ICTs*. London: Sage; 163–182.

Mitchell, C. and Reid-Walsh, J. (2002) *Researching Children's Popular Culture: The Cultural Spaces of Childhood.* London: Routledge.

Montanaro, A. (2001) 'A concise history of pop-up and movable books'. In *Pop-Up: An Exhibition of Movable Books and Ephemera from the Collection of Geraldine Roberts Lehowitz.* Fort Lauderdale: Biener Center for the Literary Arts; 9–17.

Morse, M. (2003) 'The poetics of interactivity'. In J. Malloy (ed.) *Women, Art, and Technology.* London: MIT Press; 16–33.

Muir, P. (1954) *English Children's Books 1600–1900.* New York: Frederick A. Praeger.

Murray, J.H. (1997) *Hamlet on the Holodeck: The Future of Narrative in Cyberspace.* New York: Free Press.

Murray, J.H. (2004) 'From game-story to cyberdrama'. In N. Wardrip-Fruin and P. Harrigan (eds) *First Person: New Media as Story, Performance, and Game.* Cambridge, MA: MIT Press; 2–11. http://www.electronicbookreview.com/thread/firstperson/autodramatic [21 December 2005].

Pearce, C. (2002) 'Sims, battlebots, cellular automata god and go: a conversation with Will Wright', *Game Studies,* 2(1). http://www.gamestudies.org/0102/pearce/ [21 December 2005].

Plumb, J.H. (1982) 'Commercialization of leisure'. In N. McKindrick, J. Brewer and J.H. Plumb (eds) *The Birth of a Consumer Society: The Commercialization of Eighteenth-Century England.* Bloomington: Indiana University Press; 265–285.

Reid-Walsh, J. (2006) 'Pantomime', 'toy theatre'. In J. Zipes (ed.) *Oxford Encyclopedia of Children's Literature.* New York: Oxford University Press.

Reid-Walsh, J. (in press) 'Allegorical metamorphosis and spectacular transformation: 18th century flap books for children and youth'. *Princeton University Library Chronicle.*

Shefrin, J. (1999) *Neatly Dissected for the Instruction of Young Ladies and Gentlemaen in the Knowledge of Geography. John Spilsbury and Early Dissected Puzzles.* Los Angeles: Cotsen Occasional Press.

Speaight, G. (1969) *The History of the English Toy Theatre.* London: Studio Vista.

Speaight, G. (1991) 'Harlequinade turn-ups'. *Theatre Notebook,* 45(2): 70–84.

Spencer, J. (1986) *The Rise of the Women Novelist.* Oxford: Basil Blackwell.

Stevenson, R.L. (1884) 'A Penny Plain and Two Pence Coloured'. Rpt. in *Memories and Portraits* (1917). New York: Scribner's Sons; 198–211.

Wilson, A.E. (1932) *Penny Plain Two Pence Coloured: A History of the Juvenile Drama.* London: George Harrap.

PART 2

Problematics

At least since Philippe Ariès published his now classic *Centuries of Childhood* in 1960, childhood researchers have argued over the relations between parents and children. Is parental care a particular modern invention, as Ariès seems to claim? Or, are humans more or less genetically predisposed for prolonged nursing? While such psychological issues may be difficult to determine with any accuracy given the paucity of evidence, it is evident that children are a constant cause of social concern. It is equally obvious that cultural articulations, whether self-styled or mediatized, are obvious entry points for playing out such concerns, because they are tangible manifestations of children's everyday practices and priorities. Given the increasing prominence of the media in children's everyday cultures, the social concerns over children often revolve around media as a symptom or pretext for discussion and debate.

These persistent and ongoing concerns over children and the public manifestations in relation to the media are at the heart of this part of the *Handbook*. The contributors are unanimous in arguing that public concerns over children and media are not chiefly about media, but about socio-cultural relations of authority and the negotiation of cultural and social boundaries. The chapters that follow were selected to demonstrate and illuminate the main dimensions within which these negotiations are played out. These have to do with the organization of children's time, with their spatial sites and settings and with the pushing of normative boundaries: in relation to parents, to society, to media genre or, indeed, to reality itself. Furthermore, all authors in this part demonstrate that the debates, and the underlying concerns, are ongoing social phenomena, irrespective of their overt focus on temporal, spatial or normative dimensions. These insights caution against evaluating public debates on media at face value, and they point to the necessity for contextualized empirical studies pursued across demarcations of discipline and region. Contributions range from linguistics, sociology, and media and information and communication technology studies, to film and literary studies and theoretical positions from social cognitivism to constructivism. Such interdisciplinary diversity elicits new analytical commonalities which, however, are still in the making.

That the main dimensions of negotiation over media have to do with time, space and the normative boundaries of social relations is no coincidence. Since the advent of chapbooks and penny dreadfuls, children's use of media has demanded a modicum of free time. Moreover, access to the media in question is key, and access mostly means pocket money or parental purchases, because most media are commercial from the outset. Access is not enough, however, since children also need to be able to carve out a little space so that they may use the media at hand. Free time has been sparse for most children through history, because they have worked, or because they attend school or some other form of training. Children's online engagements today push their boundaries in terms of being virtually always accessible; and new social divergences emerge between potential onliners and children who are denied, or who opt out, of the mediatized circuits of communication (Holloway and Valentine, 2003). Still, these recent conflicts with teachers and other adults of authority over time spent texting or gaming are part of a long-term struggle over who has the right to control children's leisure time and for what reasons.

With print media, producers and distributors control the cycle of output while the consumers may decide on when and mostly where to read the products. Until the advent of the VCR, broadcasters decided not only when to broadcast, but also when it was possible to listen to radio and watch television. The research literature amply demonstrates the ways in which joint watching with siblings, parents or friends in the heydays of mass communication have structured everyday life for young and old alike (Götz, 2004). Even with the current possibilities of time-shifting, the temporal structuring of spectatorship remains important for some groups and in some situations. Lemish, in her chapter, notes that young children tend to stick to the allotted TV slots, and even toddlers aged two-and-a-half know when favourite shows are shown. In her chapter on youth films, Jerslev discusses teenage video nights and the importance played there by the temporal orchestration of the film menu. It is against this backdrop of controlled audiencing that the recent debates over children's time spent with online and mobile media must be seen. Howard Rheingold (2002) speaks about mobile devices shaping social *ad-hocracies* in the sense that, for example, meeting times need not be fixed, but can be continuously rearranged. Time, at one and the same time, seems more fluid and more firm, more malleable, but also a constant presence.

Mobile devices, in particular, offer quite radical reappropriations not only of time, but also equally of children's spatial arrangements. Haddon and Ling note how the mobile operates as an ambivalent mediator between private and public spaces according to differing social arrangements: in some countries, such as Britain, perceived fears of public violence have served to domesticate and supervise children's leisure time, and so the mobile offers both a parental 'umbilical cord' and a lifeline to public space. In countries such as Finland and Japan, such fears are less pronounced and here the mobile helps structure and coordinate children's public activities. The variations in negotiating children's activities in public and private spaces are clear indications of the ambivalent ways in which media speak to, and impinge upon, particular tensions in changing definitions of childhood. For most of the previous century, 'proper' childhood in Western societies has been defined in relation to domestic spaces, and approved media uses have included reading aloud in the drawing room or alone in one's bedroom, watching TV together or listening to favourite music programmes on the radio. Most computer use is still part of domestic arrangements even if the personalization of media uses in many countries mean that families are now 'living together separately' (Livingstone, 2002).

The transmutations of temporal and spatial arrangements in children's media uses are clearly deeply embedded into a wider set of arguments about the definition of childhood and into ongoing negotiations of authority between young and old. Generally speaking, authority negotiations in Western societies have moved away from the area of work and into the spheres of school and leisure. This is essentially because children in industrialized societies gradually, and conflictually, lose control as contributors to the family economy, while they gain control over their leisure culture (Drotner, 1988). Media play an important role in this cultural struggle, first because children are often early and avid adopters of new media, and second because many media, such as television, film and latterly computer games, challenge established cultural hierarchies in which print media are at the pinnacle: playing a computer game or watching television requires very little formal training prior to being adopted and enjoyed, unlike print media, which, for the majority of children, demand some sort of formal, adult intervention and control in order to break the code of letters.

Tracing the often-heated debates following the introduction of new media, Critcher cogently notes that these moral, or media, panics may be understood as extreme instances of wider, ongoing processes of moral regulation and negotiation with anxieties over the perceived ill-effects of media violence taking pride of place, with concerns over media blurring boundaries between fantasy and reality taking second place, as noted by Messenger Davies in her chapter. Much of the more mundane negotiations are played out in the domestic context of the family. Hoover and Clark, in their chapter, chart how, in the USA, parental articulation of normative values are forms of claims-making in terms of perceived cultural hierarchies and ideals of family life, articulations that are at odds with both their own and their children's actual media practices as these could be followed through observation. Such insights help unpack prevalent notions of media discourses as monolithic givens and point to the need for more detailed studies, attuned to the often imperceptible, but significant, ambivalences involved in family negotiations over media.

Consumption is another key area in which cultural norms of child–adult relations are played out. In their chapter on child consumerism, Kenway and Bullen describe how advertising and entertainment aimed at children are currently converging, creating new ambivalences between parents and their offspring. In line with Kinder (1995), they note that commercial media and advertising industries position children as discrete, independent consumers with a 'right' to make independent choices, while at the same time cultivating adult hedonism with a 'right' to have fun.

Through the twentieth century, then, media have played a key role in negotiating normative boundaries, particularly as these are played out in children's leisure time, whether they are positioned in relation to parents and siblings in the home or as consumers in relation to entertainment and advertising corporations. But, as we noted, the transformation of children's social position in Western, industrialized societies has also entailed that schooling now operates as a central arena in children's everyday lives. Here, too, media play an important role as catalysts of cultural negotiations between pupils and teachers and, in a wider sense, between approved cultures of learning and practised cultures of leisure. Not least, computer games hold an ambivalent position here, since they are clearly developed as part of a rapidly growing entertainment industry, while at the same time being marketed as innovative forms of learning. In the blurring of boundaries between learning and leisure, between seriousness and fun, the roles played by commercial media and domestic consumption come together in children's lives. The so-called edutainment industry, including games, has been criticized for its piggybacking on parental perceptions of good parenting and proper childhood (Buckingham and Scanlon, 2003). While not discounting political–economic interventions against edutainment, Gee, in his chapter, makes a strong argument for the learning potentials to be harnessed by what he terms good video games. Such games are seen to enhance new ways of collaborating, of shaping and sharing knowledge; hence, they may teach teachers important lessons about basic principles of learning.

In conclusion, the chapters in this part address persistent and ongoing public concerns over children and the media. This introduction has mapped some of the particular tensions mobilized by these concerns. We have noted how these tensions speak to basic notions of time, space and the normative regulation of social relations – between approved cultures of adult society and the cultural practices of children, between the norms of parents and children, teachers and pupils, media industries and young consumers. In addressing and analysing these tensions, the authors demonstrate the conceptual strengths, the theoretical breadth and empirical diversity needed in order to illuminate these complex issues. In doing so, the authors also illustrate important debates for future study. Several note the urgent need for international comparative studies in order to qualify current research on, for example, panic discourses and mobile media uses. Others point to inadequacies in methodological validity and call for more contextualized accounts. This is demonstrated with particular eloquence by Messenger Davies in her chapter on traditions of studying children's distinctions between fantasy and reality as these are articulated by television, in particular.

Several authors also illuminate how the moral tensions that are catalysed by children's media cultures speak to contradictory taxonomies of childhood as innocent/evil, malleable/uncivilized, vulnerable/competent. Questions may be raised whether such dichotomies are particular to Western, industrialized societies or to frames of understanding that are deeply embedded in Christian religious traditions. Or whether they reflect more deep-seated adult ambiguities concerning power and control over offspring on whom adults will ultimately be dependent. Are struggles over authority a reflection of these more existential concerns? The chapters in this part of the *Handbook* provide no neat answers to those questions, but they offer reflexive theoretical and empirical reference points for new studies – and for contradiction.

REFERENCES

Buckingham, D. and Scanlon, M. (2003) *Education, Entertainment and Learning in the Home.* Buckingham: Open University Press.

Drotner, K. (1988) *English Children and Their Magazines, 1751–1945.* New Haven, CT: Yale University Press. (Orig. 1985.)

Götz, M. (2004) '"Soaps want to explain reality": daily soaps and Big Brother in the everyday life of German Children and adolescents'. In C. von Feilitzen (ed.) *Young People, Soap Operas and Reality Tv.* Gothenburg: The International Clearninghouse on Children, Youth and Media/Nordicom; 65–80.

Holloway, S.L. and Valentine, G. (2003) *Cyberkids: Children in the Information Age.* London: RoutledgeFalmer.

Kinder, M. (1995) 'Home alone in the 90s: generational war and transgenerational address in American movies, television and presidential politics'. In C. Bazalgette and D. Buckingham (eds) *In Front of the Children: Screen Entertainment and Young Audiences.* London: British Film Institute.

Livingstone, S. (2002) *Young People and New Media.* London: Sage.

Rheingold, H. (2002) *Smart Mobs: The Next Social Revolution.* Cambridge, MA: Basic Books.

Making Waves: Historical Aspects of Public Debates about Children and Mass Media

Chas Critcher

INTRODUCTION: OFF LIMITS

There is a symbiosis between childhood and the mass media. Both were institutionalized in the twentieth century, though with much earlier roots. Both allegedly pose dangers which must be headed off by new regulatory bodies. Both help define a modernized society. When the two coincide, there is often unease. For example, trouble has been expected in those times and places when: children are found at popular theatres or in darkened cinemas; children read comics or watch television too avidly; children spend hours with gameboys or before computer screens. The dangers identified have varied, but the sense of unease has remained constant (Drotner, 1999). Examining such debates reveals how both the new medium and childhood are relocated in the prevailing social order.

We have concentrated on those mass media which historically have most appealed to children. We begin with film, which even the illiterate child could appreciate, and end with computer-based technologies, which most children in the developed world can now access. To define childhood we have followed Smith (2005) and taken 16 as the upper age limit. New media forms have always had their supporters, apart from commercial interests. They will appear only occasionally. Nor shall we pay much attention to the regulatory efforts which often resulted from these debates. Though varied and complex, these are not our primary concern.

Some media have caused more adverse comment than others. Film is not only the best-documented case, but it also rehearses the basic arguments reproduced for later forms. The next mass medium, radio, caused very little concern in relation to children, whilst by contrast another, comics, provoked one of the largest and most international controversies of all time. By the time we reach television the usual accusations are made but are more severely contested. Later reactions to computer-based media are much narrower in scope and purchase.

Each medium will be discussed in turn as it appeared: film, radio, comics, television, video games, computing. Wherever possible, we shall refer to debates outside the English-speaking world. Unfortunately, studies available in English come predominantly from the USA and Britain. There is an urgent need for more internationally comparative work on debates around children the media. The gaps in the following account may help identify where this need is greatest.

The specific interest is not merely in whether concern over children and the media is 'motivated by a desire to protect children, or to control them' (Smith, 2005: 178). We want to identify what such debates tell us about how those involved conceptualized the nature of the new medium, the nature of childhood and, thus, the relationship between them. Towards the end we will consider explanations of recurrent controversies over the media and children. Our final concern will be with the continuing dilemmas of censorship.

POPULAR MEDIA BEFORE FILM: CURTAIN RAISER

Our main concern here is with mass electronic media of the twentieth century, but the arguments and complaints they would provoke had a history of their own. The charges to be levelled against the electronic media of the twentieth century had already been evident in reactions to mass literature. The novel was accused of overstimulating young women of nervous disposition, invited to identify with the emotional traumas of the heroines (Starker, 1989). In America in the 1870s there was a crusade against cheap dime novels for consumption by popular audiences, including children. Its leader Anthony Comstock objected to these mainly cowboy and detective stories because they affected their readers by arousing their sexual desires, inciting them to commit criminal acts and diverting their minds from hard work and thrift (West, 1988). Drotner (1999) also notes campaigns against new forms of popular literature in the late nineteenth century in Germany, France and especially Denmark, with a furore over the Nick Carter crime novels at the turn of the century.

Popular amusements other than literature also attracted criticism. In the England of the 1860s, youths congregated at nightly penny gaffs, especially in London. These provided a mixture of song, comedy, magic and dance. Middle-class observers disapproved of opportunities for lewd intercourse between the sexes. The dramatization of the exploits of highwaymen and other notorious criminals allegedly encouraged criminal thoughts and deeds. Eventually, health and safety regulations were invoked. Gaffs were forced to close or else mutate into the emerging self-regulating respectability of the music hall (Springhall, 1998), but they continued the tradition of the collective show, portraying real events as well as fantasy, on which film especially would draw (Flichy, 2002).

The encouragement of crime, disorder and sexual desires were thus criticisms of different kinds of popular culture well before the advent of truly mass media. Youth were certainly at risk, children not yet so. But electronic media would soon jeopardise their place in the social order as well.

FILM: PROJECTING FEARS

The first major media threat to children came with the advent of moving pictures. The first nickelodeons, as they were called, appeared in the USA in 1905. By 1915 the cinema was established as an internationally dominant form of popular entertainment. It expanded after the First World War, especially with the introduction of sound in 1927.

Established opinion reacted negatively. In 1907 a New York Commissioner of Police condemned the movies as a 'pernicious, demoralizing and direct menace to the young'. *Good Housekeeping*, in 1910, complained that films 'represent real-life forms', 'impart their lessons directly though the senses' and give the child 'first-hand experience'. A psychologist offered the opinion in 1916 that 'the sight of crime may force itself on the consciousness with disastrous results' (Starker, 1989).

In the USA the Catholic Legion of Decency campaigned for films to adhere to Christian morality. Using propaganda effectively and threatening to organize boycotts of 'immoral' films, they were instrumental in forcing the industry to undertake self-regulation, in the form of the Hays Code. This governed the content of American films from the late 1920s to the mid 1960s, when for the first time America introduced the age rating of films. The arguments against certification up to then had been economic; in order to maximize audiences, films should be suitable for all (Black, 1994, 1997).

British critics were more varied. Smith's analysis indicates the importance of family associations, schools and youth movements, as well as churches. Since these are 'structures traditionally considered responsible for socialisation' this suggests that such concerns 'related to unspoken issues of social control' (Smith, 2005: 86).

Not all of the middle class was necessarily antagonistic. A common reaction was to convene a committee of investigation. The outcomes were not a foregone conclusion. The 1917 Cinema Commission of Enquiry set upon by the National Council of Public Morals in Britain largely exonerated the cinema from criticism. The Payne Fund studies in America in the 1920s also, on balance, felt that films did more good than harm (Charter, 1933), despite a misleadingly sensationalist summary (Forman, 1934). Smith (2005) found that of four British local enquiries into film in the 1930s, two came out in favour of film and two against it. British police mostly approved of the cinema because it helped keep mischief off the streets (Richards, 1984).

Nevertheless the requirement for regulation, especially to protect children, was accepted and 'would drive the development of censorship and the regulation of cinema-going, both in Britain and worldwide' (Smith, 2005: 19). In came an increasingly elaborate machinery of censorship through certification: the British Board of Film Censorship in the UK, while US filmmakers themselves voluntarily complied with the strict moral precepts of their own Hays Code. As early as 1914, most countries with cinemas had introduced some form of censorship; by 1930, all regulated children's access. Unfortunately, as Smith (2005: 4) notes, 'no work has yet been published that considers the international dimension of the debate over children and film'. Essentially the same arguments, enquiries and remedial measures appeared not only in Anglophone countries, such as Australia (Bertrand, 1978), Canada (Dean, 1981) and New Zealand (Watson and Shuker, 1998), but across Europe and into Asia. Japan, for example, introduced censorship regulations in 1915, with 15 as the minimum age requirement to see adult-certificated films.

Reactions to film were shaped by the preoccupations of national elites. In Germany, for example, the questions asked about cinema related to its implications for definitions of high culture and the validity of pure pleasure (Kaes, 1987; Jelkavich, 2004). Whatever the nature of local debates, they all recognized that nothing like film had ever appeared before. Drotner (1999) identified its five unique characteristics. One was that film was the first medium not to have print as its main mode of communication, reliant initially on moving pictures, with speech and music later. A US magazine lamented in 1914 the pictorial emphasis as 'a poor exchange for the analytical elements of logical interpretation which reading and listening demand' (cited in Starker (1989: 98)).

Second, the mode of participation, unlike reading, could not be taught and channelled. Without tuition, children would automatically be led to identify with characters and to imitate their nefarious ways. The populist Payne

Fund summary stressed that the audience member

> loses ordinary control of his feelings, his actions, and his thoughts, he identifies himself with the plot and loses himself in the picture, he is possessed by the drama. (Forman cited in Starker (1989: 103))

Third, it appealed particularly to children, estimated as half the early cinema audience. The British Home Office in 1917 noted that, unlike theatre, the cinema 'audience is less intelligent and educated, and includes far more children and young people' (Jones, 2001: 337). Fourth, films were shown in cinemas, places of specialized activity which were commercial and unregulated. Film historians have demonstrated how the need to control such places (initially through health and safety, then censorship of content) often preoccupied local authorities. Fifth, films purported to show real events, likely to confuse the simple-minded into confusing fantasy and reality. For boys this meant temptation into a life of crime, for girls enticement into illicit love affairs (Black, 1997).

Later media would also be primarily visual, require few formal skills of their audiences, appeal to children and make little distinction between fantasy and reality. A crucial difference was that films were shown in public, so the location of viewing could be licensed and the composition of the audience stipulated. But new broadcasting media would send their messages directly into the home, directed at a family audience. New forms of regulation would be required.

RADIO: SOUNDING OFF

Radio started up in the late 1920s and by the mid 1930s was a common household object. Reaction to radio was low key, since, unlike film or television, it was primarily an adult medium. Programmes for children nevertheless caused concern, at least in the USA, where objections came from existing middle-class organizations of parents or women. One contemporary commentator suggested in 1936 that parents puzzled over disturbing changes in their children's behaviour because radio 'has gained an invincible hold of their children' (cited in Wartella and Jennings (2000: 33)).

But reaction was not organized. No new leaders or pressure groups emerged. The objection was not that the detective and other stories to which children could listen would encourage them to commit crime. Quite the opposite: they were likely to be frightened by the dramatic features of radio. Such comparatively mild protests had some effect in the USA, where radio broadcasters adopted a code of ethics in 1939 (West, 1988; Starker, 1989).

In studying reactions to new media, the absence of controversy is as significant as its presence. We can advance three possible reasons why radio caused less controversy than media forms before and after it. The first is that children, as an audience, were not a primary target. They were not the significant paying customers for a radio licence or for the goods advertised in commercial breaks. Second, radio was self-censoring from the beginning. Whether organized by commercial enterprise or the state, there were clear reasons to avoid giving offence, especially as the material was broadcast directly into people's homes. Third, radio broadcasting lacked what for many critics was the true power of other new media. It had no pictures. Reliant upon the power of the word, radio could not be criticized for fostering an illusion of realism or detracting from the development of proper literacy. Hence, radio was and still is regarded as the least problematic medium for child audiences.

COMICS: DRAWING LESSONS

Children's literature had its origins in eighteenth-century Britain. Periodicals spread from middle-class boys to middle-class girls to working-class boys and then working-class girls. Comic books, aimed specifically at children and emphasizing pictures as much as words, appeared early in the twentieth century.

For boys especially, stories of detectives, adventure and war proved popular, with girls' equivalents concentrating on the minutiae of boarding-school life. Sales of such comics peaked either side of the Second World War (Drotner, 1988). But in the USA a rather different kind of comic had evolved, which would prove extremely problematic for the defenders of childhood innocence.

American comics grew out of the comic strips prevalent in US newspapers in the late nineteenth century, becoming specialist supplements in the early twentieth century. Separate comic books appeared in the USA in the 1930s, grew steadily in readership before and during the Second World War and reached their widest circulation in the 1950s. Crime comics peaked in popularity between 1948 and 1950, horror comics between 1950 and 1954. Aimed at (male) teenagers and young adults, the main subjects of comics were crime, cowboys, war and horror. They soon attracted criticism.

The objectors, led by American child psychiatrist Fredric Wertham, had specific objections to each type of comic book. Superhero stories, including Superman and Batman, were criticized for presenting violence as the optimum solution to all problems; for implicit homosexuality and sadomasochism (the Batman–Robin relationship especially open to such interpretations); for racism towards outsiders; and, finally, for inviting readers to immerse themselves in a world of total fantasy. Crime stories glorified crime, encouraging its imitation, and blunted the sensibilities of readers, especially in relation to violence, often against women. Horror comics condoned grotesque acts of violence.

Wertham (1955: 118) summarized his eight basic objections to crime comics:

1 The comic book format is an invitation to illiteracy.
2 Crime comic books create an atmosphere of cruelty and deceit.
3 They create a readiness for temptation.
4 They stimulate unwholesome fantasies.
5 They suggest criminal or sexually abnormal ideas.
6 They furnish the rationalization of them, which may be ethically even more harmful than the impulse.
7 They suggest the forms a delinquent impulse may take and supply details of the technique.
8 They may tip the scales toward maladjustment or delinquency.

For Wertham, the comics were crude, the readers gullible. Again, the pictorial element was regarded as crucial. Audiences were more likely to imitate actions in comics because they could actually see them taking place, with the suffering of victims all too graphically illustrated. Boys, for this is a highly gendered debate, were likely first to endorse the attitudes and second to replicate the conduct to be found in these comics. As Barker (1984: 85) said of British opponents of comics:

> their vision of what is contained in the stories, and what therefore will transfer to the minds of the children, is tied in with their views on the nature of children and how they are influenced.

Wertham, whose views on many other social questions were highly progressive, became obsessed with comics. His influence was considerable. The American solution was increased self-regulation. The comics industry introduced a six-point industry code in 1948, revised in 1954 and again in 1971. In Britain, the characteristic response was legislation, the Children and Young Persons (Harmful Publications Act) 1955, which prohibited, on pain of fines and even imprisonment, printing, selling or otherwise distributing comics featuring violent or criminal acts 'likely to corrupt its readers'.

The comics scare occurred in at least twenty countries on four continents, with specific legislation in at least five: 'the issues were basically the same, as were the players, methods of handling the controversies and solutions' (Lent, 1999: 25). Documented cases include: USA, Canada, Australia, New Zealand, Britain, Ireland, France, Germany, Holland, Belgium, Sweden, Denmark, Norway, Finland, Italy, Brazil, Mexico, The Philippines, Taiwan, Korea and Japan. Anti-American sentiment abroad often encouraged liberal or left organizations to join in the condemnation. In Germany, for example, comics were attacked on aesthetic and ethical grounds. They invited readers to identify with characters and, thus, to imitate their actions. Comics were censored under a general law about literature for juveniles in 1953 (Jovanovic and Koch, 1999). In France, opposition to comics was part of an overall effort to create a new sense of citizenship amongst young people following the ravages of war (Jobs, 2003). In virtually every country the 1950s was perceived to be producing the new phenomenon of juvenile delinquency. In the absence of any other explanations, popular literature would do.

In retrospect, the reaction to comics seems quite bizarre. Comics were a minority pastime, not the weekly leisure pursuit of millions as film was. This whole furore was not about comics at all, 'but about a conception of society, children and Britain' (Barker, 1984: 6) or equivalent nationhood elsewhere. The febrile atmosphere of the 1950s – with the Cold War threatening violence from without and juvenile delinquency threatening violence from within – may have contributed to the tenor of the debate. Other factors also intrude; film earlier and television later had their defenders, but comics had none. The power of organized lobbying and propaganda against popular culture would never again be so effective.

TELEVISION: BOXED IN A CORNER

Mass-produced television sets first appeared in the USA in the late 1940s and by the end of the 1950s were common household items in industrialized democracies. Immediately, familiar charges were levelled against television, including 'over stimulation, creation of aggressive and destructive tendencies, passivity, eye damage, anxiety and nightmares' (Starker, 1989: 132). In Britain, a major study (Himmelweit *et al.*, 1958) investigated and rebutted criticisms of television's effects on children: that it caused aggression; displaced more worthy activities, especially reading; stopped children going out and meeting their friends, and made children more passive in habits and outlook. The study concluded that television influenced children's lives rather less than many adults supposed. Much depended on the child, their viewing habits and social context. Similar conclusions were reached in American research published 3 years later (Schramm *et al.*, 1961).

Television initially provoked no pressure groups favouring censorship. The most trenchant critics of television as a medium appeared well after television's first impact. Three critical texts focused on children.

For Winn (2002), originally published in 1977, the problem is not the content of television programmes but how the nature of television affects the development of children and relationships with significant others. She concludes that 'the television experience is at best irrelevant and at worst detrimental to children's needs' (Winn, 2002: 12). To develop properly, children need to discover their own abilities, acquire communication skills, relate to others in the family, enjoy fantasy and experience intellectual stimulation. By contrast, television induces in children passivity, capacity for instant sensory gratification and addictive behaviour, whilst decreasing levels of physical activity. Television is particularly injurious to two vital activities. The first is play. Television decreases the time for play and channels it into simulating television scenarios. The second is reading. This is perceived as quite different from and superior to the television watching which threatens to displace it. Above all, television is destructive of family life: its times, rituals, common activities and shared experiences.

Postman (1994), first published in 1982, opposes television because it destroys childhood, one of the great historical accomplishments of the late nineteenth and early twentieth centuries. Childhood, a period for learning the skills and abilities necessary in the adult world, had been institutionalized by print culture and mass schooling. This is now under threat. Television, as essentially a pictorial medium, is inferior to the process and habits of mind stimulated by language. The picture 'does not put forward a proposition, it implies no opposite or negation of itself, there are no rules of evidence or logic to which it must conform' (Postman, 1994: 72–73). Television is seen to undermine childhood because it needs no tuition to appreciate it, demands little from its watchers and recognizes no barriers between children and adults.

Kline's (1993) critique comes later, reflecting the progressive deregulation of American television in the 1980s. Kline focuses on the appropriation of children's television as a marketing tool. The inherited forms of children's culture (toys, children's literature, 'traditional' cartoons) are converted into a comprehensive marketing strategy in which programmes, videos, characters and games become indistinguishable. Lacking adult discernment, children are powerless against a mass-marketing machine. Children's television consists mainly of formulaic fantasies, especially animations, which will attract child viewers. Equally poor in quality are TV tie-ins, toys and games. All this is argued to impoverish children's play, as being a:

> cause for concern for those people who still believe that the quality and content of the stories told to young children and the way that they play are important for their socialisation. (Kline, 1993: 232)

Different in other ways, these critiques share three increasingly familiar assumptions. The first is a sense of the past as being somehow better for children, because television did not exist (Winn), childhood was an unambiguous status (Postman) or corporations had not penetrated children's television (Kline). The second is a belief that, left to themselves, children spontaneously generate innocent play which television or its corporate masters seek to undermine. The third is that words are better than pictures, reading better than viewing. It is difficult to avoid the impression that, for these and many other media critics, they would really prefer children to eschew all media and sit down to read a good book.

These arguments have, however, been dwarfed in importance by the one dominant accusation, that violence on television begets violence in real life. Some writers are explicit about their view:

> that violence, as it is dramatized on-screen in all its forms, affects our children and conditions them to be more violent than they would naturally become without being exposed to it. (Grossman and Degaetano, 1999: 10)

This debate has sidetracked media studies for decades. Summaries are available elsewhere (Barker and Petley, 1997). Two basic points are relevant to the current discussion. First is the problem of the media text. Given a consistent definition, the presence of a 'violent' act may be easy to detect; but what it means is less obvious, especially if interpreted or shown out of context. This is essentially the problem of genre, cartoon violence being the obvious example. The second problem is that of response. Children are regarded as impressionable: still learning and developing, they model their own conduct on that shown to them on screen. Yet this process is assumed, or more properly inferred, from their behaviour. There is no interest in how such material is decoded. Other problems with the violence debate include the peculiarities of the excessive violence on American television, the dubious status of experimental evidence and the apparent lack of interest in other more obvious and substantiated causes of violence in social conditions.

Such reservations do not prevent controversies such as that in Britain and Australasia, though not the USA, over 'video nasties'. In two episodes in the early 1980s and 1990s, horror movies were alleged to be reaching child audiences because they could be watched in the unregulated space of home when hired from unscrupulous retailers. Twice the British Parliament saw the need to legislate, the first time introducing and the second time tightening legislation to certificate videos on ever more stringent grounds. Australia and New Zealand followed suit (Critcher, 2003).

In the USA, acceptance of the media's effects on children became political orthodoxy. The preamble to the 1996 Communications Decency Act stated that such a link had been proven, for both violence and sex. The outcome was the V-chip amendment, requiring all new standard television sets to be fitted with a filtering device which could be activated to block identified programmes. Broadcasters would rate each programme so that adult material would not reach children (Price, 1998).

Two assumptions dominate: that children are directly affected by violent and sexual materials on television and that the responsibility for monitoring their access lies ultimately with parents. The very notion of effect is a problem here, as if the child exists outside of television to be suddenly changed by encountering this alien medium. The violence debate perpetuates a view of the normal, healthy child who is led astray by media images. This was the assumption made by early critics of film. Almost 100 years later, it is still present in the arguments about television violence.

VIDEO AND COMPUTER GAMES: SCREEN SAVERS

Video games emerged in the late 1970s, initially as coin-operated machines such as *Space Invaders* in specialist arcades and amusement parks. The early version of the table tennis game *PONG* transferred to television. Specialist consoles were produced from 1982 onwards. Some concerns were expressed, mainly in the USA, about the addictive nature of the games and the sleazy environ of the arcade (Haddon, 1993). Concern heightened when the early shooting games acquired narrative content and then transferred from arcades to consoles and on to microcomputers.

Video games prompted familiar accusations about the physical effects of extended periods of play, the moral debilitation from aggressive fantasy, the severe sexual stereotyping endorsed by the games, the displacement of other more worthwhile activities and possible thefts by addicts to support their 'habit' (Watson and Shuker, 1998). The need to act was not confined to the USA: 'video game regulation has been identified as a problem world-wide' (Watson and Shuker, 1998: 163). The US Video Game Violence Act (1993) pressurized manufacturers to label each product with suitability rating stickers (Jones, 2001), but few parents seem aware of the system (Subrahmanyam *et al.*, 2000: 123). Such concerns were reinforced by the Columbine High School shootings in 1999, when it was alleged that the perpetrators were obsessed with the violent computer game *Doom.* It seems that 'the amount of aggression and violence has increased with each new generation of games' (Subrahmanyam *et al.*, 2000: 123). In 2003 the video game *Grand Theft Auto III* caused controversy, with its apparent endorsement of attacking police officers and of sex with prostitutes.

By the turn of the century such games were an international multi-million dollar industry whose revenues exceeded Hollywood's (Buckingham, 2000). The basic fear remained that innocent children might be corrupted by exposure to their violence, while the already corrupt might be tempted to play out in real life the simulated actions on the screen. For some, the interactivity of the medium made this even more likely:

> whereas before the children were just 'passive receivers' of screen violence, with video games they push the button, click the mouse, and pull the trigger to initiate the carnage and killing. (Grossman and Degaetano, 1999: 3)

Other less polemical researchers argued that since these games are mostly violent and aggressive and given that we 'know' media violence elsewhere causes aggression, then we must assume that to be true of computer games as well (Subrahmanyam *et al.*, 2001). Research findings on this issue are typically confused. Those claiming to have found negative effects (Anderson, 2004) are countered by those who find none (Bensley and van Eenwyk, 2001), whilst yet others claim positive effects (Durkin and Barker, 2000).

The wider debate reworks familiar themes, such as the vulnerability of youth to the debilitating effects of a new medium and the consequent threat of imitative deviant behaviour. Effects are not proven, but are assumed. The text (here, the absurd and cartoon style violence) is interpreted literally for its inherent moral message (Watson and Shuker, 1998) or inserted into inappropriate typologies of 'degrees' of violence (Buckingham, 2000). The adult observers, not the young players, mistake the virtual for the real world.

HOME COMPUTERS: TIGHTENING THE NET

Games addiction apart, the personal computer, with its access to the internet and World Wide Web, was seen to pose less of a threat to children. The interactive nature of computer technology and its obvious advantages for education excused it from accusations of inducing passivity and illiteracy which had dogged previous technologies (Buckingham, 2000). It was nevertheless suggested that excessive use of computers might induce obesity, cause repetitive strain injury, encourage social isolation and detract from sports and play activities (Shields and Berman, 2000). More substantial concerns about computers and children concentrated largely on their exposure to sexual material and to sexual predators via chatrooms (Wartella and Jennings, 2000).

As a response, in 1996 and 1988 the US Congress passed laws making it a criminal offence to supply obscene or harmful material to minors, but both stalled when challenged in court as inimical to the First Amendment of the American Constitution, which guarantees freedom of expression. It has not proved viable to follow early examples of prosecutions of internet service providers in Germany and France for allowing child pornography to be accessed (Jones, 2001). Instead, the emphasis is on providing 'protected online space for children' (Montgomery, 2000: 159). The responsibility shifts to parents to monitor, with or without the help of specialist software, the sites which their children can visit (Akdeniz, 1999).

It has been argued that children's likelihood of exposure to internet pornography has been so wildly exaggerated that it constitutes a moral panic (Sutter, 2000) or 'cyberpanic' (Sandywell, 2006). Concern may have been too sporadic to justify these terms. More obvious is a general recognition that 'the "interactivity" that is the hallmark of children's use of new media enables both greatly enriched learning as well as increased risk of harm' (Wartella and Jennings, 2000: 39).

This latest medium has its dangers for children, but the benefits far outweigh the disadvantages. In a world of digital media, new technologies are no longer regarded with suspicion. Gadgets of every kind proliferate, with children as their most enthusiastic users. Adults are not far behind, credit card in hand. There are intermittently concerns about software, but the hardware is a normal not an alien presence. Children are comfortable in their relationship with new media. Adults' reservations are limited.

DISCUSSION: THREE-DIMENSIONAL IMAGES

Programme interruptions

The history of debates about children and the mass media reveals discontinuities and continuities. Some original worries no longer apply. Media are no longer accused of physically damaging children or being shown in venues which expose them to sexual temptation, nor can they now be required to uphold traditional Christian morality. Possibilities of censorship have declined. Films could be certificated and comic books banned. Terrestrial television can still be regulated, but satellite television cannot. The content of the internet is out of control. Campaigns about the dangers of new media have become narrower, such as the need to protect children from encountering pornographic materials or predatory men. Nobody could now inveigh against the whole idea of the internet as they once did against moving pictures.

Attitudes towards moral evaluation of media have also changed. Significant shifts have been identified in the discourses about children and media, moving from an initial 'pessimist elitism and censorship', through 'tacit paternalist measures' to a 'democratic pluralism' (Springhall, 1998: 156; Drotner, 1999). The nature of the debates has changed. As media technologies multiply and media have become ever more enmeshed in children's lives, media debates have become more short-lived and dispersed. Panics over media are less frequent and more localized.

Panic rules

Despite all these changes, there is a remarkable constancy in the cycle of reaction to many new media. Reviews agree that quite different media provoke essentially similar reactions (West, 1988; Starker, 1989; Springhall, 1998; Wartella and Jennings, 2000). The pattern is standard. A new medium, product of a new technology or a new application of an old one, emerges and finds a mass market. Its content is seen as criminal or violent or horrific. It constitutes a danger to children who cannot distinguish between reality and fantasy.

As an explanation, Gilbert develops the idea of an 'episodic notion'. Each has four characteristics: it reworks the theme of the innocent corrupted by culture; the debate is actually about something else than it appears to be; campaigners often have ulterior motives; and it is always bound up with anxieties about the state of social order (Gilbert, 1986). Such a pattern bears a remarkable resemblance to the classic definition of a moral panic. A 'condition, episode, person or group of persons' is identified as a 'threat to societal values and interests'. It is stereotyped by other mass media, often the press. Moral guardians pronounce upon the evil. Experts concur in denouncing the injurious effects. Measures are put in place. The issue goes away, returns in another form or is replaced by a new one (Cohen, 1973: 9). This fit has prompted Drotner (1999) to offer 'media panic' as a subspecies of moral panic.

Other writers have expressed reservations about the usefulness of the moral panic model (Barker, 1984; Springhall, 1998; Buckingham, 2000; Smith, 2005). It assumes that concerns are irrational and driven by the media, that there needs to be a folk devil and that all panics conform to essentially the same pattern. None of these seems to be true of media 'panics'. The moral panic model may have been misinterpreted (Critcher, 2003), but it remains limited. An alternative is to see moral panics as extreme instances of a wider process of moral regulation:

> practices whereby some social agents problematize some aspect of the conduct, values or culture of others on moral grounds and seek to impose regulation upon them. (Hunt, 1999: ix)

Whereas moral panics are discrete episodes, moral regulation is a continuous process. Reformers have to establish the moral dimension, often through organizations of middle-class females. In the process of moralization, distinctive discourses are generated. For children and media, one persistent discourse is the superiority of words over pictures. Upon examination, this turns out to be about class-based definitions of culture.

Words and pictures: the writing on the wall

From film onwards, mass media have been derided for their reliance on pictures. For Postman (1994), for example, print is the repository of rational thought because words enable the reader to reflect upon the ideas being expressed. By implication, primarily visual media involve us too much, enticing us to endorse our feelings which are, by definition, irrational. To forsake print, therefore, is to give up on intellect and reason. Postman is, as it were, inviting us to compare Wittgenstein with Walt Disney, in the belief that we will find it no contest. Several writers, such as Barker (1984) and Starker (1989), have noted how this perspective sets up a series of binary oppositions between literary

Table 5.1 Binary oppositions between literary and media culture.

Literary culture	*Media culture*
rational	emotional
abstract thought	concrete situations
analytical	intuitive
individual response	group response
psychological distance	psychological involvement
linearity/chronological	time reversal or fragmentation
largely verbal	largely visual
mainly factual	mainly fictional

and media culture, which can be represented as shown in Table 5.1.

Media reliant on visual messages, from comic books to television, are perceived as inherently inferior (Starker, 1989). A cultural hierarchy locates print media at the top and visual media at the bottom (Drotner, 1999). Little understanding is shown of the distinctive nature of each new medium or genre. Moral content is simply read off from the plot or an allegedly typical scene. Films, comics, television programmes and computer games have, thus, all been interpreted reductively.

Preference for the literary indexes class influence on the perceived relationship of children to the mass media. The written word forms the cultural heritage to which children should be exposed. The mass media, by contrast, offer standardized narratives, gross messages, effortless enjoyment. These are intrinsic differences: no matter what the media do, they cannot reach the heights of great literature. Cultural guardians are members of the educated class, recruited across the conventional political spectrum. Conservatives and radicals unite to condemn the latest manifestation of mass culture threatening civilization. One such threat is the collapse of distinctions between child and adult.

Adults and childhood: succeeding generations

Starker (1989) identifies class as one concern underlying views of children and media. The other is adult fear, subdivided into three. First is the challenge to cognition, when new media threaten established ways of understanding the world. Second is the loss of cultural control over media which intrude into the home and communicate directly to children. Third is a sense of psychological vulnerability. The new media are so insidious because they invite us to project our emotional selves into the story by projection and identification.

The basic insecurity is that socializing children is inherently a hazardous enterprise. It is accomplished by families and schools, despite a mass-media system which is at best indifferent and at worst hostile to the enterprise. The media are not to be trusted if 'upbringing is seen as the locus of character formation, and childhood is defined in terms of development' (Drotner, 1999: 613).

Adult reactions to children's media exposure are often about control. Initially the control they seemed to have lost and sought to restore was control over content; hence the regulation of film and TV. Then came new media, characterized by interactivity, convergence and ubiquity. Adults struggled to acquire media literacy that their children assumed effortlessly over multichannel television, computer games, websites. Now adults had lost control of the form as well as the content.

Loss of control is remedied by invoking ideologies of childhood, 'a set of meanings which serve to rationalize, to sustain or challenge existing relationships between adults and children, and indeed between adults themselves' (Buckingham, 2000: 11). Such images vacillate between the child as original innocent and original sinner. A past golden age is evoked when children and childhood were different, before the advent of whichever medium is being criticized.

The historically constructed nature of childhood is the prevailing concern of the 'new' sociology of childhood (James *et al.*, 1998) which, as Livingstone (2002) points out, pays remarkably little attention to the media. How the media are implicated in culturally constructing childhood may be indicated by two examples. One is the status of the child audience in the cinema. Examining Saturday matinees in the USA in the 1920s, deCordova (1990) has argued that they reconstructed and institutionalized the status of childhood. Initially, cinema seemed to jeopardize childhood as a separate status, since the child audience was indistinguishable from adults. Matinees (re)recognized children as a separate, special audience for whom appropriate films could be selected, around which other kinds of structured activities could take place, all subject to direct adult supervision. They managed to 'reassert traditional distinctions between child and adult by identifying, producing and preserving a children's culture within the cinema itself' (deCordova, 1990: 102).

Second, empirical studies of children's use of the media, whether television (Himmelweit *et al.*, 1958) or new technologies (Livingstone, 2002), recognize that children's media activities, at least in the developed world, take place in and around the places and times of family life. Asked when or why they use media, such children invariably reply that it prevents them being bored. This banal explanation is implicitly a claim to leisure. Children are denied this. Their play must be invested with moral qualities. Controlling children's media use is to intervene in their right to leisure.

Controversies over children's relationship to each new mass medium may thus be explained as the outcome of these three influences: the urge to moral regulation, the struggle for cultural standards and the effort to preserve a particular construction of childhood. All converge on the problem of censorship.

CONCLUSION

Censorship: licence to kill

Ideas have consequences. The main consequence of the debates about children and the media has been to regulate their access via means varying from legally enforceable censorship to voluntary codes of compliance. Balancing adult rights to free expression against the protection of children from harm is widely acknowledged, for example in the codes of regulatory bodies in Canada (MacKay, 1998) and New Zealand (Watson and Shuker, 1998) or in the EU directive on 'Television without frontiers' (Price, 1998). Millwood Hargrave and Livingstone (2006) have charted how the principles underlying media regulation have shifted from 'taste' and 'decency' towards 'harm' and 'offence', then latterly to a new risk-based public health model.

However, the viability of regulatory systems is declining, especially for computer-based media. Those who oppose censorship in principle, and those who reluctantly conclude that it is no longer practicable, fall back on two remedial strategies. The first is that parents should monitor and censor their own children's use of the media, with guidance from product ratings (Akdeniz, 1999). Unfortunately, many, if not most, parents lack the knowledge, will or capacity to censor or monitor their children's use of the media. This was discovered in the early days of television (Himmelweit *et al.*, 1958), emerging more recently for computer games (Subrahmanyam *et al.*, 2000) and the V-chip (Price, 1998). This abdication of parental control is even more likely in the case of computing. Mothers are more likely than fathers are to supervise their children's computing activities, but they are less likely to understand the technology (Buckingham, 2000). Moreover, we know so little about parent–child decisions about media use that it seems unwarranted to assume that parents can or should adopt this role (Price, 1998).

The second remedy is that children should receive media education so that they become critical media consumers (Watson and Shuker, 1998). This seems no more than a hope. It is not clear, for example, how any module on media education can counter the extent to which children's television in the USA (and increasingly elsewhere) has been hijacked by advertisements for junk food (Horegen *et al.*, 2001). Children are immersed in television long before they can be taught media literacy. There is, in any case, no evidence that media literacy increases children's resistance to media messages (Millwood Hargrave and Livingstone, 2006).

To rely, therefore, on a combination of parental responsibility and children's acumen derived from media education seems essentially to be a counsel of despair. It may be true that:

> it is far from clear how we can prevent children gaining access to 'harmful' content, while simultaneously encouraging them to make the most of the educational and cultural potential of these new media (Buckingham, 2000: 86)

but this does not mean that we have to give up on any kind of regulation. What is clear is that our ability to debate the problem of regulation will be enhanced by avoiding the kinds of moral panic, class-based cultural preferences and mythical images of childhood which have so dogged past attempts to understand children and the media. This is one repeat showing that we could do without.

REFERENCES

Akdeniz, Y. (1999) *Sex on the Net.* Reading: South Street Press.

Anderson, C. (2004) 'An update on the effects of playing violent video games'. *Journal of Adolescence*, 27(1): 113–122.

Barker, M. (1984) *A Haunt of Fears: The Strange Story of the British Horror Comic Campaign.* London: Pluto Press.

Barker, M. and Petley, J. (eds) (1997) *Ill Effects: The Media/Violence Debate.* London: Routledge.

Bensley, L. and Van Eenwyk, J. (2001) 'Video games and real-life aggression: Review of the literature'. *Journal of Adolescent Health*, 29(4): 244–257.

Bertrand, I. (1978) *Film Censorship in Australia.* St Lucia: University of Queensland Press.

Black, G.D. (1994) *Hollywood Censored: Morality Codes, Catholics and the Movies.* Cambridge: Cambridge University Press.

Black, G.D. (1997) *The Catholic Crusade Against the Movies 1940–1975.* Cambridge: Cambridge University Press.

Buckingham, D. (2000) *After the Death of Childhood: Growing Up in the Age of Electronic Media.* Cambridge: Polity Press.

Charter, W.W. (1933) *Motion Pictures and Youth.* New York: Macmillan.

Cohen, S. (1973) *Folk Devils and Moral Panics.* St. Albans: Paladin.

Critcher, C. (2003) *Moral Panics and the Media.* Milton Keynes: Open University Press.

Dean, M. (1981) *Censored! Only in Canada: the History of Film Censorship – the Scandal of the Screen.* Toronto: Virgin Press.

DeCordova, R. (1990) 'Ethnography and exhibition: the child audience, the Hays office and Saturday matinees'. *Camera Obscura*, 23(May): 90–107.

Drotner, K. (1988) *English Children and Their Magazines, 1751–1945.* Yale: Yale University Press.

Drotner, K. (1999) 'Dangerous media? Panic discourses and dilemma of modernity'. *Paedogogica Historica*, 35(3): 593–619.

Durkin, K. and Barber, B. (2002) 'Not so doomed: computer game play and positive adolescent development'. *Journal of Applied Psychology*, 23(4): 373–392.

Flichy, P. (2002) 'New media history'. In L.A. Lievrouw and S. Livingstone (eds) *Handbook of New Media.* Thousand Oaks: Sage.

Forman, H.J. (1934) *Our Movie Made Children.* New York: Macmillan.

Gilbert, J. (1986) *A Cycle of Outrage.* New York: Oxford University Press.

Grossman, D.G. and Degaetano, G. (1999) *Stop Teaching Our Kids to Kill.* New York: Crown Publishers.

Haddon, L. (1993) 'Interactive games'. In P. Hayward and J. Wollen (eds) *Future Vision: New Technologies of the Screen.* London: British Film Institute.

Himmelweit, H.T., Vince, P. and Oppenheim, A.N. (1958) *Television and the Child.* London: Oxford University Press.

Horegen, K.H., Choate, M. and Brownwell, K.D. (2001) 'Television and food advertising'. In D.G. Singer and J.L. Singer (eds) *Handbook of Children and the Media.* Thousand Oaks, CA: Sage.

Hunt, A. (1999) *Governing Morals: A Social History of Moral Regulation.* Cambridge: Cambridge University Press.

James, A., Jenks, C. and Prout, A. (1998) *Theorizing Childhood.* Cambridge: Polity Press.

Jelkavich, P. (2004) '"Am I allowed to amuse myself here?" the German bourgeoisie confronts early film'. In S. Marchand and D. Lindenfield (eds) *Germany at the Fin de Siècle: Culture, Politics and Ideas.* Louisiana: Louisiana State University Press

Jobs, R. (2003) 'Tarzan under attack: youth, comics and cultural reconstruction in postwar France'. *French Historical Studies*, 26(4): 687–725.

Jones, D. (ed.) (2001) *Censorship: a World Encyclopaedia* (four volumes). London: Fitzroy Dearborn.

Jovanovic, G. and Koch, U. (1999) 'The comics debate in Germany: against dirt and rubbish, pictorial idiotism and cultural antialphabetism'. In J.A. Lent (ed.) *Pulp Demons: International Dimensions of the Postwar Anti-Comics Campaign.* Madison Teaneck: Fairleigh Dickinson University Press.

Kaes, A. (1987) 'The debate about cinema: charting a controversy (1909–1929)'. *New German Critique*, 40: 7–33.

Kline, S. (1993) *Out of the Garden: Toys, TV and Children's Culture in the Age of Marketing.* London: Verso.

Lent, J.A. (ed.) (1999) *Pulp Demons: International Dimensions of the Postwar Anti-Comics Campaign.* Madison Teaneck: Fairleigh Dickinson University Press.

Livingstone, S. (2002) *Young People and New Media.* London: Sage.

MacKay, A. (1998) 'In search of reasonable solutions: the Canadian experience with television ratings and the V-chip'. In M.E. Price (ed.) *The V-Chip Debate: Content Filtering from Television to the Internet.* New Jersey: Lawrence Erlbaum.

Millwood Hargrave, A. and Livingstone, S. (2006) *Harm and Offence in Media Content.* Bristol: Intellect.

Montgomery, K.C. (2000) 'Children's new media culture in the new millennium: mapping the digital landscape'. *The Future of Children*, 10(2): 145–167.

Postman, N. (1994) *The Disappearance of Childhood.* New York: Vintage Books. (Originally published 1982.)

Price, M.E. (1998) 'Introduction'. In M.E. Price (ed.) *The V-Chip Debate: Content Filtering from Television to the Internet.* New Jersey: Lawrence Erlbaum.

Richards, J. (1984) *The Age of the Dream Palace: Cinema and Society in Britain 1930–1939.* London: Routledge and Kegan Paul.

Sandywell, B. (2006) 'Monsters in cyberspace: cyberphobia and cultural panic in the information age'. *Information, Communication and Society*, 9(1): 39–61.

Schramm, W., Lyle, J. and Parker, E. (1961) *Television in the Lives of our Children.* Palo Alto, CA: Stanford University Press.

Shields, M.K. and Berman, R.E. (2000) 'Children and computer technology: analysis and recommendations'. *The Future of Children*, 10(2): 4–25.

Smith, S.J. (2005) *Children, Cinema and Censorship.* London: I.B. Taurus.

Springhall, J. (1998) *Youth, Popular Culture and Moral Panics.* Basingstoke: Macmillan.

Starker S. (1989) *Evil Influences: Crusades against the Mass Media.* New Brunswick: Transaction Publishers.

Subrahmanyam, K., Kraut, R., Greenfield, P. and Gross, E. (2000) 'The impact of computer use on children's activities and development'. *The Future of Children*, 10(2): 125–144.

Subrahmanyam, K., Kraut, R., Greenfield, P. and Gross, E. (2001) 'New forms of electronic media: the impact of interactive games and the internet on cognition, socialization and behavior'. In D.G. Singer and J.L. Singer (eds) *Handbook of Children and the Media.* Thousand Oaks: Sage.

Sutter, G. (2000) '"Nothing new under the sun": old fears and new media'. *International Journal of Law and Information Technology*, 8(3): 338–378.

Wartella, E.A. and Jennings, N. (2000) 'Children and computers: new technology – old concerns'. *The Future of Children*, 10(2): 31–43.

Watson, C. and Shuker, R. (1998) *In the Public Good? Censorship in New Zealand.* Palmerston North, NZ: Dunmore Press.

Wertham, F. (1955) *Seduction of the Innocent.* London: Museum Press.

West, M.I. (1988) *Children, Culture and Controversy.* Hamden, CT: Archon Press.

Winn, M. (2002) *Television, Computers and Family Life*, second edition. London: Penguin. (Originally published 1977.)

6

Children and Media in the Context of the Home and Family

Stewart M. Hoover and Lynn Schofield Clark

INTRODUCTION

Concerned adults have long debated the significance of the media in the lives of children and youth. More than a century ago, parents, as well as authorities in education, religion and public life, wrote numerous articles and gave many a sermon criticizing penny dailies, 'dime novels' and comic books: the popular entertainment media, or 'kids culture', of their day. By the time television was introduced into the living rooms and apartments around the world at mid-twentieth century, the themes of research and criticism into media's negative effects had been well established. Similar concerns and research agendas are now emerging in relation to the internet.

These are not the only research approaches to the topic of children and media in the home, of course. We begin this chapter with an overview of this research, however, because it has been the dominant paradigm that continues to be voiced in policy debates and in family circles around the world. We then touch upon developments in what has come to be known as new audience studies, or those that insist on the consideration of social and cultural contexts when evaluating and researching the effects of media on children, families and all other media consumers. We then reflect upon some of the findings emerging from a recent in-depth study of families in the USA that we conducted, considering implications for further research.

In the USA, concerns about the negative effects of television reached a high-water mark with the Surgeon General's studies of the 1960s and 1970s. This was an effort that played a major role in the form and shape of the developing scholarly field of mass media research overall (Comstock and Rubenstein, 1972). Research on the 'effects' of the media on children continues to the present day (for comprehensive reviews of this literature, see Liebert *et al.* (1982) and Freedman (2002)).

It is impossible to do justice to the impressive array of such studies in the space available here. Instead, we would like to focus on that research specifically focused on children's media in relation to parental intentions, where we see two main approaches: (1) those studies that survey children about media (Singer and Singer, 2001; Freedman, 2002); (2) those surveys that ask parents about their practices of supervising the media consumption of their children (Dorr *et al.*, 1989; Holz, 1998; Warren, 2003). In recent years, this literature has been deepened and enhanced by studies that contextualize children's media consumption in the context of the home, often employing multiple methodologies or in-depth participant observation and interviews. In the USA, for example, Amy Nathanson has conducted surveys with parents and with children, and has also supervised experiments with children (Nathanson, 1998, 2001, 2002; Nathanson and Yang, 2003). She and her colleagues have advocated for 'active mediation' or age-appropriate discussion about television content between adults and their children as a result of this research.

Some scholars, particularly those identified with the so-called 'new audience studies' (a tradition where we would place our own work), have looked beyond the immediate issues of children and childrearing to explore issues of context, definition and interpretation in the discussion of the role of media in family life. Silverstone *et al.* (1992) were pioneers in this approach in the UK with their focus on the role of the media in the daily lives of families. In the USA, James Lull's (1980) work on the social contexts of media was equally influential. In her overview of audience research, Bird (2003) has suggested that relations to media in the context of family need to be seen as continuous with other aspects of life. Holland (2004) noted that ideas about the way media may influence children flow from certain ways of imagining childhood that themselves change across time. Messenger Davies (2001) argued that there is much to be learned by taking the perspective of children themselves as they interact with television and other media, understanding the ways in which their pleasures and other psychological satisfactions need to be understood.

Dickenson *et al.* (2001) studied the context of family life and its interaction with specific practices and genres of television, revealing much about both family life and family media. With its emphasis upon imagination and creativity as expressed in writing, Belton's (2000) studies encouraged a rethinking of the whole notion of 'influence'. Other studies have looked at specific demographic categories, such as adolescents (NB: de Bruin, 2001; Clark, 2003), and specific genres such as 'reality television' (Hill, 2000, 2002; Holmes, 2004). More recently, scholars in this tradition have looked at how policy-making in children's television and family media is rooted in ideas of democracy, civic space and democratic participation (Zanker, 2004; Van Zoonen, 2004). Still other studies have looked at particular issues in family and children's media, including sexuality (Bragg and Buckingham, 2004; Buckingham and Bragg, 2004) and even – one of the themes in our own work reported here – religion (Neumann, 2006).

As an example of work that has been particularly influential on our own, in a series of participant observational studies of children and their caregivers, Seiter (1999) observed that views about television in the family are closely related to class differences and the particular circumstances that arise in relation to limited incomes. She found that whereas the high-income preschools she studied advocated limited to no television viewing, lower-income preschools, and the parents of more modest means whose children attended them, were often more reliant upon television as a means by which busy single- or dual-income parents and overstressed caregivers could manage the demands of household management and child care. Because television is the most denigrated of media, often-strapped caregivers relied upon television but felt guilty about it, Seiter argued.

Livingstone's work has also explored the context beyond the household that shapes family media practices in ways that we have found particularly helpful (Livingstone, 1998, 2001, 2003, 2005). She has argued that concerns about children's media use cannot be separated from the fact that childhood is increasingly bureaucratized and supervised. She has also noted that the blurring of boundaries between public and private that is both an outcome and a cause of our increasingly mediated lives has made it increasingly difficult for parents to mediate, just as it has also made it more difficult for nations to regulate and for scholars to research the role of media in everyday family life.

Each of these studies has problematized the notion that it is sufficient to think of and study these matters as though specific stimuli and effects can be identified irrespective of the contexts of media use (Krendl, *et al.*, 1993; Gauntlett and Hill, 1999; Buckingham, 2000; Clark, 2003). In this way, recent research on media use in the family is part of a broader response to critiques of the decontextualized surveys of individual use and media behaviours of the past (cf.: Willis, 1974; Lindlof, 1995; Moores, 1993, 2000; Turner, 2002; but see also Barker (2003) for a critique and reflection). Studies that explore family media use have often been rooted in the assumption that children are not passive consumers of media but are actively engaged in their own media lives, and that interactions between children and their media, and between parents, children, and media, are significant – even potentially decisive (Seiter, 1999; Livingstone, 2002; Hoover *et al.*, 2004a).

In research that became the basis for the book *Media, Home, and Family*, we built upon these prior studies and their methods, combining observations with interviews of 269 parents and children in 62 families. Each family was interviewed first as a group; then, on a second visit, each family member was interviewed individually. The research sample was built employing maximum variation sampling, in which families were added to the study to represent a demographic range and to address gaps in our understandings as we became aware of them (Lindlof, 1995; Lindlof and Taylor, 2002). The families represented a cross-section of US families in income, racial/ethnic background, religious backgrounds and family structure (dual parent, single parent, multiple generation, blended and same-sex parents). Each family had at least one child living in the home who was younger than 17, and most families had multiple children between the ages of 9 and 17.

Our work is also grounded in a particular national setting, that of the USA and its cultural context. As has been widely observed, the USA is nearly unique among the Western industrial countries in the manifest role that religion plays in the articulation of normative values. We have found it logical and necessary, therefore, to foreground religion as a key dimension of our data gathering and analysis. Simply put, it is nearly impossible for Americans (even those who are not particularly religious themselves) to discuss values and ideals without discussing religion.

In addition, ideas such as the notion of a cultural 'mainstream' that emerges in a number of our cases are inflected with received ideas of religious identity and values. Consistent with our essentially 'constructivist' approach, however, we treat such claims as 'data', not necessarily as 'evidence'. American religious and spiritual self-descriptions are commonplace, and we treat them as such in our work, choosing to understand their meanings and what our informants seek to achieve by invoking those meanings rather than attempting an inductive treatment of religion as an 'independent variable'.

Our ideas in this regard have largely emerged from concrete experience in the field. As we undertook a major multi-year, multi-method qualitative study of meaning-making in the media age, we encountered systematic descriptions of media behaviour that seemed to be linked in important ways to senses of family identity. In the course of our inquiries, we soon realized that we were encountering three different ways in which people discussed the relationship between media and family life. We have called these 'levels of media engagement': 'experiences *in* the media', 'interactions *about* the media' and 'accounts *of* the media'. (Hood *et al.*, 2004b: 74). Experiences in the media are the relatively straightforward interactions people have with the media they consume. They can express in more or less detail their reasons for watching and listening, the kinds of things they have seen and heard, what they have learned or experienced there and what they think the outcomes have been.

We should note here that there are clear interactions between these levels, and that the boundaries between them are hard to describe. We do not argue, for example that they are inductive categories or would work as such. Rather, they emerged as largely distinct in our interviews as separate ways that our informants described their own interactions with media and their identities in relation to their media lives. They are themselves descriptions of interactions between individual histories, contexts, values, and patterns and practices of viewing, and we treat them as such in our interpretations.

Interactions about the media are those contexts and moments where media experience is brought into play in social relations within the household and beyond it. This has received a great deal of attention in qualitative and cultural studies audience research (see, for example, Katz and Liebes (1985) and Lull (1990)). In statements of interactions about the media, people express the ways that media practices and discussions about media are integrated into the interactions of daily life Such statements demonstrate the way in which media have become part of the 'cultural currencies of exchange' through which families develop and maintain relationships, and reinforce shared values, through interactions that draw upon shared media experiences.

These two levels of engagement, which move out from the direct experience of media to ways that media experience might be used in social relations, are now thought of as commonsensical, but it should be remembered that, before the emergence of culturalist and interpretive sensibilities a few decades ago, only the first of these was thought to be really significant in understanding the relationship between children and television. That media might also be understood in a larger context of practice and interaction is a more recent innovation. In our research, we have begun to understand that a third level of engagement is also important.

We call this level 'accounts of the media'. What we saw at first was a superficial inconsistency between the way people described media in their lives and the actual behaviours that would often be revealed elsewhere in interviews. The most obvious conflicts were between what parents would describe as their family's approach to media or the rules and policies for media in the home, and the actual viewing behaviour children described or we observed. Consistent with Warren (2003), Holz (1998) and Krendl *et al.* (1993), we found a kind of 'social desirability' effect in these matters, with parents claiming a variety of positive involvements in child television use, something that is, therefore, clearly a normative social value in the television age. But we were interested in *why* parents chose to give us certain ways in which these often-inconsistent stories seemed to tell us less about actual patterns of behaviour, and more about the desire of parents to present themselves as appropriately *accountable* for the media behaviours and actions of their children.

Rather than seeking to resolve these inconsistencies, therefore, we soon realized that there was much to be learned by *theorizing* them – seeking to understand what they told us about what it means to be a responsible or accountable parent in the context of a contemporary mediated society, and how children made sense of discrepancies between parental intentions and actual practices. It is clear that what people say reflects a set of received 'public scripts' which value certain kinds of media over others, and which further reinforces normative parental approaches to media in the home.

These 'accounts', therefore, draw upon what James Carey has called the 'publicly available stock of symbols' through which we think about social and cultural relations. 'Thinking consists of building maps of environments', Carey (1989: 29) notes. In the case of 'accounts of the media', these are maps of the ways that media should function in the home and family. But it is not enough to say only that these accounts derive from larger social discourses. Following Pierre Bourdieu's ideas about the relationship between categories of taste and value, and categories of class and social power, we began to investigate these accounts for insights into the cultural fields in which they are produced. We have described our evolving understanding of these accounts elsewhere in this way:

> With Bourdieu in mind, then, we began to look at 'accounts of the media' as including normative claims for oneself and one's family, not just an informant's notion of what the media should or should not do. This...broadened the notion of 'accounts of the media' from a convenient label for normative claims about media practice at the individual level to a broader, more significant theoretical category that would help us understand the society in which those accounts emerged (Clark and Alters, 2004: 44).

In general terms, the 'accounts of the media' we encountered focused on two areas: (1) ideas about the nature of media and the relative value of certain media over others; (2) self-descriptions of how a given family or household's media policies or practices were more strict or more lenient than others' policies or practices. Consistent with emerging theoretical and methodological directions in theory and research, specifically 'constructivist' ideas about the nature of the interactions between informants and researchers (Clark, 2004a), we have wanted to understand these accounts as normative self-descriptions through which our informants craft an ideal presentation of family identity. Asking parents to talk about media and family is, in effect, an intervention that challenges them to describe their ideal version of family life and family relationships in relation to media, thus helping to construct what Silverstone (1992) has termed the 'moral economy of the household'.

What parents *intended* to teach their children through household media rules, regulations and discussions, therefore, tells us a great deal about the way that they envision the role of media in relation to family life. We observed four different ways in which families attempted to make this negotiation between parental intentions, familial media practices and children's understandings of their family and its stance in relation to media and contemporary life.

DISTINCTIVE FAMILIES[1]

Two of the families in our study, the Ahmeds and the Paytons, focused on the *distinctions* they saw between their household/family 'cultures' and the broader media 'culture'. While these families differ, they share in common the idea that, through careful negotiation of the line between them and 'the media', they can create and maintain a distinct family identity. These families were especially interesting, for whereas many families voiced the desire to create such distinctions for their families, the children in these families were particularly adept at understanding and articulating their families' distinctiveness in ways similar to their parents. Both the Ahmeds and the Paytons are middle class in income and education terms, though for the Paytons (as we will see) there is clearly a desire to see themselves in contrast to the values of mainstream bourgeois culture.

The Ahmeds are an American Muslim family. The father, Umar, is an immigrant from Libya; the mother, Jemila, is an Anglo-American convert who was raised as a Protestant Christian. Like most American Muslims, the Ahmeds find themselves in the midst of a culture that does not readily understand or accept them and their religion. This gives the parents a multi-layered challenge with regard to television and other media. First, they find themselves needing to act in ways consistent with general norms of media parenthood, articulating and enforcing media-behavioural and viewing norms. Second, they must work to police the boundary between their culture and the 'mainstream' culture represented in media, seeking to filter out negative messages about Islam, and at the same time looking for positive messages about Islam that allow their children to have the same experience enjoyed by their non-Muslim peers: media representations that normalize them and their culture.

The Ahmeds' rules for media use resemble those from other households with two exceptions. They are more detailed than most, and they include explicit reference to Muslim prayers and family religious instruction sessions as part of the daily routine into which media necessarily would be integrated. Like other families we've interviewed, though, we found that the rules were more honoured in the breach than in the observance. When asked why it is hard to follow the family's rules, 9-year-old Sakinah replies, 'We like TV!' She and her brothers admit that they often watch television when they get home from school when their mother is not present, in spite of the rules. In a telling passage, Sakinah's brother Hasan reveals that even though they may watch prohibited programmes, they have nonetheless learned the rules and understand their parents' 'accounts of the media'. 'The whole family knows what they are supposed to watch; it doesn't mean they follow it', he notes. The rules and categories have thus been learned, but the fact that they do not result in uniform adherence in behaviour is confirmed by the fact that the Ahmeds gave up on trying to control cable television viewing and cancelled their subscription (Clark, 2004b: 86).

We contend that these rules are significant in spite of their seeming impotence. That children have come to understand parents' ideas about what is appropriate and inappropriate can and does provide important grounding in the 'moral economy of the household'. And, such common understandings are a measure of the extent to which media are integrated into the warp and woof of domestic life in a fundamental way. That such rules may be violated may well be less important than that they are understood and accepted as normative, which they seem to be by the Ahmed children.

Significantly, the children clearly saw the articulation of rules to be consistent with, and reinforcing of, their Muslim faith. But, this is a negotiated relationship. The Ahmeds are like other families, where television and other media constitute a set of attractions that are in tension with their normative values and beliefs. And, like other families, accounts of the media then constitute an important set of markers of distinction in their lives. Also like other families, the Ahmed parents realize that they could be more coercive and restrictive in prohibition of certain kinds of television, but are reluctant to do so. Their reluctance is not just based on their acceptance of the difficulty of doing so (a real issue for most families), it is also rooted in a sense that their role as parents is to prepare their children for a later life where they will be responsible for their own choices. Sheltering them will not prepare them for adulthood, where they must make their own choices based on internalized values.

As we have said, the challenge faced by the Ahmeds is larger, given that they are part of a subaltern community in American culture. The attractions of media mean that the Ahmeds are motivated to consume them while conscious of their own difference from the 'mainstream' gaze for which most media are produced. This involves certain strategies of reception that combine an active search for media material that represents Islam and their culture in a positive light (or is at least relevant) with consumption of other media in ways that 'filter' its texts according to their particular cultural perspectives. In one case discussed with our interviewer, the Ahmeds expressed profound ambivalence towards a high-profile example of Islamic culture in popular film: Disney's *Aladdin*. On the one hand, they appreciated that a popular film would represent a culture near their own, but, on the other hand, they found the representations limited and stereotypical.

The family's consumption of media in general takes place in the context of their experience of a 'two worlds' identity. On the one hand, they live in American culture and relate on a day-to-day basis with American peer groups. On the other hand, they realize they are distinct from that mainstream, and their media strategies reflect that distinction. For example, the parents act to limit the children's exposure to popular music, prohibiting MTV viewing as well as limiting their consumption of music. This means that the children are less informed about contemporary music than many of their peers. This took an ironic turn for the boys when they travelled to Libya to meet their extended family. There, they found that their cousins were much more knowledgeable about and involved in popular music than they were. Pleased that in Libya they were respected as representatives of American culture, the boys were at the same time troubled by the contradiction.

Not surprisingly, for the children there seems to be a constant struggle over the meaning of their identity as Arab-Anglo-Muslim Americans. On the one hand, they wish to be, as younger son Aziz puts it, '...a regular person...' in American culture. On the other hand, they realize the importance of the distinctions. Oldest son Hasan reflects:

> I don't know why I like this, but I don't think of myself as American, mostly. I think of myself as Libyan or Muslim. I know I'm American, but I guess I take for granted the running water, that we have water all the time, and the TV, and video games, and the stars and stuff (Clark, 2004b: 92).

This is a particularly focused case of distinction. They are bound to American culture, but media allow them ways of negotiating a unique identity in relation to that culture. This is important, in that neither their commonality nor their distinction is the whole story. It is the negotiation between these two that continues to define the situation. As mother Jemillah suggests, this is probably an important set of lessons for the children, as they will need to continue such negotiations as they move into adulthood. The fact that media are such an important element of these negotiations, so integrated into the making of family identity, is further significant.

The Paytons share with the Ahmeds the goal of maintaining distinction *vis-à-vis* media culture. They wish to live an eco-friendly, sustainable lifestyle that puts them at odds with the materialism and commercialism of the dominant culture. The mother, Corrine, defines her family's identity in terms of eco-responsibility, which she sees has having important economic and moral benefits for her family:

> ...if you don't buy a lot of this stuff, it's cheaper! And you know what? Then you don't need to have two jobs, and then you have more time to go do stuff and you don't need money to purchase things to do...going as a family for a walk (Clark, 2004b: 95).

It is important to understand that, for Corrine, as with others who identify themselves as eco-oriented, these ideas are relevant to more than discrete patterns and activities of life, but that they identify an identity that she seeks to weave into a consistent 'structure of feeling'. As with the Ahmeds, this means that the Paytons think in a certain way about the media and map themselves with reference to media consumption. Corrine is also more restrictive than the Ahmeds are, in that the Paytons do not even own a television set. This situation leads to a keenly felt sense of difference for the girls. They've experienced a sense of isolation from not knowing about current television, and have been subject to some good-natured ribbing at school. In spite of her strong feelings about television, Corrine appreciates the situation her daughters find themselves in. She's considered getting a set again, so they are not '...totally out of the loop...' she observes.

The two Payton daughters do watch television at their father's house, and so have some exposure there. Thus, they are aware of what they are missing. Like the Ahmed children, they understand and appreciate their mother's 'account of media'. They are able to relate to her desires for their media lives, even as they continue to watch television and consume other media. 'I don't want to get a TV just because somebody's bugging me about it', says Brenna, but she confirms that in her ideal future home, television and other media will clearly be part of the landscape (Clark, 2004b: 97).

The Ahmeds and the Paytons illustrate how complicated the relationship between media and family identity is. On the one hand, both families see themselves as distinct in important ways from mainstream culture, and see media as a potential antagonist to their values and identities. Both employ strategies (explicit rules in the case of the Ahmeds and the lack of a television set in the case of Corrine Payton) intended to ameliorate the impact of media in their families' lives. Both articulate 'accounts of media' that frame these strategies, and they articulate rationale for them. In both families, these accounts and structures run up against the reality of their children's lives, where they encounter media on a daily basis in their peer groups. Thus, the ever-present reality of a mainstream culture (articulated through the media) is hard to avoid or ignore. Children and parents in both households find themselves negotiating a fine line between distinction and participation. Their shared conversations about their household 'accounts of media' provide important markers and resources in that ongoing negotiation. Further, both Jemila Ahmed and Corrine Payton feel that stricter measures (such as full prohibition) would be counter-productive, as it is important for children to develop their own tools of discernment about the media, tools that will continue to serve them in later life.

AT THE HEART OF THE CULTURE[2]

Religion can define participation in the mainstream as well as in distinct subcultures. The next two cases investigate this. The Hartmans and Roelofs are much nearer, even at the centre of, the US mainstream than are the Ahmeds or Paytons, in that they are devout Christian Protestants. They differ in that the Hartmans are active in the burgeoning Evangelical Protestant movement, while the Roelofs identify with the non-Evangelical, or 'old mainline', tradition of Protestantism.

The Hartmans are upper-middle class and live in an urban setting, both parents being employed full time. Both are college educated. They own only one television set, which along with a VCR and a computer with internet access, sit in the living room of their home. Reminiscent of Jemila Ahmed, Sharon Hartman sees limiting television exposure as an important way of addressing television's challenge to parenting. They do not subscribe to cable television, and they receive only five channels of television. There are limitations on which videos are collected and viewed, as well as on internet access. These are experienced as rules and structures by the three children, the oldest a boy of 14. Also like the Ahmeds, the Hartmans describe using religious practice (daily prayer and Bible reading) as a way of constraining media use in the home.

For the Ahmeds and Paytons, the media provided a constant stream of cultural messages against which their faith or belief needed always to be articulated. The Hartmans feel the same way; though nearer the US cultural mainstream, we might have expected more of a sense of commonality with media content on their part. While the Hartmans do agree that media contain symbols and values that are significant to the moral and religious culture of their home, they make a distinction between those media messages that are 'religious' and those that are merely 'good' or 'positive'. 'There are a lot of people of different religions that are very upright in their behaviour…' says father John with reference to television shows that might contain such positive social values, 'but they're not religious' (Alters, 2004: 108). Like these others, the Hartmans articulate an 'account of the media' that defines themselves and their values in clear distinction to television. It does not inform religious belief, in their view, but provides a way of describing themselves and their values in contrast to mainstream culture.

Also like the Ahmeds and Paytons, the Hartman children seem to have understood well their parents' attitudes about media and television. At the same time though, the

Hartmans are enthusiastic and frequent television viewers. The children report watching television unsupervised when their parents are away, and the family spoke with pride and pleasure their ritual of watching reruns of the sitcom *Home Improvement* together each afternoon.[3] However, such inoffensive programmes are not the only ones they view. There was a good deal of discussion between our interviewer and the Hartmans over *The Simpsons*. While mother Sharon expressed deep reservations about this programme, the children clearly had seen it regularly and discussed it with one another and their peers. It was obvious in the interview that even Sharon had viewed and enjoyed this programme from time to time.

The Roelofs are less religiously oriented than the Hartmans. In further contrast to the Hartmans, they live in a rural area and have less disposable income, as only the father, Ryan, is employed full time. Thus, their income and education levels would place them in a 'lower middle class' category, both in social and income terms. They are not frequent church attenders, but contend that religion is an important part of their lives, and a source of important values and beliefs. Unlike the families we met earlier, the Roelofs seemed less sanguine that their ideas about appropriate media would be or could be internalized by their children. Believing that good 'religion-informed morals' are important to their children, they try to seek out media that are consistent with those morals, thus taking a slightly different approach than others.

But, as with other families, it was clear that the Roelofs' aspirations to intervention in their children's media lives are often not realized. Their oldest son, a 10-year-old, revealed in the interview that he regularly views *King of the Hill*, a programme his mother adamantly opposes (though she also admits watching it herself 'sometimes').[4] He also noted that an out-of-use television set in the basement in fact receives signals and is regularly viewed by him and his brother. Like the others we've interviewed, then, it was important for the Roelofs to articulate an account of the media as policies and practices of viewing, and that this was an important element of their sense of themselves as a family. There is some evidence that their children have learned and to an extent internalized some of these values and ideas. How the Roelofs differ from the Hartmans is in the tools that the media themselves provide to their practices of media parenting. For the Hartmans, media contained a variety of focused moments where symbols and values could be identified and their relationship to the family's values could be articulated. These were seen in terms of their relationship to a normative notion of 'religion'. For the Hartman children, these values or rules (while not necessarily followed) were accessible and easy to understand and re-articulate.

This was all more difficult for the Roelofs, for whom available discourses do not provide the kind of focused standards ideas of 'religion' provided for the Hartmans. Like many parents, the Roelofs wish to rely instead on the media industry's own rating system. Conveying the Hartmans' 'religious' values to their children resulted in a situation where the children could share the family 'account of media' (though not necessarily act accordingly). For the Roelof children, their parents' expressed attitudes about media violence (a more serious concern for them than other kinds of content) and the reliance on the media rating system left them with a less focused idea of what the family perspective on media is. For example, the younger son, Cary, revealed a good deal of confusion about what the word 'content' in the industry-ratings term 'adult content' meant. He knew he was to avoid 'adult content', but he had no idea whatsoever that might be. He and his brother thought it might have something to do with the amount of blood and gore in a given programme or video game, but that was about it (Alters, 2004: 123).

For both the Hartmans and the Roelofs, their expressed media rules face important challenges in practice. The media are too important and too attractive a part of life for their children to avoid them without cost, and in both households, the parents themselves admit to an active involvement in media, too.

The media are simply inevitable in family life. The question for all four families that we have considered is how to articulate policies and rules and identities in light of this reality.

FITTING IN WITH THE MEDIA[5]

The families we have looked at so far could be described in terms of difference and distinction *vis-à-vis* the media. For the first two families, distinction emerged from their own social positionality at the edge of mainstream culture. For the second two families, distinction still seemed to be an issue even from their position within the cultural mainstream. For all of them, giving 'accounts of the media' enabled them to map their place in the web of social relations while not directly or successfully guiding behaviour in terms of television or other media.

The broader cultural mainstream is a different issue for the next two families, the Price-Benoits and the Franzes. For these two families, the media sphere is seen as normative in a certain way, and their accounts of the media are more about how participation in the media is important and functional than it is about the media containing values or ideas that they wish to contest or teach against.

For the Franzes, television is less something to be contested than something to be used. A two-parent family with both parents employed full time, the Franzes are well educated and of higher income, living in a university town in the Midwestern USA. Their household consumes a lot of media, from magazines to radio and television. Like other families, they have only one television set, and express the common idea that television should be limited. However, for the Franzes, it is the amount of time that children watch more than it is the content that is of concern. Father Mark says that his children '…just know that a lot of TV…we don't approve of that'. Their account of media focuses more on other families than on their own, drawing distinctions between themselves and families that are less selective about media and less concerned about the amount of media their children consume.

At the same time, though, the Franzes appreciate media more than the others do. Their ideas about what is appropriate for their children to do and watch have gotten through, but in their interviews the children express the same sort of conflicted ideas about media that their parents articulate. On the one hand, they understand their parents' concerns about specific programmes (though they could not always articulate them clearly), such as *The Simpsons*; on the other hand, they like these shows and search for positive things to say about them.[6]

What seems to be most important to the Franzes, though, is a variation on a theme we heard earlier: that parenting in the media age involves equipping children to be their own best media consumers, that positive parenting is less about prohibition and more about teaching. But, for the Franzes, this takes on an additional element, the idea that media are something that is a 'normal' part of life. Mother Kirsten expresses this with reference to her decision to let her daughter see the film *Titanic* at a younger age than might have been appropriate. She saw this as a 'social issue', where for her relations with her peers, Bridget needed to have seen the film. Thus, while the Franzes see themselves as having rules about media that are more restrictive than some other families, they understand that 'normal' childhood involves media, and that adulthood will, too. Unlike families for whom a contrast between media and themselves was the driving issue, for the Franzes the media are a sphere that is inevitably part of child and adult life, and ways must be found to accommodate to them.

For the Price-Benoits, this issue of normalcy or 'fitting in' takes on a different dimension, because they are a gay family. Mark Price and Gabriel Benoit are parents to a precocious 12-year-old Lisette. Like the Franzes, Mark and Gabriel focus on time spent with media more than content. Mark makes a distinction between himself and his conservative Evangelical sister, who prohibits 'tawdry' television. For him, television is more a waste of time than a negative influence on values. The Price-Benoit media diet is much like that of other families. They speak very much in terms of their 'family' when describing their media policies and other social attitudes. Lisette gives an indirect confirmation to the normalcy of their lives when she replies to the interviewers' question of whether the structure of her family affects her media use. 'I have friends [from] all kinds of different families, and most of us have the same kinds of rules, so I don't think that really has much to do with it', she says (Hood, 2004: 141).

In fact, much of what this family says is mundane and unsurprising. Like other families of their social and educational class, Mark and Gabriel encourage Lisette to read more and use other media less. They are concerned about violence on television and try to shield Lisette from such programmes and films. Like the Franzes, they seem less concerned about specific media messages than the other families are, talking more about their own satisfactions with certain kinds of media (their 'experiences in media') than other parents do. Further, Lisette seems to have internalized their values about media. What is significant for them, though, is that they are a family outside the mainstream, and their accounts of media are thus interesting, focused as they are on a family identity so consistent with generally accepted parental 'accounts of the media'. For them, being 'normal' in media consumption is a way of understanding themselves as centred in the US social landscape, something that is particularly significant to them.

This idea of 'normalcy' stands alongside the sense from earlier families that media present a context within which family identity can be defined. For some families, that context is distinct. For others, the distinctions must be articulated with reference to focused religious or social values. For others, the media sphere is seen as a 'common culture' through which identities must be defined (for a more complete discussion, see Hoover (2006)). The media are in some ways inevitable, as we have seen, and these families demonstrate that the challenge for parents in articulating identities is to find a way of accounting for what will be the reality – that children will consume media and know about media and interact about media with their peers.

'COUCH POTATO' FAMILIES[7]

In a way, the Franzes and the Price-Benoits are examples of families whose embraced identities are consistent with a kind of normative status for media in contemporary society and culture. The last two families, the Vogels and the Carsons, are even more accepting. As we have seen, the received social attitudes that underlie our 'accounts of the media' reveal a deep ambivalence about the role of media in our lives. The opprobrium that is often attached to media use has often been expressed under the label 'couch potato', or someone who is so much a media viewer that they are best described as being in a permanent vegetative state.

The Vogels are a family of three living in a large home in the mountains. Both parents are full-time employed and the family is well educated and of higher income. They frequently watch television together, and for relaxation will also retire to the home theatre they have in their basement to watch motion pictures. They have satellite television and subscribe to independent film channels. They watch news channels almost constantly. In short, they are a media-suffused family. Their media rules also differ from those of other families. Twelve-year-old daughter Renee, for example, is free to watch anything she wants so long as she continues to earn A grades in school. Interestingly, Renee uses this freedom to watch rather esoteric films and television about social injustice and oppression.

Unlike most cases, where media was seen as by definition negative, the Vogels see media as something *positive*, a way of relaxing and refreshing themselves. Rather than adopting a stance of restriction and distinction, they actively seek programmes and media experiences that help Renee develop positive values.

Interestingly, for Isabel Vogel (the mother), Native American spirituality defines the value context through which she consumes media: such things as violence in media are actually positive, as they are parts of life that must be understood and transcended, rather than simply avoided. Whereas other families still exercised some limits, and (more importantly) articulated 'accounts of the media' around those limits, the Vogels avoid such limits, believing that their own use and enjoyment of media is something that Renee will benefit by learning and doing.

The Vogels are clearly familiar with the larger received discourses of the media. 'I think those sorts of rules are detrimental to a child's growth', says Elton. 'You have to learn to make decisions', adds Isabel. Summing up their beliefs in this area, Elton shares his judgment that parents who are overly concerned with the influence of television on their children '…are not parenting right' (Champ, 2004: 158).

A final family, the Carsons, resemble much more the classic 'couch potato' approach to television. Where the Vogels' family life is settled, comfortable and prosperous, the Carsons are a blended family with many challenges: mental illness, child abandonment, brushes with the law. An uncle, two nephews and an unrelated friend of the boys live together in a bungalow basement in a poorer section of the city. Television, video games, web surfing and music listening are nearly constant activities. Their 'accounts of the media' were far from the dominant, normative ones. In fact, they seemed to have little knowledge of the idea that media should be controlled and that parenting involves rules and restrictions on media use. Not surprisingly, none of the children could articulate a sense of rules.

Instead, media are used to help negotiate a complex maelstrom of social experience. Teenage Jacob, for example, talks in detail about using the Asian video series *Ramna*1/2 as a guide to life and relationships. In addition, the Carsons watch news, listen to music, watch popular television programmes and see the latest films. That media are normatively involved in making their lives satisfying and sensical is summed up by Jacob, who says at one point, 'video games are to forget, music is to soothe, and TV is to encourage and excite' (Champ, 2004: 166).

The Vogels and Carsons are clearly outliers in the continuum of normative models of parenting. In a way, they demonstrate how unusual it is in US society to find families that are media suffused and at the same time express 'accounts of the media' that do *not* problematize that suffusion. Very few families in everyday experience, and certainly very few families among our interviewees, would be comfortable *not* making the idea of parental intervention to control media exposure a normative ideal. The Vogels and Carsons demonstrate that it is possible to articulate such an approach to media from radically different directions, but it is significant that such exceptions require such unique conditions and identities to support them.

CONCLUSIONS

In spite of the seeming difference between these families, a set of themes links them at the level of media engagement that we have called 'accounts of the media'. *Distinction* is one such theme. For some of these families, the media provide a set of symbols by which they can chart their family in social and cultural terms. Some of them, such as the Ahmeds and the Price-Benoits, see these distinctions in a large and global way, as they inhabit social categories that are clearly understood as 'others' in the context of the larger, mainstream culture. These two families respond quite differently to the question of distinction, though, with the Ahmeds basing identity on policing the line between media culture and their culture, and the Price-Benoits seeking to see media (and to be seen) in more conventional and accepting terms, again connected to questions of identity.

Other families take a more pragmatic approach to distinction. In a way, the Hartmans and the Paytons have chosen to construct the media as an 'other' against which they create a discursive distinction. For them it is most important to inscribe distinctions and differences – to create them, in a way – within a media culture that is on other levels very much representative of *their* culture. This bears marks of the kind of rational and reflexive meaning-making described by Giddens (1991) and other theorists of late modernity, who suggest that the self and identity are central projects of modernity.

A second theme that runs through these cases is the issue of the *inevitability* of media, and the necessity of families engagement with it. In each of these families, but particularly those for whom the media were the most troubling, even the most intentional approaches at control of media use fell against the rocks of child (and parent) practices of media consumption. In some families, it was further felt that this inevitability had the status of a social fact: that participation in social life (particularly on the part of children) necessarily involved participation in media. Kirsten Franz expresses this the most explicitly, but it is a theme that runs across a range of these families, including the 'distinct' Paytons. Even the Ahmeds recognize that cultural currency involves media currency. This is consistent with the findings of some studies in the 'parental mediation' field, where parents were seen to treat television more or less as a given, but something that also could be addressed by parental 'co-viewing' (Bybee *et al.*, 1982; Valkenburgh *et al.*, 1999; Warren *et al.*, 2002) or 'active mediation' (Nathanson, 1998).

A third theme that comes into relief here is the difficulty of establishing a *normative definition of 'good media'*. As has been observed elsewhere (Clark, 2003; Hendershot, 2004; Hoover, 2006), the most consensual definition of good or quality media, even among audiences that are motivated by strict and moralistic attitudes (who have the most explicit and complex definitions of what is *not* good), is simply media that are *'inoffensive'*. For most of these families, when they describe programmes that they approve of, or watch together, they are more likely to be things like *Home Improvement* than culturally edgier material. The distinction between accounts of the media and the realities of practice then comes into play, in that those programmes about which meaningful conversations dealing with taste and value take place are programmes that are more 'offensive', such as (as we have noted) *The Simpsons*.

As we have inferred, the distance between normative beliefs about media (accounts of the media) and actual practice might have been understood simply as a failure of values, or a failure of parenting or even as moral weakness. Instead, what we see here explains why it is that these families must negotiate between their received and expressed accounts of media and their practices of viewing and consumption. There are a range of reasons why it makes sense for these parents and children to consume media the way they do.

What links these cases, then, is a parental strategy that accepts the fact of media in family life: the idea expressed by most of our families that parenting should involve *pedagogy rather than prohibition*; that good parenting should involve training children to become active media consumers. Children's exposure to a range of media, even offensive media, thus can be an important aspect of child development. Or so the logic goes.

It goes without saying that parenting and childhood in the media age are complex. What is more important here, though, is the extent to which media culture and media practice are integrated into daily life in the household, and into parenting, child development and social relations within and outside the household. As we have argued, accounts of media have evolved to make sense of what seem to be the contradictions between media culture and idealized household cultures. These strategies are more or less successful and satisfying, but they tell us a great deal about the larger reality. They also help to address ongoing concerns in the field of children and media about the role and function of household and parental mediation. Rather than the potential efficacy of parental intervention *between* media and children (cf.: Kubey, 1998; Nathanson, 2002; Warren, 2003), we argue that the whole context of the household's interaction with media needs to be understood and interpreted. This context includes, significantly, the ways that parents choose to describe their and their children's media lives. Rather than evidence of parental efficacy, such accounts tell us much more about the extent to which the media form the symbolic and values context of contemporary culture.

Thus, our research found that, despite the widespread stated desire of parents to oversee their children's media use in the home, the ways in which parental mediation strategies are worked out are far from consistent. Instead, we argue that parental mediation is part of a larger set of familial identity goals, and it is these goals – to create distinction from mainstream culture, to accept some but not all of a culture's norms, to seek media behaviour that mimics and places one within a perceived cultural norm or to challenge the very normative way in which most parents think of restricting media use – that actually influence how that mediation plays out in individual families. Ultimately, what parents want to teach their children about how to relate to the world beyond the family greatly influences the way they advocate media use within it. Whether a family wants to see themselves as mainstream or distinctive or as normal or extraordinary, the patterns of the ways in which media are discussed and experienced in family life shape the ways that children come to understand the family of which they are a part.

In methodological terms, the whole question of how parents and families wish to present themselves as media households has implications for research that depends on such accounts and treats them as 'evidence'. We recognize that less and less research on children and television today is so naïve. Nonetheless, it is common for lay and journalistic discourse about children and television to be based on opinion survey and anecdotal self-reports. To the extent that we base our assumptions about what goes on in the parent–child–media relationship on such input, we need clearly to contextualize and complexify those assumptions. The media are simply too important and integral an element of family life to take at face value the way people wish to describe their media lives.

NOTES

1 This section is excerpted from and is a review of Lynn Schofield Clark, 'Being distinctive in a mediated environment: the Ahmeds and the Paytons', in Hoover *et al.* (2004: 79–102). The Ahmed family was interviewed and analysed by Lynn Schofield Clark, and the Payton family was interviewed and analysed by Joseph Champ.

2 This section is excerpted from and is a review of Diane Alters, 'At the heart of the culture: the Hartmans and the Roelofs', in Hoover *et al.* (2004a: 103–130). The Hartmans were interviewed and analysed by Diane Alters, and the Roelofs were interviewed and analysed by Lee Hood.

3 *Home Improvement* was a situation comedy airing from 1991 to 1999 in the USA, featuring comedian Tim Allen as a father who hosts a television programme about home improvements, yet whose own home projects often went awry, much to the consternation of his wife and three sons.

4 *King of the Hill* was an animated situation comedy that aired on the Fox network from 1997 through 2006 and beyond. Created by *Beavis and Butthead*'s Mike Judge, father Hank Hill is often besieged by problems and seeks solace, sometimes successfully, in his home life with his wife, his socially awkward son and his live-in niece, as well as with his equally besieged male neighbourhood friends.

5 This section is excerpted from and is a review of Lee Hood, 'Fitting in with the media: the Price–Benoits and the Franzes', in Hoover *et al.* (2004: 131–144). The Price–Benoits were interviewed and analysed by Lee Hood, and the Franzes were interviewed and analysed by Joseph Champ.

6 *The Simpsons* is the longest-running animated programme of all time, with 17 seasons and 372 episodes since its debut on the Fox network in 1989. Its satirical humour lampoons life in 'middle America' and features underachieving Bart, precocious Lisa, baby Maggie, and parents Homer and Marge. The programme has been a lightning rod for the US culture wars, as it is the highest-rated cartoon of all time and has received numerous accolades, yet is also named as a television programme parents least want their children to watch.

7 This section is excerpted from and a review of Joseph G. Champ, '"Couch potatodom" reconsidered: the Vogels and the Carsons', in Hoover *et al.* (2004: 145–170). The Vogels were interviewed and analysed by Joseph Champ, and the Carsons were interviewed and analysed by Henrik Boes.

REFERENCES

Alters, D.F. (2004) 'At the heart of the culture: the Hartmans and the Roelofs'. In S.M. Hoover, L.S. Clark and D.A. Alters, *Media, Home, and Family*. New York: Routledge; 103–129.

Barker, M. (2003) 'Assessing the "quality" in qualitative research: the case of text–audience relations'. *European Journal of Communication*, 18(3): 315–335.

Belton, T. (2000) 'The "face at the window" study: a fresh approach to media influence and to investigating the influence of television on children's imagination'. *Media, Culture & Society*, 22: 629–643.

Bird, S.E. (2003) *The Audience in Everyday Life: Living in a Media World.* New York: Routledge.

Bragg, S. and Buckingham, D. (2004) 'Embarrassment, education and erotics: the sexual politics of family viewing'. *European Journal of Cultural Studies*, 7: 441–459.

Buckingham, D. and Bragg, S. (2004) *Young People, Sex and the Media: The Facts of Life?* Basingstoke: Palgrave Macmillan.

Buckingham, D. (2000) *After the Death of Childhood: Growing Up in the Age of Electronic Media.* Polity Press.

Bybee, C., Robinson, D. and Turow, J. (1982) 'Determinants of parental guidance of children's television viewing for a special subgroup: mass media scholars'. *Journal of Broadcasting & Electronic Media*, 26: 697–710.

Carey, J. (1989) *Communication as Culture.* Boston: Unwin-Hyman.

Champ, J. (2004) '"Couch potatodom" reconsidered: the Vogels and the Carsons'. In S.M. Hoover, L.S. Clark and D. Alters (eds) *Media, Home, and Family.* New York: Routledge.

Clark, L.S. (2003) *From Angels to Aliens: Teenagers, the Media, and the Supernatural.* New York: Oxford.

Clark, L.S. (2004a) 'The journey from postpositivist to constructivist methods'. In S.M. Hoover, L.S. Clark and D. Alters, *Media, Home, and Family.* New York: Routledge; 19–34.

Clark, L.S. (2004b) 'Being distinctive in a mediated environment: the Ahmeds and the Paytons'. In S.M. Hoover, L.S. Clark and D. Alters (eds) *Media, Home, and Family.* New York: Routledge; 79–102.

Clark, L.S. and Alters D.F. (2004) 'Developing a theory of media, home, and family'. In S.M. Hoover, L.S. Clark and D. Alters (eds) *Media, Home, and Family.* New York: Routledge; 35–50.

Comstock, G. and Rubenstein, E. (1972) *The Report of the Surgeon General's Scientific Advisory Committee on Television and Social Behavior* (5 Volumes). Washington, DC: US Government Printing Office.

De Bruin, J. (2001). 'Dutch television soap opera, ethnicity and girls' interpretations'. *Gazette*, 63(1): 41–56.

Dickinson, R., Murcott, A., Eldridge, J. and Leader, S. (2001) Breakfast, time, and 'breakfast time': television, food, and the household organization of consumption. *Television & New Media*, 2(3): 235–256.

Dorr, A. Kovaric, P. and Doubleday, C. (1989) 'Parent–child coviewing of television'. *Journal of Broadcasting & Electronic Media*, 33: 33–51.

Freedman, J. (2002) *Media Violence and its Affect on Aggression.* Toronto: University of Toronto Press.

Gauntlett, D. and Hill, A. (1999). *TV Living: Television Culture and Everyday Life.* London: Routledge/British Film Institute.

Giddens, A. (1991) *Modernity and Self-Identity: Self and Society in the Late Modern Age.* Stanford: Stanford University Press.

Hendershot, H. (2004) *Shaking the World for Jesus: Media and Conservative Evangelical Culture.* Chicago: University of Chicago Press.

Hill, A. (2000) 'Fearful and safe: audience response to British reality programming'. *Television & New Media*, 1(2): 193–213.

Hill, A. (2002) 'Big Brother: the real audience'. *Television & New Media*, 3(3): 323–340.

Holland, P. (2004) *Picturing Childhood: The Myth of the Child in Popular Imagery.* London: I.B. Tauris.

Holmes, S. (2004) '"Reality goes pop!" Reality TV, popular music, and narratives of stardom in Pop Idol'. *Television & New Media*, 5(2): 147–172.

Holz, J. (1998) *Measuring the Child Audience Issues and Implications for Educational Programming.* Annenberg Public Policy Survey Series, No. 3. Philadelphia: University of Pennsylvania, Annenberg Public Policy Center.

Hood, L. (2004) 'Fitting in with the media: the Price-Benoits and the Franzes'. In S.M. Hoover, L.S. Clark and D.F. Alters, *Media, Home, and Family.* New York: Routledge; 131–144.

Hood, L., Clark, L.S., Champ, J.G. and Alters, D.F. (2004) 'The case studies: an introduction'. In S.M. Hoover, L.S. Clark and D.F. Alters (eds) *Media, Home, and Family.* New York: Routledge; 69–77.

Hoover, S.M., Clark, L.S., Alters, D.F., Champ, J. and Hood, L. (2004) *Media, Home, and Family.* New York: Routledge.

Hoover, S.M. (2006) *Religion in the Media Age.* London: Routledge.

Katz, E. and Liebes, T. (1985) 'Mutual aid in the decoding of Dallas: preliminary notes from a cross-cultural study'. In P. Drummond and R. Paterson (eds) *Television in Transition: Papers from the First International Television Studies Conference*. London: British Film Institute.

Krendl, K.A., Clark, G., Dawson, R. and Troiano, C. (1993) 'Preschoolers and VCRs in the home: a multiple methods approach'. *Journal of Broadcasting & Electronic Media*, 37: 293–312.

Kubey, R. (1998) Obstacles to the development of media education in the U.S. *Journal of Communication* 48(1): 58–69.

Liebert, R., Sprafkin, J. and Davidson, E. (1982) *The Early Window: Effects of Television on Children and Youth*. New York: Pergamon Press.

Lindlof, T.R. (1995) *Qualitative Communication Research Methods*. Thousand Oaks, CA: Sage.

Lindlof, T. and Taylor, B. (2002) *Qualitative Communication Research Methods*, second edition. Newbury Park, CA: Sage.

Livingstone, S. (1998) 'Mediated childhoods: a comparative approach to the lifeworld of young people in a changing media environment'. *European Journal of Communication*, 13(4): 435–456.

Livingstone, S. (2001) 'Children and their changing media environment'. In S. Livingstone and M. Bovill (eds) *Children and their Changing Media Environment: A European Comparative Study*. Lawrence Erlbaum Associates.

Livingstone, S. (2002) *Young People and New Media: Childhood and the Changing Media Environment*. London: Sage.

Livingstone, S. (2003) 'Children's use of the internet: reflections on the emerging research agenda'. *New Media and Society*, 5(2): 147–166.

Livingstone, S. (2005) 'Mediating the public/private boundary at home: children's use of the internet for privacy and participation'. *Journal of Media Practice*, 6(1): 41–51.

Lull, J. (1980) 'Family communication patterns and the social uses of television'. *Communication Research*, 7: 275–294.

Lull, J. (1990) *Inside Family Viewing: Ethnographic Research on Television's Audience*. London: Routledge.

Messenger Davies, M. (2001) *'Dear BBC': Children, Television Storytelling and the Public Sphere*. Cambridge: Cambridge University Press.

Moores, S. (1993) *Interpreting Audiences: The Ethnography of Media Consumption*. London: Sage.

Moores, S. (2000) *Media and Everyday Life in Modern Society*. Edinburgh: Edinburgh University Press.

Nathanson, A.I. (1998) 'Identifying and explaining the relationship between parental mediation and children's aggression'. *Communication Research*, 26: 124–143.

Nathanson, A.I. (2001) 'Parents versus peers: exploring the significance of peer mediation of antisocial television'. *Communication Research*, 28: 251–274.

Nathanson, A.I. (2002) 'The unintended effects of parental mediation of television on adolescents'. *Media Psychology*, 4(3): 207–230.

Nathanson, A.I. and Yang, M.-S. (2003) 'The effects of mediation content and form on children's responses to violent television'. *Human Communication Research*, 29: 111–134.

Neumann, I.B. (2006) 'Pop goes religion: Harry Potter meets Clifford Geertz'. *European Journal of Cultural Studies*, 9: 81–100.

Seiter, E. (1999) *Television and New Media Audiences*. Oxford: Oxford University Press.

Silverstone, R. (1992) *Consuming Technologies: Media and Information in Domestic Spaces*. London: Routledge.

Silverstone, R., Hirsch, E. and Morley, D. (1992) 'Information and communication technologies and the moral economy of the household'. In R. Silverstone and E. Hirsch (eds) *Consuming Technologies. Media and Information in Domestic Spaces*. London: Routledge; 15–31.

Singer, D.G. and Singer, J.L. (eds) (2001) *Handbook of Children and The media*. Thousand Oaks, CA: Sage.

Turner G. (2003). *British Cultural Studies: An Introduction*, 3rd edition. London: Routledge.

Valkenburg, P.M., Krcmar, M., Peeters, A.L. and Marseille, N.M. (1999) 'Developing a scale to assess three styles of television mediation: "Instructive mediation", "restrictive mediation", and "social coviewing"'. *Journal of Broadcasting & Electronic Media*, 43: 52–66.

Van Zoonen, L. (2004) 'Imagining the fan democracy'. *European Journal of Communication*, 19(1): 39–52.

Warren, R. (2003) 'Parental mediation of preschool children's television viewing'. *Journal of Broadcasting & Electronic Media*, 47(3): 394–486.

Warren, R., Gerke, P. and Kelly, M.A. (2002) 'Is there enough time on the clock? Parental involvement and mediation of children's television viewing'. *Journal of Broadcasting & Electronic Media*, 46: 87–111.

Willis, P. (1974) 'Symbolism and practice: a theory for the social meaning of pop music'. Stencilled Occasional Paper, Centre for Contemporary Cultural Studies, University of Birmingham.

Zanker, R. (2004) 'Commercial Public service children's television: oxymoron or media commons for savvy kids?' *European Journal of Communication*, 19(4): 435–455.

7

Reality and Fantasy in Media: Can Children Tell the Difference and How Do We Know?

Máire Messenger Davies

INTRODUCTION

According to Malcolm Williams, a sociologist of science:

> An important task of science and one in which it is (I think) partially successful, is to distinguish between the real and what is socially constructed as real … gravity for example does not differentially affect cultures in time or space (Williams, 2000: 85).

A distinguished media and cultural studies scholar, Christine Geraghty, proposes:

> Semiotics was significant in work on the media because it attempted to break the notion of mediation and to show that the key relationship within a language system was not between a word and its referent …; instead it was argued that a word's meaning was established through its relationship with other words … the real world did not pre-exist language but was constructed through it (Geraghty, 2005: 47).

From these two brief quotations addressing the relationship between the real world and human constructions of it – quotations which are representative of a considerable body of contemporary scholarship – we can see that questions about the relationship of fantasy to the real are not simply (as they have often been presented) issues about anxious parents of children being bombarded with glitzy advertising. These questions are at the heart of contemporary scholarship in both the arts and sciences; indeed, they have long been at the heart of scholarship, since Plato discussed the differences between seeing shadows, reflections and the actual light of the sun, in his allegory about the acquisition of knowledge, 'The cave', in *The Republic* (*c*. 375 BC). What *is* real and is there, indeed, a difference between it and fantasy which children can be taught to 'tell'?

This chapter will approach this question from a number of perspectives. First, it will discuss psychological approaches to the study of what, and how, children come to know not only the nature of the world around them, but also, more relevantly, how to interpret it, particularly from the point of view of distinguishing true from false knowledge. These approaches come broadly under the heading of theory of mind (ToM) studies, and they are also linked to studies of language development – how children 'learn to mean' (Halliday, 1975). In the context of language development, we can see the difficulty of structuralist and poststructuralist theories of language as outlined by Geraghty: if language predetermines reality, in what form can the prelinguistic child understand the world? Through what means can the baby acquire language in the first place, if there is no reality external to language to help them to do so? Adults have the responsibility to teach the children they bring into the world how to negotiate with and live in it. Media in all their forms (words, music, pictures, moving pictures, sounds) are the means whereby adults do this. But media, too, are part of the material reality of the child's world, and to understand how they function is not just to understand their content; understanding media involves a recognition of their embodied reality in the form of institutions, codes, styles and products – an understanding that can be broadly characterized as 'media literacy'.

Second, the chapter will review studies of reality and fantasy perception as applied to media, particularly to television (the primary medium to arouse concern about this issue); however, it is obviously an issue with other media, such as traditional stories (a big worry for Plato); films, books and comics (see Starker (1991), for a good historical overview); and more recently, computers and computer games (Cassell and Jenkins, 1999; Hutchby and Moran Ellis, 2001; Livingstone, 2002). Many of these studies on children's fantasy/reality perception have been particularly concerned with teaching children to tell the difference as defined by adult experimenters, rather than investigating whether or not there is a difference, and whether, and how, children see it. Such studies have proposed reality perception as a mediating variable to protect children against harmful effects. For example, Robert Hawkins (1977: 299) suggested:

> If the social and psychological processes involved in television effects can be isolated, one can then search for ways in which those processes can be altered ... children's perception of television's reality has seemed an especially good candidate [for an intervening variable] and has stimulated much hope and considerable research.

This discourse, very pervasive in the 1970s and 1980s, has reappeared in the more recent discourses of UK Government media policy, for instance in publications from the British regulatory body Ofcom (2004) such as their 'Strategy and priorities for the promotion of media literacy'. Media literacy is defined as 'the ability to access, understand and create communications in a variety of contexts' (Ofcom, 2004: 2). The authors of the document argue that media-literate people will be 'able to exercise informed choices about content and services ... and be better able to protect themselves and their families from harmful or offensive materials' (Ofcom, 2004: 3). If people can become media literate, then there will thus be less need for governmental regulation of media content and the production companies wanting to profit from the production of potentially harmful or offensive material will be restrained from doing so primarily by consumer choice, rather than by legislation. Ofcom's Draft Annual Plan for 2006–2007 describes media literacy as one of its consumer protection goals (Ofcom, 2005: 4).

Third, the chapter will look at some more recent approaches and studies to this question, drawing on empirical data from children themselves, in which the issue of telling the difference between reality and fantasy is seen not just as a mediating variable, or form of inoculation, in order to protect children from harmful media effects. In some of these more recent studies (e.g. Goetz *et al.*, 2005) the importance and centrality of fantasy, including mass media influences, in children's lives is explored and defended. These approaches draw more on the psychoanalytic tradition of Bruno Bettelheim, in turn indebted to Freud; Bettelheim argued that fairy tales were essential to psychological health in young children, and his ideas have also been internalized by contemporary children's television producers such as Anna Home (1993) and Roger Singleton-Turner (1994). In other recent studies, children's understandings of social reality, including their responses to media news material, have been discussed. With news and factual material, the ability to tell the difference between fantasy and reality is only one aspect of a broader question about the relationship between media representations and actual events. Children's understanding of news will not be discussed in detail here, but it is clearly a pertinent component of any examination of this question. Further information can be found in Carter (2003), Carter and Davies (2005), Buckingham (2000) and Lemish and Goetz (2007).

In discussing these different approaches, differing methods of 'finding out' will be apparent. Inevitably, there has to be some discussion of aesthetics (of form and of genre) of, as John Ellis (2002: 99) put it:

> the degree to which the world beyond television has been processed by television by the pictorial qualities of the programmes in which it is worked through. Documentary images will have a more calculated sense of framing than does news footage; television fiction will be far more composed as a rule except when it is consciously striving to imitate the roughness of news material, as with a series like *NYPD Blue*.

All of these 'cues in the stimulus material', to quote James Potter (1988: x), have to be part of the methodology of research in the 'how do we know' aspect of this chapter. Those of us who study audiences need to be sensitive to the text itself, as well as to what its readers and viewers make of it. Indeed, practitioner/scholars such as Ellis would argue that it is impossible to separate the two. In qualitative studies of children's perceptions of fantasy and real material, the relationship between aesthetic features of the text (style, narrative, special effects and so on) and children's perceptions of reality are central to how they choose to speak about these issues.

THE MEANING MIND: DEVELOPMENTAL APPROACHES

Symbolic expression is innate and exclusive to humans; it is something that all human infants learn to do, without formal instruction (Bee and Boyd, 2003). Children first learn to communicate through crying, gestures, facial expressions, meaningless but highly expressive sounds such as babbling, and then, towards the end of the first and throughout their second year, in language – first single words, then combinations of two words, then complex sentences and eventually extended utterances, such as narratives and jokes (Davies *et al.*, 1987). Verbal language, as Ferdinand de Saussure ([1915] 1974), the founding father of semiotics, most clearly articulated, is arbitrary; that is, its symbols, whether of sound, or script, have no intrinsic relationship to its referents. Thus, there is a sense in which all forms of communication media, including the one most fundamental to human interaction, namely language, are not real, only representational. Children learn this massively complex arbitrary symbolic system of language relatively effortlessly, and extremely young (most grammatical rules are acquired by the age of 4), which suggests that they are particularly well equipped to handle symbolic information generally. We could hypothesize that the main job of the developing human brain is to tell the difference between reality and fantasy and that it would be very surprising, and indeed, counter-evolutionary, if children could not do it.

Barrett *et al.* (2002: 2) argue from the perspective of evolutionary psychology that cultural behaviour, of which language is the foundation, is a biologically programmed necessity. Phenotypic plasticity – the ability of human beings to adapt to different circumstances and to develop appropriate cultural patterns for dealing with them – is the most important of human evolutionary adaptations. The ability to fantasize, they argue, is one of these adaptations and is a central aspect of second-order intentionality – or the ability to recognize another's point of view:

> Storytelling is only possible with at least second-order intentionality, because composer and audience have to be able to imagine that the world could be other than as they find it. . . . if stories are more than just descriptions of fictional worlds then even more advanced mentalising abilities may be required (Barrett *et al.*, 2002: 362).

For children, stories serve many purposes, one of which, as Barrett *et al.* (2002) point out, is the fostering of the social, cultural and political skill of second-, third- and fourth-order thinking. ToM studies suggest that young human children are biologically equipped to make distinctions between different states of being, and different states of mind – their own and others'. ToM, first formulated by Premack and Woodruff (1978), is usually tested by asking children to recognize false beliefs, that is, the possibility that another person may hold a view that is contrary to the actual state of affairs. This has been, and continues to be, an extremely popular field of research in developmental psychology. In 1991, a special issue of the *British Journal of Developmental Psychology* addressed 'Perspectives on the child's theory of mind', stimulating much subsequent interest (Harris *et al.*, 1991; Samuels and Taylor, 1994; Roberts and Blades, 1995; Moore, 1996; Davies, 2001; Foote and Holmes Lonergan, 2003; Symons *et al.*, 2005). Introducing the 1991 special issue, the editors (George Butterworth, Paul Harris, Alan Leslie and Henry Wellman) defined the term 'theory of mind' as 'naive psychology – our everyday, lay notions about people as psychological beings … with a mental world of thoughts, ideas, imaginings' (Butterworth *et al.*, 1991: 1).

HOW DO WE KNOW?

The primary means of testing children's ToM about other people's mental states has been the controlled experiment, characterized rather sardonically by Butterworth *et al.* as: 'the experimental study of Anglo-European pre-schoolers understanding of the mental state of belief under laboratory conditions' (Butterworth *et al.*, 1991: 1). For example, Harris *et al.* (1991) showed children aged between 4 and 8 a series of empty boxes. They were asked to imagine that inside one of the boxes was a fierce little animal. Children were then shown the inside of the box and were able to test for themselves that imaginary creatures were not inside. But in the second stage of the experiment, children still showed reluctance to put their fingers through a hole in the box, in case their fingers were bitten by the animal, and the younger they were the more likely this was to be the case.

Such experimental studies continue to be a preferred means of testing children's developing understanding of the real and the imaginary by developmental psychologists. The irony of using controlled experiments to test children's knowledge about the difference between reality and fantasy is that the experiment itself is a form of pretence. When experimenters tell children, 'we are going to play a game where you have to guess what Teddy is thinking', they are giving false information: the experimenters are not playing a game, they are conducting research. Thus, a further measure of children's understanding of mental states could be the extent to which they understand that the tasks they are undertaking are not for real but are being carried out for some other motive not revealed to them. When children know that they are being tested, this is a potentially invalidating problem. One could argue that the truest measure of children's ability to understand another person's point of view would be if they called the experimenters' bluff and refused to play the game.

Partly because of the artifice of experimental technique (and also because of its use of numerical data), researchers in cultural studies traditions, such as Buckingham (1993a,b) and Walkerdine (1986), have been suspicious of this kind of research, preferring to carry out talk-based group studies, or ethnographic observations of children at home, to discuss children's interpretations of fictional narratives. Nevertheless, empirical research, yielding quantitative data, can be carried out in ways whereby children do understand that they are taking part in research, but are told that they are collaborators, rather than subjects, and that their views on the nature of reality are the primary focus of interest: there is no right or wrong answer. In this case, there is no deception involved. More recent research on children's media use has taken this more collaborative approach, using a combination of methods, such as questionnaires, diaries, drawings, interviews, structured tasks and so on (Livingstone and Bovill, 1999; Davies, 1997, 2001). Cross-cultural approaches using both qualitative and quantitative methods have also been effectively employed to analyse and compare children's responses to global products, such as Disney's, across different countries and cultures; see *Dazzled by Disney* (Wasko *et al.*, 2001).

METALINGUISTIC DEVELOPMENT

If we accept that the ability to tell reality from fantasy is a function of general symbolic capacity, then children's use and understanding of language – the primary symbol system of human communication – give necessary insights into their perceptions of the real. Studies of metalinguistic development indicate that around the age of 7 or 8, children become able to use language reflexively; for instance, they learn to understand irony and the use of puns (Gardner, 1991). Johnson and Pascual Leone (1989) demonstrated that metalinguistic skills, such as the ability to understand metaphor, puns, ambiguity, synonymy, figurative language and pragmatic intent, become more marked in middle childhood, at around the age of 7 or 8. Dent and Rosenberg (1990) found a similar developmental trend between ages 5 and 7 for the understanding of complex visual metaphors. Elinor Ochs (1979) pointed out the centrality of pragmatics – the study of speech acts – and the importance of formal characteristics in indicating 'the child's increasing sensitivity to the perspective of the listener'. The development of grammatical knowledge indicates how the child moves away from 'reliance on the immediate situational context ... [and develops] the tense system, the use of articles, relative clauses, reference to entities in the past, future or imaginary world... the most pervasive and fundamental speech act of all is that of reference ... successfully accomplished when the speaker believes the hearer can identify what is being referred to' (Ochs, 1979: 12–13).

MODALITY JUDGEMENTS

Thus, one of the main ways in which children demonstrate awareness of other people's mental states is through language, but more specifically through the modifications of language by grammatical and rhetorical codes and conventions. A particular cue for this understanding is through the use of modal transformations, such as 'must', 'might', 'could', which indicate degrees of certainty, or uncertainty, about mental states (Aitchison, 1983). Bob Hodge and David Tripp (1986) produced a classic study on media 'modality', which has been persistently referred to by other media researchers. Their study with Australian elementary schoolchildren adapted the concept of modality from linguistics and applied it to formal features of television, in particular to cartoons. According to Hodge and Tripp, fantasy, as found in the cartoon form, is 'weak modality'; that is, it cannot be easily confused with reality. Cartoons say 'this might be a monster', not 'this is a monster'. In Hodge and Tripp's study, children were required to interpret an animated cartoon called *Fangface* . Hodge and Tripp's goal was to demonstrate that their own semiotic analysis of the cartoon, laid out through paradigms, syntagms and various other structural markers, would be reflected in the children's interpretation of it. Their method was to show individual children the first five minutes of an episode of the cartoon and then to get them to discuss its realism, or otherwise. The children's conversations were transcribed and analysed for the use of semiotic and modality markers. By the age of 9, it was obvious that children used a large number of formal features as the basis for their modality judgements, distinguishing cartoons from films and films from real life.

Cartoons are pretty obviously not real, nor even realistic, to most children, but, as Hodge and Tripp discovered, discussing them is a very useful research tool in generating insights into children's own judgements about reality and fantasy. Striking modality awareness prompted by the cartoon form was shown by this 7-year-old girl in an outer-London primary school in a study with over 1,300 6- to 13-year-olds, which I carried out for the BBC, *Dear BBC*:

> In cartoons you can do anything, you can do anything really, you can make anything happen, as long as you can draw it. With films, I really like films, because its real people and they are doing things sort of like more clear and more firm – the colours – and you can see all the things that are happening and it makes you feel it is true. While in cartoons you know it is only drawings (Girl, 7: outer London infants school) (Davies, 2001: 225).

Learning to read the modal cues of television in this way can be seen as an aspect of developing ToM. Such readings require, in the words of Moore and Frye (1991: 4):

> representing a representation as a representation of reality, or, in other words, judging how the [*other*] person's representation relates to the world.

INOCULATION THEORY AND MEDIA EDUCATION

Most of the research most directly concerned with children's lay notions about people as psychological beings has been done with pre-school children, but, as with the 7-year-old quoted above, who produced this comment in a discussion about the cartoon *Rugrats* with members of her primary-school class, children's social relations become most developed in middle childhood, when they are at school. This is also the age when they are most avid media consumers, which is a major source of children's knowledge about social relations, the overwhelmingly favoured form being dramatic fiction (Livingstone and Bovill, 1999).

In the 1980s and 1990s, concerns about the trustworthiness of media content gave rise to a number of media literacy – or critical viewing skills – programmes in schools in the USA, designed to teach children not to trust the persuasive techniques of modern commercial communications technologies, particularly television (Hawkins, 1977; Brown, 1993). Experimental classroom programmes, such as those carried out by Aimee Dorr and her colleagues at the University of California, Los Angeles (Dorr *et al.*, 1980, 1990; Dorr, 1983), trained children in the understanding of both the techniques and the institutional economics of television production, with the hope of protecting them against possible harmful effects – the 'inoculation theory' of media education. There is some evidence that, at least in the short term, children who received this training became more sceptical about, for example, the trustworthiness of sitcom characters as role models (Dorr, 1980). According to Dorr *et al.* (1991), the perceived realism of television content plays a mediating role between exposure to television content and its social effects.

Nikken and Peeters (1988), pursuing a similar line of inquiry, asked children questions such as: 'A child told me Tommie is put in a closet until the next *Sesame Street*. Do you think that is true?' Although it was the child's 'perceptions' that were under investigation, the answer 'No' was coded as 'wrong'. Such questions are designed to uncover children's *mis*perceptions, as measured against an objective standard of reality. *Why* the child thought that Tommie was not put in a closet was not fully explored. Morison *et al.* (1981) explored children's reasoning processes about television reality in more depth. In Morison *et al.*'s study children were presented with 12 pairs of programmes, pre-chosen by the researchers, and asked to decide which were 'more real'. An example of such a pairing was *The Wizard of Oz* versus the news. In this forced-choice task, children from second to sixth grade did not differ in their choices about which were 'more real'. Nearly all made the 'right' choices. Where children of different ages did differ was in the criteria they used to explain their choices.

Morison *et al.* (1981) found significant age differences in reliance on physical features as a 'reality cue', with 52% of younger children and only 15% of older children referring to them. A useful construct developed by William Elliott and his colleagues (Elliott, 1983) is the idea of 'personal utility' in evaluating how real viewers find televised representations. If personal utility is a criterion, then, for young children, *The Wizard of Oz* may very well seem more real to children than the news, in its representation of childhood preoccupations and fantasies, such as abandonment, victimization, homesickness, friendship and overcoming danger. So, although most children quite correctly identified the news as a more realistic genre than the movie, the inoculation argument, that doubting its reality should lessen the impact, does not follow. Knowing that *The Wizard of Oz* is less real than the news does not necessarily stop children from being frightened by the Wicked Witch of the West, nor from identifying with Dorothy's desire to go home.

Potter (1988), in a useful critique of reality definitions in research, was critical of the tendency of researchers to 'know best' and to define 'perceived reality' as 'a synonym for media accuracy, isomorphic to real life experiences'. Potter laid special emphasis on what he calls 'generational issues', arguing that they involve three important factors: a person's experience with the media; a person's ability to make sense out of media stimuli; and the type of cues in the stimulus material. 'Cues in the stimulus material', Potter points out, have been 'virtually ignored in the [research] literature'. The question raised by Potter is the one mentioned by John Ellis (above): to what extent do formal and generic characteristics signal whether or not material should be taken seriously?

As many educators would argue (e.g. see Whitehead (1990)), the question of what children cannot do should not mask a recognition of what they can do. Here, Vygotzky's concept of 'the zone of proximal development' becomes a consideration in designing procedures to explore children's understanding of the nature of reality and fantasy. This concept argues that good teaching practices push a child just beyond what his/her current competence and developmental stage would appear to be. The focus is on competence, and how to extend it, and on the potential for what the child could do if given adult encouragement and resources – including media resources.

REAL-WORLD FANTASIES

Just as the ToM literature rarely addresses the contribution of children's cultural experiences, such as watching TV, to their developing knowledge of social relations, so most of the literature within communications studies on children's media literacy does not address children's beliefs about fantasy and reality derived from other sources outside the media. Children's beliefs about, for instance, mythical figures such as fairies and Santa Claus, or imaginary friends, were the subject of a whole issue of the *British Journal of Developmental Psychology* in 1994. Paul Harris, in an introductory essay, described magical events as

> events that violate everyday causal principles … The ability to classify particular events as magical allows children to develop an appropriate cognitive and emotional stance towards a wealth of cultural material. They are encouraged to participate in ritual practices such as placing a tooth under a pillow, hanging a stocking at the foot of the bed, or making a wish. In addition they are exposed to a plethora of stories, films and playground talk about ghosts and monsters (Harris, 1994: 1–2).

Harris and the other researchers published in this edition of the *British Journal of Developmental Psychology* were particularly interested in children's understanding of causality – of what normally makes things happen, as compared with what does *not* normally make things happen. 'The understanding that these magical practices and supernatural beings are special depends on a prior appreciation of the mundane' (Harris, 1994: 2). To appreciate 'magic', children need to know what is normal and not magic. They need, in other words, to be able to 'tell reality from fantasy'.

This indicated the importance of not confining concerns about children's beliefs in true or false phenomena only to television and other media. Rosengren *et al.* (1994: 70) in this edition of the *British Journal of Developmental Psychology* refer to the Piagetian term 'magical causality' as 'a type of reasoning in which children believe in their own efficacy to cause some event merely through the power of their own gestures or thoughts'. Rosengren *et al.* (1994: 69) also point out that parents and 'other non-psychologists' (although many psychologists are also parents and will share parental assumptions) 'have a common belief … that children believe in the reality of such fictional characters as magicians, ghosts and Santa Claus'. Rosengren *et al.* tested children between ages 4 and 5 by showing them pictures of events that could and could not happen. Children were shown still images of animals getting bigger, smaller, or more or less complex, and asked if these transformations were possible. Most children correctly answered that animals could get bigger, but not smaller or less complex. Children were then asked, in a second stage, whether a magician could make these things happen. In contrast to the first stage, children *did* agree that these impossible things could happen if a magician worked magic on the animals. The study demonstrated both children's knowledge of everyday mundanity and their willingness to suspend disbelief when a magician was involved.

In a study I carried out in Philadelphia (Davies, 1997) I wanted to look at the relationship of TV reality perception with these other kinds of magical beliefs. I gave children aged between 6 and 11 years (39 boys and 43 girls) a questionnaire on the perceived reality of TV formal features, such as special effects, editing, staging and acting. The questionnaire was read to the youngest children (6- and 7-year-olds) and the 8–11-year-olds filled it in themselves. In addition to demographic information, including age, gender, school, and information about TV viewing, liking and favourite programmes, most of the questions consisted of multiple-choice statements requiring the child's opinion (true/not true/not sure) about television reality or non-reality; for instance: 'TV shows like *The Cosby Show* and *Full House* happen in somebody's real house' or 'Superman and Batman can't really fly in the movies; it's a trick'. It also included multiple-choice questions about non-TV reality beliefs; for instance: 'Santa Claus is a real person who brings us gifts at Christmas time'. There were also questions about the morality, or otherwise, of showing realistic violence or deceptive commercials on TV; for example: 'It's OK to show violence in programs on TV because it makes the program exciting'. Tables 7.1 and 7.22 show the age differences in responses to these questions (scores are grouped).

As these tables indicate, the oldest children were the most sceptical, but there was no

Table 7.1 Children's awareness of TV illusions: percentage of true, untrue and not sure answers in each age group[a]

	1st grade (6–7 years), $n = 28$	*3rd grade (8–9 years),* $n = 25$	*5th grade (10–11 years),* $n = 29$
Answering 'Not true', i.e. aware that the show took place on a TV set (%)	76.5	74.5	86.5
Answering 'True'(%)	12.5	11	9
Answering 'Not sure'(%)	11	14.5	4.5

[a] Sample base: n=82. Sample question format: 'Shows like *The Cosby Show* and *Full House* happen in somebody's real house. Circle one answer: True; Not True; Not sure'

Table 7.2 Children's awareness of real-life illusions: percentage of true, untrue and unsure answers, by age group[a]

	1st grade	*3rd grade*	*5th grade*
'Not true'(%)	31	45	88
'True'(%)	32	32	4
'Not sure'(%)	37	23	8

[a] Sample question format: 'Santa Claus is a real person who brings us presents at Christmas time: Circle one answer: True; Not true; Not sure'

significant age difference on the scores for the TV reality questions. In contrast, there was a very significant difference between younger and older children in the incidence of 'not true' answers to the three questions probing children's beliefs about non-television fantasy/reality – Santa Claus, the tooth fairy and birthday wishes. As psycholinguistic studies of children's increasing metalinguistic capacity with age would predict, age was associated with greater awareness of illusion in my study. Younger children were significantly more likely than older ones to say that Santa Claus really existed, but, in contrast, none of them believed that Superman could really fly. From a ToM perspective, this supports Paul Harris and colleagues' finding of a conflict between younger children's rational ability to recognize another person's false belief (that there is an animal inside a box) and their emotional response to the *idea* of the animal (they refused to put their fingers inside the box, in case they were bitten) – a response not found in older children.

In contrast, the measures designed to test the children's understanding of TV reality in my study showed no statistically significant differences between age groups. These children did not have media education in school and in the qualitative discussions during the interview stage of the research, they were asked where they got all this information about how TV worked; for virtually all of them it was from TV itself, although one child had a parent who worked as a TV producer and had visited a studio. A key point from these findings is that the contrast between the responses to the TV reality questions, and to the real-world reality question (about Santa, etc.), suggests that knowing the difference between fantasy and reality on TV does not protect young children from being taken in by other sorts of fantasy. It is possible for a 6-year-old to be a media-wise viewer and still hang up their stocking hopefully on Christmas Eve.

QUALITATIVE INTERVIEW TASKS

The second stage of the study involved individual interviews with 18 children, three boys and three girls from each age group. The interviewer showed the child four short clips from four different TV shows, each containing a variety of more or less unexpected events and effects: *Sesame Street*; *The Cosby Show*; *Real News for Kids; The Sand Fairy* (the BBC drama based on Edith Nesbit's book, *Five Children and It*). Children were asked to press the pause button on the remote control every time they saw something that 'couldn't happen in real life'. Across the four clips, each lasting two or three minutes, 67 different events were identified as 'couldn't happen in real life'. For the purposes of comparison between the three age groups, the television events which led to each child pausing the tape for 'couldn't happen in real life' were combined into four overall categories: (i) Special Effects; (ii) Literary/Theatrical (including references to narrative and genre); (iii) Impossibility (objects' behaviour) and (iv) Improbability (human behaviour). The distribution of these categories across the three age groups can be seen in Figure 7.1.

Both younger and older children persistently chose special effects as a mark of unreality; this is in contrast to Dorr and colleagues' findings (Dorr, 1983; Dorr *et al.*, 1990), which showed that surface features such as special effects were more salient for younger viewers than for older ones. Younger children sometimes used the construct 'magic' to explain special effects, whereas older children never did.

These analyses suggest that second-order pragmatic judgements about other people's motives and reactions are partly a function

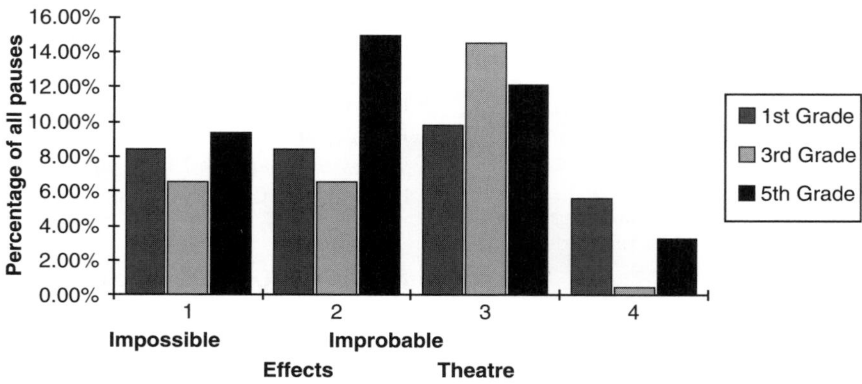

Figure 7.1 'Not real': reasons for pausing the tape, by grade

Key

1. **Impossible: reasons based on physical impossibility, e.g. blocks can't move by themselves.**
2. **Effects: reasons based on television special effects, e.g. fast editing.**
3. **Improbable: reasons based on real life probability, e.g. shopkeepers don't lend you money.**
4. **Theatre: reasons based on awareness of acting and performance: Big Bird is a guy dressed up.**

of age. TV effects and deceptions, on the other hand, were generally recognized by nearly all the children, in each age group, to be 'fake'. Indeed, such was the cynicism that these children had about TV that even where locations and settings *were* real, and not a studio set, they insisted: 'That's fake'. For example, the castle used in one of my video clips, *Five Children and It*, was a real castle and the episode was filmed on location. One fifth-grader argued that it was 'all a set. They're just trying to express to you that this film is supposed to be set in a castle, but you know it really isn't' (Davies, 1997: 120). A first-grade boy explained: 'The castle is not made out of bricks. It would cost too much money' (Davies, 1997: 120). Some British children in the BBC study (Davies, 2001) were shown the same sequence in a class group, not individually. They lived in rural Co. Durham, which has many historical remains, and they were asked by the interviewer: 'If I told you that the castle wasn't true, it was just in a studio, they put pretend bricks up and the windows weren't real? Would you believe it?' They all replied 'No, no, no'. The interviewer asked, 'What made it look real?' and the children specified: 'The knights, the clothes, there were no pictures on the walls, the stairs'. (Davies, 2001: 209).

These differences in response raise the question of the cultural capital (Bourdieu, 1984) which children bring to the viewing situation and on which they inevitably draw for making reality judgements. For North American children, the dominant cultural expectation was that castles would be built in studios – Universal Studios, as one boy suggested. For the British children, used to period drama in both children's and adults' schedules, castles used in location shooting could be encoded as authentic. The distinction here was not between one group of children who were wrong and another who were right, with the implication that the children who were wrong could not tell the difference between reality and fantasy. Both groups were quite capable of understanding the constructed nature of the setting of the drama – but the cues in the stimulus material interacting with their prior cultural knowledge and expectations produced interestingly different, but equally valid, interpretations of the setting. Again, to emphasize the lack of one-to-one correlation between children's awareness of media constructions and real-world knowledge, it should be noted that it was the more sceptical 'media-savvy' group who were, in fact, wrong about the actual reality status of the castle.

The interviews with the children in the Philadelphia study showed that the deceptions of TV aesthetics were accepted by most interviewees, as requirements of the medium, and hence were seen as justified. The animation in *Sesame Street* was universally identified as 'couldn't happen in real life' – but it was seen as legitimate, because it made knowledge more appealing for 'little kids'. In contrast, animation in the news programme was seen as less justifiable. Many children also accepted the generic requirements of comedy in *The Cosby Show*; in real life, older brothers do not let little sisters beat them at checkers (third-grade girl), but in a situation comedy this is allowable because 'it's supposed to be funny'. The suspension of disbelief was similarly in evidence in their explanations of why magic was appropriate in *The Sand Fairy*: 'it's supposed to be a fairy tale' (fourth-grade girl). This ability to make social judgements about the legitimacy of deception within the internal context of the particular story, or genre, provides another dimension of reality judgement to the taxonomies provided by earlier researchers such as Hawkins (1977) and Potter (1988). Where a programme appeared to be breaking its own internal generic rules, a number of children objected: a striking example was the response to the use of the letter T to mark the spot where there was buried treasure in *Sesame Street*. A number of children said this was not real because, according to the generic rules of treasure-hunting stories, 'it should be an X'.

In the BBC study, a group of 11–12-year-olds in Buckinghamshire defended fantasy particularly explicitly in terms of its power to provide escape. In doing so, one of the group quite clearly delineates the difference between fantasy and reality. Indeed, if there were no such difference, fantasy would not have this power:

> Girl 1: Children don't just want to watch what is real, they want fantasy; they don't just want to watch what happens every day – they know what happens because they see it in their own home – they want to see something that is really unbelievable (Davies, 2001: 223).

This group made a further generic proviso. For them, when a programme was classified as 'children's', children watching were able to feel safe. This sense came partly from a generic knowledge of children's programmes as stories which do not, as a rule, include terrible, irretrievable events. Through being defined as 'children's', they are fantasies, no matter how many signifiers of realism they may include. The discussion of 'children's' versus 'adults' thus constantly returned to the question of realism. Several children in the BBC study pointed out that the whole function of stories, whether realistic or fantastic, is precisely to get away from the mundane, but this judgement would not be possible (as with the psychology experiments) if the mundane were not clearly understood to be 'what normally happens':

> Boy 2: Not everybody wants to watch things that happen every day, because things like *Cracker* or *The Bill* have always got drugs or someone trying to kill someone else, but in programmes like *The Demon Headmaster*, if someone says they are going to try and kill somebody you know they are just making it up. There are programmes like *Byker Grove*, and they are just all about real life, but this is like fantasy and what doesn't happen – you can't really believe it, but you just want to watch it....
>
> Girl 2: You don't just want to watch all soaps and dramas and things, because you want to have something to let your mind just escape (Davies, 2001: 224).

THE NECESSITY OF FANTASY

'Letting your mind escape' could be seen as a rephrasing of the title of Bruno Bettelheim's (1976) book *The Uses of Enchantment*. It reiterates the point that stories for children are expected to be useful for them. One of these uses is supposedly to educate them in the established codes and values of their society, whether to reinforce or to subvert. Another use, as Bruno Bettelheim argued of fairy tales, is to help children come to terms with psychic inner conflicts and the struggles of development. Yet another use, related to Bettelheim's, is educational. For progressive educationists the value of cultural experience is child-centred and essential to person-formation; art and literature are ways of promoting optimum intellectual and creative development.

In *Potent Fictions* (Hilton, 1996), a collection of essays by media educators about their work with primary-school children, Mary Hilton points out the large emotional and imaginative investment made by children in narratives and cultural material invented for them. For Hilton, pleasure is part of the pedagogic value of children's relationship with storytelling:

> if we wish to connect children with literature … the ends will have served out their wonderful, predictable measure of pleasure. But children, like adults, want to sustain that pleasure, to return again and again to the dilatory space in the grand narrative as *agents and authors* of their own satisfaction (Hilton, 1996: 42).

For Hilton, the pleasure of abandoning oneself to storytelling is an end in itself. Other media researchers have explored the role of television rather than literature in the positive stimulation of imaginative behaviour and play; for instance, Singer and Singer (1976, 1981), Schmitt and Anderson (2002) and Valkenberg (1994, 2001). Imaginative play was defined by Singer and Singer (1976: 76) as 'whether or not the child used an object or toy in a way different from what its appearance suggested, e.g. calling a toy giraffe a 'spaceman' or indicating … some kind of story line … behaving in an *as if* dimension'. Their study was experimental, with four groups of nursery children, some watching a children's television programme under different conditions, some not watching and then being evaluated for imaginative play and positive affect afterwards. The study found little significant differences between the groups and no obvious negative effects of TV viewing. It concluded that:

> a program such as *Mister Rogers' Neighborhood* may serve as the basis for stimulating increased imaginative play, subject to careful qualification if viewed by smaller groups in the company of an adult (Singer and Singer, 1976: 80).

Valkenburg and Van Der Voort (1994) provide a very extensive review of research on the influence of TV on imaginative play; on daydreaming (internal mental processes such as musing); creative imagination (such as generating novel ideas) and reviewing a range of hypotheses (effects, functions) and methods (correlational, experimental). They cite over 100 studies on these questions. And their conclusion is that 'although there is no evidence that TV stimulates creative imagination, it cannot be ruled out that specific types of TV programmes may foster creative imagination' (Valkenburg and Van Der Voort, 1994: 336). It would appear from this abundance of research that the negative effects 'inoculation' model has been a major stimulus to scholarship: television has been seen as potentially inhibiting to children's cognitive and emotional development, and evidence has been intensively sought to support this. But, as Valkenburg and Van Der Voort conclude, the evidence is not particularly compelling one way or the other, and this would suggest that more fruitful explorations are needed.

Chandler (1997) provided an extensive review of children's understanding of what is 'real' on television – again, the quotation marks indicating the difficulty of establishing the exact nature of 'reality' when discussing this question. Gerard Jones (2002) in a popular text called *Killing Monsters: Why Children Need Fantasy, Super Heroes and Make Believe Violence* confronts the inoculation theory head on and robustly defends children's attraction to violent stories. Jones makes frequent references to his own young son's behaviour, a technique which is controversial, but of necessity sometimes used in this field of study. To avoid the artifice of experimentation, the unobtrusive observation of children in their normal environment can be a better way of evaluating their spontaneous responses to everyday media experiences. Observation of their own children was pioneered by Jean Piaget and Charles Darwin, and more recent media scholars (e.g. Kinder, 1991; Kline 1993; Buckingham, 1995) have also used this method.

THE RELEVANCE OF METHOD

In a more traditionally scholarly study than Jones', Goetz *et al.* (2005) also raised questions about the positive role of fantasy in children's emotional and cognitive development. Both the Jones study and the Goetz *et al.* study are examples of how posing different research questions will generate different methodologies – or 'how do we know' techniques. Jones and Goetz *et al.* proceeded from a hypothesis that media fantasies and stories served particular necessary cognitive and emotional purposes for children and, hence, needed to be 'taken seriously' by researchers, even if the content of these stories might seem alarming to adults.

Goetz *et al.* (2005) constructed an international study in four nations (USA, Germany, Korea and Israel) in which children were positively encouraged to fantasize. The researchers' goal was to determine the extent to which popular media was involved in these fantasies, and also in what ways. They were particularly interested in 'daydreaming', and part of their study involved requiring children to lie down and deliberately enter into a favourite fantasy world and then to describe it later. As well as referring to recent psychological research (e.g. Singer and Singer, 1990), in using such a methodology, they also invoke Freud ([1908] 1995: 146): 'The motive forces of phantasies are unsatisfied wishes and every single phantasy is the fulfilment of a wish, a correction of unsatisfying reality'. Hence, the issue of whether or not children could 'tell the difference between fantasy and reality' was not the primary question. The primary question was: what can children's fantasies tell us about their developmental needs and what part do media fantasy narratives and characters play in this?

These researchers (Goetz *et al.*, 2005) drew on cross-cultural materials and samples in four distinct environments, and also used a variety of methods: a fantasy journey; drawing and writing about a make-believe world; individual interviews and a questionnaire with parents and educators. Their basic research question was: 'to understand these make-believe worlds in children's everyday lives and to examine the nature of the relationships between children's media pleasures and these make-believe worlds' (Goetz *et al.*, 2005: 17) They were particularly interested in whether, and how, children incorporate media texts into their make-believe worlds. As is obvious, there is no sense here that having make-believe worlds might be harmful to children, or that the role of media in influencing and constructing elements of these make-believe worlds was something to be resisted. Texts which turned up repeatedly in the 193 children's make-believe products (stories, drawings and interviews) included Harry Potter, Pokemon, movies such as *Armageddon*, Disney films such as *Cinderella* and locally specific stories such as *Sissi* (Germany), *Mashimaro* (Korea) and local news (Israel), where children's media traces reflected current states of conflict.

The study found cross-cultural and gender differences, but all children drew on media, in what the authors considered to be a functional and healthy way, to build and interpret their fantasy worlds. An example was 11-year-old Sandro (Germany) talking about his make-believe world:

> I'm in Pokemon land. I have seen Muk who wanted to attack me ... I'd love to be a trainer for my favourite Pokemon Electrode. This one can do thunderstruck. Then I could only throw my Pokeball and shout 'go for it Electrode, thunderstruck.' I'd love to be a trainer in reality. (Goetz *et al.*, 2005: 135)

The researchers interpret this as allowing him to 'legitimately combine the desire to fight with the desire to nurture. By combining masculine and feminine narratives he finds a positive path for himself on the ambivalent road to boyhood' (Goetz *et al.*, 2005: 137). These writers explicitly dissociate themselves from the idea that, by deconstructing children's belief in fantasy, they are protecting, or inoculating, them from 'harmful effects' They argue: 'For his educators to deny Sandro these imaginary Pokemon fights may serve to additionally intensify his feeling of having his identity threatened' (Goetz *et al.*, 2005: 137).

Their conclusion is that

> media do play a central role in children's make-believe worlds… in ways that are used mainly to help children symbolise their own experiences and self image and as a springboard for their own narration of a world that allows them a personal space for developing who they wish to be (Goetz *et al.*, 2005: 199).

This benign view of the relationship between children's psychological well-being and media fictions is some way from the 1970s and 1980s view of teaching children to 'tell the difference between reality and fantasy' in special inoculatory educational programmes. The idea that undermining make-believe can be an 'intervening variable' in helping children to negotiate a media world that is seen primarily as damaging and threatening appears to have no purchase in this most recent in-depth research on children and their media. According to these researchers, in our multi-channel, globalized, glocalized world, German and Korean children quite comfortably use Japanese fantasy figures to negotiate their identities and whether or not they can 'tell the difference between reality and fantasy' is not, any longer, the primary issue for many researchers.

This does not mean that further controlled developmental studies will not be needed to explore children's understanding of the world and the various symbolic means whereby the reality of the world is expressed. We also need further research exploring how children's and others' perceptions of fantasy and reality are shaped by the hyperreal fantasy worlds of video and computer games and the interactive domains of the internet. Given the challenges to research posed by increasingly 'realistic' technological representations of both the real world and of fantasy worlds, it would seem necessary for the main scholarly traditions in the field of media studies to collaborate more closely. The first tradition concerns whether not knowing the difference between fantasy and reality is harmful to children, and whether this can lead to anti-social perceptions and behaviours, particularly in the very young – giving rise broadly to experimental studies, many very valuable, but many of which lack conclusive findings. The second approach explores in what ways media fantasies are beneficial to children and promote their 'proximal development' – these are more likely to be qualitative and, although persuasive in their imaginative techniques and in their sympathetic approach to children's needs and rights, may be dismissed by more hard-line social scientists as lacking rigour and social representativeness. Both traditions of research involve value judgements on the part of adult researchers, derived from their own views of the media: scholars who don't like television or contemporary popular culture and who think we are 'amusing ourselves to death' (Postman, 1985) are likely to be drawn to the first 'inoculation' tradition; scholars who do like popular culture or who have ideological objections to elitism in cultural education are more likely to be drawn to the second. Both traditions and their accompanying methodologies need to be grounded in knowledge of social-scientific developmental studies about children's growth and upbringing, Similarly, the field of developmental psychology could perhaps pay more attention to the importance of culture in children's cognitive and affective learning. All scholars need to be reflexive about their own views on the pervasive, increasingly realistic and even more increasingly commercial media environment in which we all live.

REFERENCES

Aitchison, J. (1983) *The Articulate Mammal.* London: Hutchinson.

Barrett, L., Dunbar, R. and Lycett, J. (2002) *Human Evolutionary Psychology.* Basingstoke: Palgrave.

Bee, H. and Boyd, D. (2003) *The Developing Child.* Allyn and Bacon.

Bettelheim, B. (1976) *The Uses Of Enchantment.* London: Thames And Hudson.

Bourdieu, P. (1984) *Distinction: A Social Critique of the Judgement of Taste*, R. Nice (transl.). Cambridge, MA: Harvard University Press.

Brown, J.A. (1993) *Television Critical Viewing Skills' Education: Major Media Literacy Projects in the United States and Selected Countries.* Hillsdale NJ: Lawrence Erlbaum Associates.

Buckingham, D. (1993a) *Children Talking Television: The Making of Television Literacy.* London: Falmer Press.

Buckingham, D. (1993b) *Reading Audiences: Young People and the Media.* Manchester: Manchester University Press.

Buckingham, D. (1995) *Moving Images.* Manchester: Manchester University Press.

Buckingham, D. (2000) *The Making of Citizens: Young People, News and Politics.* London: Routledge.

Butterworth, G., Harris, P., Leslie, A. and Wellman, H. (1991) 'Editorial preface: theory of mind'. *British Journal of Developmental Psychology*, 9(1): 1–4.

Carter, C. (2003) 'Scary news: children's responses to news of war'. In J. Rutherford (ed.) *Mediactive:Media War.* London: Barefoot Publications, Lawrence and Wishart; 67–84.

Carter, C. and Davies M.M. (2005) ' "A fresh peach is easier to bruise": Children and traumatic news'. In S. Allan (ed.) *Journalism: Critical Issues.* Maidenhead: Open University Press; 224–235.

Cassell, J. and Jenkins, J. (eds) (1999) *From Barbie to Mortal Kombat.* Cambridge, MA: MIT Press.

Chandler, D. (1997) 'Children's understanding of what is 'real' on television: a review of the literature'. *Learning, Media and Technology*, 23(1): 65–80.

Davies M.M. (1997) *Fake, Fact and Fantasy: Children's Interpretation of Television Reality.* Mahwah, NJ: Lawrence Erlbaum Associates.

Davies, M.M. (2001) *'Dear BBC': Children, Television-Storytelling and the Public Sphere.* Cambridge: Cambridge University Press.

Davies, M.M. (1989, 2nd edition 2001) *Television is Good for Your Kids.* London: Hilary Shipman.

Davies, M.M., Lloyd, E. and Scheffler, A. (1987) *Baby Language.* London: Unwin Hyman.

De Saussure, F. ([1915] 1974) *Course in General Linguistics*, J. Culler (ed.). London: Harper-Collins.

Dent, C. and Rosenberg, L. (1990) 'Developmental Accounts of Children's Processing of Non-literal Material, Visual and Verbal Metaphors: Developmental Interactions'. *Child Development.*

Dorr, A. (1983) 'No shortcuts to judging reality'. In J. Bryant and D. Anderson (eds) *Children's Understanding of Television.* New York: Academic Press.

Dorr, A., Graves, S.B. and Phelps, E. (1980) 'Television literacy for young children'. *Journal of Communication*, 30(3): 84–93.

Dorr, A., Kovaric, P. and Doubleday, C. (1990) 'Age and content influences on children's perceptions of the realism of television families'. *Journal of Broadcasting and Educational Media*, 34(4): 377–397.

Ellis, J. (2002) *Seeing Things: Television in an Age of Uncertainty.* London: I.B. Tauris.

Foote, R.C. and Holmes-Lonergan, H.A. (2003) 'Sibling conflict and theory of mind'. *British Journal of Experimental Psychology*, 21(1): 45–58.

Gardner, H. (1993) *The Unschooled Mind: How Children Think and How Schools Should Teach.* New York: Basic Books.

Geraghty, C. (2005) 'Representation, reality and popular culture: semiotics and the construction of meaning'. In J. Curran, J. and M. Gurevich (eds) *Mass Media and Society.* London: Hodder Arnold; 46–59.

Goetz, M., Lemish, D., Aidman, A. and Moon, H. (2005) *Media and the Make Believe Worlds of Children: When Harry Potter Meets Pokemon in Disneyland.* Mahwah, NJ: Lawrence Erlbaum Associates.

Halliday, M. (1975) *Learning How to Mean: Explorations in the Development of Language.* London: Edward Arnold.

Harris, P.L., Brown, E., Marriott, C., Whittall, S. and Harmer, S. (1991) 'Monsters, ghosts and witches: testing the limits of the fantasy–reality distinction in young children'. *British Journal of Developmental Psychology*, 9: 105–124.

Hawkins, R. (1977) 'The dimensional structure of children's perceptions of TV reality'. *Communication Research*, 4(3): 299–320.

Hilton, M. (ed) (1996) *Potent Fictions: Children's Literacy and the Challenge of Popular Culture.* London: Routledge.

Hodge, R. and Tripp, D. (1986) *Children and Television.* Cambridge: Polity Press.

Home, A. (1993) *Into the Box of Delights: A History of Children's Television.* London: BBC Books.

Hutchby, I. and Moran Ellis, J. (2001) *Children, Technology and Culture: The Impacts of Technologies in Children's Everyday Lives.* London: Routledge.

Johnson, J. and Pascual-Leone, J. (1989) 'Developmental levels of processing in metaphor interpretation'. *Journal of Experimental Psychology*, York University, Ontario.

Jones, G. (2002) *Killing Monsters: Why Children Need Fantasy, Super Heroes and Make Believe Violence.* New York: Basic Books.

Kinder, M. (1991) *Playing with Power in Movies, Television and Video Games from Muppet Babies to Teenage Mutant Ninja Turtles.* Berkeley: University of California Press.

Kline, S. (1993) *Out of the Garden: Toys and Children's Culture in the Age of TV Marketing.* London: Verso.

Lemish, D. and Goetz, M. (eds) (2007) *Children and Media in Times of Conflict and War.* Cresskill, NJ: Hampton.

Livingstone, S. (2002) *Young People and New Media.* London: Sage.

Livingstone, S. and Bovill, M. (1999) *Young People and New Media.* London: LSE.

Moore, C. (1996) 'Theories of mind in infancy'. *British Journal of Developmental Psychology,* 14(1): 19–40.

Moore, C. and Frye, D. (1991) 'The acquisition and utility of theories of mind'. In D. Frye and C. Moore (eds), *Children's Theories of Mind: Mental States and Social Understanding.* Hillsdale, NJ: Lawrence Erlbaum Associates.

Morison, P., Kelly, H. and Gardner, H. (1981) 'Reasoning about the realities on television: a developmental study'. *Journal of Broadcasting,* 25(3): 229–242.

Ochs, E. (1979) *Developmental Pragmatics.* New York: Academic Press.

Ofcom. (2004) *Ofcom's Strategy and Priorities for the Promotion of Media Literacy: A Statement.* London: Office of Communications.

Ofcom (2005) *Draft Annual Plan 2006/7: Consultation Document.* London: Office of Communications.

Postman, N. (1985) *Amusing Ourselves to Death: Public Discourse in the Age of Showbusiness.* New York: Penguin.

Potter, W.J. (1988) 'Perceived reality in television effects research'. *Journal of Broadcasting and Educational Media,* 32(1).

Premack, D. and Woodruff, G. (1978) 'Does the chimpanzee have a theory of mind?' *Behaviour and Brain Sciences,* 1: 515–526.

Roberts, K.P. and Blades, M. (1995) 'Children's discrimination of memories for actual and pretend action in a hiding task'. *British Journal of Developmental Psychology,* 13(4): 321–333.

Rosengren, K.S., Kalish, C.W., Hickling, A.K. and Gelman, S.A. (1994) 'Exploring the relation between preschool children's magical beliefs and causal thinking'. *British Journal of Developmental Psychology,* 12(1): 69–82.

Samuels, A. and Taylor, M. (1994) 'Children's ability to distinguish fantasy events from real-life events'. *British Journal of Developmental Psychology,* 12: 417–427.

Singer, J.L. and Singer, D.G. (1976) 'Fostering creativity in children: Can TV stimulate imaginative play?'. *Journal of Communication,* 26(3): 74–80.

Singer, J.L. and Singer, D.G. (1981) *Television, Imagination and Aggression: A Study of Preschoolers.* Mahwah, NJ: Lawrence Erlbaum Associates.

Singleton-Turner, R. (1994) *Television and Children.* London: BBC.

Starker, S. (1991) *Evil Influences: Crusades Against the Mass Media.* New Brunswick, NJ: Transaction.

Symons, D.K., Peterson, C.C., Slaughter, V., Roche, J. and Doyle, E. (2005) 'Theory of mind and mental state discourse during book reading and storytelling tasks'. *British Journal of Developmental Psychology,* 23(1): 81–102.

Valkenberg, P.M. and Van Der Voort, T.H. (1994). 'The influence of television on daydreaming and creative imagination: a review of research'. *Psychological Bulletin,* 116(2): 316–339.

Van Der Voort, T.H. and Valkenberg, P.M. (1994). 'Television's impact on fantasy play: a review of research'. *Developmental Review,* 14(1): 27–51.

Walkerdine, V. (1986) 'Video reply: families, films and fantasy'. In V. Burgin J. Donald and C. Kaplan (eds) *Formations of Fantasy.* London: Routledge and Kegan Paul.

Wasko, J., Phillips, M. and Meehan, E.R. (eds) (2001) *Dazzled by Disney: The Global Disney Audiences Project,* London: Leicester University Press.

Whitehead, M.R. (1990) *Language and Literacy in the Early Years.* London: Paul Chapman.

Williams, M. (2000) *Science and Social Science: An Introduction.* London: Routledge.

8

Children, Youth and the Mobile Phone

Rich Ling and Leslie Haddon

INTRODUCTION: WHY STUDY CHILDREN AND TEENS?

In its short life, a surprisingly large literature on the use of mobile communication among children and teens has been written. Indeed, in recent years there has hardly been a conference or a collection of readings that did not include work in this area. The iconic status of the mobile telephone among children and teens has been one of the big surprises associated with this form of communication. While originally conceived as a way to allow business people to interact, mobile telephony has become, perhaps more than anything else, a phenomenon of teens and young people. Reports from Japan (Hashimoto, 2002; Ito, 2005), the Philippines (Ellwood-Clayton, 2005) the broader Asian context (Castells *et al.*, 2007; Kim, 2004), Norway (Ling, 1999, 2000, 2001a,b; Ling and Yttri, 2002; Skog and Jamtøy, 2002), the UK (Green and Smith, 2002), Finland (Rautiainen and Kasesniemi, 2000; Nurmela, 2003; Oksman and Rautiainen, 2003a), the broader European scene (Mante-Meijer *et al.*, 2001; Castells *et al.*, 2007) and the USA (Grinter and Palen, 2002; Katz and Aakhus, 2002) all underscore this. In Malaysia, for example, students reported that the mobile telephone was among their most prized possessions (Abdullah, 2004) and material from the USA shows that teens would be loath to give up their cell phone (University of Michigan, 2006).

It is perhaps not surprising to find this amount of commentary, since children's wide-scale adoption of mobile communication exposes taken-for-granted assumptions as to who should talk to whom and when. It shows the gaps in parental control and the yearning (or perhaps confusion) regarding adolescents' press towards emancipation (Park, 2005). However, teens' use of mobile communication also allows us to focus on more conceptual issues. These include the wider context social construction of childhood, issues around child–parent relations and peer relations, diversity amongst youth and some of the social consequences of young people's mobile phone practices.

The first part of this chapter looks at elements within the mobile phone and children/youth literature, organized around, on the one hand, parent–child relationships and, on the other hand, on peer relationships, although there are links between the two. The second part of the chapter looks more critically at how we might frame this material and suggests some considerations for future research.

PARENT–CHILD RELATIONSHIPS AND THE MOBILE PHONE

Although the amount of coverage of parent–child relationships around the mobile phone is substantial, it is not as large as the literature on the role of the mobile within peer relationships. One key underlining theme of this material is that both parents and children using the technology as a way to manage the child's growing independence. But some of the research also acknowledges the scope for conflict within this process, in the same way as has been documented in relation to other information–communication technologies (ICTs), such as television viewing. This will be developed in the second half of the chapter.

To set the scene, many parents first purchased the mobile phone as a way to ensure their children's safety as they move into the broader society. In the UK, the adoption of the mobile is sometimes linked to when the teen starts driving 'in case the car breaks down' (Nafus and Tracey, 2002: 212). It allows for remote parenting, or, to provide the original gender inflection, 'remote motherhood' (Rakow and Navarro, 1993). The child can be contacted in the early afternoon and plans can be laid as to where they will be after school (visiting friends, at home) and what responsibilities need to be attended to (school work, household chores, etc.).

One metaphor that has been employed is that the mobile can allow a type of 'umbilical cord' between parent and child. However, some writers in this field have highlighted how the device provides the child with a type of cautious independence or autonomy *vis-à-vis* their parents (Castells *et al.*, 2007). For their part, parents may be more or less active in using the mobile telephone as a control device, checking up on their children's activities remotely, but they may also use it to push their children on the road towards independence.

While the general trend is towards emancipation, it is also important to note that at times the adolescent also seeks reassurance that the parental bond is operative. The children of divorced parents, for example, might need to know that the non-resident parent is emotionally available (Castelain-Meunier, 1997; Ling, 2005b; Russo Lemor, 2005). We can also see this in the context of less permanent separations, such as when the child is at a summer camp or at a weekend retreat. In some of these cases they seek out the contact with their parents that the mobile telephone provides. Thus, while the general trend is away from intense parental interaction, it is by no means a one-way street.

More practically, there is the question of familial coordination between parents and mobile-phone-equipped teens. Döring *et al.* (2005) found that parents were frequent telephonic interlocutors with adolescents, particularly via voice mobile communication. This is the adolescents alerting parents as to when they are done with free-time activities and thus optimalizing transportation. Certainly when it is expedient for them, children also use the device for coordination; for example, if it is more convenient to ask for a parent to come and retrieve them than having to deal with the public transport system. But of course, 'coordination' can also sometimes involve the exercise of parental power, as in the case of parental requests/commands that the child comes home for dinner, etc. (Ling, 2005a).

As with the case of other ICTs, including rules about television watching and the strategies children use to evade those rules, children also resist such parent control and surveillance. For example, when distance from their parents is important, teens deploy strategies through which they limit parents' access (Oksman and Rautiainen, 2003b).

Guises such as 'my battery was dead' or 'I didn't hear it ring' are ways of erecting barriers and the child establishing a separate identity. On the other hand, we find the conflicts over the costs of children's mobile telephony. On the one hand, negotiations about the mobile phone bill may be used by the parent to give children object lessons in independent economic responsibility; for example, as a way to give the child a better understanding of money and consumption (Ling, 2004: 112). But it also clearly leads to tensions, pressures and also arguments, as we will see later.

PEER RELATIONSHIPS AND THE MOBILE PHONE

Once again, while there is a functional aspect to peer-to-peer communications and indeed the organization of meetings, this literature has also noted the role of peers in the process of emancipation, especially in identity formation. The reorientation away from family to peers in adolescence especially had already been shown by research on the use of the fixed telephone line (Claisse, 2000). So one question is that of how the mobile phone fits into this pattern. Another question is how it enhances it. Part of this process involves the emergence of peer norms in relation to the mobile and, as will be clear in the next section, in relation to texting in particular.

Research in the USA (Choi, 2004), Malaysia (Abdullah, 2004), Scandinavia (Ling and Yttri, 2002; Ling and Haddon, 2003) and Germany (Roessler and Hoeflich, 2002) shows how important mobile communication is for the coordination of everyday affairs, and this applies to peer groups of youth as well. Indeed, the device allows for a type of so-called 'micro-coordination' that is nuanced and fine-tuned to the immediate needs of the individuals (Ling and Yttri, 2002). Taken in the context of teens, interactive coordination has often developed into a form of diffuse social arrangements that become negotiated and more concrete as the time for the event approaches; for an example of this using the landline telephone, see Manceron (1997). It is also sometimes the case that the individual keeps several opportunities open, choosing one or the other only as the time for the event nears. The implications of this will emerge later.

Turning to the mobile's more expressive role, various researchers have paid attention to how the mobile can assist in the adolescent's development of identity in its role as a fashion object. The mobile phone can function as a form of display much in the same way as a piece of jewellery (Henin and Lobet-Maris, 2003). It becomes a part of the individual's façade or look (Ling, 2001b; Fortunati *et al.*, 2003; Fortunati, 2005). This may be calibrated to fit into a style that is shared in a peer group or can be used in the individual's pursuit of class transcendence (Nafus and Tracey, 2002). Yang (2004), for example, discusses how college students at Beijing University used the mobile telephone as a marker of current as well as assumed future status. Finally, some people can overinvest themselves in the mobile telephone. That is, the device becomes too central to the individual's sense of self. Chen (2004), for example, links mobile telephony with depression and Park (2005) talks about mobile phone addiction.

As developed above, a part of the emancipation process is the teen's development of a self-identity. The mobile telephone plays a role here by being providing adolescents with a more direct link to peers, compared with the fixed line, which any household member may answer (Castells *et al.*, 2007). The arrival of texting went a stage further, by making that communication cheaper, given that teens and young people often use mobile communication on a limited budget. This was one key motivation, along with the willingness to try innovative forms of mediation (Kangas, 2003), that lay behind the diffusion of texting among teens.

Social forces are also seen in the newly coined ethics regarding the use of the mobile telephone. Studies have shown that teens have tacit understandings of when texting is appropriate, as opposed to voice or face-to-face interaction. This comes up, for example, when considering the 'correct' way to end a romantic relationship. Thus, it is not honourable to dump someone by sending a text message (Taylor and Harper, 2001). The fact that it is a topic of debate at all means that there is not necessarily a consensus and that some teens make choices that others think inappropriate (Haddon, 2005).

PEERS AND TEXTING

It is no overstatement to say that texting has been a phenomenon that was developed among teens (Kasesniemi and Rautiainen, 2002; Skog and Jamtøy, 2002; Ellwood-Clayton, 2003). Texting arose when it was still free to use. Teens' discovery of this meant that the use of texting went from nothing to a huge amount of traffic in only a few months time. The operators were quick to set up tariff systems in order to capture the revenue from this form of interaction, but by then the cultural die had been cast. For many parts of the world, but interestingly not the USA (Broege, 2004; University of Michigan, 2006), texting had become a type of talisman for the teens of the late 1990s, driven perhaps by a type of generational *élan* (Oksman and Rautiainen, 2003a).

Perhaps because of this, adolescents also derived various types of lingo and jargon when using texting (Skog and Jamtøy, 2002; Ling, 2005d). Even though this phenomenon is often overplayed in the press, teens are the largest users of slang and emoticons (Ling, 2005d). However, teens' interpretation of messages goes beyond the content of the text and can include the timeliness of a response. In some cases this is as carefully calibrated and interpreted as the actual text of the message (Laursen, 2005). Responding too quickly may be seen as being overeager, whereas waiting too long is seen as being too casual when, for example, interacting with a potential new boy/girlfriend.

The wider social nature of texting, beyond particular person-to-person communications, is indicated when specific messages that these youth receive are shown to others and shared in the co-present peer group (Rautiainen and Kasesniemi, 2000). There are also reports on how messages are collectively composed and circulated among friends and how fitting phrases are borrowed and baked into new messages as needed (Johnsen, 2002; Kasesniemi and Rautiainen, 2002; Haddon, 2005). Another example would be the case of asking friends which text messages are appropriate for being saved (those that evoke memories of fun times) and which can be erased (messages from earlier boy- or girl-friends). At a more abstract level, some research indicates that intense use of texting can be an element in the formation of cliques (Cardon and Granjon, 2002; Licoppe, 2004; Reid and Reid, 2004) that are ideologically unified (Gergen, 2003) and that can, in some cases, play into various forms of boundary testing and deviance (Pedersen and Samuelsen, 2003; Ling, 2005c).

Even though texting is often used for traditionally instrumental forms of interaction such as coordination ('where are you?') or delivering messages ('come by at 9:00'), there are also phatic messages where the main point of making contact is that it is a type of gifting (Johnsen, 2002). In this way the individuals confirm their common status and that they are part of the same network. This form of gifting may be of particular importance for teens, since the friendships marked by the giving and reciprocity can be a fixed element in an otherwise turbulent period of life (Taylor and Harper, 2001; Bakken, 2002; Johnsen, 2002; Ling and Yttri, 2002).

Finally, it is clear that the texting can provide a direct and discreet channel between (potential) partners in matters of intimacy, dating and sexuality (Dietmar, 2005; Döring *et al.*, 2005; Prøitz, 2006). Both genders have reported the use of multimedia messaging service (MMS) to photograph what they consider to be attractive members of the opposite sex (Scifo, 2005).

Turning to dating and eventual sexuality, analysis has shown that during the early exploratory phases of a relationship teens use texting as a way to get to know their new love interest. These can be in the form of innocent flirting between teens who have met at some social function (Ling, 2004). As the push for intimacy develops, the intensity and the familiarity of the text messages might increase. Prøitz (2004) discusses texting in which the thoughts and impulses that are too loaded to express verbally find an outlet in text messages. These include quite frank discussions about the desire to kiss, have sex, etc. There can also be full-fledged courting that is arranged via third-party matchmakers. This is carried out with the use of texting that is outside the traditional, more staid courting behaviours (Ellwood-Clayton, 2003). Meanwhile, adolescents who are steadily dating use texting and voice mobile communication as a direct (and often well-used) channel (Lin and Lo, 2004). It allows them to plan for trysts beforehand and to draw out enchantment of the event afterwards (Ito and Okabe, 2005) and it allows them to develop ritual forms of interaction, such as a quasi-obligatory 'good-night' or 'good-morning' text message (Ling, 2004). In those cases where there is some question as to the loyalty of a boy/girlfriend, Dietmar (2005) found that the mobile is used to monitor partners. This can be done, for example, by checking on their availability to exchange text messages or willingness to take calls. The partner who is no longer interested can also use the lack of response to these appeals as a not-so-subtle description of their feelings.

THE CHANGING EXPERIENCE OF CHILDREN AND YOUTH

If these previous sections describe the results of research on children, youth and mobiles pretty much using the frameworks of the studies themselves, we now need to reflect upon these patterns of behaviour, contextualizing them in various ways. One starting point is the literature on the social construction of childhood (Ariès, 1973; Gillis, 1981; James and Prout, 1997). This approach draws attention to fact that the experiences of children and youth, as well as expectations of their roles, their independence, their knowledge, etc., are relative: they change over time and vary cross-culturally.

It is worth noting that in these discussions of social construction the exact details of how childhood and youth are changing are themselves debated. For instance, one view, reflected in a Norwegian study, is that there has been a move from children having autonomy and responsibility to being more protected, making less decisions and experiencing making more restrictions in their daily activities (Vestby, 1994). Another view, reflected in British work, is that not only we see more autonomy being experienced by children, more domestic democracy and the individualization of childhood, but also increased regulation and risk management of children by adults (Livingstone, 1997: referring to Giddens' analysis). These two characterizations cover some similar points, but they are not identical.

However, the implication is that in the earlier section reviewing parent–child interaction in relation to the mobile phone, the negotiations, the rule setting, the way in which children's independence is managed, etc. are in part influenced by these wider and constantly evolving perceptions of what is appropriate for children and, indeed, what is appropriate parental behaviour (which signals we should also consider the social construction of parenthood). This provides a new insight into the question of how much is 'new' about parent–children interactions around the mobile phone. Before the mobile phone appeared, did not parents and children have similar interactions around other issues? If we take a short timescale, the answer is probably yes in general. But would the interactions have been a little more different if the mobile had appeared much earlier, say 40–50 years earlier. Moreover, this perspective also requires us to think about the cross-cultural dimension. On the face of it, we seem to have studies from different parts of the world that show similar processes. But one would at least have to ask to what degree the interactions of parents and children around mobiles are slightly different in different countries or cultures, because of any cross-cultural variation in how the interactions are managed more generally.

To take another example in the same vein, we noted how the mobile is used for coordination when youth are mobile (e.g. arranging to be picked up by parents). But children's mobility has itself changed (or, rather, it has in some countries), with various writers noting arguments about children's greater absence from unsupervised public spaces (Büchner, 1990; Livingstone, 2002). That mobility has a number of facets. In some countries, like the UK, many children spend a fair amount of time in organized post-school activities (in other words, in supervised spaces), and it appears that this is increasing, creating part of the need for parents to ferry children around and, hence, the interest in coordination (Haddon, 2004). Reflecting concerns about children's safety in public spaces, we now have a situation where the vast majority of children in Britain are now driven to school and many are picked up from school, sometimes involving mobile phone coordination if there are changes in plans. Lastly, and this is perhaps truer in some Western countries than in others, it has been argued that many social activities that in the past took place in public are increasingly taking place in the home. The home is itself becoming more public, more open to outsiders (Wellman, 1999). Children also experience this, having their friends around to interact with in their homes, in their own rooms, part of a phenomenon identified as 'bedroom culture' (Livingstone, 2002). Once again, this creates an interest in the coordination where it involves dropping off and picking up children from friends' homes.

In other words, the mobility patterns of youth are not a constant: we can see how it has changed in some areas, in some respects, and this has a bearing upon the role and usefulness of the mobile phone for managing the related coordination. But in all these cases, there is cross-cultural variation. For example, the concerns about safety and the degree of ferrying children around is not the same in all countries. And even the bedroom culture described above applies more to some parts of the world than to others, with studies in various Asian countries indicating that this does not exist, partly because of the size and nature of homes (Lim (2005) on China and Yoon (2002) on Korea).

A slightly different angle on this social construction of childhood involves asking how the arrival of ICTs like the mobile phone (and the internet), as well as the related practices that emerge among children themselves, can lead to re-evaluations of children's circumstances and roles, certainly from parents' perspectives. What new rules should relate to this technology? At what stage are children responsible enough to manage the mobile phone? We have a more concrete illustration of changing expectations in a study commenting on Norwegian debates about the minimum age that children should be to have access to a mobile phone (Ling and Helmersen, 2000). After the mobile had spread widely amongst the teenage population, the new phenomenon in the late 1990s was mobile acquisition by pre-teens. This created some unease, as shown in interviews with parents about the age at which it was appropriate to have a mobile. In fact, even some contemporary teenagers commented that nowadays children were receiving mobile phones when they were 'too young', given that these youth had only acquired a mobile themselves when they were first in their teens. During this period in the late 1990s the mobile phone became an 'appropriate' coming-of-age gift for children, suggesting a broader social (though perhaps temporary) fixing of the correct age for the consumption of this technology.

A different framework in which to consider the changing experience of children is cohort or generational analysis. Much has been made of the fact that it was the youth of the 1990s who were pioneers in the use of mobile technology for texting. There is actually some evidence that this could contribute to a sense of identity in this respect. One Italian study looking at young people's reactions to the MMS service being offered found that while some saw sending multimedia messages as the next step on from texting, others rejected it. In part, this because it was an industry-driven service, whereas, they argued, it was they and not industry that had helped to created the culture of the short message service or SMS (Colombo and Scifo, 2005).

In which case, what happens with the next cohort of teens who by now are encountering a pre-existing set of practices, rather than pioneering them. In one sense, there is always scope for them to develop innovatory practices, just as Japanese high-school girls had created unforeseen social uses of the pager before the mobile appeared (Ito, 2005). Maybe there will be new practices relating to images taken using the mobile phone or some combination of mobile phone and internet use – both are seen in case of the Korean *Cyworld*, where pictures taken with camera phones are posted to web-pages. In other words, in future studies of children's mobile use, we would expect to see some changes from the picture painted in the earlier description at the start of this chapter. But we can also ask the question of whether some forms of innovation in the practices of mobile use by one cohort of youth are more wide reaching than the innovation of another at another time period. The other side of coin is the question of what happens when the youth who pioneered texting themselves grow older. What changes because of entering a different life stage and what remains because it was introduced at this stage in their lives? Obviously, this no longer involves research on youth per se.

TENSIONS IN PARENT–CHILDREN AND PEER RELATIONSHIPS

The picture painted so far does not quite do justice to negative elements in parent–child and peer relationships, whether these are to be characterized as conflicts, tensions, issues or by using some other label. If we start with parent–children relations, a five-country European study demonstrated the considerable tensions arising because of the costs of children's use of the fixed line when this was paid for by parents (Haddon, 1998, 2004). Subsequent research has shown how some of these issues continue with the mobile phone, as parents attempt to impose limitations on their children's calls and texts when they are paying the bill (Haddon and Vincent, 2004). Another continuity from the fixed line is that incoming calls to the mobile can be disruptive, as when they arrive during mealtimes, and so in at least some households this gives rise to another set of rules. Finally, there is the issue, relating to the section above, of when children are allowed to have mobiles at all, where details of current 'negotiations' in households has received little attention in a period when the age at which children have mobile phones is falling.

When we turn to the case of peers, animated text messages as well as MMS images of nudity and pornographic sexuality are a flourishing phenomenon among teens, particularly with males (Brandtzæg, 2005). Further, illicit and covertly captured MMS images of unclad people in showers, toilets, etc. (Tikkanen and Junge, 2004). In one sense, the illicit use of MMS discussed above is in reality a type of chicanery that has been a part of telephony that also includes obscene and threatening telephone calls. However, in the case of landline telephony there may be ambiguity as to who is the intended target. The targeting is more precise with mobile telephony (Katz, 2005). Kury *et al.* (2004) found that 11% of German women (of all age groups) reported receiving obscene calls via their mobile telephone. Then there is the work on the use of the mobile phone as an element in bullying (Tikkanen and Junge, 2004; Campbell, 2005) and so-called happy slapping (Brough and Sills, 2006). This is obviously a serious problem, but it is also a problem that is easily played upon in the tabloid press.

Finally, analysis has shown that, for a small portion of teens, there is an interaction between the mobile telephone and various forms of criminal, or at least illicit, behaviour. In some cases this has the character of testing boundaries. However, in other cases the link is between mobile phones and drug use, fighting and theft, including the theft of mobiles from peers (Ling, 2005c).

It is important to keep a critical eye on parent–children and peer interactions in order to avoid the trap of painting too rosy a picture of these relationships. As these, for the most part relatively recent, references show, the mobile phone becomes involved in family and peer relationships that are not always harmonious.

DIVERSE YOUTH

In the 1960s, in many Western countries, the increased spending power of youth and related transformations in cultural industries to cater for them (e.g. the music industry) led to a discussion of whether there was a new 'youth culture'. We can learn the lessons of research in that period, which, understandably, noted a certain diversity in the experience of children and youth even within countries. Class or socio-economic status still made a difference to young people's experience, as did such ethnicity. Occasionally, contemporary studies of children, youth and mobile phones pick up on this diversity, but many of the studies in this field do not, emphasizing instead the commonalities in the experience of young people, especially within countries. Yet, even such a dimension as the sociability of teenage peers, singled out in mobile phone studies, varies. For example, one French study produced a typology of relationships between teens and patterns of phone use, including teens who socialized little with their peers (Martin and de Singly, 2000).

Two dimensions of the diversity of children's mobile phone experience in particular warrant further attention: cross-cultural variation and gender. As regards the first of these, different cultural norms, values, social structures, communications traditions, time structures, material culture, etc. can have a bearing on how we experience information and communication technologies in general (Thomas *et al.*, 2005). For example, the heavy regulation of mobile phones in public space in Japan, such as in the transport system, means that, since voice calls are prohibited, many Japanese youth resort to using solely text in those circumstances (Ito, 2005).

Apart from 'cultural' considerations, the technology supply side is also important. For example, many observers have noted how mobile phone use and texting is less developed in the USA than in Europe and Asia, but this in part reflects the whole development of the mobile in the USA and related policy decisions that shaped that history, including a lack of standardization (Agar, 2003). From the start the user paid for mobile communication in Europe and Asia, whereas the receiver paid in the original US system, meaning users were less likely to leave the mobile on all the time. To take a Korean example, the homepage system *Cyworld* arguably encouraged more use of camera phone, as people posted pictures from everyday life and to some extent encouraged the use of the mobile for checking up on what was happening on this online world. Meanwhile, the availability of the Japanese iMODE offered youth e-mail rather than facing the constraints, but also creativity, of SMS. In other words, different youth have varied experiences because of the different services and technological possibilities open to them.

Turning to gender, much of the work noted earlier in this chapter focused on adult women, rather than girls, especially noting the role of mothers maintaining links with family and wider social networks. This pattern was empirically demonstrated in a European five-country, but this research also drew attention to how the different gendered patterns of communication with the fixed line changed according to life stage and circumstances (Claisse, 2000). There was actually much less difference between male and female teenage phone use compared with later periods of life, with girls making slightly more calls than boys (to parents); and since they are chatting more, there was a slightly longer duration of calls. But the emphasis is on 'slightly' and the point is that one cannot automatically read off gender patterns in children from a knowledge of adult behaviour.

Surveys on the use of the phone by youth and mobiles regularly have a section on gender; in addition, some qualitative studies refer to this dimension. But, given the common finding of different gender patterns of ICT use, if by the late 1990s and early years of new century adoption rates are pretty much the same for boys and girls, maybe this itself needs explaining (Henin and Lobet-Maris 2003). The reason probably lies in a process that appears to be equally true for adults. Early in the adoption cycle, males are often more likely to adopt mobile telephony (Ling, 2005b). Males have also been seen as the innovators with regard to various services. This has been reported as reflecting an interest in technology as such (Henin and Lobet-Maris, 2003; Lobet-Maris, 2003).

However, shortly afterwards women catch up when the artefact is seen less as a technology and more as a tool for maintaining social interaction. This seems to be true also for other technologies, such as internet access (Haddon, 2004). The whole argument is given further credence in a Norwegian study that asked what youth valued in a mobile (Skog, 2002). Boys were more likely to mention technical features, while girls referred to functions such as ringtones. More generally, other studies have argued that girls are more interested in the interactive side of mobile communications, seeing the potential for social networking (Skog, 2002) as well as the aesthetic dimensions (Oksman and Rautiainen, 2003a). Girls' practices, such as decorating their phones, in particular noted as 'Technocute' in an Asian context (Hjorth and Kim, 2004), also underline the effort to downplay the technology dimension. This has been characterized as performing gender when appropriating the object, detaching some technological connotations.

In the literature, a number of other gender dimensions have been noted, such as the manner and basis of mobile phone acquisition. For example, in an early Norwegian study, girls were more likely to loan the mobile than were boys. Parents were also more likely to pay for girls' use (Ling, 1998). In a Belgian study, girls more often than boys received the mobile as a gift from parents (Henin and Lobet-Maris, 2003). It remains to be seen whether these turn out to be features solely applicable to the early years of the mobile mass market, more true in some countries than others. Various studies have noted gender differences in the style and content of communication – i.e. girls' more 'expressive' communications, longer texts messages, expressions of friendship and love, etc. These patterns may well fit patterns of communications by the fixed line. Lastly, differences in the amount of use are perhaps more intriguing. A number of studies suggest more 'intense' use by girls. For example, German and Belgian studies have noted more calls by girls and more SMS communications (Ling, 2004; Döring *et al.*, 2005). However, before speculating whether this somehow reflects differences in boys' and girls' networking, one would have to ask why such gender differences exist in relation to the mobile phone, when only 'slight' differences existed in relation to the fixed line, as noted above. Moreover, to put gender into an age context, we must always remember that we are discussing the specificities of gender differences within youth; for example, both boys and girls text more than adult men and women.

SOCIAL CONSEQUENCES

Various potential social consequences of new mobile phone practices have been noted in the literature, some applying more specifically to youth. The first argument is that mobiles have changed the nature of (teenage) meetings in various ways. One analysis of Japanese youth shows the use of mobile communication to anticipate and to summarize physical encounters, as young people phone in advance to talk about the meeting, and continue talking about it on the mobile after they have departed (Henin and Lobet-Maris, 2003). In a sense, the boundaries of the meeting can become less clear. But probably the dimension discussed a little more is the spontaneous, fluid nature of planning of if, where and when to meet that was noted earlier in this chapter.

While this development may well be common, this flexibility is probably itself affected (both enabled and limited) by the particular time constraints and time commitments of (different kinds of) youth (Haddon, 2004). This needs more exploration. Moreover, is the change always welcomed? One Singaporean study showed how, in certain circumstances, this process of negotiating meetings on the fly can also be problematic and frustrating (Chung and Lim, 2005).

Next there is the argument that there is now greater mutual awareness among teens because of the mobile, as indicated in Licoppe's (2005) idea of 'connected presence'. The low threshold for interaction allowed by the mobile phone (the ease and low cost of texting in particular) means that teens are in connection with each other on a quasi-perpetual basis. There is a greater degree of insight into each other's affairs and there is a willingness to report on thoughts and situations that would not, were contact more irregular, survive the vetting process as to things that would be discussed. In other words, the ability to fill the gaps between co-present sessions is greatly facilitated by the mobile phone (Lobet-Maris, 2003; Henin and Lobet-Maris, 2004), something that could also be accomplished in the pre-mobile world with various combinations of pagers, telephones, answering machines, etc. (Lobet-Maris, 2003). While this may be so, what is lacking in this field of research is some discussion of the fact that teenagers might also want some privacy from their peers, not just from their parents. Hence, we have questions of for whom privacy is more important and of how youth manage, at times, to escape what can also be considered to be mutual surveillance.

Third, there is the suspicion that mobile communication leads to bounded social networks or a type of 'ghettoization'. For example, de Gournay and Smoreda (2003: 69) write

> At a local level [the] homogeneity of social circles produces a 'ghetto-like' social form: we discover some of the elements of the ghetto phenomenon, but without the cultural and ethnic characteristics of its traditional urban form.

If we are seeing more intensive communications between smaller social networks, does this kind of sociability excludes other forms? The notion of 'walled community' (Ling, 2004) conveys the idea that when communication is increasingly aimed at a limited number of people we know well, this limits our opportunity to 'establish new ties in one's co-located situation'. As French researchers arguing in a somewhat similar vein have pointed out, since people's attention is limited, this shift in the balance to a more 'connected' relationship with an intimate few can be at the expense of making the effort to interact with strangers (Rivère and Licoppe, 2003). The jury may be out on how much this process is developing, but it is an interesting line of enquiry that merits further research.

CONCLUSIONS

Like all reviews, this is a snapshot covering the mobile research literature of the last few years. But the mobile phone as an artefact is itself evolving, as are the services associated with it. The mobile telephone already has the potential to be our personal calendar, personal music player, call history, message centre, to-do list, photographic album and, in the future, it can conceivably even have the function of our pocket book and identity card. Add to this the ongoing initiatives to develop the mobile platform for TV and internet access, and in a few years time we might well expect some new strands of research on mobile phones in general and their relation to children and youth in particular.

That said, the review has attempted to summarize the common strands in this literature, as well as to raise questions about that research, identifying frameworks, noting gaps and indicating directions for future work. We have seen how children's experience of the mobile phone can be contextualized by understanding how children's experiences (and perceptions of childhood) change more generally over time. We need to be more sensitive to the problematic sides of parent–child and peer interactions. It is important to be aware of the diversity of youth, their circumstances and their experiences. And there are a range of potential social consequences that deserve not only more research, but also critical attention.

To end on a slightly different note, this literature on children, youth and the mobile phone has arguably put youth especially on the academic map in a new way. There has been a tradition of studying children and ICTs, with perhaps the research on television being the most obvious example. In the late 1980s and early 1990s there was some, but relatively little, research on children and fixed-line telephony and some material on children and PCs. But the mobile literature has arguably picked up on the innovatory nature of youth, as they established new practices and hence the range of studies of this group across a number of countries. Moreover, there activities have even had ramifications for theoretical frameworks. Within the social shaping of technology tradition, for example, SMS practices are often cited as the best and most widespread contemporary example of unanticipated innovation from users. Meanwhile, the domestication framework, or certain strands of it, was forced to look beyond the household, to understand some of what could be considered to be the collective domestication processes taking place within these peer networks as they interacted around the mobile phone (Haddon, 2003, 2004). Clearly, then, the mobile phone and children/youth literature has already made a significant contribution to the wider ICT literature, even if there is considerable scope for further development.

REFERENCES

Abdullah, M.Y.H. (2004) 'Adoption of cellular phone among young adults: a study among youths in the Klang Valley, Malaysia'. In S.D. Kim (ed.) *Mobile Communication and Social Change*, Seoul: SK Telecom; 305–312.

Agar, J. (2003) *Constant Touch. A Global History of the Mobile Phone*. Cambridge: Icon Books.

Ariès, P. (1973) *Centuries of Childhood*. Penguin: Harmondsworth.

Bakken, F. (2002) 'Telenærhet: en studie av unge døve og hørendes bruk av SMS'. Sosiologi, Universitetet i Oslo, Oslo.

Brandtzæg, P. (2005) 'Children's use of communications technologies'. In G. Stald (ed.) *Mobile Media, Mobile Youth*. Copenhagen: University of Copenhagen.

Broege, S. (2004) 'CU on IM: the instant messaging generation: young adult motivations for synchronous mediated communication in Germany and the United States'. In S.D. Kim (ed.) *Mobile Communication and Social Change*. Seoul: SK Telecom; 273–296.

Brough, R. and Sills, J. (2006) 'Multimedia bullying using a website'. *Archives of Disease in Childhood* 91: 202.

Büchner, P. (1990) 'Das Telefon im Alltag von Kindern'. In F. Telefonkommunikation (ed.) *Telefon und Gesellschaft 2*. Berlin: Volker Spiess; 263–274.

Campbell, M. (2005) 'The impact of the mobile phone on young people's social life'. In *Social Change in the 21st Century*. Queensland University of Technology.

Cardon, D. and Granjon, F. (2002) 'Eléments pour une approche des pratiques culturelles par les réseaux de sociabilités'. In *Le(s) public(s). Politiques Publiques et Équipements Culturels*. Paris: Auditorium du Louvre.

Castelain-Meunier, C. (1997) 'The paternal cord: telephone relationships between 'non-custodian' fathers and their children'. *Reseaux* 5: 161–176.

Castells, M., Fernandez-Ardevol, M., Qiu, J.L., et al. (2007) *Mobile Communication and Society: A Global Perspective*. Cambridge MA: MIT.

Chen, Y.-F. (2004) 'The relationship of mobile phone use to addiction and depression amongst American college students'. In S.D. Kim (ed.) *Mobile Communication and Social Change*. Seoul: SK Telecom; 344–352.

Choi, J. (2004) 'Exploring characteristics of cellular phone communication of the US college students'. In S.D. Kim (ed.) *Mobile Communication and Social Change*. Seoul: SK Telecom; 353–365.

Chung, L.-Y. and Lim, S.-S. (2005) 'From monochronic to mobilechronic. Temporality in the era of mobile communication'. In K.E. Nyíri (ed.) *A Sense of Place. The Global and the Local in Mobile Communication*. Vienna: Passagen Verlag.

Claisse, G. (2000) 'Identités masculines et féminines au Telephone. Des rôles, des pratiques des perception contrastés'. *Reseaux* 18: 51–90.

Colombo, F. and Scifo, B. (2005) 'Social shaping of new mobile devices. Representations and uses among Italian youth'. In L. Haddon, E. Mante-Meijer, B. Sapio, K.-H. Kommonen, L. Fortunati and A. Kant (eds) *Everyday Innovators. Researching the Role of Users in Shaping ICTs*. Dordrecht: Springer; 86–103.

Dietmar, C. (2005) 'Mobile communication in couple relationships'. In K. Nyiri (ed.) *A Sense of Place: The Global and the Local in Mobile Communication*. Vienna: Passagen Verlag; 201–208.

Döring, N., Hellwig, K. and Klimsa, P. (2005) 'Mobile communication among German youth'. In K. Nyiri (ed.) *A Sense of Place: The Global and the Local in Mobile Communication*. Vienna: Passagen Verlag; 209–217.

Ellwood-Clayton, B. (2003) 'Virtual strangers: young love and texting in the Filipino archipelago of cyberspace'. In K. Nyiri (ed.) *Mobile Democracy: Essays on Society, Self and Politics*. Vienna: Passagen Verlag; 35–45.

Ellwood-Clayton, B. (2005) 'Desire and loathing in the cyber Philippines'. In R. Harper, A. Taylor, and L. Palen (eds) *The Inside Text: Social Perspectives on SMS in the Mobile Age*. London: Klewer; 195–222.

Fortunati, L. (2005) 'Mobile phones and fashion in post-modernity'. *Telektronikk* 3(4): 35–48.

Fortunati, L., Katz, J.E. and Riccini, R. (eds) (2003) *Mediating the Human Body: Technology, Communication and Fashion*. London: Lawrence Erlbaum.

Gergen, K. (2003) 'Self and community and the new floating worlds'. In K. Nyri (ed.) *Mobile Democracy: Essays on Society, Self and Politics*. Vienna: Passagen Verlag; 61–69.

Gillis, J. (1981) *Youth and History: Tradition and Change in Age Relations, 1770–Present*. London: Academic Press.

Green, N. and Smith, S. (2002) ' "A spy in your pocket"? Monitoring and regulation in mobile technologies'. In *Third Wireless World Conference*. University of Surrey: Digital World Research Centre.

Grinter, R. and Palen, L. (2002) 'Instant messaging in teen life'. In *Proceedings of the ACM Conference on Computer Supported Cooperative Work (CSCW 2002)*. New Orleans, LA: ACM Press.

Haddon, L. (1998) 'Il controllo della comunicazione. Imposizione di limiti all'uso del telefono'. In L. Fortunati (ed.) *Telecomunicando in Europa*. Milano: Franco Angeli; 195–247.

Haddon, L. (2003) 'Domestication and mobile telephony'. In J.E. Katz (ed.) *Machines that Become Us: The Social Context of Personal Communication Technology*. New Brunswick, NJ: Transaction; 43–56.

Haddon, L. (2004) *Information and Communication Technologies in Everyday Life*. Oxford: Berg.

Haddon, L. (2005) 'Research questions for the evolving communications landscape'. In R. Ling and P. Pedersen (eds) *Mobile Communications: Renegotiation of the Social Sphere*. London: Springer; 335–349.

Haddon, L. and Vincent, J. (2004) 'Making the most of the communications repertoire – mobile and fixed'. In K. Nyiri (ed.) *A Sense of Place: The Global and the Local in Mobile Communication*. Vienna: Passagen Verlag; 231–240.

Hashimoto, Y. (2002) 'The spread of cellular phones and their influence on young people in Japan'. In S.D. Kim (ed.) *The Social and Cultural Impact/Meaning of Mobile Communication*. Chunchon, Korea: School of Communication Hallym University; 101–112.

Henin, L. and Lobet-Maris, C. (2003) 'Communication without speaking or speaking without communicating? Youths, mobile phones and SMS'. In L. Haddon, E. Mante-Meijer, B. Sapio, K.-H. Kommonen, L. Fortunati and A. Kant (eds) *The Good, the Bad and the Irrelevant: The User and the Future of Information and Communication Technologies*. Helsinki, Finland: Media Lab, University of Art and Design; 13–17.

Hjorth, L. and Kim, H. (2004) 'Being there: society of the phoneur. Gendered customising of mobile telephonic new practices in Seoul'. In S.-D. Kim (ed) *Proceedings of the Conference 'Mobile Communication and Social Change*. Seoul: Korea.

Ito, M. (2005) 'Mobile phones, Japanese youth and the replacement of social contact'. In R. Ling and P. Pedersen (eds) *Mobile Communications: Renegotiation of the Social Sphere*. London: Springer; 131–148.

Ito, M. and Okabe, D. (2005) 'Intimate connections: contextualizing Japanese youth and mobile messaging'. In R. Harper, L. Palen and A. Taylor (eds) *The Inside Text: Social, Cultural and Design Perspectives on SMS*. Dordrecht, Netherlands: Springer; 127–146.

James, A. and Prout, A. (eds) (1997) *Constructing and Reconstructing Childhood: Contemporary Issues in the Sociological Study of Children*. London: Falmer Press.

Johnsen, T.E. (2002) 'The social context of the mobile phone use of Norwegian teens'. In J. Katz and M. Aakhus (eds) *Perpetual Contact: Mobile Communication, Private Talk, Public Performance*. Cambridge: Cambridge University Press; 161–170.

Kangas, S. (2003) 'Youth as innovators: utility games advance local user innovations'. In L. Haddon, E. Mante-Meijer, B. Sapio, K.-H. Kommonen, L. Fortunati and A. Kant (eds) *The Good, the Bad and the Irrelevant: The User and the Future of Information and Communication Technologies*. Helsinki, Finland: Media Lab, University of Art and Design; 174–177.

Kasesniemi, E.-L. and Rautiainen, P. (2002) 'Mobile culture of children and teenagers in Finland'. In J. Katz and M. Aakhus (eds) *Perpetual Contact: Mobile Communication, Private Talk, Public Performance*. Cambridge: Cambridge University Press; 170–192.

Katz, J. (2005) 'Mobile phones in educational settings'. In K. Nyiri (ed.) *A Sense of Place: The Global and the Local in Mobile Communication*. Vienna: Passagen Verlag; 305–317.

Katz, J.E. and Aakhus, M. (eds) (2002) *Perpetual Contact: Mobile Communication, Private Talk, Public Performance*. Cambridge: Cambridge University Press.

Kim, S.D. (2004) 'Mobility, communication and generation'. In S.D. Kim (ed.) *Mobile Communication and Social Change*. Seoul: SK Telecom.

Kury, H., Chouaf, S., Obergfell-Fuchs, J. and Woessner, G. (2004) 'The scope of sexual victimization in Germany'. *Journal of Interpersonal Violence* 19: 589–602.

Laursen, D. (2005) 'The replying norm in adolescent SMS communication'. In R. Harper, A. Taylor and L. Palen (eds) *The Inside Text: Social Perspectives on SMS in the Mobile Age*. London: Kluwer, 53–73.

Licoppe, C. (2004) 'Connected presence: the emergence of a new repertoire for managing social relationships in a changing communications technoscape'. *Environment and Planning D: Society and Space* 22: 135–156.

Lim, S.S. (2005) 'From cultural to information revolution: ICT domestication by middle-class Chinese families'. In T. Berker, M. Hartmann, Y. Punie and K. Ward (eds) *Domestication of Media and Technologies*. Maidenhead: Open University Press; 185–204.

Lin, A. and Lo, J. (2004) 'New youth digital literacies and mobile connectivity: Text messaging among Hong Kong college students'. In S.D. Kim (ed.) *Mobile Communication and Social Change*. Seoul: SK Telecom; 297–312.

Ling, R. (1998) *'It Rings all the Time': The Use of the Telephone by Norwegian Adolescents*. Kjeller: Telenor R&D.

Ling, R. (1999) ' "We release them little by little": maturation and gender identity as seen in the use of mobile telephone'. In *International Symposium on Technology and Society (ISTAS'99) Women and Technology: Historical, Societal and Professional Perspectives*. New Brunswick, NJ: Rutgers University.

Ling, R. (2000) ' "We will be reached": the use of mobile telephony among Norwegian youth'. *Information Technology and People* 13: 102–120.

Ling, R. (2001a). 'Adolescent girls and young adult men: Two sub-cultures of the mobile telephone'. Telenor R&D, Kjeller.

Ling, R. (2001b). ' "It is 'in'. It doesn't matter if you need it or not, just that you have it". Fashion and the domestication of the mobile telephone among teens in Norway'. In L. Fortunati (ed.) *Il Corpo Umano tra Tecnologie, Comunicazione e Moda* (*The Human Body between Technologies, Communication and Fashion*). Milano: Triennale di Milano.

Ling, R. (2004) *The Mobile Connection: The Cell Phone's Impact on Society*. San Francisco: Morgan Kaufmann.

Ling, R. (2005a) 'The complexity of everyday life: the car, the mobile phone and other factors that contribute to and alleviate the sense of time pressure and stress'. In S.D. Kim (ed.) *Beyond Phones: Mobility and the Future of Media*, Seoul, South Korea.

Ling, R. (2005b) 'The "divorce" mobile phone: mobile telephones and the children of divorced parents'. In *Mobile Media, Mobile Youth*. Copenhagen.

Ling, R. (2005c) 'Mobile communications *vis-à-vis* teen emancipation, peer group integration and deviance'. In R. Harper, A. Taylor and L. Palen (ed.) *The Inside Text: Social Perspectives on SMS in the Mobile Age*. London: Kluwer.

Ling, R. (2005d) 'The socio-linguistics of SMS: an analysis of SMS use by a random sample of Norwegians'. In R. Ling and P. Pedersen (eds) *Mobile Communications: Renegotiation of the Social Sphere*. London: Springer; 335–349.

Ling, R. and Haddon, L. (2003) 'Mobile telephony, mobility and the coordination of everyday life'. In J.E. Katz (ed.) *Machines that Become Us: The Social Context of Personal Communication Technology*. New Brunswick, NJ: Transaction.

Ling, R. and P. Helmersen. (2000) ' "It must be necessary, it has to cover a need": the adoption of mobile telephony among pre-adolescents and adolescents'. In *The Social Consequences of Mobile Telephony*, Oslo.

Ling, R. and Yttri, B. (2002) 'Hyper-coordination via mobile phones in Norway'. In J.E. Katz and M. Aakhus (eds) *Perpetual Contact: Mobile Communication, Private Talk, Public Performance*. Cambridge: Cambridge University Press; 139–169.

Livingstone, S. (1997) 'Mediated childhoods: a comparative approach to young people's changing media environment in Europe'. *European Journal of Communication* 13: 435–456.

Livingstone, S. (2002) *Young People and New Media*. London: Sage.

Lobet-Maris, C. (2003) 'Mobile phone tribes: youth and social identity'. In L. Fortunati, J. Katz and R. Riccini (eds) *Mediating the Human Body: Technology, Communication and Fashion*. Mahwah, NJ: Lawrence Erlbaum Associates; 87–92.

Manceron, V. (1997) 'Get connected! Social uses of the telephone and modes of interaction in a peer group of young Parisians'. In A. Kant and E. Mante-Meijer (eds) *Blurring Boundaries: When Are ICTs Coming Home?* Stockholm: Telia; 171–182.

Mante-Meijer, E., Haddon, L., Concejero, P., Klamer, L., Heres, J., Ling, R., Thomas, F., Smoreda, Z. and Vrieling, I. (2001) 'Checking it out with the people – ICT markets and users in Europe'. *EURESCOM*, Heidelberg.

Martin, O. and de Singly, F. (2000) 'L'évasion amicable. L'usage du Téléphone familial par les adolescents'. *Reseaux* 18(103).

Nafus, D. and Tracey, K. (2002) 'Mobile phone consumption and concepts of personhood'. In J.E. Katz and M. Aakhus (eds) *Perpetual Contact: Mobile Communication, Private Talk, Public Performance*. Cambridge: Cambridge University Press; 206–221.

Nurmela, J. (2003) 'A "great migration" to the information society? Patterns of ICT diffusion in Finland in 1996–2002'. In K.-H. Kommonen (ed.) *The Good, the Bad and the Irrelevant, COST 269*. Helsinki: Finland.

Oksman, V. and Rautiainen, P. (2003a) 'Extension of the hand: children's and teenagers' relationship with the mobile phone in Finland'. In L. Fortunati, J. Katz and R. Riccini (eds) *Mediating the Human Body: Technology, Communication and Fashion*. Mahwah, NJ: Lawrence Erlbaum Associates; 93–102.

Oksman, V. and Rautiainen, P. (2003b). ' "Perhaps it is a body part": how the mobile telephone became an organic part of the everyday lives of Finnish children and teenagers'. In J.E. Katz (ed.) *Machines that Become Us: The Social Context of Personal Communication Technology*. New Brunswick, NJ: Transaction; 293–308.

Park, W.K. (2005) 'Mobile telephone addiction'. In R. Ling and P. Pedersen (eds) *Mobile Communications: Renegotiation of the Social Sphere*. London: Springer; 259–272.

Pedersen, W. and Samuelsen, S.O. (2003) 'Nye mønstre av seksualatferd blant ungdom'. *Tidsskrift for den Norske Lægeforeningen* 21: 3006–3009.

Prøitz, L. (2004) 'The mobile fiction: Intimate discourses in text message communication amongst young Norwegian people'. In S.D. Kim (ed.) *Mobile Communication and Social Change*. Seoul: SK Telecom; 230–236.

Prøitz, L. (2006) 'Cute boys or Game Boys? The embodiment of femininity and masculinity in young Norwegian's text message love-projects'. *Fibreculture*. http://journal.fibreculture.org/issue6/_proitz.html [6 October 2006].

Rakow, L.F. and Navarro, V. (1993) 'Remote mothering and the parallel shift: women meet the cellular telephone'. *Critical Studies in Mass Communication* 10: 144–157.

Rautiainen, P. and Kasesniemi, E.-L. (2000) 'Mobile communication of children and teenagers: case Finland 1997–2000'. In R. Ling and K. Thrane (eds) *Sosiale konsekvenser av mobiletelefoni: proceedings fra et seminar om samfunn, barn og mobile telefoni*, vol. FoU N 38/2000. Kjeller: Telenor FoU; 15–18.

Reid, D. and Reid, F. (2004) 'Insights into the social and psychological effects of SMS text messaging'. *160 characters*. http://www.160characters.org/documents/SocialEffectsOfText/Messaging.pdf [10 February 2005].

Rivère, C. and Licoppe, C. (2003) 'From voice to text: continuity and change in the use of mobile phones in France and Japan'. In R. Ling and P. Pedersen (eds) *Front Stage/Back Stage*. Grimstad: Norway.

Roessler, P. and Hoeflich, J. (2002) 'Mobile written communication, or e-mail on your cellular phone'. In S.D. Kim (ed.) *The Social Cultural Impact/Meaning of Mobile Communication*. Chunchon, Korea: School of Communication Hallym University; 133–157.

Russo Lemor, A.-M. (2005) 'Making a "home". The domestication of information and communication technologies in single parents' households'. In T. Berker, M. Hartmann, Y. Punie and K. Ward (eds) *Domestication of Media and Technologies*. Maidenhead: Open University Press.

Scifo, B. (2005) 'The domestication of cameraphone and MMS communication'. In K. Nyiri (ed.) *A Sense of Place: The Global and the Local in Mobile Communication*. Vienna: Passagen Verlag; 305–317.

Skog, B. (2002) 'Mobiles and the Norwegian teen: identity, gender and class'. In E. Katz and M. Aakhus (eds) *Perpetual Contact: Mobile Communication, Private Talk, Public Performance*. Cambridge: Cambridge University Press; 255–273.

Skog, B. and Jamtøy, A.I. (2002) 'Ungdom og SMS'. ISS NTNU, Trondheim.

Taylor, A. and Harper, R. (2001) 'The gift of the gab? A design oriented sociology of young people's use of "MobilZe!"'. Working Paper, Digital World Research Centre.

Thomas, F., Haddon, L., Gilligan, R., Heinzmann, P. and de Gournay, C. (2005) 'Cultural factors shaping the experience of ICTs: an exploratory review'. In L. Haddon (ed.) *International Collaborative Research. Cross-Cultural Differences and Cultures of Research*. Brussels: COST.

Tikkanen, T. and Junge, A. (2004) 'Realisering av en visjon om et mobbefritt oppvekstmiljø for barn og unge'. Rogalandsforskning, Stavanger.

University of Michigan (2006) 'On the move: the role of cellular communication in American life: Pohs report on mobile communication'. Department of Communication Studies, University of Michigan, Ann Arbor.

Vestby, G.M. (1994) 'Constructing childhood: children interacting with technology'. In A. Berg and M. Aune (eds) *COSTA4 Workshop Domestic Technology and Everyday Life: Mutual Shaping Processes.* Norway: University of Trondheim, Centre for Technology and Society. Trondheim; 97–118.

Wellman, B. (1999) 'The network community'. In B. Wellman (ed.) *Networks in the Global Village.* Boulder: Westview; 1–48.

Yang, S. (2004) 'College student's self-positioning and the cell-phone consumption'. In S.D. Kim (ed.) *Mobile Communication and Social Change.* Seoul: SK Telecom; 335–343.

Yoon, K. (2002) 'Extending familialism through the mobile: young people's re-articulation of traditional sociality through mobile phones in Seoul, South Korea'. In *Third Wireless World Conference The Social Shaping of Mobile Futures Location! Location!*, Guildford: Surrey University.

9

The Mediated Playground: Media in Early Childhood

Dafna Lemish

INTRODUCTION

Newborns joining our world are characterized by a unique personal genealogy, characteristics, and traits. They are born into different family structures, cultures, religions, histories, languages, and economic situations, to name just a few differences. Their parents may have different dreams and aspirations for their children's future. Yet, many of these babies share the fact that they make their entry into a taken-for-granted, highly meditated environment. They listen to music and sounds while still in the uterus; they learn to crawl and sit in front of the TV screen; they bang on their special baby-keyboard when they are barely uttering their first words; they sing and dance to their favorite video-tape; they drag 'my first' tape-recorder (or game-console, or play-phone, or speaking stuffed animal) with them to bed. They sit on mom's lap in front of the computer, fall asleep on the sofa with dad during a late-night show, join brother at the movie theater, and play with the keys of sister's mobile phone. Media are as natural to them as are any other features of their everyday environment. They are there to be explored and enjoyed. They are part of being and of growing up.

THE CHANGING PLAYGROUND

Clearly, this trend has not escaped the eyes of many entrepreneurs who have saturated the market in recent years with media and media-related products aimed specifically at the very young, including special television programs, video-tapes/DVDs, computer keyboards and games, and interactive books and 'play-stations'. Motivated by this booming market of media products for very young children, a Kaiser Foundation initiative set out to map media exposure and use of a US national representative sample of over 1000 parents of children aged 6 months to 6 years (Rideout *et al.*, 2003). The main findings of this first comprehensive study highlighted the following. Nearly all children of this age group in the USA were raised in a home with a TV, half had three or more TV sets, and a third had a TV in their own bedroom.

Three-quarters of the children had a computer at home, two-thirds had internet access, about half had a video game player, and nearly all of them had products (clothes, toys, games) based on characters from TV shows and movies. Nearly all of the children in the study listened to music and were read stories to; 9 out of 10 watched television, videos, and DVD. Half of children had used a computer (70 percent by the time they were 4–6 years old), and close to a third had played video games. According to the parents, they spent an average of about 2 hours daily with screen media (as much as the time spent playing outside, and three times more than reading or being read to). As active media consumers, they turned television on (77 percent), asked for particular shows (67 percent), used the remote control to switch channels (62 percent), asked for specific videotapes and DVDs (71 percent), put in their own CDs or music tapes into the Walkman (36 percent), climbed up on a chair to access the computer by themselves (33 percent), loaded their own CD-ROMs (23 percent), and even asked for specific websites while surfing the net (12 percent).

The study pointed to some predictors of media access and use. For example, young children who had media in their bedroom actually spent more time using them. Demographic factors seemed to play a role as well. For example, children being raised in heavy-television households watched more television and read less than other children (Vandewater *et al.*, 2005a). Children with less-educated parents and those from African-American background tended to use media more frequently. Age, however, was the strongest predictor of overall use: as children grow older, they spend more time with various media (Anad and Krosnick, 2005). Gender, however, was not a significant predictor of media use in this age group, except for the fact that boys play more video games than girls. As Rideout *et al.* (2003: 12) chose to conclude:

> This study has documented a potentially revolutionary phenomenon in American society: the immersion of our very youngest children, from a few months to a few years old, in the world of electronic and interactive media. The impact that this level of media exposure has on children's development is unknown, but one thing is certain: it is an issue that demands immediate attention from parents, educators, researchers, and health professionals.

Three years later, a second Kaiser survey of over 1,000 USA parents with children aged 6 months to 6 years old and a series of focus groups across the country found very similar results (Rideout and Hamel, 2006), reconfirming the centrality of screen media in the lives of young viewers and the important role they serve for parents struggling through the hardships of joggling intensive work and family lives.

THE DEVELOPING CHILD

Indeed, it is this very reality illuminated in the Kaiser report that has been at the center of much controversy. It seems that every theme of concern raised in regard to the lives of children exists in an even greater measure when it comes to young, preschool-age children. They are perceived as the most vulnerable, the most needing of protection and adult guidance, the most under-developed, unknowledgeable, unskilled. The 'moral panic' that typically accompanies the introduction of each new medium into Western societies (Drotner, 1992) is particularly predominant with this age group: concerns for proper physical, cognitive, social, and emotional development; anxieties over the violent and sexual nature of a large portion of media content; concerns for advertising and consumerism; predictions of current general moral deterioration; and the like.

There are also several concerns that are particular to the main developmental tasks facing this age group, including the continuous physical development of the brain in early years of life; development of language, communication, and social skills; and general motor and physical development. These worries were reinforced by a highly controversial recommendation by the

American Academy of Pediatrics Committee on Public Education (1999) that discouraged all forms of television viewing before the age of 2 years and suggested limiting the viewing time of older children to less than 2 hours a day. Although this recommendation was based on very limited research evidence, it assumed that television viewing hinders physical, emotional, social, and cognitive development, as young viewers are presumed to be bombarded with too much audio-visual stimulation and are placed mostly in quite passive situations. Echoing earlier concerns over television's 'displacement effect' (Vanderwater *et al.*, 2006), the overriding assumption was that viewing takes time away from social interactions with adults and children alike which are so crucial to children's healthy development.

Indeed, developmental theory that has been applied widely in studies of young children and television (Valkenburg, 2004; van Evra, 2004) does emphasize that children's cognitive, emotional, and social skills develop over time. Children use, make meaning, and derive pleasure out of television with the skills and tools that they acquire with age and experience. As they mature, their tastes as well as the nature of their interactions with television change dramatically, along with what they take away with them in the process. More specifically, during the first 2 years, the baby-toddler passes through what has been termed by Piaget the 'sensory-motor stage', during which mental schemas are shaped by the infant's senses and actions. As they move into the 'pre-operational stage' between 2 and 7 years of age, their development is characterized by the acquisition of language, which frees the youngster from the sensory-motor experiences of the 'here and now' and allows representative thought. However, in comparison with more mature thinking, their cognitive processes are bound by several limitations: limited information-processing capacity; difficulty distinguishing between fantasy and reality; tendency to center attention on the immediate and concrete; difficulty understanding causal relationships and transformations over time; as well as difficulty in assuming others' points of view (e.g. see Piaget (1969) and Piaget and Inhelder (1969)).

According to Piaget and his followers, as children grow they continue to construct knowledge through their actions on the world through a process of assimilation of new experiences and accommodation to existing ones. Alternatively (and, many would argue, additionally), Vygotsky (1962, 1978), another major theorist of developmental psychology, emphasized the role of social interaction in the development of children's cognition. According to his theory, engagement with adults and peers allows for much better fulfillment of one's potential for cognitive development (known as ZPD: zone of proximal development) than what can be attained alone. This attempt to explain consciousness as the end product of socialization is particularly useful in our discussion of media in the lives of young children, as we will argue in the discussion that follows.

An additional reason why this age group provides researchers with an exciting challenge is that we are confronted with complicated methodological concerns in our efforts to study the many research questions associated with these many concerns. That is, studying the centrality of media in our everyday lives is a complicated task, which becomes even more so when we focus on very young children. On the one hand, in comparison with adults, their linguistic and self-reflexive skills and abilities are more limited, their attention span is shorter, and they are less prone to social pressure to cooperate and conform with unfamiliar adult researchers. On the other hand, they are much more open to engage in a variety of creative play activities that bypass language and formal means of testing. As a result, studying young children requires experimenting with a variety of creative means (observations, free play, role-playing, drawings, and plastic art) in addition to talking with children and recruiting their parents as cooperative informants.

What, then, do we know about the constructed nature of early childhood in this mediated world? What roles do media play in the lives of young children? In what ways do media contribute to their personal and social development? We turn now to examine the main issues that have been investigated so far, and to the many questions yet to be pursued.

ROAMING AROUND THE MEDIATED PLAYGROUND

With all the possibilities available to children as they enter this rich media playground of activity and stimulation options, what choices do they make? What do they attend to and how? How do they make sense of these playful experiences?

The development of attention and viewing preferences

Attention to television develops from birth. Newborns of a few weeks have been observed reacting to sounds coming from the TV set by stopping their feeding and turning their heads towards it. Babies continue to be dependent mostly on audio cues in directing limited attention to television, for a few seconds at a time during their first few months of life. Here, researchers distinguish between 'foreground television,' television content to which young viewers attend closely, and 'background television', which may operate as background noise in a room where the young child is engaged in other activities (Anderson and Paempek, 2005). As they mature, 'foreground' viewing by young viewers becomes more dominant, particularly in regard to television programs and videotapes that are clearly more comprehensible to them. Programs designed for them can hold a baby's attention for much longer stretches of time.

Particularly attractive television contents are peppy music, sound effects, animation, lively pacing that is not overwhelming, humor and noises of laughter, pleasing colors and shapes. Babies seem to react, too, to content that looks and makes sense to them: short verbal outputs, smiling faces, loveable animals, as well as female and children's voices. Home observation of babies, as well as reports from care-givers, suggest that from the age of a few months babies will often stop their activities, move to the music, clap their hands, make happy gurgling sounds, toddle toward the television set, and point at objects and characters on it. Preference for familiar contents viewed with pleasure over and over again intensifies during the second year of life. Observations have documented high levels of attention and active viewing of toddlers, which included singing and dancing along, pointing to the screen, imitating behaviors, speaking back to the television, and generally reacting enthusiastically with great joy (Lemish, 1987; Cupitt *et al.*, 1998; Lemish and Tidhar, 2001; Valkenburg and Voorone, 2004).

Babies' and toddlers' attention to television is greatly influenced by the behaviors of people around them. For example, placing a baby on one's lap or cuddling together in front of the television will significantly lengthen the baby's attention period. Food, too, seems to ensure longer periods of satisfied concentration. Babies offered a bottle or a snack while viewing continued to be relaxed, attentive viewers. By the end of their second year, toddlers' viewing sessions gradually lengthen with signs of growing interest in animation. While accurate measurement of attention to television in young viewers is a complicated matter (Anderson *et al.*, 2001), researchers claim that the amount of time spent with television grows dramatically, particularly during the second year of life, but with great diversity: some babies do not watch any television, whereas others may be viewing 1–2 hours daily regularly.

In contrast to some populist claims that young viewers are 'hooked' on or 'hypnotized' by television, research has found that preschool viewers clearly demonstrate very frequent changes in orientation, moving back and forth between the screen and the surrounding environment. Attention to television continues to grow as a function of the child's development, personality, program content, and environment. The ability to sustain interest in the television program for longer stretches of time and to manipulate one's own attention to television, as well as to competing activities, is gradually strengthened and modified.

As children mature into the preschool years of 3–5, their access and use of the media, as well as their content preferences and tastes, change dramatically. Television remains the most central medium for this age group (including broadcast, cable, satellite, videotapes, DVDs), but there is variability in the amount of viewing time reported for this age group (NB: this may be a result of diversity of child demographics, the operational definition of what constitutes 'viewing', as well as the measures applied, such as parental reports, observations, or computerized rating measures). As a result, it is difficult to generalize from the results, since findings may fluctuate from an average of 1–4 hours of daily viewing, depending on the particular study.

Around the average age of 2½ years many youngsters are capable and willing to stay fully tuned to a program that interests them. They have favorite programs and tend to know when and in which channel they are broadcast. As toddlers grow into preschoolers, around the age of 3 years, they gradually become more interested in and able to comprehend narratives as well as diverse magazine formats. However, they continue to need more time than adults to process television images and language and, thus, prefer slower-paced programming and enjoy lots of repetition than do older children. They show a strong preference for programs produced specially for them that combine segments of animation, puppets, documentaries, and drama and use age-sensitive language, including appropriate vocabulary, sentence length, and pace (for example, the internationally known *Sesame Street*, *Blue's Clues*, *Teletubbies*, *Barney and Friends*,[1] as well as many locally produced programs) (Valkenburg and Cantor, 2000). Such programs are designed with the understanding that young viewers' attention span and viewing preferences develop gradually. Thus, often a 'quilted' magazine format is adopted that offers a variety of segments providing each child the opportunity to interact according to individual needs and abilities (Fisch, 2004).

As they mature and gain experience with the medium, young children become attracted to more fast-paced and stimulating programs, including cartoons and commercials, as well as family genres such as situation comedies that also require a better mastery of language and deeper understanding of characters and social relationships. Gender taste differences start to become more evident: while boys are becoming attracted to action-adventure genres in all screen media and gradually disassociate themselves from educationally oriented television, girls 'hang on' to this preschool television environment a lot longer. By the time they are in school, children seem to have internalized a gender-appropriate preference for contents and role models, and an ability to distinguish between commercials designed for boys (for example, action packed, employing figures and technology) and for girls (for example, pastel and glittery colors, cute and sweet animals) (Hoffner, 1996; Roe, 1998; Lemish *et al.*, 2001). These socially constructed gender differences are, of course, fueled by economic interests in the potential of specialized marketing to young audiences.

It is important to note that habits of media use formed at this age are important not only for the time being, but also because they set the stage for future behavioral patterns and attitudes towards media. In addition, there is research evidence coming from both the psychological and medical literature to suggest that early exposure to television, for example, has long-term effects on behavior, achievements at school, and even attention disorders (e.g. Huessman and Miller, 1994; Anderson *et al.*, 2001; Christakis *et al.*, 2004; Borzekowski and Robinson, 2005; Hancox *et al.*, 2005; Zimmerman and Christakis, 2005). Thus, studying children's early experiences with media may well help us understand many behavioral patterns in later years.

The development of comprehension of television content and genres

During the first 2 years of 'sensory-motor' stage, the baby-toddler mental schemas are shaped by their senses and actions. For example, a baby may learn about the unique world of television by such actions as touching the screen when a favorite puppet appears, clapping hands to the music, or by playing with the power button. These sensory-motor experiences are gradually integrated within the youngster's developing understanding of television and social reality. Thus, the child understands that puppets on television feel very differently when 'touched' on the TV screen than does a favorite stuffed animal cuddled in the crib and that television can be turned on and off at will (Lemish, 1987).

With experience, and by the time they move into the preschool years of 3–5, children have a fairly good grasp of some audio-visual conventions and are able to discriminate between different program genres, including the distinction between programs and commercials. Yet, an integrative review of the developmental literature (Valkenburg and Cantor, 2000; Valkenburg, 2004; van Evra, 2004) suggests that preschoolers (around 3–5 years old) and kindergartners (around 5–6 years old) differ from older children in their ability to understand television and that with maturation they gradually acquire cognitive skills in the following areas: (a) the understanding of storylines and narratives, including the ability to reconstruct events, understand sequence, distinguish between central and incidental information, connect causes to consequences; (b) the understanding of characters such that they are able to describe characters not only by exterior appearance, but also by personality traits, motivations, feelings, personal history, and social orientation, as well as the contexts in which they interrelate with others; (c) the understanding of audio-visual language, including the ability to identify and to understand the codes and conventions of audio-visual expressions such as special effects, shooting angles, slow and fast motion; (d) the understanding that all forms of television are a production, even realistic genres, and that each television text involves the work of many professionals.

For example, young viewers under 5 years old are capable of reconstructing individual episodes or scenes of programs, but they have difficulty connecting them into a coherent story. Most of their thinking centers on the present; thus, they also have difficulty following a chronological development. They assess whether information is central or incidental in a manner different from adults and, thus, they may pay less attention to what adults consider to be primary information and may not be able to remember it as adults do. Similarly, in terms of prognostication (that is, when their viewing is interrupted and they are asked to project future developments in the program), they may propose quite different suggestions than those of an average adult viewer.

Generally, they do not understand that television is an industry that functions within a complicated system of economic, social, political, legal, and human constraints that influence content in various ways. Nor do they understand the interrelationships between television and reality, including its selective nature, its role in creating and representing certain parts of reality, and its contribution to the construction of our worldview.

One particular area that attracted research interest is in changes that develop in young children's ability to distinguish between real and fantasy dimensions of television (Dorr, 1983; Chandler, 1997; Messenger Davies, 1997). Most children by the time they are 4–5 years old are able to distinguish between real objects and televised images, as well as between human actors and cartoon characters. They recognize the factuality of news, but only gradually make correct judgments about fictional dimensions of television entertainment as they mature. In general, they lack the understanding that television programs are staged and that actors portray television characters. They believe and trust adults portrayed on television and have only a partial understanding of the persuasive intent of television commercials, to which they are highly attracted.

Related difficulties inherent in understanding the constructed nature of television at this age group have been the concern of several studies. In one study that focused on the development of visual literacy, 4–6 year-old children were found to gradually develop some understanding as they move from no awareness whatsoever of its constructed nature and perceive television to mirror reality to a recognition that television programs are produced by people. They also move from having no perception of the role of the camera in creating the television world to a growing understanding of the relationships between cameraperson, the camera, the subject of photography and an ability to associate specific camera movements with specific effects. It seems that the understanding of television conventions is indeed an acquired skill influenced by cognitive development and, therefore, is rather incomplete even for children who grow up in a television-rich environment (Tidhar and Lemish, 2003).

Yet, it has also been found that knowledge about television conventions accumulated through prior experience with particular program formats can be applied to new episodes and to new series even at this age group (Crawley *et al.*, 2002). Similarly, there is also evidence suggesting that the prior experience with television, as well as general social and cultural attitudes towards it, influence some aspects of even young children's comprehension of television genres and contents. For example, lack of familiarity with commercials in Israel (at the time of the study) elicited much more naïve and uninformed attitudes towards this genre, in comparison with the budding cynicism already evident in the discourse of American kindergartners. At the same time, while both groups of children already had a clear understanding that the genre of news deals with reality, and is 'bad' and 'sad' in nature, Israeli children perceived it to be concerned with the national collective and 'important people', while American children were more concerned at the time with personal safety and the weather (Lemish, 1997, 1998). It follows that one cannot study children in isolation from the context in which they are being raised. As cultural circumstances change, so does the children's understanding of the role that the media play in their lives. In this regard, one might wonder how American kindergartners would have responded had they been interviewed following the events of 9/11 or the war in Iraq.

THE BENEFITS OF THE MEDIATED PLAYGROUND

So what is the value of all this roaming around the mediated playground, particularly television? Do young viewers learn from it? Does it help promote any skills: cognitive, social, emotional, and behavioral? In what ways do the media contribute and/or hinder the development of youngsters?

Viewing and language development

A common criticism of excessive television viewing at the very young age is that it hinders the development of language, a most central cognitive task for babies and toddlers. The argument is that the quality of verbal engagement with television is low, since most of its popular programs are linguistically underdeveloped and use a limited vocabulary with dialogues consisting of short sentences (this, for example, has been a common critique of the BBC series *The Teletubbies* that is popular worldwide). Furthermore, the visual aspects of television often dominate the viewing experience. Finally, the nature of the viewing experience does not allow for reciprocal interactions; that is, language on television is incapable of adjusting itself to meet the needs or interests of each particular viewer or to provide feedback and appropriate reinforcements. There is some research evidence to support these claims, as the quality and quantity of parent–child interactions were found to be significantly reduced in the presence of background television (Anderson and Pempek, 2005). However, the current literature on the development of language skills presents an accumulation of research evidence that suggests that it is also possible to acquire language through observation of the verbal interactions of others. Such interactions are plentiful on television, take place in a wide variety of social situations, and in formats that repeat themselves, become familiar, and are thus easily learned by the child.

The distinction between background and foreground television is useful here, too, as other studies point to the possibility that viewing of age-appropriate programs with parental mediation may even stimulate language viewing. For example, studies that examined educational programs designed to enrich young children's lives and facilitate linguistic development demonstrate significant achievements. Such programs adopt linguistic styles that facilitate learning: repetitiveness, clear yes and no questions, specific 'W' questions (who, what, where, when, and why), verbal descriptions that are synchronized with the visuals presented, pacing similar to that often used by parents reading a story, and the like. These presentation styles were found to be effective in research situations: young viewers learned unfamiliar vocabulary (both nouns and verbs) following exposure to television programs, both in short-term experiments (where children were presented with a video segment only once) as well as in more long-term ones (where children were exposed to a series of programs for several weeks) (Rice and Woodsmall, 1988; Rice *et al.*, 1992, 1994).

In a longitudinal study of *Sesame Street* illustrative of this line of research, American researchers examined the vocabulary of 3 and 5 year olds in mid-America as well as viewing logs filled in by parents once every 6 months (Rice *et al.*, 1990). The most interesting finding for the purpose of our discussion is that 3 year olds who viewed *Sesame Street* frequently improved their vocabulary in much more significant ways in comparison with those who viewed it much less. These findings remained valid even when other related variables that could affect both the viewing of *Sesame Street* and language development were considered (such as parents' education, number of siblings, initial score on the vocabulary test, and the like). The researchers have suggested that this may be an indication of the direction of causality: viewing of *Sesame Street* contributed to vocabulary development, not the other way around. Interestingly, these findings were not found for the older group that started the study at the age of 5 years. Since the program's linguistic level was aimed at 3–7-year-old children, it is possible that it did not contribute in a significant manner to older children.

Aimed at even younger children, a longitudinal study by Linebarger and Walker (2005) found that infants and toddlers benefited most from viewing programs that applied specific linguistic strategies that are appropriate for this target age group, such as the actors speak directly to the child-viewer, encourage their participation, engage in object naming, and provide opportunities for the child to respond (e.g. *Blue's Clues*, *Dora The Explorer*[2]). Watching programs that use attractive storytelling formats was also found to be associated with positive language development. Interestingly, another popular program of this age group, *Barney and Friends*, was found to be negatively associated with the acquisition of vocabulary, but at the same time positively associated with the production of expressive language in play situations.

The few observational studies that focused on the language development of babies and toddlers in their home environment suggest that some parents use television as a 'talking book' with their young ones (Lemish and Rice, 1986). They practice linguistic skills during television viewing, particularly with programs aimed at the very young. For example, both children and parents designate objects and characters on the screen by name (e.g. 'Here is a balloon!' 'This is a butterfly'), they ask questions (e.g. 'Where did they go?' 'What is she doing?'), repeat messages, including commercials and slogans; and describe what they see (e.g. 'He is sad'. 'They are playing with the dog').

As a whole, the studies of incidental language learning from television viewing at an early age suggest that there is clear evidence for the acquisition of vocabulary, but this does not appear to be the case for a much deeper learning of grammar (Naigels and Mayeux, 2001). In addition, they highlight the importance of paying attention to specific program types and content in considering the effects on language development, as well as to the active role parents may be playing in making television content accessible and relevant to their children's linguistic development.

Cognitive development and learning

A central concern in this area focuses on cognitive development and learning from early media experiences. For example, one large study claimed that it found a relationship between the presence of background television noise in the first few years of life and less involvement in reading (Vandewater *et al.*, 2005a). A few experimental studies that examined learning from videos presented to viewers under 2 years of age were quite consistent in indicating that there is very little learning occurring under such conditions, and what is taking place is dramatically less than that found for equivalent live displays of behavior. Such was the case for experimenting with learning imitation from televised behavior, for searching for hidden objects, and for learning positive versus fearful emotional reactions (Schmitt and Anderson, 2002; Anderson and Pempek, 2005). While these studies are too few and far between, when taken together they do suggest that learning from television by children under the age of 2 years is poor, probably due to their limited symbolic and perceptual and linguistic skills.

At the same time, there is evidence from evaluative research of older, preschool children's viewing of educational television that documents positive learning. This is most notably the case with regard to the heavily studied, world-famous *Sesame Street*. Such studies suggest that viewing the program on a regular basis helped 3–5 year olds perform better in tests of skills such as number and letter recognition and understanding various concepts (such as near–far, wide–narrow), learning pro-social behavior and attitudes (such as tolerance towards various minorities and disabilities), and dealing with emotions (such as anxiety over new experiences). Furthermore, the more children viewed the program, the more their scores improved. These findings were found to hold for all children – both boys and girls, from a variety of ethnic groups, cultures, and geographical areas (Fisch and Truglio, 2001; Fisch, 2004).

Still, even with these impressive results, the series is not without its strong critics. One line of argument claimed that it was really the parents' intervention in encouraging viewing that was the main factor in improving performance and not the viewing itself. Further, since it can be assumed that more well-to-do families have encouraged their children to view the program more often than did those from lower class families, the gap between the two populations of children widened. Another line of criticism has referred to the fast pace of the program. It was argued that this pace does not allow children enough time to process information, that it encourages the development of impatience for the more structured, slower paced school setting, and that it makes it harder for children to learn to delay the need for gratification. Finally, concern was also expressed that parents invest most of their efforts in assisting viewing of the program, rather than spending quality time with their young children away from television.

Two major research projects in the early 1990s in the USA challenged these critics. The first, 'The Early Window Project', followed about 250 children from diverse backgrounds, aged 2 and 4 years, for 3 years, until they reached the ages of 5 and 7 years respectively (Wright *et al.*, 2001). The children's viewing habits, family characteristics, linguistic skills, and school readiness were monitored and tested periodically. The results presented persuasive evidence that viewing of *Sesame Street* did indeed improve viewers' achievements over time and that the more the program was viewed the greater the achievement. The effect was stronger for the younger group, suggesting that viewing *Sesame Street* improves younger viewers' chances of success in the educational system. Positive achievements were documented even without parental intervention, and children from lower classes benefited from viewing just as much as their peers from higher classes. The main difference, however, was that, on the average, lower class children viewed the program less than children from higher socio-economic status classes. This led to the conclusion that, in order to narrow the knowledge gap, it is necessary to find more effective ways to encourage disadvantaged children to watch the program more often.

In concluding this project, the researchers suggested that television is not a monolithic entity that affects children in a unified manner. On the contrary, the content of viewing makes a big difference in children's lives. Heavy viewers of *Sesame Street* who were light viewers of other television contents popular at that age group (particularly animation programs) benefited most from *Sesame Street*. Even more striking was the claim made possible due to the longitudinal nature of the study that the positive contribution of viewing *Sesame Street* (in interaction with other background variables, such as parents' education) reached beyond the specific skills acquired during those early viewing days: as they mature, young viewers developed a more positive set of attitudes towards learning in general, as well as a higher level of self-confidence in their ability to learn.

The second project applied a very different method of study: a phone survey of a representative sample of about 11,000 parents of kindergarteners, first- and second-grade children (approximately 5–8 years old) (Zill, 2001). The survey examined the more general issue of school readiness, but included some specific questions regarding viewing *Sesame Street*. The results suggested that most children in all demographic groups, including disadvantaged children, were viewing the program at the time. That is to say, in contrast to other educational means available at this young age group, *Sesame Street* is accessible to children even in areas of poverty and distress. Regular viewers demonstrated early signs of reading and writing skills already in kindergarten, were more able to read on their own in first and second grades, and needed less assistance when faced with reading difficulties. However, this did not hold true for children with particularly low achievements or learning disabilities. The results of the survey thus reinforced the claim that viewing educational programs during the preschool years is associated, even if only partially, with better scores on school-readiness tests, with the exception of children with particularly low learning achievements.

The accumulative evidence from *Sesame Street*, as well as other pre-school programs (Fisch, 2004), suggests that educational television can and does teach at this age group. However, it does not provide convincing proof that educational television can replace other socializing agents in closing substantial gaps between different populations. Children from all strata of society and cultures are attracted to successful programs, but children living in more culturally enriched environments who receive parental and other types of reinforcement seem to gain a lot more from sustained viewing. Educational television, so it seems, is incapable of addressing the deeper social and economical deprivation of disadvantaged groups in our respective societies.

A special case in point is learning from early computer use. While very little is known to date on this part of young children's mediated world, it is nevertheless clear that a majority of parents assign positive values to giving their children an early start with computers. For example, 72 percent of parents in the Kaiser study answered that using a computer 'mostly helps' youngsters' learning (Rideout *et al.*, 2003). The interactive nature of the computer experience, in comparison with viewing television, for example, seems particularly attractive to parents and educators. So, do young users actually benefit from computer content?

Analysis of the Kaiser study data (Calvert *et al.*, 2005a) indicated that, in discussing computer-related learning, much like learning from television, it is not the medium alone that makes the difference, but perhaps more the type of content with which the child interacts. For example, no correlations were found between time spent playing computer games and parents' reports of their child's ability to read, but such relationships were reported in regard to non-game computer use, which may be indeed facilitating reading skills.

In addition, an exploratory experiment with 4–6-year-old children presented preliminary evidence that children were less attentive and less interested in a computer story when control of the mouse was in the hand of an adult rather than in their own. At the same time, however, there were no differences in memory of the content as a function of who controlled the mouse (although there was a gender difference: boys tended to remember visual content better). The findings also reinforced the 'visual superiority effect' according to which computer players remembered visual content better than verbal content, regardless of adult mediation (Calvert *et al.*, 2005b).

These studies represent only the initial steps in what is sure to develop into an exciting research agenda in the next few years. It is nevertheless evident, even at this stage, that the issues involved in learning from a medium, whichever medium, are much more complicated than any simple causal explanation would lead us to believe.

PARENTAL MEDIATION IN THE MEDIATED PLAYGROUND

Are youngsters left alone in the mediated playground? Is there an adult supervision of their whereabouts, activities, and safety, and in what form and shape? Our discussion so far has clearly pointed to the important role that parental mediation at this young age may be playing in language, as well as in cognitive development and learning. To date, research suggests that parents' involvement in their children's media-related activities may be related to three levels (Tidhar and Levinson, 1997; Valkenburg *et al.*, 1999; Warren 2003). First, the level of 'awareness and co-viewing/playing': the degree to which parents are around during viewing and game playing; the degree to which parents are familiar with the contents of the programs, computer and video games, and the like that their children are spending time with; the degree to which parents offer their children role models of media-consumption habits; and even view and play with them. Second, the level of 'supervision,' also termed 'restrictive mediation,' is the degree to which parents supervise and restrict the media activities of their children, the temporal quantity of engagement, and the contents; the use of media for reward or punishment; and the degree of monitoring secondary behaviors (e.g. reading or eating while viewing). Here, parents may also take advantage of available program rating in designing their content-related viewing rules (Warren, 2002). Finally, the 'instructive mediation' level relates to the degree to which parents mediate between their children and the content attended to, through conversation, explanation, value judgments, processing of emotions, understanding information, application of learning, critical evaluation, and the like. Research evidence suggests that it is much easier for parents, in terms of allocation of their personal resources of time and effort, to design viewing rules, for example, than to be involved in co-viewing and active interactions. The result is that apparently not much co-viewing happens during these early years of socialization.

We have seen that viewing television together with children has been demonstrated to be a desirable activity. In doing so, parents are able to assist their children to understand the medium of television as well as its contents, to encourage them to internalize messages selectively and critically, to intervene immediately when children are exposed to objectionable content in their opinion, to handle emotional reactions of children and the like. The fact that more and more children are engaged in individual viewing, in the privacy of their own room or when there is no adult supervision at home, restricts the possibilities for such parental contributions.

Parental viewing rules were found in the Kaiser study in the USA to develop as children grow older and to be associated with higher socio-economic status (Calvert *et al.*, 2005a). Overall, a majority of parents (88 percent) reported that they have program rules (i.e. rules about the types of program viewed), and less parents, but still a majority (67 percent), reported holding to viewing-time rules (i.e. rules about the amount of viewing time). Children who were raised in homes that hold to viewing-time rules tended to spend less time in front of the screen. However, this was not the case for children who were raised in homes that hold to program rules, who were more likely to hold positive attitudes towards television and to be present during the viewing itself (Vandewater *et al.*, 2005b).

These three dimensions of potential parental intervention, i.e. awareness, supervision, and instructive mediation, are intertwined with parents' own attitudes towards television. Some perceive television to be a destructive force in their children's lives, even to the point of believing in the addictive power of the medium, and so take a protective position towards it. Others may see the positive sides involved in viewing television and its role in providing entertainment, relaxation, and information to their kids. Yet another group of parents may find that television assists them in the task of raising and socializing their children. While still others my take a liberal stance towards their children's viewing, allowing them the freedom to determine their own viewing habits. On the whole, various studies have reported that many parents have faith in the educational value of media designed for their preschoolers (Rideout *et al.*, 2003; Fisch, 2004; Rideout and Hamel, 2006).

Parental mediation has also proven to be valuable in regard to emotional responses to television, not only cognitive ones. In particular, the effects that television viewing might have on anxiety and fear reactions of children have elicited both public and research concern. As preschoolers grow older they do not become less easily frightened. Rather, what seems to happen is that they are less bothered by some stimuli that concerned them in the past, while other stimuli that had never elicited reactions in the past do so as they mature. More specifically, young viewers are typically scared of animals, dark, supernatural forces (such as ghosts, witches, and monsters), and things that look anomalous or move unexpectedly. They might be more afraid of something that looks dangerous, but which in fact is not, than of something that does not look dangerous, but which in fact is. Thus, young children react more fearfully to strong visuals and imaginary programs (e.g. cartoons, monsters) than to real but abstract dangers (e.g. news reports about an anticipated natural disaster). This process will be reversed during school years. In addition, cognitive comforting strategies spontaneously used by parents, such as explanations that 'this is not real' or that 'this is happening very far away', have been proven to be less effective for this age group than behavioral comforting strategies, such as a hug or offering a snack (Cantor, 2001, 2002; Moyer-Guse and Smith, 2007).

The research on parental mediation of children's television use emphasizes the importance of understanding the place of media in the lives of young children as an integral part of the socialization processes taking place in the family as a social unit (Warren, 2003). Parents convey implicit messages to children about the way media should be used through their own habits (e.g. books for learning and television for entertainment; Jordan, 2005). On their part, parents derive their attitudes towards media from a much more general public discourse related to their perception of children's developmental processes and their own role as parents and educators.

CONCLUDING NOTE

Overall, it is undeniable that the mediated playground is growing rapidly and in diverse ways, some of which we are unable to anticipate today. Is it a better or a worse playground than the familiar swing-jungle gym-sandbox one is not the question. It is certainly a different kind. The pleasures obtained there may be different; and so, too, are the dangers, as no playground is without its pitfalls, sharp edges, or run-down equipment. But the main question remains, of how to turn this playground into a safe, friendly, and beneficial environment that is age appropriate, and one that offers our children opportunities for healthy growth and development.

What research tells us with a relative degree of certainty is that media experiences should be age appropriate – taking into consideration the child's cognitive, emotional, social, behavioral, and physical needs and abilities. Some of the difficulties that young children experience in dealing with and understanding media texts are a result of the complexity and abstract nature of content that is not produced with them in mind; that is removed from their experiences and, thus, is more difficult to relate to and understand; that is intended for an older, very diverse audience (such as family television programs and movies, computer games and internet sites).

This relates to our second conclusion: it is not necessarily the medium itself that should be the focus of our concern (e.g. Should youngsters be allowed to view television? Are computer games good for preschoolers? Is early control of the mouse a desired skill?), but rather the specific content with which the child interacts that makes the real difference. As Anderson *et al.* (2001: 134) stated in their conclusion: 'Marshall McLuhan appears to have been wrong. The *medium* is not the message. The *message* is the message!'

Third, it is also quite clear that the interactions of the child's individual traits with characteristics of the family and the preschool environment, as well as the macro characteristics of society, are central in forming and understanding media-related experiences and outcomes. The study of the mediated playground cannot take place outside of the contextualizing social neighborhood. This having been said, it should be noted that we have very limited knowledge of research on this age group conducted outside of the Westernized world (beyond some research conducted in relationship to *Sesame Street*). Thus, our conclusions are inherently based on approaches developed in the West. As such research becomes available, we hope it will help us challenge our notions of what the mediated playground looks like around the world.

Finally, our review of the literature highlights, once again, the importance of cultivating media literacy skills in children of all ages. Media literacy, in general terms, is commonly understood to refer to the ability to access, analyze, and evaluate messages, as well as the ability to communicate creatively in a variety of ways. It is perceived to be a form of critical literacy necessary for participation in civic and cultural life that requires an informed, critical, and creative citizenry (Lemish, 2007: 182). The research presented above makes it clear that children need guidance in developing these skills from the first encounter they have with media and throughout their life.

In summary, our accumulated knowledge to date suggests that no young child should be left unattended in any playground, let alone one as rich and vast as the media world. Adults in charge of children's well being also have the responsibility of making the most out of their children's daily experiences with media. We already have some knowledge about how to be engaged in such efforts, but we need to continue to pursue the many questions yet to be addressed and that are emerging rapidly as a result of the expanding and changing nature of the mediated playground.

NOTES

1 *Sesame Street* is a magazine format program produced by Sesameworkshop (formerly Children Television Workshop – CTW), which presents a variety

of forms of short segments: animation, theater, documentary, and Muppets. *Blue's Clues* is an animated program produced by Nickelodeon featuring a live-action host and his puppy Blue. *Teletubbies* features four colorful dressed-up characters in animated scenes and is produced by the BBC. *Barney and Friends* features Barney, the large purple-like dinosaur character and his colorful friends, produced by the PBS.

2 *Dora the Explorer* is an animated adventure program produced by Nickelodeon, featuring Dora and her animal friends.

REFERENCES

American Academy of Pediatrics Committee on Public Education (1999) 'Media education'. *Pediatrics*, 104: 341–343.

Anand, S. and Krosnick, J.A. (2005) 'Demographic predictors of media use among infants, toddlers, and preschoolers'. *American Behavioral Scientist*, 48(5): 539–561.

Anderson, D.R. and Pempek, T.A. (2005) 'Television and very young children'. *American Behavioral Scientist*, 48(5): 505–522.

Anderson, D.R., Huston, A.C., Schmitt, K.L., Linebarger, D.L. and Wright, J.C. (2001) 'Early childhood televiewing and adolescent behavior'. *Monographs of the Society for Research in Child Development*, 66(1): 119–134.

Borzekowski, D.L.G. and Robinson, T.N. (2005) 'The remote, the mouse, and the no. 2 pencil: the household media environment and academic achievement among third grade student'. *Archives Pediatrics and Adolescent Medicine*, 159: 607–613.

Calvert, A.L., Rideout, V.J., Woodlard, J.L., Barr, R.F. and Strouse, G.A. (2005a) 'Age, ethnicity, and socioeconomic patterns in early computer use'. *American Behavioral Scientist*, 48(5): 590–607.

Calvert, S.L., Strong, B.L. and Gallagher, L. (2005b). 'Control as an engagement feature for young children's attention to and learning of computer content'. *American Behavioral Scientist*, 48(5): 578–589.

Cantor, J. (2001) 'The media and children's fears, anxieties, and perceptions of danger'. In D.G. Singer and J.L. Singer (eds) *Handbook of Children and the Media*. Thousand Oaks, CA: Sage Publications; 207–221.

Cantor, J. (2002) 'Fright reactions to mass media'. In J. Bryant and D. Zillmann (eds) *Media Effects: Advances in Theory and Research*. Mahwah, NJ: Lawrence Erlbaum; 287–306.

Chandler, D. (1997) 'Children's understanding of what is "real" on television: a review of the literature'. *Journal of Educational Media*, 22(1): 65–80.

Christakis, D.A., Zimmerman, F.J., DiGiuseppe, D.L. and McCarthy, C.A. (2004). 'Early television exposure and subsequent attentional problems in children'. *Pediatrics*, 133(4): 708–713.

Crawley, A.M., Anderson, D.R., Santomero, A., Wilder, A., Williams, M., Evans, M.K. and Bryant, J. (2002) 'Do children learn how to watch television? The impact of extensive experience with *Blue's Clues* on preschool children's television viewing behavior'. *Journal of Communication*, 52(2): 264–280.

Cupitt, M. Kenkinsonh, D., Ungere, J. and Waters, B. (1998). *Infants and Television*. Sydney, Australia: Australian Broadcasting Authority.

Dorr, A. (1983) 'No shortcuts to judging reality'. In J. Bryant and D.R. Anderson (eds) *Children's Understanding of Television: Research on Attention and Comprehension*. New York: Academic Press; 190–220.

Drotner, K. (1992) 'Modernity and moral panics'. In M. Skovmand and K.C. Schroeder (eds) *Media Cultures: Reappraising Transnational Media*. London: Routledge.

Fisch, S.M. (2004) *Children's Learning from Educational Television: Sesame Street and Beyond*. Mahwah, NJ: Lawrence Erlbaum Associates.

Fisch, S.M. and Truglio, R.T. (eds) (2001) *'G' is for Growing: Thirty Years of Research on Children and Sesame Street*. Mahwah, NJ: Lawrence Erlbaum Associates.

Hancox, R.J., Milne, B.J. and Poulton, R. (2005) 'Association of television viewing during childhood with poor educational achievement'. *Archives Pediatrics and Adolescent Medicine*, 159: 614–618.

Hoffner, C. (1996) 'Children's wishful identification and para-social interaction with favorite television characters'. *Journal of Broadcasting and Electronic Media*, 4: 289–402.

Huessman, L.R. and Miller, L.S. (1994) 'Long term effects of repeated exposure to media violence in childhood'. In L.R. Huessman (ed.) *Aggressive Behavior*. New York, Plenum Press; 153–186.

Jordan, A. (2005) 'Learning to use books and television: an exploratory study in ecological perspective'. *American Behavioral Scientist*, 48(5): 523–538.

Lemish, D. (1987) 'Viewers in diapers: the early development of television viewing'. In T. Lindlof (ed.) *Natural Audiences: Qualitative Research of Media Uses and Effects*. Norwood, NJ: Ablex; 33–57.

Lemish, D. (1997) 'Kindergartners' understandings of television: a cross cultural comparison'. *Communication Studies*, 48(2): 109–126.

Lemish, D. (1998). 'What is news? A cross cultural examination of kindergartners' understanding of news'. *Communications: European Journal of Communication Research*, 23, 491–504.

Lemish, D. (2007). *Children and Television: A Global Perspective.* Oxford, UK: Blackwell.

Lemish, D. and Rice, M. (1986). 'Television as a talking picture book: a prop for language acquisition'. *Journal of Child Language*, 13: 251–274.

Lemish, D. and Tidhar, C. (2001) 'How global does it get? The *Teletubbies* in Israel'. *Journal of Broadcasting and Electronic Media*, 45(4): 558–574.

Lemish, D., Liebes, T. and Seidmann, V. (2001) 'Gendered media meanings and uses'. In S. Livingstone and M. Bovill (eds) *Children and their Changing Media Environment: A European Comparative Study.* Mahwah, NJ: Lawrence Erlbaum; 263–282.

Linebarger, D.L. and Walker, D. (2005) 'Infants' and toddlers' television viewing and language outcomes'. *American Behavioral Scientist*, 48(5): 624–645.

Messenger Davies, M. (1997) *Form, Fake and Fantasy.* Hillsdale, NJ: Erlbaum Associates.

Moyer-Guse, E. and Smith, S.L. (2007) 'TV news and coping: parents' use of strategies for reducing children's news-induced fears'. In D. Lemish and M. Götz (eds) *Children and Media at Times of War and Conflict.* Cresskill, NJ: Hampton Press; 267–286.

Naigels, L.R. and Mayeux, L. (2001) 'Television as incidental language teacher'. In D. Singer and J. Singer (eds) *Handbook of Children and the Media.* Thousand Oaks, CA: Sage; 135–152.

Piaget, J. (1969) *The Origins of Intelligence in the Child.* New York: International University Press.

Piaget, J. and Inhelder, B. (1969) *The Psychology of the Child.* New York: Basic Books.

Rice, M.L. and Woodsmall, L. (1988) 'Lessons from television: children's word learning when viewing'. *Child Development*, 59: 420–429.

Rice, M.L., Huston, A.C., Truglio, R. and Wright, J. (1990) 'Words from "Sesame Street:" learning vocabulary while viewing'. *Developmental Psychology*, 26(3): 421–428.

Rice, M.L., Buhr, J. and Oetting, J.B. (1992) 'Specific language-impaired children's quick incidental learning of words: the effect of a pause'. *Journal of Speech and Hearing Research*, 35: 1040–1048.

Rice, M.L., Oetting, J.B., Marquis, J., Bode, J. and Pase, S. (1994) 'Frequency of input effects on word comprehension of children with specific language impairment'. *Journal of Speech and Hearing Research*, 37: 106–122.

Rideout, V. and Hamel, E. (2006). The media family: electronic media in the lives of infants, toddlers, preschoolers and their parents. The Henry J. Kaiser Family Foundation Report, USA.

Rideout, V.J., Vandewater, E.A. and Wartella, E.A. (2003) Zero to six: electronic media in the lives of infants and preschoolers. The Henry J. Kaiser Family Foundation Report, USA.

Roe, K. (1998) '"Boys will be boys and girls will be girls:" Changes in children's media use'. *Communications: The European Journal of Communication Research*, 23(1): 5–25.

Schmitt, K.L. and Anderson, D.R. (2002) 'Television and reality: toddlers' use of visual information from video to guide behavior'. *Media Psychology*, 4: 51–76.

Tidhar, C.E. and Lemish, D. (2003) 'The making of television: young viewers' developing perceptions'. *Journal of Broadcasting and Electronic Media*, 47(3): 375–393.

Tidhar, C.E. and Levinson, H. (1997) 'Parental mediation of children's viewing in a changing television environment'. *Journal of Educational Media*, 23(2–3): 141–155.

Valkenburg, P.M. (2004) *Children's Responses to the Screen: A Media Psychological Approach.* Hillsdale, NJ: Lawrence Erlbaum Associates.

Valkenburg, P.M. and Cantor, J. (2000) 'Children's likes and dislikes of entertainment programs'. In D. Zillman and P. Vorderer (eds) *Media Entertainment: The Psychology of its Appeal.* Mahwah, NJ: Lawrence Erlbaum Associates; 135–152.

Valkenburg, P.M. and Vroone, M. (2004) 'Developmental changes in infants' and toddlers' attention to television entertainment'. *Communication Research*, 1(1): 288–311.

Valkenburg, P.M., Krcmar, M., Peetrs, A.L. and Marseille, N.M. (1999) 'Developing a scale to assess three styles of television mediation: "Instructive mediation," "restrictive mediation" and "social coviewing"'. *Journal of Broadcasting and Electronic Media*, 43(1): 52–66.

Vandewater, E.A., Bickham, D.S., Lee, J.H., Cummings, H.M., Wartella, E.A. and Rideout, V.J. (2005a). 'When the television is always on: heavy television exposure and young children's development'. *American Behavioral Scientist*, 48(5): 562–577.

Vandewater, E.A., Park, S.-E. and Wartella, E.A. (2005b) '"No – you can't watch that": parental rules and young children's media use'. *American Behavioral Scientist*, 48(5): 608–623.

Vandewater, E.A., Bickham, D.S. and Lee, J.H. (2006) 'Time well spent? Relating television use to children's free time activities'. *Pediatrics*, 117(2): e181–e191.

Van Evra, J. (2004) *Television and Child Development* (third edition). Mahwah, NJ: Lawrence Erlbaum Associates.

Vygotzky, L.S. (1962). *Thought and Language.* Cambridge, MA: MIT Press.

Vygotsky, L.S. (1978). *Mind in Society.* Cambridge, MA: Harvard University Press.

Warren, R. (2002) 'Preaching to the choir? Parents' use of TV ratings to mediate children's viewing'. *Journalism and Mass Communication Quarterly,* 79(4): 867–887.

Warren, R. (2003) 'Parental mediation of preschool children's television viewing'. *Journal of Broadcasting and Electronic media*, 47(3): 394–417.

Wright, J.C., Huston, A.C., Scantlin, R. and Kotler, J. (2001) 'The Early Window Project: *Sesame Street* prepares children for school'. In S.M. Fisch and R.T. Truglio (eds) *'G' is for Growing: Thirty Years of Research on Children and Sesame Street.* Mahwah, NJ: Lawrence Erlbaum Associates; 97–114.

Zill, N. (2001) 'Does *Sesame Street* enhance school readiness: evidence from a national survey of children'. In S.M. Fisch and R.T. Truglio (eds) *'G' is for Growing: Thirty Years of Research on Children and Sesame Street.* Mahwah, NJ: Lawrence Erlbaum Associates; 115–130.

Zimmerman, F.J. and Christakis, D.A. (2005) 'Children's television viewing and cognitive outcomes'. *Archives Pediatrics and Adolescent Medicine*, 159: 619–625.

10

Dividing Delights: Children, Adults and the Search for Sales[1]

Jane Kenway and Elizabeth Bullen

INTRODUCTION

Consumption is now recognized as a defining characteristic of the lifestyle of the Western world. Consumption and information and communication media *together* hold a powerful and privileged position in today's culture, society and economy. We call the cultural form that arises from the blending of consumption and information and communication media 'consumer-media culture'. Advertising, diverse media forms and other meaning-making (semiotic) practices are central to consumer-media culture. They remake the meaning of goods in order to sell them. In complex and contradictory ways, consumer-media culture in its many forms has transformed the lives of children, the family and the school and, ultimately, the 'nature' of childhood (Kenway and Bullen, 2001).

Entertainment, advertising and education were once understood as separate, but they are increasingly coalescing – not as one or all at once. Diverse convergences of the consumer form have implications for different generations and for different types of cross-generational relationships. This creates both possibilities and predicaments for today's kids, parents and teachers.

We begin by considering the ways in which children's entertainment and advertising are converging. We show how child and youth markets are now distinct from and 'other' to adult markets, noting that they also offer children and youth positions as adult-like consumers. We then consider adult culture's responses to kids' cultures, arguing that adult concerns are cultivated by the media and also entail 'othering' practices. These translate into an adult consumer form that hybridizes advertising, entertainment and education. We conclude with a brief discussion of the production of adult-like children and child-like adults. Our overall purpose is to point to some of the patterns that underlie the rapidly changing world of children's consumer-media culture.

KIDS' CULTURE

Advertainment: hybridizing entertainment and advertising

Children's and young people's culture/entertainment has its own aesthetic. It is flashy, fast, frenetic, fantastic, funny, fun, colourful and catchy. It privileges visual communication over verbal, and so do the commercials that target children. Indeed, a British qualitative study of children's responses to advertising found that children rarely mention the product; they like particular advertisements because of 'the personalities, the gimmicks, the humour and the songs' (Cullingford, 1984, cited in Seiter, 1995: 105). These elements constitute, in Williams' (1989) classic words, 'a magic system of inducements' rather than a rational appeal. Market researchers know that children's preferred mode of information processing is visual (their ability to process it being far superior to that of adults) and that advertising is most effective when key points are presented to them in this way (Smith, 1997: 3). Of course, entertainment is not solely visual; but, in television and online advertising, what is shown has greater impact than what is said. This is because the 'response of children to brand advertising is largely based in its symbolic content, its metaphorical meaning' (Dell Clark, 1999: 82).

Advertisements are increasingly presented as entertainment, as enjoyable in their own right rather than 'as consumer information' (Seiter, 1995: 105). The resulting hybridization of entertainment and advertising which distinguishes young people's culture and media manifests in a variety of ways which we will now discuss.

Marketers have long known that characters sell products, and they sell particularly well to kids. The elves Snap, Crackle and Pop were developed specifically to market Kellogg's Rice Krispies, originating in a radio jingle in the 1930s, appearing on packaging and later as animated characters in television commercials. Ronald McDonald has been the face of McDonald's restaurants since 1963. Hello Kitty originated in the 1970s as a symbol on Japanese design company Sanrio's character-branded stationery and accessories for adolescent girls. The mouth-less white kitten is now used to market merchandise as diverse as clothing and bed linen, jewellery and furniture, toys and collectibles, kitchen utensils and car accessories.

The history of using characters originating in print, film and television media to sell unrelated products is just as long. The first Mickey Mouse cartoons were released in 1928, and by 1929 its characters were being used to sell Disney-licensed merchandise, including school writing tablets. The first Mickey Mouse dolls came on the market in 1930 (James, 1997: 3). In the twenty-first century, Disney Interactive produces software tie-ins to promote its film and new media products. Children who enjoy Disney/Pixar's *Monsters Inc.* (2001) can also play *Monsters Inc. Scare Island*, while software titles like *Disney's 102 Dalmatians: Puppies to the Rescue* and *Disney's Extremely Goofy Skateboarding* promote older character brands. Furthermore, these character icons are used to promote traditional or otherwise generic products for children, with obvious benefits to both the manufacturer and the licence holder of the characters. Parker Brothers, for instance, now manufactures Star Wars, Spongebob Squarepants, and Disney editions of Monopoly. Characters from *Cars* (2006) appeared on boxed confectionery released by Nestlé for the 2006 Christmas season. Characters from earlier favourites, like *Toy Story* (1995), *Tarzan* (1999), and *A Bug's Life* (1998), continue to appear on its flavoured yoghurts, custards and mousses.

Cross-advertising of this sort encourages the young to associate a brand-name product automatically with the entertainment texts which they enjoy. Indeed, it normalizes the advertising and entertainment blend and presents it as a source of pleasure. The pleasures of entertainment thus become the pleasures of consumption.

With characters and media texts increasingly marketed as brands in their own right, children's and youth media formats often function as full-length commercials for toys and music. Kids recognize the persuasive intent of commercials. Children under five are able to distinguish commercials from programmes and, thus, between entertainment and selling intent, even if they cannot articulate the difference between them (Roedder, 1999: 6). However, programme-length commercials are designed to make it difficult for children to differentiate content from marketing of the likes of *Pokémon*, *My Little Pony*, *Strawberry Shortcake*, *The Care Bears*, *The Power Rangers*. Indeed, it has now become equally common for the toy 'characters' to be created first and the media format to be then developed around the 'characters'. Barbie's burgeoning movie career is a case in point, with titles including *Barbie as Rapunzel* (2002), *Barbie of Swan Lake* (2003), *Fairytopia* (2005). *Barbie in the 12 Dancing Princesses* (2006) and *Mermaidia* (2006). Barbie CD ROMs were the best selling children's software titles in 1996, 1997, 1998 and 1999, likewise acting as advertising for this ubiquitous doll. Hello Kitty features in a range of interactive software and, in the 1990s, in a number of animated features. Sam Toucan, the promotional character for Froot Loops since 1963, currently appears in *Pirates of the Carribbean*-style video clips on Fun K. Town, Kellogg's online gaming site (Kirkham, 2006).

As our examples suggest, the conflation between advertising and entertainment is intensified by media convergence and the various ways in which characters, originating in different genres and media, cross over. In addition to the advertising, toy and feature-film characters we have mentioned, the advertising–entertainment blend draws on characters originating in books (*Winnie the Pooh*, *Harry Potter*, and *Lemony Snicket*) and comics (*Batman*, *Ghost World* and *X-Men*), TV cartoon (*The Simpsons* and *Bugs Bunny*) and puppet (*Sesame Street* and *Teletubbies*) series. Both the media producers and the manufacturers of tie-in products enjoy mutually reinforcing exposure for their products at the same time as the boundaries between advertising and programming, entertainment and consumption are blurred.

In background action to a scene in the 1997 remake of Disney's 1965 *That Darn Cat*, a young girl sitting in a diner tells her grandma that she feels sick. Presumably this is to avoid eating what is on her plate, because, having been told she doesn't have to finish her meal, almost immediately she asks if she can have a Big Mac on the way home. Grandma agrees. Marketers are increasingly introducing brands into the sets and, as we have just seen, into the scripts of children's films and television, in this case altering the original narrative. This ranges from the strategic placement of products that are normalized within the setting or context and add to the illusion of reality in film, TV, print, games and toys, to flagrant advertising and, as we will explain, ad-parodies which rely on children's brand literacy.

In live-action films for the young, product placement contributes to the realism or naturalness of the characters' fictive world. It is assumed that audiences will be familiar with the repertoire of skills, knowledge and interests required to read the text. For instance, the implied viewer of *Mean Girls* (2004), a tween (age 7–14) girl is expected to recognize products like Coca-Cola, Red Bull, Cheetos and Doritos, the consumption of which presumes a shared experience between the characters and audience. The endorsement of the product is therefore linked to the way in which the viewer is invited to identify with the characters that consume the products or the actor who plays the role, in this case Lindsay Lohan. In another Lindsay Lohan feature film, a remake of Disney's *The Parent Trap* (1998), Nabisco's Oreo biscuits are the subject of discussion, a switch from the Fig Newtons in the original.

Of course, such movies also offer models for identity formation to their audiences, and the integration of brand usage and characterization reinforces certain brands and modes of consumerism as hip identity markers. References to high fashion brands – Fendi, Louis

Vuitton and Burberry in *Mean Girls*; Versace, Hugo Boss, Jimmy Choo and Vera Wang in the TV series *The OC* – naturalize aspirational luxury consumer desire in young men and women. Indeed, consumerism has become so normalized that brands are appearing in fiction for the young, without fees being exchanged. Jonathan in J. Minter's *Insiders* (2004) has a designer shoe fetish to rival Carrie Bradshaw's in *Sex and the City*, while this 16-year-old's girl friend wears Gucci and Marc Jacobs. Rockport shoes are the object of desire for 9-year-old Damien's classmates in Frank Cottrell Boyce's *Millions* (2004).

The themes of films aimed at younger children and the prevalence of animation for this audience makes product placement for this audience somewhat more difficult. Themes that do offer opportunities for product placement include films about toys, for instance, *Elf* (2003) and *Toy Story 1* and *Toy Story 2* (1995 and 1999). According to Brandchannel.com, sales of Etch A Sketch went up a reported 4500% after the release of *Toy Story 2*. Fish-out-of-water stories also offer scope for product placement that contributes to the viewers' pleasure. Seeing the animal characters in *Madagascar* (2005) encounter brands like Krispy Kreme Donuts, Denny's and Toys'R'Us is part of this film's appeal. The same might be said of the delight of the forest creatures' first encounter with a range of junk foods in *Over the Hedge* (2006), and which undercuts the film's overt anti-consumer theme.

Of course, many children's films involve fantasy scenarios in which it is seemingly impossible to place products. However, this does not prevent puns on brand name products. In *Shark Tale* (2004) there are references to Coral-Cola, abbreviated to Coke, and Burger Prince (Burger King). In *Shrek 2* (2004), the pleasure of recognizing the fairy tale intertexts is linked with the pleasures of recognizing Versarchery, Farbucks and Baskin Robinhood. Malibu Stacey, Laramie cigarettes and Krusty burgers in *The Simpsons* operate the same way. Such parodies of brand names nonetheless reinforce consumer awareness. They present advertising as entertainment, which is also the purpose of the 'fake' advertisements on the Nickelodeon.com website. According to Austin and Reed (1999: 596) this 'could cause children to be misled when they visit other sites that have real advertisements'. Whether or not children are misled, this treatment naturalizes advertising in the world of children's entertainment and, thus, contributes to the socialization of young consumers.

There are, of course, films for children which avoid product placement, but which, instead, engage in what is known as reverse product placement. This refers to the marketing of a formerly fictional brand product. Harry Potter fans can buy Bertie Bott's Every Flavour Beans, while Nestlé's Wonka chocolate confectionary originated in Roald Dahl's *Charlie and the Chocolate Factory*. The two film adaptations have supplied ample advertising, most recently the 2005 version with Johnny Depp. And, of course, children's exposure to the covert form of advertising of both direct and reverse product placement has become far more sustained. The growth in the children's home video and DVD market means that many films and TV series are subjected to multiple viewings. In a sense, such repeated exposure mimics the operation of advertising itself.

The repetition and reiteration of the repeated viewing, the sequel, the series, the recurring appearance of characters across media and genre and via licensed merchandising, cross-selling and product placement – these are also a source of pleasure. Umberto Eco believes it is the 'foreseen and awaited reappearance' of the known that provides the pleasure taken in the repetition of a popular song, a TV commercial, and the iterations of narrative patterns and characters in comic strips, genre fiction or series in which there is 'any character obsessively repeating his/her standard performance' (Eco, 2005: 192, 196). In the following section, we look more closely at the sorts of pleasure the entertainment and advertising blend offers to children.

Pleasing children and othering adults

Pleasure is at the core of children's consumer-media culture, and the pleasures that it offers are multiple and have various benefits and costs for children. The consumer form blurs boundaries and so does the pleasure it produces.

In *The Pleasure of the Text*, Roland Barthes (1975) describes two distinct, but intermingled, types of pleasure: the text of pleasure (*plaisir*) and the text of bliss (*jouissance*). He describes the former as the text that 'contents, fills, grants euphoria; the text that comes from culture and does not break with it is linked to a *comfortable* practice of reading' (Barthes, 1975: 14). By contrast, the text of bliss 'imposes a state of loss, the text that discomforts ... unsettles the reader's historical, cultural, psychological assumptions, the consistency of his [sic] tastes, values, memories' (Barthes, 1975: 14). To elaborate on this distinction, *jouissance* or bliss is a 'pleasure without separation', a pleasure which 'knows no bounds' and involves a 'momentary loss of subjectivity' (Grace and Tobin, 1997: 177). It is a far more voluptuous and less discriminating pleasure than *plaisir*, which 'produces the pleasures of relating to the social order' (Grace and Tobin, 1997: 177).

Barthes is convinced that mass culture cannot evoke *jouissance*, in part because the nature of *jouissance* is 'asocial' and breaks with social norms against which mass culture stands as a logical contradiction. He argues that bliss only comes of the experience of the absolutely new and in mass culture, the new is merely fashion, superficial novelty, a repetition. Repetition, as stereotype, is a major instrument of ideology. Like Eco, Barthes concedes that mass culture produces pleasure, but it is not bliss.

However, we argue that consumer-media culture constructs texts which promote both *jouissance* and *plaisir*, indeed, which appropriates *jouissance* in the interests of consumer ideology. As we will explain, it does so by situating children's culture in opposition to the authority, values and social norms of adult culture, thus disrupting the 'proper' order of relations between adult and child.

This has been largely driven by the separation of the adult and child market segments. This came about, Kline (1993) suggests, because marketers were dissatisfied with family viewing. Neither schools nor families were seen by the world of commerce to be adequate providers of consumer skills, knowledge and attitudes. Marketers wanted the market to have a more central place in the 'matrix of socialization' (Kline, 1993: 13); indeed, the market wanted to talk directly to children. In separating the child and youth from the adult market, consumer-media culture needed to construct distinct consumer identities for the young. Such identities transgress adult norms and authority and, in our view, give rise to the affective pleasures of *jouissance*, which Barthes (1975: 31) links with 'a state of becoming' and which we link with the state of 'becoming a consumer' and, thence, the *plaisir* of conformity to a community of consumers.

Children and youth are encouraged to delight in the impertinent and the forbidden, to transgress adult codes, to live only in the present. Consumer-media culture offers them a picture of the world from a kid's perspective. To children, their media represents resistance and subversion, or what McDonnell (1994: 33) calls 'speaking the forbidden'. And, because there is much in consumer and media culture generally which adults see as being unfit for children, they come to represent 'the irresistible aura of power and danger' (McDonnell, 1994: 42). Seiter (1995: 11–12) argues that children's consumer culture often involves a:

> subversion of parental values of discipline, seriousness, intellectual achievement, respect for authority and complexity by celebrating rebellion, disruption, simplicity, freedom, and energy. .... Children's mass culture rejects the instrumental use of toys and television for teaching and self-improvement preferred by parents.

As such, consumer-media culture inverts many ideas associated with adult culture and binds children together as an audience defined in opposition, even resistance, to adults. It thus partakes of the *carnivalesque*.

The concept of the *carnivalesque* has attracted scholars for the possibilities it holds to explain resistance to, and transcendence and reversals of, dominant discourses and institutions of power. The carnival is characterized by 'subversion, inversion, diversion, and perversion', but it is highly controlled, involving 'ordered disorder, regulated deregulation, organized chaos, authorized antiauthoritarianism, controlled decontrol of the emotions, and ultimately reinforcement rather than subversion of the status quo' (Brown *et al.*, 1999: 15). Children's media-consumer culture inverts the power relationship between kids and adults; but, as we will show, it is selective in its subversion of adult authority and the particular status quo it reinforces.

In their research, Aronowitz and Giroux (1985: 54) argue that 'almost all students grow up in two worlds: one of school and family where they feel that they are not in control of their lives, and the other, with friends and by themselves, which they see as more autonomous'. While teachers and parents may be, and often are, constructed as a problem, they are seldom, if ever, constructed as providing solutions. Children's and, indeed, youth media represent parents and teachers as dull or too earnest, usually disapproving, slightly ridiculous, unworthy of emulation and as being subjected to well-justified rebellion and rejection. They are only occasionally heroic. Davies (1996) draws on Gerbner (1973) and O'Brien (1990) to show how the representation of teachers has evolved from idealized images of noble professionals – albeit subverted by the 'hidden curriculum' which constructs schools as ineffective – to caricatures of them. As O'Brien (1990: 33) explains, 'The media ... provide a "hidden curriculum" that supersedes the learning process in school' and caricatures teachers 'as incompetent nincompoops or rigid authoritarians. It is bad enough that teachers have been *displaced* by the media, but worse that their image ... has been distorted' (quoted in Davies, 1996: 78).

Advertising and television construct school education as an old-fashioned, puritanical, drab and overdisciplined place where, dreadfully or ridiculously, children must be governed by others or be self-restrained – in other words, as a dystopia. Audiences are exposed daily to the image of Lisa Simpson's jazz saxophone-playing exit from school orchestra practice under the disapproving gaze of a teacher in the opening credits of *The Simpsons* and the recurrent game of one-upmanship between Bart and Principal Skinner. In images such as these, the generation gap is simultaneously exacerbated and collapsed and the pleasures of adults and children polarized. In children's culture, entertainment and advertising are constructed as separate from, and superior to, education and adult values – at least for children.

However, if consumer culture turns the generational hierarchy upside-down, ultimately it can be seen as a form of 'ordered disorder' designed to socialize children into consumer-media culture. With the aid of advertising and new media forms, the market has offered children consumption as a primary motivating force and cultural artefacts with which to construct their dreams, set their priorities and solve their problems. It has offered them the basis upon which to build their group's commonalities and their sense of others' differences, and upon which to establish their personhood.

Seiter, however, maintains that the desire for its artefacts need not be understood as mainly a function of greed and hedonism. It may also be an expression of desire for common bonds with the child community. She contends that 'Consumer culture provides children with a shared repository of images, characters, plots and themes: it provides the basis for small talk and play' and stresses the agency of the child audiences of children's commercials (Seiter, 1995: 7). She emphasizes the meanings and images which children derive from advertisements, their preoccupation with pleasure, their appreciation of the fantasy element, their enjoyment of the humour and their use of commercials as a cultural resource with their friends. Drawing from the Marxist philosopher Ernst Bloch, she also identifies a utopian sensibility, noting the way in which children's mass culture represents an escape from or an alternative to the everyday – the image of something better. It stands in direct and extreme contrast to the inadequacies of the Real. However, as Bauman (2005) says in 'Living in Utopia', escape is not utopia; it's simply the only available substitute. And what consumer-media culture offers as a means of escape is the purchase, the fetish object and the momentary pleasure it brings.

The pleasure that children derive from consumer culture is designed to ensure they uncritically consume rather than reflect on the objects of their desire or media that promotes them. *Jouissance* produces a surge of affect, not the reflexive pleasure of knowing about what is happening as it happens. By its very nature, children's consumer-media culture seeks not to operate at this level of the rationality. As Lee (1993: 143) says of the postmodern aesthetic, children's media culture 'invites a fascination, rather than a contemplation, of its contents; it celebrates surfaces and exteriors rather than looking for or claiming to embody (modernist) depth'. It also 'transforms all cultural content into objects for immediate consumption rather than texts of contemplative reception or detached and intellectual interpretation'. Indeed, consumer media culture blurs the boundaries between the Real and Imaginary, and entertainment and advertising. It bombards children with simulations (images) and simulacra (signs) which often have no referents.

According to Baudrillard's (1983) concept of simulation and simulacra, hyperreality results when the simulated images or models and signs presented by the media begin to determine reality and our perception of it rather than represent it. Giroux (1997: 55) discusses hyperreality in relation to Disney movies, working from Baudrillard's thesis that 'Disneyland is more "real" than fantasy because it now provides the image on which America constructs itself'. He says that 'Unlike [an] often hard-nosed, joyless reality ... children's films provide a high-tech visual space where adventure and pleasure meet in a fantasy world of possibilities and a commercial sphere of consumerism and commodification' (Giroux, 1997: 53–54). Indeed, Kincheloe believes that the postmodern child cannot avoid the effects of the hyperreality produced by electronic media saturation. As he explains it, in postmodernity, 'media-produced models replace the real – simulated TV kids on sitcoms replace real-life children as models of childhood' (Kincheloe, 1997: 45). We may well ask, as Kinder (1991: 35) does: what of 'the impact [on children] of seeing an imaginary world so full of rich visual signifiers before having encountered their referents or acquired verbal language'?

Seldom are children offered the pleasures of reflexive knowing or of having a sense of agency derived from recognizing how their meanings, identities and affective investments are produced. The potential pleasures of becoming informed and active citizens within the politics of consumption are usually overridden by the pleasures of fantasy. Equally, in anti-political correctness–youthful revenge genres, the pleasures of knowing are outweighed by those of retaliation, reversal and transgression. Further, the historically decontextualizing and self-referential processes of consumer-media culture also mean that the knowledge that children do achieve is contained within the bubble. This means that a critical insider/outsider stance is difficult to gain even when the text itself is potentially what Fiske (1996) calls 'a rebellious space'. Instead, children are led to believe that they can gratify their needs, wants and desires and solve their problems through consumption.

ADULTS' CULTURE

If adults and education are the 'negative other' of children's culture, then the reverse is also true. Children's culture is often constructed by adults as trivial, if not noxious, and this is informed by a range of assumptions about the nature of childhood. According to Christian-Smith and Erdman (1997: 131–132):

> In Western societies, children are often regarded as low-status, economically dependent, incompetent individuals who achieve competency and normality through their interactions with adults who initiate children into larger cultural values. Adult society is constructed as the norm and the desirable state, whereas children's society seems to be different and often aberrant.

Consumer-media culture challenges this central idea.

There has long been a standoff between the two ideological apparatuses of the media and school education and, thus, between the differently inflected generational or adult/child power relations within which they are both immersed. Corporate 'pedagogues', including child marketing experts such as Kid Power Xchange in the USA, construct themselves as simply responding and appealing to the child's stage of development – stages that they closely manufacture as well as monitor. In so doing they offer themselves to the young as the friend of children's culture. In contrast, parents, teachers and the 'child experts' associated with the state often express anxiety about children's play, pleasure and desire, and about those media which can be said to characterize children's commercial culture on various screens (TV, the web, the mobile phone, games) and advertising directed at children. With the web, games and mobile phones converging and becoming the favoured media forms amongst the young, concerns have emerged about 'mbranding' and 'adver-games'. Increasingly, however, educational consumption of various sorts also reinforces consumerism. Many education and entertainment (edutainment) and education and advertising (edverts) mutations tap into the contradictory consciousness of the current generation of adults, especially with regard to consumerist 'solutions' to 'governing' children.

Uneasy adults othering children

Many adults are suspicious about the quality of children's media and consumer culture. They fear its effects on reading and print (the so-called literacy crisis) and the child/youth body (the so-called obesity crisis), they object to its hedonism and violence, and oppose its race, gender and class stereotypes (the so-called values crisis). They worry that it will lead to the triumph of individualism over community, corrupt children's morals, undermine their creativity and result in passive (and overweight) children. Indeed, they fear it will result in what Postman (1994) has called the 'disappearance of childhood'. In their concern, adults cling to the notion of childhood innocence and ignorance and, by extension, adult wisdom and enlightenment (see Buckingham, 1995).

Despite its claims that it speaks to age-related developmental stages, children's/youth consumer-media culture is understood to threaten the developmental order of generations: children are seen to 'learn about life out of sequence'. It also taps into the adult generation's concern that children are defiant and hard to control. Adults are concerned about children's individualistic and maverick styles of behaviour, what they see as children's bad manners, impudence, bravado and egotism. There is a general adult anxiety about the *ungovernability* of young people.

Holland (1996: 157) suggests that adults' 'Concern about *what* kids know is equaled by concern about *how* they get to know it'. Postman (1994: chapter 6) offers one answer when he describes television as a 'total disclosure medium' which 'effectively undermines adults' control over the knowledge and experiences that are available to children' (Bazalgette and Buckingham, 1995, quoted in Holland, 1996: 157). According to Holland (1996: 157):

> Many share his [Postman's] fear that knowledge is no longer in the hands of adults who pass it on to children, drip by drip, monitoring its use. Now it is grabbed by them, wholesale and without understanding. They by-pass parents and teachers in the name, not of a children's culture, but of a futurist cyber-culture where the contact is with less responsible adults.

These fears have been exacerbated by the access to adult knowledge which the new media and media convergence have given children.

Indeed, 'the grown-up world, far from being somewhere children are permitted to graduate only when they have jumped through a fixed course of educational hoops, now appears to be morphing into the image of the Net Generation – fluid and hybrid' (Bagnall, 2000: 24). Often possessing greater electronic competence than their parents, children's sense of themselves as 'incompetent and dependent entities' has been subverted (Steinberg and Kincheloe, 1997: 17). Advertising's sensitivity to this sensibility is evident in a print advertisement for Aptiva (2000) showing two adolescent girls and the caption

> i have
>
> friends I tell everything
>
> parents I tell enough
>
> e mail
>
> an aptiva

As Steinberg and Kincheloe (1997: 17) observe:

> Such a self-perception does not mix well with institutions such as the traditional family or the authoritarian school, institutions both grounded on a view of children as incapable of making decisions for themselves.

Children and youth are not only seen to be in danger, but to be 'dangerous' to themselves and to the integrity of the adult order.

Clearly, there are very real social and economic reasons for the altered face of family life and cross-generational relationships. According to Mackay (1997) in *Generations*, parents have had to adapt to new family forms, work patterns and technologies in the context of the declining influence of traditional agencies of socialization like the Church, family and school. At the same time as they juggle the demands of their complicated lives, they try to 'connect' with their children, to give them 'quality time' and 'the good life', to be 'responsible parents' and also to lead fulfilling lives of their own. Because they are time-poor, they worry that their children have too little of their time and energy. They thus involve them in more and more supervised purchased activities. At the same time, they fear that they are overindulging their children, overcompensating for their own parental deficiencies through consumer goods, overexposing them to the more adult themes of life. They fear that they have left their kids to grow up too fast and without clear moral codes. Some question the merits of materialism as a system of personal and family values, but find it hard to retreat from it for themselves or their children. They thus turn with nostalgia to their own childhoods, which, even if dull and conventional, they associate with well-established intergenerational codes and values, respect for elders and for discipline, and also with child safety.

It is Kinder's (1995) contention that this parental mood has been exacerbated by media culture. She argues that an 'exaggeration of generational conflict and conflation' (Kinder, 1995: 77) has come to serve as a form of trans-generational address for commercial television, film and advertising. The dual process of exaggerating and conflating age differences performs the role of functional differentiation for commercial products. By exaggerating generational warfare so that trans-generational products can 'come to the rescue', the same product can be marketed to multiple age groups. The focus on generational conflict, Kinder argues, has many unfortunate effects.

With its focus on the white middle-class, heterosexual family as the norm, it represses matters of class, race, gender and sexuality. It implies that generational wars and dysfunctional families are at the heart of such major social problems as crime, drug abuse and even national productivity. Kincheloe (1997: 39) makes the point that 'the battle to ascribe blame for family dysfunction in general, and childhood pathology in particular, plays out on a variety of landscapes', including popular culture. In his analysis of *Home Alone*, he identifies the mother as the target for blame. These themes produce and promote parental guilt and anxieties about their children and their parenting and enhance the attraction of consumerist solutions. Kinder (1995: 77) reports fears that 'the simultaneous exaggeration of generational conflict and conflation' also 'threatens to erode the formerly "naturalised" boundaries between adults and minors, parents and children, and the patriarchal laws and incestuous taboos that are propped on these distinctions'.

As Sibley (1995: 132) has argued:

> "family" tensions represent a clash between adults' desire for order and young people's for disorder; and between adults' preference for firm boundaries in contrast to young people's disposition for more lax boundaries.

These tensions are part of the negotiation of identities as the subject-in-progress moves towards independence. As we have seen, representations of transgression of boundaries in media and consumer culture can be a source of *jouissance* for children. However, adults tend to believe the blurring of boundaries leads to contamination and corruption of innocence. These effects have been exaggerated by media and consumer culture.

The trans-generational address used to manipulate adult consumers has a number of contradictory effects. The considerable ambivalence and diversity with which adult culture treats children's and youth consumer-media culture is one of many flow-on effects. Some teachers and, indeed, educational policy makers, for instance, mirror the 'othering' practices of the media towards education, seeing the media as mainly trivial and/or manipulative – particularly with regard to food. They relegate children's/youth culture to the field of low culture and image, and locate 'proper' education within high culture and print. Other teachers, especially in primary schools, may use toys, TV and the web somewhat unproblematically as motivational learning aids. Yet other teachers, along with educational researchers, have reinvented notions of literacy so that multimedia, multimodal texts become central; indeed, some argue that such things as video games have much to teach about 'learning and literacy' (Gee, 2003). The title of Prensky's (2006) book seeks to promote this view to parents: *Don't Bother Me Mom – I'm Learning*. In one way or another they all become vulnerable to policy and media panics about the literacy, obesity and values 'crises' noted earlier, and to negative representations of teachers, schools and parents.

This suggests that it is not just a question of adult controls over children, but of which adults seek to control them and for what purposes. Clearly, these various stances adopted in relation to children's consumer culture both challenge and mask certain adult–child power relations, as well as power relations between adults themselves – the corporate and the educational pedagogues for instance (Kenway and Bullen, 2007). These masking practices are reflected in the hybridization of entertainment, education and advertising.

Hybridizing advertising, entertainment and education

Whereas children are more attracted to a blend of entertainment and advertising than education and entertainment, adults prefer children's entertainment to be educational. According to the promotional brochure for a children's toy shop in New York, 'Our mission is to provide families with a HUGE selection of creative and stimulating products in a customer-friendly entertaining and interactive shopping environment because we believe kids learn best when they're having fun'. Children's television programmes such as *Sesame Street* promote the comforting belief that they are educational as well as entertaining. Fisher-Price promotes its products in precisely this way by, for example, claiming to promote activities that improve language skills or stimulate the senses. Tamagotchi (the virtual pet) develops nurturing skills. Parents buy their children lunch-box snacks that have been marketed as 'nutritious' treats or as making good nutrition fun. Food company websites incorporate edverts – educational quizzes accompanied by logos.

Goods and entertainment are sold to parents for their instrumental, cognitive and motivational value in the child's educational and social development. Indeed, teachers and child psychologists may well be employed as part of market research teams to offer an educational gloss to products and services – hence the reference to such things as age-related 'skill sets' or 'cognitive stages', or visual, textual and kinaesthetic literacy. As Block (1997: 154, italics in original) says, this is all about 'fun *with a purpose*'.

'Fun with a purpose' suggests a particularly adult conception of pleasure. The pleasures of 'fun with a purpose' are much more like *plaisir* than *jouissance*. As Grace and Tobin (1997: 177) explain:

> Plaisir represents conscious enjoyment and is capable of being expressed in language. It is more conservative, accommodating, and conformist than jouissance. ... Plaisir produces the pleasures of relating to the social order; jouissance produces the pleasures of evading it.

Grace and Tobin argue that much which passes for fun in school conforms to Barthes' definition of *plaisir*. We suggest that while children may experience *plaisir* as a consequence of the way they use consumer culture to construct a sense of community and solidarity, adult and child pleasures are polarized along the axes of *plaisir* and *jouissance* respectively.

Parents are persuaded to buy goods more for their serious utilitarianism than the pleasure factor. Parents use entertainment to sell education to children. And as noted, marketers use education to sell goods and commodified entertainment to parents who then also sell on to children, including books, toys and electronic gadgets of all sorts. Purely functional goods, such as school lunch-boxes and stationery, are enhanced with Wiggles, Star Wars and Barbie images. Collectable toys from fast-food outlets become clipped-on attachments to school bags. Sportswear brands, like Nike and Adidas, and surf brands, like Rip Curl and Billabong, market footwear and backpacks to target the education market. The extensive range of entertaining educational software taps into adult anxieties about ensuring their child the competitive edge in education and the job market. Indeed, like much before it, electronic media forms have been sold to parents on educational and family entertainment grounds. Given the ambivalence that many adults express about children in the information era, it is ironic that 'Education is the cover that gives kids' their passport to play in the digital world' (Bagnall, 2000: 24). But further, parent's anxieties about children's safety have provided marketing openings for the mobile phone industry. For instance the 'Gecko mobile phone for kids' (quite young kids actually) is marketed to parents in the following manner at http://www.geckoworld.com.au/phone-parents.htm:

> Gecko for parents
>
> Hugh's an independent gecko, so it's a big relief knowing his Dad and I are on speed dial when he's out and about. We helped Hugh program his mates' details into his Gecko, so we know who he's calling and who's calling him. Costs are controlled with the SMS Gecko-lerts I'm sent – genius! What parents love:
>
> * Parent text alerts to control costs
> * Mum and Dad speed dial keys
> * 22 parental programmed numbers
> * Optional call screening
> * Emergency call button

Further, via global positioning systems, the mobile phone has the potential to become a form of digital tracking device to enable apprehensive parents to monitor the child's every location.

In buying such goods and services, parents clearly demonstrate a contradictory consciousness. As Mackay's (1997: 82) research indicates, they act out their anxious and nostalgic concerns about 'the responsible parent' and 'quality time' and their fear for their children's safety and success. Through consumer goods they not only overprovide and overcompensate, but also seek consumerist solutions to parenting problems and, in this respect, reinforce the consumer socialization of their children.

THE ADULT-LIKE CHILD AND THE CHILD-LIKE ADULT

The *Home Alone* (1990 and 1992) movies are typical of the trend in entertainment and advertising that shows adults as irresponsible, immoral and, above all, easily outwitted by kids. This, in itself, is nothing new. Fairy tales and literary classics abound with adult characters that are wicked, foolish or neglectful and child characters who get the better of them. If such child characters transgress the rules of the social or generational order, it is to expose the folly of adults or the corruption of society. It is implied that the moral purity of the child characters gives them access to more fundamental 'truths' or values. This is not always the case in the particular world of children's consumer culture of which the *Home Alone* films are representative.

Young people today are offered identities as pleasure-seeking, self-indulgent, autonomous, rational decision-makers. The category now deployed is 'kids getting older younger' – KYOG. They are more often precocious than innocent. For instance, Kinder (1995) and Kincheloe (1997) regard the *Home Alone* movies as emblematic of postmodern childhood and the social and generational relationships which underpin it. Kinder discusses these films as typical of a trans-generational address noted earlier. Kincheloe foregrounds what he describes as the adult ambivalence towards children.

As indicated, much in children- and youth-targeted marketing contradicts the values of the adult world. This is in part due to the fact that:

> market values have themselves come together with childish values. The marketing of goods, particularly toys and other goods which are purely for fun and make no pretence at usefulness, depends on the creation and potential gratification of desires. The belief that libidinous pleasure is indeed possible and the ability to throw off constraints in the interests of pure enjoyment are seen as characteristics of childish spontaneity (Holland, 1996: 161).

Children's and youth culture are emblematic of the childhood identifications expelled in order to construct an adult identity. As such, it can evoke a sense of nostalgia and loss in adults which consumer–media culture manipulates, encouraging them to indulge in such libidinous pleasures. The transgenerational address has created:

> subject positions for a dual audience of infantilised adults and precocious children. These subject positions seem to provide an illusory sense of empowerment both for kids who want to accelerate their growth by buying into consumerist culture and for adults who want to retain their youth by keeping up with pop culture's latest fads. (Kinder 1995: 77)

Both Postman (1994) and Meyrowitz (1985) attribute the rise of the child-like adult to the effects of the electronic media. In Postman's view, the presentation of information as entertainment and the irrational appeal of commercials have led to a 'dumbing-down' of adult sensibilities. He defines the child-like adult as 'a grown-up whose intellectual and emotional capacities are unrealized and, in particular, not significantly different from those associated with children' (Postman, 1994: 99). Children, on the other hand, are depicted in the media as 'miniature adults' whose 'interests, language, dress or sexuality' do not differ substantially from adult tastes or style (Postman, 1994: 122–123).

Meyrowitz (1985) offers a more critical reading. He argues that at the same time as electronic media have offered children 'adult' knowledge, demystified adult authority and wisdom, and invited children to 'revolt', they have also created 'the feeling among adults that they cannot maintain their traditional adult performances' (Meyrowitz, 1985: 154). As a result, 'both adult and child roles shift towards a "middle region", all-age role' (Meyrowitz, 1985: 154). While the representation of precocious children getting the better of adults may be more pronounced today than in the early days of television, he says that television has always subverted adult roles. Unlike Kincheloe (1997) and Postman (1994), Meyrowitz (1985: 236) argues that even programmes like *Father Knows Best* exposed children to the hidden aspects of adult life, showing them the 'backstage reality' of adult 'fears, doubts, anxieties, and childish behaviours, and "privately" discuss[ed] techniques for handling children'. Parents who were the original child viewers of such programmes have clearly had *their* perception of adult authority undermined.

These feelings of uncertainty have been compounded by the massive social, economic and technological changes over the late twentieth and early twenty-first centuries. As parent's lives have become increasingly complex, the morals, values and mood of adult generations have become ambiguous. It is little wonder that today's adults not only experience doubts about the parental role, but also an 'envy of children's impulsive egoism and their ability to indulge without guilt in pure, selfish pleasure' (Holland, 1996: 161). They are likely to take advantage of the 'greater license to explore emotions, act "spontaneously" and depart from former stricter controlled parental roles' (Featherstone, 1992: 59). The advertising industry, talks of 'extended youth' and Mackay (1997: 65) explains adults' 'elastic adolescence' and their use of consumer goods and services (sex, travel, food health, diet, personal growth and self-therapies and information) to attempt to stay young for as long as possible.

At the same time, adult nostalgia for their own youth is reinforced by the market success of feature-length movie versions of popular television series of their childhood and youth. Examples include *The Flintstones* (1994), *The Brady Bunch* (1995), *Mr Magoo* (1997) and *Inspector Gadget* (1999), as well as updated versions of Disney films like *Flubber* (1997) and re-released animated classics like *Sleeping Beauty* and *Bambi*. As Giroux (1997: 57) says in relation to Disney's films, they 'work because they put children and adults alike in touch with joy and adventure'. However, Disney now also produces:

> prototypes for model schools, families, identities, communities, and the way the future is to be understood through a particular construction of the past (Giroux, 1997: 55).

In its ideological conservatism, Disney offers a reassuring alternative to the post-traditional world in the guise of entertainment. It is part of a cultural pedagogy which, Giroux says, parents and teachers underestimate or, like children, uncritically consume. Complex processes of de-traditionalization and re-traditionalization are at work here.

CONCLUSION

Consumer-media is central to the construction of childhood and child–adult relationships; and, as we have argued, the fusing of advertising, entertainment and education is central to this. The separation of child and youth consumers from their parents and in opposition to adults has allowed the child and youth market to grow into one of the most profitable and powerful market segments which, we might add, is constantly further segmented, inviting fresh psychological and financial investments. The search for sales always leads to the production of new (or revived) consumer goods, new sites for promotion and consumption and new consumer identities, identifications and dis-identifications. This animates, polarizes and complexifies pleasures and anxieties and relationships as adults and children use and are used by consumer-media formations.

NOTES

1 An earlier version of this chapter was originally published in Kenway and Bullen (2001). We acknowledge Calvin Taylor from Monash University for his valuable contribution.

REFERENCES

Aronowitz, S. and Giroux, H.A. (1985) *Education Under Seige: The Conservative, Liberal and Radical Debate Over Schooling.* Massachusetts: Bergin & Garvey.

Austin, M.J. and Reed, M.L. (1999) 'Targeting children online: internet advertising ethics issues'. *Journal of Consumer Marketing*, 16(6): 590–602.

Bagnall, D. (2000) 'Born to be wired'. *The Bulletin*, 15 August.

Barthes, R. (1975) *The Pleasure of the Text*, R. Miller (transl.). New York: Hill and Wang.

Baudrillard, J. (1983) *Simulations*, P. Foss, P. Patton and P. Beitchman (transl.). New York: Semiotext(e).

Bauman, Z. (2005) 'Living in Utopia'. Ralph Miliband Public Lecture, London School of Economics, http://www.lse.ac.uk/collections/LSEPublicLectures AndEvents/pdf/20051027-Bauman2.pdf [27 October 2006].

Bazalgette, C. and Buckingham, D. (1995) 'The invisible audience'. In C. Bazalgette and D. Buckingham (eds) *In Front of the Children: Screen Entertainment and Young Audiences*. London: British Film Institute.

Block, A.A. (1997) 'Reading children's magazines: kinderculture and popular culture'. In S.R. Steinberg and J.L. Kincheloe (eds) *Kinder-Culture: The Corporate Construction of Childhood*. Boulder, CO: Westview Press.

Brown, S., Stevens, L. and Maclaran, P. (1999) 'I can't believe it's not Bakhtin! Literary theory, postmodern advertising, and the gender agenda'. *Journal of Advertising*, 28(1): 11–24.

Buckingham, D. (1995) 'The commercialisation of childhood? The place of the market in children's media culture'. *Changing English*, 2(2): 17–40.

Christian-Smith, L.K. and Erdman, J.I. (1997) '"Mom, it's not real!" Children constructing childhood through reading horror fiction'. In S.R. Steinberg and J.L. Kincheloe (eds) *Kinder-Culture: The Corporate Construction of Childhood*. Boulder, CO: Westview Press.

Cullingford, C. (1984) *Children and Television*. Aldershot: Gower.

Davies, J. (1996) *Educating Students in a Media-Saturated Culture*. Lancaster, PA: Technomic Publishing Co.

Dell Clark, C. (1999) 'Youth, advertising, and symbolic meaning'. In M.C. Macklin and L. Carlson (eds) *Advertising to Children: Concepts and Controversies*. Thousand Oaks, CA: Sage Publications.

Eco, U. (2005) 'Innovation and repetition: between modern and postmodern aesthetics'. *Daedalus*, 134(4): 19–40.

Featherstone, M. (1992) *Consumer Culture and Postmodernism*. London: Sage Publications (first published 1991).

Fiske, J. (1996) *Media Matters: Everyday Culture and Political Change*. Minneapolis, MN: University of Minnesota Press.

Gee, J. (2003) *What Video Games Have to Teach Us About Learning and Literacy*. New York: Palgrave Macmillan.

Gerbner, G. (1973) 'Teacher image in mass culture: symbolic functions of the hidden curriculum'. In G. Gerbner, L.P. Gross and W.H. Melody (eds) *Communications Technology and Social Policy*. New York: Wiley.

Giroux, H.A. (1997) 'Are Disney movies good for your kids?' In S.R. Steinberg and J.L. Kincheloe (eds) *Kinder-Culture: The Corporate Construction of Childhood*. Boulder, CO: Westview Press.

Grace, D.J. and Tobin, J. (1997) 'Carnival in the classroom: elementary students making videos'. In J. Tobin (ed.) *Making a Place for Pleasure in Early Childhood Education*. New Haven, CT: Yale University Press.

Holland, P. (1996) '"I've just seen a hole in the reality barrier!" Children, childishness and the media in the ruins of the twentieth century'. In J. Pilcher and S. Wagg (eds) *Thatcher's Children? Politics, Childhood and Society in the 1980s and 1990s*. London: Falmer Press.

James, C. (1997) 'From *Rugrats* to *Spice Girls*: the role of characters and personalities in lateral marketing to child and youth markets'. *European Society for Opinion and Marketing Research*, http://www.warc.com/fulltext/esomar/9270.htm [20 October 2006].

Kenway, J. and Bullen, E. (2001) *Consuming Children: Education–Entertainment–Advertising*. Buckingham: Open University Press.

Kenway, J. and Bullen, E. (2007) 'The global corporate curriculum and the young cyberflâneur as global citizen'. In N. Dolby and F. Rizvi (eds) *Youth Moves: Identities in Global Perspective*. Critical Youth Studies Series, G. Dimitriadi (ed.). New York: Routledge.

Kincheloe, J.L. (1997) '*Home Alone* and "bad to the bone": the advent of a postmodern childhood'. In S.R. Steinberg and J.L. Kincheloe (eds) *Kinder-Culture: The Corporate Construction of Childhood*. Boulder, CO: Westview Press.

Kinder, M. (1991) *Playing with Power in Movies, Television and Video Games: From Muppet Babies to Teenage Mutant Ninja Turtles*. Berkeley, CA: University of California Press.

Kinder, M. (1995) '*Home Alone* in the 90s: generational war and transgenerational address in American movies, television and presidential politics'. In C. Bazalgette and D. Buckingham (eds) *In Front of the Children: Screen Entertainment and Young Audiences*. London: British Film Institute.

Kirkham, C. (2006) 'Marketers package sugary cereals with online fun'. *Washingtonpost.com*, 20 July, D03.

Kline, S. (1993) *Out of the Garden: Toys and Children's Culture in the Age of TV Marketing*. London: Verso.

Lee, M.J. (1993) *Consumer Culture Reborn: The Cultural Politics of Consumption*. London: Routledge.

Mackay, H. (1997) *Generations: Baby Boomers, Their Parents and Their Children.* Sydney: Pan Macmillan.

McDonnell, K. (1994) *Kid Culture: Children & Adults & Popular Culture.* Toronto: Second Story Press.

Meyrowitz, J. (1985) *No Sense of Place: The Impact of Electronic Media on Social Behavior.* New York: Oxford University Press.

O'Brien, T. (1990) *The Screening of America: Movies and Values from Rocky to Rainman.* New York: Frederick Ungar.

Postman, N. (1994) *The Disappearance of Childhood.* New York: Vintage Books (first published 1982).

Prensky, M. (2006) *Don't Bother Me Mom – I'm Learning.* Minnesota, MN: Paragon House.

Roedder John, D. (1999) 'Through the eyes of a child: children's knowledge and understanding of advertising'. In M.C. Macklin and L. Carlson (eds) *Advertising to Children: Concepts and Controversies.* Thousand Oaks, CA: Sage Publications.

Seiter, E. (1995) *Sold Separately: Children and Parents in Consumer Culture.* New Brunswick, NJ: Rutgers University Press.

Sibley, D. (1995) 'Families and domestic routines: constructing the boundaries of childhood'. In S. Pile and N. Thrift (eds) *Mapping the Subject: Geographies of Cultural Transformation.* London: Routledge.

Smith, G. (1997) 'How to advertise effectively to children and youth'. *European Society for Opinion and Marketing Research,* http://www.warc.com/fulltext/esomar/9267.htm [20 October 2006].

Steinberg, S.R. and Kincheloe, J.L. (1997) 'Introduction: no more secrets – kinderculture, information saturation, and the postmodern childhood'. In S.R. Steinberg and J.L. Kincheloe (eds) *Kinder-Culture: The Corporate Construction of Childhood.* Boulder, CO: Westview Press.

Williams, R. (1989) 'Advertising: the magic system'. In R. Williams (ed.) *Problems in Materialism and Culture: Selected Essays.* London: Verso (first published 1962).

11

Youth Films: Transforming Genre, Performing Audiences

Anne Jerslev

INTRODUCTION

Much research about youth films takes as its point of departure that Hollywood cinema has been *juvenilized* (Doherty, 1988) since the 1950s, where the moviegoers shifted from a familial to a teenage audience. The many youth films in the 1950s are regarded as both a symptom and a result of this 'juvenilization' with respect to themes, style and address. Since the 1950s, the American film industry in particular, but also other national cinemas, has continued their effort to target the youth audience by producing films drawing on aspects of teenagers' problems, culture and life styles. Whereas the majority of films as a whole are targeted at a broad, youthful audience, the youth film specifically, most studies agree, has as its main characters a group of young people. Youth films are about young people, and the focus of most research on youth films is either on filmic themes or how the films represent the social reality of young people. Even though Steven Neale (2000) reminds us that films about young people are not necessarily addressed at this group and, conversely, films targeted at a youth audience do not necessarily involve young protagonists, much research about youth films, whether rooted in the humanities or the social sciences, implies as part of their critical argument that youth films are watched by young people.

The origin of at least the American youth film is connected to the socio-economic changes and media developments in the US after World War 2. The decline of the studio system and the classical Hollywood film, the decline in ticket sales due to the competition from television and the suburbanization and changes in the demographics of the audience forced the industry to think of ways of addressing this new and distinct group in more direct ways. The rise of specific films about youth in the 1950s in other countries, such as the UK and Scandinavia, may be indicative of the same process of social and cultural modernization and the rise of a modern youth culture. Yet, the films are labelled and marketed differently in different national film contexts, and there may be many different explanations as to the continued production of these films. Some of these have to do with the whole question of genre development and generic inertia, the power of American genres on a global scale and the transport of genre formulas into a national film context, as well as different national film economic situations, national cultural traditions and different national policies for financial support of film production.

Even though this chapter uses the term *youth film* to refer to films with young people as their main characters, different studies of youth film use different terms, and single studies may also use alternate terms. The terms used are *teenpics* (Doherty, 1988; Neale, 2000; Schmidt, 2002; Shary, 2002), *cinema of adolescence* (Considine, 1985), *teen films/movies/cinema* (Lewis, 1992; Bernstein, 1997; Dixon, 2000; Schmidt, 2002; Shary, 2002, 2005; Kaveney, 2006), *high-school films* (Wood, 1986), *youth films/movies* (Neale, 2000; Schmidt, 2002; Shary, 2002). The chosen term may point to the delimited focus of the material, either historically or thematically, or a term may be preferred to demarcate a body of films by way of the protagonist's age. However, the terminological diversity illustrates the heterogeneity of the films collected under the label youth films and points to questions of defining and selecting the works under scrutiny.

YOUTH FILM AS A GENRE

Whereas genre is not an issue in David Considine's seminal book on youth films from 1985, it is the methodological point of departure or reference point for most of the other scholarly studies that carefully try to define and, not least, to outline the confines of the group of films they are including in their study. Steve Neale (2000) claims that youth films have been multi-generic right from the start and include a range of other genres, like drama, musicals, horror films and social-problem films. This understanding of youth films as a sort of general label or umbrella label for building upon other genres is recurrent in the research literature. New subgenres are, for example, appointed along the line of gender. We have terms such as 'female teenpics' and 'girl power movies' (Kearney, 2002), 'tough girls' films (Shary, 2002) and '"angry girl" films' (Roberts, 2002), all subgenres indicative of what Frances Gateward and Murray Pomerance designate a shift in 'the industry's primary demographic from young men to young women' (Gateward and Pomerance 2002: 15; see also Orenstein (1996)). The horror film subgenre of 'slasher films' (starting with *Halloween* (1978), *A Nightmare on Elm Street* (1984) and *Friday the 13th* (1980)) is labelled as youth films by Neale, Shary, Doherty, Schmidt and Lewis. Dance films like *Flashdance* (1983), *Dirty Dancing* (1987) and *Save the Last Dance* (2001) are included in, for example, Kaveney (2006) and Shary; and 'teen comedy' is a commonly used label, not least by the industry. Some studies use 'trend' or 'cycle' for further subdivisions; for example, Wood (1986) in his discussion of what he calls the 1980s 'high school cycle' – most importantly, Amy Heckerling's classic *Fast Times at Ridgmont High* (1982)) or the 'John Hughes cycle' (Bernstein 1997), including famous 1980s youth films like *Sixteen Candles* (1984), *Pretty in Pink* (1986), *Ferris Bueller's Day Off* (1986) and *Some Kind of Wonderful* (1987).

Studies tend to be either exclusive or inclusive. Robin Wood is easily able to describe the common features of the 1980s high-school cycle; what unites his small body of films are narrative features (multi-character movies), the focusing on sex and on the fight for the elimination of male sexual innocence as the essential coming-of-age ritual, the lack of parents as filmic characters and the repression of homosexuality. At the other end of the spectre, Timothy Shary has collected an impressively large number of films during the period 1980–1999 having youth issues in the front – in Shary (2005) the scope is even extended to the beginning of film history. He systematizes his material into five subgenres, which develop in the first part of the period, but are more or less still valid, he argues:

youth in school, delinquent youth, the youth horror film, youth and science, and youth in love and having sex. The juvenile delinquency subgenre is the largest, which he traces back to the American films about troubled youth in the 1930s, and the school film is 'the most foundational' (Shary, 2002: 9), mainly because the school setting provides the backdrop for having young people flaunt their basic identity trait, i.e. stylistic distinction.

Genre studies cover almost exclusively American youth films. Even though it goes without saying that mainstream films abound, the material selected often also crosses institutional lines between studio productions and independent films as well as artistic lines between auteur films and mainstream, formula films. What mainly unites the collected films is the age of their protagonist and their construction of images of teenage life.

Even though there is an extensive body of studies of American youth films (for a bibliography on American 'teen films' until 1995, see Benton *et al.*, 1997) which makes it stand out as, essentially, an American genre, the term is not, as pointed out by Timothy Shary, common in standard works on American film history. Neither is the term youth film common in books on national cinema outside the American production system. Thus, it seems that *youth films* or other corresponding labels may be rightfully used for the American genre tradition, whereas the last 60 years have regularly seen the production of *films about youth* in the UK, in other European countries and in Australia, for example.

There is, however, an exception to this pattern. In English language writings about Scandinavian films, a unique tradition for producing (children's and) youth films is accentuated; Norwegian film historian Gunnar Iversen claims straight out that 'since the 1970s all Nordic cinemas have depicted every phase of childhood and adolescence in numerous films about growing up' (Iversen, 2005: 272); and there are similar statements in Elkington (2005), Cowie (1999, 2005) and Widding (1998).

The tradition of addressing youth issues in the Nordic countries goes back to the post-World War 2 cinema. In the wake of 1940s realist cinema, Nordic countries produced an array of juvenile delinquency films in the 1950s, borrowing heavily from the American subgenre and also bringing fame to new national teenage idols (Bengtsson, 1998; Jerslev, 1998). Even though production of children's films go even further back, this 1950s wave of films about troubled youth – which eventually gave way to representations of youth as having more fun by the end of the decade – demarcates historically a tradition which in Denmark has been supported by the state since the beginning of the 1980s. Public funding and appointment of a children's film consultant, whose job it was to distribute the funds to production of children's and youth films (Zeruneith, 1995), secured the blooming of the films.

The Nordic youth films are extremely diverse in style and themes and, apart from the troubled youth films of the 1950s, it is hardly relevant even to discuss 'subgenres'. The Danish film-support system has launched an array of 'quality' youth films being as much auteur films as youth films, most notably in Denmark with Nils Malmros' *The Tree of Knowledge* (*Kundskabens Træ*, 1981) and Bille August's Oscar-winning *Pelle the Conqueror* (*Pelle Erobreren*, 1987). In Sweden, Lukas Moodysson's *Show Me Love* (*Fucking Åmål* 1998) is another example worth mentioning. The impact of American genre formulas on the Danish film is, of course, undeniable, and there have been recent adaptations of American youth film genre formulas, such as the slasher film *Midsummer* (*Midsommer* 2003). A film like *Triple Dare* (*Supervoksen* 2006) is obviously marketed as a girly comedy 'teenpic' by borrowing the poster iconography of three girls posing on a white background from a film like *Mean Girls* (2004). However, the Danish youth film is generally more inclined towards the Danish realist tradition, which has never been characterized by either the humorous or satirical or by the light comedy, feel good and only slightly embarrassing modality of at least many popular American mainstream youth films from the 1960s onwards.

RESEARCH TRADITIONS

The literature on youth films agrees that youth films are basically films about youth, but studies differ as to research traditions and they ask different research questions. Overall, two approaches prevail: a social scientific and a humanistic. The social science perspective deals with the films as *mirrors of youth* and asks what cultural function the films perform. From either a sociological or a cultural studies angle they discuss the dynamics between film industrial considerations, social changes and the development of filmic representations of youth. Humanistic youth film studies are primarily interested in *images of youth* and genre studies prevail. Thus, we have studies concerned with social and cultural questions, which discuss whether films about youth reflect the social and psychological problems, identity construction or desires and life styles of actual groups of youths or teenagers in American society. These studies often take an explicit critical stance to the films. And then we have studies primarily interested in the actual films as texts. These studies provide an overview of the development of narrative forms, motifs and themes over time and discuss how youth film as a genre constructs and develops cinematic archetypes. However, many genre studies combine the two approaches. Even though they may primarily be interested in genre development and the systematization of films into subgenres, they do pose questions as to how the constructed images of youth reflect and influence the development of real youth.

This is, for example, the case with Timothy Shary's genre study of American youth films in the last two decades of the twentieth century. Shary studies generic patterns and their development, considering 'how American films about teenagers have utilized different techniques and stories to represent young people within a codified system that delineates certain subgenres and character types within the "youth film" genre' (Shary, 2002: 11). A subgenre may, therefore, develop textual strategies that afford its youth characters more space for trying out different identities. Despite his textual approach, he explicitly points out that he is studying 'social representations'. Besides being aesthetic artefacts and produced for specific commercial purposes, films are also bearers and co-producers of cultural meaning and may tell about the struggle for identity among young people and the changing social conditions of being young.

Representations of youth, as well as their historical differences, tell us something about the conditions and tensions through which the real social category of youth is constructed. The question remains, however, as to what precisely they 'tell' us and how we should validate answers to such questions. Here, Shary relies on the theoretical notion of cultural artefacts as social seismographs and argues that his combined approach permits him to nuance the range of possible explanations to a subgenre's rise and decline.

He asks, for example, for cultural explanations to the rise of youth horror films by the end of the 1970s and their decline at the beginning of the 1990s and enumerates tentatively a range of possible and related answers. The rise of the genre might follow from a general occupation with violence in the late-1970s films, he proposes; it might join in the general critique of consumer society at the time or answer to the fear of AIDS through narratives where the ones who have sex are also the ones that die. The decline might be part of the general decline in teen films, or the genre ran out of ideas and was, therefore, brought down by the studios. But this leaves an important theoretical and methodological question, namely about at what point and on what grounds a sample of films may be elevated to tell something culturally significant. Is it on the level of trend? In that case, when is a trend a trend and enter into the realm of cultural significance?

Because Shary is primarily interested in youth films from the point of view of genre, his sketching of socio-cultural explanations is held on a general level. He explicitly positions his study as a follow-up to David Considine's work on 'the cinema of adolescence'. However, it may be as much in line with David Doherty's study of 1950s 'teenpics', where he carefully and empirically well-informed considers the relationship between this new genre, changes in the American film industry, the need of new market strategies and the rise of a new teenage audience for popular culture.

Informed by the social sciences, David Considine's study takes a very different point of departure than Shary's, and his approach is critical and normative. Drawing on the mirror metaphor, his overall aim is to discuss whether the cinema of adolescence reflects or distorts the image of actual youth; his conclusion is that the image is primarily distorted: the 'American film industry has been spectacularly unsuccessful in realistically depicting adolescence' (Considine, 1985: 9), 'always producing an image that is out of proportion to physical reality' (Considine, 1985: 276).

Considine believes strongly that the more films deliver representative and true images of actual youth the better; therefore, his study is as much about emphasizing the issues and angles the films are not touching upon as what they are about. *The Cinema of Adolescence* is rich with references to sociological and social psychological literature and empirical studies which form the basis for his general points: the films fail to present an adequate and precise image of society or contemporary youth problems, for example of juvenile delinquency or changing family patterns, and the distorted image is often bleaker than necessary. This regards, for example, the image of the American school system, which, to Considine, presents school as a battleground instead of as a space for education and support (Considine, 1985: 144). Yet, Considine also outlines broader and more general theses; for example, that schools on film function 'as a mere microcosm of society' and the depicted tensions reveal broader currents in 'the American psyche' (Considine, 1985: 125). The depiction of the school in the influential *The Blackboard Jungle* (1955) may not only mirror actual problems in the American inner-city schools, but may also, just like Shary argues, reflect wider social anxieties, '[f]ear, uncertainty, suspicion, hysteria, corrupt authority, and the struggle of the individual to survive are key elements not only of the school film, but of almost every genre the decade delivered' (Considine, 1985: 125).

Even though the mirror metaphor does not lead Considine to believe that the young audience are merely passive vessels to be filled with distorted images of themselves, he maintains a belief in popular cultural images of youth as potentially endangering for the development of a youthful identity. His book is founded on a feeling of solidarity with actual youth and a critical attitude towards a film industry, which more often than not produces stereotypical images of youth. This stance leads him by the end of the book to adopt a more critical view upon the mirror metaphor as a sociologically precise term; it is too symmetrical and lacks sensitivity to power structures and questions of media influence.

Finally, Jon Lewis's (1992) often-cited book about American and English youth films from the 1950s and onwards may stand as representative of the cultural studies approach. Lewis is theoretically informed by English youth culture studies and critical theory; the purpose is to study the ways teen films as mass-mediated representations of youth contribute to a youth culture which is dynamically produced and negotiated in a field between cultural autonomy and cultural commercialization. To Lewis, youth is not constructed outside the media, as Considine implies, but in and through popular media culture; therefore, his study alternates between enumerating cultural and sociological data about American youth and society and focusing on the way films construct images of youth.

Lewis takes a critical view upon youth films and even though there are exceptions, he regards them as more or less restorative and conformist. His main thesis is that the youth film in general is about the dissolution of traditional authority structures and claims that whereas analyses of youth cultures since World War 2 have demonstrated how they were basically about the questioning and rejection of authority, the films seem to restore authority, conformity and the adult culture – from *Rebel Without a Cause* (1955) at one end of the historical spectre to *Heathers* (1989) at the other. In Lewis's view this poses a paradox, since youth must be regarded as a contradictory and multifaceted socio-cultural entity, which will always enter into a dialogic, at once appropriating and contesting relationship to popular media culture and other youth cultural expressions. Why do young people go to see slasher films which 'punish behaviour the teenagers themselves are either engaging in or dreaming about' (Lewis, 1992: 68), he asks? And he continues: 'Through these films, teenage audiences experience a euphoria at their own punishment' (Lewis, 1992: 68). However, Lewis's theoretical and methodological approach makes it impossible for him to acquire grounded knowledge of the ways a teenage audience watches slasher films and whether there is a paradox. Or the critic merely forgets the cultural sensitivity that is one of the prerequisites for the analysis of youth culture when it also involves commercial cultural products.

YOUTH FILM, YOUTH AUDIENCES, AND YOUTHFUL AUDIENCES

No matter whether youth films are conceptualized as a genre or merely as films about youth, the different studies, although with different emphasis, regard them as reflections of social and cultural tensions, changes or topics. The films make meaning, but different studies understand how the films are informative of youth in different ways. It goes for some of the studies that they, in one way or another and more or less sceptical, raise the question as to whose fantasy is enacted in the films, implying that they are constructed by grown ups and may essentially reflect grown-up anxieties. Other studies take for granted that, because the films are targeted at a youth audience, they are also attended by a youth audience and should be made responsible to this group. The many studies of youth film raise at least two important questions, the answers to which may point towards other fields of youth research. One is *who* actually watches these films and finds them enjoyable? That is, does the audience to youth films actually mirror the screen images demographically? The other question is *in what ways* actual young people experience these 'genre' films and in what ways do they find them enjoyable? Youth film research is still in need of both empirical studies of the reception of youth films by a youth audience and more knowledge about youthful reception strategies to fiction films in general. Not much empirical research has been done on young people's reception of fiction films, either in the cinema house or at home, since the Payne Fund Studies of movies and their effect on children and youth at the beginning of the 1930s.

The suggestions that Steve Neale made as to possible lacks of symmetry between the ages of film characters and the age of the audience have not been followed up or elaborated upon, even though it is most likely that there is an asymmetry considering the many studies that show how childhood is diminishing as a cultural and psychological stage. If we turn to studies of reception of television teen series, then one could, by comparison, estimate, too, that there might be a difference. Dominique Pasquier's (1996a,b) empirical studies of the reception of the French high-school/college series *Helène et les garcons* broadcast in France at the beginning of the 1990s shows that the series was targeted at the 13- to 17-year-olds but it had its largest market share among the 4–11 group. An important part of Pasquier's material was fan mail sent to the actress who played the title character. The large majority of the passionate letters came mainly from girls under 13 years old, many written by little girls no older than 6 years. Pasquier concludes that the French series may appeal to children because of its narrative simplicity and uncomplicated character construction. It offers scenarios of more adult life and may, therefore, function as a kind of aid in discussing the young viewers' anxieties and hopes related to growing up.

Pasquier's reception study does not ask questions as to likeness to or distortion of realities of 1990s French youth, or whether the series construction of youth is conformist or not. She is not so much interested in the meaning of the programme as to how it makes meaning to its viewers. Timothy Shary's collection of cinematic images of youth in contemporary American films may, by its mere size, imply that youth films as bearers of meaning are traces of social and personal concerns and exert an influence on young people. Quantitative studies of young people's *choice of* films may tell another story. They may show that youth films are not especially important contributors to the cultural life of young people; for example, a Danish survey of youth and media use from the late 1990s showed that youth films were not among the eight highest-ranking genres (Jerslev, 1999) with regard to attendance. (I am aware, though, that there may be reasons for this result which have got nothing to do with preferences – for example, that the data were collected before the boosting production of youth films around the year 2000 – and youth films may be included in some of the other 'genre' categories in the questionnaire, one of them being 'romance and love').

What needs to be elaborated further upon in both the social sciences and the humanities branch of youth film research is the much-quoted notion of *juvenilization* which Thomas Doherty coined in the late 1980s. The same goes for the concept of youth which is the founding distinctive term in these studies. Here, too, youth film studies might be inspired by studies of youth television. In order to expand in new and fruitful directions and not just add another decade's core examples to existing genre studies, youth film studies need to call attention to *the interrelationship between* youth films and youth as audiences. Humanistic youth film studies should attend much more than hitherto to how certain films not only thematically, but also by way of aesthetics and address, *construct their viewers as youth*, thus trying to understand their *youth appeal* – or lack of youth appeal. Youth films should be understood and worked upon not merely as films with *young* protagonists, but studied also for the ways they construct a *youthful* audience through style and address. This would leave, for example, Timothy Shary with new and challenging parameters for selecting his body of films. Shary notes in passing that contemporary youth films have their counterparts in a range of youth (high-school) series on television targeted at a youth audience from the 1990s onwards, for example *Beverly Hills 90210* (1990–2000), *Buffy the Vampire Slayer* (1997–2003), *Dawson's Creek* (1998–2003), *Gilmore Girls* (2002–2007), *One Tree Hill* (2003–) and *Veronica Mars* (2004–). Cross-media comparisons might shed light on exactly how notions of youth and youthfulness are constructed in similar or different ways in films and television fiction. How is the 'filmicity' of youth films constructed, how do the films relate to the television series and in what ways do they communicate a youthful sensibility to their audience?

Media scholars such as Celia Lury (1996), Karen Lury (2001), Simon Frith (1993) and film scholar Jonathon Oake (2004) have argued that 'youth' and 'young' or 'youthful' may not necessarily coincide in the same audience today. Youth may not even be a specific age group or it may be more than that, a *viewing sensibility* which responds to new aesthetic forms (Lury, 2001) and may or may not be adopted by the young generation – or may equally be adopted by other groups of viewers. Thus, as Celia Lury (1996: 216) points out:

> young people are principally defined as an audience [...] but this is an audience of a new kind. In this view, then, it is the distinctive activities of young people as members of an audience that both marks them out as young, or at least youthful, and makes them key cultural intermediaries.

Youth is constituted by certain viewing practices. Celia Lury is here, like the other authors mentioned, expanding on Simon Frith's (1993) argument that consumer culture and the intensification of competition among the media tend to construct youth as primarily an *audience position*; the notion of youth, thus, becomes inseparable from the notion of media. Whoever watched what television scheduled as youth programmes, became youth. Therefore, youth became an attitude which, since the mid 1980s, expanded demographically downwards into childhood and upwards into adulthood both by programmers and media advertisers.

The discussion of how to understand 'youth' in a media-saturated environment has not been influential in youth film studies. With few exceptions, age is continually a prominent parameter of selection, and studies of strategies of audience address are understudied in favour of sociological discussions of realism and verisimilitude. Nevertheless, the large amount of what Timothy Shary names youth horror films, from *Halloween* (1978) to the *Scream*, *I Know What You Did Last Summer* and *Scary Movie* cycles from the mid 1990s and onwards, are interesting examples of how a youth film subgenre and youth appeal coincide. Besides exemplifying the juvenilization of the American cinema and offering a strangely consistent imagery of puritanical slaughtering of sexually active young people, they are also innovative for their striking construction of a youthful viewing sensibility by means of an innovative aesthetic attention to graphic violent scenes, gory details and sex – and by means of their ironic sensibility to their own ritualistic seriality. Thus, the teen horror films from the late 1970s and onwards may be specifically suited for optimizing sensory pleasure and arousal to a youth audience (Sparks and Sparks, 2000), thus offering by these very means a filmic example of the youthful attitude that Karen Lury discussed in British television.

Though in a less obvious manner, other subgenres may exactly by their constancy point to changes in ways of understanding youth from primarily being an age group to being a cultural sensibility and a certain way of enacting spectatorship. It seems remarkable that many youth films released around the year 2000 still use the high school as the primary topos and construct the prom as the final and highly overdetermined narrative event, for example *She's All That* (1999), *10 Things I Hate About You* (1999), *American Pie* (1999), *Whatever It Takes* (2000), *Drive Me Crazy* (1999), *Never Been Kissed* (1999) and *Clueless* (1995). Or put another way, it is striking how little the 'school film subgenre' has changed over the past decades. The repetitiveness in the construction of the topos and its conflicts seems to beg the question why the setting and the narratives it allows are still so important a means of representing youth – aside from the obvious sociological fact that the location mirrors the everyday of the majority of American teenagers. Provided that this question makes meaning, one answer could be that the high-school setting *is necessary in order to construct these young people as youth*. The young protagonists are young because they attend high school, not because they act or think fundamentally different than the parental generation. Psychologically and culturally defined demarcations between generations are more or less eliminated in many of the films. Therefore, the high school is *the single differentiating topos* and the textually overdetermined prom becomes a kind of mental topos which represents the rite of passage to adulthood. The subgenre may thus, despite its generic consistency, point to changes in the definition of 'youth'. But still, this does not say anything about the films' potential youth appeal, aesthetically or otherwise.

GIRLS WATCHING HORROR FILMS TOGETHER

Film may be regarded as an emotion-producing machine (Grodal, 1997; Tan, 1996). Audiences choose films on the basis of preferred and expected emotional impact, and different genres produce different kinds of emotion. Dominique Pasquier's studies of mostly girls' fan mail showed how the series functioned as a kind of initiation rite to the functioning of romance and love for the girls. The only way it could do so was because the highly stereotypical staging of romantic intrigues in the series was felt by the girls as emotional realism. As such, emotions were the entry points into each of the girls' personal exchange with the series' more adult conflicts. In the final part of this chapter I shall go more into the question of emotional response to youth films. I shall focus on the subgenre of youth horror films and reference findings from a qualitative study of young people watching films in groups that I conducted in the late 1990s (Jerslev, 2001). According to a large-scale quantitative survey of media use among Danish young people aged 15 to 18 years (Fridberg *et al.*, 1997), more than 50 per cent watch films together with friends. In my qualitative reception study I wanted to go more into communal viewing practices. I focused on film viewing in the home and particular 'video evening events' where groups of young people watched several films in a row. I am going to concentrate on interviews with five girls between the ages of 14 and 18 who liked horror films and each vividly and enthusiastically recounted their experiences with watching horror films together with other girls in a home context. My first aim is to show that the paradox Jon Lewis outlined above is not a paradox by describing how the affective environment the girls created in and through their creation of a specific kind of viewing was *both communal and collective*. My second aim is to show how character, plot and narrative development may be a means to another end by a youthful audience. And finally, I want to shed light on a specific gendered viewing practice. Some horror film studies have underlined that horror films, despite persistent claims to the opposite, have a female audience as well (Clover, 1992; Berenstein, 1996; Buckingham, 1996; Cherry, 1999; Boyle, 2005); however, I have been particularly interested in studying the collective interplay when girls watch horror films together with other girls.

Even though horror films might not be the five girls' favourite genre, they watched horror films at regular intervals – similar to eight per cent of Danish girls who watched horror films at least once a week and 26 per cent who watched at least once a month in the late 1990s (Jerslev, 1999). The horror film nights I have studied are different both from distinctive young males' fan communities around horror films (for example, as studied by Vogelgesang (1991) and Eckert *et al.* (1991)) and from female horror film fans of different ages (studied empirically by Cherry (1999)), simply because the girls did not consider themselves horror film fans. Their choice of films was pragmatic and their sense of filmic and emotional quality contextually determined. What was good and bad to the five girls, might, in another context (e.g. when they watched films alone), be replaced by different criteria.

Choosing horror films in the rental store or from their private collection was a means to quite specific experiences. All five girls told in detail about their creation of a kind of *collective spectatorship* where each individual viewing became part of a mutually choreographed spectatorial play. They performed an almost ritual play of submission and mastery by means of scary movies in order to create certain emotional experiences. Through their collective performance in a homely context they orchestrated different levels of heightened arousal and emotional distress at the same time as managing to be in control of their fear. In this way they created 'quality thrills' as one girl put it, and they could only do this together.

To all girls, the meaning and pleasure of horror film nights – they often saw more than one horror film, but at other times they chose to watch a horror film together with, for example, a romantic comedy and a comedy – was to be scared together and enjoy bodily sensations and strong emotional arousal. Their essential collective viewing was about daring to be afraid and enacting their fear together with the other girls. But horror film nights were also about confronting fear and challenging their ability to endure. Horror film nights were about exploring boundaries and testing themselves. The girls confront the scary scenes on the screen and if they do not feel scared enough they use the homely space and different props to orchestrate shock-arousing performances that may reinforce the level of tension and, consequently, the pleasurable enactment of their fear. They tried to heighten emotional arousal not because habit made them immune to horror films, as suggested by Zillmann and Weaver (1996), but because their viewing was planned as a collective experience. One of the girls recounted how she and her girl friends orchestrated a horror film evening in the following manner:

> It has to be evening and dark outside. We light lots of candles and maybe we put garlic around the room – or other funny stuff. We also try to work up each other beforehand to get in the right mood to watch scary movies. And we may bring pillows and blankets so that you can sit there and hide yourself under the blanket. We used to do this more than we do now. But, you know, it is pleasant at the same time as it is really scary.

Another girl described the event as follows, her phrasing underlining the event as a sort of ritualized and highly orchestrated enactment:

> One of my friends brought films and we brought pop corn and coke and sweets. So we sit there and watch films and then, sometimes, some of us go to the bathroom and then, when they are finished, they tear the door open with a big booh! And then we all jumped to our feet because we got so scared and it was so fun!

Horror film spectatorship in this specific context is *a collectively orchestrated viewing behaviour where strong emotions of fear are at once produced and tested.* The chosen horror films – most of the films mentioned by the girls could be labelled youth horror films, in Shary's terminology – is just one part, although, of course, an important part, of the girls' conscious and skilled staging of *a thrilling environment* which may co-produce *quality thrills*. The prerequisite for a quality thrill, contrary to a bad one, was watching them together with friends and not alone. A quality thrill is a pleasurable feeling of transcending the body at the same time as bodily sensations are enlarged, just like how you feel right before jumping from the five-meter springboard, as one of the girls put it. Working each other up is part of the play, it is creating the same kind of bodily tension like before an important sports event: 'Working each other up, it's like the same you do before you are going to play an important football or handball match', to quote another of the girls.

Part of the girls' play is to transform their well-known environment into an unfamiliar space and work each other up to be frightened by the noise of a branch zipping on the window or being overpowered by a friend coming back from the bathroom, like they were all the stalker's victims in a horror movie. At the same time they have their sweets and soda and pillows, necessary props in order to anchor the unknown in the well known. Also, they have the next film in the evening's super flow which is, if necessary not a horror film but a romantic comedy or a funny film. Thus, the girls' enactment of communal film nights may be overall orchestrated in the same manner as the scheduled horror film, like a kind of affective roller-coaster ride where physiological excitation is replaced by relaxation.

On the background of experiments conducted in 1986 with girls and boys who watch horror films together, cognitive psychologists Dolf Zillmann and James B. Weaver (1996) argue that being spectators functions as a kind of contemporary mediated initiation rite to both girls and boys. According to Zillmann and Weaver, spectatorship is one ritualized practice through which boys and girls are provided with mastery of gender-specific behaviour, being undisturbed and calm or disturbed and disgusted in the face of fearful experiences respectively.

In their experimental testing of 'intergender effects' they had made participants of both genders watch a horror film together with one person of the opposite sex. One of the two participants was hired by the researchers to act different emotional conditions, 'gender-appropriate emotions', 'gender-inappropriate emotions' or 'no emotions'. The film shown was *Friday the 13th Part III*. The research team concluded that enjoyment of the horror film was greatly affected by the emotional reactions of their opposite-gender co-viewer. Male participants enjoyed the film twice as much in the company of a girl who showed that she was afraid compared with viewing the film together with a girl who demonstrated no sign of being afraid. Correspondingly, the researchers concluded that female participants enjoyed the film the least in the company of a male who displayed fear and dismay. The same pattern was found in male and female attraction to the opposite sex. Males were most attracted to females who showed fear and distress and, conversely, females were more attracted to males who showed mastery. So, the viewing experience was most pleasurable for both male and female participants who were in the company of a peer who exhibited the adequate gender behaviour.

My qualitative interviews may suggest that there is more to horror film viewing than the Zillmann and Weaver experiments can show. They may also tell about changed gender roles since the mid-1980s (see also Clark (2003: 7), where she briefly refers to communal television viewing of horror films and gender roles). The girls certainly told about watching horror films with boys and conform to expected roles by showing fear and distress, but they also recounted how they were often laughed at because they were afraid and, thus, in a sense were *subjected* to their male peers' need to demonstrate mastery. They also talked about how it was considered cool in their intergender peer groups to watch certain horror films and how they might choose to watch horror films *in order to* be accepted and respected by the boys. But mostly they talked about choosing to watch horror films in girls' groups and the joy of not being embarrassed at displaying distress. The five girls agreed that when together with the boys they had to be cool, which was not the most pleasurable way of watching horror films.

The girls' horror film evenings are neither about getting a medal for bravery nor for acting fear most convincingly 'girlishly'. Watching horror films together with other girls is to each of these girls about the collective creation of a space where they are allowed to be afraid and show that they are afraid. It is equally a space where they never run the risk of being afraid in a bad way. They see to it that their play at being spectators in distress never runs out of control. Thus, it seems as if the girls are able to occupy pleasurably both *girls*' and *boys*' roles in the gendered balance that Zillmann and Weaver outlined in their experiments. The girls I interviewed 'refuse to refuse to look' (Cherry, 1999), but they also dare to hide their eyes behind cushions, exactly because they are together with other girls.

Both the girls and the boys I interviewed stated that it made a difference whether they watched films in mixed gender groups or not. Both girls and boys told that they preferred to watch certain kinds of films with peers of their own gender. Which films are chosen for the evening's event is contextually determined, dependent upon whom they are together with and what kind of emotional space is preferred. The chosen films, whether youth horror films or other genre films, take part in an interactive play and are made to mean different things depending upon the group's interaction. Likewise, gender is performed differently according to different reception situations. When the girls watched together they performed male as well as female parts. Thus, gendered positions were not a given but were dependent upon what kind of emotional script the group of young people and the chosen films constructed.

REFERENCES

Bengtsson, B. (1998) *Ungdom i fara – ungdomsproblem i svensk spelfilm 1942–62.* Stockholm: Stockholms Universitet.

Benton, M., Dolan, M. and Zisch, R. (1997) 'Teen films. An annotated bibliography'. *Journal of Popular Film and Television*, 25(2): 83–88.

Bernstein, J. (1997) *Pretty in Pink. The Golden Age of Teenage Movies.* New York: St. Martin's Press.

Berenstein, R. (1996) *Attack of the Leading Ladies. Gender, Sexuality and Spectatorship in Classic Horror Cinema.* New York: Columbia University Press.

Boyle, K. (2005) *Media and Violence.* London: Sage.

Buckingham, D. (1996) *Moving Images. Understanding Children's Emotional Responses to Television.* Manchester: Manchester University Press.

Cherry, B. (1999) 'Refusing to refuse to look: female viewers of the horror film'. In M. Stokes and R. Maltby (eds) *Identifying Hollywood's Audience. Cultural Identity and the Movies.* London: British Film Institute.

Clark, L.S. (2003) *From Angels to Aliens. Teenagers, the Media, and the Supernatural.* Oxford: Oxford University Press.

Clover, C. (1992) *Men, Women and Chain Saws. Gender in the Modern Horror Film*. London: British Film Institute.

Considine, D.M. (1985) *The Cinema of Adolescence*. Jefferson, NC: McFarland.

Cowie, P. (1999) *Straight from the Heart. Modern Norwegian Cinema 1971–1999*. Oslo: Norwegian Film Institute.

Cowie, P. (2005) *Cool and Crazy. Modern Norwegian Cinema 1990–2005*. Oslo: Norwegian Film Institute.

Dixon, W.W. (2000) '"Fighting and violence and everything, that's always cool": teen films in the 1990s'. In W.W. Dixon (ed.) *Film Genre 2000*. Albany, NY: State University of New York Press; 125–143.

Doherty, T. (1988) *Teenagers & Teenpics. The Juvenilization of American Movies in the 1950s*. London: Unwin Hyman.

Eckert, R., Vogelgesang, W. and Wetzstein, T.A. (1991) *Grauen und Lust – Die Inszenierung der Affekte*. Pfaffenweiler: Centaurus Verlagsgesellschaft.

Elkington, T. (2005) 'Costumes, adolescence, and dogma: Nordic film and American distribution'. In A. Nestingen and T. Elkington (eds) *Transnational Cinema in a Global North*. Detroit, MI: Wayne State University Press.

Fridberg, T., Drotner, K., Schultz Jørgensen, P., Nielsen, E. and Scott Sørensen, A. (1997) *Mønstre i Mangfoldigheden. 15–18-Åriges Mediebrug i Danmark*. København: Borgen.

Frith, S. (1993) 'Youth/music/television'. In S. Frith, A. Godwin and L. Grossberg (eds) *Sound and Vision: The Music Video Reader*. London: Routledge.

Gateward, F. and Pomerance, M. (2002) 'Introduction'. In F. Gateward and M. Pomerance (eds) *Sugar, Spice and Everything Nice. Cinemas of Girlhood*. Detroit, MI: Wayne State University Press.

Grodal, T. (1997) *Moving Pictures. A New Theory of Film Genres, Feelings, and Cognition*. Oxford: Clarendon Press.

Iversen, G. (2005) 'Learning from genre: genre cycles in modern Norwegian cinema'. In A. Nestingen and T. Elkington (eds) *Transnational Cinema in a Global North*. Detroit, MI: Wayne State University Press.

Jerslev, A. (1998) 'Farlig ungdom'. In K.B. Jensen (ed.) *Dansk Mediehistorie*. Copenhagen: Samleren; 238–244.

Jerslev. A. (1999) *Det er Bare Film. Unges Videofællesskaber og Vold på Film*. København: Gyldendal.

Jerslev, A. (2001). 'Video nights'. Young people watching videos together – a youth cultural phenomenon'. *Young. Nordic Journal of Youth Research*, 9(2): 2–18.

Kaveney, R. (2006) *Teen Dreams. Reading Teen Films and Television from Heathers to Veronica Mars*. London: I.B. Tauris.

Kearney, M.C. (2002) 'Girlfriends and girl power: female adolescence in contemporary U.S. cinema'. In F. Gateward and M. Pomerance (eds) *Sugar, Spice and Everything Nice. Cinemas of Girlhood*. Detroit, MI: Wayne State University Press.

Lewis, J. (1992) *The Road to Romance and Ruin. Teen Films and Youth Culture*. London: Routledge.

Lury, C. (1996) *Consumer Culture*. Cambridge: Polity Press.

Lury, K. (2001) *British Youth Television. Cynicism and Enchantment*. Oxford: Clarendon Press.

Neale, S. (2000) *Genre and Hollywood*. New York: Routledge.

Oake, J.I. (2004) 'Reality bites and Generation X as spectator'. *The Velvet Light Trap*, (53, Spring): 83–97.

Orenstein, P. (1996) 'The movies discover the teenage girl'. *New York Times*, 11 August.

Pasquier, D. (1996a) '"Dear Helène". Social uses of college series'. *Reseaux. The French Journal of Communication*, 4(1): 87–116.

Pasquier, D. (1996b) 'Teen series' reception. Television, adolescence and culture of feelings'. *Childhood*, 3: 351–373.

Roberts, K. (2002). 'Pleasures and Problems of the "Angry Girl"'. In F. Gateward and M. Pomerance (eds) *Sugar, Spice and Everything Nice. Cinemas of Girlhood*. Detroit: Wayne State University Press.

Schmidt, M.P. (2002) Coming of age in American cinema: modern youth films as genre. Dissertation.

Shary, T. (2002) *Generation Multiplex. The Image of Youth in Contemporary American Cinema*. Austin, TX: University of Texas Press.

Shary, T. (2005) *Teen Movies. American Youth on Screen*. London: Wallflower Press.

Sparks, G.G. and Sparks, C.W. (2000). 'Violence, mayhem, and horror'. In D. Zillmann and P. Vorderer (eds) *Media Entertainment: The Psychology of Its Appeal*. Mahwah, NJ: Lawrence Erlbaum Associates.

Tan, E. (1996) *Emotion and the Structure of Narrative Film. Film as an Emotion Machine*. Mahwah, NJ: Lawrence Erlbaum Associates.

Vogelgesang, W. (1991) *Jugendliche Video-Cliquen. Action- und Horrorvideos als Kristallisationspunkte einer neuen Fankultur*. Opladen: Westdeutscher Verlag.

Widding, A.S. (1998) 'Denmark'. In T. Soila, A.S. Widding and G. Iversen (eds) *Nordic National Cinemas*. London: Routledge.

Wood, R. (1986) *Hollywood from Vietnam to Reagan.* New York: Columbia University Press.

Zeruneith, I. (ed.) (1995) *Wide-Eyed. Films for Children and Young People in the Nordic Countries 1977–1983.* Copenhagen: Tiderne skifter.

Zillmann, D. and Weaver, J.B. (1996) 'Gender-socialization theory of reactions to horror'. In J.B. Weaver and R. Tamborini (eds) *Horror Films: Current Research on Audience Preferences and Reactions.* Mahwah, NJ: Lawrence Erlbaum Associates.

12

Learning Theory, Video Games, and Popular Culture

James Paul Gee

INTRODUCTION

Today, children's popular culture is more complex than ever before (Johnson, 2005). A game like *Yu-Gi-Oh* – a card game played by children as young as 7, either face-to-face or on a *GameBoy* handheld game machine – involves the sorts of complex language, vocabulary, and thinking skills we associate with the advanced grades in school (Gee, 2004). Children today 'multi-task' across multiple modalities, playing a video game like *Age of Mythology*, reading and writing about mythology, researching it on the internet, and, maybe, even contributing to websites devoted to the game and wider topics in mythology (Jenkins, 2006).

Concentrating on good modern video games, I will argue that children today often engage in cutting-edge learning in their popular cultural practices, learning of a sort that fits well with what the Learning Sciences have discovered about optimal human learning, but not necessarily well with how current schools operate (Bransford *et al.*, 2000; Gee, 2003, 2004, 2005). At the same time, good video games (like contemporary research in the Learning Sciences) challenge us to truly integrate cognition, language, literacy, affect, and social interaction in our ideas about learning and the organization of learning inside and outside schools (Damasio, 1994; Gee, 1996, 2004).

Much of what I have to say here about video games is equally true when comparable games are played face-to-face with no digital technology involved, whether this be *Yu-Gi-Oh* or *Dungeons and Dragons*. However, digital technology does add certain features to the learning, features that are, we will see, reminiscent of how scientists use simulations to learn and to produce new knowledge.

But we need to discuss two points before starting our discussion of games and learning: content and technological determinism.

First, content. Media discussions of video games often focus on the content of video games, especially if that content is violent (though many games are not violent, including the best-selling game of all time, *The Sims*). More generally, non-gamers tend to view video games in the same way in which they view films and novels: content is what determines the nature and value of the work. However, in video games (unlike in novels and films) content has to be separated from game play. The two are connected, but, to gamers, game play is the primary feature of video games; it is what makes them good or bad games (Salin and Zimmerman 2003; Koster, 2004; Juul, 2005).

The content in a game like *Grand Theft Auto: San Andreas* involves poverty, an African-American community, and crime. However, the game play involves solving problems strategically, problems like how to ride a bike through city streets so as to evade pursuing cars and follow a map to end up safely where you need to go. In games like this, elements of content could be changed without changing the game play; for example, in some cases, taking pictures of people instead of shooting them or secretly planting a message rather than a bomb in their car would leave the problem solving and its difficulty pretty much the same. Critics of games need to realize that players, especially strategic and mature players, are often focusing on game play more than they are on content *per se*.

Content in a game sets up, but does not fully determine, game play. It is also determines the basic themes, metaphors, and emotional valences of the game, beyond the emotions of challenge, frustration, competition, and accomplishment that are determined by game play. However, the two interrelate in complex ways; for example, in a role-playing game one's pride in accomplishment or regret for poor decisions can easily be projected onto the character the player is playing in the game. Equivalently, the power, problems, or fascinating features and accomplishments of a character in a game can be transferred as emotions to the player (e.g. feeling 'cool' while being Solid Snake in *Metal Gear Solid* or empathy with the main character in *Grand Theft Auto: San Andreas*).

Then, too, video games, like most popular culture media, reflect back to us, in part, the basic themes and even prejudices of our own society. The *Grand Theft Auto* series is made in Scotland, but it clearly recycles US media images from television and film. In this respect, games are no different than popular films and television. Some people think they are more powerful than these other media, because the player acts in games. But the fact is that while humans react emotionally to images (television, film, games, even pictures) in much the way they do to real life (Reeves and Nass, 1999), this does not mean they are tempted to act on these emotions in real life: people do, after all, have higher thought processes in terms of which they make decisions and decide what is and is not real.

We also need to realize that video games involve content in a quite broad sense. Video gaming has turned out (despite early predictions to the contrary) to be a deeply social enterprise (Steinkuehler, 2006; Taylor, 2006). Even single-player gaming often involves young people in joint play, collaboration, competition, sharing, and a myriad of websites, chat rooms, and game guides, many of them produced by players themselves. But the social nature of gaming goes much further. Multiplayer gaming (i.e. games where small teams play against each other) is very popular among many young people. And massively multiplayer games (i.e. games where thousands or millions of people play the same game) have recently (thanks, in part, to the tremendous success of *World of WarCraft*) become mainstream forms of social interaction across the globe. Such games are introducing new 'states' (six million people worldwide for *World of WarCraft*) or 'communities' into the world. In such games, people are learning new identities, new forms of social interaction, and even new values, which is a broad form of 'content' indeed (Steinkuehler, 2006; Taylor, 2006).

There is, indeed, much space for critique and critical theory in regard to video games, though that is not my topic here. My remarks about content are meant to suggest some of the issues particularly germane to video games as media that need to be considered for such a critique, not to mistake games for books or films. But there is another issue relevant to anyone who wants to engage in critical theory in regard to games, and that is technological determinism.

The media often discuss video games as if they are inherently good for people or bad for them. This is a form of technological determinism. Technologies (including television, computers, and books, as well as games) are neither good nor bad and have no effects all by themselves, though, like all tools, they have certain affordances (Greenfield, 1984; Sternheimer, 2003). Rather, they have different effects, some good, some bad, some neutral, depending on how they are used and the contexts in which they are used (Hawisher and Selfe, 2007). As I have already mentioned, one important aspect of use is the way in which the player engages with the game's game play as opposed to its content or graphics ('eye candy'). Players can be more or less reflective, strategic, and focused on game play rather than content or graphics. Critics of games need to consider how games are 'consumed' by different people in different contexts. Blanket general claims (either for the good or the bad effects of games) are close to useless.

Finally, let me say that my discussion below, about the powerful ways in which video games can recruit learning as a form of pleasure, is as much about the potential of games as we spread them to new contexts and design new types of game as it is about the present games. Video games are a relatively new form of popular culture, and no one should mistake their present state (for example, deeply influenced as it is by a Hollywood blockbuster mentality that often drives out innovation) for their future potential in the context of a diverse array of new technologies, designers, players, and learning and playing situations.

VIDEO GAMES ARE GOOD FOR LEARNING, BUT NOT JUST BECAUSE THEY ARE GAMES

Video games are good for learning (Gee 2003, 2005; Shaffer *et al.*, 2004). What I mean by this is that good commercial video games build in good learning principles, learning devices that are supported by recent research in the Learning Sciences (Gee, 2003; Sawyer, 2006). Of course, how these learning principles are picked up will vary across users and contexts, as I pointed out above. This claim does not just mean we should use video games for learning in and out of schools. It also means that we should use the learning principles built into good video games in and out of schools even if we are not using games. These learning principles can be built into many different curricula.

What makes video games good for learning is not, by any means, just the fact that they are games. Furthermore, the video games that are most interesting for learning are not just any video games. Different types of game can have different effects. Puzzle games like *Tetris* and *Bejeweled* may very well exercise pattern recognition capacities; *Trivial Pursuit* games may well make learning facts fun. But these are not, in my view, the sorts of video game which are most interesting in regard to learning.

Before I say what makes video games good for learning, let me be clear about just what type of video game I am interested in in this chapter. First, consider simulations in science, say a digital simulation of an electromagnetic field, a solar system, or an ecological system. Sometimes scientists use such simulations to test hypotheses, but very often they use them to examine systems that are so complex that it is hard to make specific predictions about outcomes ahead of time (take weather, for example). In this case, they design these simulations ('virtual worlds'), 'run them' (i.e. let many variables interact across time), and see what happens. Then they seek explanations for the outcomes, build new theories about the complex system being simulated, run the simulation again and again in order to improve the theory, and, maybe, eventually, get better at making actual predictions.

These scientific digital simulations are not video games. However, the video games in which we are interested here – for example, in the case of commercial games, games like *Deus Ex*, *Half-Life*, *The Sims*, *Rise of Nations*, *SWAT IV*, *Civilization*, *The Elder Scrolls III: Morrowind* – are, indeed, simulations. They are worlds in which variables interact through time. What makes them interestingly different from scientific simulations is that the player is not outside, but, rather, inside the simulation (the virtual world). There are also cases like flight simulators and games like *Full Spectrum Warrior* which are used, in one form, as professional training devices and, in another form, as games for the commercial market.

The player has a surrogate in the simulation (game), namely the virtual character or characters the player controls in the virtual world (e.g. Solid Snake in *Metal Gear Solid*, a Sim family in *The Sims*, or citizens, soldiers, and buildings in *Rise of Nations*). Through this character or characters the player acts and interacts within and on the simulation. The player discovers or forms goals within the simulation, goals that the player attributes to their surrogate in the world. In order to reach these goals, the player must recognize problems and solve them from within the inside of the simulated world. This essentially means that the player must figure out the rule system (patterns) that constitutes the simulation (the rules that the simulation follows thanks to how it is designed). The player must discover what is possible and impossible (and in what ways) within the simulation in order to solve problems and carry out goals. Achieving these goals constitutes the win state for the player.

So the video games in which I am interested, the ones that I think are most interesting for learning, are digital simulations of worlds that are 'played' in the sense that a player has a surrogate or surrogates through which the player can act within and on the simulation and that have 'win states' (reachable goals that the player has discovered or formed through their surrogate). By the way, in augmented reality games, a person can be playing a virtual role (e.g. urban planner, toxic spill specialist, detective) in a rule system that is designed to play out partly in a virtual world and partly in the real world (Klopfer and Squire, in press).

Take *Thief: Deadly Shadows* as an example. *Thief* is a simulated world that is built around light and dark spaces, places good for hiding (dark) and places where one is exposed to detection (light). The world is medieval, filled with police and guards, as well as citizens, some of them well armed. Players must move through this world to accomplish specific goals, but they have little physical power and no powerful weapons for melee combat. Face-to-face confrontations are possible, but difficult and can quickly lead to defeat. The player plays the master thief Garrett, the player's surrogate in the virtual world. Using Garrett's body (which comes equipped with the ability to meld into the shadows), players must move carefully and hide often, engaging in stealth. All the while they are trying to figure out how best to get where they need to be and how best to accomplish their goals; for example, infiltrating a museum and stealing a well-protected precious object. Using and understanding this world (spaces, light conditions, virtual people and objects) and understanding the rule system it incorporates – a system that facilitates some actions, defacilitates others, and makes some others downright impossible – to accomplish various smaller and bigger goals successfully is the win state for the player.

So why would a learning theorist be interested in video games like these? For all sorts of reasons. A good number of these reasons have nothing to do with the fact that video games are games. I will first discuss a few such reasons that have little to do with the fact that video games are games and then turn to some reasons directly connected to the fact that video games are games.

EMBODIED EMPATHY FOR A COMPLEX SYSTEM

Let us go back to those scientific simulations – simulations of things like weather systems, atoms, cells, or the rise and fall of civilizations. Scientists are not inside these simulations in the way in which players are inside the simulated worlds of games like *Thief: Deadly Shadows*. The scientist doesn't 'play' an ant in his or her simulation of an ecosystem. The scientist doesn't discover and form goals from the perspective of the ant in the way I do from the perspective of Garrett in *Thief*.

However, it turns out that, at the cutting edge of science, scientists often talk and think *as if* they were inside not only the simulations they build, but also even the graphs they draw. They try to think from within local regions of the system being simulated, while still keeping in mind the system as a whole. They do this in order to gain a deeper feel for how variables are interacting within the system, for the range of possibilities and impossibilities in the system. Just as a player becomes Garrett, a scientist can talk and think as if they were actually an electron in a certain state or an ant in a colony. For example, consider the following from a physicist talking to other physicists while looking and pointing to a graph on a blackboard (Ochs *et al.*, 1996: 328–369):

> But as you go below the first order transition you're
> (leans upper body to right) still
> in the domain structure and you're still trying to get
> (sweeps right arm to left) out of it.
> Well you also said
> (moves to board; points to diagram) the same thing
> must happen here.
> (Points to the right side of the diagram) When
> (moves finger to left) I come down
> (moves finger to right) I'm in
> (moves finger to left) the domain state (pp. 330–331).

Notice the instances of 'you' and 'I'. The scientist talks and acts as if he and his colleagues are moving their bodies not only inside the graph, but also inside the complex system it represents. In reality he is talking about atomic particles and the states they can be in. So, though video games and scientific simulations are not the same thing, a video game can, under the right circumstances, encourage and actually enact a similar 'attitude' or 'stance'. This stance involves a sort of 'embodied empathy for a complex system' where a person seeks to participate in and within a system, all the while seeing and thinking of it as a system and not just local or random events. Squire's (Squire and Jenkins 2004; Squire, 2005) work on *Civilization III* and other games has shown that even young learners can enter a game as a complex system and learn deep conceptual principles about history and the social sciences. Halverson (2005) is designing a video game in which adult educational leaders can use the game to understand modern principles of school leadership within a framework that sees schools as complex systems interacting with a variety of other complex systems.

'ACTION-AND-GOAL-DIRECTED PREPARATIONS FOR, AND SIMULATIONS OF, EMBODIED EXPERIENCE'

Video games don't just carry the potential to replicate a sophisticated scientific way of thinking. They actually externalize the way in which the human mind works and thinks in a better fashion than any other technology we have.

In history, scholars have tended to view the human mind through the lens of a technology they thought worked like the mind. Locke and Hume, for example, argued that the mind was like a blank slate on which experience wrote ideas, taking the technology of literacy as their guide. Much later, modern cognitive scientists argued that the mind worked like a digital computer, calculating generalizations and deductions via a logic-like rule system (Newell and Simon, 1972). More recently, some cognitive scientists, inspired by distributed parallel-processing computers and complex adaptive networks, have argued that the mind works by storing records of actual experiences and constructing intricate patterns of connections among them (Clark, 1989; Gee, 1992). So we get different pictures of the mind: mind as a slate waiting to be written on, mind as software, mind as a network of connections.

Human societies get better through history at building technologies that more closely capture some of what the human mind can do and getting these technologies to do mental work publicly. Writing, digital computers, and networks each allow us to externalize some functions of the mind. Though they are not commonly thought of in these terms, video games are a new technology in this same line. They are a new tool with which to think about the mind and through which we can externalize some of its functions. Video games of the sort I am concerned with are what I would call 'action-and-goal-directed preparations for, and simulations of, embodied experience'. A mouthful, indeed, but an important one, and one connected intimately to the nature of human thinking; so, let us see what it means.

Let me first briefly summarize some recent research in cognitive science, the science that studies how the mind works (Bransford *et al.*, 2000). Consider, for instance, the remarks below (in the quotes below, the word 'comprehension' means 'understanding words, actions, events, or things'):

> … comprehension is grounded in perceptual simulations that prepare agents for situated action (Barsalou, 1999a: 77)

> … to a particular person, the meaning of an object, event, or sentence is what that person can do with the object, event, or sentence (Glenberg, 1997: 3)

What these remarks mean is this: human understanding is not primarily a matter of storing general concepts in the head or applying abstract rules to experience. Rather, humans think and understand best when they can imagine (simulate) an experience in such a way that the simulation prepares them for actions they need and want to take in order to accomplish their goals (Clark, 1997; Barsalou, 1999b; Glenberg and Robertson, 1999).

Let us take weddings as an example, though we could just as well have taken war, love, inertia, democracy, or anything. You don't understand the word or the idea of weddings by meditating on some general definition of weddings. Rather, you have had experiences of weddings, in real life and through texts and media. On the basis of these experiences, you can simulate different wedding scenarios in your mind. You construct these simulations differently for different occasions, based on what actions you need to take to accomplish specific goals in specific situations. You can move around as a character in the mental simulation as yourself, imaging your role in the wedding, or you can 'play' other characters at the wedding (e.g. the minister), imaging what it is like to be that person.

You build your simulations to understand and make sense of things, but also to help you prepare for action in the world. You can act in the simulation and test out what consequences follow, before you act in the real world. You can role-play another person in the simulation and try to see what motivates their actions or might follow from them before you respond in the real world. So I am arguing that the mind is a simulator, but one that builds simulations to prepare purposely for specific actions and to achieve specific goals (i.e. they are built around win states).

Video games turn out to be the perfect metaphor for what this view of the mind amounts to, just as slates and computers were good metaphors for earlier views of the mind. Video games usually involve a visual and auditory world in which the player manipulates a virtual character (or characters). They often come with editors or other sorts of software with which the player can make changes to the game world or even build a new game world (much as the mind can edit its previous experiences to form simulations of things not directly experienced). The player can make a new landscape, a new set of buildings, or new characters. The player can set up the world so that certain sorts of action are allowed or disallowed. The player is building a new world, but is doing so by using and modifying the original visual images (really the code for them) that came with the game. One simple example of this is the way in which players can build new skateboard parks in a game like *Tony Hawk Pro Skater*. The player must place ramps, trees, grass, poles, and other things in space in such a way that players can manipulate their virtual characters to skate the park in a fun and challenging way.

Even when players are not modifying games, they play them with goals in mind, the achievement of which counts as their 'win state'. Players must carefully consider the design of the world and consider how it will or will not facilitate specific actions they want to take to accomplish their goals. One technical way that psychologists have talked about this sort of situation is through the notion of 'affordances' (Gibson, 1979). An affordance is a feature of the world (real or virtual) that will allow for a certain action to be taken, but only if it is matched by an ability in an actor who has the wherewithal to carry out such an action. For example, in the massive multiplayer game *World of WarCraft* stags can be killed and skinned (for making leather), but only by characters that have learned the skinning skill. So a stag is an affordance for skinning for such a player, but not for one who has no such skill. The large spiders in the game are not an affordance for skinning for any players, since they cannot be skinned at all. Affordances are relationships between the world and actors.

Playing *World of WarCraft*, or any other video game, is all about such affordances. The player must learn to see the game world – designed by the developers, but set in motion by the players, and, thus, co-designed by them – in terms of such affordances (Gee, 2005). Broadly speaking, players must think in terms of 'What are the features of this world that can enable the actions I am capable of carrying out and that I want to carry out in order to achieve my goals?'

The view of the mind I have sketched argues, as far as I am concerned, that the mind works rather like a video game. For humans, effective thinking is more like running a simulation in our heads within which we have a surrogate actor than it is about forming abstract generalizations cut off from experiential realities. Effective thinking is about perceiving the world such that the human actor sees how the world, at a specific time and place (as it is given, but also modifiable), can afford the opportunity for actions that will lead to a successful accomplishment of the actor's goals. Generalizations are formed, when they are, bottom up from experience and imagination of experience. Video games externalize the search for affordances, for a match between character (actor) and world, but this is just the heart and soul of effective human thinking and learning in any situation. They are, thus, a natural tool for teaching and learning.

As a game player you learn to see the world of each different game you play in a quite different way. But in each case you see the world in terms of how it will afford the sorts of embodied actions you (and your virtual character, your surrogate body in the game) need to take to accomplish your goals (to win in the short and long run). For example, you see the world in *Full Spectrum Warrior* as routes (for your squad) between cover (e.g. corner to corner, house to house), because this prepares you for the actions you need to take, namely attacking without being vulnerable to attack yourself. You see the world of *Thief: Deadly Shadows* in terms of light and dark, illumination and shadows, because this prepares you for the different actions you need to take in this world, namely hiding, disappearing into the shadows, sneaking, and otherwise moving unseen to your goal.

While commercial video games often stress a match between worlds and characters like soldiers or thieves, there is no reason why other types of game could not let players experience such a match between the world and the way a particular type of scientist, for instance, sees and acts on the world (Gee, 2004). Such games would involve facing the sorts of problems and challenges that type of scientist does and living and playing by the rules that type of scientist uses. Winning would mean just what it does to a scientist: feeling a sense of accomplishment through the production of knowledge to solve deep problems.

I have argued for the importance of video games as 'action-and-goal-directed preparations for, and simulations of, embodied experience'. They are the new technological arena – just as were literacy and computers earlier – around which we can study the mind and externalize some of its most important features to improve human thinking and learning.

DISTRIBUTED INTELLIGENCE VIA THE CREATION OF SMART TOOLS

Consider how good games distribute intelligence (Brown *et al.*, 1989). In *Full Spectrum Warrior*, the player uses the buttons on the controller to give orders to two squads of soldiers (the game *SWAT 4* is also a great equivalent example here). The instruction manual that comes with the game makes it clear from the outset that players, in order to play the game successfully, must take on the values, identities, and ways of thinking of a professional soldier: 'Everything about your squad', the manual explains, 'is the result of careful planning and years of experience on the battlefield. Respect that experience, soldier, since it's what will keep your soldiers alive' (p. 2). In the game, that experience – the skills and knowledge of professional military expertise – is distributed between the virtual soldiers and the real-world player. The soldiers in the player's squads have been trained in movement formations; the role of the player is to select the best position for them on the field. The virtual characters (the soldiers) know part of the task (various movement formations) and the player must come to know another part (when and where to engage in such formations). This kind of distribution holds for every aspect of military knowledge in the game.

By distributing knowledge and skills this way – between the virtual characters (smart tools) and the real-world player – the player is guided and supported by the knowledge built into the virtual soldiers. This offloads some of the cognitive burden from the learner, placing it in smart tools that can do more than the learner is currently capable of doing by themselves. It allows the player to begin to act, with some degree of effectiveness, before being really competent – 'performance before competence'. The player thereby eventually comes to gain competence through trial, error, and feedback, not by wading through a lot of text before being able to engage in activity.

Such distribution also allows players to internalize not only the knowledge and skills of a professional (a professional soldier in this case), but also the concomitant values ('doctrine' as the military says) that shape and explain how and why that knowledge is developed and applied in the world. There is no reason why other professions – scientists, doctors, government officials, urban planners (Shaffer, 2004) – could not be modeled and distributed in this fashion as a deep form of value-laden learning (and, in turn, learners could compare and contrast different value systems as they play different games). Shaffer's (2004, 2005) 'epistemic games' take this principle much further and demonstrate how even young learners, through video games embedded inside a well-organized curriculum, can be inducted into professional practices as a form of value-laden deep learning that transfers to school-based skills and conceptual understandings.

'CROSS-FUNCTIONAL AFFILIATION'

Consider a small group partying (hunting and questing) together in a massive multiplayer game like *World of WarCraft*. The group might well be composed of a Hunter, Warrior, Druid, Mage, and Priest. Each of these types of character has quite different skills and plays the game in a different way. Each group member (player) must learn to be good at his or her special skills and also learn to integrate these skills as a team member within the group as a whole. Each team member must also share some common knowledge about the game and game play with all the other members of the group – including some understanding of the specialist skills of other player types – in order to achieve a successful integration. So each member of the group must have specialist knowledge (intensive knowledge) and general common knowledge (extensive knowledge), including knowledge of the other member's functions.

Players – who are interacting with each other in the game and via a chat system – orient to each other not in terms of their real-world race, class, culture, or gender (these may very well be unknown or, if communicated, made up as fictions). They must orient to each other, first and foremost, through their identities as game players and players of *World of WarCraft* in particular. They can, in turn, use their real-world race, class, culture, and gender as strategic resources if and when they please, and the group can draw on the differential real-world resources of each player, but in ways that do not force anyone into preset racial, gender, cultural, or class categories.

This form of affiliation – what I will call cross-functional affiliation – has been argued to be crucial for the workplace teams in modern 'new capitalist' workplaces, as well as in contemporary forms of social activism (Gee *et al.*, 1996; Beck, 1999; Gee, 2004). People specialize, but integrate and share, organized around a primary affiliation to their common goals and using their cultural and social differences as strategic resources, not as barriers.

Let me say here, too, that what is really important about today's massive multiplayer games, like *World of WarCraft*, *Lineage*, *EverQuest*, *City of Heroes*, and *Guild Wars*, is the ways in which, sometimes for better and sometimes for worse, people are creating new ways to build and share knowledge. They are also forming new forms of learning communities. We have much to learn from these games about new ways to organize learning socially in tomorrow's classrooms, libraries, workplaces, and communities (Steinkuehler, 2005, 2006).

SITUATED MEANING

Words have different and specific meanings in different situations in which they are used and in different specialist domains that recruit them (Gee, 2004). This is true of the most mundane cases. For instance, notice the change in meaning in the word 'coffee' in the following sentences which refer to different situations: 'The coffee spilled, go get the mop' (coffee as liquid), 'The coffee spilled, go get a broom' (coffee as grains), 'The coffee spilled, stack it again' (coffee in cans). Or notice the quite different meanings of the word 'work' in everyday life and in physics (e.g. I can say, in everyday life, that I worked hard to push the car, but if my efforts didn't move the car, I did no 'work' in the physics sense of the word).

A good deal of school success is based on being able to understand complex academic language (Gee, 2004) – like the text printed below from a high-school science textbook. Such a text can be understood in one of two different ways: either verbally or in a situated fashion. When students understand such language only verbally, they can trade words for words; that is, they can replace words with their definitions. They may be able to pass paper-and-pencil tests, but they often cannot use the complex language of the text to facilitate real problem solving, because they don't actually understand how the language applies to the world in specific cases for solving such problems. If they do understand how the words apply to specific situations and for specific problem solutions, they understand the words in a situated fashion. We have known for years now that a great many school students can get good grades on paper-and-pencil tests in science, but they can't use their knowledge to solve actual problems (Gardner, 1991).

> The destruction of a land surface by the combined effects of abrasion and removal of weathered material by transporting agents is called erosion. ... The

production of rock waste by mechanical processes and chemical changes is called weathering.

People acquire situated meanings for words – that is, meanings that they can apply in actual contexts of use for action and problem solving – only when they have heard these words in interactional dialogue with people more expert than themselves (Tomasello, 1999) and when they have experienced the images and actions to which the words apply (Gee, 2004). Dialogue, experience, and action are crucial if people are to have more than just words for words, if they are to be able to cash out words for experiences, actions, functions, and problem solving. They must be able to build simulations in their minds of how the words are used in talk and action in different specific contexts. As they can do this for more and more contexts of use, they generalize the meanings of the word more and more, but the words never lose their moorings in talk, embodied experience, action, and problem solving.

Since video games are 'action-and-goal-directed preparations for, and simulations of, embodied experience' they allow language to be put into the context of dialogue, experience, images, and actions. They allow language to be situated. Furthermore, good video games give verbal information 'just in time' (i.e. near the time it can actually be used) or 'on demand' (i.e. when the player feels a need for it and is ready for it) (Gee, 2003). They do not give players lots and lots of words out of context before they can be used and experienced or before they are needed or useful. This is an ideal situation for language acquisition, for acquiring new words and new forms of language for new types of activity, whether this is by being a member of a SWAT team or a scientist of a certain sort.

OPEN-ENDEDNESS: GOALS AND PROJECTS THAT MELD THE PERSONAL AND THE SOCIAL

We need to say more about goals, since this leads to yet another good reason why video games are good for learning. In a video game, the player 'plays' a character or set of them. The player must discover what goals this character has within the game world and carry them out, using whatever abilities the character has (remember affordances and smart tools). In *Thief: Deadly Shadows*, the player comes to realize that Garrett has specific goals that require stealth, for which Garret is well suited, to carry out. These are the 'in-game' goals the player must discover and carry out.

But in good open-ended games, games like *The Elder Scrolls III: Morrowind*, *Arcanum*, *The Sims*, *Deus Ex 2*, *Mercenaries*, *Grand Theft Auto*, and many more, players also make up their own goals, based on their own desires, styles, and backgrounds. The player must then attribute these personal goals to the virtual character and must consider the affordances in the virtual world (psych out the rule system) so as to get these personal goals realized along with the virtual character's more purely 'in-game' goals.

For example, in *The Elder Scrolls III: Morrowind*, a player may decide to eschew heavy armor and lots of fighting in favor of persuasive skills, stealth, and magic, or the player can engage in lots of face-to-face combat in heavy armor. The player can carry out a linear sequence of quests set by the game's designers or can make up his or her own quests, becoming so powerful that the designer's quests become easy and only a background feature of the game. In *Grand Theft Auto III* , the player can be evil or not (e.g. the player can jump in ambulances and do good deeds), can do quests in different orders, and can play or not play large pieces of the game (e.g. the player can trigger gang wars or avoid them altogether). Even in less open-ended games, players, even quite young ones, set their own standards of accomplishment, replaying parts of the game so that their hero pulls things off in the heroic fashion and style the player deems appropriate.

This marriage of personal goals and 'in-game' goals is a highly motivating state. When a person is learning or doing science, they must discover and realize goals that are set up by the scientific enterprise as a domain and as a social community. These are equivalent to 'in-game' goals. But they also, when effective, marry these goals to their own personal goals, based on their own desires, styles, and backgrounds. They try to be scientists of a certain type. When they do this, there is no great divide between their scientific identity and their 'life world', their personal and community-based identities and values. Good video games readily allow such a marriage; good science instruction should, too.

This issue of marrying personal and 'in-game' goals leads to the issue of identity. Video games are all about identity. The player 'plays' some character; the player takes on, carries out, and identifies with some special identity in a virtual world. When I have married my personal goals and values to the virtual character's 'in-game' goals, I see the game as both a *project* that the game designers have given to me and, simultaneously, I *project* my own goals, desires, values, and identity into the game world, melded with the 'in-game' identity and goals of the virtual character. The 'project' now becomes 'mine' and not just something imposed on me, because I have 'projected' myself into it.

Good science instruction should involve, as well, a marriage of *science's* goals and mine. I should see the project given to me by the classroom or the current state of science as something into which I can also project my own goals, values, desires, and identities. Good science instruction should, then, be 'open ended' in the way in which some good video games are.

LEARNING FEATURES CONNECTED TO GAMES AS GAMES

In addition to the learning features we have discussed thus far – features that are not directly connected to the fact that video games are games – there is a bevy of learning features (features that make video games good examples of good learning) that are more directly connected to the fact that video games are games. I will briefly discuss some of these features here.

First, good learning requires that learners feel like active agents (producers), not just passive recipients (consumers). In a video game, players make things happen. Players don't just consume what the 'author' (game designer) has placed before them. Video games are interactive. The player does something and the game does something back that encourages the player to act again. In good games, players feel that their actions and decisions – not just the designers' actions and decisions – are co-creating the world they are in and the experiences they are having. What the player does matters, and each player, based on their own decisions and actions, takes a different trajectory through the game world.

The Elder Scrolls: Morrowind is an extreme example of a game where each decision the player makes changes the game in ways that ensure that each player's game is, in the end, different from any other player's. But at some level this is true of most games. Players take different routes through *Castlevania: Symphony of the Night* and do different things in different ways in *Tony Hawk's Underground*.

Second, people cannot be agents of their own learning if they cannot make decisions about how their learning will work. At the same time, they should be able (and encouraged) to try new styles. Good games achieve this goal in one (or both) of two ways. In some games, players are able to customize the game play to fit their learning and playing styles. In others, the game is designed to allow different styles of learning and playing to work. For example, *Rise of Nations* allows players to customize myriad aspects of the game play to their own styles, interests, and desires. *Deus Ex* and its sequel *Deus Ex: Invisible War* both allow quite different styles of play and, thus, learning, to succeed.

Third, deep learning requires an extended commitment, and such a commitment is powerfully recruited when people take on a new identity they value and in which they become heavily invested (diSessa 2000), whether this be a child 'being a scientist doing science' in a classroom or an adult taking on a new role at work. Good games offer players identities that trigger a deep investment on the part of the player. They achieve this goal in one of two ways. Some games offer a character so intriguing that players want to inhabit the character and can readily project their own fantasies, desires, and pleasures onto the character. Other games offer a relatively empty character whose traits the player must determine, but in such a way that the player can create a deep and consequential life history in the game world for the character.

For example, *Metal Solid Gear* offers a character (Solid Snake) that is so well developed that he is, though largely formed by the game's designers, a magnet for player projections. *Animal Crossing* and *The Elder Scrolls: Morrowind* offer, in different ways, blank-slate characters for which the player can build a deeply involving life and history.

Fourth, given human creativity, if learners face problems early on that are too free-form or too complex, they often form creative hypotheses about how to solve these problems, but hypotheses that don't work well for later problems, even for simpler ones, let alone harder ones (Gee, 2004). They have been sent down a 'garden path'. The problems learners face early on are crucial and should be well-designed to lead them to hypotheses that work well, not just on these problems, but as aspects of the solutions of later, harder problems, as well. Problems in good games are well ordered. In particular, early problems are designed to lead players to form good guesses about how to proceed when they face harder problems later on in the game. In this sense, earlier parts of a good game are always looking forward to later parts.

Fifth, learning works best when new challenges are pleasantly frustrating in the sense of being felt by learners to be at the outer edge of, but within, their 'regime of competence' (diSessa 2000). That is, these challenges feel hard, but doable. Furthermore, learners feel (and get evidence) that their effort is paying off in the sense that they can see, even when they fail, how and if they are making progress. Good games adjust challenges and give feedback in such a way that different players feel the game is challenging but doable and that their effort is paying off. Players get feedback that indicates whether they are on the right road for success later on and at the end of the game. When players lose to a boss, perhaps multiple times, they get feedback about the sort of progress they are making so that at least they know if and how they are moving in the right direction towards success.

Sixth, expertise is formed in any area by repeated cycles of learners practicing skills until they are nearly automatic, then having those skills fail in ways that cause the learners to have to think again and learn anew (Bereiter and Scardamalia, 1993). Then they practice this new skill set to an automatic level of mastery only to see it, too, eventually be challenged. In fact, this is the whole point of levels and bosses. Each level exposes the players to new challenges and allows them to get good at solving them. They are then confronted with a boss that makes them use these skills together with new ones they have to learn, and integrate with the old ones, to beat the boss. Then they move on to a new level and the process starts again. Good games create and support the cycle of expertise, with cycles of extended practice, tests of mastery of that practice, then a new challenge, and then new extended practice. This is, in fact, part of what constitutes good pacing in a game.

Seventh, failure works very differently in good video games than it does in school, for example. In a good video game, players are encouraged to take risks, explore, and try new things, because the price of failure is not terribly high. If the player fails, then they can start back at the last game save or checkpoint. Furthermore, failure in games is seen by players as crucial to learning. No player expects or even wants to beat a boss on the first try. Rather, the player expects to learn from failing to kill the boss initially what patterns to look for and how to do better on the next chance.

CONCLUSION: BEYOND COMMERCIAL GAMES

None of this is to say that video games do these good things all by themselves. It all depends on how they are used and what sorts of wider learning systems (activities and relationships) they are made a part of. None of these reasons why video games are good for learning stems primarily from a game's great three-dimensional graphics and many of them do not stem from the fact that a video game is a game in the general sense of 'game'. The cutting edge of games and learning is not in video game technology – although great graphics are wonderful and technical improvements are important. The cutting edge is realizing the potential of games for learning by building good games into good learning systems in and out of classrooms and by building the good learning principles in good games into learning in and out of school whether or not a video game is present.

Our discussion has centered around commercial games. However, thanks to the fact that commercial industry is part of the larger global media entertainment complex, such games stress content that is, for the most part, not academic or socially activist (though there are exceptions like *Civilization*). So called 'serious games' devoted to such content are beginning to appear, games like *A Force More Powerful* (devoted to the spread of democracy), *Re-Mission* (a game to help and inform young cancer patients), or *Dimenxian* (a shooter recruiting algebra learning). One key question for some educators has been whether the learning principles in commercial games can be moved effectively into games teaching more school-based content, though not in ways traditionally associated with formal schooling.

One of many current examples of such games, and the research associated with them, is an 'epistemic game' designed by David Shaffer called *Madison 2020*. In this project, Shaffer and Kelly Beckett at the University of Wisconsin have developed, implemented, and assessed a game and accompanying learning system that simulates some of the activities of professional urban planners (Beckett and Shaffer, 2004; Shaffer, 2007; see also Shaffer *et al.* (2005)).

Shaffer and Beckett call their approach 'augmented by reality', since a virtual reality (i.e. the game) is augmented or supplemented by real-world activities, in this case further activities of the sort in which urban planners engage. As in the commercial game *SimCity*, students in Shaffer and Beckett's game make land-use decisions and consider the complex results of their decisions. However, unlike *SimCity*, they use real-world data and authentic planning practices to inform those decisions.

Shaffer and Beckett argue that the environmental dependencies in urban areas have the potential to become a fruitful context for innovative learning in ecological education. Cities are comprised of simple components, but the interactions among those components are complex. Altering one variable affects all the others, reflecting the interdependent, ecological relationships present in any modern city. For example, consider the relationships among industrial sites, air pollution, and land property values: increasing industrial sites can lead to pollution that, in turn, lowers property values, changing the dynamics of the city's neighborhoods in the process.

Shaffer and Beckett's *Madison 2020* project situated student experience at a micro level by focusing on a single street in their own city (Madison, Wisconsin):

> Instead of the fast-paced action requires to plan and maintain virtual urban environments such as *SimCity*, this project focused only on an initial planning stage, which involved the development of a land use plan for this one street. And instead of using only a technological simulation [i.e., the game, JPG], the learning environment here was orchestrated by authentic urban planning practices. These professional practices situated the planning tool in a realistic context and provided a framework within which students constructed solutions to the problem (Beckett and Shaffer, 2004: 11–12).

Professional urban planners must formulate plans that meet the social, economic, and physical needs of their communities. To align with this practice, students received an informational packet addressed to them as city planners. The packet contained a project directive from the mayor, a city budget plan, and letters from concerned citizens providing input about how they wished to see the city redesigned. The directive asked the student city planners to develop a plan that, in the end, would have to be presented to a representative from the planning department at the end of the workshop.

Students then watched a video about State Street, featuring interviews with people who expressed concerns about the street's redevelopment aligned with the issues in the informational packet (e.g. affordable housing). During the planning phase, students walked to State Street and conducted a site assessment. Following the walk, they worked in teams to develop a land-use plan using a custom-designed interactive geographic information system called MadMod built into a *SimCity*-like game.

MadMod allows students to see a virtual representation of State Street. It has two components, a decision space and a constraint table. The decision space displays address and zoning information about State Street using official two- or three-letter zoning codes to designate changes in land use for property parcels on the street. As students made decisions about changes they wished to make, they received immediate feedback about the consequences of changes in the constraint table. The constraint table showed the effects of changes on six planning issues raised in the original information packet and the video: crime, revenue, jobs, waste, car trips, and housing. Following the professional practices of urban planners, in the final phrase of the workshop, students presented their plans to a representative from the city planning office.

Students are gaming at two levels in *Madison 2020*: within a virtual *SimCity*-like world and via role-playing in the real world. Of course, *Madison 2020* in some respects stretches the notion of a game. In my view, video games are simulations that have 'win states' in terms of goals that players have set for themselves. In this case, the students have certain goals and the game lets them see how close or far they are from attaining those goals. At the same time, the game is embedded in a learning system that ensures that those goals and the procedures used to reach them are instantiations of the professional practices and ways of knowing or urban planners.

Shaffer and Beckett show, through a pre-interview/post-interview design, that students learning through the game were able to provide more extensive and explicit definitions of the term 'ecology' after their learning experience than before it. The students' explanations of ecological issues in the post-interview were more specific than they were in the pre-interview about how ecological issues are interdependent or interconnected. Concept maps that the students drew showed an increased awareness of the complexities present in an urban ecosystem. Thus, students appear to have developed a richer understanding of urban ecology through their work in the project.

All of the students said the workshop changed the way they thought about cities, and most said the experience changed the things they paid attention to when walking down a city street in their neighborhood. Better yet, perhaps, Shaffer and Beckett were able to show transfer: students' responses to novel, hypothetical urban planning problems showed increased awareness of the interconnections among urban ecological issues. All these effects suggest, as Shaffer and Beckett argue, 'that students were able to mobilize understanding developed in the context of the redesign of one local street to think more deeply about novel urban ecological issues' (Beckett and Shaffer, 2004: 21).

We seem now far from a commercial game like *Thief*, though not so far from *SimCity*; but, in reality, all these games cause players to look at and live in a world in a distinctive way, to find patterns, and to solve problems. And these games give players the tools with which to accomplish these goals. *Madison 2020* simply builds a more comprehensive learning system around the game and more integrally relates the game to the real world. In the end, however, it is an open research question as to how far we can go in moving the learning principles in good commercial games outside the entertainment sphere those games inhabit and the distinctive pleasures they offer.

REFERENCES

Barsalou, L.W. (1999a) 'Language comprehension: archival memory or preparation for situated action'. *Discourse Processes*, 28: 61–80.

Barsalou, L.W. (1999b) 'Perceptual symbol systems'. *Behavioral and Brain Sciences*, 22: 577–660.

Beck, U. (1999) *World Risk Society*. Oxford: Blackwell.

Beckett, K.L. and Shaffer, D.W. (2004) 'Augmented by reality: the pedagogical praxis of urban planning as a pathway to ecological thinking'. University of Wisconin–Madison. http://www.academiccolab.org/initiatives/gapps.html [August 2007].

Bereiter, C. and Scardamalia, M. (1993) *Surpassing Ourselves: An Inquiry into the Nature and Implications of Expertise*. Chicago: Open Court.

Bransford, J., Brown, A.L. and Cocking, R.R. (2000) *How People Learn: Brain, Mind, Experience, and School: Expanded Edition*. Washington, DC: National Academy Press.

Brown, J.S., Collins, A. and Dugid, P. (1989) 'Situated cognition and the culture of learning'. *Educational Researcher*, 18: 32–42.

Clark, A. (1989) *Microcognition: Philosophy, Cognitive Science, and Parallel Distributed Processing*. Cambridge, MA: MIT Press.

Clark, A. (1997) *Being There: Putting Brain, Body, and World Together Again*. Cambridge, MA: MIT Press.

Damasio, A.R. (1994) *Descartes' Error: Emotion, Reason, and the Human Brain*. New York: Avon.

DiSessa, A.A. (2000) *Changing Minds: Computers, Learning, and Literacy*. Cambridge, MA: MIT Press.

Gardner, H. (1991) *The Unschooled Mind: How Children Think and How Schools Should Teach*. New York: Basic Books.

Gee, J.P. (1992) *The Social Mind: Language, Ideology, and Social Practice*. New York: Bergin & Garvey.

Gee, J.P. (1996) *Social Linguistics and Literacies: Ideology in Discourses*, second edition. London: Routledge/Taylor & Francis.

Gee, J.P. (2003) *What Video Games Have To Teach Us about Learning and Literacy*. New York: Palgrave/Macmillan.

Gee, J.P. (2004) *Situated Language and Learning: A Critique of Traditional Schooling*. London: Routledge.

Gee, J.P. (2005) *Why Video Games Are Good for Your Soul: Pleasure and Learning*. Melbourne: Common Ground.

Gee, J.P., Hull, G. and Lankshear, C. (1996) *The New Work Order: Behind the Language of the New Capitalism*. Boulder, CO: Westview.

Gibson, J.J. (1979) *The Ecological Approach to Visual Perception*. Boston: Houghton Mifflin.

Glenberg, A.M. (1997) 'What is memory for'. *Behavioral and Brain Sciences*, 20: 1–55.

Glenberg, A.M. and Robertson, D.A. (1999) 'Indexical understanding of instructions'. *Discourse Processes*, 28: 1–26.

Greenfield, P. (1984) *Media and the Mind of the Child: From Print to Television, Video Games and Computers*. Cambridge, MA: Harvard University Press.

Halverson, R. (September, 2005) 'What can K-12 school leaders learn from video games and gaming?' *Innovate* 1.6. http://www.innovateonline.info/index.php?view=article&id=81 [August 2007].

Hawisher, G.E. and Selfe, C.L. (2007) *Gaming Lives in the Twenty-First Century: Literate Connections*. New York: Palgrave/Macmillan.

Jenkins, H. (2006) *Convergence Culture: Where Old and New Media Collide*. New York: New York University Press.

Johnson, S. (2005) *Everything Bad for You Is Good for You: How Today's Popular Culture is Actually Making Us Smarter*. New York: Riverhead.

Juul, J. (2005) *Half-Real: Video Games Between Real Rules and Fictional Worlds*. Cambridge, MA: MIT Press.

Klopfer, E. and Squire, K. (in press) 'Developing a platform for augmented reality gaming'. *Educational Technology Research & Development*.

Koster, R. (2004) *A Theory of Fun for Game Design*. Scottsdale, AZ: Paraglyph Press.

Newell, A. and Simon, H.A. (1972) *Human Problem Solving*. Englewood Cliffs, NJ: Prentice-Hall.

Ochs, E., Gonzales, P. and Jacoby, S. (1996) 'When I come down I'm in the domain state'. In E. Ochs, E. Schegloff, and S.A. Thompson (eds) *Interaction and Grammar*. Cambridge: Cambridge University Press; 328–369.

Reeves, B. and Nass, C. (1999) *The Media Equation: How People Treat Computers, Television, and New Media Like Real People and Places*. New York: Cambridge University Press.

Salin, K. and Zimmerman, E. (2003) *Rules of Play: Game Design Fundamentals*. Cambridge, MA: MIT Press.

Sawyer, R.K. (ed.) (2006) *The Cambridge Handbook of the Learning Sciences*. Cambridge: Cambridge University Press.

Shaffer, D.W. (2004) 'Pedagogical praxis: the professions as models for post-industrial education'. *Teachers College Record*, 10: 1401–1421.

Shaffer, D.W. (2005) Epistemic games. *Innovate* 1.6. http://www.innovateonline.info/index.php?view=article&id=79 [August 2007].

Shaffer, D. (2007) *How Computer Games Help Children Learn*. New York: Palgrave/Macmillan.

Shaffer, D.W., Squire, K., Halverson, R. and Gee, J.P. (2005) 'Video games and the future of learning'. *Phi Delta Kappan*, 87(2): 104–111.

Steinkuehler, C.A. (2005) Cognition and learning in massively multiplayer online games: a critical approach. Doctoral dissertation, University of Wisconsin–Madison (unpublished).

Steinkuehler, C.A. (2006) 'Massively multiplayer online videogaming as participation in a discourse'. *Mind, Culture, & Activity*, 13: 38–52.

Sternheimer, K. (2003) *It's Not the Media: The Truth about Pop Culture's Influence on Children*. Cambridge, MA: Westview Press.

Squire, K.D. (2005) 'Changing the game: what happens when videogames enter the classroom?' *Innovate* 1.6. http://www.innovateonline.info/index.php?view=article&id=82 [August 2007].

Squire, K. and Jenkins, H. (2004) 'Harnessing the power of games in education'. *Insight*, 3(1): 5–33.

Taylor, T.L. (2006) *Play Between Worlds: Exploring Online Game Culture*. Cambridge, MA: MIT Press.

Tomasello, M. (1999) *The Cultural Origins of Human Cognition*. Cambridge, MA: Harvard University Press.

PART 3

Cultures and Contexts

A central premise of this *Handbook* is that difference and diversity is central to childhood. Understanding the importance of media and culture in the lives of children and young people, therefore, demands an engagement with theories of globalization and transnational media flows, and with the methods of cross-national comparative and ethnographic research (Alasuutari, 1995; Morley and Robins, 1995; Tomlinson, 1999; Rantanen, 2004). Children and childhood (and, further, processes of learning and development, family dynamics, peer relations, consumption, media engagement and play) are not the same everywhere. Nor, evidently, are the institutions, forms and practices associated with the media and communication environment. The following 10 chapters begin to sketch the range of children's experience with media and culture worldwide. What is children's experience of media and culture in different countries? Are there commonalities across cultures? And what are the significant or intriguing points of divergence? The view offered in this *Handbook* is inevitably partial: there is much research we lacked the space to include and there are many countries where little research has yet been conducted.

Nonetheless, these chapters span the continents of the world. Those writing in a European context reflect not only the increasingly dominant English-speaking tradition (Buckingham), but also its northern limits in Greenland (Rygaard) and its recent integration of East and West (Heller). Childhood in Africa is addressed from the perspective of South Africa (Strelitz and Boshoff) and also the Arab countries' African interface with Asia (Kraidy and Khalil). Several chapters focus on Asia itself, a region whose rapid economic development is now attracting growing research interest both internally and from the rest of the world: Wei writes about China, Nayar and Bhide about India, and Donald considers the Asian region from China to Australia in comparative perspective. Last, we include two chapters that exemplify contrasting methodological approaches to this global diversity: one takes an intensive ethnographic approach to the richness of everyday life in South America (Wildermuth) while the other takes in a broad sweep across continents by employing cross-national comparative methods (Caronia and Caron).

The very focus on contextualization demands that, in this introduction, we consider each chapter in turn, not least because, since basic information regarding national, cultural and political information is a necessary background, as is that regarding the media system and everyday consumption patterns, the chapters in this part of the *Handbook* are particularly rich in detail. While together they scope the range of contexts within which children engage with media, we begin with the most general chapter precisely because it sets out the case for cultural and contextual specificity. Buckingham outlines a cultural studies approach to children and media, drawing on a particularly British tradition of theory, though one that has both strong European counterparts and a wider influence internationally. This focuses a critical lens on the relations between specific cultural practices and the broader social analysis of processes of power. Contrary to abstract claims regarding media power or political economy, though sensitive to the merits of such perspectives, cultural studies insists on grounding its analysis in particular cultural forms in particular contexts in order to reveal both the power relations embedded in those experiences, forms and contexts and to guide theoretical conclusions that transcend the particular.

Cultural studies has produced insightful research in several areas relevant to our present concerns: a long tradition of work on youth subcultures (especially informing the accounts of Jerslev, of Dahlgren, and of Ling and Haddon in this volume), a critique of mediated moral panics regarding children and media (also see both Critcher and Holland in this volume) and a semiotically informed account of audiences' interpretations of media texts (e.g. Reid-Walsh, Pasquier, and others in this volume) (Hall and Jefferson, 1976; Buckingham, 1987; Barker and Petley, 2001). More contentiously, cultural studies has critiqued the dominant psychological tradition regarding children and media, though some have sought to move beyond this culture/individual polarity (Hodge and Tripp, 1986; Livingstone, 1998; Turkle, 1995). Some scholars are now seeking an integration of the micro and macro of cultural and political economy approaches (e.g. Kenway and Bullen, Kraidy and Khalil, and Wasko in this volume).

As Buckingham argues, the 'cultural circuit' linking processes of the production and consumption of mediated meanings is inherently social and dynamic, demanding a multidimensional and multilevel analysis that respects people's agency while recognizing the significant degree to which institutions, culture and political economy shape the contexts within which people (including children) act. So, although the constraints of children's media provision are largely set institutionally, children's interpretations may reflexively reposition as childish or patronizing those texts considered appropriate for them by adults; one consequence is the emergence of children's tastes which, as Jenkins (2003) has shows, may then be reappropriated by profit-hungry content providers. The implications of such analyses extend beyond a specialized focus on children's media: Buckingham reviews the recent controversy following the launch of *Teletubbies* in the UK, a programme that updated the pedagogy of traditional public service with a distinctly surreal dressing, showing how this occasioned public debate not only about children's experience or even the legitimacy of pre-school television, but also, more fundamentally, about the ambitions of public service broadcasting in an increasingly global and commercial age.

Widening our gaze from the national to the global, while retaining a contextualized sensitivity to the cyclic dynamics linking political economy, text and audience, is a demanding task. The hotly contested theory of media imperialism remains a common starting point, with several authors in this part challenging the assumption that the main effect of globalization is the unidirectional flow of cultural images from the West to the rest. By examining the South African context, itself related to other African research, Strelitz and Boshoff directly contest this view both empirically and theoretically (see also Ito and Takahashi, this volume). They observe that, for many of today's youth, there is no unified national identity to be challenged, undermined or reshaped by imported media. In South Africa, class and ethnicity remain closely linked, marking major social divisions in (among other things) the interpretative resources with which young people interpret media contents. For example, a young black man reinterprets American rap music in terms of his turbulent experience in Soweto while middle-class white students read techno music as offering an identity of 'global whiteness' which they prefer to a specifically African identity.

Strelitz and Boshoff suggest that youth's pleasurable engagement with imported media is often due to an intense negotiation with local contexts of experience, resulting in both a reimagining of life's possibilities and also, simultaneously, a reaffirmation of the traditional. So, although one group of black working-class students in Grahamstown reject global media for lacking 'cultural proximity', instead preferring local drama as offering a 'haven' from the threat of the modern, others, positioned at the hybrid intersection of the global and local, use media to negotiate competing identities. Examples include the Indian students in South Africa who try to reconcile traditional family values with the pleasure of watching the American series *Friends* or, involving a different kind of cultural negotiation, Bollywood movies; consider, too, the interpretative demands on South African youth as American television confronts them, sometimes for the first time, with images of successful middle-class black people or of young women with the right to publicly voice their experiences.

To those on the margins of the Arctic North, the critique of globalization as a cultural and economic threat to a traditional way of life receives sparse attention. Moreover, debates that resonate elsewhere – should children watch national or imported television programmes, for example? – make little headway in a country where the costs of producing domestic content for a population of 57,000 are prohibitive, making imported content the norm. Notwithstanding a centuries-long history of imperialism, for young people in Greenland the prospect of the globalization of culture and lifestyle is welcomed as an exciting opening up to the world, even though, for the rest of the world, Greenland barely figures on the map. Rygaard's portrait of youth culture in Greenland reveals that, as so often, it is youth who lead the way, particularly grasping the global connections afforded by the internet. She concludes that globalization carries distinct risks for so small a population, but that these are far outweighed by the frustrations of being located within so marginal a context.

While youth 'lead the way' in cultural globalization, the media and culture provided by a nation for its children often focus contestation over social values, especially when the society is itself under pressure to change. The values embedded in children's media culture Heller terms the 'hidden curriculum': childhood games are shown to reinforce social roles, societal hierarchies and the importance of winning, whether they prioritize inventiveness and intellectual mastery, memory and knowledge, warfare and opposition or even, as in Snakes and Ladders, the very course of human life with its path of trials and successes, accompanied by good and evil. Individual economic competition, as epitomized by Monopoly, posed a particular problem for socialist Hungary when the game first marketed in the 1960s, and the refashioning of the game (with the board divided into 'good' socialist institutions of pedagogy, culture and trade unions and the 'bad' places of bars, tobacconists and pubs) captures the tacit recognition that children's play matters. Youthful resistance to such ideology is equally well demonstrated by the case of Monopoly, for Heller notes the secret and pleasurable circulation of the original capitalist version among Hungarian households.

Control over media, culture and, of course, education by the state shapes children's experiences in many parts of the world. Donald traces the Chinese state's efforts to socialize children through education and media to fulfil a vision of a new and sustainable modernity, for example, through the insistence on broadcasting children's programmes in Mandarin despite the plethora of languages and dialects spoken at home. Rejecting the othering of Asia implied by the dominance of Western approaches in the (English-language) research literature, Donald examines children and media in the Asia-Pacific region through the idea of 'regional modernity', seeking to understand the negotiation between local and global through its contextualization in the geography, culture and politics of the region. This brings into focus some of the tensions in Asia's modernity that fit poorly with a Western modernity centred on individualism, secularism, freedom of speech and equality and allows us to avoid what Donald terms 'the lure of ungrounded cosmopolitanism'. Revealing a strongly anti-modern tendency in China, Australia and elsewhere, Donald is concerned to show that Asian modernity is characterized significantly by stark and growing differences in social class, typically mapped onto the crucial geographic distinction between urban and rural and thus dividing the experiences and life chances of children across the region.

Not only social class, but also gender divides children's experiences in many countries. Wei also focuses on China, but her concern is both less theoretical and more urgent than Donald's, for she focuses on the persistent gender inequalities evident in, indeed reinforced by, mass media representations of girls and boys, women and men. Her self-appointed task is first to persuade the reader that media representations matter, especially given the many other pressing tasks for feminists and social reformers to address in China, and then to identify a strategy for media change. So, notwithstanding the many doubts raised in Western media and communications theory regarding the putative harmful effects of mediated images, and in rejection of the Government view that the Communist Party has brought about gender equality, Wei argues that the highly stereotyped portrayal of femininity – as passive, irrational and inferior – is inextricably linked to the shocking statistics of an imbalanced sex ratio at birth, the inequality in girls' education and the incidence of trafficking of girls and women. Indeed, she shows that not only are news reports often stereotyped, but they also repeat myths about violence against women, dramatizing sexual violence against women and children, framing rape in terms of sex rather than abuse of power and portraying the low rate of female births as a problem for men ('Who will they marry?' wail the headlines) rather than one of (girls') human rights. Wei concludes with a call for feminist activism that capitalizes on the already existing linkages between media institutions and other established agencies of power, including journalists' organisations, non-governmental organizations and women's advocacy groups, and international organizations concerned with human rights.

The tasks – for researchers, for policy-makers, for child welfare bodies – are considerable. Responding to rapid change in India is equally demanding, as Nayar and Bhide note when scoping children and young people's relation to the media in a country in which they represent some half of the population. The potent combination of youthfulness, social change and new media developments has several consequences in India: one is 'the politics of anxiety', in Salman Rushdie's phrase, another is the generational divide between parents and their children in terms of their experiences of media in childhood (see Kraidy and Khalil). Like Strelitz and Boshoff, Rygaard and Donald, Nayar and Bhide trace the connection between geography and consumption, contextualizing consumption, lifestyle and youth culture in relation to both world geography and also the spaces of the nation, especially the urban/rural divide so striking in Asia. Too often, they argue, the world's image of Indian youth – as fast changing, successfully integrating Western and traditional values, ready to adapt to global capitalism, wired via the internet cafés – is an urban image, barely touching the daily experience of millions of rural youth, though their aspirations may be very similar. It is also, to a considerable degree, a masculine one in India (and, arguably, elsewhere), though the signs of a new image of technologically skilled Indian womanhood can also be discerned in the emerging discourse of mediated modernity. This demands some clever footwork from young women (and their families), for, as Nayar and Bhide observe, they remain the bearers of traditional values but added to this is today's expectation of achievements commensurate with a globalized and commercialized individualism – exemplified by *Indian Idol*, a popular televised singing competition which is a far cry from the call for a Spartan lifestyle expected of youth by Nehru's Government half a century ago.

Similar demands fall on the shoulders of Arab youth, although, as elsewhere, the opportunities offered by new media technologies are enthusiastically welcomed by these young people, as they seek to participate in global youth culture. Kraidy and Khalil argue that the consequence is less cultural homogenization but rather a cultural hybridity, albeit one marked by the growing 'detraditionalization' or individualism of family life (especially insofar as global influences are locally appropriated by Islamic culture – examples include the growth of religious channels on satellite television and the emergence of religious stars or *tele-muftis*). Such a hybridization is hampered, however, by the paucity of indigenous cultural production for children in many Arab states, making reliance on Western imagery and ideas a practical necessity. Kraidy and Khalil trace how one Lebanese programme, *Mini Studio*, pioneered a multilingual cultural space for children but combined this with an equally pioneering approach to encouraging the advertising industry to target children – leading to the programme being popularly dubbed 'Mini Market'. They are more optimistic about Al-Jazeera Children's Channel and its promise to counter the relentless commercialization of children's culture by harnessing the interactive potential of the media to educate, engage and empower children.

What is meant, in the foregoing, by 'global youth culture'? Giddens argues that young people are, in globalized late modernity, fundamentally absorbed in 'the project of the self', a continual biographization of identity for which today's complex, intertextual and reflexive media environment provides the symbolic resources for the never-completed task of drafting and redrafting (Giddens, 1991). Acknowledging Buckingham's insistence on the recognition of structure, especially political economic and institutional constraints, as well as on the dynamics of the creative reappropriations of given meanings, Wildermuth integrates audience reception analysis of interpretative practices with a notion of the mediated imagination in his rich, ethnographic account of youth's creative appropriation of media resources in Brazil in order to 'draft' and redraft the self. Again, this is a far from comfortable account, for Brazilian youth suffer the contradictory demands of a 'periphery country', expected to 'progress' rapidly, especially via new media technologies, while still caught in the familiar trap of inequality, poverty and a considerable underclass. As ever, these tensions are made visible through the stratified acquisition and display of media goods and in the far greater choices available to middle-class youth whose possessions and media activities thereby mark (and perpetuate) social distinction. As Wildermuth concludes, these inequalities are all but impossible to escape from, despite the deployment of media by underprivileged young people to seek individual tactics for identity, resistance and social mobility.

We conclude this part of the *Handbook* with a chapter whose geographic scope encompasses several continents. Caronia and Caron pursue the methodological challenge of comparative research that accompanies the theoretical challenge of globalized media flows (see also Livingstone and Bovill (2001)). Like others in this *Handbook*, they take as their starting point the assumption that talking about media grounds children in their lifeworld, providing them with the symbolic resources to negotiate some of the factors that constrain them and aiding their co-construction with others of a common culture in which they have a meaningful place. Using an intriguing device – the broadcasting of a short announcement entitled, 'TV, this is how I'd like you to be…', Caronia and Caron collected children's letters, drawings and email responses to explore children's engagement with television in seven countries. While their local cultures vary, this analysis points to a cross-national 'community of viewers' within which children find 'a possible universe of common references'.

Clearly, for the contributors to this *Handbook*, universalistic claims should be critically interrogated, for the 'same' phenomenon evidenced in different contexts often requires a different explanation. In particular, this *Handbook* refuses as its starting point the dominant American research tradition on children and media, for diversity in theory and method is vital if we are to recognize the diversity of our research domain and avoid obscuring or 'othering' the non-American experience (Curran and Park, 2000). Donald offers some stern warnings to the research community, warning against uncritically applying findings from one culture or subculture to another, or against building assumptions into our methodologies that blind us to certain dimensions of children's experience or ignore the values embedded in language when we translate (literally or figuratively) across contexts. Nor can the contemporary researcher take their own experience as primary and project this unwittingly onto the rest of the world. Even one's 'home' culture can be misunderstood. As editors, our conception of European childhood may be too middle class, grounded in a particular moment of the twentieth century, blind to the experiences of diasporic or disadvantaged children, for example. And of course, the so-called 'American experience' is also, in reality, diverse, contested and dependent on the local as well as the national context, as Hoover and Clark illustrate in this volume).

At a minimum, the careful hedging of claims with qualifications and contextualization is, perhaps, a necessary strategy for researchers in a fast-globalizing space of knowledge production. But at its best, a view that spans cultures, balancing both range and depth, offers the excitement of new questions and insights, critical reflections and challenging problems that stimulate a rethinking of long-held assumptions regarding children, media and culture (see also Lemish (2007)).

REFERENCES

Alasuutari, P. (1995) *Researching Culture: Qualitative Methods and Cultural Studies*. London: Sage.

Barker, M., and Petley, J. (2001) *Ill Effects: The Media/Violence Debate* (2nd edition). New York City, New York: Routledge.

Buckingham, D. (1987). *Public Secrets: EastEnders and its Audience*. London: British Film Institute.

Curran, J. and Park, M. (eds) (2000). *Dewesternising Media Studies*. London: Routledge.

Giddens, A. (1991) *Modernity and Self-Identity: Self and Society in the Late Modern Age*. Cambridge: Polity Press.

Hall, S. and Jefferson, T. (eds) (1976) *Resistance Through Rituals: Youth Subcultures in Post-War Britain*. London: Hutchinson & Co.

Hodge, R. and Tripp, D. (1986) *Children and Television: A Semiotic Approach*. Cambridge: Polity.

Jenkins, H. (2003) 'Quentin Tarantino's Star Wars? Digital cinema, media convergence, and participatory culture'. In D. Thorburn and H. Jenkins (eds) *Rethinking Media Change: The Aesthetics of Transition*. Cambridge, Mass.: MIT Press; 281–312.

Lemish, D. (2007) 'Setting new research agendas'. *Journal of Children and Media*, 1(1), 1–4.

Livingstone, S. (1998) *Making Sense of Television: The Psychology of Audience Interpretation* (2nd edition). London: Routledge.

Livingstone, S. and Bovill, M. (eds) (2001) *Children and their Changing Media Environment: A European Comparative Study*. Mahwah, NJ: Lawrence Erlbaum Associates.

Morley, D. and Robins, K. (1995) *Spaces of Identity: Global Media, Electronic Landscapes and Cultural Boundaries*. London: Routledge.

Rantanen, T. (2004) *The Media and Globalization*. London: Sage.

Tomlinson, J. (1999) *Globalization and Culture*. Chicago, IL: University of Chicago Press.

Turkle, S. (1995) *Life on the Screen: Identity in the Age of the Internet*. New York: Simon & Schutser.

13

Children and Media: A Cultural Studies Approach

David Buckingham

WHAT IS CULTURAL STUDIES?

Attempting to define Cultural Studies is a task that is fraught with difficulties (see Storey (1996)). It invokes claims and counter-claims for disciplinary territory of the kind that often preoccupy academics, yet which must appear to the wider world rather like debates about the precise number of angels that can dance on the head of a pin. In this chapter, I provide a personal perspective on the contribution of Cultural Studies to analysing children's relationships with media. I outline a simple theoretical model, review a range of relevant research, and then describe a particular research project of my own that sought to apply this model in practice. I make no claim to be definitive: this will be *a* Cultural Studies approach, rather than *the* approach.

The history of what is now commonly termed 'British' Cultural Studies has been well documented, and does not need to be rehearsed in any detail here (e.g. see Tudor (1999) and Turner (2002)). The origins of Cultural Studies lie in the study of English literature and its encounter with the emergent discipline of sociology. The work of Raymond Williams and Richard Hoggart in the late 1950s represented a significant challenge to the elitism of traditional literary criticism: in different ways, both argued for a broadening of the concept of 'culture', and for the need to study not simply the received canon of literary texts, but a much broader range of cultural practices (Williams, 1958, 1961; Hoggart, 1959). Hoggart went on to establish the Centre for Contemporary Cultural Studies at the University of Birmingham, which became the key institution in the field, particularly under its subsequent director, Stuart Hall. The Birmingham Centre was the focus both for sustained empirical work on aspects of popular culture (most notably on youth culture) and for a critical engagement with major theoretical developments, particularly in Marxist and post-Marxist theories of ideology. During the late 1970s and 1980s, it struggled to accommodate new challenges deriving from feminism and anti-racism, as well as struggling to responding to contrary theoretical tendencies, for example in the emergence of psychoanalytically informed 'screen theory'.

Broadly speaking, Cultural Studies is defined by its concern with the relationships between particular cultural practices and broader processes of social power. It looks at how cultural meanings and pleasures are produced and circulated within society, at how individuals and social groups use and interpret cultural texts and at the role of cultural practices in the construction of people's social identities. In this sense, Cultural Studies is primarily concerned with the *political* dimensions of cultural practice; and it has paid particular attention to the ways in which power relationships – for example, based around social class, gender and 'race' – are reproduced, resisted and negotiated through acts of cultural production and reception (key early texts here would include those of the Centre for Contemporary Cultural Studies, University of Birmingham (1982), the Centre for Contemporary Cultural Studies, University of Birmingham, Women's Studies Group (1978) and Hall *et al.* (1979, 1980)).

'Media', in the sense of 'mass' media such as television, film, advertising and the press, are thus only one element of the broader field of Cultural Studies. Some of the more ethnographic work undertaken here has looked in a more holistic way at social and cultural practices – for example, those of youth 'subcultures' – of which the use and interpretation of media form only a part. Nevertheless, there is a strong tradition of empirical research on media within the Cultural Studies tradition, which incorporates the analysis of media texts alongside the study of audiences. Such work is typically qualitative, and in the case of audience research there is a strong emphasis on analysing the ways in which different social groups talk about what they watch and read (key early examples of such work would include those of Ang (1985), Hobson (1982) and Morley (1980)).

In terms of our focus here, it is worth noting that children were almost entirely absent from the empirical research conducted at Birmingham. Social class, gender and 'race' were key concerns; but age, as an equally significant dimension of social power, was strangely neglected. However, there was a strong focus on aspects of *youth* culture (e.g. Hall and Jefferson, 1975; Hebdige, 1979; Willis, 1990; MacRobbie, 1991); and while this work has subsequently been challenged on several grounds (e.g. Bennett, 2000), it remains a basic point of departure for a great deal of contemporary research in this field. Significantly, the Birmingham researchers regarded 'youth' as a category that was cut across by other social differences, particularly class and gender; and while this work sometimes tended to romanticize forms of youth cultural 'resistance', it should caution us against essentialized conceptions of youth – or indeed of childhood.

The 'Birmingham tradition' occupies a near-mythical status in accounts of Cultural Studies; but most acknowledge that the discipline (if such it is) has become significantly more dispersed and heterogeneous over the past 20 years. The 1990s saw the growing institutionalization of Cultural Studies, particularly in the USA, via the establishment of degree programmes, scholarly journals, publishers' lists, conferences and academic associations (Hall, 1992). European Cultural Studies has also expanded via the delineation of nationally focused traditions (e.g. Forbes and Kelly, 1995; Jordon and Morgan-Tamosunas, 2000; Phipps, 2000); and there has been a growing international dialogue, with the emergence of regional variants such as Latin American and Asian Cultural Studies, and powerful calls for the 'de-Westernizing' of the field (e.g. Curran and Park, 2000).

In many respects, this has been a success story, although there are some who still pine for the days when Cultural Studies saw itself as a form of political activism, waging war on the academic establishment. Even so, the institutionalization of Cultural Studies does not appear to have resulted in greater coherence about its fundamental aims and methods. Perhaps the most damaging development, in my view, is the tendency for Cultural

Studies to be seen as synonymous with Cultural Theory, and for the strongly empirical emphasis associated with the Birmingham tradition to be dissipated. Yet despite these developments, it is still relatively straightforward to differentiate Cultural Studies from what it is *not*.

Research on children and media, particularly in the USA, continues to be dominated by conventional approaches drawn from developmental psychology, social psychology and communication studies. Exponents of these approaches typically ignore or denigrate Cultural Studies, while also taking little account of innovative theoretical developments within their own disciplines (e.g. Singer and Singer, 2002). Cultural Studies presents several fundamental challenges to this 'business as usual' approach. Epistemologically, it questions positivist and empiricist approaches, for example as embodied in conventional forms of media content analysis: it does not assume that meaning is self-evident or immanent in media texts, or that it is simply transmitted or delivered to readers. It disputes normative models of child development, focusing attention instead on the changing social, historical and cultural construction of childhood. It seeks to understand children's media practices in their own terms and from their own perspectives, rather than comparing them with those of adults; and it seeks to explore the *social* experiences of children, not least as these are constructed through the operation of other dimensions of social power, such as social class, gender and ethnicity. In these respects, Cultural Studies approaches to children and media draw on recent work within the sociology of childhood (see Chapter 1), on critical psychology and (more broadly) on forms of poststructuralist theory.

Perhaps the clearest illustration of this difference is in the debate about the effects of media violence. While most mainstream psychologists (at least in the USA) tend to proclaim that there is academic consensus about this issue, Cultural Studies researchers have directly and persistently challenged the basic theoretical and methodological assumptions of effects research (e.g. see Barker and Petley (2001)). These critics dispute the reliability of laboratory experiments as a guide to real-life behaviour; they challenge the use of correlational surveys as a means of proving causal connections between media use and behaviour; they argue that effects researchers typically define 'violence' in inconsistent and simplistic ways; and they claim that notions of causal 'effect' are a highly inadequate way of conceiving of the relationships between media and their audiences. From a Cultural Studies perspective, effects research is seen to operate with a naïve and inadequate theory of *meaning*; and it largely denies the agency of audiences as active makers of meaning, rather than merely as recipients of predefined 'messages' (Barker, 2001). However, this dispute also has a political dimension: Cultural Studies academics argue that the construction of 'media violence' as a social problem effectively permits politicians to avoid addressing more fundamental causes of violent crime, such as the easy availability of lethal weapons – and that effects researchers are largely colluding in this process. This sustained deconstruction of the discourses of 'media effects' is, for the most part, simply ignored by mainstream researchers. However, some critics of Cultural Studies, such as Kline (2003) and Kubey (1996), have attempted to strike back: they accuse Cultural Studies of pretending that media have no effects whatsoever, or of claiming that such effects are merely benign – a charge that can only be described as an absurd misrepresentation.

While by no means wishing to defend everything that purports to be Cultural Studies, I would argue that it offers a distinctive set of theories and a methodological orientation towards the study of children and media that is very different from that of mainstream disciplines, particularly psychology. The central emphasis here is not on the *effects* of the media on behaviour or attitudes, but on the ways in which *meanings* are established, negotiated and circulated. The media are not seen merely as vehicles for delivering 'messages' to passive audiences; nor is the emphasis simply on the isolated encounter between mind and screen. On the contrary, this research regards children's uses and interpretations of the media as inherently *social* processes; and it understands these processes to be characterized by forms of power and difference. The 'child' is not primarily seen here in developmental terms, as a category defined merely by age. On the contrary, there is an emphasis on the diversity of childhood*s* (in the plural), not least in terms of social class, gender and ethnicity. From this perspective, what it means to be a child is not something fixed or given, but something that is socially constructed and negotiated.

A CULTURAL STUDIES APPROACH

The Cultural Studies approach I propose in this chapter is in some respects a traditional one. It derives partly from a seminal article published more than 20 years ago by Richard Johnson, subsequently Director of the Birmingham Centre (Johnson, 1985, 1996). Johnson outlines a circular model of cultural analysis with four key dimensions (see Figure 13.1). I have simplified this in my naïve model to three (see Figure 13.2).

In his article, Johnson makes an important case for the multidimensional nature of cultural analysis. He argues that culture is a social process, and that we can identify a series of 'moments' in that process which can usefully be isolated for analysis. The moment of *production* is that in which cultural objects or texts are brought into being; these *texts* take specific forms that can be analysed in their own right; the meanings of these texts are then actualized in the moment of *reading*; and readings subsequently feed into what Johnson terms *lived cultures*, which then in turn impact back on the process of production.

Social conditions and relations impinge on this process at each point. For example,

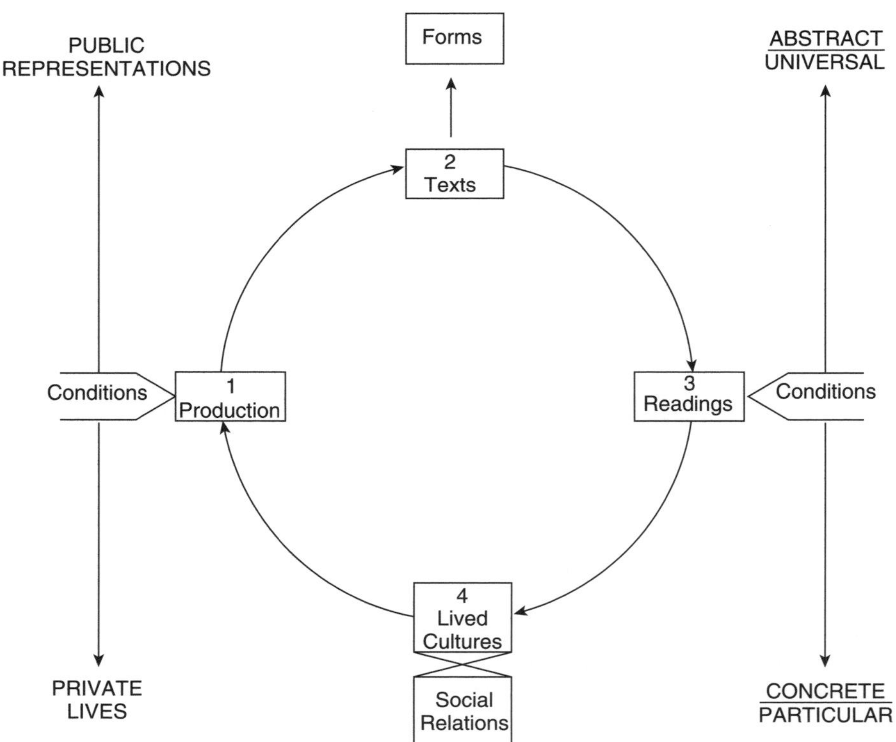

Figure 13.1 Richard Johnson's 'circuit' of Cultural Studies (reproduced from Johnson (1985))

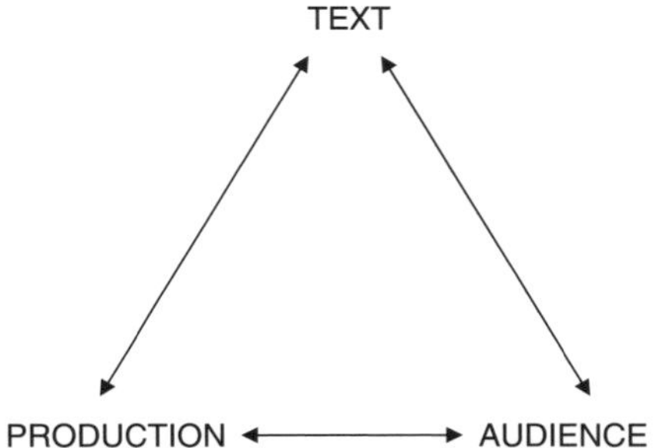

Figure 13.2 Cultural Studies: a 'naïve' theoretical model

production is not seen here merely as an individual 'creative' activity, but as one that is subject to specific institutional, social and economic conditions. Likewise, reading is not seen as a self-contained encounter between the individual reader and the text; on the contrary, it, too, occurs in a particular social context, which partly influences which readings are likely to be made. These broader social conditions do not wholly determine particular acts of production or of reading; however, they do set constraints and create possibilities which systematically favour the generation of particular meanings rather than others.

How is this model any different from the well-known 'sender–message–receiver' model of communication first proposed by Shannon and Weaver (1949)? The crux, in my view, is that it is a dynamic model. In Johnson's diagram, the arrows flow in a circuit, linking each of the four elements in turn; in my triangle, however, each element connects reciprocally with the other. Theoretically, this implies that none of the moments in the process should necessarily be privileged. Meaning does not flow in one direction, from sender to receiver, and the power to determine meaning does not lie at any one of these points, but in the relationships between them. In my simplified model, the bidirectional arrows imply that the relations between audiences, texts and producers are mutually determining. Texts do not simply 'contain' meanings that they impose on readers, any more than readers make of them any meaning they happen to wish. Likewise, producers may 'target' audiences – or seek to construct and define them in particular ways – but audiences also 'speak back' to producers, and their behaviour constrains what it is possible for producers to do or achieve. Finally, producers do not simply insert meanings into texts: textual forms and genres exert their own constraints on what it is possible to say, and what is ultimately 'said' may not correspond to what producers consciously intend.

Johnson argues that each of these moments in the process is deserving of a specific form of analysis, but that none of them is necessarily determining of any of the others and that there are risks in taking each of them in isolation. Focusing solely on production, for example, may lead us to overestimate the power of the producers – for example, of the large corporations that typically dominate the media market. Focusing exclusively on texts can result in one of the familiar fallacies of textual analysis: that the critic's interpretation necessarily tells us how the text will be read (and, indeed, the effects it may have on its readers). Focusing only on the moment of reading can result in a romanticized celebration of the power and activity of the reader, as though the meaning of any text were simply determined by the reader. Likewise, focusing solely on 'lived cultures' can lead us to place too great an emphasis on individual agency and to neglect the ways in which everyday experiences are shaped by wider social forces. The history of media research in Cultural Studies is replete with examples of such fallacious assumptions; and part of the purpose in returning to this early account is that it provides some way of overcoming the internal disputes that have characterized the field.

Richard Johnson's basic model has been challenged and refined in various ways in recent years. For example, the Open University's Cultural Studies undergraduate course (partly led by Stuart Hall) is based on a five-point 'star', whose elements are defined more conceptually (these elements are: production, regulation, representation, consumption and identity). In practice, however, I would argue that the instances or 'moments' of analysis in the course itself are still very close to those proposed in Johnson's original model (see du Gay *et al.* (1997)). More recently, Nick Couldry (2004) has proposed a 'new paradigm' in media research, based on an account of 'media as practice'. He argues that this approach will 'decentre' media research from its preoccupation with texts and production, and redirect it towards 'the study of the open-ended range of practices directly or indirectly focused on media' (Couldry, 2004: 117). In some respects, Couldry seems to be calling for renewed attention to the elements that Johnson refers to as 'lived cultures' – in other words, for a more 'anthropological' attention to the diverse range of 'media-oriented practices' that go beyond those in which people are explicitly constituted (or constitute themselves) as an 'audience'.

These reformulations are certainly useful, although they beg broader questions that cannot be explored in detail here. Ultimately, I would argue that conceiving of production, text and reading as 'moments' in a broader ongoing process is not necessarily incompatible with the reformulation that Couldry is proposing. The 'moment' of reading, for example, should not be understood simply as a matter of the isolated encounter between the reader and the text: this encounter takes place in specific social settings, in the context of various social and institutional relationships, and forms part of a history of other encounters with other texts. While the text itself may appear as a fixed object, it is surrounded by other texts to which it relates and refers, and which in turn form part of the 'symbolic resources' readers use to make sense of it. Likewise, the 'moment' of production is, of course, also much more than a moment: it is often a collaborative process that evolves over time, within specific institutional and political settings. Analytically, it may be necessary to isolate 'moments' for analysis, but these moments are always inevitably part of a broader social and cultural practice.

The attentive reader will no doubt have recognized that the dimension of 'lived culture' from Johnson's model is effectively missing from my own. This is not because of any desire to avoid the messy realities of everyday experience; it merely reflects a desire to delimit the boundaries of *media* research, as distinct from a more broad-ranging and inclusive anthropology of everyday life (or 'culture'). Focusing on the audience as a 'moment' in this broader practice implies that media research needs to concentrate primarily on the points at which people come to be constituted (or to constitute themselves) as audiences – as readers or users of particular media. Of course, people are never *only* audiences; and 'audiencing' (being a member of an audience) is merely a part of their broader social experience. Yet, while acknowledging that our behaviour as members of (multiple) audiences is necessarily situated in this wider context, analysing the specific place of *media* in that context simply means that we have to draw a line at some point.

CULTURAL STUDIES, CHILDREN AND MEDIA: A BRIEF REVIEW

Over the past two decades, childhood has gradually emerged as a focus of concern in academic Media and Cultural Studies, although it still remains fairly marginal to the field, at least in English-speaking countries. The following brief review draws attention to some of the more significant studies relating to children and media in each of the three areas identified on my triangular model. Inevitably, much of this work focuses on television (which is also my primary concern in this chapter), although there is a growing concern with new media such as the internet and computer games.

Production

Critical academic studies of media production for children are relatively few and far between. Early studies of children's television, such as those by Melody (1973) and Turow (1981), adopted a broad 'political economy' approach, focusing on questions of ownership, marketing and regulation. Aside from the work of Buckingham *et al.* (1999) and Hendershot (2004a), there has been very little analysis of producers' assumptions and expectations about the child audience; and while there has been some historical and international comparative research on the evolution of regulatory policy on children's television (e.g. Hendershot, 1998; Keys and Buckingham, 1999; Lisosky, 2001), this, too, has remained underresearched. Even in the case of cinema, historical research has been relatively underdeveloped, although there are important studies relating specifically to cinema exhibition and distribution (Staples, 1997) and to questions of censorship (Kuhn, 2002; Smith, 2005).

Perhaps the most interesting work in this field in recent years has related to broader concerns about the commercialization of children's culture (see Chapter 27). This issue has generated a growing body of popular commentary (e.g. Linn, 2004); and while much of this has been driven by a view of children as especially vulnerable to influence and exploitation, it has also shed light on the increasingly sophisticated and often 'invisible' practices of children's marketers. There have also been some important historical studies of marketing to children – for example, of goods such as clothing (Cook, 2004) and toys (Cross, 1997) – and of marketing practices more broadly (Seiter, 1993; Cross, 2004). While advocates of a traditional 'political economy' approach tend to regard the market as inherently inimical to children's best interests (e.g. Kline, 1993), others have adopted a more sanguine approach, arguing that critiques of consumer culture are often driven by implicitly elitist conceptions of taste and cultural value (Seiter, 1993). Our own research on the political economy of children's television (Buckingham *et al.*, 1999) and of 'edutainment' media (Buckingham and Scanlon, 2005) also suggests that success in the marketplace is far from secure or guaranteed, and that producers often face considerable challenges in identifying children's wants and needs in the first place.

Texts

Of course, children's use of media is far from confined to material that is specifically designed for them; yet, the analysis of children's media provides interesting insights into some of the broader tensions that surround dominant definitions of childhood. For example, research on children's television has focused on well-established concerns such as gender representation (Seiter, 1993; Griffiths, 2002), as well as on more novel issues such as its implicit models of adult citizenship (Northam, 2005), how it handles the relationship between 'information' and 'entertainment' (Buckingham, 1995), and how it addresses the child viewer (Davies, 1995). There have also been fruitful discussions of specific genres of children's programming, such as costume drama (Davies, 2002), news (Buckingham, 2000), action-adventure shows (Jenkins, 1999) and preschool programming (Oswell, 2002). Likewise, in relation to film, there have been important studies of the ways in which contemporary 'family films' are seeking to redefine (if only superficially) the relationships between adults and children (Allen, 1999; Morris, 2000). As in research on children's literature, the analysis suggests that the position of the medium as a 'parent' or 'teacher' and the process of attempting to 'draw in' the child are fraught with difficulties and uncertainties (Rose, 1984).

Some of the most interesting work in this area has focused on the widely denigrated area of children's cartoons. As against the continuing use of quantitative content analysis (e.g. Kline, 1995), there have been several studies that have applied semiotics (Hodge and Tripp, 1986), psychoanalysis (Urwin, 1995) and postmodernist theory (Kinder, 1991) in qualitative analyses of this apparently simple genre. This work raises interesting hypotheses about the ways in which cartoons offer the potential for 'subversive' readings and enable viewers to explore and manage anxiety, thereby perhaps bringing about more protean forms of subjectivity (Hendershot, 2004b; Wells, 2002). Disney has proved a particularly fertile ground for textual studies, generating competing analyses informed by a range of theoretical perspectives, including feminism (Bell *et al.*, 1995), poststructuralism (McQuillan and Byrne, 1999) and more conventional forms of ideological critique (Dorfman and Mattelart, 1975).

More recently, analyses of new media have also begun to address texts specifically targeted at children. There have been several productive studies looking at specific genres of computer games (Cassell and Jenkins, 1998; Carr *et al.*, 2006), entertainment websites for children (Seiter, 2005), 'edutainment' games and websites (Buckingham and Scanlon, 2003, 2004) and the interface between games and more traditional forms of children's media, such as books (Burn, 2006).

Audiences

It is in the area of audience research that Cultural Studies researchers have made the most significant contribution to this field; and several of the other chapters in this volume illustrate this in different ways. As I have suggested, Cultural Studies challenges the positivist epistemology of mainstream psychology, as well as seeking to develop a more fully *social* account of the child audience. Its primary emphasis in terms of audience research is in understanding the social processes through which the meanings and pleasures of media are constructed, defined and circulated. While Cultural Studies research is not necessarily qualitative (see Murdock (1997)), it often relies either on focus-group or individual interviews or on 'ethnographic' observation.

In their ground-breaking study, Hodge and Tripp (1986) applied a social semiotic perspective, both to the analysis of children's programming and to audience talk. Although they regard children as 'active' producers of meaning, they are also concerned with the ideological and formal constraints exerted by the text. In the process, they explore how children's talk about television depends upon the context in which it occurs, and how it enacts social relationships with others (including researchers themselves). This approach has been pursued in my own work, where there is a central emphasis on the ways in which children define and construct their social identities through talk about television and other media (Buckingham, 1993a,b; 1996; 2000; Buckingham and Bragg, 2004). Rather than applying a narrowly semiotic approach, this research uses arguments drawn from discourse analysis to challenge the positivist use of audience data within mainstream research: rather than regarding what children say at face value, as some kind of self-evident reflection of what they 'really' think or believe, it argues that talk should itself be seen as a form of social action or performance (Potter and Wetherell, 1987). Children's judgments about genre and representation, and their reconstructions of television narrative, for example, are studied as inherently social processes; and the development of knowledge about television ('television literacy') and of a 'critical' perspective are seen in terms of their social motivations and purposes.

In parallel with this work, some researchers have adopted a more 'ethnographic' approach to studying children's uses of media, based primarily on observation. Thus, there have been studies of the use of television and other media both within the home (e.g. Palmer, 1986; Richards, 1993) and in the context of the peer group (Sefton-Green, 1998; Wood, 1993), as well as studies of children's engagement with new media such as computer games (Schott and Horrell, 2000) and the internet (Beavis *et al.*, 2005; Davies, 2006). Several studies have observed the use of media in schools and informal educational settings, mainly in the context of media education programmes (e.g. Buckingham and Sefton-Green, 1994; Buckingham *et al.*, 1995; Richards, 1998; Marsh, 1999; Bragg, 2000; Burn, 2000). However, the term 'ethnographic' is perhaps best reserved for studies that have entailed long-term immersion in a particular community; and work of this kind is comparatively rare in media research more broadly. Marie Gillespie's (1995) study of the use of television among a South Asian community in London is a rare exception, which combines an analysis of the role of television within the family and the peer group with an account of children's responses to specific genres such as news and soap opera.

While this is a developing body of research, there are several broader issues within it that remain to be resolved. Like sociologists of childhood, Cultural Studies researchers are broadly inclined to regard children as 'active' participants in the process of making meaning – as competent social actors, rather than as passive and incompetent victims. This kind of argument offers an important challenge to many of the assumptions that typically circulate in public debate, particularly in arguments about media violence. Yet there is a risk of adopting a rather simplistic 'child-centred' approach, which seeks to celebrate the sophistication of the 'media-wise' child and to prove (endlessly) that children are not as gullible or as passive as they are made out to be. There is often an implicit assumption that if children are 'active', then they are somehow not going to be influenced by what they watch. Yet this does not necessarily follow; indeed, one could argue that in some instances to be 'active' is to be more open to influence – and 'activity' should not in itself be equated with agency, or with social power. Furthermore, this kind of celebration of children's sophistication as users of media can lead us to neglect the fact that there are areas they need to know more about – which is inevitably a key concern both for educators and for media regulators.

This reflects a broader tension here between 'structure' and 'agency' that is characteristic of the human sciences in general (see Buckingham and Sefton-Green (2004)). The temptation to celebrate children's agency – and, in doing so, to speak 'on behalf of the child' – can lead researchers to neglect the broader economic, social and political forces that both constrain and produce particular forms of audience behaviour or meaning-making. The intellectual, cultural and, indeed, material resources that children use in making meaning are not equally available to all. The actions of media producers and the structures and forms of media texts clearly delimit, and to some extent determine, the possible meanings that can be made. From the perspective of 'structuration theory' (Giddens, 1984), we would argue that structure works through agency, and agency works through structure: in order to create meanings and pleasures, the media depend upon the active agency of audiences; and yet (to paraphrase another well-known commentator) audiences can only make meanings in conditions that are not of their own choosing.

This is why, in my view, it remains crucially important for researchers to combine the different areas of investigation identified here. Yet, while there have been significant contributions in each of these areas, there have been comparatively few attempts to bring them together or to theorize the relationships between them. Janet Wasko's studies of Disney (Wasko, 2000; Wasko *et al.*, 2001) do address the economic, textual and audience dimensions of the phenomenon and look across a range of media; and Stephen Kline *et al.* (2003) provide a similarly multidimensional analysis of video games, albeit one that is significantly more effective in its analysis of the industry than in accounting for other aspects. Yet, while both studies cover the relevant bases, neither offers a convincing theoretical reconciliation of the different perspectives. However, Joseph Tobin's edited volume on the Pokemon phenomenon manages to combine these elements more effectively (Tobin, 2004a): the contributions by Tobin (2004b) and by Buckingham and Sefton-Green (2004) seek to move beyond polarized accounts of the operation of 'media power', combining each of the three aspects identified above. As we suggest, this is not simply a matter of balancing the equation and thereby finding a happy medium between the 'power of the text' and the 'power of the audience'. Nor is it something that can be achieved in the abstract. Ultimately, the relationship between children and the media can only be fully understood in the context of a wider analysis of the ways in which both are constructed and defined.

RELOCATING THE CHILD AUDIENCE

In the final part of this chapter, I would like to provide a brief outline of a research project I undertook some years ago that tried to develop these connections. The project focused primarily on children's television and how children themselves use and interpret it. Further information about this research can be found in Buckingham (2002a), Buckingham *et al.* (1999), Davies *et al.* (1999, 2000) and Kelley *et al.* (1999).

Our starting point here was to question the category of 'the child' and particularly 'the child audience'. We wanted to make explicit and to deconstruct the assumptions that are made about children: about who children are, about what they need, and about what they should and should not see. These assumptions derive in turn from a whole range of moral, political, economic, psychological and educational theories. Our basic research question, therefore, was: how do the media (particularly television) *construct* the child audience? And how do children negotiate with these constructions – how do they define themselves and their needs as an audience? We also wanted to consider how those definitions and constructions have changed historically, and how they do or do not reflect changing social constructions of childhood more broadly.

The key point in terms of my argument here is that these questions cannot be answered by looking at only one aspect of the picture – for example, just by looking at television itself or just by looking at the audience. On the contrary, we need to understand the relationships between producers, texts and audiences. We need to analyse how these different assumptions about children circulate and are manifested at different levels: in policy, in production, in regulation, in the practice of research, in scheduling, in choices about content, in textual form, in children's own perspectives on and uses of media, and in how those uses are regulated and mediated within the home. It is vital to emphasize that none of these levels is determining; on the contrary, there is an ongoing struggle over meaning. Texts position readers, but readers also make meanings from texts. Media institutions create policies that are manifested in texts; but policies are not simply implemented, since producers exercise their own kinds of creativity and professional judgment. Likewise, media producers imagine and target audiences; but audiences are elusive, and the changing behaviour of audiences in turn produces changes in the practices of media institutions.

Furthermore, all these relationships evolve over time. Policies and institutions evolve historically, in response to other forces; texts also bear histories of intertextual or generic relations with other texts, which themselves are subject to change; and readers do not come to texts either as blank slates or as wised-up critical viewers: they also have reading histories, histories of engagements with other texts, which have enabled them to develop certain kinds of competencies as readers.

CHANGING CONSTRUCTIONS OF CHILDHOOD: PRODUCTION, TEXT AND AUDIENCE

In terms of *production*, our research explored three main areas. We looked historically at the evolution of children's television and the kinds of institutional struggles that went on in attempting to claim and preserve a specific place for children in the schedules; we explored the contemporary political economy of children's television, and the fate of public service television in the light of the move towards a more commercial, multichannel, global system; and we gathered and analysed instances of policy discourse, in the form of official reports and interviews with policy-makers, broadcasters, regulators, lobbyists and others (see Buckingham *et al.* (1999)).

In very broad terms, what we find here is a complex balance between the fear of doing harm (a protectionist discourse) and the attempt to do children good (a pedagogical discourse); and these are discourses that in each case draw on broader discourses about childhood. There are also, obviously, some significant historical shifts, as established traditions and philosophies come under pressure in the changing media environment. At present, for example, older philosophies of child-centredness, which were very dominant in the UK in the 1960s and 1970s, are being rearticulated through their encounter with more consumerist notions of childhood, and with notions of children's rights.

Yet, far from enjoying an absolute power to define the child audience, producers and policy-makers in fact display a considerable degree of uncertainty about it. Changing social and economic conditions often appear to have precipitated a much broader set of doubts about the changing nature of childhood. In the 1950s, for instance, the advent of commercial television, and the subsequent dramatic decline in the ratings of the BBC (the public service channel), led to a thoroughgoing process of soul searching. Those responsible for children's programmes at the BBC were dismayed by their loss of the child audience and increasingly came to doubt the somewhat middle-class, paternalistic approach they had been adopting. Ultimately, after a period of internal crisis, the BBC's Children's Department was abolished in the early 1960s and was subsumed by a new Family Department. When it re-emerged, later in the decade, it did so with a much less paternalistic view of its audience.

Similar doubts and uncertainties are apparent in the present situation, as terrestrial broadcasters try to come to terms with the threat of competition from new cable and satellite providers, and (more broadly) with the challenges of globalization and commercialization. Since the late 1990s, children in Britain (or at least those whose parents subscribe to pay-TV) have gained access to a vast range of new specialist channels (there are 31 at the time of writing in 2007); and while the generic range of new programming is comparatively narrow, much of it appears distinctly fresh and innovative, and there is a great deal more for children to choose from.

Contrasting the publicity material produced by the BBC with that produced by the US-based specialist channel Nickelodeon provides a symptomatic indication of the different definitions of childhood that are at stake here (see Buckingham (2002c)). The BBC still tends to hark back to the past, invoking (or indeed reinventing) tradition and, in the process, playing to parents' nostalgia for the television of their own childhoods. By contrast, Nickelodeon does not have to achieve legitimacy with parents (and, hence, secure their continued assent for the compulsory licence fee): it can address children directly, and it does so in ways that emphasize their anarchic humour and their sensuality. What we find here, and in the statements of its executives (e.g. Laybourne, 1993), is a rhetoric of empowerment: a notion of the channel as giving voice to kids, taking the kids' point of view, as the friend of kids. This is typically aligned with a form of 'anti-adultism', which defines adults as necessarily boring and conservative. This is a very powerful rhetoric, albeit one that could be accused of disguising its fundamental commercialism under a superficial affectation of 'children's rights'.

In terms of *texts*, we were interested in how these assumptions and ideologies of childhood are manifested or negotiated in the practices of producers, and in the form of texts themselves. There were two aspects to our research here. First, we tried to develop a broad view of the range of material that has been offered to children over time, through an audit both of the children's television schedules over the past four decades and of the programmes that are most popular with children. The schedules for children's TV in the 1950s embody a very different construction of the space of childhood, and of the nature of children's viewing, compared with the diversity of material that is on offer today; and they implicitly propose a very different phenomenology of the viewing experience itself (Lury, 2002). Our analysis questions some of the myths of cultural decline that often characterize discussions of children's television: the notion that we once lived in a kind of golden age of quality, and that we are now being swamped by trashy

American programming, simply does not hold up in the face of the evidence.

Second, we undertook a series of qualitative case studies of particular texts or genres, as well as talking to their producers. We were particularly interested in texts or areas of programming that have a long history, where we can see clear indications of historical change. We looked at how texts address and construct the child viewer – for example, the various ways in which the viewer is spoken to; how the viewer is or is not invited to be involved; the function of children as actors or participants within the programmes; how adult–child relations are represented or enacted; and more formal devices, such as how the visual design of the studio, the camerawork, graphics and music imply assumptions about who children are, and what they are (or should be) interested in. This analysis is also, of course, about content, namely about which topics are seen to be appropriate for this audience and how the perceived interests of the child audience are demarcated from or overlap with those of the adult audience.

The BBC preschool series *Teletubbies*, and the debates that surrounded it, provide an interesting case study of some of these changes (see Buckingham (2002b)). *Teletubbies*, which began broadcasting in 1997, combines elements that are very familiar in programmes for younger children, such as songs, dances and playful sketches, with more innovative components, such as short documentary sequences narrated from the child's viewpoint. The overall scenario of the programme – which features four brightly coloured creatures resembling babies in diapers, who live in an underground science-fiction bunker – is, to say the least, somewhat quirky and surreal. *Teletubbies* is an outsourced, independent production that has generated strong overseas sales and a vast range of ancillary merchandising. It has been accused by critics of abandoning the 'great tradition' of educative programming (and thereby of 'dumbing down' its audience), of commercially exploiting children, and (by some overseas critics) of cultural imperialism, in terms of pedagogy and social representation. The controversy it has aroused can be seen as a highly symptomatic reflection of the BBC's current dilemmas, as it attempts to sustain national public service traditions while simultaneously depending on commercial activities and global sales.

In terms of both form and content, *Teletubbies* is an amalgam of two historical traditions within British preschool children's television: the more didactic (albeit play-oriented), 'realist', adult-centred approach of *Playdays* and its predecessor *Playschool* on the one hand, and the more surrealistic, entertaining tradition of many animation and puppet shows on the other hand. While it is the latter that immediately confounds and surprises many adult critics, it is important to recognize the particular forms of education that are being offered here, and the different ways in which they construct the child viewer. Thus, the 'child-centred' pedagogic approach is manifested in documentary inserts shot and narrated from the child's point of view, in the manipulation of knowledge via narrative, and in the slow pace and 'parental' mode of address. This contrasts with the more didactic elements, relating to pre-reading and counting skills and the modelling of daily routines.

Teletubbies almost instantly became extremely popular with its immediate target audience of 1–3-year-olds, but it also briefly attained a kind of cult status among older children and among some adults. The programme was a frequent topic of conversation in our audience research, although our sample was much older than the target audience. The 6–7-year-olds were often keen to disavow any interest in the programme, while the 10–11-year-olds seemed to relate to it with a kind of subversive irony – although it was often passionately rejected by those with younger siblings. As this implies, the children's judgments about the programme reflected their attempts to project themselves as more or less 'adult'. Combined with more anecdotal information about the programme's popularity with older children and young adults, this suggests that its (passing) cult popularity may have been symptomatic of a broader sense of irony that suffuses contemporary television culture – and one that often reflects ambivalent investments in the *idea* of 'childishness'.

What we find at the level of institutions and texts, then, are some very powerful definitions of the child, definitions which are partly coercive, but also partly very pleasurable, and often quite awkward and contradictory. The obvious question here is how children negotiate with these definitions; that is, how they define themselves as an *audience*. This was the third dimension of the project, and again there was a quantitative and a qualitative dimension.

Audience ratings can clearly tell us a fair amount about how children define themselves as an audience; and however unreliable or superficial they may be, they clearly show (for example) that children are increasingly opting to watch adult programmes and not children's programmes. At the same time, children do choose to watch particular kinds of adult programmes; and it is interesting to look at the versions or aspects of 'adulthood' that they choose to buy into and those they reject or resist.

These kinds of questions were the focus of our more qualitative investigations of the child audience, which focused on children aged 6–7 and 10–11. Through a series of focus-group discussions and activities, we investigated how children negotiate with these adult definitions of childhood, how they define themselves as children, and as children of a particular age – and how they do this in different ways in different contexts and for different purposes.

In the children's exploration of what makes a programme 'appropriate' for children, the strongest arguments were negative ones. Programmes featuring sex, violence and 'swearing' were singled out by both groups as being particularly 'grown-up'. Likewise, children's programmes were predominantly defined in terms of absences; that is, in terms of what they do *not* include. One area of our analysis here concerned children's discussions of sex and sexuality on television. On one level, it was clear that 'adult' material on television could function as a kind of 'forbidden fruit'. In discussing this kind of material, the children displayed a complex mixture of embarrassment, bravado and moral disapproval. Discussions of sex and romance in genres such as dating game shows, soap operas and sitcoms often served as a rehearsal of projected future (hetero-)sexual identities, particularly among girls. Boys were less comfortable here, with the younger ones more inclined to display disgust than fascination; although the older ones were more voyeuristic.

The children were very familiar with adult definitions of appropriateness, although they were inclined to displace any negative 'effects' of television onto those younger than themselves, or onto 'children' in general. While some of the youngest children expressed a more censorious rejection of 'adult' material, this was much less common among the older children, who aspired to the freedom they associated with the category of the 'teenager'; and these discussions could serve as a form of mutual policing, particularly among boys. Overall, the analysis here suggests that, in discussing their responses to television, children are performing a kind of 'identity work', particularly via claims about their own 'maturity'. In the process, these discussions serve largely to reinforce normative definitions both of 'childhood' and of gender identity (see Kelley *et al.* (1999); and for subsequent research on this issue, see Buckingham and Bragg (2004)).

Another aspect of our investigation here concerned the issue of children's tastes. We were interested to discover whether children have distinctive tastes as an audience, and how these tastes are articulated and negotiated in the context of peer-group discussion. We analysed the social functions and characteristics of children's expressions of their tastes using a set of overlapping paradigmatic oppositions which emerged from their attempts to categorize programmes: parents/children, grannies/teenagers, boring/funny, and talk/action. In each case, the children generally favoured the latter element (associated with children) and disavowed the former (associated with adults). However, they frequently distinguished here between the tastes attributed to parents in general and those they observed in the case of their *own* parents – again, suggesting a recognition that broad discursive categories may not always be directly applicable in everyday life. The older children were inclined to aspire to the identity of the 'teenager', via the display of particular tastes, notably in comedy. By contrast, the tastes of some adults were dismissed as belonging to the category of 'grannies', who were parodied as hopelessly 'old fashioned' and 'uncool'. The children were highly dismissive of programmes featuring 'talk' and enthusiastic about those featuring action – not least action of a violent or otherwise spectacular nature. As this implies, they frequently inverted cultural hierarchies and resisted adult notions of 'good taste'.

Contemporary debates about children's television have emphasized the need for factual programmes, literary adaptations and socially responsible contemporary drama. Without disputing this, our analysis suggests that there is also a need for entertainment programming – and indeed for programmes that a majority of adults would consider 'infantile', 'puerile' or otherwise 'in bad taste'. The complex and playful nature of children's judgments of taste, and their understanding of taste as 'cultural capital', is certainly apparent in the popularity of such self-consciously ironic and 'tasteless' texts as *South Park* and *Beavis and Butthead*. Nevertheless, children's tastes cannot be defined in an essentialist way, any more than adults' can: both groups are more heterogeneous than is typically assumed (see Davies *et al*. (2000)).

CONCLUSION

In this chapter, I have proposed a particular approach to studying children and media that is squarely located within the tradition of Cultural Studies. It is an approach that directly challenges the positivist assumptions of mainstream psychology and of media effects research. Rather than seeing meaning as something that the media simply deliver to passive audiences, it focuses on the diverse ways in which meanings and pleasures are constructed, defined and circulated. It begins from the assumption that audiences are indeed 'active', but that they act under conditions that are not of their own choosing – and to this extent, it challenges the tendency to equate 'activity' with *agency* or power. In the case of children, their relationships with media are structured and constrained by wider social institutions and discourses, which (among other things) seek to define 'childhood' in particular ways. The child audience (or at least the specific characteristics of that audience) is thus constructed through an ongoing process of social negotiation.

Of course, there is a great deal that is not included within this account. The primary focus of the research I have described has been on television; and while I have referred to some research on other media, there is a great deal more that might said, particularly about the ways in which Cultural Studies might contribute to an analysis of 'new' media such as the internet and computer games (see Buckingham (2005)). I am also very conscious that my account has been 'Anglo-centric', and I have been unable to take full account of the contributions to Cultural Studies emerging from non-English-speaking countries, although I am confident that this absence will be made good by my fellow contributors to this volume.

The crucial question that remains, however, is to do with the connections between the different areas of research I have discussed. The 'cultural circuit' model and my simplified triangle identify several key areas of study that, when taken together, should provide a comprehensive account of children's relationships with media. Even so, this kind of multifaceted approach is not easy to achieve in practice; and theorizing the relationships between the different 'moments' or elements is a complex matter. In practice, it is often difficult to take account of the 'balance of forces' between structure and agency. On the one hand, there is a view of childhood (and, by extension, of the subjectivity of children) as somehow inexorably produced by powerful institutional and textual discourses; on the other hand, there is the view that real children somehow automatically and inevitably evade those constructions. Accounting for the real slippages and inconsistencies here, and doing so *in empirical terms*, rather than simply through recourse to a series of 'in principle' theoretical qualifications, is a continuing endeavour.

ACKNOWLEDGEMENTS

The project 'Children's media culture: education, entertainment and the public sphere' was funded by the Economic and Social Research Council UK (ref.: L126251026). I would like to thank my colleagues Hannah Davies, Ken Jones and Peter Kelley for their contributions.

REFERENCES

Allen, R. (1999) 'Home alone together: Hollywood and the family film'. In R. Stokes and R. Maltby (eds) *Identifying Hollywood's Audiences: Cultural Identity and the Movies*. London: British Film Institute; 109–131.

Ang, I. (1985) *Watching 'Dallas': Soap Opera and the Melodramatic Imagination*. London: Methuen.

Barker, M. (2001) 'The Newson report: a case study in "common sense"'. In M. Barker and J. Petley (eds) *Ill Effects: The Media/Violence Debate*, 2nd edition, London: Routledge; 27–46.

Barker, M. and Petley, J. (eds) (2001) *Ill Effects: The Media/Violence Debate*, 2nd edition, London: Routledge.

Beavis, C., Nixon, H. and Atkinson, S. (2005) 'LAN cafes as liminal spaces for new literacies, identities and communities in formation'. *Education, Communication, Information*, 5(2): 41–60.

Bell, E., Haas, L. and Sells, L. (1995) *From Mouse to Mermaid: The Politics of Film, Gender, and Culture*. Bloomington, IN: Indiana University Press.

Bennett, A. (2000) *Popular Music and Youth Culture*. Basingstoke; Palgrave Macmillan.

Bragg, S. (2000) 'Media violence and education: a study of youth audiences and the horror genre'. PhD thesis, Institute of Education, University of London.

Buckingham, D. (1993a) *Children Talking Television: The Making of Television Literacy*. London: Falmer.

Buckingham, D. (ed.) (1993b) *Reading Audiences: Young People and the Media*. Manchester: Manchester University Press.

Buckingham, D. (1995) 'On the impossibility of children's television'. In C. Bazalgette and D. Buckingham (eds) *In Front of the Children*. London, British Film Institute; 47–61.

Buckingham, D. (1996) *Moving Images: Understanding Children's Emotional Responses to Television*. Manchester: Manchester University Press.

Buckingham, D. (2000) *The Making of Citizens: Young People, News and Politics*. London: University College London Press.

Buckingham, D. (ed.) (2002a) *Small Screens: Television for Children*. Leicester: Leicester University Press.

Buckingham, D. (2002b) 'Teletubbies and the educational imperative'. In D. Buckingham (ed.) *Small Screens: Television for Children*. Leicester: Leicester University Press; 38–60.

Buckingham, D. (2002c) 'Introduction: the child and the screen'. In D. Buckingham (ed.) *Small Screens: Television for Children*. Leicester: Leicester University Press; 1–14.

Buckingham, D. (2005) 'Children and new media'. In L. Lievrouw and S. Livingstone (eds) *Handbook of New Media*, 2nd edition. London: Sage; 75–91.

Buckingham, D. and Bragg, S. (2004) *Young People, Sex and the Media: The Facts of Life?* London: Palgrave Macmillan.

Buckingham, D. and Scanlon, M. (2003) *Education, Entertainment and Learning in the Home*. Buckingham: Open University Press.

Buckingham, D. and Scanlon, M. (2004) 'Connecting the family? "Edutainment" websites and learning in the home'. *Education, Communication and Information*, 4(2–3): 271–291.

Buckingham, D. and Scanlon, M. (2005) 'Selling learning: towards a political economy of edutainment media'. *Media, Culture and Society*, 27(1): 41–58.

Buckingham, D. and Sefton-Green, J. (1994) *Cultural Studies Goes to School: Reading and Teaching Popular Culture*. London: Taylor and Francis.

Buckingham, D. and Sefton-Green, J. (2004) 'Gotta catch 'em all: structure, agency and pedagogy in children's media culture'. In J. Tobin (ed.) *Pikachu's Global Adventure: The Rise and Fall of Pokemon*. Durham, NC: Duke University Press; 12–33.

Buckingham, D. Grahame, J. and Sefton-Green, J. (1995) *Making Media: Practical Production in Media Education*. London: English & Media Centre.

Buckingham, D., Davies, H., Jones, K. and Kelley, P. (1999) *Children's Television in Britain: History, Discourse and Policy* . London: British Film Institute.

Burn, A. (2000) 'Repackaging the slasher movie: digital unwriting of film in the classroom'. *English in Australia* 127–128: 24–34.

Burn, A. (2006) 'Multi-text magic: Harry Potter in book, film and videogame'. In F. Collins and J. Ridgman (eds) *Children's Literature in Performance and the Media.* Bern: Peter Lang; 227–250.

Carr, D., Buckingham, D., Burn, A. and Schott, G. (2006) *Computer Games: Text, Narrative and Play.* Cambridge: Polity.

Cassell, J. and Jenkins, H. (eds) (1998) *From Barbie to Mortal Kombat: Gender and Computer Games.* Cambridge, MA: MIT Press.

Centre for Contemporary Cultural Studies, University of Birmingham (1982) *The Empire Strikes Back: Race and Racism in 70s Britain.* London: Hutchinson.

Centre for Contemporary Cultural Studies, University of Birmingham, Women's Studies Group (1978) *Women Take Issue: Aspects of Women's Subordination.* London: Hutchinson.

Cook, D. (2004) *The Commodification of Childhood: The Children's Clothing Industry and the Rise of the Child Consumer.* Durham, NC: Duke University Press.

Couldry, N. (2004) 'Theorising media as practice'. *Social Semiotics,* 14(2): 115–132.

Cross, G. (1997) *Kids' Stuff: Toys and the Changing World of American Childhood.* Cambridge, MA: Harvard University Press.

Cross, G. (2004) *The Cute and the Cool: Wondrous Innocence and Modern American Children's Culture.* Oxford: Oxford University Press.

Curran, J. and Park, M.-J. (eds) (2000) *De-Westernizing Media Studies.* London: Routledge.

Davies, H., Buckingham, D. and Kelley, P. (1999) 'Kids' time: television, childhood and the regulation of time'. *Journal of Educational Media,* 24(1): 25–42.

Davies, H., Buckingham, D. and Kelley, P. (2000) 'In the worst possible taste: children, television and cultural value'. *European Journal of Cultural Studies,* 3(1): 5–25.

Davies, J. (2006) ' "Hello newbie! **big welcome hugs** hope u like it here as much as i do! " An exploration of teenagers' informal on-line learning'. In D. Buckingham and R. Willett (eds) *Digital Generations: Children, Young People and New Media.* Mahwah, NJ: Erlbaum; 211–228.

Davies, M.M. (1995) 'Babes 'n' the hood: pre-school television and its audiences in the United States and Britain'. In C. Bazalgette and D. Buckingham (eds) *In Front of the Children.* London, British Film Institute; 15–33.

Davies, M.M. (2002) 'Classics with clout: costume drama in British and American children's television'. In D. Buckingham (ed.) *Small Screens: Television for Children.* Leicester: Leicester University Press; 120–140.

Dorfman, A. and Mattelart, A. (1975) *How to Read Donald Duck: Imperialist Ideology in the Disney Comics.* New York: International General.

Du Gay, P., Hall, S., Janes, L., Mackay, H. and Negus, K. (1997) *Doing Cultural Studies: The Story of the Sony Walkman.* London: Sage.

Forbes, J. and Kelly, M. (eds) (1995) *French Cultural Studies.* Oxford: Oxford University Press.

Giddens, A. (1984) *The Constitution of Society: Outline of the Theory of Structuration.* Cambridge: Polity Press.

Gillespie, M. (1995) *Television, Ethnicity and Cultural Change.* London: Routledge.

Griffiths, M. (2002) 'Pink worlds and blue worlds: a portrait of infinite polarity'. In D. Buckingham (ed.) *Small Screens: Television for Children.* Leicester: Leicester University Press; 159–184.

Hall, S. (1992) 'Cultural Studies and its theoretical legacies'. In L. Grossberg, C. Nelson and P. Treichler (eds) *Cultural Studies.* London: Routledge; 277–286.

Hall, S., Critcher, C., Jefferson, T., Clarke, J. and Roberts, B. (1979) *Policing the Crisis: Mugging, the State and Law and Order.* London: Macmillan.

Hall, S., Hobson, D., Lowe, A. and Willis, P. (eds) (1980) *Culture, Media, Language.* London: Hutchinson.

Hall, S. and Jefferson, T. (eds) (1975) *Resistance Through Rituals: Youth Subcultures in Post-War Britain.* London: Hutchinson.

Hebdige, D. (1979) *Subculture: The Meaning of Style.* London: Methuen.

Hendershot, H. (1998) *Saturday Morning Censors: Television Regulation Before the V-Chip.* Durham, NC: Duke University Press.

Hendershot, H. (ed.) (2004a) *Nickelodeon Nation: the History, Politics and Economics of America's Only TV Channel for Kids.* New York: New York University Press.

Hendershot, H. (ed.) (2004b) 'Nickelodeon's nautical nonsense: the intergenerational appeal of *Spongebob Squarepants*'. In H. Hendershot (ed.) *Nickelodeon Nation: the History, Politics and Economics of America's Only TV Channel for Kids.* New York: New York University Press; 182–208.

Hobson, D. (1982) *Crossroads: The Drama of a Soap Opera.* London: Methuen.

Hodge, B. and Tripp, D. (1986) *Children and Television: A Semiotic Approach.* Cambridge, Polity.

Hoggart, R. (1959) *The Uses of Literacy.* London: Chatto and Windus.

Jenkins, H. (1999) ' "Her suffering aristocratic majesty": the sentimental value of *Lassie*'. In M. Kinder (ed.)

Kids' Media Culture. Durham, NC: Duke University Press; 69–101.

Johnson, R. (1985) 'What is Cultural Studies anyway?' *Social Text*, 16: 38–80.

Johnson, R. (1996) 'What is Cultural Studies anyway?' In J. Storey (ed.) *What is Cultural Studies? A Reader*. London: Edward Arnold; 75–114 (republished from Johnson (1985)).

Jordon, B. and Morgan-Tamosunas, R. (2000) *Contemporary Spanish Cultural Studies*. Oxford: Oxford University Press.

Kelley, P., Buckingham, D. and Davies, H. (1999) 'Talking dirty: children, television and sexual knowledge'. *Childhood*, 6(2): 221–242.

Keys, W. and Buckingham, D. (eds) (1999) *International Perspectives on Children's Media Policy*. Special issue of *Media International Australia/Culture and Policy* 93.

Kinder, M. (1991) *Playing with Power in Movies, Television and Video Games*. Berkeley, CA: University of California Press.

Kline, S. (1993) *Out of the Garden: Toys and Children's Culture in the Age of TV Marketing*. London: Verso.

Kline, S. (1995) 'The empire of play: emergent genres of product-based animations'. In C. Bazalgette and D. Buckingham (eds) *In Front of the Children*. London, British Film Institute; 151–165.

Kline, S. (2003) 'Media effects: redux or reductive?' *Participations* 1(1) http://www.participations.org/volume%201/issue%201/1_01_kline_reply.htm [August 2007].

Kline, S., Dyer-Witheford, N. and de Peuter, G. (2003) *Digital Play: The Interaction of Technology, Culture and Marketing*. Montreal: McGill-Queens University Press.

Kubey, R. (1996) 'On not finding media effects: conceptual problems in the notion of an "active" audience'. In J. Hay, L. Grossberg and E. Wartella (eds) *The Audience and its Landscapes*. Boulder, CO: Westview; 187–205.

Kuhn, A. (2002) 'Children, "horrific" films and censorship in 1930s Britain'. *Historical Journal of Film and Television*, 22(2): 197–202.

Laybourne, G. (1993) 'The Nickelodeon experience'. In G.L. Berry and J.K. Asamen (eds), *Children and Television*. London: Sage.

Linn, S. (2004) *Consuming Kids: The Hostile Takeover of Childhood*. New York: New Press.

Lisosky, J. (2001) 'For *all* kids' sakes: comparing children's television policy-making in Australia, Canada and the United States'. *Media, Culture and Society*, 23(6): 821–845.

Lury, K. (2002) 'A time and place for everything: children's channels'. In D. Buckingham (ed.) *Small Screens: Television for Children*. Leicester: Leicester University Press; 15–37.

MacRobbie, A. (1991) *Feminism and Youth Culture*. London: Macmillan.

Marsh, J. (1999) 'Batman and Batwoman go to school: popular culture in the literacy curriculum'. *International Journal of Early Years Education*, 7(2): 117–131.

McQuillan, M. and Byrne, E. (1999) *Deconstructing Disney*. London: Pluto.

Melody, W. (1973) *Children's Television: The Economics of Exploitation*. New Haven, CT: Yale University Press.

Morley, D. (1980) *The Nationwide Audience: Structure and Decoding*. London: British Film Institute.

Morris, T. (2000) *You're Only Young Twice: Children's Literature and Film*. Urbana, IL: University of Illinois.

Murdock, G. (1997) 'Thin descriptions'. In J. McGuigan (ed.) *Cultural Methodologies*. London: Sage; 178–192.

Northam, J. (2005) 'Rehearsals in citizenship: BBC stop-motion animation programmes for young children'. *Journal of Cultural Research*, 9(3): 245–263.

Oswell, D. (2002) *Television, Childhood and the Home: A History of the Making of the Child Television Audience in Britain*. Oxford: Oxford University Press.

Palmer, P. (1986) *The Lively Audience*. Sydney: Allen and Unwin.

Phipps, A. (2000) *Contemporary German Cultural Studies* Oxford: Oxford University Press.

Potter, J. and Wetherell, M. (1987) *Discourse and Social Psychology*. London: Sage.

Richards, C. (1993) 'Taking sides? What young girls do with television'. In D. Buckingham (ed.) *Reading Audiences: Young People and the Media*. Manchester: Manchester University Press; 24–47.

Richards, C. (1998) *Teen Spirits: Music and Identity in Media Education*. London: UCL Press.

Rose, J. (1984) *The Case of Peter Pan: Or the Impossibility of Children's Fiction*. London: Macmillan.

Schott, G. and Horrell, K. (2000) 'Girl gamers and their relationship with the gaming culture'. *Convergence*, 6(4): 36–53.

Sefton-Green, J. (ed.) (1998) *Digital Diversions: Youth Culture in the Age of Multimedia*. London: UCL Press.

Seiter, E. (1993) *Sold Separately: Parents and Children in Consumer Culture*. New Brunswick, NJ: Rutgers University Press.

Seiter, E. (2005) *The Internet Playground: Children's Access, Entertainment and Mis-Education*. New York: Peter Lang.

Shannon, C.E. and Weaver, W. (1949) *The Mathematical Theory of Information*. Urbana, IL: University of Illinois.

Singer, D. and Singer, J. (2002) *Handbook of Children and the Media*. New York: Sage.

Smith, S. (2005) *Children, Cinema and Censorship: From Dracula to the Dead End Kids*. London: I.B. Tauris.

Staples, T. (1997) *All Pals Together: The Story of Children's Cinema*. Edinburgh: Edinburgh University Press.

Storey, J. (ed.) (1996) *What is Cultural Studies? A Reader*. London: Edward Arnold.

Tobin, J. (2004a) *Pikachu's Global Adventure: The Rise and Fall of Pokemon*. Durham, NC: Duke University Press.

Tobin, J. (2004b) 'Conclusion: the rise and fall of the Pokemon empire'. In J. Tobin (ed.) *Pikachu's Global Adventure: The Rise and Fall of Pokemon*. Durham, NC: Duke University Press; 257–292.

Tudor, A. (1999) *Decoding Culture*. London: Sage.

Turner, G. (2002) *British Cultural Studies: An Introduction*. London: Routledge.

Turow, J. (1981) *Entertainment, Education and the Hard Sell*. New York: Praeger.

Urwin, C. (1995) 'Turtle power: illusion and imagination in children's play'. In C. Bazalgette and D. Buckingham (eds) *In Front of the Children*. London, British Film Institute; 127–140.

Wasko, J. (2000) *Understanding Disney*. Cambridge: Polity.

Wasko, J., Phillips, M. and Meehan, E. (eds) (2001) *Dazzled by Disney?* London: Leicester University Press.

Wells, P. (2002) ' "Tell me about your id, when you was a kid, yah?" Animation and children's television culture'. In D. Buckingham (ed.) *Small Screens: Television for Children*. Leicester: Leicester University Press; 61–95.

Williams, R. (1958) *Culture and Society*. London: Chatto and Windus.

Williams, R. (1961) *The Long Revolution*. London: Chatto and Windus.

Willis, P. (1990) *Common Culture: Symbolic Work at Play in the Everyday Cultures of the Young*. Buckingham: Open University Press.

Wood, J. (1993) 'Repeatable pleasures: notes on young people's use of video'. In D. Buckingham (ed.) *Reading Audiences: Young People and the Media*. Manchester: Manchester University Press; 184–201.

14

The African Reception of Global Media

Larry Strelitz and Priscilla Boshoff

INTRODUCTION

This chapter engages debates concerning the impact of global media on local youth audiences in Africa. Recognizing the profound rootedness of media consumption in everyday life, the chapter specifically examines the way selected South African youth audiences, differentially embedded in their particular economic and ideological formations, use local and global media texts as part of their ongoing attempts to make sense of their lives. The chapter will point to the complex individual and social reasons that lie behind media consumption choices and will argue the deficiencies of the media imperialism thesis with its definitive claims for cultural homogenization, seen as the primary, or most politically significant, effect of the globalization of media. The latter part of this chapter gives a brief overview of some of the sparse but suggestive research conducted on youth and global media in other countries in Africa.

THE SOUTH AFRICAN SOCIAL AND POLITICAL CONTEXT

Despite the transition to democracy that followed the 1994 South African elections, the social effects of apartheid are very much still in evidence. (Leibrandt *et al.*, 2000: 31; Seeking, 2000: 53).[1]

The socio-economic inequalities in South Africa correspond largely, but not exclusively, to racial divisions, and huge disparities have opened among Africans.[2] As a result, South Africa is currently witnessing the emergence of a differentiated class structure among the African population, which includes a strong middle class and professional stratum, and a tiny economic elite. In other words, the country's income mal-distribution is increasingly shifting from being 'race' based to class based (Marais, 2001: 106).

Besides the racial and class divides in South Africa, another fundamental cleavage is that between 'modernity' and 'tradition', with some authors arguing that it ranks as the most fundamental, unresolved contradiction in much of post-colonial Africa (Marais, 2001: 303).[3]

South African youth

South Africa is thus a deeply divided society. These structural inequalities are reflected in the lives of young people – the focus of our research – in contemporary society.[4] Writing on the social and educational inequalities that exist amongst South African youth, van Zyl Slabbert *et al.* (1994: 56–60) have noted that social dynamics have placed most white South African youth in middle-class urban areas, quite distinct from the world of African youth. While van Zyl Slabbert *et al.* (1994: 57–58) distinguish between poor rural and urban middle-class Africans, they feel that, on the whole, theirs is a world of unemployment, poverty, high population growth rate, inadequate schooling and largely unavailable basic social amenities. Coloured and Indian youth in South Africa appear to be positioned between African and white youth. While we accept this, given the rapid changes in class composition that have occurred since the 1994 elections, it is no longer possible, as interviews below indicate, to identify clear 'racial' identities. For example, in many instances black middle-class youth have more in common with white middle-class youth, in some areas of their identities, than with black working-class and peasant youth.

THE MEDIA IMPERIALISM THESIS

It is within the above deeply divided and even contradictory socio-political scenario that media imperialism is said to operate and have its effects. The media imperialism thesis evolved to deal with questions which earlier theoretical international communications models generally ignored (Fejes, 1981: 281; Sreberny-Mohammadi, 1991: 119). Where the earlier models perceived modern media as tools for development, the media imperialism approach, by placing the media in a transnational context, viewed them as an obstacle to meaningful socio-economic progress. In essence, the thesis argues that the transnational media provide the necessary cultural context for the reception of Western countries' economic policies and thus serve Western economic and political interests (Fejes, 1981; Schiller, 1991: 14; Lemish *et al.*, 1998: 540; White, 2001).

A central tenet of the media imperialism thesis is that media globalization is resulting in global cultural homogenization or, according to Hamelink (1983: 3), an unprecedented 'cultural synchronisation'. As Lemish *et al.* (1998: 540) write: 'Globalisation has been perceived as a form of Western ethnocentric and patronising cultural imperialism, which invades local cultures and lifestyles, deepens the insecurities in indigenous identities and contributes to the erosion of national cultures and historical traditions'.[5]

'Authenticity' in local and global cultures

An assumption that runs consistently through the media imperialism thesis is that before the US-led media/cultural invasion, Third World cultures were largely untouched by outside influences (Tunstall, 1977: 57–59; Massey, 1992: 9; Thompson, 1995: 169; Hannerz, 1996: 66). This bipolar vision pits a culturally destructive and damaging 'global' against the 'local', with the latter seen as a site of 'pristine cultural authenticity' (Ang, 1996: 153).[6] As Morley (1994: 151) observes, the conventional model of cultural imperialism presumes 'the existence of a pure internally homogeneous, authentic, indigenous culture, which then becomes subverted or corrupted by foreign influence'.

However, as Morley (1994: 151) reminds us, 'every culture has ingested foreign elements from exogenous sources with the various elements becoming "naturalised" within it'. Cultural encounters (often backed by coercive political and military power) have, after all, been taking place for centuries, and as Appiah (2006) argues, hybridity and creolization have historically characterized adaptive, living cultures the world over. Given this, encounters between these societies and globalized forms of electronic media represent only the latest such cultural encounter.

The threat posed to national cultures by global media

A corollary to the refutation of the 'contamination' of 'pure' or 'authentic' local cultures by global media is the argument against the belief that contemporary forms of global media pose a major threat to 'national cultures' (Tomlinson, 1991: 68). This idea is so widespread that, over the years, it has profoundly influenced national media policies in a number of countries, including South Africa.[7]

However, as Tomlinson argues, it is difficult to define national cultures and relate these in any unproblematic way to the nation state because, as he notes, '... within nation-states, and even possibly across national boundaries, there exist patterns of cultural identification which are quite different from, and often in direct conflict with, the "national culture"' (Tomlinson, 1991: 68–69; see also Ang (1990: 252), Hall (1991b) and Ferguson (1992: 80)). Given the already-discussed deep social divisions in South Africa (both historical and current) along lines of 'race', class, tradition, and modernity, it is not surprising to find that a unified national identity does not exist.[8]

It is these existing social divisions, and the lack of a unified national identity, which give credence to Massey's (1992: 11–15) claim that places should no longer be seen as internally homogeneously bounded areas. She writes that we should see places as 'spaces of interaction' where local identities are constructed out of material and symbolic resources which may not be local in their origins, but should still be considered 'authentic' (Massey, 1992: 11–15). Similarly, Miller (1992: 164–165) writes that it is unproductive to think about cultural imperialism as a process in which a set of external or corrupting forces impinges on the pure sphere of the local, which must then be protected from their destructive influences. Rather, he believes, we should understand the ways in which people construct their identities from the symbolic resources at hand (including foreign media products), which are then subjected to a process of 'indigenization'. It is more useful, he argues, to assess these cultural resources in terms of their *consequences*, not their *origins* (Miller, 1992: 164–165).

One student interviewee, Mandela, grew up in the black urban township of Soweto during the 1980s at the height of the armed resistance to the apartheid regime. His parents were members of the then-banned African National Congress (ANC). In an interview, he discusses the resonance and authenticity that American rap music had for him during these turbulent times:

> There used to be a lady living in our street who was an MK [Umkonto weSizwe, the armed wing of the ANC] cadre. In fact, there used to be quite a lot [of MK operatives] because they used to come to our home and ask if they could sleep over for two days. I used to see these guys and my mom used to say, 'That guy can fire an AK' [the Russian-made rifle most often used by members of Umkonto weSizwe and synonymous with liberation struggles around the world] and I used to say like 'damn!' The thing is that Ice-Cube [a rap artist] and those guys from America wrote about AK 47s. And here was a guy in my house with a trench-coat and he's sleeping under the table, or some woman and she can fire an AK 47.

Thus, Mandela inserted the meanings of rap music into his experience of Soweto and his experience of Soweto into the meanings of rap music – each was influenced by and validated the other.

For many white students, on the other hand, their identification with Western/European culture (in South Africa the term 'European' is often applied to whites as a way of denoting their historical roots in Europe rather than Africa) means that it is foreign, rather than local media, which have a 'local' relevance. From her research into the uses and meanings of popular culture in the mid-1990s at newly multi-racial Fernwood High School in Natal, Dolby (1999: 298) argues that white middle-class students, instead of projecting a 'South African whiteness', 'cling to the styles and tastes of global whiteness, [specifically techno music], to consolidate an identity about which the feel and express passionate attachments'. Dolby (1999: 305) further argues that, throughout the school, popular culture does not merely reflect, but is actively constitutive of the dynamic, lived relations of race and class, and the consequent social groupings, that the students inhabit.

As Tomlinson (1991: 61) reminds us, media messages are mediated by other modes of cultural experience. Tomlinson (1991: 61) argues that we view the relationship between 'media' and 'culture' as a 'subtle interplay of mediations'. On the one hand, we have the media as the dominant representational aspect of modern culture; on the other hand, we have 'lived experience' of culture which may include the discursive interaction of families, friends, and peers and so on. As Tomlinson (1991: 61) notes, the relationship implied in this is the constant mediation of one aspect of cultural experience by another: what we make of a media text is influenced and shaped by what else is going on in our lives. Equally, he continues, our lives are lived as representations to ourselves in terms of the representations present in our culture. In other words, our biographies are, partly, 'intertextual'.

THE ETHNOGRAPHIC CRITIQUE OF THE MEDIA IMPERIALISM THESIS

The above discussion about 'authentic' local and nation cultures has brought into focus the need to examine more closely the particular and situated interactions between global cultural influences and local subjects. In recent years, a significant development in media studies has been the attempt by researchers to chart the sense that media consumers make of the texts and the technologies they encounter in everyday life (Stald and Tufte, 2002; Murphy and Kraidy, 2003). Drawing on qualitative research methods, this consideration of consumption practices represents, according to Moores (1993: 1), an 'ethnographic turn' in media studies. Skovmand and Schroder (1992: 3) note: 'The basic premise [of this approach] has been to try and understand popular cultural practices as meaningful activities: as part of people's ongoing attempts to make sense of their lives and the specific class, gender, race, and other identities they inhabit'.

This focus on the ongoing subjective 'use' of media products by consumers also underpins Thompson's (1995: 164–178) critique of the media imperialism thesis. According to Thompson (1995: 172), the thesis:

> fails to take account of the fact that the reception and appropriation of cultural phenomena are fundamentally hermeneutical processes in which individuals draw on material and symbolic resources available to them, as well as on the interpretative assistance offered by those with whom they interact in their day-to-day lives, in order to make sense of the messages they receive and to find some way of relating to them.

These observations by Skovmand and Schroder (1992) and Thompson (1995) are part of what Moores (1993: 1) has referred to as 'the ethnographic "turn"', and Murdock (1997: 179) as 'the "turn" towards interpretation' in media studies.

Central to the qualitative research into the local consumption of global media has been its highlighting of 'the complexity of the modes in which [American] cultural power is both exercized and resisted' (Morley, 1994: 143). Furthermore, empirical research into media consumption has led to the realization that the role that texts play in either helping to sustain or resisting existing relations of cultural power cannot be ascertained from the properties of the text alone. Rather, the texts need to be analysed *in situ*, in relation to the structured patterns of power, which they may (or may not) help to establish and sustain (Thompson, 1990: 56). Accordingly, at the centre of qualitative approaches to the investigation of textual reception is the appreciation that the social conditions of reception of symbolic forms are as important a moment in one's analysis as are the formal properties of the forms themselves. In line with this position, Ang (1996: 70) has called for a 'radical contextualism' in media studies which entails understanding the media's meanings for its audiences within the context of the 'multidimensional intersubjective networks in which the object is inserted and made to mean in concrete contextual settings'.

Within qualitative approaches to media consumption, this focus on the interplay between text and context in the production of meaning has provided an important corrective to the textual determinism underpinning the media imperialism thesis (Skovmand and Schroder, 1992). In particular, it has resulted in a re-examination of the claims for cultural homogenization and synchronization (Schiller, 1976; Hamelink, 1993) seen to follow in the wake of the spread of global (primarily American) media.

This chapter so far has outlined the media imperialism thesis and problematized its reputed power to affect local South African youth audiences: the always, already hybrid nature of South African culture in general, and the specific lack of a distinct national culture to be so influenced. The remaining sections of part one of this chapter look through the lens of the ethnographic approach in order to understand the nuanced readings of local and global media by particular South African youth audiences.

The uneven penetration of global media into local cultures

Global media are not necessarily attractive to local audiences, nor are they the only media consumed by such audiences. In his study of media consumption practices in Latin America, Straubhaar (1991: 51) coined the term 'cultural proximity' to describe the desire by the 'lower classes' to consume nationally or locally produced media that is more reinforcing of traditional identities. He further observed that this desire for 'cultural proximity' may not be as strong for elites, who seem much more internationalized, as dependency theory would predict (also see Abu-Lughod (1995)).

Straubhaar does not clarify what constitutes 'cultural proximity' for local audiences: it could refer to the use of language, the narrative construction or the thematic concerns of the text. But the concept is useful for the understanding of South African radio and television consumption patterns. For example, local music content averages for the public broadcaster radio services in South Africa indicate that the urban-based, English-language stations play a much lower percentage of local music than do the rural, indigenous-language stations. Two radio stations, 5 FM and Ukhozi FM, provide cases in point. Some 59% of 5 FM's listeners are white, while 99% of Ukhozi FM's listeners are black. According to the South African Broadcasting's 2003 annual report, 23% of the music played on 5 FM was local. By contrast, 80% of the music played on Ukhozi FM was of local content.[9]

What these statistics indicate is that the penetration of foreign cultural forms into local cultures is a far more complex process than the media-cultural imperialism thesis would predict. In some sectors of society the global media resonate with local audiences (although this still begs the question of the meanings audiences make of these media), while in other sectors of society the global media is less popular than local forms. This is not to deny that locally produced content does not sometimes follow imported Western generic structures. For example, in her discussion of the popularity of locally produced soap operas, Flockemann (2000: 143) notes that *Generations* 'deliberately employs the staple ingredients of American serials and soaps such as *Dallas* and *Dynasty* – corporate intrigue, love interests and "the family" as structural and thematic focus of plots and subplots'.

The 'homeland' students

Interviews conducted with African students, on the Rhodes University campus in Grahamstown, who come from rural working-class or peasant backgrounds, confirmed these national trends.[10] The research revealed that many of them relied on an 'empiricist' understanding of 'realism' (Ang, 1982: 36; Ellis, 1982: 6–7) – in that at the level of denotative meaning they sought a literal resemblance between the fictional world of the text and the 'real' world as they experienced it – in rejecting global media. This antipathy towards foreign television and film productions, a result of their lack of empirical realism, is evidenced in following extract from a focus group interview:[11]

> Andile: My personal response to *Isidingo* [a South African soap opera which at the time of viewing dealt primarily with the experiences of the black working class] is one that is informed by my background. The very fact that our fathers and brothers were working on the mines... they used to come back and talk and relate these stories to us. So now what is happening in *Isidingo* is the confirmation of that. So every time I see that setting I reflect back on those things they used to tell us... working at Iscor [steel refinery], things like that. Tribal conflicts, faction fights... within that setting. So it's a confirmation of those things that I used to hear.

These students believe that the majority of African middle-class students are no different to their white counterparts. They refer to them as 'coconuts': black on the outside but white on the inside. One of the most obvious signs of the perceived assimilation of middle-class African students into white culture is their preference for the English language, interpreted as a denial of traditional black culture. This is their perception of many South African black middle-class students, and also many black Zimbabwean students. As Michael noted, everything African middle class and (African) Zimbabwean students do 'is something that is done by whites... I've never seen them being proud of their (African) culture'.[12]

Their cultural isolation from the black and white middle-class students on campus is reflected in the fact that a number of the students from African working-class or peasant backgrounds prefer to watch television in their own viewing space, attached to one of the university residences, which they have named the 'homeland' (Strelitz, 2002b).[13] Every evening, with the regularity of the ritual it has become, 15 to 20 of these students gather to watch their favourite programmes. The viewing sessions start at 18:30, when they gather to watch *Isidingo*: the local African drama set on a goldmine. At 19:00 they disperse for supper in the residences, returning at 19:30 for the African-language news. At 20:00 they view a local black drama *Generations*, set in an advertising agency. At weekends they often meet to watch South African soccer. Missing from their daily television diet are any foreign productions.

The 'homeland', where only Xhosa is spoken, allows these students to interact with each other confidently, free from the ridicule of the better educated, more urbane, middle-class 'modern' students. In this space their traditional cultural identities are confirmed. It provides a haven from the threat of the 'modern'. Faced with an institutional culture in which they feel white and black middle-class norms dominate, they have felt the need to consolidate and signify their difference from such a culture and to reconfirm their traditional African identities. The nightly ritual of local television consumption in the 'homeland' is one of the means of achieving this. As Thompson (1995: 204) notes, migrant populations – these students have 'migrated' to Rhodes University – often display a strong quest for roots.[14]

Of significance is the fact that many of these students, before entering the 'alien' space of Rhodes University, were consumers of global media. Interviews revealed that, in many cases, within a rural context of reception, such media conveyed the 'promise of modernity'. Now, in contrast, within the context of Rhodes University, these students indicated a preference for local dramas which, they pointed out, raised issues of cultural concern for further discussion, which in turn helped solidify an identity rooted in traditional African culture.

The existence of the 'homeland' students provides not only an example of the rejection of global media by a sector of South African youth, but also lends some support to Ang's call that we need to understand the media's meanings for its audiences within the context of the 'multidimensional intersubjective networks in which the object is inserted and made to mean in concrete contextual settings' (Ang, 1996: 70). This approach, Ang (1996: 70) argues, entails a form of 'methodological situationalism', which recognizes the importance of context – from the macro context of South African to the micro context of Rhodes University – in trying to make sense of how people interact with the media in everyday life.

THE HYBRID INTERSECTION OF GLOBAL AND LOCAL

Not all South African youth see themselves as exclusively 'modern' or 'traditional' subjects. Many occupy a hybrid space, articulating their identities at a juncture between these two competing discourses. This hybridity of identity is reflected in a deep ambivalence towards global popular culture.

Kraidy (1999) describes a similar phenomenon in his research into the ways in which cultural identities are reconstructed by Christian Maronite youth in Lebanon at the intersection of global and local discourses. Kraidy (1999: 464) writes: 'An overriding concern among my interlocutors was their inability and unwillingness to exclusively belong to one or the other of what they saw as two irreconcilable worldviews'. Identifying the Arab world with tradition and the West with modernity, '...young Maronites articulated both discourses with the cultural matrices permeating their consumption of media and popular culture' (Kraidy, 1999: 464). The consumption of American television in the local cultural space of Christian Maronite youth both reflected and helped these young people to construct hybrid identities – caught between 'the West' and 'the Arabs', modernity and tradition.

The process, discussed by Kraidy (1999: 464), of simultaneous identification with two very different cultural traditions, was strongly evidenced in Strelitz's interviews with Indian students on campus. For many of these youth, the student culture of Rhodes University contrasted strongly with their more traditional and conservative family values and, as a result, they felt they had to continuously move back and forth between two very different sets of cultural expectation. This was clearly expressed by Amichad, a second-year pharmacy student from KwaZulu-Natal:

> Amichad: Rhodes has got to me. When I came here I had everything that I learnt at home and I embraced all my culture. In the first day that I came here I was faced with every single situation that went against everything that I believed in. But over the years I've learned to actually make a blend between what I believe in and what is here... I've made a negotiation... So we do our ritual prayers in our room and we go to the temple on Sundays, fasting at the appropriate time... and come to fun days, we take a break from our work and we go for it.

Depending on the dictates of their family cultures and religious traditions, students found it easier or more difficult to move between what they perceived to be as two irreconcilable sets of cultural expectations. Despite many of these students staying 'within the traditions' of their family cultures, many admitted to enjoying American teenage drama series, such as *Friends*. They were interested in the clothing the characters wore and the fact that it centred on the lives of young people: 'we can identify more because it's a young crowd... the things they speak about are things that we as teenagers can identify with'.

Multiple identities

This tension was reflected in the television consumption practices of the Indian interviewees, as many admitted to being drawn to programmes which promoted values at odds with those of their parental culture. A recurrent response was to deny the cultural significance of these programmes by dismissing them as 'mere entertainment' (and, therefore, as culturally insignificant). However, as the following interview extract illustrates, this neat separation of 'entertainment' from 'cultural significance' was often difficult for the students to sustain:

> Khavita: It's entertainment, I mean it's TV...it's not something you're going to live by... it doesn't affect our lifestyle.
> Kirti: It's nice to look. Just see like them wearing the short skirts or not wearing anything...like just

> covering the bare necessities. It's just nice to see the different ideas people have... Like I've been to a fashion show and it's nice to see the different ideas people have... yeah, how ridiculous people can be.

The simultaneous attraction and rejection of Western values expressed in Kirti's final statement – attracted to different expressions of fashion while at the same time rejecting such displays as 'ridiculous' – reflects the difficulty students face in attempting to reconcile the opposing pulls of tradition and modernity.[15] As Kraidy (1999: 166) found with his Maronite youth, the Indian students admitted to being 'entertained' by American media and attracted to certain of the values it espouses, while simultaneously remaining critical of the lack of social values they felt was evidenced in American culture; for example, what they viewed as excessive materialism and disrespect towards parents and the institution of marriage. This general antipathy towards American culture (when compared with their own traditional cultural values) by Indian students often translated into criticism of the values conveyed by American mass-mediated popular culture (which, however, they continued to consume). Indian students' simultaneous identification with traditional parental values and the Western youth values of youth-oriented American television dramas echoes Kraidy's (1999: 464) finding that Maronite youth displayed an inability and unwillingness to belong exclusively to one or other irreconcilable worldviews. Their experience reminds us that we are composed of multiple identities, that our subjectivities are 'nomadic' in that, as Fiske (1989: 24) has observed, we realign '[our] social allegiances into different formations...according to the necessities of the moment'. (Also see Hall (1991b: 57).)

Bollywood and the construction of a South African diasporic identity

Similar themes emerge in Boshoff's (2006) study of Indian students on the Rhodes University campus. South African Indians are mostly descendants of the British colonial labour diaspora of the late 19th and early 20th centuries (Bhana and Brain, 1990; Ebr.-Vally, 2001). Their social and political positions in South Africa as a visible but discriminated and marginalized minority group under colonial and apartheid governments has recently begun to change as young people take advantage of the discourse of multiculturalism promoted by the post-apartheid government:

> Radha: I mean, you remember your grandparents or great-grandparents did come from [India] but it's just, ja, South African. I think it's multicultural, multiracial, multi everything, it's quite an amazing place, I think.

Despite an unequivocal (thought not untroubled) allegiance to a South African national identity, interviews with Indian youth at Rhodes University by Boshoff (2006) support Strelitz's findings discussed earlier. They suggest that Indian youth are unwilling to abandon core cultural values despite exposure to Western ways of life and media. Away from the sureties of home and community life, Indian youth on Rhodes University campus engage in collective social and ritual activities in order to maintain a sense of 'home'. As Boshoff's (2006) study reveals, one of the ways in which they do this is by watching Bollywood movies. Ironically, the movies produced by the Mumbai movie industry are also accused of a kind of 'media imperialism', by promoting a form of 'diasporic nationalism' in tune with the modernizing project of recent conservative Indian governments. Bollywood's images of modern, cosmopolitan (yet traditional) youth of the Indian diaspora who return home to embrace the values of the Indian homeland are said to promote an idea of an essentialized middle-class Hinduism (Alessandrini, 2001; Gillespie and Cheesman, 2002; Rajadhyaksha, 2003). Boshoff's (2006) research indicates that Indian youth do use Bollywood images of young, 'modern', yet 'traditional' diasporic Indian subjects in order to represent to themselves a way of being both 'modern yet traditional'. However, the idea of a return to an Indian homeland is not what attracts these youth to the Bollywood movies. Rather, young Indians use Bollywood to teach themselves Hindi and to reflect on their local community values:

> Sanjay: The movies I like are family movies, they teach you family values like the movie *Bagbhan*... it teaches you family values that should happen normally in Indian family lives [in South Africa].

In addition, their imaginative participation in the international award ceremonies and concerts held in South Africa by the Bollywood industry has awakened an interest in their unique membership within a global community of diasporic Indians (rather than a desire to return to the motherland).

> Parveen: Before about 10 years ago Bollywood stars would come to South Africa once in a blue moon. Now it is huge... I can't even tell you how many Indian actors that I've read interviews with and heard them say they love this country, and many of them have established ties here... I think Bollywood is a big influence on South African society and South Africa's a big influence on the industry.

Indian students reproduce the songs and dances from popular movies in marked social and ritual occasions – for example, weddings, and the local 'Culture Show' staged by the Indian student society – and consciously reinforce a sense of belonging to a unique diasporic community. By incorporating Bollywood's dance, music and fashions into lived local culture, they are thus able both to draw affirmation from participation in a common cultural pool and to respond to international interest in, and acceptance of, a modern and highly fashionable entertainment phenomenon.

GLOBAL MEDIA AND THE PROCESS OF 'SYMBOLIC DISTANCING'

As we see, ambivalence reigns in the valuation and reception of global media. In his critique of the media imperialism thesis, Thompson (1995: 175) points out that part of the attraction of global media for local audiences is that their consumption often provides meanings which enable '... the accentuation of symbolic distancing from the spatial-temporal contexts of everyday life'. The appropriation of these materials, he further notes, enables individuals '... to take some distance from the conditions of their day-to-day lives – not literally but symbolically, imaginatively, vicariously' (Thompson, 1995: 175). Through this process, he writes, '[I]ndividuals are able to gain some conception, however partial, of ways of life and life conditions which differ significantly from their own' (Thompson, 1995: 175). Thus, global media images can provide a resource for individuals to think critically about their own lives and life conditions (Thompson, 1995: 175); for examples, see Deswaan (1989: 720), Appadurai (1990: 7), Morley (1992: 78), Davis and Davis (1995) and Hannerz (1996: 169).

Evidence of such symbolic distancing through the media emerged in a number of interviews conducted with youth. One such theme was the way American media representations of Afro-Americans helped puncture the 'reality' of being black in South Africa. In particular, these images provided young middle-class black students with role models of successful blacks: 'It was sort of like black people have suddenly become like white people... like a sense of freedom, inspiration'; '[B]efore, to be successful you had to be a white person. Now you see that blacks can also get the money'; 'It gives you a hope that if a black person is given a chance he can succeed in anything'. The media here provide a way to imagine a possible way of life that differs from the harsher realities of lived experience as black youth in South Africa.

Depictions of middle-class Afro-Americans may understandably resonate with middle-class black South African youth, but the process of symbolic distancing is not restricted to class. Khulani is a male student who grew up in a traditional community in KwaZulu-Natal, in a family which still adheres proudly to a particular way of life in which 'we use our cultural way of doing things. Everything is traditional'. This is a patriarchal culture, which obliges its members to adhere to formal ways of relating to family members, particularly the father:

> Khulani: I can't go to my father with any problems. I can ask from him, but only through my mother.

There was no television in the household when Khulani was growing up, as his father decided that Western media would be detrimental to their home culture. As a result, his first sustained exposure to Western culture came after he finished school and moved to Johannesburg to look for work. There, he lived in a men's hostel, where he avidly watched the American soap operas, *Days of Our Lives* and *The Bold and the Beautiful*:

> Khulani: What I saw [in *Days of Our Lives*] was so amazing actually because in our culture a girl can't approach you and say what she feels about you... I liked that programme because I learnt that everyone has got a right, if they feel strongly about something, to express it.

Soap operas not only provided a space for Khulani to consider more satisfying ways to conduct personal relationships, he also felt compelled by the soap operas' portrayals of parental relationships to reflect on what he felt were shortcomings in his own experience of relating to his father:

> Khulani: After watching these programmes, I realised that I should be allowed to speak to my father, he should be my friend rather than just my father... just to dismantle that wall of formality. I think that if we can adopt that, it will be great, because the manner in which we relate is not satisfactory at all.

Despite these deep impressions, the American media that Khulani consumed did not supplant or obliterate his Zulu identity, but rather caused shifts in perception and understanding in which traditional and Western values could coexist:

> Khulani: I feel I am a very strong Zulu man. I feel I know what is good for the Zulu nation. Our national will be very progressive and strong should we address those imbalances like having a woman just sit and care for her kids only. I will address those imbalances by starting with my own family and will talk with other people from my own culture.

Khulani's words remind us that Western culture does not constitute an indivisible package that is either adopted or rejected by local cultures. Rather, aspects of mediated Western culture are adopted while others are found irrelevant and are resisted (Tomlinson, 1991: 74). This is reflected in Khulani's rejection of certain aspects of Western culture which did not accord with respected Zulu values, such as beginning relationships too young and sending elderly relatives to old-age homes. It is also a reminder that foreign materials have a subversive, but potentially progressive, role by undermining the certainties of established national or local cultural hierarchies.

A further example of this was provided when Khulani matter-of-factly discussed the educative value pornographic movies have played for his friends in rural KwaZulu- Natal.

> Khulani: Some of my friends back home they like those blue movies. They like to explore new ways of making love and all that. That's something that is not there in our culture because a woman is expected to just lie back and a man must do his thing. But guys back home, they like to get the woman involved as well.

For Khulani we see that the 'progressive' meanings he derived from American soaps and the pornographic movies derived from the interplay between the context of reception and the formal properties of the text (while, for other audiences, the meanings derived might be culturally and politically regressive). Morley (1994) argues that one of the problems with this 'defensive' model of resistance to foreign cultural imperialism concerns the fact that the 'foreign' should not be necessarily equated with cultural regression. It can be argued, he believes, that 'foreign' materials often play a subversive (and potentially progressive) role, by undermining the certainties of established national or local cultural hierarchies (Morley, 1994; Ang, 1987).

What we also witness in Khulani's interview is the role played by Western media as *carriers of modernity* (Berger *et al.*, 1973). Berger *et al.* (1973: 15) argue that while modernization can be defined as the 'growth of a set of institutions rooted in the transformation of the economy by means of technology', these then give rise to a set of discourses and ways of seeing the world – the 'modern world view' (Berger *et al.*, 1973: 43) – which is diffused through a multiplicity of channels (and here the media play a central role) and which is no longer dependent upon any direct connection with the actual processes of technological production. Thus, they write that: 'Like other fully developed world views, the world view of modernity takes on a dynamic of its own' (Berger *et al.*, 1973: 43).

ASSESSMENT: THE LOCAL AND THE GLOBAL

Khulani's understanding of how global media products have transformed aspects of his life show that the 'essentialist' approach to the globalization of the media is not necessarily an accurate description of consumers' experience (Morley, 1992: 77). Gripsrud (1995: 9) notes the need for media theorists to develop 'more nuanced ideas about how socio-cultural structures and forces on the one hand and individuals and their minds and choices on the other work in relation to each other in the reception of media texts'. Accepting both the cognitive and the cultural provides us with a more complex picture of how media are incorporated into the lives of individual consumers. The meanings that 'global' and 'local' media take on for individual consumers are more subtle than their textual content alone would suggest.

Our research has led us to agree with Bonfadelli (1993: 232), that media use and competency has to be perceived as the result of biographical experience with various media and that these processes are embedded in the ecological contexts of family, neighbourhood, school and so on. The interview evidence leads us to consider that global media, far from producing homogenized audiences, itself becomes part of the many kinds of materiel whereby local subjectivities are forged (Appadurai, 1996; Nuttall and Michael, 1999; Savage *et al.*, 2004). The rich symbolic resources of global media flows are woven into the construction of particular localities and local identities: as Appiah (2006: 3) comments, 'globalisation can produce homogeneity. But globalisation is also a threat to homogeneity'.

Nuttall's (2004) exploration of the forms of 'Y' (youth) culture in contemporary Johannesburg is an apt illustration of this argument. Nuttall points to the way in which black middle-class youth, in their self-conscious search for an idiom of the modern (and future) South Africa, both appropriate and resist (and remake) local and foreign (US) urban visual, sartorial and music culture. The 'delicate balance between actual emerging lifestyles of middle class black youth and the politics of aspiration' (Nuttall, 2004: 439) has resulted in a unique 'stylizing of the self', an accessorization of the body that, Nuttall (2004: 449) argues, 'represents one of the most decisive shifts of the post-apartheid era'.

OTHER AFRICAN RESEARCH

The findings above with regard to South African responses to international media are, interestingly, borne out quite independently by much of the (albeit limited) research conducted thus far with widely differing local youth audiences upon the broader African continent.[16] These investigations fall into two broad sections: those influenced by the media imperialism thesis and others which engage with more or less ethnographic interpretations of what young people do with foreign media.

Media imperialism and the globalization of youth culture are cited as motivating academic research to protect the 'African' identities of local youth. Lloyd and Mendez's (2001) quantitative study of the consumption of American music videos by Botswana youth, however, leaves unasked the many important questions that arise from the actual complex socio-cultural milieu within which such local youth watch music videos and incorporate particular aspects of their imagery into their lives. Research premised on such *a priori* interventionist objectives – effectively, a self-appointed cultural guardianship – would perhaps benefit by adopting a less essentialized understanding of local African cultures and a greater openness to the immense variety (and changing nature) of the 'traditions' by which they are partly characterized (Appiah, 2006). Such a stance is advocated by Nyamnjoh (2002: 49), who argues that 'as researchers, we must … be creative, negotiating, dynamic and realistic in attributing Africanity to the children we study'.

Studies by Davis and Davis (1995) in Morocco and Assefa (2005) in Ethiopia exemplify the advantages of employing the ethnographic method in media research. Both deal with global media consumption and the engagement by youth audiences in the 'symbolic distancing' which this affords. Both emphasize the importance of the local conditions of reception, and argue that superficial similarities in media exposure '*suggest* a universal experience mediated by Western television, films and popular music – but it prove[s] difficult to establish that [all] youth [are] in fact using these media in similar ways' (Davis and Davis 1995: 578, emphasis added). Their research findings bear out this claim by emphasizing the particularities of the local cultural context within which reception takes place.

In the Moroccan study, global media are not necessarily more popular than local content: Davis and Davis (1995: 590, italics in original) state that about half both male and female youth prefer to watch '*both* Arab and Western programmes'. Although television consumption has a gendered dimension, with men having more private access to a variety of media than women, Davis and Davis point out that the overall effect for both young men and women has been a re-imagining of their social selves:

> The rapidly expanding array of media was used by adolescents in a period of rapid social change to re-imagine many aspects of their lives, including a desire for more autonomy, for more variety in heterosexual interactions, and for more choice of a job and a mate (Davis and Davis, 1995: 578).

As was discussed earlier in this chapter, re-imagining does not necessarily mean enacting: local youth, especially women, by and large respect and conform to local customs and religious values, despite their vicarious and imaginative participation in alternative ways of life through the media: 'young women are "caught between several worlds whose borders the new media technologies can cross but most individual lives cannot"' (Abu-Lughod, 1995: 47, in Davis and Davis (1995: 592)).

Davis and Davis (1995) and Assefa (2005) similarly emphasize the importance of the local socio-cultural milieu. Assefa locates her study within the post-1991 urban context, and interprets the communal consumption of American action movies by unemployed male youth in informal video houses as a means of simultaneously affirming a masculine identity while protesting against their social alienation from normative patriarchal culture. A marginal youth identity in opposition to authority is created by consciously attending screenings in these illegal video houses. They become a space for the operation of an 'oppositional semiosis' (Fiske, 1989: 83–84), a counter-hegemonic male youth culture that speaks to the deprivations and limitations of their lives (Assefa, 2005: 75).

Examined from within this socio-economic context, American action movies cannot be seen simply as agents of Western cultural imperialism. Assefa (2005: 73) shows that, although American movies are symbolic "carriers of modernity", Ethiopian youth are easily able to distinguish between the representation of life in the West and its (in)appropriateness to their own lived reality. Similar to findings by Strelitz (2002b), and Davis and Davis (1995), Assefa concludes that global media have an uneven penetration into local culture, as the meanings that the youth made of action films are differentiated according to their various lived realities.

CONCLUSION

Locating itself within the qualitative research tradition, what we have referred to as the ethnographic critique of the media imperialism thesis, this chapter has highlighted the deficiencies of this thesis with its definitive claims of cultural homogenization as the most politically significant effect of the globalization of media. The focus on the interplay between text and context in the production of meaning provides an important corrective to the textual determinism underpinning this thesis. Furthermore, such an approach recognizes that the social conditions of reception by youth of symbolic forms are as important a moment in one's analysis as are the formal properties of the forms themselves. As Ang (1996: 70) argues in calling for a 'radical contextualism' in media studies, we need to understand the media's meanings for its youth audiences within the context of the 'multidimensional intersubjective networks in which the object is inserted and made to mean in concrete contextual settings'.

NOTES

1 Statistical indicators show the racial dimension of poverty and inequality in South Africa: 95% of the very poor are African and 5% are Coloured (mixed race). Poverty has a rural dimension, with 75% of the poor living in rural areas. Poverty also has an age dimension, with 45% of the poor being children below the age of 15 (Jennings *et al.*, 1997: 8). Some 49% of African youth live in households that at some point during 1994–1995 were unable to feed their children. This applies to 35% of Coloured youth, 11% of Indian and 6% of White youth (Jennings *et al.*, 1997: 23). Similar ratios are borne out by life expectancy rates amongst the different population groups. For the years 1996 to 2001, the average life expectancy for Africans is 64.5 years, for Indians 70.2 years, for Coloureds 64.4 years and for Whites 73.6 years (SAIRR, 2003).

2 Marais (2001:106) points out that the mean income of the lowest-earning 40% of African households declined by almost 40% between 1975 and 1991, while that of the richest 20% of African households rose by 40%. Subsequently, African professionals, skilled workers and entrepreneurs benefited from the collapse of apartheid making them the most upwardly mobile 'race' group.

3 Millions of rural inhabitants still live under local chiefs, operating under customary law (Marias, 2001: 3). There have been ongoing disputes between the ANC-led government and the Congress of Traditional Leaders of South Africa (Contralesa) over the place of traditional culture, norms, and customs, and the role of traditional (non-elected) leaders in post-apartheid South Africa in their traditional rural strongholds (e.g. see Gevisser (1996: 14)). Thus, for example, at the 1992 Convention for a Democratic South Africa (Codesa) negotiations at the Johannesburg World Trade Centre, Contralesa's delegations insisted on exemptions for customary law and from gender equality clause in the Bill of Rights (Gevisser, 1996: 14).

4 In South Africa, the problems of the definition of youth are especially acute. According to van Zyl Slabbert *et al.* (1994: 12), the unstable socio-political conditions in South Africa have made any attempt at gaining conceptual clarity when talking about youth '... a frustrating and enigmatic exercise'. They write:

> Whilst it is trite to say that life itself is a process and not an event, this observation gets specific meaning when one tries to pin down youth as a social category. Infancy, adulthood, old age, marriage, birth, death are concepts that enable us to identify clear patterns of social interaction and institutional organisation. In relatively stable societies, organised education provides the best arena in which to explore the transient characteristics of youth; but in unstable, unequal and deeply polarised and divided societies, problems in educational organisation very often add to the difficulties in coming to grips with youth as a social category (van Zyl Slabbert *et al.*,1994: 12).

Because of these considerations, these authors advocate adopting the broadest possible definition of youth, namely to South Africans of all population groups between 15 and 30 years of age. The authors admit that this conceptual definition of youth is much more one of operational convenience than of any philosophical substance (van Zyl Slabbert *et al.*, 1994: 13). However, as they note, this broad definition '... enables us to cluster and clarify research results which relate to young people who fall in this age category and who, from different points of view, and for varying purposes, are referred to as "youth"' (van Zyl Slabbert *et al.*, 1994: 13).

The broad definition of youth is echoed in the National Youth Commission Act (No. 19 of 1996), which takes into account the fact that people between the ages of 25 and 30 bore the brunt of the recent political struggles in South Africa in the 1970s and 1980s. The National Youth Commission (NYC), therefore, defines the range of youth from 14 to 35 (NYC, 1997: 7). In my own research I interviewed students aged between 18 and 24.

5 Whether media imperialism is a result of 'inevitable' market laws, unaffected by ideological motives, or whether it needs to be seen as a deliberate political and ideological process is open to dispute amongst theorists (Biltereyst, 1995: 4).

Biltereyst (1995: 4) refers to these as the 'free-market' and 'dependency' paradigms respectively.

6 Similarly, Hannerz (1989: 70), Kraidy (1999: 459), and Thompson (1995: 170) point to the romanticism inherent in this purist position.

7 For a discussion of the impact that such assumptions have had on European media policy, see Schlesinger (1991, 1993). As Baines (1998: 2) points out, the South African Independent Broadcasting Authority's (IBA) 1994 report on the need for local content quotas in South African media was premised on the need to preserve South Africa's national cultural identity.

8 One reason is the lack of a sense of common descent, culture and language necessary for the creation of a communal/national culture (Degenaar, 1994: 23). Another is the primordial view of ethnic identity promoted by segregationist and apartheid ideologies and social policies which created a divided society (Steenveld and Strelitz, 1998: 610). The discourse of 'nation-building' and the image of the 'rainbow nation' much in evidence after the first democratically held elections in 1994 reflected the desire amongst politicians and social theorists to create a composite national identity. Such an identity, it was felt, would help South Africa transcend its deep social divisions and the ongoing and yet-to-be resolved internal conflict of who is and is not 'African'.

9 There are distinct class and race dimensions to these statistics: 70% of 5 FM's listeners earn R4000 or more a month compared with 10% of Ukhozi FM's listeners. In fact, over one-third of Ukhozi FM's listeners earn less than R500 a month. While there are no specific figures for an urban/rural split in listenership, we can get some indication if we take into account that 81% of 5 FM listeners live in communities of 40,000 or more, while the corresponding figure for Ukhozi FM is 39%. In fact, over half (53%) of Ukhozi FM's listeners live in communities of less than 500 in size. It appears that local music has a strong resonance for rural, black, relatively poor and ill-educated South Africans, while the opposite is true for white, urban, well-educated and relatively affluent South Africans. The national broadcaster, SABC, reports similar trends in television viewing practices (SAARF, 2002).

10 At the time of research, Rhodes University, Grahamstown, had 4,411 registered students: Indian (10%), African (36%), Coloured (4%) and White (50%). This despite the fact that African students make up 83% of the total school population in South Africa. The historical reason for this anomaly lies in the poorly funded Apartheid era 'Bantu' education system, administered by the Department of Education and Training (DET). Most Black South African students are still schooled within the old Apartheid school system, with disastrous consequences: in 1996, only 12% of African students passed grade 12, compared with 41% of Whites (SAIRR, 1999).

11 According to Ang (1982: 36),'empiricist realism' is cognitively based and works primarily at the level of denotative meaning, in which a literal resemblance is sought between the fictional world of the text and the 'real' world as experienced by the audience member. Judgements are made accordingly, and as Ang (1982: 36) explains, '...a text which can be seen as an "unrealistic" rendering of social reality (however that is defined) is "bad"'.

12 Because the Zimbabwean students are not eligible for bursaries at South African universities, the majority tend to come from middle-class families who can afford the fees.

13 Apartheid was premised on the classification of people into different race groups and their segregation into different residential areas, educational systems and public amenities. Under this policy, the reserves, known as Bantustans or the Homelands, saw land, which had been set aside in 1913 and 1936 (by the 1913 Land Act and the 1936 Native Land and Trust Act), consolidated into 10 ethnic geo-physical units. These 'national states' were the only places where Africans were allowed to exercise political and economic 'rights' (Stadler, 1987: 34). Disenfranchised from the South African state, it was here that Africans were supposed to express their political, economic and cultural aspirations – no longer as South Africans, but as citizens of these independent states. However, since the first national democratic elections in 1994, the ANC-led government has promoted the idea of a unified South African national identity (Steenveld and Strelitz, 1998). The voluntary return to a symbolic 'homeland' by these students, and their rejection of foreign television, therefore, signifies the students' continuing sense of 'disenfranchisement' on the campus of Rhodes University.

14 As Thompson (1995: 204) points out, the appeal of the quest for roots is that it offers a way of recovering and, indeed, inventing traditions which reconnect individuals to (real or imaginary) places of origin.

15 See Fiske (1987: 175) for a discussion of the process of simultaneous attraction and rejection of Western values by non-Western audiences, and Song (2003) for the complex personal and intra-communal negotiations that surround the changes implied by the adoption of Western value systems.

16 Web-based searches on the Rhodes University library electronic database http://www.ru.ac.za/library/electronic_resources/ in March 2006 reveal few articles on the intersecting topics of African youth, global media and local culture (and none on children *per se*). Much more research has been conducted into the effects of *local* media production on youth culture, especially local 'edutainment' programmes aimed at educating youth about HIV/AIDS (e.g. see Barnett (2002)).

REFERENCES

Abu-Lughod, L. (1995) 'The objects of soap opera: Egyptian television and the cultural politics of modernity'. In D. Miller (ed.) *Worlds Apart: Modernity through the Prism of the Local.* London: Routledge; 190–210.

Alessandrini, A. (2001) ' "My heart's Indian for all that": Bollywood film between home and diaspora'. *Diaspora,* 10(3): 315–340.

Ang, I. (1982) *Watching Dallas: Soap Opera and the Melodramatic Imagination.* London: Routledge.

Ang, I. (1987) 'The vicissitudes of "progressive television"'. *New Formations,* 2: 91–106.

Ang, I. (1990) 'Culture and communication: towards an ethnographic critique of media consumption in the transnational media system'. *European Journal of Communication,* 5: 239–260.

Ang, I. (1996) *Living Room Wars: Rethinking Media Audiences for a Postmodern World.* London: Routledge.

Appadurai, A. (1990) 'Disjuncture and difference in the global cultural economy'. *Public Culture,* 2(2): 1–24.

Appadurai, A. (1996) *Modernity at Large.* Minneapolis, MN: University of Minnesota Press.

Appiah, K.A. (2006) 'The case for contamination'. *The New York Times,* Magazine, 1 January. http://select.nytimes.com/gst/abstract.html?res=FB0812F839540C728CDDA80894DE404482 [13 March 2006].

Assefa, E. (2005) An investigation into the popularity of American action movies shown in informal video houses in Addis Ababa, Ethiopia. MA thesis, Rhodes University, Grahamstown, South Africa.

Baines, G. (1998) 'National identity, cultural policy and popular music in the "new" South Africa'. Unpublished paper, Rhodes University, Grahamstown, South Africa.

Barnett, C. (2002) ' "More than just TV": educational broadcasting and popular culture in South Africa'. In C. von Feilitzen and U. Carlsson (eds) *Children, Young People and Media Globalisation.* Gothenburg: Nordicom/The UNESCO International Clearinghouse on Children, Youth and Media; 95–110.

Berger, P.L., Berger, B. and Kellner, H. (1973) *The Homeless Mind.* New York: Penguin.

Bhana, S. and Brain, J. (1990) *Setting Down Roots: Indian Migrants in South Africa, 1860–1911.* Johannesburg: Witwatersrand University Press.

Biltereyst, D. (1995) 'Qualitative audience research and transnational media effects: a new paradigm'. *European Journal of Communication,* 10(2): 245–270.

Bonfadelli, H. (1993) 'Adolescent media use in a changing media environment'. *European Journal of Communication,* 8: 225–256.

Boshoff, P. (2006) Diasporic consciousness and Bollywood. South African Indian youth and the meanings they make of Indian film. MA thesis, Rhodes University, Grahamstown, South Africa.

Davis, S.S. and Davis, D.A. (1995) 'The mosque and the satellite: media and adolescence in a Moroccan town'. *Journal of Youth and Adolescence,* 24(5): 577–593.

Degenaar, J. (1994) 'Beware of nation building'. In N. Rhoodie and I. Liebenberg (eds) *Democratic Nation-Building in South Africa.* Pretoria: HSRC Publishers; 23–30.

Deswaan, A. (1989) 'Platform Holland: Dutch society in the context of global cultural relations'. *International Spectator,* 43(11): 718–722.

Dolby, N. (1999) 'Youth and the global popular. The politics and practices of race in South Africa'. *European Journal of Cultural Studies,* 2(3): 291–309.

Ebr.-Vally, R. (2001) *Kala Pani: Caste and Colour in South Africa.* Cape Town: Kwela Books.

Ellis, J. (1982) *Visible Fictions.* London: Routledge and Kegan Paul.

Fejes, F. (1981) 'Media imperialism: an assessment'. *Media, Culture and Society,* 3(3): 281–289.

Ferguson, M. (1992) 'The mythology about globalisation'. *European Journal of Communication,* 7: 69–93.

Fiske, J. (1989) *Understanding Popular Culture.* Boston, MA: Unwin Hyman.

Flockemann, M. (2000) 'Watching soap opera'. In S. Nuttall and C.-A. Michael (eds) *Senses of Culture: South African Culture Studies.* Oxford: Oxford University Press; 141–154.

Gevisser, M. (1996) 'That other Holomisa'. *Mail and Guardian,* 13 September; 14.

Gillespie, M. and Cheesman, T. (2002) 'Media cultures in India and the South Asian diaspora'. *Contemporary South Asia,* 11(2): 127–133.

Gripsrud, J. (1995) *The Dynasty Years: Hollywood Television and Critical Media Studies.* London: Routledge.

Hall, S. (1991) 'Old and new identities, old and new ethnicities'. In A.D. King (ed.) *Culture, Globalisation and the World System.* London: Macmillan; 41–69.

Hamelink, C.J. (1983) *Cultural Autonomy in Global Communications.* New York: Longman.

Hamelink, C.J. (1993) 'Globalism and national sovereignty'. In K. Nordenstreng and H.I. Schiller (eds) *Beyond National Sovereignty: International Communication in the 1990s.* Norwood, NJ: Abex Publishing; 371–393.

Hannerz, U. (1989) 'Notes on the global ecumene'. *Public Culture,* 1(2): 66–75.

Hannerz, U. (1996) *Transnational Connections: Culture, People, Places.* London: Routledge.

Jennings, R., Evaratt, D., Lyle, A. and Budlender, D. (eds) (1997) *The Situation of Youth in South Africa*. Johannesburg: Community Agency for Social Enquiry (CASE).

Kraidy, M.M. (1999) 'The global, the local and the hybrid: a native ethnography of glocalisation'. *Critical Studies in Mass Communication*, 16: 456–476.

Leibrandt, M., Woolard, I. and Bhorat, H. (2000) 'Understanding contemporary household inequality in South Africa'. *Studies in Economics and Econometrics*, 24(3): 31–51.

Lemish, D., Drotner, K., Liebes, T., Maigret, E. and Stald, G. (1998) 'Global culture in practice: a look at children and adolescents in Denmark, France and Israel'. *European Journal of Communication*, 13(4): 539–556.

Lloyd, B.T. and Mendez, J.L. (2001) 'Botswana adolescents' interpretation of American music videos: so that's what that means!' *Journal of Black Psychology*, 27(4): 464–76.

Marais, H. (2001) *South Africa: Limits to Change: the Political Economy of Transition*. Cape Town: University of Cape Town Press.

Massey, D. (1992) 'A place called home'. *New Formations*, 17: 3–15.

Miller, D. (1992) 'The young and the restless in Trinidad'. In R. Silverstone and E. Hirsch (eds) *Consuming Technologies: Media Information and Domestic Space*. London: Routledge; 163–182.

Moores, S. (1993) *Interpreting Audiences: The Ethnography of Media Consumption*. London: Sage.

Morley, D. (1992) 'Electronic communities and domestic rituals: cultural consumption and the production of European cultural identities'. In M. Skovmand and K.C. Schroder (eds) *Media Cultures: Reappraising Transnational Media*. London: Routledge.

Morley, D. (1994) 'Postmodernism: the highest stage of cultural imperialism'. In M. Perryman (ed.) *Altered States: Postmodernism, Politics, Culture*. London: Lawrence and Wishart.

Murdock, G. (1997) 'Thin descriptions: questions of method in cultural analysis'. In J. McGuigan (ed.) *Cultural Methodologies*. London: Sage.

Murphy, P.D. and Kraidy, M.M. (eds) (2003) *Global Media Studies. Ethnographic Perspectives*. London: Routledge.

Nuttall, S. (2004) 'Stylizing the self: the Y generation in Rosebank, Johannesburg'. *Public Culture*, 16(3): 430–452.

Nuttall, S. and Michael, C.A. (1999) 'Re-imagining South African Cultural Studies'. *African Sociological Review*, 3(2): 54–68.

Nyamnjoh, F.B. (2002) 'Children, media and globalisation: a research agenda for Africa'. In C. von Feilitzen and U. Carlsson (eds) *Children, Young People and Media Globalisation*. Gothenburg: Nordicom/The UNESCO International Clearinghouse on Children, Youth and Media; 43–52.

NYC (1997) *Youth Policy 2000*. Pretoria: National Youth Commission.

Rajadhyaksha, A. (2003) 'The "Bollywoodization" of the Indian cinema: cultural nationalism in a global arena'. *Inter-Asia Cultural Studies*, 4(1): 25–39.

SAARF (2002) *All Media and Products Survey: Amps 2002a*. Johannesburg: South African Advertising Research Foundation.

SAIRR (1999) *South African Survey 1998/9*. Johannesburg: South African Institute of Race Relations.

SAIRR (2003) *South African Survey 2002/3*. Johannesburg: South African Institute of Race Relations.

Savage, M., Bagnall, G. and Longhurst, B.J. (2004) *Globalization and Belonging*. London: Sage.

Schiller, H.I. (1976) *Communication and Cultural Domination*. New York: M.E. Sharpe.

Schiller, H.I. (1991) 'Not yet the post-imperialist era'. *Critical Studies in Mass Communication*, 8: 13–28.

Schlesinger, P. (1991) *Media, State and Nation: Political Violence and Collective Identities*. London: Sage.

Schlesinger, P. (1993) 'Wishful thinking: cultural politics, media and collective identities in Europe'. *Journal of Communication*, 43(2): 6–17.

Seeking, J. (2000) 'Visions of society: peasants, workers and the unemployed in a changing South Africa'. *Studies in Economics and Econometrics*, 24(3): 53–71.

Skovmand, M. and Schroder, K.C. (eds) (1992) *Media Cultures: Reappraising Transnational Media*. London: Routledge.

Song, M. (2003) *Choosing Ethnic Identity*. Cambridge: Polity Press.

Sreberny-Mohammadi, A. (1991) 'The global and the local in international communications'. In J. Curran and M. Gurevitch (eds) *Mass Media and Society*. London: Edward Arnold; 93–119.

Stadler, A. (1987) *The Political Economy of Modern South Africa*. Cape Town: David Philip.

Stald, G. and Tufte, T. (eds) (2002) *Global Encounters: Media and Cultural Transformation*. Luton: University of Luton Press.

Steenveld, L. and Strelitz, L. (1998) 'The 1995 Rugby World Cup and the politics of nation-building in South Africa'. *Media, Culture and Society*, 20(4): 609–629.

Straubhaar, J.D. (1991) 'Beyond media imperialism: asymmetrical interdependence and cultural proximity'. *Critical Studies in Mass Communication*, 8: 39–59.

Strelitz, L. (2002) 'The "homeland" students: identity formation and cultural consumption'. In T. Tufte and G. Stald (eds) *Global Encounters: Media and*

Cultural Transformation. Luton: University of Luton Press; 151–172.

Thompson, J.B. (1990) *Ideology and Modern Culture*. Stanford: Stanford University Press.

Thompson, J.B. (1995) *The Media and Modernity: A Social Theory of the Media*. Cambridge: Polity Press.

Tomlinson, J. (1991) *Cultural Imperialism*. London: Pinter Publishers.

Tunstall, J. (1977) *The Media are American*. London: Constable.

Van Zyl Slabbert, F., Malan, C., Marais, H., Olivier, J. and Riordan, R. (eds) (1994) *Youth in the New South Africa*. Pretoria: HSRC.

White, L.A. (2001) 'Reconsidering cultural imperialism theory'. *Transnational Broadcasting Studies*, 6: 1–17.

15

Let the World In! Globalization in Greenland

Jette Rygaard

INTRODUCTION

When a female student graduates from Ilisimatusarfik (the University of Greenland), she receives her diploma in her richly coloured traditional costume and receives a beautiful bouquet of flowers, in a country which, for the greater part, is covered by inland ice and the remainder is above the timberline. Her parents snap her photograph with their digital *Nikon*. And barely has the ceremony ended before she is sending SMSs with her *Sony Ericsson* cell phone to friends to make reservations for the night's party at the Thai restaurant where the New Zealand white wine goes well with the Greenlandic sushi. Later, at the discothèque *Manhattan*, she dances in her *Replay* designer jeans, a diminutive sealskin top and her *Nike* shoes to the DJ's music from the local band *Chilly Friday*, the German *Rammstein* or the American *Marilyn Manson*. Her drink is mixed with *Coca-Cola*. The taxi that takes her home is a *Toyota* 4WD. In her weekly paper she reads about global warming threatening to melt the icecap, the hole in the ozone layer making the strong Arctic sun dangerous or the pollution having degenerative effects on polar bears and marine mammals. Every day she 'meets' her friends in cyberspace on the Danish web-meeting place Arto.dk, where she refines her profile to become a 100% VIP or she surfs or e-mails via Microsoft Messenger. With a certain familiarity, she feels at home watching American films and TV series. Her little brother, anxious to get to Denmark on a school exchange in 2005, was forced to stay behind because of her parents' fear of riots in repercussion for the Danish so-called 'cartoon crisis'.[1] Instead, he had to console himself with the television series *24*(2001–). The memory of the 9/11 terror is still much on her mind, especially since she experienced standing at the Ground Zero monument in New York in spring 2005, as part of the promotional campaign *A Greenlandic Week* held at the Smithsonian Institute in Washington, DC.

In lifestyle and consumerism, the marriage of globalization and traditionalism seems to be rather unproblematic in Greenland, as demonstrated by the above example. Among the top 20 global/American (Kjeldgaard: 2004: 213) brands, we here recognize the three that usually score exceptional high: Nike, Coca-Cola and Sony. The local papers revel in the buzzword 'globalization' as a new way to describe Greenland *vis-à-vis* the world. But if you try googling the Greenlandic word for globalization – *nunarsuarmioqataaneq*,[2] meaning 'making something world-embracing' – you get only 26 hits gleaned from speeches made by the former Minister of Culture,[3] yet globalization is all-pervasive in everyday life in Greenland: in its goods, products, merchandise, culture products, news and media, which attracts young people to surf, study or travel abroad in the world and in cyberspace surrounding the enormous island, and to adapt themselves to real life via the socializing effects of the Internet.

Greenland, on the other hand, is in some aspects barely on the global map. If you want to buy goods from some World Wide Web site, like *Amazon.com*, you cannot choose Greenland as a country, but have to register yourself as residing in Denmark: the postal code DK3900 is Nuuk![4] Furthermore, when you wait for transportation to Denmark in the airport at Kangerlussuaq, you can divert yourself with dreaming of such faraway places as The North Pole, Paris, Moscow and Frankfurt where you can arrive in around 5 hours time by airplane. The sky above you is roaring with airplanes; however, all routes pass it by! What a young female student replied when I asked her in a 2006 survey about Greenland's relation to the world seems true: 'Most confined! The rest of the world does not know much about Greenland, but we know a lot of the global world' (woman, Nuuk, 27).

In the following, I will focus on some cultural aspects of globalization as seen through the eyes of young people in Greenland. We will listen to their statements in Rap music, their opinions of Greenland as a global partner in the world, and we will examine their tastes and preferences in the three-course (American, Danish and Greenlandic) media dinner served on their local table. Finally, we will see how they use their time in relation to media habits, listen to their travel wishes, and close by asking how all this global and local interconnectedness affects their self-image.

Because young people do not exist in a vacuum, I will touch upon a few features of Greenland's history in, and with, the world. Greenland's history of globalization is intimately linked with Greenland's status as a colony, which lasted for more than 250 years. Whether it is the older generation's problems, the younger generation's impatience to leave this drawback-start behind, or today's media, no one is unaffected by this fact. The battle-fields have included the economy, language, self-determination, and the individual and national Greenlandic identity. Until recently, the leaders and scholars of Greenland did not engage in debates on the pros and cons of globalization. Today, however, the politicians are well aware of the many advantages – not to mention the necessity – of both letting the world in and getting Greenland *out* into the world.

Before the advent of modern media technology, the country's geographic location and climate almost predestined Greenland to isolation. Although the global flow of information has, undeniably, been mainly one-way traffic, the media have played an essential part in making this gigantic island smaller and synchronic and have sped its development.

MATERIAL AND METHODS

As part of the project 'Children, Youth and Media in Greenland 1996–1997', a pilot survey in Nuuk in 1996 was carried out among 220 young people between the ages of 12 and 19 (Rygaard, 1999). This was followed in 1997 by a nationwide qualitative survey (454 young people between 12 and 19 years of age) and quantitative studies (120 from the entire group) carried out by a colleague[5] and me. The questions dealt with lifestyle, media use and attitudes towards media (Rygaard and Pedersen, 1999).

During 1999–2001, we proceeded with an audience study: 'Young People's Media Cultures in a Reception Perspective'. A camera/diary project (Cam/Di-project) was sent to Nuuk, Sisimiut and Ittoqqortoormiit. A total of 101 informants aged between 12 and 19 were supplied with disposable cameras and with diaries to be used during one week in the fall of 2000. We asked them to describe 'their life with media' and received 696 pictures and 313 related diary texts (Pedersen and Rygaard, 2003). A second Cam/Di-project was carried out with the aid of graduate students. This time, the focus group was 'tweens' (10–12 years of age) from Nuuk (Rygaard, 2006) who were asked to describe their lives as consumers of both media and other consumer goods. We received 221 pictures and 40 brief descriptions.

Another nationwide survey was carried out in November 2004, involving the age group 12–25 with 319 informants from five communities around Greenland dealing with the same issues as in the 1997 survey. Finally, in the summer of 2006, I asked 100 university undergraduate and graduate students (aged 20 and older) 12 qualitative questions about globalization. Because the questions were e-mailed during the summer break, the response rate was rather low: 41 answers. The data received from all these surveys form the background material for this chapter.

GLOBALISM AND GLOBAL YOUTH CULTURE

From a certain perspective, globalization is as old as the first interconnectedness around the world, but, in the wake of modernization (Giddens, 1990: 55ff; Robertson, 1992: 20; Waters, 1995: 48) and the inventions of modern technologies, globalization has really peaked. And, more places are constantly being drawn into its reach, raising debates about its pros and cons. Several perspectives on the by now almost exhausted term are at play, dividing advocates and antagonists in the continued debate.

Thomas Ziehe, a German youth researcher, sees the cultural extinction of modernization, and hence globalization (Giddens, 1990: 55ff; Robertson, 1992: 20; Waters, 1995: 48), penetrating society at three levels: society/history, culture/media and the individual (Ziehe and Stubenrauch, 1993).

Greenland has been attracting attention from adventurers, explorers, travelling sales representatives and exploiters during a period marked by a strong undercurrent of imperialism and colonization. The cultural products of the global world are seen from a Greenlandic perspective pretty much as one-way traffic (Rygaard, 2002), both concerning consumption and media. But, as will become apparent, the individuals, namely the young people in the surveys, are not in danger of becoming homogenized with the USA, as the older American imperialist critic Herbert Schiller (1976) and others feared could be the case when the primary supplier of media in Greenland, as in many countries, *was* and *is* the USA.

As was demonstrated in the so-called 'Dallas research' (Liebes and Katz, 1993) and by other researchers (Ang, 1985), the homogenization idea was looked upon as a superficial 'stopover in an airport' (Tomlinson, 1999: 6), denying the complex reception process justice. Theories purporting that globalization is nothing but another 'colonial discourse' (Nilan and Feixa, 2006: 3) have been repudiated in one study after another in recent years (Inda and Rosaldo, 2002; Nilan and Feixa, 2006). Also in Greenland, there are absolutely no traces of 'colonial discourse': the Greenlanders participate eagerly in becoming part of the global world.

Other fears have been expressed that, in the end, the global will eclipse the local (Nilan and Feixa, 2006: 3). Zygmundt Bauman (1998) has been one of the most ardent representatives of those pointing out the fragility of the local cultures which are in danger of annihilation resulting from globalization. When asked if local cultures were disappearing in Greenland, a young female respondent answered that Greenland's exceptional location would prevent local cultures from disappearing: 'Greenland is, and always will be, a district marginal to the rest of the world' (NN, 19, Nuuk, 2001; from Rygaard (2003)). The 2006 survey confirms this point of view.

Bauman (1998, 25–29), who further claims that to be local in a global world is a sign of social deprivation and degradation, represents yet another fear that is relatively more difficult to reject in Greenland. Being a young person in some of the outer districts in Greenland results in some repercussions concerning leisure and educational possibilities, as well as prospects related to tourism. Free media access is strongly related to parents' income levels (Rygaard, 2003: 299). Studies from Greenland reveal that this drawback situation further affects the young people's dreams for and faith in the future (Rygaard, 2003), as is the situation of minority youths elsewhere (Evenshaug and Hallen, 2001: 291). Although the Greenlanders are not a minority in their own country, the colonial history renders them vulnerable to discrimination, prejudice and the blight of not enough challenge in the outer districts. However disastrous these conditions might be, my argument is that without globalization the situation for these youngsters would be the same. However, scholars claim (Ziehe and Stubenrauch, 1993; Rygaard and Pedersen, 1999; Jørgensen, 2002: 123) that a feeling of being deprived, of being jealous and of missing opportunities may exist. The feeling of 'nothing is happening here in my society' (boy, 14 years of age, in Upernavik, 1997 interview) is prevalent in all the investigations during later years. It is difficult to be online with the world if you want to have a tactile relationship with the society around you. As a replacement, being online with the world is not so bad either – and the internet really is *made for* Greenland.

For advocates like Anthony Giddens (1990), globalization involves a profound reorganization of time and space in social and cultural life. The confines of locality disintegrate and make way for relations between absent others. In Giddens' words, it disembeds social relations from the local context and rearranges them across time and space (Giddens, 1990) as we see enacted with the help of media-stuff and on the internet (Christensen, 2003).

In much the same way, we see a 'de/territorialism' of the reception of foreign media content. Inda and Rosaldo (2002: 10) explain the term 'de/territorialism' like this:

> The key to the meaning of this term is the slash. [...] this means that the root of the word always to some extent undoes the action of the prefix, such that while the 'de' may pull culture apart from place, the 'territorialization' is always there to pull it back in one way or another. So ... there is no dislodging of everyday meanings from their moorings in particular localities without their simultaneous reinserting in fresh environment.

As we shall see later, this de/territorialization works for the Greenlandic students who 'feel at home' in the everyday meanings of attitudes in American movies.

New technology and media are, however, much more than information technologies. They are technologies of entertainment, communication, leisure, social intercourse and play – a total mixture of work and recreation – and although all members of the society profit from these technologies and new media, the youth are among the most eager users.

Globalization and youth are a perfect match. The way global cultures are assimilated in the locality as seen in such visual practices as graffiti (Rygaard, 2006), as internationally similar forms of music and as online/offline peer groups (Christensen, 2003) makes youth culture 'a laboratory' for hybrid cultures (Canclini, 1995) and young people the forerunners of new ways of living. As young people in a changing and global world try to search for, adapt to or negotiate identities with the help of rich and available media and consumer cultures, they create generational identities that are delocalized (Nilan and Feixa, 2006) and embedded from cyberspace into real life and vice versa (Christensen, 2003) in an 'emancipatory' use of culture (Bannerji, 2000).

For a country like Greenland, the technological possibilities and the cultural flow of globalization could be seen as the major inventions that changed Greenlandic life from being isolated and cut off from the outside world for many months at a time. People expect, now, to be able to travel whenever they feel like it, buy whatever they need and to tap into the global information network by a variety of means almost without regard for location. Assisted by time–space compression, we are also able to be part of 'the global village' (McLuhan and Powers, 1989) and, as such, to see and hear anything as it happens no matter where we live. For arctic regions, such as Alaska, Canada and Greenland (with their expensive infrastructure and strenuous living conditions), technology, media and globalization have meant technological progress, extended intercommunication and an invitation to participate in a world in motion.

GREENLAND AND THE WORLD: A BRIEF HISTORICAL OVERVIEW

In Greenland's interconnection with the world several epochs stand out: the last and most desired, offering independence from Denmark, is yet to come. Every new period has been the harbinger of new times and testifies to an expansion of consciousness among the Greenlanders. All of these periods are cases of 'intensification of global interconnectedness' (Inda and Rosaldo, 2002: 5).

A long history of exchange until the sixteenth century existed between Inuit, Northern, Arctic, Polar populations, the Vikings and the Dutch whalers. With the arrival of the Norwegian priest Hans Egede in 1721, Greenland entered a new and decisive phase as a Danish colony. For 220 years this connection with Denmark was the umbilical cord that provided the Greenlanders with food, supplies and money in exchange for sealskins, blubber, baleen and cryolite. A statute from 1925 stipulated that Greenland should be economically self-contained and that its economy should exist as a closed business isolated from the outside world (Gad, 1954: 462). Seen from a Danish point of view, this organization was interpreted as an attempt to protect the indigenous culture. Later, Greenlandic interpretations conceived of the statute rather as a case of colonialist imperialism (Olsen, 2005: 11).

During World War II, when Denmark was occupied by Germany, the fear of losing the now-needed supplies from Denmark contributed to opening the Greenlanders' eyes to the surrounding world. Five years of new and exciting supplies from the USA in exchange for cryolite, and the establishment of four military bases, introduced a hitherto unknown global connectedness. As the administration of Greenland now had to be managed *from* Greenland (Bruun, 1946: 40), the Greenlanders experienced a kind of national sovereignty and a greater self-determination in line with the French philosopher Jean Paul Sartre's existentialist logic claiming that he was never freer than when he was in jail during World War II (Sartre, 1966: 770f).

In addition to freedom, the Greenlanders tasted the sweet temptations of consumption and technological progress. New experiences had found their way into a country used to living a simple life. Exciting new mail-order catalogues, like 'the farmer's bible' from *Sears & Roebuck* (Fleischer, 1996: 96), were distributed all over the country. The first car ever seen in Greenland wheeled ashore (Fleischer, 1996: 84) with the subsequent demand for establishing roads. A visit from Marlene Dietrich in 1944 in high-heeled gold slippers, singing Lili Marleen and leaving one of her shoes behind like another Cinderella (Fleischer, 1996: 89), seemed like a fairy tale from abroad.

This new connectedness to the global society led to a noticeable economic growth and a lust for the exciting new products which they were unwilling to give up afterwards. Certainly, the shipping of cultural goods and merchandise was an asymmetric one-way traffic and could be seen as a manifestation of the 'imposition and dominance' (Inda and Rosaldo, 2002: 13) of American culture. But to think of this traffic as resulting in a cultural homogeneity is not to bear in mind the reality of 'otherness' and 'difference', the climate and location that were and still are the hallmarks of Greenland.

A strong wish to maintain Greenland's development and openness to the world led to the G-50 negotiations about modernization and new status as Danes for Greenlanders. At the same time, decolonization really became an issue internationally that helped the Greenlanders to fight monopolism, discrimination and isolationism as the status of a 'closed country' (Hedtoft: 1949: 28). Much can be said about the ensuing Danization of Greenland: skilled craftsmen from Denmark occupied positions at construction sites, building houses, schools, hospitals, factories and roads; and afterwards, technicians, teachers and experts took over the operations – all these activities demanding a substantial rise in the Danish block financial grant. The results were evident. Health conditions improved, infant mortality declined and people moved to the cities (Rygaard, 2006: 154).

In just 50 years, Greenland and the Greenlanders were forced to undergo a modernization process that the Europeans had had 200 years to develop (Rygaard, 2006: 157). Consequently, the development had repercussions for large parts of the indigenous population, corroborating some of the dire predictions made by the critics of modernization. By changing the former Greenlandic way of life to new and 'civilized' forms, Christianity and colonization contributed to rendering people tangled, rootless and with a lack of self-confidence. They were not skilled artisans, and most of them were without any education. In many ways the hasty modernization process reduced Greenlanders to onlookers to what took place in their own country. A class system emerged, separating people who learned Danish and got an education, from the people of the 'lost generation' – i.e. the Greenlanders who did not take part in the development and who were, consequently, marginalized.

The after-effects of this process introduce the subject of Greenland's disturbing statistics (Bjerregaard *et al.*, 1995) on subjects such as people on transfer income, various forms of misery and one of the highest suicide rates in the world (Sørensen, 2006: 10).

A PROSPECT OF FREEDOM: HOME RULE

While under Danish rule, the Greenlanders established connections with fellow Inuit in Canada and Alaska, gained status to address the UN as a non-governmental organization and became active partners for the global connection of indigenous people of the world – which could be seen as 'an embryo to a global civil society' (Kaspersen, 2005: 18).

In 1972, in an attempt to control their own relations, they voted 'no' to the European Economic Community, as it was then called, which brought them into conflict with the interests of their Danish 'motherland'. Weary of distant controls, this controversial 'no' demonstrated their actual influence – which was perceived as none at the time.

Although the way for establishing Home Rule was cleared in many ways, the battles were to be fought on a number of fronts. Winning general sympathy for the idea of self-government was complicated by one of the tragic consequences of colonization, as emphasized by the Greenlandic politician Aqqaluk Lynge, in a reference to Frantz Fanon (1968), '... as other colonized people, the Greenlanders reacted by defending their colonizers' (Olsen, 2005: 209).

During the years of subdued, internal struggle to gain self-determination in Greenland, many revolutions and upheavals took place in the outside world: the war in Vietnam, Women's Liberation, student revolts, etc. The Greenlanders in these years were busy looking inward, living the 'colonial discourse' so to speak, and were not really affected by these subversive events, as expressed with pawkish humour by one of the impatient young politicians, Lars Emil Johansen: 'Upheavals boiled everywhere while we in Greenland peacefully were eating guillemots' (Olsen, 2005: 156).

The Home Rule Government did become a reality in May 1979, and in February 1985 the Greenlanders for the second time voted 'no' to joining the European Union – a declination that was, however, mainly meant to protect their fishing quotas and not their relationship to the world as such.

While the Greenlanders were previously busy looking inward, today, the politicians know that in order to make actual self-government a reality in the future, they have to promote Greenland as a part of the world economy – turning their back once and for all on their history of imperialism and colonial ways of thinking. The Minister of Economic Affairs, however, is very realistic about Greenland's difficult and extraordinary situation as a market partner: '... with its geographical location, its climate and its enormous area in addition to a modest population and an imperceptibly small domestic market, Greenland's possibilities to win keen competition in a global market is more than difficult' (Motzfeldt, 2006: 6).

Greenlanders are still striving to become independent of the Danish block grant of 3.006 billion Danish kroner, to adjust the trade balance and to get self-government, and new and creative ways are being sought to achieve this. A series of sales drives and promotional campaigns have been launched to 'brand' Greenland; see www.greenland.com. Greenlanders stopped eating guillemots long ago. In the process, globalization has turned into an everyday Greenlandic concept, and nobody asks anymore ... '*Branding sunaana*?' ('What is branding?').

YOUTH AND MEDIA IN GREENLAND: VIDEO, MOVIES AND TELEVISION

The impact of modern media (film, television, video and the internet) has played an essential role in the globalization process in Greenland, not least in the way in which today's Greenlandic youth see themselves as citizens of the world.

Radio news was launched during World War II. And in the sixties (1964–1965), video emerged as a medium in itself, not as a recording device for television. Video soon became very popular because 'cinemas' were not really an alternative before Greenland opened its first cinema, *Katuaq*, in Nuuk in 1997. Although the boom of American movies gradually declined with the soldiers leaving after the war, American movies continued to be highly valued.

Television sneaked in through a backdoor in the late 1960s by way of private organizations which each hired a Dane to record television in Denmark from DR (the public-service Danish Broadcasting Corporation) for distribution in Greenland. The first private television association, *Godthåb lukkede telenet* (Godthåb[6] closed telecommunications network), did not fulfil the requirements of the copyright act, but the authorities, including DR, turned a blind eye. Rumours about the new and wonderful form of entertainment spread rapidly, and so did television associations. In 1982 there were 25 private television associations established around Greenland (Rygaard, 2004: 174–176).

These private beginnings were not, however, without start-up problems, such as sledge dogs eating the cables, months of waiting for the videotapes, interruptions in the programmes because the playback person fell asleep, and never seeing the endings of the films because the one 'taping', a little old lady in Denmark, '... always goes to bed at ten o'clock (Rygaard, 2004)!

With the introduction of Home Rule Government, the road was paved for a national Greenlandic television. Through a very amicable settlement between The Danish Radio (DR) and *Kalaallit Nunaata Radioa* (KNR), the so-called simultaneity TV started on 1 November 1982, but the agreement meant that the Greenlanders still watched almost solely Danish television – even though some people did not understand Danish. Still, the intention of the newly established KNR was to rapidly reach a language use ratio similar to that of the radio, with 80:20 Greenlandic:Danish programmes. The reality now, 24 years after, is very different, as seen in Figure 15.1 and Table 15.1, where there is a declining home production and 91% foreign content, with the attendant problems of always having to identify oneself with

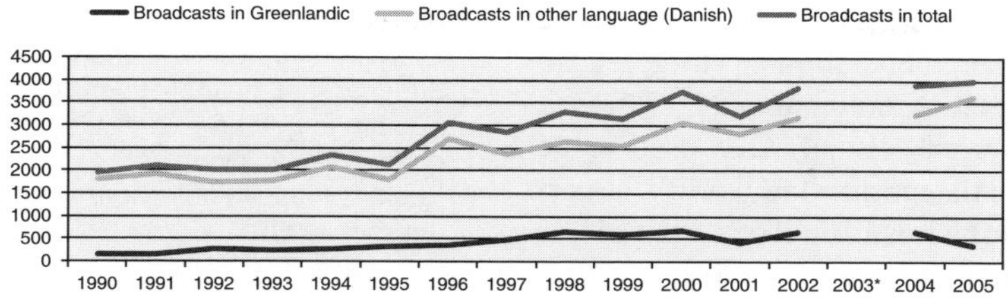

Figure 15.1 Graphic representation of KNR-TV broadcasts (hours), 1990–2002. Figures are from Greenlandic Statistics for all years mentioned using my own calculations (Rygaard, 2004: 173)

Table 15.1 Broadcasts of KNR-TV, 1990–2005, from Greenlandic Statistics.

Language	*Broadcasts per day (h:min)*													
	1990	1991	1992	1993	1994	1995	1996	1997	1998	1999	2000	2001	2002	2003	2004
Greenlandic	0:23	0:27	0:43	0:38	0:44	0:55	0:58	1:17	1:49	1:39	1:54	1:08	1:49		1:29
Other	4:58	5:17	4:46	4:50	5:39	4:58	7:23	6:29	7:15	6:58	8:21	8:42	8:41		8:54
Total	5:20	5:43	5:28	5:28	6:23	5:52	8:21	7:46	9:04	8:37	10:14	9:50	10:30		10:41

foreign cultures and people (Rygaard, 1999) and also the presence of foreign language, i.e. Danish or English/American with Danish subtexts.

Until 2002, local production had steadily increased year after year, from 23 minutes a day in 1990 to 1 hour and 49 minutes in 2002. For 2003, the numbers are missing from KNR and the following years, 2004 and 2005, are assessed in an opaque manner, maybe to conceal that the numbers for Greenlandic production, and hence in the native language, had dropped to 59 minutes, as seen in the Figure 15.1 and Table 15.1.

Producing television in a country with only 57,000 inhabitants is expensive. The price of each minute here is ten times the price in Denmark (Rygaard, 1999), so the government usually turns a blind eye to language problems and foreign and ethnically unfamiliar programme content.

Since 1 August 2002, a competing decoder television station, *Nuuk TV*, has experienced a boom which corresponds to KNR's gradual reduction in its own productions. *Nuuk TV* sells packets of 19 or 23 digital TV channels: all Danish, English and American, with or without Danish subtitles. These sleek programmes of film, series, sports, documentaries and news easily compete with the 'hand-held' and 'dogma coloured' Greenlandic programmes from KNR-TV, especially among the young people, who state repeatedly: 'We want more channels' (high-school girl, one of 22 in Qaqortoq) or 'More programmes from other countries' (boy, 17, born in Sisimiut). The wide array of foreign and very professional infotainment makes for eager viewers. Most people, not least young people, value options, professionalism and entertainment above nationality (Drotner, 2001a,b). In so doing, they turn their backs on 'the old' and somewhat patronizing assumption held by the critiques of cultural imperialism (Garofalo, 1993: 18), that 'authenticity' is everything and that the encounter with Western media puts it at risk. For national television and its centre-to-periphery flow, as well as the West-to-Greenland flow, there is, however, a truth in the statement that 'the centre speaks and the periphery listens' (Hannerz, 1992: 219). But the Greenlandic youth actively choose what they think is good from the West.

YOUNG GREENLANDERS AND THE GLOBAL CONNECTION

To most young Greenlanders, the connection to the global world occurs at a pace that is too slow. They are losing their patience with the older generation's struggles to overcome previous colonial hardships, and they want to break out of what used to be a segregated existence on the world's largest island 740 kilometres from the North Pole.

The majority of the 41 university students participating in the 2006 survey came up with rather depressing answers to the question, 'How do you perceive Greenland's relationship to the rest of the world?' Many of them indicated feelings of enclosure and charged the politicians with being too slow and not competent enough: 'It appears as if the country is still looked upon as a colony' (woman, 27, born in the capital Nuuk); 'Feeble, I feel that our politicians are behind in relation to the rest of the world. They are narrow-minded and are not taken seriously' (woman, 30, Uummannaq, small city in the north of Greenland); 'As a frail start, nothing much has happened between Greenland and other countries [...]' (woman, 30, born in Qaqortoq, larger city in South Greenland).

This disillusionment with the politicians runs parallel to many young Greenlanders' critique of their parents and families – especially those of the so-called lost generation mentioned above. For instance, the members of the rap band Prussic scold their parents for being drunk and for not caring for or loving them. They explain in a new short feature, *Nipersoneq Sakkugalugu*, 2006 (*Music as Mouthpiece*), that they want to write a song that hits their parents' generation really hard, using their own and other children's experiences and touching on some of the strongest taboo subjects in Greenland: suicide, child abuse and neglect. The song is called *Angajoqqaat* (*Parents*):

> My parents don't care about me,
> They are going on a binge and leaving me to myself
> I'm alone every day; they use their money on booze instead of food
> I envy other children with happy parents
> Fuck, why don't I feel better, maybe it's their fault
> My daddy loves hash more than me
> How will I be when I'm grown up?
> Will I end up like my parents?
> Do listen to me and raise me!
> I have asked them to stop their abuse
> But they refuse to listen to reason
> Because I'm only a child and I have nothing to say
> But does that mean that I must be alone?
> You are forgetting your children; take care of your children like anybody else
> You are wrapped up in booze and hash only ...
> (Prussic, 2005).

Today, many previously strong taboos are broken by the younger generations, who, tired of the elders' stories of the old Greenland, of colonial misery and of their lack of self-confidence, look ahead to a new Greenland as a valid part of the world and a nation that stands up to its own problems.

Some of the young generation's critical attitudes can be seen as a sign of health: a departure from colonial ways of thinking. Individualism and wishes for change now take precedence over national solidarity, and the media flow contributes to diffusing trend events and processes of democratization around the world, forcing individuals '... to negotiate lifestyle choices among a diversity of options' as claimed by Anthony Giddens (1993).

Among the Greenlandic television programmes, the news programme *Qanoroq* (*What is happening*?) tends to become *the* Greenlandic programme that almost everybody watches. In 1997, 87% of the 12–19-year-olds claimed an interest (Rygaard, 2002: 179), and in both 2004 and 2006 as well, 'News is important to keep oneself posted' (woman, 30, born in Uummannaq, 2006 survey). However, a slight slipping is seen between the young people's explicit preference for *Qanoroq* in 1997 to more vague remarks on news, TV-news or *Qanoroq* as such in 2006. Television news *has* become global.

Until 1997, the news was only in Greenlandic, with no Danish speakers, no subtitles and no news items from abroad. In 1997, KNR gave in to the pressure from the local Danes who wanted to know what was going on in the country in which they paid their taxes, namely Greenland. However, the change that forced open the Greenlandic window to the world was the terror attack on the Twin Towers in New York, 11 September 2001,

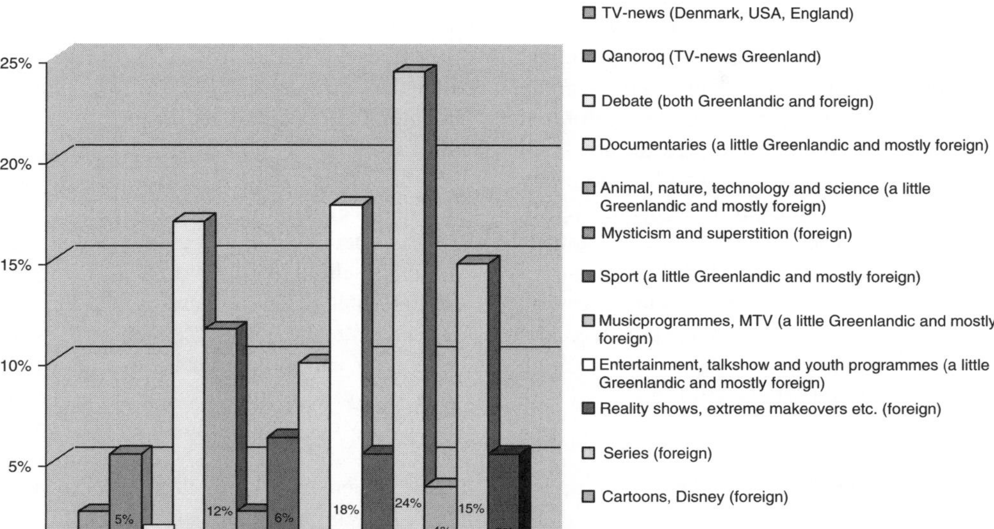

Figure 15.2 Preferred TV programmes, 2004 survey (*N* = 319)

when KNR switched to CNN's live broadcast. That disaster became the tangible proof of 'a world getting closer' and from that time on *Qanoroq* has had news headlines from abroad interspersed with the local news.

When we asked young people in the 1997 survey if they were interested or not interested in a number of programmes shown on KNR-TV, the top scorers were detective, gangster and action series, youth series and movies (Rygaard, 2002), most of which are 'made in America'. A similar question was posed, but this time phrased as an open-ended question, in the 2004 survey, 'Which television programme/programmes do you prefer?' Although the open-ended form invites a broader range of answers and, thereby, produces results which are not immediately compatible with the former survey, the tendencies were the same. The top scorer was series, in second place was entertainment, talk shows and youth programmes, with films running fourth. The third place was occupied by documentaries, a rather diffuse, but generally very popular group containing both docu-soaps, lost-person documentaries and real documentaries; see Figure 15.2.

The answers to the question 'Which programmes do you prefer to watch on television?' in the 2006 survey were overwhelmingly similar: movies, series such as *Desperate Housewives* (2004–), *Sex and the City* (1998–2004), *Star Trek* (1966–2005), *Alias* (2001–2006), *Frasier* (1993–2004), *Friends* (1994–2004), etc., and news – in that order. When asked about their favourite movie(s), the answers were a range of American movies (79%) with titles such as *Face/Off* (John Woo, 1997), *Seabiscuit* (Gary Ross, 2003), *Pirates of the Caribbean: Dead Man's Chest* (Gore Verbinski, 2006),[7] *In America* (Jim Sheridan, 2002), *Moulin Rouge* (Baz Luhrmann, 2001), *Braveheart* (Mel Gibson, 1995), etc. besides Danish movies (7%) and genre forms as indicated (14%).

The young women, not surprisingly, were very keen on romantic, emotional and dramatic films: 'Love movies with a big "K"' (*Krig, Kærlighed and Kaos – War, Love and Chaos*) (woman, 27, Nuuk). Generally, they prefer movies that nurture fantasies, escapism and daydreams, but they also like 'true stories'[8] and recognition of everyday life: 'I like films where the everyday life and problems are comparable to my own' (woman, 26, Nuuk). Most important, however, foreign languages and ethnic otherness do not seem to bother them: content outweighs nationality (Drotner, 2001a,b). Both these women speak of the recognition of the American culture, which reassures them. This feeling is not an expression of a cultural homogenization, rather it testifies to a certain disembeddedness or de/territorialization – they are inscribing the global into their local culture.

ONLINE WITH THE WORLD

Much as the war made Greenlanders covet the American dream, and much as the outside world was made familiar via television, the internet has opened the door wide to the global community. It began at the end of 1997 with very few subscribers; but, in 1998, the percentage of Greenlanders connected to the internet increased to be almost identical to that of Danes: in Greenland, 13% were connected to the internet, whereas in Denmark the figure was 16%.

What really proves that the Greenlanders' 'go' is still intact are the answers to the question, 'Do you plan to purchase a computer and connect to the internet?' (Statistics Greenland, 2000–2001: 90): 27% of the Greenlanders answered 'yes' as opposed to only 3% of the Danes. This may say something about the strong wish for an open window to the world, a place where 'you can buy anything and find anything' (girl of 13 in Ittoqqortoormiit, 2001). Almost all the young people we have asked about the internet gave similar responses. It may seem to be quite an advantage to have the World Wide Web to choose from when you are living in a small community, with a single co-op selling everything from diapers to bullets.

In 1997 and 1998, telecommunications and broadband services boomed in Greenland, and during 1998–1999 the number of internet users increased by 50% (Statistics Greenland, 2004: 91) to reach 10,210 in 2003 (Statistics Greenland, 2004: 182). This meant that every other household had access to the internet (Statistics Greenland, 2004: 73), placing Greenland on a par with France (Nielsen, 2002: 132).

In the survey from 1997, only a few months after the internet adventure began, we asked to which media the young people had access. Although schools and libraries in the cities and the outer districts found it important to get PCs with internet access as soon as the technology and economical situation would allow it, we, nevertheless, saw a significant discrepancy between social groups (Rygaard, 2003).

Tele Greenland claims that 99% coverage is possible in Greenland, but the signal does not reach some of the outer districts in the north and some of the sheep-farming homesteads in the south (Greenland Statistics, 2004: 180). Out there, where telephone communication, television or internet access is not possible, globalization is not what one fears the most.

In the 2006 survey, I asked my respondents whether they all had access to or owned a PC with internet access through ADSL (internet broadband service), which was made available in 2003. They all had. To the question 'Which do you prefer, TV or PC?' (Figure 15.3), 24% answered that they could not live without either of them, but, if they had to choose, the PC would win: 'You can't live without any of them! ... But if I had to choose I could do better without television. Today a PC with a proper access to the Net is almost as good as television' (man, 34, x-town).

All the same, the old medium of television scores a small success: 42% absolutely could not do without their television '... as long as it has a decoder' (woman, 27, Nuuk), meaning having access to 23 channels; 34%, however, were wholeheartedly for the PC: 'PC – because you are in control' (man, 48, Y-town).

In the 2004 survey, we asked young people what they actually did on their PCs, and for how long. The answers reflect

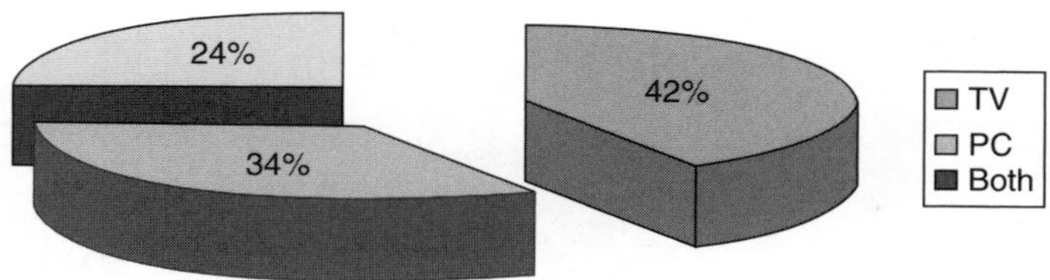

Figure 15.3 Preferences for TV or PC, 2006 survey ($N = 41$)

Table 15.2 Activities on PC, 2004 survey ($N = 319$).

	No time		*<0.5 hour*		*1–2 hours*		*3–4 hours*	
	Nuuk	*Qaqortoq*	*Nuuk*	*Qaqortoq*	*Nuuk*	*Qaqortoq*	*Nuuk*	*Qaqortoq*
Seek information on the internet (%)	6	2	42	18	42	51	11	29
Downloads programs or music (%)	38	29	36	16	21	31	6	24
Buy things (%)	48	32	33	36	19	26	0	6
Play games (%)	40	33	32	29	21	18	8	20
Chats (%)	55	39	30	24	13	31	2	6
E-mails (%)	6	2	77	65	13	31	4	2

the geographical diversity of the country. With its 16,000 inhabitants, the capital Nuuk (which is also a centre for education) contains a wide range of possibilities for leisure activities. Qaqortoq, in the south, has 3,200 inhabitants, a high school and a rich art life – a unique sculpture park carved in granite rocks by Scandinavian artists[9] – but, all the same, Qaqortoq is short of the kinds of leisure possibilities that young people crave.

In Table 15.2 we see that writing e-mails is one of the most important activities for both Nuuk and Qaqortoq youths; they do it every day for up to half an hour (marked in bold).

The next conspicuous leisure activity is that both groups spend a lot of time, about 1–2 hours a day, seeking information or 'surfing' – on the Internet (in italics). From the structural differences between Nuuk and Qaqortoq in terms of shopping potentials, one might expect the Qaqortoq youth to shop more on the Internet, as seen in former research (Rygaard, 2003). And they did. For 1–2 hours a day, 26% of them claim to be on the outlook for things to buy, against the Nuuk youth's 19%. Judging by their possession of new electronic gadgets, new films and music, and fancy clothes that revealed their very smart daily life, I believe their claims. Generally, we can sum up that the missing opportunities in Qaqortoq *vis-à-vis* Nuuk increase the time spent on the computer, as we see shown in the last two columns of Table 15.2 (1–2 hours and 3–4 hours).

In the 2004 survey we also asked for the most popular site on the internet. In November 2004 the Danish meeting place www.Arto.dk seemed to be *the* place (Figure 15.4) to socialize with friends, both inside and outside Greenland, while many of the discussions in cyberspace – like in *R*eal*L*ife (RL) – also centre around problems of being a Greenlander in relation to language, discrimination and identity (Rygaard, forthcoming).

GREENLANDER OR GLOBAL [CITIZEN]? THE INNER FEELINGS

According to Zygmunt Bauman (1998), globalization creates social stratification – not everyone has the means to be a global traveller and tourist. For Greenland, this is certainly true, at least in part. The price of an airline ticket to Copenhagen, which *is* the route to the world, so to speak, since one has to go via Copenhagen to get anywhere else, is equal to that for a ticket with five 'hops' round the world. Globalization is not the culprit, though. Rather, the geography, the remoteness

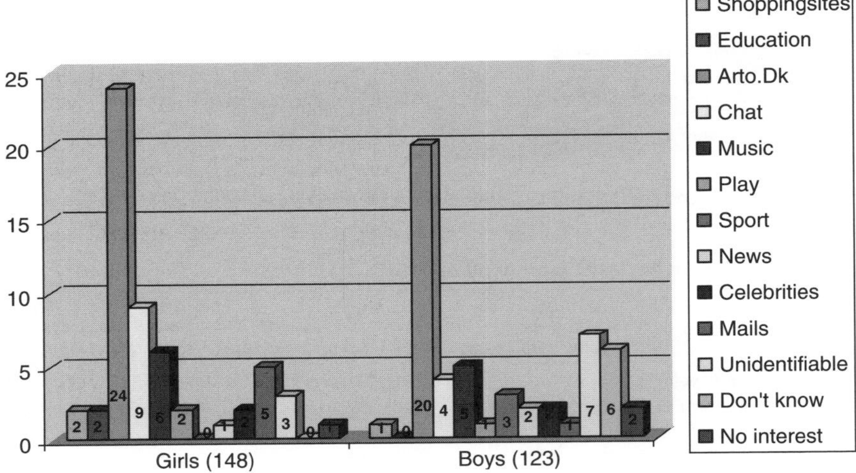

Figure 15.4 Favourite sites on the internet, 2004 survey ($N = 271$)

and Greenland's impassability are to blame, together with Air Greenland's monopoly. With the summer air route from Kangerlussuaq to Baltimore which opened in May 2007 as part of the politicians' renewed fight for global interaction, competition and lowered prices will encourage Greenlanders, at least those living in the urban centres (Rygaard, 2002, 2003), to be world travellers and tourists; they certainly long for it!

In the 2006 survey, I asked the students about their preferred holiday destinations. Although it was an open question, the answers were very similar to those obtained in the 1997 survey (Rygaard, 2003) and could be classified into four groups as seen in Figure 15.5. One group (13%) wants to go to undefined big cities; the second (33%) is keen on visiting family in Denmark, whereas the third group (13%) wishes for undefined warm countries and the majority (41%), dream of exotic places and adventures, such as 'Greece or the Pacific Islands' (man, 31, small settlement), 'driving a car through the USA' (woman, 21, Ilulissat), 'visiting China and Russia' (woman, 20, Nanortalik), 'Panama and Spain – I would like to travel and experience other places. So many things are to be seen in the world!' (woman, 24, Narsaq). The big cities are exciting with many possibilities and swarms of people: 'I love the buzzing of the big cities' (woman, 27, Nuuk).

The wish to visit family is not surprising, because most Greenlanders are still very connected to their family (Tróndheim, 2004), and when visiting relatives in Denmark, one can easily 'go anywhere from Denmark' (woman, 30, Uummannaq). The group that just wishes for warm places sounds a little displeased with the Arctic climate: 'I want to go where the climate is warm; here in Nuuk it is so cold!' (woman, 25, n-city).

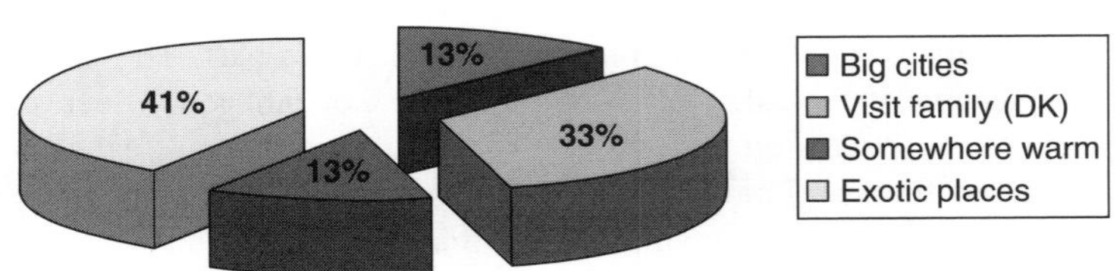

Figure 15.5 Preferred holiday destinations, 2006 survey ($N = 39$)

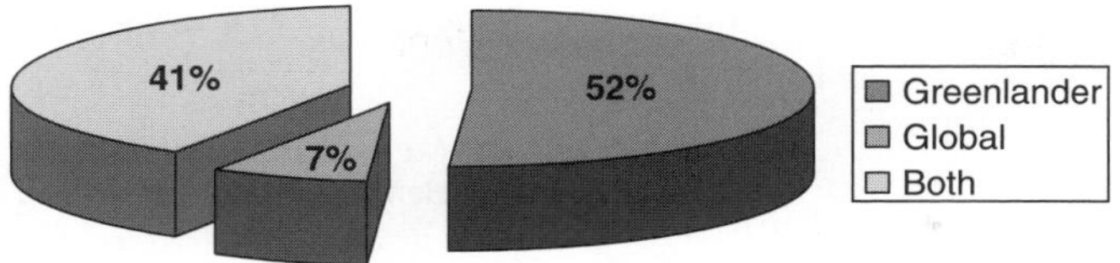

Figure 15.6 Greenlander or global? 2006 survey (*N* = 41)

Unfortunately, the climate is getting still warmer due to global warming, which is yet another instance of globalization (International Polar Year, 2007).

However, as much as the young people want to go away as tourists, thrive on their 'McMedia-use' and long for exciting new things, products and experiences, they are, in their inner feelings, Greenlanders, strongly connected to tradition, family and close human relations in their local societies. That view is much in line with the finding of Neil Blair Christensen (2003), who claims that although the Arctic people are eager 'onliners', their 'virtual interaction' is seen as a mere adjustment to their contemporary world and their sense of belonging (Christensen, 2003: 14–17).

In line with debates in the 1990s (Ziehe and Stubenrauch, 1993; Bauman, 1998), we tried to figure out in our 1997 survey whether globalization, foreign influences and media flow had a detrimental effect on the young Greenlanders. We asked them of their dreams for and faith in the future regarding job possibilities and places to live, both as real opportunities and as 'wild' dreams (Rygaard, 2003). These young people were sadly realistic and non-demanding. For the most part, they were not yearning for exotic places to live and they were (again for the most part) content to move to a larger city in Greenland or to wish for a job they already knew someone to have. They were very dependent on personal experiences (Rygaard, 2003). For a country and a people that needed the new generation to secure an independent national future, these young people's shortage of ambitions to be social climbers could be a problem that could cause further stratification between centre youths in the capital and periphery youths in the outer districts. Inspiration from the outside *was* and *is* sorely needed, even though it would come mediated through foreign media flow (Rygaard, 2003).

In the 2006 survey, I asked the students if they felt as inhabitants of the global village or as 'just Greenlanders' (Figure 15.6). More than half of them were Greenlanders – full stop! Most of them talk about the parents, language and inner feelings that connect them to their country, and some feel as 'other' for instance, when Danish men consider Greenlandic females 'promiscuous' (woman, 27, Nuuk).

Another young woman had the same feeling of being Greenlander in relation to foreigners: '... others make me feel that I am a Greenlander' (woman, 25, Nuuk). A few do not at all connect to the idea of being a global citizen: 'I feel that I am much unlike other young persons elsewhere in the world. We have some quite unique conditions up here, concerning both nature and the struggle we are fighting to find our identity and our position in the world' (woman, 30, Uummannaq).

Some 7% of the respondents feel as global citizens: 'I see my life as being part of the world ... My way of life with cellular phone, internet and my personal consumption is pretty much the same as the young, self-confident consumer in Europe' (man, 35, Sisimiut), 'I am a global Inuit, [he giggles] ...' (man, 31, Qaqortoq); 41% feel both as Greenlanders and as global citizens: 'I am Greenlander but I am also a fellow citizen in the world' (woman, 33, Aasiaat).

Although none of the young people in these two groups, the 'global perceivers' and the 'Greenland-global perceivers', mention television as one of their links to 'the global village', their feelings seem to be those of 'tribal emotions' that the late McLuhan wrote about (McLuhan and Fiore, 1967: 63). They are very much aware of being Greenlanders whether they are on the internet (Christensen, 2003), on one of their preferred chat rooms (Rygaard, forthcoming) or in their contemporary consumer life (Kjeldgaard, 2004).

CONCLUSIONS

For the most part, Greenland and its inhabitants try really hard to connect to the world, to let the world in through products, media, inspiration, travels and world connections. Even though sceptics and critics are certainly right in blaming globalization for much irreversible environmental damage; and however asymmetric the cultural traffic has been, the exchanges with Denmark, the USA, northern Europe and, increasingly, with the Far East, have been an eye-opening advantage to Greenland, not least to the young generation, who wants to break isolation and take what the world has to offer. The Greenlanders love all of it. Let the world in!

On the other hand, Greenland is also eager to let Greenland out into the world! The government's 'branding' endeavours seek not only to attract foreign tourists and investors to Greenland, but also to draw the world's attention to the 'Greenlandishness' of Greenland – an objective also shared by all the young people in their media habits and leisure pleasures. To be a Greenlander and *how* to be a Greenlander is still a very hot subject in spite of almost 28 years of Home Rule. In Greenland, globalization has thus far primarily been a story of successfully embedding the global into the local. The task now is for Greenland to turn the predominantly one-way cultural traffic into a two-way street in a climate yet based on what is still an extremely strong local identity.

NOTES

1 On 30 September 2005, the Danish Paper *Jyllands-Posten* published an article 'The faces of Muhammed' with 12 satiric drawings of the prophet. Subsequently a 'war' between Muslims and the paper and later Denmark spread. http://da.wikipedia.org (visited 2.12.2006).

2 *Nunarsuup*: the world, the globe.

3 Henriette Rasmussen (visited 2.12.2006).

4 Greenland has been a colony of Denmark since 1721. On 1 May 1979 the Home Rule Government became a reality and Greenland obtained its own flag in 1985. These years Greenland aims at sovereignty.

5 Associated professor, Birgit Kleist Pedersen, Ilisimatusarfik.

6 The former 'colonial' name for Nuuk.

7 The title was given as two different movies several times.

8 The weakness for 'true stories' presumably is a trace of tradition like in other indigenous societies (Inda and Rosaldo, 2002: 16–17).

9 The projects are called *Rocks and People* http://www.greenland.com/Byer_og_regioner/Sydgroen/andQaqortoq.php

REFERENCES

Ang, I. (1985) *Watching Dallas. Soap Opera and the Melodramatic Imagination*. London: Methuen.

Bannerji, H. (2000) *The Dark Side of the Nation: Essays on Multiculturalism, Nationalism and Gender*. Toronto: Canadian Scholars Press.

Bauman, Z. (1998) *Globalization: The Human Consequences*. Cambridge: Polity Press.

Bjerregaard, P., Curtis, T., Senderovitz, F., Christensen, U. and Pars, T. (1995) *Levevilkår, Livsstil og Helbred i Grønland* (*Living Conditions, Life Style and Health in Greenland*). Copenhagen. DIKE.

Bruun, E. (1946) 'Grønlands administration i adskillelsens aar' (The administration of Greenland in the year of separation'). In *Det Grønlandske Selskabs Aarsskrift* (*The Greenland Society Yearbook*). København: Munksgaards Forlag.

Canclini, N.G. (1995) *Hybrid Cultures. Strategies for Entering and Leaving Modernity*. Minneapolis, MN: University of Minnesota Press.

Christensen, N.B. (2003) *Inuit in Cyberspace. Embedding Offline Identities Online*. Museum Tusculanum Press.

Drotner, K. (2001a) *Medier for Fremtiden: Børn, Unge og det Nye Medielandskab* (*Media for the Future: Children, Youth and the New Media*). København: Høst & Søn.

Drotner, K. (2001b) 'Global media through youthful eyes'. In S. Livingstone and M. Bovill (eds) *Children and their Changing Media Environment: A European Comparative Study*. New York: Erlbaum.

Evenshaug, O. and Hallen, D. (2001) *Barne- og Ungdomspsykologi* (*Children and Youth Psychology*). Oslo: Gyldendal Norsk Forlag.

Fanon, F. (1968) *Fordømte her På Jorden* (*The Wretched of the Earth*). Copenhagen. Rhodos.

Fleischer, J. (1996) *Forvandlingens År. Grønland fra Koloni til Landsdel* (*The Years of Transformation. Greenland from Colony to Province*). Nuuk: Atuakkiorfik.

Gad, F. (1954) 'Grønlands historie IV 1925–1954' ('The history of Greenland IV 1925–1954'). In *Grønland 1954* (*Greenland 1954*). Charlottenlund/Minneapolis, MN: The Greenlandic Society/University of Minneapolis Press.

Garofalo, R. (1993) 'Whose world, what beat: the transnational music industry, identity and cultural imperialism'. *The World of Music*, 35(2).

Giddens, A. (1990) *The Consequences of Modernity.* London. Polity Press.

Giddens, A. (1993) *Modernity and Self-Identity. Self and Society in the Late Modern Age.* Oxford: Polity Press.

Hannerz, U. (1992) *Cultural Complexity. Studies in the Social Organization of Meaning.* New York. Columbia University Press.

Hedtoft, H. (1949) 'Grønlands fremtid' ('The future of Greenland'). In *The Greenland Society Yearbook 1949.* København: Munksgaards Forlag.

Inda, J.X. and Rosaldo, R. (2002) *The Anthropology of Globalization. A Reader.* Oxford. Blackwell.

International Polar Year (2007) http://www.ipy.org/development [August 2006].

Jørgensen, C.R. (2002) *Psychologien i Senmoderniteten* (*Psychology in Late Modernity*). Copenhagen: Hans Reitzels Forlag.

Kaspersen, L.B. (ed.) (2005) *Globalisering På Vrangen* (*The Reverse Side of Globalization*). Copenhagen: Frydenlund.

Kjeldgaard, D. (2004) *Consumption and the Global Youth Segment. Peripheral Position, Central Immersion.* University Press of Southern Denmark.

Liebes, T. and Katz, E. (1993) *Export of Meaning. Cross-Cultural Reading of Dallas.* Cambridge: Polity Press.

McLuhan, M. and Fiore, Q. (1967) *The Medium is the Massage: An Inventory of Effects.* New York: Random House.

McLuhan, M. and Powers, B.R. (1989) *The Global Village.* New York: Oxford University Press.

Motzfeldt, J. (2006) Sermitsiaq (Greenlandic paper) no. 12. Nuuk.

Nielsen, J.K. (2002) 'Udenrigspolitik, globalisering and bæredygtighedens dilemmaer' ('Foreign politics, globalization and dilemmas of sustainability'). In *Grønlandsk Kultur- og Samfundsforskning 2002* (*Greenlandic Research of Culture and Society 2002*). Nuuk: Ilisimatusarfik/Atuagkat.

Nilan, P. and Feixa C. (eds) (2006) *Global Youth? Hybrid Identities, Plural Worlds.* London: Routledge.

Olsen, T.R. (2005) *I Skyggen af Kajakkerne* (*In the Shadows of the Kayaks*). Nuuk: Atuagkat.

Pedersen, B.K. and Rygaard, J. (2003) 'Grønlandske unge mellem tradition og globalisering' ('Greenlandic youth between tradition and globalization'). In H. Helve (ed.) *Ung i Utkant. Aktuel Forskning om Glesbygdsumdomar i Norden* (*Youth in Outskirts. Current Research about Young People in Small Settlements in the North*). Copenhagen. Nordic Council: Children and Youths.

Prussic (2005) *Nipersomeq Sakkugalugu* (*Music as a Mouthpiece*). Nuuk: Atlantic Music.

Robertson, R. (1992) *Globalization. Social Theory and Global Culture.* London: Sage.

Rygaard, J. (1999) 'Fjernsyn og identitet i et bikulturelt samfund' ('Television and identity in a bilingual society'). In C.L. Christensen (ed.) *Børn, Unge og Medier. Nordiske Forskningsperspektiver.* Göteborg: Nordicom.

Rygaard, J. (2002) 'Grønland og den kulturelle globalisering' ('Greenland and the cultural globalization'). In E. Janussen, B.K. Pedersen, D. Thorleifsen, K. Langgård and J. Rygaard (eds) *Grønlandsk Kultur- og Samfundsforskning 2000/01* (*Greenlandic Research of Culture and Society 2000/01*). Nuuk: Ilisimatusarfik/Atuagkat.

Rygaard, J. (2003) 'Youth culture, media and globalization processes in Greenland'. *Young. Nordic Journal of Youth Research*, 11(4): 291–308.

Rygaard, J. (2004) En TV-historie. In B. Jacobsen, B.K. Pedersen, K. Langgård and J. Rygaard (eds) *Grønlænder og Global – Grønlandsk Sprog, Litteratur og Medier i 25-Året for Hjemmestyrets Indførelse* (*Greenlander and Global: Greenlandic Language, Literature and Media in the 25th Year since the Establishment of Home Rule*). Nuuk: Ilisimatusarfik.

Rygaard, J. (2006) 'Proksemik Nuuk'. In *Grønlandsk Kultur- og Samfundsforskning 2004–05* (*Greenlandic Research of Culture and Society 2004–05*). Nuuk: Ilisimatusarfik/Atuagkat.

Rygaard, J. (forthcoming) *New Communities and Identity Works on the Internet.* Copenhagen: North Atlantic 'Brygge'.

Rygaard, J. and Pedersen B.K. (1999) 'Feltarbejde, metode og teori' ('Fieldwork, method and theory'). In *Grønlandsk Kultur and Samfunds Forskning 98/99.* Nuuk: Ilisimatusarfik/Atuagkat.

Sartre, J.P. (1966) *Being and Nothingness.* New York: Washington Square Press.

Schiller, H. (1976) *Communication and Cultural Domination.* New York: International Arts and Science Press.

Sørensen, A. (2006) '40 selvmord i årets første ni måneder' ('Forty suicides in the first nine months of the year') In *Grønlandsposten* (*The Greenlandic Post*) 21 September, Nuuk.

Statistics Greenland (2000–2004) Home Rule Government. Nuuk.

Tomlinson, J. (1999) *Communication and Culture.* Nottingham: The University of Chicago Press.

Tróndheim, G. (2004) 'Kinship in contemporary urban settings'. In *Dynamics and Shifting Perspectives. Arctic Societies and Research. Proceedings of the First IPPSSAS Seminar (International PhD School for Studies of Arctic Society).* Nuuk: Ilisimatusarfik.

Waters, M. (1995) *Globalization.* London: Routledge.

Ziehe, T. and Stubenrauch, H. (1993) *New Youth and Unusual Learning Processes: Cultural Release and Subjectivity.* Copenhagen: Politisk Revy.

16

Games and the Media: The Acquisition of Social Structure and Social Rules

Maria Heller

SOCIALIZATION PROCESSES AND YOUTH CULTURE

Socialization is a complex process of adaptation of the individual (child) to rules and norms of the surrounding society. It involves the control of instincts and affection (Elias, 1939), the subordination of behaviour to norms of embracing groups, the acquisition of social knowledge, of symbolic structures (language being the most important one), and skills and competences (like communication). Socialization takes place in various social spaces (family, school, peer groups and increasingly through media), through various channels (oral communications, written texts, personal experiences, and more and more through different cultural products and processes accessed through new information and communication technologies (ICTs)). Although basic knowledge about social structure and rules and norms of social behaviour have always been transmitted to young generations through different social institutions and cultural forms, activities and procedures, these mechanisms have recently been radically modified by the quick development of media and ICTs. Public discussions of these phenomena mainly testify to the growing uneasiness and dismay of adult generations with respect to youth culture, to media use by children and youngsters (Werner, 1998; Ling and Thrane, 2002; Livingstone, 2002, 2003a) and to the growing generation gap and frequent problems of behaviour and social integration. Most of these debates put the blame on aggressive movies, TV programmes and video games. Quickly increasing advertising activity is also pinpointed, especially when it directly targets children (and tries to influence parents through their offspring) or when children are used as attractive components of ads (Müller, 1997).

The acquisition of societal rules and norms has always relied on culture. This process has always been based on cultural products and activities of the surrounding society, even in ancient times: mythology, legends, story-telling and songs transmitted beliefs and knowledge about social order and authority, about social structure, the origin of the group (ethnic, national, religious, etc.), the prevalent roles and their characteristic constituents.[1] The various cultural genres enhance the acquisition of values, skills, procedures or strategies that are necessary for adequate participation in society: collaboration, competition, understanding and other patterns of human activity. Since ancient times, games, plays and toys have been an important part of the socialization process, just as have different feasts, celebrations and rituals. With the appearance, however, of ever-newer forms of media that facilitate access to diverse forms of culture, the socialization process has become more complex and more controversial.

While it is widely accepted that toys and games have an important function in teaching and consolidating social rules and norms, in establishing skills and transmitting social knowledge, in creating and reinforcing human relations and providing relaxation and entertainment, the appearance of new ICTs and the games they introduced do not meet such undivided recognition and acceptance. Both specialists and the wider public struggle with the problem that new games available through new devices do not fit into the traditional role of games reinforcing accepted social values. Anxieties focus around the aggressive character of many electronic games, just in the same way as in the cases of other genres of electronic entertainment (action movies, cartoons, certain types of popular music, etc.). There are also worries concerning the huge amount of time spent watching films or playing video games, which, in some cases, can reach addiction.

The use of electronic media blundered into a traditionally established system of socialization which was mainly realized through direct personal experience (close to the adults' everyday reality), tales (that introduced supernatural and unreal worlds and contributed to smoothing or deconstructing children's fears and scares) (Bettleheim, 1975), and toys and games, all of which closely imitated the adults' world and helped children to acquire a range of social roles with their complementary constituents (behaviour, language, habitus, problem-solving techniques, etc.)

The earliest electronic media had already introduced radical changes in these processes. According to Meyrowitz (1986), television destroyed the walls that separated different social situations; in particular, offstage settings and behaviour became open to access for diverse social groups. Television uncovered the closed and protected micro-world of the family to be accessible from outside, but it also let into the family circle so-far inexperienced behaviours, problems, settings and experiences. Television not only opened up completely new possibilities in information management, education and culture, but also led to a continual search for compensatory entertainment and leisure, voyeurism, gossiping and evasion from reality's hardships. The spread of new ICTs, although they provide different patterns of usage (interactivity), did not reverse this latter tendency.

International statistics show that people's media usage has greatly increased even if free time has not increased as much as it was foreseen by social scientists at the beginning of the period of the so-called information economy. Still, time spent on media compared with overall time-budget has increased internationally. Television occupies a large part, but other new media and communication devices also show an increasing time share.[2] Children start to use ICTs at an ever-earlier age; they not only have access to common family devices, but also often have their own.[3]

The use of new ICTs, digital network communication and access to multimedia information, culture and entertainment can contribute to making people's lives richer and more comfortable. Access to all new devices, however, stirs up many problems, fears and worries about their misuse and their negative influence. The increase of violence and violent entertainment, the disturbed time-balance of many media-addicted youngsters or the blurring of the dividing line between reality and virtual worlds are often cited dangers introduced by ICTs.

For various reasons, childhood and young age have gained more value and have even become overvalued in the 20th century. This new and very suggestible consumer group is kept in high esteem in the quickly changing consumption culture because, nowadays, youngsters have their own budget for consumption. This cohort has become a preferential target for different forces and ideologies, serving political, religious or economic interests. Communications aiming at this age group are manifold; and with the spreading of old and new ICTs, many new communicative genres and forms have been invented to reach them. In the following, some aspects of these old and new forms and their social message will be examined.

The changing structure of socialization and youth culture in the new media environment raises many debates among theorists, but also among practitioners (e.g. educators) and the lay public (parents confronted with problems of youth culture). Socialization processes in traditional and contemporary societies will be examined in the following, with special focus on how toys and games throughout the ages contributed to teaching social rules to young generations. Special emphasis will be laid on the transmission of value structures, social order and social norms. The theoretical approach will be complemented by recent empirical data and enlightening examples. The media usage of youngsters and the most recent media-based, electronic or virtual-reality games will be examined in the light of contemporary controversies. Young generations' media usage in the new EU member states will be examined and compared with EU15 data.

THE HIDDEN CURRICULUM: SOCIAL ORDER IN GAMES AND CELEBRATIONS

Archaeological findings of ancient cultures have revealed small objects found either in graves or in ancient dwelling places. Their function is not always very clear. Some of them are clearly representations of gods, goddesses or other supernatural forces and might have had the function of worship or magic, but at the same time they also communicated the spiritual order of the society they originated from. Prehistoric cave-paintings are thought to have had magical or aesthetic functions, but some researchers also explain the red and black dots and hands painted next to the pictures of domesticated animals as ancient 'book-keeping',[4] and many of these pictographs that represent hunting scenes might have been used to organize hunting strategies and to teach young hunters of the horde. Some ancient archaeological objects are clearly toys: articulated dolls and carts were found in Mesopotamia.[5] They might have been tools to teach children (probably girls) their future social roles in the family.

While it is easy to understand the socializing function of dolls or toy soldiers throughout history, it is important to remark that other toys and games, less directly related to future roles of the individual, also contribute to socialization by inculcating social order, social hierarchy and symbolic subordination to rules. Many globally practised board and card games today originate from ancient Asia: they certainly had either religious functions or were used as oracles or devices for predictions. But the representations that are found in ancient tombs, pictures or books also testify that they were widely used as means of leisure or competition. They comprised the worldview of the society they stemmed from and, thus, were able to transmit symbolic messages. In this way, they also fulfilled the role of teaching the prevailing rules of society and its social structure. Researchers agree that most games have a 'hidden curriculum', containing relevant social knowledge and norms, and by their interiorization the games serve to inculcate and reinforce social order.

Toys and games, whether they are aimed at children and/or adults, clearly have different functions. They not only provide entertainment or amusement, letting people get away from everyday problems and relaxing, but also provide for social occasions and enhance human relationships, even when games involve competition and agonistic functions among players. It is important to note that the time and space reserved for games is always clearly marked, and actions realized in this separated space and time do not necessarily interfere with 'real life'. Certain capitals amassed during games, however, can be transferred to real society.[6] Toys and games also help in acquiring physical and intellectual skills: dexterity and rapidity (Mikado, etc.) inventiveness, cunning (memory games, Mastermind, etc.) or intellectual knowledge in various fields (Trivial Pursuit, Scrabble, etc.). But as a most important and less evident function, toys and games effectively contribute to socializing children, and it has been so since the oldest of ages. Many games that are widely known and used nowadays all over the world have long, traditional lineages.

Games like 'Pachisi', the 'goose game', and 'snakes and ladders' symbolize the course of human life, its hardships and successes. They are rich in symbols and enhance the education of ethical norms. They often divide the world of the game (as the real world) into two opposing forces: and the game itself represents the struggle of the good and the bad and the power of fate.

'Snakes and ladders' was born in ancient India. It represents a symbolic journey through the terrestrial world aiming at fulfilment in ultimate perfection. Good and bad are represented throughout the game together with the idea of reincarnation: the player's bad moves are punished when they glide back from the snake's head to its tail, being reborn into the body of some animal. Thus, the bad moves deviate the player from the goal, while the good moves advance them to fulfilment. In ancient 'Pachisi', also an Indian game, players had to go through a path driving into the four main directions; if they met obstacles that prevented them

from continuing on their way, they had to go back to the middle of the board to be reborn in order to continue. This game was described being played in the Middle Ages in the garden of the grand Mogul Akbar, who was sitting in the middle of a marble playing space and the playing figures were young slave women, dressed in the four traditional colours. Similar games were played in different parts of the world, like 'Patolli' among inhabitants of ancient Mexico, the Aztecs and the Toltecs; and modern versions of it are still widely used everywhere, representing the ups and downs of human life. The labyrinth of the 'goose game', its sacred number of 63 (taken for the ideal human age in the Antique world), and the positive and negative steps representing fortune and misfortune also symbolize human advancement in the surrounding objective and ethical world and teach social tasks: obligation to pay taxes when crossing the bridge, punishment when entering the inn, encountering the prison and sometimes death; all these events in the game have practical, spiritual or ethical meanings and messages.

Another type of game mainly symbolizes warfare. Games like the Asian 'Go', which dates back to more than 4000 years, represent the world as a battlefield. Go opposes two armies of common soldiers surrounded by the sea on four sides. Other widely known games, like 'chess', depict two opposing armies with different social ranks or military grades. Chess also originates from India (it was called 'Chaturanga' in Sanskrit, meaning 'four branches of military': artillery, elephant raiders, cavalry and infantry). The game reached Europe through Persia, where it was modified according to the dominant social structure there: staging the shah, the vizir (and not queen), etc. Later, new modifications were introduced according to the medieval social structure in Europe: king, queen or dame, knight, peasants, etc.[7] Many historical and literary sources prove the popularity of the game throughout the ages, among which is the most extraordinary book of Alphonse X the Wise, King of Castille and Leon (1221–1284). The game's hidden message affirms that different social roles have different values and powers and they are permitted different moves or activities.

Other board games originating in ancient cultures comprise socially relevant knowledge of their time (like 'backgammon', 'Mankala', 'Senet' and others). 'Senet' was found in Egyptian tombs (like Tuth-anch-Amon's, more than 5300 years old) and must have been a game used also for predicting the dead person's path in the world of gods. It has 30 spaces, certainly in relation to the length of a month. Backgammon and its variants are highly representative of knowledge of temporal structure, with their 24 spaces (12 on each side) 30 stones, 2 colours and 7 sides; all important temporal divisions are represented: the year, the months, the days, the zodiac, the night and the day, etc.

Card games, these widely used but often blamed and forbidden games, also have a hidden curriculum. Their origin goes back to painted sticks and arrows and later paper strips used in ancient times in Korea for divination. Cards were used for performing prophecy and they quickly spread everywhere. Being used in organized sets, they could easily be used for representing social order. Several different types exist even today: cards used in southern Europe (Spain, Italy) go back to Indian traditions, those in central (Germany, Austria, Hungary) and western Europe (France, Britain) preserve different traditions.[8] Many card games convey intellectual knowledge: quartets teach geographical notions; rummy card-backs often represent royal successions. A rare Belgian card series, edited in 1945, represents the four victorious armies of World War II, with real historical figures (Stalin, Churchill, De Gaulle and Truman as 'kings', with the most famous buildings of their capitals for aces and a caricature of Hitler as Jolly Joker, sitting on bombs).

Different role games, as well as rituals performed at festivities and carnivals at certain well-defined periods of the year, also have their hidden social message. Detailed analyses about these rituals agree that their main function was teaching social rules: although

celebrations, rituals and carnivals reverse normal social order (the election of an Easter king or queen, fool king, etc.) and bring about excess (eating, drinking, dancing, ecstatic events, etc.), their main function is to let the tensions sweep away like through a valve and reinforce the underlying social order. This function explains why heavy stress was put on the separated time and space coordinates of such rituals and festivities. They were often performed at special places: the inn, the outskirts of a city or a village, and at special times of the year, which all had their social meaning (struggle between good and bad at winter–spring junction, solstice, etc.) (Huizinga, 1944; Fabre and Camberoque, 1977; Supka, 1989; Fabre 1992).

Examples can be cited endlessly, but all these cases witness the social role of games. In different societies, at different geographical points and in different times, they were used to teach and reinforce societal roles and rules, social hierarchy and values. Although differences can be found among cultures and epochs, the overall pattern is the same, functions and messages are similar. In more recent times, and in more liberal societies, the rules may have become less binding, but the 'hidden curriculum' is still there. New games also follow the structure and function of ancient ones. Not only Halma, Dames and others are conceived in similar ways as Go or chess, but popular games like Barbi or Matchbox contribute to the acquisition of the values of today's consumer society, putting the emphasis on a middle-class way of life and private property. Barbi is a perfect model of the modern capitalist world of consumption, where the child learns the importance of physical attraction, changing fashion, abundance in consumer goods and a wide range of leisure activities. Pets, cars, holidays, fashionable sports, outings and fashionable jobs are represented by the accessories available for Barbi and they are appealingly depicted in the catalogues. Matchbox cars and transformer collections have the same functions in boys' consumer training. Duplo and Lego, Polly Pocket and other 'worlds' convey the image of modern middle-class townships[9] with all their *public and private* buildings: hospital, school, fire station, little shops, playgrounds, nice family houses, camping cars, etc.

The most outstanding type of game that has to be mentioned here for the important 'message' and 'training' it provides about a modern capitalist economy and society is Monopoly, although it is a new game in the sense that it does not have centuries old history going back to ancient times. It became famous and widespread in the 20th century. And although many games later tried to borrow rules of certain restricted areas of economy (Burse-game, Auction-game, etc.), it still is the basic game of its sort. The central role of Monopoly in 'teaching' modern (monopole-) capitalist economy becomes evident by the fact that it was adapted to all countries of the modern world: it exists in all national versions (with national street names, etc.). In Hungary before the Communist period, it existed in its Hungarian version, named Capitaly(!). After World War II, the game was never re-edited in Hungary and official ideology considered it as a game conveying adversary propaganda. For ideological reasons, no doubt, the state socialist game industry was expected to propose some similar games introducing the rules of socialist economy and ideology instead of the 'rotten capitalist' ones. 'Gazdálkodj okosan!' ('Economize wisely!') appeared in the Hungarian market in the 1960s. It was a poor, socialist version of Monopoly: the playfield where the players had to evolve depicted Hungarian monuments and institutions classified in two categories: the good socialist institutions, which were either free for their great pedagogical value (visit to the National Gallery, sight-seeing in Budapest, zoo and sporting activities) or inexpensive (institutions for everyday private life, like food shops, public transport, holidays in trades-union hotels). Other places represented a negative moral: the pub, the tobacconist, the night bar (where the player had to pay a month's salary), etc. Work was represented with high esteem: Ózd, the newly constructed industrial city, symbol of socialist heavy industry, was the place where the player earned their wages. The goal the players could attain was not buying more and more streets, houses and hotels and making others pay when they entered their property; the ultimate goal in this socialist 'Monopoly' was to buy a block flat, with one drawing room, a bedroom, a kitchen and a bathroom, and to buy some basic furniture and simple household devices: a sewing machine, a washing machine, a stove, a radio and a TV. In order to be able to buy a flat, the player had to 'economize', regularly place money in the state bank. The game had relatively high success among youngsters, as this was the only version available of the yearned-for Western game. Later, in the 1970s, some improved and enriched versions of the game also appeared, where the players could also buy a car and personal belongings that were somewhat more attractive than in the first version (and more attractive typographically).

Still, the few old versions of Capitaly that outlived the war in private ownership were secretly borrowed by friends and acquaintances for a day or two, to play in the intimacy of their home. Thus, the new generations of kids were 'taught' the same rules and principles of capitalism as their Western peers. Private game-copying was also a 'system-resistant' activity: in research back in the 1980s, we found many hand-made, copied versions of Monopoly, Capitaly and other similar games, which were unavailable in a socialist country but which had an aura of 'liberty' at that time.

In the West, as a counter reaction to mainstream games, certain marginal game producers edited games with different 'messages'. Several mock-Monopolies were published: 'Anti-Monopoly', a game emphasising anti-racism, and values of equality and social justice; 'Mad Max', where the ultimate aim was to lose all one's own fortune. Games with alternative political and ideological messages also appeared: 'Mai 68'; 'Chomageopoly', using the example of the Paris student riots or the famous Lip factory's strike to teach equality, workers' solidarity and other values of counter-culture. Other games, like 'Cité, élus et citoyens construisent leur ville', tried to transmit the message of a democratic society with active and responsible citizens. Games elaborated by different civil society groups attempt to transmit knowledge and values that are highly valued by their members, e.g. the American 'Made for Trade'

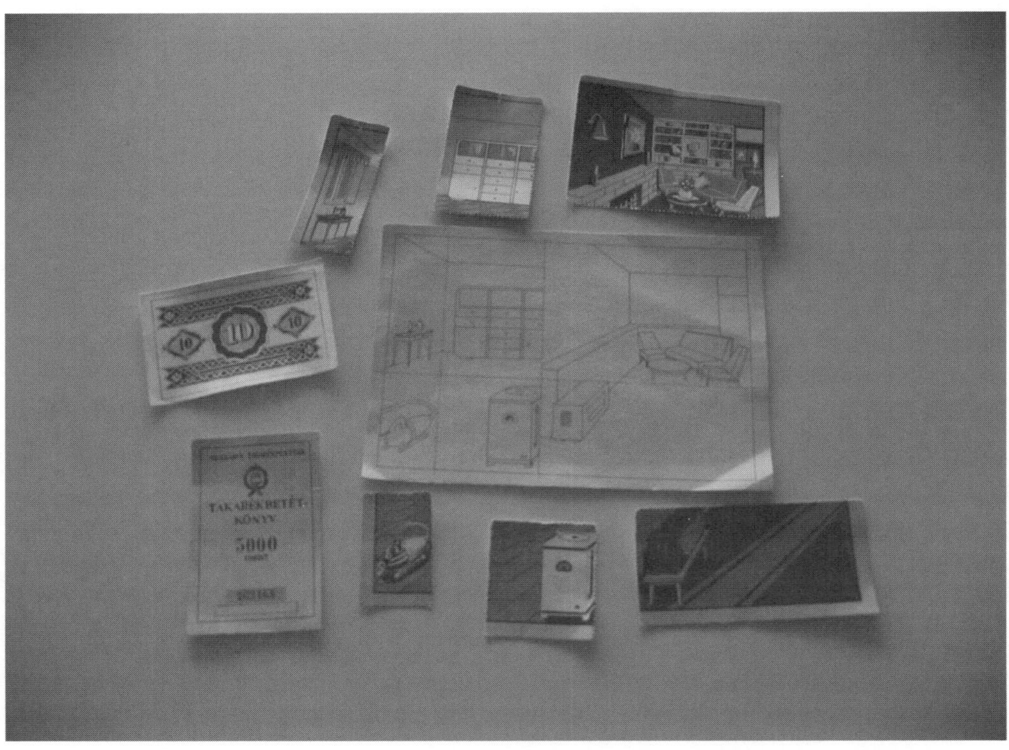

GAZDÁLKODJ
OKOSAN!
SZERENCSE
KÁRTYÁK
VILLAMOS
TÜZIFA
SZÉN
NEMZETI
GALÉRIA
KÖZÉRT
CSEMEGE
SZERENCSE
KERÉK
SÖR
OTP

ANTI-MONOPOLY
Ce jeu n'est ni une licence
ni une production de Parker Brothers,
les producteurs du jeu MONOPOLY
350 écus
Boîte aux lettres
Boîte aux lettres
ALLEZ AU
TRIBUNAL
DÉSOLÉ
CAISSE
ANTI-TRUST
100
écus
DÉPART
100
écus

ce jeu a été conçu et réalisé par les travailleurs de LIP
ont participé à la réalisation de ce jeu
S.I.T.R.A.B. (Vosges)
C.I.P. (Nord)
CHOMAGEopoly

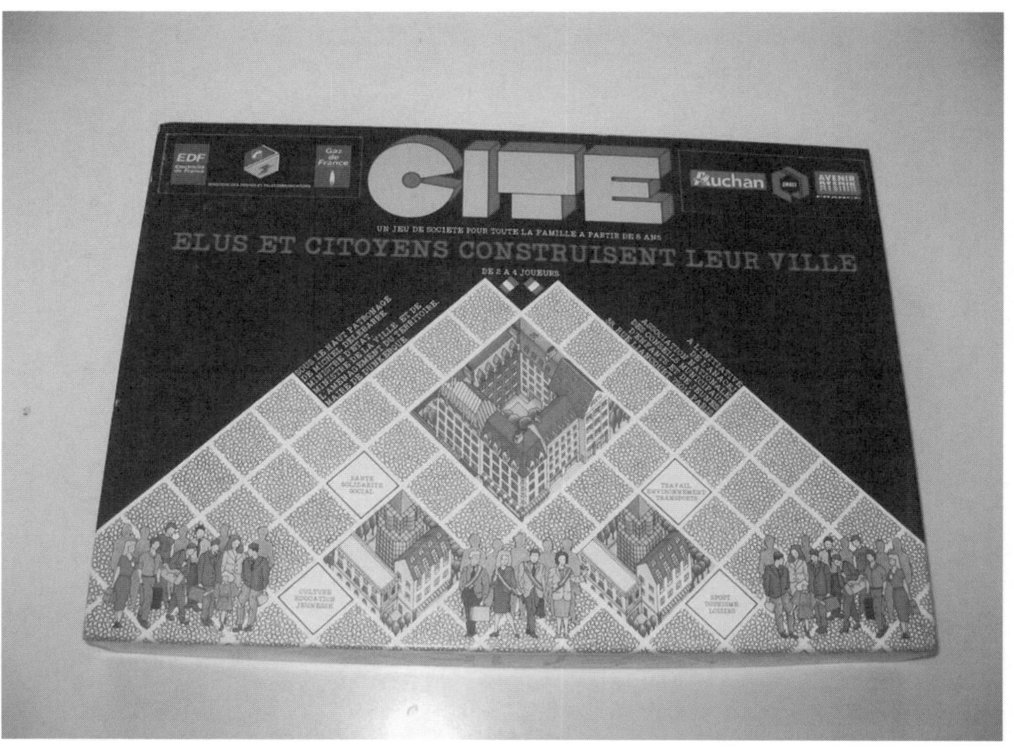
EDF
Gaz de France
CITE
Auchan
UN JEU DE SOCIETE POUR TOUTE LA FAMILLE A PARTIR DE 8 ANS
ELUS ET CITOYENS CONSTRUISENT LEUR VILLE
DE 2 A 4 JOUEURS

game, depicting traditional American society, or the Basque game Ziunta, created, produced and distributed by cultural activists in the French Basque country.

The hidden ideological message of the games was well recognized by playful people in central and eastern Europe. During our research, we found several home-made games, which did not just copy existing foreign games. Private people, groups of friends, made their own versions of games depicting the world around them using the typical narrative structure of some of the well-known games. The most striking one we found was a completely designed game (only one original exists!) called 'Socialy' with Lenin's pictures and other socialist imagery on the playground. The philosophy of the game was inspired by Monopoly: the players had to collect the most important 'good' in order to succeed in a state-socialist society; they had to have the greatest amount of 'socialist relations', patronage, favouritism, but they could also use baksheesh, tipping, social influence, wire-pulling, etc.

INFORMATION AND COMMUNICATION TECHNOLOGIES IN CENTRAL AND EASTERN EUROPE

The use of the new devices follows a particular pattern in central and eastern Europe and, thus, the above-mentioned worries concerning their predominance in youth culture are particularly strong in this region.

Economic, sociological, historical and cultural factors play an important role in the way consumption and related processes have developed in eastern and central Europe, and this closely affects media use as well. Several recent surveys have shown that, because of the delayed economic, political and social development of the countries in the region,

differences of attitude, of expectance and of trust in institutions and in social development exist between western and eastern European societies, as well as differences in self-image, identity formation and belief in the future. Central/eastern Europe has been hampered in its social, economic and political development in comparison with the West. The century-old dilemma of how to catch up with the West and especially with the Western model of consumption gave increased importance to possessing Western-type consumer goods, Western entertainment and liberty of choice in leisure activities.

Another important factor that affects the use of new ICTs in central/eastern Europe comes from the fact that their tumultuous past decades and frequent political and ideological changes and the tendencies of state socialism resulted in an effort of the population to severely separate private life from public scrutiny, to try and preserve some private freedom, at least in consumption and leisure. All these attempts provided an increased importance attached to private life and consumer goods.

The penetration of new media technology played an important role in the political changes that occurred in central/eastern Europe at the end of the 1980s. They communicated Western lifestyle and images of consumption, obstructed the smooth functioning of censorship,[10] enhanced liberal, pluralist communication flows and accelerated the changes. The spreading of the new devices clearly demonstrated the unsustainability of the former political system.

During the Kádár regime in Hungary, in the context of a tacit compromise between the central political power and the population, there existed a certain 'restricted public sphere', relatively free private life and slowly growing consumption possibilities. The population carefully preserved every bit of private freedom. Private life, Western consumption goods and signs of private wealth were highly valued by the population, and sociologists took account of a special sort of 'consumption tourism': Hungarian state holidays, especially in the last decade before the system change, gave occasion to thousands of Hungarian families to purchase consumption goods in neighbouring Austria.[11] Information and communication channels free from the control of central authorities also exercised strong appeal on the Hungarian population, mainly as signs of private freedom. Products of Western technology appeared quickly in Hungary, mostly through private import. These products (like home videos, the first mobile phones, Commodore computers in the early 1980s) had a clear function of signalling social status. These devices were put in the 'saint corner' of homes to be seen by all incoming persons, or worn ostensibly by quickly enriching entrepreneurs.[12]

Sociologists acknowledged a strong value-crisis in central/eastern European societies. It was considered to result from the many unsolved problems of the past, but also because of the political system of the countries of the region. Constraints of political ideology and lack of Western-type consumer choice reinforced an extremely privatizing individualism aiming at individual consumption, leisure and a strongly growing appeal of hedonistic values. Hankiss (1982) characterized this development as 'negative modernization'.

Because of economic hardships, consumer goods are valued highly in the region and are strongly used as indicators of social success. They often serve as status symbols and their possession is sometimes more important than their use. This is often the case with the older generations, who sometimes seem to be satisfied with acquiring the latest devices without being able to use them appropriately (or use only the simplest functions, e.g. receiving cell phone calls but not actively calling or using WAP or SMS; word-processing with a computer without using the internet or other more complicated software, etc.) Young generations, however, are quick to adopt the newest technologies: a form of the generation gap between youngsters and their parents.

Even after the changeover, the requisites of a Western lifestyle and consumption continued to attract people. New ICTs became the symbols of the newly acquired freedom[13], even if people had to spend a much higher proportion of their income on them than their Western homologues (Table 16.1 helps to compare GDP among EU countries).

Several sociological surveys have proved that all devices enhancing entertainment (TVs, CD, DVD and video-players) and representing social status show quicker penetration than devices necessitating active participation and/or user competence (like PCs,

Table 16.1 GDP in Europe.[a] *Source*: Eurostat: Key Figures on Europe, Statistical Pocketbook 2006, p. 15

	GDP at current prices (EUR 1000 million)[b]			*GDP per capita (PPS)*[c]		
	2000	*2005*	*Share of EU-25, 2005 (%)*	*2000*	*2005*	*Rel. to EU-25, 2005 (EU-25 = 100)*
EU-25	9,090.5	10,793.8	100.0	20,100	23,400	100.0
Euro area	6,708.8	7,973.8	73.9	21,800	24,800	106.0
BE	251.7	299.9	2.8	23,500	27,600	117.9
CZ	60.4	98.4	0.9	12,800	17,200	73.5
DK	173.6	208.7	1.9	25,400	28,900	123.5
DE	2,062.5	2,245.5	20.8	22,500	25,300	108.1
EE	5.9	10.3	0.1	8,200	12,800	54.7
EL	125.9	181.1	1.7	14,600	19,600	83.8
ES	630.3	902.7	8.4	18,600	22,900	97.9
FR	1,441.4	1,696.8	15.7	22,800	25,500	109.0
IE	104.4	160.1	1.5	25,400	32,299	138.0
IT	1,191.1	1,417.2	13.1	22,800	24,200	103.4
CY	9.9	13.4	0.1	16,300	19,600	83.8
LV	8.5	12.8	0.1	7,100	10,900	46.6
LT	12.4	20.0	0.2	7,700	11,900	50.9
LU	21.3	27.2	0.3	43,300	53,900	230.3
HU	51.0	87.8	0.8	10,600	14,500	62.0
MT	4.2	4.5	0.0	15,600	16,200	69.2
NL	402.3	500.2	4.6	24,100	28,900	123.5
AT	210.4	246.5	2.3	25,300	28,600	122.2
PL	185.8	240.5	2.2	9,400	11,600	49.6
PT	122.3	147.2	1.4	16,200	16,600	70.9
SI	20.8	27.4	0.3	14,600	18,900	80.8
SK	21.9	37.3	0.3	9,500	12,700	54.3
FI	130.9	155.3	1.4	22,700	26,300	112.4
SE	262.6	288.0	2.7	23,900	27,700	118.4
UK	1,564.6	1,770.2	16.4	22,600	27,100	115.8
BG	13.7	21.3	0.2	5,300	7,400	31.6
HR	20.0	29.7	0.3	8,200	10,900	46.6
MK						
RO	40.3	80.6	0.7	5,000	7,800	33.3
TR	216.7	289.9	2.7	6,000	6,800	29.1
IS	9.2	12.4	0.1	25,200	29,800	127.4
NO	181.1	238.0	2.2	31,900	36,000	153.8
CH	266.7	295.1	2.7	26,700	30,800	131.6
JP	5,037.4	3,674.9	34.0	22,400	25,900	110.7
US	10,629.1	10,035.9	93.0	30,600	35,600	152.1

[a]EU-25: European Union of 25 Member States; BE: Belgium; CZ: Czech Republic; DK: Denmark; DE: Germany; EE: Estonia; EL: Greece; ES: Spain; FR: France; IE: Ireland; IT: Italy; CY: Cyprus; LV: Latvia; LT: Lithuania; LU: Luxembourg; HU: Hungary; MT: Malta; NL: Netherlands; AT: Austria; PL: Poland; PT: Portugal; SI: Slovenia; SK: Slovakia; FI: Finland; SE: Sweden; UK: United Kingdom; BG: Bulgaria; HR: Croatia; MK: Former Yugoslav Republic of Macedonia; RO: Romania; TR: Turkey; IS: Iceland; NO: Norway; CH: Switzerland; JP: Japan; US: United States.

[b]Belgium, Estonia, Spain, France, Ireland, Lithuania, Luxembourg, UK, Bulgaria, Croatia, Romania, Turkey, Iceland, forecasts.

[c]Forecasts, 2005.

internet or video/digital cameras) (Heller, forthcoming). While more traditional ICTs offering entertainment are widespread in all EU countries, new member states are lagging behind EU15 countries in the spread and use of the more complex devices. Table 16.2 shows differences between the saturated state of TV sets, fixed and mobile phones and the lower penetration of home PCs and internet. Recent Hungarian statistics also prove that 41% of Hungarian households own more than one TV set. In 2004, 16.6% of Hungarian households owned a DVD player, but their number doubled in 2005.

Table 16.3 shows the spread of household computers and internet access in EU countries from 2002 to 2005, and Table 16.4 gives insight to the penetration process by showing the relevant social groups and age groups that enhanced the increases.

Statistics prove the increasing penetration of new ICTs and their growing use in the countries of central/eastern Europe. Although the costs are relatively higher than in western Europe, new technologies steadily gain terrain in the new member states, with young generations of the population leading the process. Table 16.5 clearly affirms this tendency by showing figures in the growth of users for each country.

Entertaining media are very popular and largely spread in Hungary. It is worth remarking on the high score of the country (and also other central and eastern European countries)

Table 16.2 ICTs in European households 2005. *Source*: Eurobarometer (E-communication, Household Survey, 2006)[a]

	ICTs (%)				
	TV	*Fix phone*	*Mobile phone*	*Home computers*	*Home Internet*
EU25	97	78	80	58	48
EU15	97		81	63	53
BE	96	73	80	57	47
CZ	97	53	84	41	23
DK	97	78	87	77	64
DE	95	86	74	52	46
EE	98	58	81	45	36
EL	100	86	81	33	18
ES	99	74	78	46	37
FR	96	85	78	56	40
IE	99	80	84	44	36
IT	98	67	85	47	29
CY	100	90	85	46	27
LV	96	43	81	35	19
LT	98	54	78	36	14
LU	98	91	87	68	61
HU	97	61	75	36	18
MT	99	97	82	53	44
NL	99	96	91	83	81
AT	99	70	79	49	37
PL	97	63	67	41	20
PT	99	54	78	34	18
SI	98	85	86	59	47
SK	99	54	76	35	11
FI	97	57	93	66	54
SE	99	100	93	79	76
UK	98	85	85	58	47
BG	96	67	52	13	7
HR	98	90	79	40	30
RO	96	53	57	30	10
TR	98	75	78	12	5

[a]See Table 16.1 for country code list.

Table 16.3 Evolution of households' access to PCs and Internet 2002–2005[a]

	Access to PCs (%)				*Access to Internet (%)*			
	2002	*2003*	*2004*	*2005*	*2002*	*2003*	*2004*	*2005*
EU25			55	58			43	48
EU15	50	56	58	63	39	43	46	53
BE								50
CZ		24	30	30		15	19	19
DK	72	79	79	84	56	64	69	75
DE	61	65	69	70	46	54	60	62
EE			36	43			31	39
EL	25	29	29	33	12	16	17	22
ES		47	52	55		28	34	36
FR	37	46	50		23	31	34	
IE		42	46	55		36	40	47
IT	40	48	47	46	34	32	34	39
CY			47	46			53	
LV			26	30			15	42
LT	12	20	27	32	4	6	12	16
LU	53	58	67	87	40	45	59	77
HU			32	42			14	22
MT								
NL	69	71	74	78	58	61	65	78
AT	49	51	59	63	33	37	45	47
PL			36	40			26	30
PT	27	38	41	42	15	22	26	31
SI			58	61			47	48
SK			39	47			23	23
FI	55	57	57	64	44	47	51	54
SE				80				73
UK	58	63	65	70	50	55	56	60

[a]See Table 16.1 for country code list.

in international statistics concerning time spent watching TV (Tables 16.6 and 16.7). Children's scores are especially outstanding. The time spent playing electronic games, either in game-casinos or in private places, is also very high.

The actual spread of new ICTs in *Hungary* is both the result of the population's various needs as described above and of a late but definite governmental policy to introduce digital network technology in schools and public places. Huge sums were recently spent to provide equipment in all Hungarian schools, to establish e-points in towns and villages and to instigate software and content development to attract new users. Some 55% of internet-using Hungarian young people connect to the web at school or at university and 43% use the internet at home. E-governance has also been developed. But according to statistics the main attraction for users is e-mails and discussion fora, and for young people it is chat and gaming. Recent statistics prove that young generations are more active in using new technology. Computers are more frequently present in Hungarian households with one or two children: 57% of these households had a home PC in 2004 (29% in 2000). Internet access is also higher in these households: 24% (9% in 2000) versus 14% in all households in 2004. Table 16.8 gives a clear image of the generation gap and young people's interest with respect to digital culture.

Figure 16.1 shows the role played by young generations in the spread of Internet use and the rapidity of penetration in the Hungarian society. Besides digital culture, young people in Hungary spend relatively much of their free time listening to music or radio and watching TV and video. Time spent on reading declined steadily in the 1970s and 1980s, but

Table 16.4 EU individuals' computer use (population 16–74 having used a computer in the last 3 months)[a]

	Computer use (%)								
	Total	*Male*	*Female*	*Age range*			*Education*		
				16–24	*25–54*	*54–74*	*None/low*	*Medium*	*High*
EU25	58	62	65	85	66	29	38	66	88
EU15	82	88	67	88	70	33	37	73	87
BE									
CZ	42	45	40	77	50	12	33	40	79
DK	83	84	81	96	92	59	72	84	93
DE	73	77	69	97	85	43	65	74	83
EE	60	64	58	89	68	24	53	56	74
EL	29	31	26	55	34	6	9	39	67
ES	52	57	47	84	60	16	26	74	87
FR									
IE	44	42	46	52	49	21	26	49	72
IT	41	45	35	71	49	12	19	62	80
CY	41	41	40	75	44	9	17	45	73
LV	47	48	47	88	51	12	31	44	77
LT	42	42	41	81	44	7	31	33	76
LU	77	87	68	98	84	49	64	85	95
HU	42	42	42	66	49	15	16	59	82
MT									
NL	83	87	79	98	90	58	66	90	96
AT	63	68	58	91	74	25	39	68	85
PL	45	46	44	84	46	12	36	40	82
PT	40	43	36	78	44	9	24	86	90
SI	52	54	50	92	60		25	55	92
SK	63	65	60	89	70	18	35	70	88
FI	76	78	75	98	88	44	63	78	92
SE	84	87	81	98	93	60	71	82	97
UK	72	76	70	89	80	46	40	79	92

[a]See Table 16.1 for country code list.

reading books and magazines in recent years has gained importance due to certain editors' policies, nationwide competitions (The Big Book), Harry Potter and other popular books. It is worth noting the differences between men and women: young Hungarian women read substantially more than men do, whether books or newspapers and magazines. On the other hand, computer and internet use show slighter differences among Hungarian men and women than among the two sexes in other European countries. Table 16.9 shows the results of research on spare-time activities of Hungarian youth (from 14 to 24) in 2000.

The internet is used for various activities: information gathering, leisure, studying, creative activities, chatting and handling social relations. Among leisure and free-time activities, gaming is widespread all over the world. Among young Hungarians, 42% play online games or download games from the internet.

CHILDREN AND THE NEW MEDIA

New technological developments have greatly affected children's media use. Socialization is increasingly governed by television and other media. Computer and video games continue to have similar functions as toys and games had before. It is beyond doubt that new media can provide increasingly more comfortable and appropriate ways of acquiring new knowledge and reinforcing social values (Livingstone, 2003b,c). They can provide more effective methods of learning and communicating and of enhancing personal interest, participation

Table 16.5 Internet usage in the EU. *Source*: http://www.internetworldstats.com/stats.htm (September 2006)

	Population (2006 est.)	*Internet users, latest data*	*Penetration (% population)*	*Usage (% in EU)*	*User growth, 2000–2006 (%)*
Austria	8,188,806	4,650,000	56.8	1.9	121.4
Belgium	10,481,831	5,100,000	48.7	2.1	155.0
Cyprus	961,154	298,000	31.0	0.1	148.3
Czech Republic	10,211,609	5,100,000	49.9	2.1	410.0
Denmark	5,425,373	3,762,500	69.4	1.6	92.9
Estonia	1,339,157	690,000	51.5	0.3	88.2
Finland	5,260,970	3,286,000	62.5	1.4	70.5
France	61,004,840	29,521,451	48.4	12.3	247.3
Germany	82,515,988	50,616,207	61.3	21.1	110.9
Greece	11,275,420	3,800,000	33.7	1.6	280.0
Hungary	10,060,684	3,050,000	30.3	1.3	326.6
Ireland	4,065,631	2,060,000	50.7	0.9	162.8
Italy	59,115,261	28,870,000	48.8	12.0	118.7
Latvia	2,293,246	1,030,000	44.9	0.4	586.7
Lithuania	3,416,941	1,221,700	35.8	0.5	443.0
Luxembourg	459,393	315,000	68.6	0.1	215.0
Malta	385,308	127,200	33.0	0.1	218.0
Netherlands	16,386,216	10,806,328	65.9	4.5	177.1
Poland	38,115,814	10,600,000	27.8	4.4	278.6
Portugal	10,501,051	7,782,760	74.1	3.2	211.3
Slovakia	5,379,455	2,500,000	46.5	1.0	284.6
Slovenia	1,959,872	1,090,000	55.6	0.5	263.3
Spain	44,351,186	19,204,771	43.3	8.0	256.4
Sweden	9,076,757	6,800,000	74.9	2.8	68.0
UK	60,139,274	37,600,000	62.5	15.7	144.2
European Union	**462,371,237**	**239,881,917**	**51.9**	**100.0**	**157.5**

Table 16.6 Yearly average TV watching in Hungary for population over the age of 4 years. *Source*: AGB Hungary

Year	*Time watching TV (h:min/day)*
1995	3:30
1996	3:32
1997	3:42
1998	3:56
1999	4:00
2000	4:09
2001	4:11
2002	4:16
2003	4:22
2004	4:31
2005	4:25

Table 16.7 Average TV watching in Hungary in 2004 by age. *Source*: Kósa (2004)

Age group	*Time (h:min)*
4–12	3:52
13–17	3:28
18–29	2:58
30–39	3:49
40–49	4:03
>50	5:08

Table 16.8 Proportion of PC users and Internet users in Hungary according to age group in 2004. *Source*: WIP 2005

Age group	*PC use (%)*	*Internet use (%)*
14–17	96	89
18–29	68	54
30–39	54	33
40–49	40	24
50–59	27	17
>60	5	2

and individual choice (hobbies, etc.). But developments in media offer and usage seem to reinforce quite opposite trends. Old and new media mainly multiply choice in entertainment and distraction. There is also much concern about the educational content, 'the hidden curriculum' of ICTs, new ways of usage (p2p downloading, online gambling), new media genres (reality TV, soap operas) and popular content (violent video games); the communicated message in popular genres or games has reinforced anxieties. New forms

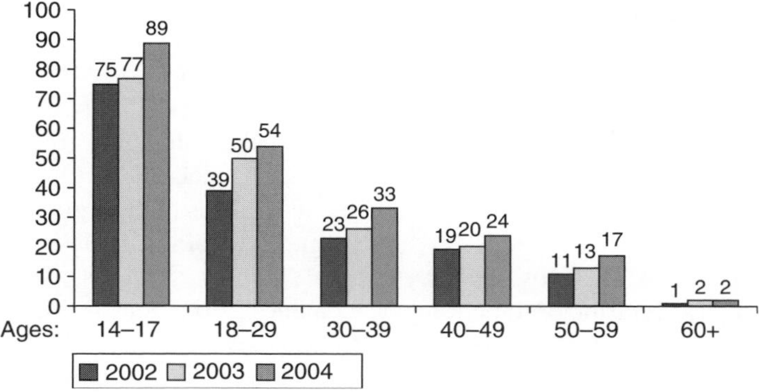

Figure 16.1 Internet users (%) in different age groups in Hungary, 2004.
***Source*: www.tarki.hu/**

Table 16.9 Spare-time activities of Hungarian youth (from 14 to 24) in 2000.
***Source*: GfK Hungária PiackutatóIntézet**

Cultural activity	*Spare time use (%)*		
	Average	*Men*	*Women*
Listening to music (radio, tape, CD)	81	82	80
Watching TV and video	72	69	74
Reading newspapers and magazines	49	46	53
Listening to radio	66	61	71
Reading books	34	26	43
Dancing, disco	20	22	17
Going to movie	16	15	18
Pop concert	4	4	3
Theatre and opera	3	2	5
Museums and exhibitions	2	1	3
Concerts of classical music	1	1	1

of social violence, especially among children and youngsters, have put on the agenda the problem of socialization through the new devices. Many international studies have tackled the problem of violence in the media and pointed to the modified value structure of popular culture (Drotner, 2000; Millwood Hargrave and Livingstone, 2006). However, the advantages and the dangers of new media and ICTs and their increased use by children have to be approached from different sides.

Children and youngsters are in the avant-garde of the use of new ICTs and quickly develop the necessary *skills and competences*. While older generations may have aversions or difficulties getting used to new technologies, it is very often the younger generations who attract their elders to use the devices, showing and teaching them how to proceed. Psychological experiments proved that youngsters approach the new devices with more curiosity and more ingenuity.

A computer game from 1994, *Alice: An Interactive Museum* by Kuniyoshi Kaneko, a Japanese painter, gave evidence of this fact (Kaneko and Toshiba–EMI Ltd, 1994). At the beginning of the game, the player finds him/herself in an unknown house with peculiar paintings on the walls (Kaneko's own paintings). To be able to proceed one has to search through all the rooms to find clues without knowing at first, what to look for. During the game, among other adventures, one gradually finds out that a deck of cards has to be found, one by one, clues which will lead eventually out of the house. Kaneko's artwork on the walls is very interactive, resulting in different surprises and clues. In an experiment conducted in Budapest in the late 1990s, adults often did not even know how to start the game and then how to proceed:

they had difficulties in reaching the end of the game. Children, however, tried all possible moves with a joystick, the keyboard and the mouse and scrolling across the screens, quickly finding the hidden objects that had to be gathered in order to proceed. Gaming experience, computer skills and knowledge of *Alice in Wonderland* by Lewis Carroll was of help to reach the goal.

Frequent usage of ICTs helps the user acquire skills and also contributes to building up a certain *techno-culture*. It is supposed that computer games enhance the acquisition of certain skills (like rapidity) and teach a certain concentration of attention. Certain functions of mobile phones (like SMS) even modify the way we use our fingers and thumbs or apply linguistic innovativeness, but there is no evidence so far as to whether these skills can easily be transferred to other spheres of life.

The technological possibilities of ICTs, and especially television, provide a *double mission* that is sometimes hard to harmonize: information transmitting, education and culture on the one hand, and entertainment, leisure and distraction on the other hand. This double function is even stronger and intermingled in more recent electronic culture. It is without doubt that new ICTs contribute to a more comfortable life for those who have access to them and have the necessary competence to use the possibilities offered by mobile, digital, networked devices. Information gathering, handling, storage and retrieval become easy and more effective, whether in the public or the private domain (home accounting, studying, word processing, handling statistics and databases, information searching, etc.).

While most ICTs and media could in principle offer a wide range of cultural products enhancing education, information and entertainment, this multiple function has been modified during the past decades. The early period of electronic media constituted a rich cultural environment (with poor technological possibilities when compared with contemporary media) with more cultural engagement. In the early years of radio and even more so of television, cultural programming was more ambitious: televised literary works, radio and TV dramas and quizzes on knowledgeable topics were offered to large populations and they met the audience's interest and popularity. The development of global media and growing competition among channels, mass cultural production and audience measurement gradually modified the offer. Entertainment has become the main goal, with less and less demanding cultural content. 'Infotainment' came to blur the borders and managed to swallow real information and culture or mix into a cocktail of light production where former value structures were replaced by values of consumption, easy compensation, glamour and fame of the star system, the boulevardization of public life with private topics and gossips to meet public liking. The enlarged media choice did not enlarge or diversify the offer of content and displaced certain cultural products into small subcultural niches.[14]

This development is especially problematic with young generations, as they lack the opportunity to get acquainted with forms of culture in the large sense that are not part of popular media. While the role of former socializing systems, especially family and school, is decreasing, the importance of the media in communicating social roles and values is becoming stronger. The type of media young people have access to and are inclined to use may be of great importance, and this is where not only the well-known digital gap among regions of the world may be decisive, but also among layers of the same society and among age groups. The digital gap in this respect depends very strongly not only on physical and technological access, but also on the acquisition of the necessary skills and competences to use ICTs and use the vast capacities they offer. The generation gap in cultural reception is especially serious, because youth culture strongly enhanced by ICTs offers a new distraction to youngsters as opposed to their parents' culture with its devalorized experiences (unemployment, depreciated competences, etc.), thus segregating even more the different generations within the family. The lack of common media and ICT experiences will entail a lack of common topics and communication fallacies inside the family[15] and reinforce the 'escape' use of media and ICTs by both generations.

A Hungarian study (László, 1999) investigated the socialization process of children between 12 and 18. It proved the growing importance of TV and video games in their lives: not only the time spent using these devices was found to be growing, but children's value structure also proved to be strongly influenced by them. An interesting aspect of the study was to find out what persons the children regarded as their heroes and where they found these models. Although differences were discovered according to types of school and family social status, the main results showed that 49% of the heroes were influenced by family (family members, persons in family narratives), 38% by the media and only 13% by the school (teachers, famous scientists, artists, politicians, etc.).[16] The most preferred values were also investigated and the results showed that values attached to lifestyle, wealth, and physical attractiveness were highly appreciated and most of the preferred values were related to private life (62% private life, 12% personal relations, 7% social coexistence and 19% others).

The quick accessibility and easy handling of all kinds of information and cultural products offer the possibility of radically *new approaches to culture and education*. Technological development enables users to reach easily and to connect creatively different cultural products. Hypertext links and accessibility through the same devices (especially computer-mediated communication) multiply the possible relationships and influence among genres, individual oeuvres, different discourses and media contents. Texts, data, pictures, music, voices and films are not only processed through the same devices, but also get into meta-cultural discourse with each other, introducing a new notion of 'intertextuality of culture'. Surfing through different cultural fields reinforces the innovativeness of cultural reception and of production. New forms and ways of access contribute to new cultural concepts: contemporary literature keeps experimenting with non-linear expressions[17] and the metaphor of cultural reception is increasingly changing from a 'path' metaphor to a 'labyrinth' metaphor. The digital networked accessibility may lead to an extremely rich and active attitude to culture and education and enhance individual and collective interactivity and creativity, as can already be seen in weblog writing, personal webpages and discussion fora. The strong *interactivity* potential characteristic of new ICTs may contribute to more activity and engagement in communal and public affairs. Public institutions, education and many other forms of culture and entertainment can build up an active and participating citizen attitude in young generations. Education of youngsters should include the use of ICTs in community affairs, in participation, in interactive decision-making, authentic production (participation in the life and decisions of the school, of the local community, of cultural institutions, producing school electronic journals, community blogs, new forms of active participation offered by theatres and museums) (Drotner, 1998; Tan *et al.*, forthcoming).

Many attempts have already been made to enhance active participation and creativity: radio or TV discussion programmes[18] where interested public can join in through new media on political, cultural, moral affairs. Local self-governments offer similar possibilities on their websites, and many cultural programmes and competitions try to reinforce children's sensibility to public issues (e.g. digital photo competitions concerning their own local region). The Hungarian version of the British *The Big Book* was a great success with the participation of several media, ICTs and an active population. Sulinet, a web portal created by the Hungarian Ministry of Education that offers all kinds of materials for children, teachers and schools, proposed a nationwide computer contest after the publication of the Hungarian translation of the fourth book of the Harry Potter series. The contest (five questions every day) was planned to last for 1 month, but the organizers were obliged to continue because of the huge interest and because of the number of participants with 100% solutions after more than 3 months. When the contest finally stopped there were still 15 people having 100% accuracy. The popularity of the competition was amazing, especially as the questions became more and more difficult and contestants had to look for solutions in the translated and the original version of all the Harry Potter volumes, as well as looking for help on the internet. It was found out at that stage that a high number of Harry Potter webpages existed in English and other languages, and some Hungarian youngsters even created interactive Harry Potter webpages where very vivid activities took place: games, literary criticism, creative writing and illustration, musical creation, aesthetic development, etc., forming, in some cases, long-lasting communities.

The technological possibilities of the new ICTs also enhance the blurring of creation. Digital technology not only simplifies creation, it also makes it possible to recreate a finished product continually in a modified form or version. Cultural production in this sense is never complete; products are open to re-elaboration. Consequently, a cultural product today can only be characterized by its time coordinates.[19]

But there is a worse problem: the technological possibilities offered by new ICTs also facilitate the *blurring of authorship*. They not only provide good possibilities to individual creativity, but also to falsification and plagiarism. This problem not only concerns p2p downloading, but also any misappropriation of digitally accessible products. The multiplication of cases of pirated theses in higher education, of internet-copied homework and other forms of 'digital stealing' prove the importance of the issue. And although legal frameworks are not yet ready to tackle the whole problem, children do not necessarily realize the norm-breaking attitude they often perform when using ICTs.

Facilitated information gathering through new ICTs also faces the users, and especially children, with the problem of *information sources*. Because of the free character of new ICTs, especially the internet, the sources of information have become more uncertain and less traceable, which makes the content less creditable. For reasons of laziness and handiness, children and youngsters tend to choose the internet instead of books, encyclopaedias and dictionaries when looking for information, but they are not aware of the liability problem they are facing. Research with schoolchildren in Hungary proved that they were not aware of the differences in credibility of information content between various media. The production-easing capacity of the new media is not paralleled with the filtering capacity that is provided by editorial boards, scientific or artistic communities and other cognitive and administrative institutions that are related to older forms of production. This fact and the problem of blurred authorship give the false impression to users that information gathered through the internet (blogs websites, etc.) is sufficiently reliable. The problem is especially strong with young users, who may lack, even more than adults, the necessary background information to be able to judge about form and content with certainty.

In certain well-established internet communities, collective filtering activities have already appeared, but the liberty and uncontrolled character of the internet does not provide for this function everywhere. Wikipedia, the global digital networked encyclopaedia, contains more than 1 million entries (versions in 39 different languages) and has been growing continually since 2001. Its content is freely produced, completed and edited by volunteers and non-professional contributors. It is a good example both of free and collaborative knowledge producing activity and of the need for filtering and controlling the content produced. The vast international project has elaborated its own rules and norms, which rely on NPOV (neutral point of view) and also peer control.

All types of communicative relationships have also greatly profited from ICT development, whether in strong or weak ties. Communication studies have revealed that people's communicative needs have strongly increased, with the new devices enhancing all forms and types of communicative activity and increasing their frequency (contacting old friends or chatting with unknown people on the net, mobile phone calls, e-cards, discussion forums on public or private topics, online gaming and gambling, etc.) These *new communicative needs* are very strong with children and youngsters. Psychology has long since been aware of the communicative difficulties of youngsters with their immediate environment, especially family. New ICTs offer a wide range of possibilities for them to escape: chatrooms, blogs and discussion fora are widely used by youngsters, where they can create new relationships, even friendships. Anonymous use is also very popular with children and youngsters: they chat with unidentifiable people or play all kinds of identity games, changing identities, sex, age, etc. in communicative actions where only nicknames are used. The new forms of communications have become so essential for young people that being cut off from them may cause serious neurotic feelings or psychological problems (Csépe, 2003). They quickly adopt new forms of communication and the skills that are necessary to cope with them (quick typing, using abbreviated forms, thumbing, etc.) The friend-seeking, relation building and dating functions of these devices are clearly visible when one enters chatrooms, either on the internet or WAP.

A research experiment involving observation of the functioning of Hungarian WAP showed that young people spend a huge sum of money and energy on WAP chats trying to find friends and dating partners. They need to have extremely quick skills to write and react, because chatting activity in the evenings and especially on weekends occurs very rapidly. Because of the use of nicknames, the first question they pose to a new entrant is 'nem/kor/lax' (sex/age/town – with unofficial abbreviated mock-spelling), the three more important pieces of information which may contribute to a decision on dating a person (Heller, 2005).

The importance of the communicative function of the new ICTs can also be seen from statistics. In most countries, e-mail activities are ranked first among user preferences. It is not without doubt that new ICTs successfully contribute to increasing one's *social capital*. The popularity of 'social websites' permitting one to find former classmates, distant relatives, etc. all testify to this function.

The surprising Hungarian website iwiw[20] (which depicts and maps social relations among fully identifiable persons) has been a great success among young Budapest-based intellectuals. It now has 424,798 members in Budapest alone, with 35,606,451 relationships among them, but the site is open to users in 27 languages living in a great number of countries. Although any new member needs an invitation from somebody already in the network, it grows very quickly because its social function is highly appreciated, especially by young people. The site functions like a communications centre for a large community, enabling members to represent their social relations (it has become quite a competition among members to show how many friends and relations they have), find acquaintances and view the acquaintances of their own acquaintances, but the system is also used to send messages and seek information; and it has other useful functions, like small ads, free places in cars, exchanging unwanted property, etc.

While new ICTs may have positive consequences on the acquisition of new skills, on the easy access and new forms of education and culture and on enhancing interactivity and active engagement in private and public causes, there are also many dangers and drawbacks, some of which have already been mentioned above. The extreme competition for consumers and the often one-sided, unreflecting use of the new devices presage dangers both for individuals' private lives and for society by deepening social cleavages and hampering the elaboration of social consensus.

CHILDREN, GAMES AND NEW MEDIA

These negatives signs are well discernible in the new media forms and games that ICTs offer for the young generations and that are massively consumed by them as parental control gets weaker and as common media usage in the family declines. An analysis of contemporary media content and games' 'hidden messages' proves that the audience, and especially children, is bombarded with a strong unified value structure that praises not only consumption (with fashionable brands, enforcing lifestyles, etc.), but also physical glamour (strength, beauty, everlasting youth) and *violence* in all forms (thrillers, horror and action films, cartoons, animated films and computer or video games delectating in scenes of slaughter and catastrophe). While scary plots in former genres for children led to reinforcement of social and moral order and concluded to distributing well-deserved rewards or punishment (cf. folk tales, Grimms' tales, etc.), most of the new production aiming at children does not contain any ethical aspect and abandons the educational or social content. Psychologists warn that not only sex and violence prevail, but also that most of the time good and bad are blurred and that this contributes to the erosion of social values, to the proliferation of negative or anti-heroes. Most televised series, action films and video games only want to provide for fun, distraction or escape. They successfully enhance time killing, and the 'educational' function they perform contributes to training young people to become obedient subjects in a society of consumption and entertainment. The interest of global cross-media corporations can easily be detected in this trend. Game consoles and more cutting-edge technology reinforced the integration of media and youth culture (MacTavish, 2002). And the message is all the more strong and efficient as the training in the above-mentioned value structure and lifestyle reaches children from different media and different activities.

Like traditional games, computer and video games can also be divided into several categories according to the required skills, the narrative, the ludological structure, etc. (Lindley, 2002). However, the trends in new games show that elements of mass culture have become predominant, and games with violent narratives, aggressive characters and destruction-centred plots occupy ever larger parts of the market. Games aim at killing the enemy, occupying his (and nearly never her) territory, destroying his allies and property. The popular 'First Person Shooter' (FPS) games (Klevjer, forthcoming) rely on rapid action (shooting) and do not even try to conceal the aggressive character of the game by bothering to create aesthetical background, interesting scenarios, or offering possibilities to build up strategies to cooperate with fellow players, etc. (Putnam, 2000). While there are many online game centres where players can play in real time against participants from the global world, a fact that could enhance the appreciation of cultural diversity, cooperation among the players is extremely rare, while in the games themselves they often fight against enemies depicting 'the other': different nationalities, different cultures and races from one's own. By daily training in these games, children get accustomed to banalized violence: trivial aggression, merciless extermination.[21] Lack of empathy, cunning and strategy building make most of these games anti-social. Death is also trivialized, as the player may earn several lives; thus, the irreversible character of human acts is veiled in a game world where body-action, bodily qualities, force and aggressiveness constitute the kernel part of the player's identity. The highly developed technology of games and films makes aggression crudely experienced because it is represented in detail and with force. These types of 'natural' representation of violence are far more influential than the symbolic aggression of folk tales or traditional games. Although there are debates among specialists as to whether violence in the media accustoms children to aggression or, on the contrary, enhances letting out one's own aggressiveness, social psychological experiments show that media cultivation represents violence as omnipresent, an inescapable part of everyday life. When playing these games, the gamer does not need to reflect, justify, calculate, verbally or morally weigh the actions; they just have to be quick. These games do not teach various problem-solving strategies; there is only one, and very basic: aggression. Although ICT games often contain different coexisting worlds, and the possible interactions between them would permit a colourful and rich game-world which could easily develop children's fantasy and creativity, quick killing is the main aim and these other possibilities stay unexploited.

Certain types of new game depart from the 'hidden curriculum' of the slaughtering type. Human 'knowledge and attitudes' of all types also appear. Certain computer games (most of which have also existed for long in non-digital forms) reintroduce logical and cognitive elements, like Scrabble, Othello, etc. Others reinvent quiz-like competitions. This form is sometimes used with more or less nationalistic content: players can occupy their own country then continue colonizing neighbouring countries by giving the right answers to cognitive questions. Still other games (like 'Civilization', 'Settlers', etc.) induce reflection on the development of culture and civilization and introduce the player into strategy building, planning and measuring the effects of their own decisions, contributing in this way to acquiring social knowledge as in many traditional games. Even more 'instructive' are games reintroducing important *social sensibility* concerning social differentiation and segregation. Here again the 'message' may go in diverse directions: certain seemingly FPS games only borrow the form, but vehicle extremist social content: xenophobia, racism, etc.

In spite of disallowance, a controversial computer game keeps on appearing on the net in revised forms but with the same racist content. 'Olah action' the game with the subtitle 'The goal is to cleanse all Hungarian regions from Gipsies'[22] is an FPS where targets to shoot at are Gipsies in the streets or other public places. When eliminated, a little spot remains to mark where the Gipsy was shot. When all the regions are 'cleaned', the map of the country becomes white. The game stirred up many discussions. Authorities claim that while it does not generate immediate violent actions, there is no need to take any preventive actions and prohibition. The game also resulted in long online discussions on different internet fora, some of which gave rise to such violent discourse that most of the interactions have been censored by the forum mediator.

The problem of ethnic hatred and social exclusion rarely constitutes the central topic of game narratives. A fantasy-game book, which uses the Dungeons and Dragons form, however, tries to transmit the feelings of being an outcast. The book is called *Gipsy Labyrinth* (Kardos and Nyári, 2004) and the reader-player has to take up a young Hungarian villager's role who happens to be a Gipsy and the game explores the ways that are open to a contemporary Gipsy in order to survive: skinheads, ethnic prejudices, poverty, discrimination, stealing etc. are part of the possible choices that are available for them. The best solution that can be attained in the game is ordinary life with stable work, a wife and two kids; all the other possible endings finish in crime, tragedy, poverty and segregation. Through role-playing, the game helps the experiencing of social exclusion and draws attention to the serious social problems that exist in central and eastern Europe, and certainly other regions of the world as well.

CROSSROAD TO FUTURE

New technology, new devices cannot, however, be blamed for the negative effects they are causing by misuse, profit-chasing or social irresponsibility. It is important that social sciences conduct more in-depth research into children's usage of new ICTs and the effects that these devices may have on their socialization process, the acquisition of knowledge and skills, and the handling of their social relations. Social scientific research should investigate more in detail and in depth the immense capacities offered by multimedia devices and digital networks, but also their drawbacks and the problems they introduce in different spheres of social and individual life. Multidisciplinary efforts are needed in social scientific research to highlight problems of social cohesion, digital divide, necessary skills for appropriate use, group relationships, cultural productivity, value-structures and -conflicts, individual psychological affects, addiction, etc. Characteristics of new group-formation and participation have to be examined, because networking, virtual groups and communities are gaining weight in peoples' experiences, and youngsters are leading the way in these processes. International research on patterns of reception of new media genres and game contents should enhance new knowledge about the functioning of new media and ICTs and their effect on various social and age groups. New ways of accessing cultural products in the broadest sense have to be investigated in order to reorganize educational and cultural institutions. While the technology-based innovation in the field is extremely quick for economic reasons and technological possibilities, social sciences should keep pace with this rapidly changing and globally spreading technological environment.

The radically increased possibilities offered by new media and ICTs can only be put in use in a socially effective way if the different social institutions and the public are aware of the advantages and the dangers. Therefore, not only is social scientific research needed, but also appropriate national and EU policies based on social scientific research. Such policies, in order to be effectively implemented, need to undergo large public discussion and public adherence. Public and private actors, civil society and individuals can contribute to introducing and spreading appropriate uses of the wide choice offered by various media and new ICTs. Social institutions, whether official or self-organized, should be able to show ways of good practice and necessary knowledge and should be able to help avoid the worst traps. Educational and cultural institutions and families should carefully observe and help children in their choices and uses (Kafai, 2006). Common activities and mutual, self-reflexive discussions among friends and family, together with a wide range on offer in interactive pastimes and suggestive recreation through the media and especially the internet, could be good ways of fighting against social problems like declining families, youth delinquency, the generation gap and a narcissistic and insensitive consumer society.

New media and ICTs offer great possibilities and constitute serious danger at the same time; society should be aware of both.

NOTES

1 See examples like Kalevala, Greek mythology, Aesopus's tales, Dante's *Divina Commedia*, etc.

2 According to American statistics, adults spent an average of 264.5 minutes per 24 hours watching TV, compared with 125.5 minutes for radio, 85 minutes for the internet, 20 minutes for newspapers and 16.3 minutes for magazines in 2005. Source: US Federal Communications Commission. Hungarian research from 2005 for the whole adult population shows the following usage: 265 minutes/day TV watching (decreasing for the first time in 10 years!), 213 minutes for radio (strongly decreasing!), 77 minutes for the internet (strongly increasing!) 21.4 minutes for newspapers and 8.5 minutes for magazines.

3 In the USA, 69% of children (6–14) have TVs in their bedrooms, 49% have video games, 46% VCRs, 37% DVD players, 35% cable or satellite TVs, 24% PCs and 18% internet access. These figures are closely related to the fact that, in 2005, TV viewing among children was at its highest in more than 20 years (23 hours and 3 minutes a week). Source: http://www.progress.org/2005/tv02.htm.

4 For example, see the famous Pêch Merle cave in the south of France with coloured dots and hands painted in negative or positive close to the animals.

5 Such toys are on display, for example, in the 'Musée du Père Noël' in Canet Plage (France).

6 Knowledge gained through games, wealth gained in gambling, but also social relations, like self-confidence gained by being good at intellectual games, etc.

7 Expressions used in chess also testify to its Persian origin: sakk = shah, vezér = vizir (in Hungarian), shah-mat (meaning the shah is lost).

8 For example, the four sets in the southern version are said to go back to the different forms of Vishnu: calix, sword, sceptre/stick and ring/coin. They are said to represent the four social layers: the clergy, the military, the bourgeois and the peasant, each order having their king, queen, (cavalier) and servant. The colours of the French cards represent a military organization: with spade and diamond as spear and arrowhead, heart representing courage and club the food given to horses (the French denominations: pique, carreau, coeur and trèfle are even more expressive). Tarot cards, especially the series of the 22 trumps, represent well-defined social roles, symbols of human values and some mythical or scary creatures.

9 I have gathered interviews of young Hungarians who were amazed to see, during their first trips to western Europe, how much the towns and villages resembled the ones they knew from Lego.

10 All devices enabling duplication of texts or photocopying played an important role in this process.

11 Western TVs immortalized the images of trashy Trabants carrying huge deep-freezers on their top on 7 November 1988 (commemoration day of the Great Soviet October Revolution).

12 These gadgets received at that time rather ironical nicknames by the rest of the population: 'blockhead phone', 'bully-phone', etc.

13 See the quick proliferation of satellite dishes, cable TVs and mobile phones.

14 Compare the actual debate in Hungary on whether the opera should be state subsidized with the argument that it only serves the interest of a thin subculture.

15 Interviews by children with excessive gaming activities testify to this process.

16 Heroes were enumerated with decreasing importance: sportsmen, actors, father, mother, relatives, pop musicians, artists, scientists, other adults, siblings, teachers, grandfather, friends, grandmother.

17 Just to mention some famous Hungarian contemporary writers: Péter Esterházy, Ferenc Temesi, Mihály Korniss and others experimenting with non-linear literature, where not only the story is related in a non-linear structure, but even the requested forms of reception are not necessarily linear, like in Dungeons and Dragons-type games or in 'programmed' educational materials.

18 Compare 'Beszéljük meg' [Let us discuss it…], an extremely popular programme on a commercial radio channel in Hungary where private persons call in to discuss strictly public and political problems.

19 Writers' original corrected hand-written manuscripts, painters' first etches, etc. will cease to exist in contemporary culture.

20 http://www.iwiw.hu/pages/main/index.jsp.

21 It is often said about FPS games that blood is trickling from the computer.

22 http://www.romnet.hu/hirek/hir0505272.html.

REFERENCES

Bettleheim, B. (1975) *The Uses of Enchantment. The Meaning and Importance of Fairy Tales.* New York: Alfred A. Knopf.

Csépe, V. (2003) 'Children in the mobile information society'. In K. Nyiri (ed.) *Mobile Communication. Essays on Cognition and Community.* Vienna: Passagen Verlag.

Drotner, K. (1998) 'Youthful media cultures: challenges and chances for librarians'. *The New Review of Children's Literature and Librarianship*, 4: 17–30.

Drotner, K. (2000) 'Difference and diversity: trends in young Danes' media cultures'. *Media, Culture and Society* 22(2): 149–166.

Elias, N. (1939) *Über den Prozeß der Zivilisation. Soziogenetische und psychogenetische Untersuchungen. Zweiter Band. Wandlungen der Gesellschaft. Entwurf einer Theorie der Zivilisation.* Basel: Verlag Haus zum Falken.

Fabre, D. (1992) *Le Carnaval ou la Fête à l'Envers.* Paris: Gallimard.

Fabre, D. and Camberoque, C. (1977) *La Fête en Languedoc.* Toulouse: Privat.

Hankiss, E. (1982) *Kényszerpályán? A Magyar Társadalom Értékrendszerének Alakulása 1930 és 1980 Között* (*On Constrained Pathways. Modifications of the Value System of the Hungarian Society Between 1930 and 1980*). Budapest: MTA Szociológiai Kutató Intézet.

Heller, M. (2005) 'A diskurzus rehabilitációja' ('Chatting rehabilitated'). *Jelkép*, 2005(2): 25–54.

Heller, M. (forthcoming) 'Global and European information society. Convergence, divergence and fragmentation'. In P. Ludes (ed.) *Convergence and Fragmentation.* Bristol: Intellect.

Huizinga, J. (1944) *Homo Ludens.* Budapest: Athenaeum. (Original: *Homo Ludens*, 1938.)

Kafai, Y.B. (2006) 'Playing and making games for learning: instructionist and constructionist perspectives for game studies'. *Games and Culture*, 1(1): 36–40.

Kaneko, K. and Toshiba-EMI Ltd (1994) *Alice: An Interactive Museum.* Synergy Interactive Corp.

Kardos, P. and Nyári, G. (2004) *Cigánylabirintus.* Budapest: Jonathan Miller Kft.

Klevjer, R. (forthcoming) 'The cultural value of games'. In P. Ludes (ed.) *Convergence and Fragmentation.* Bristol: Intellect.

Kósa, É. (2004) http://www.mindentudas.hu/kosa/20041109kosa.html.

László, M. (1999) 'Példa-kép: a tizenéves korosztály értékválasztásai és a média' ('Heroes: value choices of teenagers and the media'). *Jelkép*, 1999(3): 33–47.

Livingstone, S. (2002) *Young People and New Media: Childhood and the Changing Media Environment.* London: Sage.

Livingstone, S. (2003a) 'Children's use of the internet: reflections on the emerging research agenda'. *New Media and Society* 5(2): 147–166.

Livingstone, S. (2003b) 'Les enjeux de la recherche comparative internationale sur les médias'. Special issue: *Frontiers in Scientific Communities.* In P. Hert, (ed.) *Questions de Communication*, 3: 31–43.

Livingstone, S. (2003c) 'Mediated childhoods: a comparative approach to the lifeworld of young people in a changing media environment'. In J. Turow and A.L. Kavanaugh (eds) *The Wired Homestead: An MIT Sourcebook on the Internet and the Family.* Cambridge, MA: MIT Press; 207–226.

Lindley, C. (2002): 'The gameplay gestalt, narrative and interactive storytelling'. In F. Mäyrä (ed.) *Computer Games and Digital Cultures – Conference Proceedings.* Tampere: Tampere University Press.

Ling, R. and Thrane, K. (2002) '"I don't watch TV to like learn anything": the leisure use of TV and the internet'. *First Monday* 7(1).

MacTavish, A. (2002): 'Technological pleasure: the performance and narrative of technology in half-life and other high-tech computer games'. In G. King and T. Krzywinska (eds) ScreenPlay. *Cinema/Videogames/Interfaces.* London: Wallflower Press; 33–49.

Meyrowitz, J. (1986) *No Sense of Place*. New York: Oxford University Press.

Millwood Hargave, A. and Livingstone, S. (2006) *Harm and Offence in Media Content: A Review of the Evidence*. Bristol: Intellect Press.

Müller, M. (1997) *Die Kleinen Könige der Warenwelt – Kinder um Visier der Werbung*. Frankfurt: Campus Verlag.

Putnam, R. (2000) *Bowling Alone: The Collapse and revival of American Community*. New York: Simon and Schuster.

Supka, G. (1989) *Kalandozás a Kalendáriumban és más Érdekességek* (*Wandering in the Calendar and other Peculiarities*). Budapest: Helikon. (1st edn 1942.)

Tan, E., Chisalita, C., Raijmakers, B. and Oinonen, K. (forthcoming) 'Learning and entertainment in museums: a case study'. In P. Ludes (ed.) *Convergence and Fragmentation*. Bristol: Intellect.

Werner, A. (1998) *A Tévé-kor Gyermekei*. Budapest: Nemzeti Tankönyvkiadó. (Original: Barn i Fjernsynsalderen, Ad Notam Gyldendal AS, 1994.)

17

Children, Media and Regional Modernity in the Asia Pacific

Stephanie Hemelryk Donald

THE REGION

> In Asia today, state projects of modernity are engaged in the production of national subjects, whereas alternative modernities associated with flexible accumulation celebrate self-propelling subjects (Ong, 1997: 173).

This chapter suggests a potential framework for research in children's media and media use in the Asia-Pacific region. It does so by emphasizing the need to recognize regional particularities of children's media lives. In this scenario, an exploration of modernity, and anti-modernities, is proffered in order to signal the problems inherent in accurately capturing the historical contexts in which media use occurs. The term in which this chapter is couched is the idea of *regional modernity*, characterized by regional responses to internal and external conditions of possibility and constraint. It draws, therefore, on both the 'state' and 'alternative' exemplars which Ong (1997) laid out in her seminal work on transnational Chinese identities (see above). This field of definition is based on the observation that media institutions, whilst their content is *globally* oriented and *nationally* regulated, are phenomenally linked to regional contingencies. Therefore, in beginning to research children's media, and children *in* media, we should recognize that there is an actual geography of where and how children live – both as national subjects and as regional residents. Putting the region first, as a category in which regions are equivalent if not identical, avoids the conceptual blockage of 'core and periphery' which inflects thinking about Asia-Pacific nations (and the 'South' in general) from Europe and the USA. In terms of global influence and real politik, regional 'borders' are undoubtedly subject to the same scepticism levelled at nation states, but (like nation states) they have a viability and imaginative power which persists. It is this power that underlines Asia-Pacific as a globally meaningful entity.

Focusing on China and Australia, the discussion foregrounds the importance of history, culture, and language in how we understand the uses and affect of media for young people. Specifically, the chapter suggests how questions of relative cultural and political value, and of uneven and unexpected experiences of modernity and development, may be recognized and interpreted as they occur in media worlds outside the hegemonies of Western discourse. China and Australia have been chosen as key interpretative sites in this discussion, as between them they represent a great deal of what is confusing – for those located elsewhere – about what is locally termed 'the region'. Asia-Pacific and Oceania amount to 'the region' to those who live there, but that idea is sometimes confused with regional*ism*, and conflated with the organizing trope of the periphery or the unsophisticated, or both. Here, China and Australia will be presented as discrete, and yet mutually implicated, locations for childhood and media.

The relationship between Australia and Asia is overly determined by colonial histories of white settlement and by both parties' fluctuating sense of the other's geographic relevance. The adult political world is not at all clear about where Australia *is* in geopolitical terms and whether Asia is a neighbour or an 'Other' to be managed with caution. That suspicion goes both ways of course. For children and their families, however, Asia and Australia are becoming increasingly intertwined by virtue of kin connections and mediated links across the region. Classrooms in major cities in Australia are populated by children with relatives in mainland China, Singapore, India, Japan, Hong Kong, Vietnam, Indonesia, Thailand and Taiwan. Children in a mobile phone study conducted by the author in Sydney in 2005 were asked to use concept-mapping techniques to visualize points of communicative activity in their worldview. The results showed clearly that the region was important to many children of Chinese origin who included China in their visual accounts of ordinary communications, whilst the rest of the non-Asian world (with the single exception of Bristol in the UK) was absent from their maps. Thus, the connections between media, communications and a child's sense of place might well be a starting point for understanding how the world is experienced by the region's young people, and suggests why Media Studies research needs to start *in situ* as well as from theoretical premises developed elsewhere in response to other contingencies of the modern.

This is not to say that there are no differences between and across Asian and Australian territories, and that children's media use is not highly inflected by language and cultural expectations. The regional focus should not replace one 'media hegemony' with another. Taking China (PRC) as the major case study in the present account, it is for instance a necessary truism to point out that the construction of children's media subjectivity, a peculiarly modern activity even without 'media' (Luke, 1990: 20–22), is sharply defined by a national agenda of political coherence, which is presumed to support the uncontested power of the Party State. At the same time, China's movement towards a 'comprehensive' (*quanfa*) education system, wherein 'comprehensive' refers to media literacy and ability to think creatively in Chinese *and English*, indicates a move to familiar tropes of modernity: 'innovation, communicativity, flexibility, mobility and multi-literacy'.[1] The challenge for researchers outside the Chinese world view is to understand that these competing versions of modernity do not constitute a contradiction but a situated and contingent example of how media use is managed instrumentally by national authorities to further the benefits of contemporary flows of information. Or one might take up Ulrich Beck's insight that, whilst reflexive modernity throws out the barriers of class, nation and race, modernity as a governmental process nonetheless repositions 'anti-modernities' through its institutions, as part of the technology of maintaining and creating social hierarchies and order: 'Gegenmodernierung behauptet, zieht, shafft, befestigt alte Grenzen neu'

('Anti-modernization throws up old barriers anew') (Beck, 1993: 100; see also Ewers (1998: 27)). So, whilst it is undeniable that China's political culture renders modernity a different object from the conflations that arise from Western understandings of freedom of expression, it is also arguable that such internal contradictions are themselves a feature of the modern that will and must occur elsewhere, albeit in different formations. Nonetheless, Asia's diverse political and social structures particularly challenge everyday Western precepts of modernity and identity as achieved through individualism and equality. A key text in the few that study children's media in Asia is the late Anura Goonasekera's (2001) collection on children in the news. This book contains mainly survey material and content analysis from media outlets across the region, organized by country, but it is not a set of equivalent value-neutral accounts of the portrayal of children in the news. Each case study is written from a national perspective, and many also contain a number of implicit or overt cultural claims which demonstrate the breadth and tenacity of values and norms underpinning the researchers' perspectives. The Pakistan entry argues that identity and Islam are not reducible and that the integration of both ensures that 'a child in a typical Pakistani set-up gets a chance to develop all the basic components of his personality', and that family breakdown and alternative family units as experienced in the USA 'are not feared in a society like Pakistan' (Zuberi, 2001: 241). Zuberi later claims in his news analysis that 'children are grossly neglected by the community which does not ... protest ... the way their children are kept illiterate' (Zuberi, 2001: 249). The author is, in other words, highly critical of children's opportunities in Pakistan, but is very concerned to separate those issues from their upbringing in Islam, even though the claim is made that the religious aspect of their lives is all-embracing, 'a comprehensive way of life, continuously and intensely pervading belief and behaviour, public conduct and private experience' (Zuberi, 2001: 239). This contradiction arises mainly from the perceived need to defend Islam (and at the same time impugn Western family morality as akin to that of liberal alternatives in the USA) against the projected criticism of the Western Other. Although understandable in, say, a newspaper like Murdoch's *The Australian*, in this particular collection the approach seems oddly self-defeating. I would suggest that this perceived need is symptomatic of the regional expectation that any published work on children's media, or any media, will rest on the hegemony of a Western reading of modernity. Whilst that is not actually the case in Goonasekera's work, where the benchmark is an international treaty (UN Convention on the Rights of the Child), Zuberi demonstrates the problem by an equally problematic rebuttal.

In the same collection, the chapter on children in the news in Indonesia is also highly localized and politicized, but in a rather different fashion (Guntarto, 2001: 97ff). Here, it is not the Islamicization and segregation of the country's media and political culture which is discussed (although that is a focus of debate elsewhere: see Hill and Sen (2005: 118–122) for a secular appraisal and Ahmad (2003: 3ff) for an Islamic perspective), but a potted history of Soeharto's tyranny over the media, of post-Soeharto disappointments, and of President Habibie's attempts in 1999 to alleviate the constraints of media freedom. These general comments are followed by detailed descriptions of the heroic fashioning of particular papers and media outlets from the perspective of investigative journalism. The account of children in the media follows this lengthy introduction, noting that basic rights are transgressed (for instance, children who have suffered rape are identified (Guntarto, 2001: 117)) and commenting on the effects of advertising inappropriate children's foods to poor families (Guntarto, 2001: 112). The section is remarkably short compared with the historical scene-setting, for the point of Guntarto's contribution is to educate the reader on Indonesia's recent (and continuing) fight for public space for critical journalism, whilst his interest in children is mainly associated with his concern for the internationalization of Indonesian modernity through adherence to developmental regulations (here, the Convention on Children's Rights). Again, accepting a regional approach to the fashioning of modernity in time and space is crucial to reading this chapter. This writer is not concerned with 'constructing' the child viewer as a subject in the modernity of contemporary media theory, but he is very anxious to chart a history of media deprivations and rights in order to claim a national benchmark for Indonesian modernity.

The two examples I have cited from Goonasekera's collection demonstrate a shared perception that basic national, cultural or political information must be given to the reader in English before embarking on the job in hand: to analyse the place of children in the news in particular Asian countries. This information is imparted and narrative trajectories are selected according to very different interests in each case. One defends national-religious identity, the other stakes a claim on the history of the past 15 years of journalism. Both, however, manifest a regional insecurity about the amount of prior knowledge pertaining to their national circumstance, the political capital which they may or may not possess by virtue of writing from without the USA (or Europe) and, therefore, assume that they must begin by educating the reader on the nature of the world and the state of modernity in which their 'children' live and grow. It is that conundrum in which I am also somewhat caught in constructing a discourse for this chapter, and in placing Australia both outside and within the region, both implicated in and peripheral to the 'West'. I take comfort from Ong's work in particular. The value of insisting on regional as well as national perspectives as counterbalance to the dominance of the US–European nexus of academic and theoretical power is given weight by Ong's dismissal of another alternative, which has otherwise found favour in the mainstream academy. She has argued that a publicness of 'the diasporic' claimed in cyberspace by (especially) people of Chinese descent worldwide (*Huaren*), and led mainly by American Chinese (or, notably, Chinese Americans), is leading to a re-racialization of identity across Asia, cutting against important local structures of regional and national interdependence (Ong, 2006: 53–55). She cites Rey Chow, who warns against 'academic (and especially cultural and media studies researchers) gathering [of] endangered authenticities' (Ong, 2006: 60). Although not explicit in Ong's remarks, it is arguable that regionalism as a basis for academic enquiry is likely to produce more tenable grounds for the future than the lure of ungrounded cosmopolitanism.

On that note, I recently attended a cocktail party in Sydney, given in honour of a British parliamentary delegation on higher education. In one bemusing conversation with a young Conservative Member of Parliament from Essex I was foolish enough to make an argument for regionalism in Asia/Oceania. I was informed rather sternly that I misunderstood the way the world was turning and that Britain needed to leave the European Union and form a union of English-speaking trading nations, namely the UK, India, Australia, Canada, Singapore and Japan. I will trust this readership to note the wonderful conflation of linguistic identity, colonial traces and economic attractiveness embedded in his project. Whilst it was downright funny that India, Singapore and Japan (in particular) should be included in an Anglosphere, it was also typical that Australia should be a presumed partner in this exciting UK adventure. Australia's geographic mobility is part and parcel of the discursive power of the contemporary global imagination wielded by the North, and this MP was simply doing what the region expects and only sometimes resists. Australia, a large island in the South, and closest to Asia and the Antarctic, is both of the 'West' and a particular case in itself; it is a territory which is expected by its allies and former colonists to conform to Anglo-American patterns of analysis and outlook, despite in actuality having a strong orientation to the region as much as to colonial relationships in Europe. The commonplace elision of Australia's locational complexity is a problem coming from without and within, whereby Australia is both correctly classified as Western, and yet misplaced by a pigeonhole that defies its contemporary geopolitics and diversity of population. Importantly though, this is a slippage which obscures the life stories of the many Australian children who are not first- or second-generation European or American migrants. A first principle for regional media research in a settler post-colonial society is to take note of the facts of geography, proximity and the logic of human migrations. The peripheral in the Western imagination, although still inherited by mainstream Australian culture, is often the centre and origin of young Australian lives.

A regional approach to the study of children's media is not an easy option, however. As the writers from the Goonasekera collection show, once the hegemony of a globally acceptable theoretical framework is challenged, a great deal of information has to be shared in order to make sense of data or to embark on textual analysis. The results may be parochial, overemphasizing the particularities of place and underestimating the usefulness of discursive power in making larger, globalizing theoretical claims about the state of the world, or, in this case, the meaning of a relationship between children and the media. But such parochialism is in part at least a defensive reflection of the other parochialism which gives such spatial and temporal confidence to global theory. An exception to that observation, Beck's concept of anti-modernity as a common feature of the governmental modern, assists in seeing that the limitations to reflexivity posed by ideology or politics both defy and support the various forms of modernity worldwide. Ewers further suggests that children are the obvious fulcrum of anti-modernity in modern societies, and in his work on children's literature seeks 'to differentiate between a non-modernity which has been handed down or is traditional and a newly developed one created by the process of modernization itself' (Ewers, 1998: 27). Ewer's observation of the invention or maintenance of 'anti-modernities' may be brought to bear in respect to how certain images of children define the perfected state of social order. The image of the child in late Revolutionary China was crucial to national narratives of the future (Donald, 1999), whereby the tragedies and failures of revolutionary modernity are eclipsed by the ideal child who will carry national and spiritual principles forward, but without in itself achieving a social or political subjectivity that might challenge the status quo. In Chinese poster art, the affective power of the child refers to a number of sustaining political tropes: socialist discourses of revolutionary succession, nationalism and Han ethnic hegemony, and to styles of popular art which related the rhythm and coherence of the 'traditional' Chinese year. Tina Chen has shown how the dressing of children in these posters indicates a 1950s–1960s class status and proximity to the revolutionary elite (Chen, 2003: 382–384). The dressing of children in earlier traditions of visual representation, and evident in the symbolic trappings of New Year (*nianhua*) prints, indicates the stylistic gesture of continuity which characterizes much media for and about children in China. In film, the figure of the child is similarly central to the visual identity of the Revolution (as in *Shanshan hongxing*, *Shining Red Star*, 1974), and that pattern translates more recently into child characters who experience and transcend the downsides of modernity in the Reform era (*Bieku mama*, *Don't Cry Mama*, 1986). The films insist on the responsibility of the child to carry forward the values of social cohesion, even when their adult contemporaries, at least on screen, fail to do so.

David Kennedy (2006: 98–100) has traced a similar trajectory through Platonic infantilism, the Romantic 'counter-modern' and the child within Freudian psychoanalysis. The strategies of thought which Kennedy charts are not dissimilar to the idealization of the formation of a child's Islamic character deployed by Zuberi (above), and are also evident in the discourse of social class and media effects used by anti-media groups in Australia (see below). For Kennedy, the child is finally placed in Western philosophical and literary thought as part of a dialogic self which, once recognized, confuses the easy hierarchies of modernism (Kennedy, 2006: 109). But, seeing the child as a post-modern avatar within the modern adult is exceptionally self-knowing, and, unfashionably secular. If we take our cue from Luke (1989) in her earlier work on Lutheranism, printing and the evolution of a humanistic discourse on childhood, we might see these more common, strategic idealizations of the child-as-non-subject as a 'field of emergence' (Luke, 1989: 50), where religion, pedagogy, politics and class are converging on childhood not to produce humanism and modern precepts, but as a globally prevalent discourse of *anti-modernity*, which has regional specificities in Asia-Pacific that must be noted. In the following section I will discuss the ways in which class is implicated in these strategies: how, indeed, children are classed and declassed to bolster the boundaries of anti-modernity which sustains a hierarchy of the modern adult subject. I will also refer to instances of media use which counteract the logic of quality and class pursued by dominant national discourses in both China and Australia.

CLASS, QUALITY AND THE RURAL CHILD

China is at the other extreme of the East–West continuum from Australia. Globally, China is seen as *the* place that exemplifies difference and extremity for those outside its national or (multi)ethnic boundaries. So, whilst contemporary China falls into analytical paradigms of modern media (Lynch, 1999), its political system, cultural diversity and accelerated modernization all require that researchers constantly revisit their fieldwork, and their preconceptions, whilst holding fast to cultural knowledge and well-founded trajectories of historical understanding. In a good example of such revision, recent work (Brady, 2006) on the *tifa* (propaganda discourse) in China uses fieldwork to challenge many of the claims made by Lynch's earlier work on the demise of the propaganda state in the mid 1990s. She argues persuasively that there is no necessary propulsion towards normative modernity in an era of reform. At the same time, newspaper accounts report increased associational activity online, as the so-called middle classes seek to bolster property laws and values in Shenzhen. China's internal borders, provincial conditions and extreme disparities of wealth make it impossible to classify it sensibly and without exception as a single entity (Goodman, 2006); but, at the same time, the power of the state in China requires that some notion of China as an entity is inevitable. If we read Ong's (2006) critique of 'the diasporic' in the context of migrating peoples within China itself, we will note the actually existing cosmopolitanism of the Mainland, where over 100 million people belong to minority groups, many of which are active internal migrants across provincial borders in search of work for themselves and educational opportunities for their children (Wang, 2003: 32ff; Donald and Benewick, 2005: 30–31). As such, Ong's (1997) bifocal concept of modernity is pertinent to China's internal organization and difference, as much as to the transnational China which she was then seeking to describe.

The movement of peoples within China, the development of strong educational infrastructure in richer zones and the beginnings of bilingual education for some minority schools all indicate the State imperative to build a sustainable modernity in China and for children to be inscribed and recruited through education and media to that vision. The recruitment processes occur through schools (where there is still emphasis on patriotic education as well as efforts to boost media competencies), film education, approved children's channels on television, and occasional poster and television campaigns to promote health, environmental protection and a national ethos of development (Sayers, 2004). Meanwhile, children in China respond flexibly to the local conditions in which they are educated and use media, conditions which are differentiated by personal income, the state and manner of development in their province or county, ethnicity, access to education and language group. A 10-year-old child in Shenzhen attending a school which teaches immersion English, whose estranged father regularly travels to Hong Kong for business and to Chengdu to place investments in a new 'creative industries corridor', and who has a great number of technical gadgets brought back as gifts has a different concept of media use to a 12-year-old rural child in Anhui, only two provinces away, who attends school when it is not flooded, has never used a digital camera, and whose parents work as growers in the bamboo industry. I know both children. They are modern in outlook, ambitious for their futures (both have the capacity to attend university, and want to do so) and both enjoy electronic games (although the second only has an opportunity to play with them when entertaining foreign guests). The first child is likely to be sent to university overseas, or to a private college in Ningbo, if she does not pass the highly competitive national exams for entry to Chinese universities. The second child is aware that her parents may not even be able to afford local fees and living costs if she can stay at school long enough to try her luck at the entrance tests. She may, nonetheless, be already the more globally sophisticated once she gets online – looking for buyers for bamboo products outside the province is one activity – but getting online in the first place is hard when the electricity supply is hardly assured from one day to another even in the local non-governmental organization's offices where computers are occasionally available. If we move further afield into impoverished western provinces of China (Gansu, Xinjiang for example), children will not only be disadvantaged by their complete lack of global English, but they will also be studying in a second Chinese language (putonghua, Mandarin). Children from the Uyghur and other nationality groups in predominantly Muslim areas will actually speak Turkic languages at home and will find Chinese tones and script difficult. Despite some moves towards bilingual education (Wang, 2003), mainly for purposes of patriotic education in vulnerable border territories (Mackerras, 2004, 148), it is extremely uncommon for children's television or radio shows to be broadcast in any language or dialect other than Mandarin, as that defeats the national purpose in using media to bring a collective modernity into as many homes and communities as possible in the current infrastructure. Language, therefore, is a crucial factor in determining access to the field of emergence of modern nationalism, which resides in integration with mediated cultural and popular competencies, secular patriotism and economic development.

Similarly, Australians have differential access to the axis of modernity, although national status is not overdetermined by such access as it is in China. An Australian in Sydney's eastern suburbs may have a laptop in her bedroom, and a desktop downstairs in case the wireless connection breaks down. The broadband speed is slow in comparison with European and Singaporean servers, and the lack of competitive digital television networks or an adequately funded public netcaster make the experience less than state of the art. But, in comparison with her rural compatriots, she is very lucky indeed. She speaks English and may well have a 'community language' spoken at home (i.e. Chinese, Italian, Greek). Two states away, an indigenous resident of Port Augusta in South Australia will probably need to get to a public library or to an access centre (Government of South Australia, 2003) to use the web outside school. She may not speak English as a first language, or she may have family who are not English speakers. If she does use English it may be an indigenous 'global English' not valued in school performance tests. Also, despite the excellent access initiatives in that state, transport into town is likely to be difficult for those in remote communities, particularly the young. Again, her media use may be sophisticated once online, but the starting point for this very modern activity is uneven.

The rural or 'remote' child is at the cutting edge of class discrimination in the region. Ironically, just as global cities are indexed across Asia, so the 'anti-modernity' of class division is growing, and rurality is a common factor in 'making' class (Thompson, 1966). Also, as income disparities increase after brief twentieth century interludes of social welfare on the one hand, and of communism on the other hand, class is reinvented 'neu' by factors of improbable wealth in the global cities. Of course, wealth at some scale is necessary to the success of the creative and media industries. Many of the media products (from cartoons to adverts) that make the entertainment and information industries profitable are made for the use of child audiences; therefore, the children of middle-class (in Australia; *xiaokang* in China) parents are extremely valuable to commercial interests that supply and distribute content. The shock of child-as-consumer is, however, counter-intuitive to anti-modern ideals of childhood in contemporary societies, and so the fact of children's commerce underpins a great deal of the effort put into children's media research, and in its uptake outside academic circles. Part of the impetus for the shock is the recognition that children are both on a modern continuum to adulthood (notwithstanding the doubtful status of that hierarchy noted above), developing as social beings through their contact with adult products and social norms, and are yet quite different from adults in their ways of perceiving and encountering the world they share with their elders. Panic, and confusion, over how that development is furthered or corrupted by these encounters and perceptions lies at the heart of much discussion by media outlets themselves, and concerned adults. The separate but popularly conflated issues of commercial value and social values are most apparent in work on media effects and on the thin line between academic research and moral activism that 'effects' discourse in particular can engender. These debates rely on a 'norms and values' chain associated with psychology and socialization. The fact of class privilege, and wealth in particular, as the main driver in creating consumption-oriented media for children is not emphasized. Indeed, it is elided by many media effects activists, who prefer to blame lower-class parental ineptitude for the failure of taste in society. This twist allows the ideal of a middle-class child to remain central to the national ideal in a glocal paradigm of mediated consumption.

In late 2000, in Western Australia, I shared a platform with a leading spokesperson for an activism group, *Young Media Australia* (YMA). There were teachers and several young people and children in the audience. The YMA speaker, Barbara Biggins,[2] is well known in Australia for conservative views on media content. In this talk she denounced television and film for having produced a 'lost generation', and waving a small figurine-toy of *The Mummy* (a pseudo-horror film character) in the air she showed us its plastic innards to prove her point. Her arguments were that media damage children, that certain parents cannot manage their own children's media consumption and need to be regulated and that the state of the world is perilous due to the moral dysfunctioning of those who disagree with this stance. The main planks of her position are published on the YMA website through a series of fact sheets and other recommended publications (YMA, 2006). She was supported on the platform by an oral storyteller who argued that young people could no longer 'hear' narrative and were indeed 'lost'. These remarks were made in the context of a panel speaking to members of this generation, and to their teachers. The analysis offered by Biggins was apparently based on selective US academic research into violence and media marketing, but the attack on children's media was relocated in Australia by her classically anti-modern turn of introducing class and moral degeneracy as rhetorical weapons in a rather modernist impulse to control media space in a national context.

An understanding of regional (anti) modernity must take into account the local specificities of the return to class. The YMA argument in 2000 was couched, rhetorically and inferentially, in a class-based discourse of control, wherein poor parenting was assumed to be located in lower socio-economic groups and, especially, amongst indigenous people.

The 'lost' generation was not *really* supposed to mean the young people in the room, as they were (by default of being chosen to sit amongst middle-class educators) able to distinguish between 'good' and 'bad' media content. The subtleties of class were being deployed to undermine unrepresented populations within Australia, who were condemned by their absence. YMA did not show evidence of having asked young people in South Australia what they watched and how they watched it; the presumption given was that class dictated faulty choices and required no further interrogation. Meanwhile, the class and ethnicity nexus addressed by American researchers was used to prove particular media relationships between audience, text and 'real world' activity, thus ignoring the significant differences between Australian social cultures and those of the USA.

Anti-media organizations (and they are of course disturbingly representative of a number of activists, parental groups and opinion formers) depend not just on class exceptionalism and selective transnational claims, but on a distinct moral agenda, based on a conservative version of Christian values, to carry their points. Whilst it might be argued that Australia is a predominantly Christian country, it is certainly not a homogeneous one, and is rapidly shifting to a more complicated pattern of belief and tradition both in Christian groupings and in its several other religions. Perhaps the dismissal of a generation was a neurotic response to such complexity, but certainly the use of Christian morality to re-inscribe class criticism is a problematic habit which besets the national agenda to this day. On that panel in 2000, only 4 years into what has now become a decade of conservative power, the resurgence of a particular brand of Australian values was strident. Children were incorporated into a doctrine of conservatism through critiquing their entertainment choices, but without affording them space to respond, to explain or to counter their dismissal.

Characterized through 'quality' (*suzhi*), class division in China is fundamental to the functioning of the rural–urban divide, and to the political infantilization of the poor (Anagnost, 2004). In media representations such as feature films and documentary, rural children are often portrayed not as equivalent members of the national project, but as a catachresis of the inequalities inherent in accelerated development. Mainstream culture supports this declassing of the rural poor. In the internationally lauded director Zhang Yimou's early works, rural children function as ciphers in the historical memory of the nation. They serve as agents of oppression (as in *Ju Dou*, 1990), as the unrequited potential of revolution to effect change (*Yellow Earth*, 1984) and as victims of endless war (*Red Sorghum*, 1987). They never escape their predicament. As such, they take up the literary mantle of the classic twentieth-century writer Lu Xun, whose work on the 'lost generation' of peasant children – personified by Runtu in *My Old Home* (1921) – spoke to a generation of China's backwardness prior to Liberation in 1949.

An example of how rural children are inscribed as 'valuable strangers' (Harding, 1991, cited in Kennedy (2006: 98)) within self-confident urban modernities may be drawn from the canonization of children's film in Chinese primary education. A mid-1990s initiative, the *Film Course*, was an example of urban sensitivities imposing a particular set of narratives of the modern, and the contemporary, on schoolchildren nationwide. Many of these children's lives and historical contexts were far removed from the Beijing offices of the film selectors (the Love Children Society). Films from Western and Chinese traditions were chosen for cultural, aesthetic, social or ideological value and thematically bundled for use as a curriculum package in primary schools across 20 provinces in China. The selectors indicated that they wanted to improve media access for children in remote areas, an objective which has been welcomed by parents, who now press for their children to attend schools involved in the project. When discussing the kinds of film that are 'canonical' according to the criteria of the scheme, selectors do not consider that rural children's concerns might entail specific, 'alternative' content. The motivation for the education psychologists involved in the project at its inception was tied to improving the overall 'quality', and potential for modernity, of the students through social, political and moral learning. This is hardly surprising, as Chinese cultural discourse is organized around an elite and literate value chain of reference and historical credibility, which competes strongly with here-and-now analyses of media use, or the idea of investigating media use and preferences – such as children's feelings about cartoon characters such as Pikachu or Blue Cat.

In a perverse echo of the Western Australian panel in 2000, a meeting of rural economists and communications educators in Beijing in 2005 to discuss the space of communications in rural China provoked a speaker from the floor to argue that peasant children were once again becoming 'like Runtu', full of promise when very young and then 'lost', deadened by despair and lack of opportunity as they went through the poor schooling available for children in the poorest areas of rural China. Quality (*suzhi*) may be glossed in the contemporary Chinese lexicon as possessing a level of national culture (*wenhua*) sufficient to indicate the capacity to be modern. The damning phrase, 'like Runtu' is axiomatic of the place of rural children in the taxonomies of quality, and 'without quality' (*mei you suzhi*), in the minds of urban Chinese; it is an effective and anti-modernist literary conceit which relegates yet another generation of children to the ranks of the unmodern.

Nevertheless, given the porosity and susceptibility of film texts to local interpretation, some of the selected films in the *Film Course* were meaningful to rural children and to their teachers, allowing them to show off unexpected formations of modernity. The breakthrough came through the *Film Course* leaders' decision to allow teachers to develop local pedagogical approaches to using film in the classroom. The richer, usually urban, schools assumed that the students were already attuned to Chinese national culture. Teachers, therefore, did not work with the texts to make them 'relevant'. Rather, they emphasized technology, skills and classic formal interpretations of texts in the classroom response to film. The poorer, more remote schools tied the narratives of the films presented to actually occurring events in the students' lives. I have discussed this in detail elsewhere (Donald, 2005). In this discussion two further reflections are relevant. First, the *Film Course's* multiple locations enabled flexible creativity in media use, which yet occurred within the overall discourse of state modernity and the improvement of 'quality'. Second, the children's location ensured uneven approaches to a modern curriculum; but, although it had roots in a core–periphery sensibility amongst schools in richer areas in the east, nonetheless that unevenness was not an indication of relative sophistication in classroom practice.

The media worlds of these two large countries, China and Australia, one with a minute but diverse population and the other with a very large and diverse population base, are inflected by the hegemony of the *idea* of the West and the *idea* of China, but neither conform exactly to these imagined constraints. In both Australia and China, the rural populations have more obviously in common transnationally than they do with urban residents in the same country. Yet, as we know, that conclusion depends very much on what questions we ask when on fieldwork and what conditions we privilege in assessing media use. The rural child in a modern state, as both China and Australia definitely are, has some awareness of the urban alternative to their lives. That knowledge is inflected by the ways in which the power of the state is manifest in local conditions: through education, public information, development opportunities, disadvantage or neglect. At the very least, the contemporary rural child knows that, however declassed, she is inevitably hailed as a national subject by the imposition of state authority, Chinese or Australian, whether or not that is acceptable to her heritage and whether or not that brings benefit or loss. With such self-knowledge she also becomes modern.

Children in the news: class, politics, and anti-modernity

Since 2000, what I would term the mediated infantilization of Australian politics has continued apace. It included the 'children overboard' affair or 'a certain maritime incident', an event in Australian maritime waters in 2001. A child, wearing a life jacket, on a sinking boat, SIEV 4, was held up by an adult man, presumed his father, as if to throw the child overboard. The action was either threatened in supplication or in despair, or as a stage of a decision to get off the boat together before it went down. Several pictures of the ongoing events were taken by officers of Australian Navy; *HMAS Adelaide* was in attendance at the scene. At the point at which one particular photograph was taken, a number of people had already ended up in the sea and were subsequently picked up by the naval vessel. The Government of the day claimed that boat people were threatening to drown their children as a political gesture and to make the Navy rescue them. The Government used the photograph, cropped to show only the parent with the child, not the people already in the water or of the clear sight of the boat sinking rapidly, to help win an election. It is not possible to do the story justice here, and it is well documented in the press and online comment; I simply to note it as the quintessential example of what may occur when media, and by the same token, anti-media activists, divide children into classes of the visible, the named, the articulate and the necessary victim. These boat children are unnamed, they and their parents consigned to long stays in detention centres (Glendenning and Dodson, 2005), their access to media is limited to their status as photographic and affective subjects (in a furore which resulted in 2006 in a Government defeat at the hands of its own backbenchers). Meanwhile, the campaigns against media violence in cartoons and film continue as though these posed the greater threat to social cohesion.

'Children overboard' was a low point in a recent history of the incarceration of 'unclassed' children in detention centres, and the proliferation of the values debate, which includes the effective political ostracization of many children due to ethnicity, origin and presumed religious practice. Dismissal is a central tactic in prevailing political techniques of infantilizing the political aspirations and democratic rights of all sectors of the community. The deployment of children in the process is structurally core to such diminution, and rests on the classing of children as visible, Australian, and relevant, or not. Kennedy's conclusions make political, mediated, and pedagogic sense here: 'it makes sense ... to put childhood and adulthood in dialogue, that education would be the first of our institutions to devote itself to the broad cultural emergence of the subject-in-process' (Kennedy, 2006:110). The way we treat and respond to our children indicates something about the way we treat ourselves as adults in the political sphere and elsewhere in our lives. The response of researchers to that challenge should be, one hopes, to model the best possible relationship between adult power and children's perspectives.

Such events indicate the need for a careful balance of specificity and inference in undertaking research about children's media, and in cross-cultural or inter-regional studies in general. Certainly, the drift to rhetoric about media violence and the way that plays into violence within representation as in the 'children overboard' affair is not unusual and has provoked rebuttals (Barker and Petley, 1997; Lumby and Fine, 2006). These writers point to the banality of making the roots of social dysfunction reside in representation, without taking account of the flaws in the lived environments of the audience. Media violence in itself may be justifiably concerning, but the issue at stake is the way in which the effects debate is used to class children and their parents into modern, sophisticated *us* and a 'like Runtu', declassed *them*. *Them* is an elastic category organized around children as victims, children as potential dangers to society, children as déclassé by the fact of migration or birth. The ease with which a generation was declared *lost* in both China and Australia reminded one that academic research has a responsibility, first, to recuperate children from classification and, second, to avoid the error of assuming or declaring children to be *pre-political*, whilst all the time using them for structural or explicit political ends in the construction of debate – or making them prey to such use by adult activists. University Ethics committees make strong demands on the researcher to prove that they will not do the child-respondent harm. As important, however, should be a demand that the child is respected as an actor and participant in their own story. Political respect as much as probity underpins research-oriented conversations between subject and researcher, and that respect must itself be based on thorough knowledge and understanding of the conditions and contingencies affecting those with whom we work.

CONCLUSION: REGIONAL ANTHROPOLOGIES

It is neither ethical to take the results of work done in another place and non-reflexively apply them to different populations, nor is it intellectually sustainable to pick up the ideal of childhood as it is created and used in socio-political realms and assume that real children should aspire to the resulting constraints of their elders' neuroses. That said, it is realistic for researchers to understand that the figure of the child is a potent actor in social relations and moral structures, and that we should expect to deal with that potency, in the opinions of others, in the structural options available to children in different spatio-temporal planes, and in the design of our own work. In cross-cultural, intra-regional situations it is all too easy for a well-intentioned researcher to re-infantilize the subject by applying blanket theoretical judgements to the condition of others' lives. Children in communist (post-socialist) China, for instance, have as much right to be asked about their consumption preferences as children in London or New York. The fact that their national government is more severely regulative than the British or the American when it comes to media content does not deprive children of their intelligence or of their ability to use media in specific contexts, with particular cultural values in train. Media researchers negotiate their internal anti-modernities of classification and hierarchy every time they go 'in-country' to look at media, an activity that has been termed 'a legitimate sub-field within anthropology' (Askew, 2002: 1). Even when they investigate home-grown phenomena, they tread a thin line between the ethnographic and the judgemental. This is especially so in multi-ethnic communities, and when intra-generational populations (children and young people) are the subject of the research. In addition, not only do media researchers necessarily work in a multimedia and, thus, multiliterate environment – after all their work is to discover articulated connections between social, cultural and economic phenomena – but they must translate their findings into terms accessible to the various communities of interest to whom they speak. Talal Asad (1984: 141–152) has discussed the challenges of translating meaning from one linguistic realm to another, as a core skill for anthropologists. He argues, 'The translation is addressed to a very specific audience, which is waiting to read *about* another mode of life and to manipulate the text it reads according to established rules, not to learn to *live* a new mode of life' (Asad, 1984: 159).

Despite the difficulties posed, it is worth taking the region seriously. Research which categorizes the geo-political regimes of Asia-Pacific as local, glocal and regional will discover contingencies of the modern that would be missed if only the local and global were taken into account. Those whose work involves searching new regional media-spaces are used by children and young people (Anagnost, 1997; Bloustein, 2004; Goggin, 2006) find both detail and the possibility of wider theoretical extrapolation. Goggin could not comment effectively on mobile media in Australia if he were not aware of how this contrasts with that of Australia's immediate neighbours. Bloustien uses longitudinal ethnography to understand the formation and limits of youth cultures amongst female adolescents in South Australia. Her careful narratives tease out the relationship between highly self-aware expectations of the future, ethnicity, gender, class advantage and educational opportunity in a diverse group of young women. Whilst all their lives intersect with a generalized mainstream, Bloustein shows how the transactions of indigeneity and social class have profound effects on the degree to which her subjects can make the most of modern Australian life.

In China, the American anthropologist Ann Anagnost consistently explores the connections between social development, childhood and media. Her work on nationalism, children and the everyday politics of media clarifies the relationship between socialization and the adult world, elucidating both the prospects of modernity introduced by Ong and the ways in which children's lives as national subjects may be systematically routed through media use. Film and media have changed in the three decades of reform economics, but children's media has remained a fulcrum of political and social attention. In August 2006, the State Administration of Radio, Film and Television let it be known that local animation should take preference over unsuitable imports (*The Simpsons* was cited as a particular problem). This sporadic descrying of US product is familiar, and the call for more local animation on television for children has been growing since the then Premier Jiang Zemin first noticed its lack in 2002. Underlying these announcements is not just a will to control national culture through the metonymic hotspot of children, but also a wary recognition that children's media could lead the way in some content industries. So, by following children's media policy we see both reiterations of the spiritual purification campaigns whereby the Party takes back what it has let slip through the rush to capital, and of the commercial rationale of support for the creative industries. Both versions of the story indicate that children are crucial actors in the politics of national renewal and economic reform.

If media analysis in China draws on a chain of cultural value based in narratives of loss, succession and rural backwardness, then one might hypothesize that media use by Chinese in the region is affected by this pattern. Australia is a multi-ethnic society with competing regimes of value playing out across generations and arrival groups. If there are pre-eminent structures of feeling at work in any particular group, how will this emerge and play out in the multicultural situation of migrancy? Adult competencies are thrown into question by the very fact of arrival. Whilst, for instance, British arrivals have the advantage of language and the arrogance of a carefully remembered imperial status, other groups have a more immediate challenge to their presumed competencies as adults – learned in another place with other histories and interests. The loss of competency, both within a presumed mainstream and within the multiple ethnic nuances that make it dynamic, is very frightening for adults. It is as though they, too, have been returned to a pre-political status, infantilized by displacement.

Thus, in order to understand Australia as a regional player in media flows and content generation, one must constantly interrogate assumptions of belonging, cultural and political competency and indeed the very character and time-scales of modernity as evinced in the ordinary processes of everyday life. Children and their use of media are central to these processes, and to understanding the regional status of modernity. Those who attend selective schools in North Sydney and who will form the educational elites of the nation, have access at home to VCD copies of long-running Korean soaps, dubbed or subtitled in Mandarin and sold through video stores in downtown Chinatown, probably owned and run by a third generation Chinese from Zhongshan, or perhaps a new migrant from Shanxi. Cultural value is dependent on the conditions of its making and to the relative power of those young people who negotiate meaning across worlds of content and delivery.

The Simpsons, so disapproved of in China at the moment, is also off limits in a friend's house in Greenacres, western Sydney. Her family is Arabic, English and French speaking, Sunni, first-generation Lebanese Australian. The two teenage boys in the family, who speak Arabic at home and English at school, are constantly asked to 'turn it [*The Simpsons*] off', and constantly respond by just turning it down. These same boys regularly attend mosque, and are likely to spend time in Yemen studying scripture once their secondary and university education is completed. In first-generation British-Australian households, and my own is an example, in an inner west suburb of Sydney, there is deep suspicion of the 'quality' of Australian TV for children. 'Quality' here also refers to the capacity to be modern, in so far as it educates children into understanding British tastes, wit, accents and political sophistication. It is similar to the Chinese usage, in that it is a discourse of class, based on culture, a regional modernity and a migrant structure of taste.

The study of children and media in the Asia-Pacific region lends itself to a regional perspective, which in turn allows national, transnational and regional views of modernity and requires an appreciation of uneven stages and formations of development as seen through the prism of media use. In particular, the flows of population between China and the rest of the region are long standing and continuing. A recognition of the regional impacts and affect in media use amongst young Chinese populations invokes not just a broader conception of China itself, but also induces unexpected insights into corresponding experiences within structures of global class; the urban rich and rural poor are two cases where Australia and China have strikingly respondent situations. These larger observations must, however, rest in micro-studies of use patterns and local circumstance. None of this sets the media or children of the Asia-Pacific region apart from those of any of the other great regions of the world. Micro difference and macro correspondence are not confined to previously anthropological sites of interest. A regional approach does, however, declare a geographic and experiential equivalence and, thus resist the core–periphery model of analysis for the next generation.

NOTES

1 List adapted from Ewers (1998: 30).

2 An indication of her status is given by her inclusion on the libertus.com website, which also gives details of the Office of Film and Literature Classification, a Government body which has banned films (including Ken Park, Larry Clark, 2003) for sale in Australian states. http://libertus.net/censor/know.html#bb [18 September 2006].

REFERENCES

Ahmad, C.M. (2003) 'Mass media in Indonesia: a short historical journey through five centuries'. In M.Y. Hussain (ed.) *Mass Media in Selected Countries*. Kuala Lumpur: International Islamic University Malaysia; 1–35.

Anagnost, A. (1997) *National Past-Times: Narrative, Representation, and Power in Modern China*. Durham, NC: Duke University Press.

Anagnost, A. (2004) 'The corporeal politics of quality (suzhi)'. *Public Culture*, 16(2): 189–208.

Asad, T. (1986) 'The concept of cultural translation in British social anthropology'. In J. Clifford and G.E. Marcus (eds) *Writing Culture: The Poetics and Politics of Ethnography*. Berkeley: University of California Press; 141–164.

Askew, K. (2002) 'Introduction'. In R. Wilk and K. Askew (eds) *The Anthropology of Media: A Reader*. Oxford: Blackwell; 1–13

Barker, M. and Petley, J. (eds) (1997) *Ill Effects: The Media Violence Debate*. London: Routledge.

Beck, U. (1993) *Die Erfindung der Politischen: Zu einer Theorie reflexiver Modernisierung*. Frankfurt am Main: Suhrkamp.

Bloustein, G. (2004) *Girl Making: A Cross Cultural Ethnography of the Process of Growing Up*. London: Berghahn Books.

Brady, A. (2006) 'The rebirth of the propaganda state: China's modernised propaganda system'. Paper given at ARC Asia Pacific Futures Research Network signature conference: *Media: Policies, Cultures and Futures in the Asia Pacific*, 27–29 November.

Chen, T. (2003) 'Proletarian white and working bodies in Mao's China'. *Positions – East Asia Cultures Critique*, 11(2): 361–393.

Donald, S.H. (1999) 'Children as political messengers: space and aesthetics in posters and film'. In H. Evans and S. Donald (eds) *Picturing Power in the People's Republic of China: Posters of the Cultural Revolution.* Lanham, MD: Rowman and Littlefield; 79–100.

Donald, S.H. (2005) *Little Friends: Children's Film and Media Culture in China.* Lanham, MD: Rowman and Littlefield.

Donald, S.H. and Benewick, R. (2005) *The State of China Atlas: Mapping the World's Fastest Growing Economy.* Berkeley, CA: University of California Press.

Ewers, H.-H. (1998) 'Children's literature in the process of modernization. Some preliminary results from a current research project'. In U. Boëthius (ed.) *Modernity, Modernism and Children's Literature,* vol. 29. Stockholm: Centrum för Barnkulturforskning; 25–47.

Glendenning, L. and Dodson, L. (2006) 'Meet the barcode kids in detention' *Sydney Morning Herald,* 31 May 2005. http://www.smh.com.au/news/National/ Meet-the-barcode-kids/2005/05/30/1117305563811.html [18 September 2006].

Goggin, G. (2006) *Cell Phone Culture: Mobile Technology in Everyday Life.* London: Routledge.

Goodman, D.S.G. (2006) 'Exiled by definition: the Salar and economic activism in northwest China'. *Asian Studies Review,* 29(4): 325–344.

Goonasekera, A. (ed.) (2001) *Children in the News: Reporting of Children's Issues in Television and the Press in Asia.* Singapore: Asian Media and Information Communication Centre.

Government of South Australia (2003) 'Talk about'. *DAIS broadsheet,* October.

Guntarto, B (2001) 'How Indonesian news report news about children'. In A. Goonasekera (ed.) *Children in the News: Reporting of Children's Issues in Television and the Press in Asia.* Singapore: Asian Media and Information Communication Centre; 97–121.

Hill, D.T. and Sen, K. (2005) *The Internet in Indonesia's New Democracy.* London: Routledge.

Kennedy, D. (2006) *Changing Conceptions of the Child from the post-Renaissance to Post-Modernity: A Philosophy of Childhood.* Lewiston, NY: The Edwin Mellen Press.

Luke, C. (1989) *Pedagogy, Printing, and Protestantism: The Discourse on Childhood.* New York: SUNY.

Luke, C. (1990) *Constructing the Child Viewer: A History of the American Discourse on Television and Children, 1950–1980.* New York: Praeger.

Lumby, C. and Fine, D. (2006) *Why TV is Good for Kids: Raising 21st Century Children.* Sydney: Macmillan.

Lynch, D. (1999) *After the Propaganda State.* Stanford, CA: Stanford University Press.

Mackerras, C. (2004) 'China's minorities and national integration'. In L.H. Liew and S. Wang (eds) *Nationalism, Democracy and National Integration in China.* London: Routledge; 147–169.

Ong, A. (1997) 'Chinese modernities: narratives of nation and of capitalism'. In A. Ong and D.M. Nonini (eds) *Ungrounded Empires: The Cultural Politics of Modern Chinese Transnationalism.* New York: Routledge; 171–202.

Ong, A. (2006) 'Cyberpolitics and the pitfalls of diasporic Chinese politics'. In A. Ong (ed.) *Neoliberalism as Exception.* Durham, NC: Duke University Press; 53–72.

Sayers, J. (2004) 'Start with the little things: environmental education as political participation in contemporary China'. PhD thesis, University of Melbourne.

Thompson, E.P. (1966) *The Making of the English Working Class.* New York: Vintage Books.

Wang, S. (2003) 'Minority movement and education'. In R. Iredale, N. Bilik and F. Guo (eds) *China's Minorities on the Move: Selected Case Studies.* Armonk, NY: ME Sharpe; 32–50.

YMA (2006) http://www.youngmedia.org.au/ [September 2006].

Zuberi, N.A. (2001) 'Newspaper reporting and children's television in Pakistan'. In A. Goonasekera (ed.) *Children in the News: Reporting of Children's Issues in Television and the Press in Asia.* Singapore: Asian Media and Information Communication Centre; 235–271.

18

Girls' Issues, Gender and the Media: Feminist Activisms in China

Bu Wei

INTRODUCTION

China has undergone a rapid transformation in gender awareness and practice in the decade since the 1995 United Nations Women's Conference, which took place in Beijing. To what extent have these changes affected perceptions on issues such as the imbalance in the sex ratio at birth, girls' education, trafficking of girls and women, and violence against girls and others in society? How have the mass media reflected calls for more sensitivity to gender issues? What new methods have emerged to promote gender issues in the media and what are the challenges that remain? In this chapter I will first provide an overview of current gender issues/inequalities in relation to media representation. Based on a feminist perspective, I will then examine how mass media reporting on girls' issues is gendered. Finally, I will present and discuss recent activisms aimed at achieving change in the Chinese media's reporting on gender. Moreover, the limitations of such activisms and future challenges will be outlined.

BACKGROUND: GIRLS' ISSUES, GENDER AND THE MEDIA

After the so-called 'Reform and Opening Policy' in China was implemented at the end of 1970s, the issue of the 'girl child' was raised publicly through the mass media beginning in the mid-1980s. In the 1980s and 1990s, media reports on the girl child issue mainly concentrated on equal opportunities for school enrolment (Wei, 2006c: 358–359). For example, the initiation of the 'Spring Bud Project' at the end of the 1980s focused public attention on the issue of girls' education after a sample investigation of the Fourth Population Census showed that, in 1989, 4.8 million 7–14-year-old school-age children were not attending school and, of these, 83% were girls.

In order to address this issue, in 1989 the China Children and Teenagers' Fund (CCTF) set up the Spring Bud Project to provide stipends to aid female dropouts in poverty-stricken regions to return to school. From 1989 to 2004, the Spring Bud Project collected more than 600 million Yuan, covered 30 provinces and cities, contributed to 300 Spring Bud Schools, and supported nearly 1.5 million girl-child dropouts (Cheng, 2004). Through mass media coverage of the project, the general public was informed about how poverty specifically affects girls. In addition to education, other issues, such as the sex ratio imbalance at birth[1] and violence against girls, including trafficking, have also been discussed since the 1980s and 1990s by the media.

However, in the Chinese mass media, girls' issues are usually represented as girls' problems and are not connected to broader gender inequalities. For example, girls' education is mainly valued for its instrumental outcome, as seen in the campaign catchphrase 'The Girl of Today is the Mother of Tomorrow'. Thus, girls who receive an education are not enjoying the right to education as independent citizens, but because of their future role in the family as mothers.

Before the 1995 UN Women's Conference, media and gender were not included in the Chinese women's/feminist movement's agenda, nor was gender an issue addressed by communication studies. The *Almanac of Chinese Women's Studies (1991–1995)* does not include a single article about media and gender. This fact alone demonstrates that, in the field of Chinese media studies, media and gender had not gained attention before 1995 (Wei, 2004a: 169). However, during the preparation for the UN Women's Conference (1992–1995), feminist studies researchers, activists, and journalists had opportunities to participate in various international conferences and workshops, such as the *Women Empowering Communication Conference* held in Bangkok, 12–17 February 1994, and the *World Women and the Media Workshop* held at Iowa University in March 1995. Such interaction with international women's movements changed their ideas and actions. Because the Beijing Declaration and Platform for Action included the media as one of 12 critical areas of concern, the intersection of media and gender issues became a legitimate area of action for the women's movement in China.

As mentioned above, the 1995 Beijing Women's Conference introduced international feminist thought and practices to China. Since then, gender, as a key word of feminism, has been gradually used as an analytic tool in various academic fields. In comparison to the term 'sex', which refers to the physiological distinctions between males and females, gender refers to the socially and culturally constructed perceptions of the differences between men and women, as well as socially and culturally shaped attributes and behaviors given to the female or the male (Hom and Xin, 1994: 144). Theories of gender are united in highlighting how social identity and gender are constructed through language and naming practices. These practices are not only complex, but also are layered and use differences in consciousness and socialization as their starting points. Gender theorists further agree that naming and labeling involve classification processes in which power and meaning categories are involved. It is well known that gender inflects meaning categories negatively for females, whereas it tends to inflect them positively for males. And finally, when gender functions as an ideology, where 'difference' is equated with 'lesser rationality', as in Enlightenment discourse, then all kinds of unequal treatment for women and minorities become justifiable (Robinson, 2005: 20).

Using a gender perspective, many researchers and female activists have criticized the sexist stereotypes presented in the Chinese mass media. In common usage, the stereotype can be seen as an ideological discursive strategy that demarcates an us–them binary which then functions to reinforce the dominant discourse. For example, patriarchy often operates at the level of the stereotype in order to categorize the roles and characteristics of women, which are viewed as essentially different to those of men. Within this dichotomous opposition, the feminine is categorized as inferior while the masculine is valorized. The stereotyped ideal woman is a nurturing wife, mother or muse constructed through the scopic gaze of the male (Gamble, 2000: 323). Gender stereotyping is typically a summing-up of the female sex from the point of view of the male-dominated culture. Thus, an aggressive attitude, rational thinking and leadership ability are all admired by mainstream culture and are generally seen to be male characteristics, while the traits of passivity and irrationality are seen to belong to women.

Many researchers have also noted that children's culture in the mass media is highly gendered and that boys and girls are often portrayed as 'naturally' and fundamentally different. Not surprisingly, children's media (like their toys) are among the first contexts where girls and boys learn how masculinity and femininity 'ought' to be performed (Carter and Steiner, 2004b: 12). In famous modern Chinese fairytales, such as 'Pipi Lu and Lu Xixi'[2] and 'Boy Jia Li and Girl Jia Mei',[3] the male characters are described as tough, brave, naughty, aggressive, active, independent and taking the lead, whereas the female characters are portrayed as beautiful, emotional, passive, timid, and hoping for a male to come to their rescue. In 2005, a children's publishing house even published two versions of Hans Christian Andersen's fairytales, one for boys and one for girls. The boys' collection of ,His Fairytales, included titles like 'The Hardy Tin Soldier' while the girls' volume of 'Her Fairytales' contained 'The Little Mermaid', 'Little Ida's Flowers', and 'The Wild Swans'. Thus, in China, the famous fairytales served to further solidify gender stereotypes.

In 1996, Media Watch (a women's non-governmental organization (NGO)) was established in China to promote media criticism, and its members have been involved in publishing collections on media criticism, sponsoring advocacy activities, and holding seminars and gender training workshops for journalists in order to help reduce the use of gender stereotypes in the media (Wei, 2006b: 314–315). Though these women activists and feminist researchers have criticized sexism in the mass media, the majority of those working in the Chinese media are still rather blind to such issues. The myth that the triumph of the Communist Party in 1949 brought gender equality to China has been used to hide the fact that women are not equal with men. Moreover, most people in China believe news is 'objective' and hence cannot represent sexism. However, as we know, media texts never simply mirror or reflect 'reality'; instead, they construct hegemonic definitions of what should be accepted as 'reality'. Thus, media images conceal the extent to which they are aligned with the interests of powerful groups in society. Feminists have redeployed the notion of hegemony in order to argue that most of us cannot see how patriarchal ideology is actively made to appear as 'non-ideological', 'objective', 'neutral', and 'non-gendered' (Carter and Steiner, 2004a: 2). They have also argued that the 'communication process is a symbolic process in which reality is produced, maintained, repaired, and transformed' (Robinson, 2005: 15).

GIRLS VISIBLE AND GENDER INVISIBLE: THE REPRESENTATION OF GIRLS' ISSUES IN THE NEWS

Whereas a lot of content analysis on media representation has been conducted in China since 1996, there has been very little criticism of the manner in which girls are stereotyped by the media. In this section I will focus on how girls and issues pertaining to girls are presented in news stories of the mainstream media. Most of my examples come from three research reports: (1) 'The image of girls as reported by mainstream Chinese newspapers'[4] (Wei, 2003); (2) 'Single male issue or girls' rights issue – gender analysis on the sex ratio at birth in the Chinese media' (Wei, 2004b);[5] and (3) 'Media study on child protection issues in China'[6] (Wei, 2006a). These reports discuss the basic and essential issues related to girls' development in China, including girls' education, the sex ratio imbalance at birth and violence against girls.

Issue of girls' development

How are girls' issues raised in news stories? According to Wei (2003), which is a content analysis of girls' images in the *People's Daily* from 1996 to 1999, most reports that included girls actually only mentioned girls while reporting on other topics. Reports about national development and children's development which mentioned girls' issues made up around 34% of the total; articles on women's development and gender equality that touched on girls' issues accounted for 18%; stories that focused solely on girls only comprised 28%; and nearly 20% of reports on girls were unrelated to gender. Such articles contained the word 'girls' but were not actually about girls' development.

This same study also found that girls' issues appeared on the front page and as important news if they related to issues of national development, educational development, women's development, or children's development. When 'development issues' were discussed, girls' protection, education, and development were often mentioned. Thus, on the one hand, women's development, national development, and children's development included girls' development and identified progress in, and obstacles to, girls' development as development issues. On the other hand, we can see that the category 'girls' as an independent news item in the media is very rare and inadequate. Reporting that focuses solely on girls is disproportionate to the extent and scope of the issues in social reality.

Furthermore, in news stories, children's development or women's development issues often cover up the impact of gender inequality on girls. As Elisabeth Croll (2000: 9) has pointed out:

> girls are probably the most under-studied of all social groups in most societies. There has been much interest and activity around the issues of women and gender but very rarely is this extended routinely to include girls.

She continues by noting that:

> there has been a great deal of attention to and progress in programmes to do with children, but very rarely are children either divided into boys and girls or seen to have different needs and interests in the family, community and society. It is presumed that work with children, like work with women, will benefit girls automatically. Yet the statistics show that there are vulnerable points in girls' lives different from those of boys or older women.

Thus, we lose sight of the way specific constructions of gender and social reality affect girls. Along with the catchphrase that is meant to support the girl child, 'The Girl of Today is the Woman of Tomorrow', we have to recognize that, because the girl child is the woman of tomorrow, she does not have gender issues today (Elisabeth Croll, 2000: 9).

Issue of girls' education

Another finding in Wei (2003) was that a large majority of 'reports on girls' focused on girls' absence from school. Statistics showed that at least 82% of the news reports on girls were related to girls' school enrolment. Also, the media often highlighted 'poverty' as the sole reason for girls dropping out of school and used images of poor girls and their tears as a 'weapon' to capture readers' attention and move them emotionally. The problem with such reporting, however, is that not only is the issue of gender equity ignored, but also other gender issues related to girls' development in China are missing, including prenatal sex selection, higher rates of female infant mortality, female infanticide, discrimination against the girl child in her access to nutrition and physical and mental health services, and heavy domestic work. Sexual and gender-based violence (including physical and psychological abuse) also go unreported, such as trafficking in women and girls, other forms of abuse and sexual exploitation that place girls and women at high risk of physical and mental trauma, and girls' unprotected and premature sexual practices that can often result in their contracting HIV/AIDS and other sexually transmitted diseases.

In China, girls are less encouraged than boys to participate in and learn about the social, economic and political functioning of society and others. When the media report on education, they are likely to ignore other gender issues, for example that curricula and teaching materials remain gender biased to a large degree and are rarely sensitive to the specific needs of girls and women. Gender-biased educational processes, including curricula, educational materials and practices, and teachers' attitudes and classroom interaction, reinforce existing gender inequalities and undermine girls' self-esteem. The girl child issue has not obtained the value which it should have in the Chinese media.

Girls are also shortchanged in the number of times they appear in the 'leading role' of a news stories. Here, the leading role refers to the protagonists of news reports. More specifically, it refers to the major instigators or participants in events, whose voices are reflected in the stories. We have found that most of the time girls do not assume the leading role in a news report but rather are assigned to passive roles as victims or recipients of assistance. When we divided news roles into two categories, active participatory roles and passive roles, in 82% of news reports girls appeared in passive roles. Their voices were also absent in the media. Only 2% of all news items described girls as actors. Even when such an image emerged in real life, reporters were hardly able recognize it as a positive one. This attitude repeats the stereotypical image of the girl as a passive victim.

Wei (2003) showed that most leading roles in the news stories analyzed tended to be occupied by adults, specifically donation makers who included government officials, business executives, and others. Compared with these adults, girls were usually depicted as passive recipients of donations, guests at events, or vulnerable victims. Most news reports told stories of girls losing their opportunity to receive an education or of dropping out of school. In contrast to the image of a child victim, or a 'pathetic child', the media preferred to use donation makers as the main source of news.

Issues of violence against girls

According to Wei (2006a), media reporting on sex-related violence against girls has recently increased. This study found that, among 1,509 reports on protection of vulnerable children in the six mainstream newspapers, 324 reports mentioned violence against children, accounting for 21.5% of the total. As shown in Table 18.1, media mainly expose physical and sexual violence against children.

Among 342 reports, 108 mentioned more than one type of violence; 79 reports dealt with two types of violence at the same time, amounting to 24.4% of the total violence reports; 29 reports mentioned three types of violence at the same time, accounting for 9.0% of the total violence reports. The total 29 reports which covered three types of violence were all related to sexual violence. Most sexual violence against children was related to adults raping young girls between 12 and 16 years old.

Most of the news stories on such sex-related violence against girls repeated rape myths such as 'rape is sex', 'the assailant is motivated by lust', 'the assailant is perverted or crazy', 'women provoke rape' (because rape is believed to be sex, victims are

Table 18.1 Reports in six newspapers of violence against children

Type of violence	*No. of times reported*	*Percentage (%)*	*Percentage in total 324 reports (%)*
Physical violence	210	45.6	64.8
Mental violence	77	16.7	23.8
Sexual violence	174	37.7	53.7
Total	461	100.0	142.3

portrayed as having enticed their assailants by their looks and sexuality), and 'only "loose" women are victimized' (Benedict, 1992: 13–19). The most powerful myth perpetuated about rape is that rape is sex. It ignores the fact that rape is a physical attack and leads to the mistaken belief that rape does not hurt the victim any more than does sex. The idea that rape is a sexual rather than an aggressive act encourages people not to take it seriously as a crime (Benedict, 1992: 14).

In these news stories, women are habitually defined in terms of their relations to men rather than as separate individuals (Benedict, 1992: 21). Especially when the sexual persecutors are fathers, stepfathers, or teachers, the reports often use such language as 'beast', 'animal', or 'more cruel than the tiger which loves its whelp'. Such expressions are related to incest and moral requirements, but they have nothing to do with the rights of children and the law. The angry expressions such as 'beast' are actually used to regard the sexual violence as a kind of personal affair instead of as a violation of the human rights of children in a wider sense. Furthermore, such sex-related violence against girls is usually regarded as 'inhumane' and as a domestic matter. Thus, many girls are forced to keep silent under the intangible pressure of the cultural perceptions of virginity and the idea of 'keeping the scandal within the household'. Through defining what is 'natural' and 'normal' behavior (for example, that raping one's own daughter is not normal and that it is a 'beastly' act) and emphasizing sex issues rather than violence, the media unwittingly help to maintain the existing social order.

Issue of the sex ratio imbalance at birth

Since 2000, the high sex ratio imbalance at birth has become a hot topic in the mass media in China. It also serves as anther example of how the media represents gender stereotypes.

In the Wei (2004b) study, 117 online news stories (from 1 January 2003 to 20 June 2004) on the high sex ratio imbalance were examined from a feminist perspective. Most of these news stories were from mainstream media, including national and local newspapers.

This study revealed that among all the headlines, 45 were male focused, accounting for 38.5%, and 72 were 'neutral', accounting for 61.5%. No headlines were found with a focus on the human rights of girls or gender issues. The story with the headline 'Population alarm set for Beijing – Whom are they going to marry?' serves as a typical example. Other male-focused headlines included 'Concern for our future single males';[7] 'Imbalanced sex ratio at birth, 50 million men in China are going to be single';[8] 'Whom will our sons be marrying in 20 years – should we or should we not worry about this?';[9] 'No wives for 40 million men in 15 years';[10] and 'How can we help you, 40 million "single males"?'[11]

In Chinese the word single male (*guang-gun*) indicates a man's pathetic situation as being poor, left alone without a wife to take care of him, and as being scorned by others and even himself. It is used to label those with a low living standard and low social status. A headline such as '50 million *guanggun* will occur in China – Won't find wives' exemplifies the self-mockery by indicating that the high sex ratio at birth will bring men into a 'pathetic' *guanggun* life. With such headlines, however, the human rights of girls are completely ignored. In the study cited above, not a single headline focused on women, but instead on 'wives', 'brides', or 'sex partners', as if women were part of men's desires and merely objects that men needed for marriage. The unconscious message is that the goal of young women's lives is to meet men's demands, benefits and interests.

If we see prenatal sex selection and female infanticide as violence against women and girl children, our primary focus should be on the negative impact of the high sex ratio on the girl child's birth right and health rights, as well as the effect on women's development and the achievement of gender equality. The issue of the high sex ratio is primarily an issue of women's and girl children's human rights. However, the messages that most news reports are conveying is that the impact of the high sex ratio at birth will be mainly on men and their marriages. One expert even suggested that the high sex ratio at birth should not be a cause for concern, since young Chinese men could 'look for brides' in other parts of the world 'in the era of globalization'.[12]

The 'Single male issue or girls' rights issue' report (Wei, 2004b) also discussed how the Chinese media tend to explain the high sex ratio. The one child policy, an underdeveloped economy, lack of education for rural women, lack of social welfare in rural areas, and the cultural tradition of 'valuing men and belittling women' are causes that were often quoted by experts in the media. However, according to Croll's studies on the high sex ratio in Southeast Asian countries, this kind of discrimination occurs at different levels of economic development both in regions that are rich and poor and in locations that are urban and rural; it crosses levels of education so that discrimination is not just common among those who are illiterate and uneducated, but also among educated city families. Moreover, discrimination occurs in countries where there are strict birth control programs, such as in China, and also in countries where there is very little in the way of a birth control policies and contraception is scarce (Croll, 2000: 8–11). The phenomenon is related to beliefs about gender that make up some of the most important attributes of culture or legitimating ideologies of patriarchy, and most journalists failed to report this point.

From this analysis, we can see that many of the news stories reported on issues and solutions highlighting men's benefits and interests while overlooking structural gender inequality and girl children's human rights.

In this part, we have discussed the representation of girls in the media. Even when issues related to girls were visible, gender inequalities and gender issues were invisible, revealing that Chinese media portrayals are very backward compared with reality. Sexism and stereotyped gender roles are prevalent in the male and female representations in the mainstream Chinese media.

FEMINIST ACTIVISMS

Activism, in a general sense, can be described as intentional action to bring about social or political change. This action is in support of, or opposition to, one side of an often controversial argument (www.answer.com/topic/activism). Feminist activism is very related to gender issues, such as reproductive rights, domestic violence, maternity leave, equal pay, sexual harassment, discrimination and sexual violence.

In China, feminist activisms on girls' issues in the media must track the activisms on gender issues in the media. As mentioned above, even when we recognize gender issues that are connected to women, men, and the relationship between them, it is very possible that we still ignore gender and girls. Usually, a discussion of gender issues in relation to women and men is viewed as primary, while gender issues related to girls are viewed as secondary.

Based on the experience of the international women's movement, Carolyn M. Byerly and Karen Ross have suggested a Model of Women's Media Action that includes four paths: politics to media; media profession to politics; advocate change agent; and women's media enterprises (Byerly and Ross, 2006: 124–126). Since 1995, Chinese activisms have been undertaken along the above four paths, yet with distinct Chinese characteristics.

The first path, 'politics to media', is represented by feminists' decision to begin to use the media as a component of their feminist political work. This became very significant for Chinese popular women's organizations working at the grassroots level in the 1990s. In China, most mainstream media are sponsored by central or local governments; therefore, when the government media report on the activities of women's non-governmental groups, such coverage is viewed as a form of recognition of these groups by the government. This form of legitimacy granted by the media to NGOs can help women's NGOs to gain greater social influence. According to one study, among the 22 Beijing women's NGOs examined, most organizations got along well with the media and actively utilized the media to spread new knowledge and experience in the 1980s and 1990s, through publishing articles, being interviewees on TV stations, or developing some programs with journalists (Wei and Milwertz, 2004). Most activists are not media professionals; however, they were able to promote more women's voices in the media and reinforce women's experience and culture.

The second path in the Byerly and Ross model is 'media profession to politics'. It describes the strategy followed by women employed in media industries who use their vantage point as insiders to expand women-related content, or to reform the industry's policies to improve women's professional status. As mentioned earlier, one Chinese women's NGO, Media Watch, is actively involved in deploying this strategy. Established in 1996, Media Watch originally consisted of journalists from a variety of mainstream media in Beijing. They developed a strong identity with feminism and began to explore ways of increasing information about women in media content. On 24 February 2000, the Capital Women's Journalists Association presented a proposal to media organizations in Beijing based on the idea of 'giving women news workers a gift for International Women's Day – the right to decide media content'. This was their response to UNESCO's proposal that 8 March be a day when 'women create the news', and some mainstream newspapers were responsive to their proposal. In addition, the Association held a seminar titled 'Gender, Media and Development: Dialogue between Women Peasants and Women Journalists' in 2001. This activity raised awareness of media participation by rural women and also raised the level of concern on the part of journalists for rural women's development.

The third path, 'advocate change agent', is a strategy of putting outside pressure on the media to improve treatment of women in one or more ways, or to disseminate information with a feminist perspective. These change agents in China are usually women's NGOs and feminist individuals. Their concerns and goals focus on changing the media and shifting the agenda in media reports. The major activities they have undertaken since 1995 are presented in Table 18.2.

From Table 18.2, it is clear that the All-China Women's Federation (ACWF)

Table 18.2 Feminist activisms for media advocacy

Institution		*Actions and methods*
Women's Federations	1.	Media Workshop in the Beijing+5 and Beijing+10 Forums
	2.	Conference on Mass Media and Women's Development in 2001
	3.	Proposals for mainstream media leaders to improve media content and reinforce women journalists' positions, especially in decision-making
	4.	Organizing women activists to evaluate Chinese government's implementation of the Beijing Platform for Action (the media was one of the topics addressed)
	5.	Initiating some research programs on media and gender
Media Watch	1.	Media monitoring
	2.	Cultural criticisms
	3.	Participatory gender training workshops
	4.	Negotiation with media to develop fair representations in the media
	5.	Awards for media with fair representations
Popular Women's groups or organizations	1.	Negotiation with media to report special concerns or issues with a feminist perspective
	2.	Participatory gender training workshops
Individuals		Articles and speeches

plays an important role in the promotion of gender equality in media reporting. Similarly, Media Watch has become an active force for professional journalists from a variety of media. Their goal is to push for change not only in their own particular media outlet, but also in other media outlets. Organizing from below, they have documented how the mass media do not provide a balanced picture of women's diverse lives and contributions to society in a changing world, and how the media continue to reinforce stereotypes of men and women. They have also pointed out how advertisements and commercial messages often portray women primarily as consumers and in traditional gender roles. Media Watch has concluded that the mass media should be changed through media monitoring, cultural criticism, gender training for journalists, negotiations with media and the distribution of awards for gender equity. They have worked with media to stop sexist and inaccurate representations, to reshape media policies, and to amplify the voices of grassroots women though mediated communications. They are also involved in the Global Media Monitoring Project (GMMP) and jointly sponsored the 'Beyond Media Monitoring: Strategies for Gender Advocacy in Asia' workshop with the Asian Network for Women in Communication in Tianjin, China, in 2006.

Byerly and Ross's fourth path, 'women's media enterprises', allows women the maximum control over message production and distribution. In China, the most popular women's media enterprises are usually book and video publishing. They are very small outlets where women activists can retain the greatest degree of control over messages. Up to now we still have not established women's media enterprises such as syndicated radio programming, women's news agencies, and independent film. As media, the *China Women's News*, sponsored by the ACWF, *Rural Women*, sponsored by *China Women's News*, and the *Half the Sky* program on CCTV are seen as women's channels with gender sensitivity because they disseminate many kinds of information related to women's needs from a gender perspective and also publish women's voices from different social groups in China. Even *Rural Women* invited readers to contribute to the small magazine. However, this kind of media is still sponsored by a governmental system. Moreover, *Half the Sky* and *China Women's News* strive to survive under the pressures of the market economy, which has forced them to compromise in terms of some of their content.

Carolyn M. Byerly and Karen Ross's Model of Women's Media Action is part of the international women's movement that has been adapted to a certain extent to fit the Chinese context. Unlike other countries, most Chinese women activists have a very good relationship with the mass media. As an important partner for NGOs, the mass media often disseminate feminist voices and information from women's NGO websites, newsletters, performances, and publications. Actually, Chinese women activists tend to synthesize Byerly and Ross's four paths. To take the Domestic Violence Network as an example, we could say that they 'do media'. The network includes a journalists' group so that these journalists can use their position to raise concern about the issue of violence against women. The network also monitors representations of violence against women, conducts gender training for journalists and has developed its own publications and videos.

In their Model of Women's Media Action, Byerly and Ross mention very little about participatory gender training for journalists by women's NGOs. In China, however, participatory training on gender issues has been employed as a main method to initiate change in the media. This training method originated from a 1997–1998 UNDP development project in China, where six experts created a manual for participatory training on gender and development issues. Since then, many participatory training programs (1 or 3 days) have been conducted by feminists and activists from Media Watch.

In addition to journalists, this type of participatory training targets those in leadership roles in the media. For example, in

March 1999 the Capital Women Journalists Association and the Journalism and Communication Institute of the Chinese Academy of Social Sciences provided gender training for leaders and anchors of women's programs. In February 2004 a United Nations Population Fund (UNFPA) project offered training to media leaders in the central and Beijing governments on 'Optimizing the Media Environment for Women's Development and Raising Gender Consciousness for Mainstream Media Leaders'. Other training workshops have been on very specific topics, such as how to report on issues related to girls, women's health issues, or domestic violence. As a result, a number of media reports showing gender consciousness have begun to emerge. The special focus on media and gender issues by the *Beijing Youth Daily* on 8 March 2004, following participation in the UNFPA project, is one such example.

Although there are very few feminist media activisms related to girls, in recent years two activities on girls' issues and the media were launched by UNICEF China. At the '99 National Symposium on the Girl Child', Edwin Judd, a representative of UNICEF China, proposed that 'an annual national media day for girls could direct more media attention to girls' issues' and make fuller use of the mass media to shape societal views and promote equal opportunities for girls (Judd, 2000a: 4). In 2000, UNICEF and the ACWF held a joint 'Workshop on Media and Girls in China' to promote the visibility of girl children's issues in the mass media from a gender perspective. At this workshop, international and domestic experts conducted a training workshop on gender issues for 200 media people. Also, Edwin Judd suggested that all journalists approach the challenge of changing media reports in many ways, including: (1) communicating about China's successes in promoting the rights of girls; (2) communicating about the problems that reflect the existing gaps in respect to the rights of girls; and (3) being alert to emerging issues that face girls (Judd, 2000b). Most activists believe that the mass media could make an even more strategic impact in changing societal gender stereotypes and encouraging equal opportunities for girls.

Another important activity is training workshops on girls' issues for journalists. Since May 2004, UNICEF and the Chinese government have implemented a 'Multi-sectoral Girls' Education Program' in four counties of Guangxi Zhuang Autonomous Region, Ningxia Hui Autonomous Region, and Qinghai Province. The project aimed to improve girls' living environments, provide educational opportunities for girls in difficult situations, ensure that girls can study in schools full of love and without sex discrimination, and guarantee that they can complete their schooling successfully, receive high-quality education, and further their study in schools of higher education. UNICEF and the National Working Committee on Children and Women included 'Participatory Multi-step Training Workshops about Gender and the Media' (hereafter referred to as 'Multi-step Training Workshops') in the 'Girls' Education Program'. This means that the mass media is seen as a tool for promoting gender sensitivity in society. A total of 26 journalists or managers of local media from Guangxi, Ningxia, and Qinghai were involved in this training.

Most gender training for media workers is short (1- to 3-day courses). However, the multiple step approach requires more than one session of training, as outlined below:

Step 1 The first-phase participatory training workshop (3 days). In this period, participants discuss the issues of children's rights, gender issues, and Chinese girls' development, and work out reporting plans from the perspective of children's rights and gender.

Step 2 Field reports about girls are produced (6 months). Participants make use of their knowledge and skills to report about girls in local areas. During this period, facilitators work with participants in the localities.

Step 3 The follow-up participatory training workshop (3 days). The concepts and knowledge of gender and children's rights learned in the first phase are reviewed by taking the participants' news stories about girls as examples. Discussions are undertaken on how to report girls' issues with a gender perspective and develop a guideline for such reporting.

A fourth step or even more steps are proposed. The basic assumption of multistep training is that the improvement of gender consciousness is a long-term process from gender understanding (theory) to report practice, and once again from report practice to gender understanding (theory).

There have been several positive results of the training process: journalists have increased their probability of understanding the complexity of gender and their reports have already had an impact on local communities. Moreover, participants have formed a network, and they are providing training to other media workers in the local area. As a pioneer project, participatory training for media workers provided many positive experiences and more space for changing the mass media in the Chinese context. It has become a main advocacy instrument in China as part of the third path in the model of women's media action. On the base of gender training workshops, the first *Multi-Step Training of Trainers Manual on Gender and Media Reporting for Children*[13] was published in 2006.

It is impressive that the media and feminist activists do not usually oppose one another, though activists have leveled much criticism at the media. In China, most mainstream media are controlled by the government (central and local), and the government has promised that China will carry out the state policy 'Equality Between Men and Women' and implement the Beijing Platform for Action. Sometimes feminist activisms receive the support of the government, and in some cases they even become a governmental action. Also, activities or actions launched by UN agencies have an influence on the government and mass media. The UN has legitimated feminist activism, which has allowed such activism to enter the mainstream media more easily. In addition, most feminist activists are intellectuals with strong social capital in society, and their points are very new and critical. This attracted the attention of the mass media, which wants access to them and their activities. The important advocacy activity '*Gender Equity Media Awards*', which happened in 2006, embodied the friendly partner relationship between feminist activists and the media. The feminist activists and experts from communication fields gave awards to eight mainstream media because of their outstanding contributions to gender equity. It is this kind of partner relationship that makes participatory gender training in media very possible.

Undoubtedly, this kind of training is aimed at changing ideas and attitudes of individual media workers. One of its basic assumptions is that media content can be changed through changing attitudes of individual media workers. Yet, according to Shoemaker and Reese (1996), the individual media worker (including journalists' backgrounds and characteristics, personal attitudes, values, and beliefs, and professional roles and ethics) is only one of the influences on media content. Other more important factors are: media routines (including audience orientation, consumers, media organizations, processor, and news source); organizational influences on content (including organizations and their goals, as well as the organizations' roles and structures); influences from outside of media organizations (including influences on content from advertisers and audiences, government controls, and the marketplace); the influence on content from individual media workers; and ideology.

Training projects target individual media workers and only influence their personal attitudes, values, and beliefs. Thus, this kind of training project may have relatively minor effects on the overall society. However, 'it is possible that when communicators have more power over their messages and work under fewer constraints, their personal attitudes, values, and beliefs have more opportunity to influence content' (Shoemaker and Reese, 1996: 91). Though Shoemaker and Reese's argument is not based on research rooted in the Chinese context, it is at least a reminder to us that more complex factors influence media content and should be considered when we try to change mass media through training projects. Many participants have suggested that training projects should be conducted for leaders in the media, because most media decision-makers lack gender sensitivity and seldom support reporting on girls. Generally, changing the influence of media routines, organizational influences, influences from outside of media organizations and ideology may be much more difficult than changing personal attitudes. We need more creative ways to respond to this challenge. This could include establishing more alternative feminist media, organizing girls' issues reporting networks, developing professional education on gender and the rights of the child into departments of journalism and communication in universities and holding workshops for media leaders. While this would not change the media system, such efforts could potentially lead to an increased visibility of feminist voices in the media.

CONCLUSION

Girls' development has become a big issue in China. UNICEF has elaborated the necessity of putting value on girl child issues from two aspects. First, women's rights and girls' rights are mutually dependent for their existence. Only in a society where woman enjoy the right of equality can the girl child attain the same kind of rights. At the same time, the girl child's rights to survival, development, protection and participation, and how much these are realized or violated in the process of her growing up are all factors deciding her future living condition as a woman. Second, 'no girl child's rights, no children's rights' means that no discrimination against any child is the fundamental principle of children's rights. The girl child makes up half of the child population. If her right of equality cannot be guaranteed, we will never achieve the goal of the realization of children's rights (UNICEF, 2000: 94). If we want to reduce discrimination against women, then we must prevent discrimination against girls. The political solution is first employed to improve girls' development, and then changing traditional culture will be one of the most significant solutions. In this respect, mass media will play an important role.

Though most Chinese media are controlled and sponsored by the government, and the Chinese government proclaims the state policy 'Equality Between Men and Women', the Chinese media engages in gender stereotypes, sexism and discrimination against girls and women, just as in other countries. After 1995, Chinese feminist activists initiated many media campaigns or activities to stop sexist representations in the media. If there can be one single achievement of feminist activism over 10 years, 'it is that it is now impossible to make any sense of the mass media without paying attention to gender' (Fenton, 2000: 115). These campaigns or activities have converged with the international women's movement, as discussed above with Carolyn M. Byerly and Karen Ross's model of women's media action. Unlike other countries, the participatory gender training for media workers has become one of the most important instruments for changing the mass media in China.

Since 1995, like most feminist projects and actions, media campaigns or activisms have considered gender issues on women and men, but overlooked gender issues on girls and boys. UN-sponsored advocacy for gender issues on girls has legitimated feminist activisms and pioneered 'participatory gender training' projects for changing the mass media. Such advocacy has proven to be an effective means of bringing a positive influence on the media. However, more investigation as to how activism influences media organizations or systems to improve their representation of gender issues and have more concern for girls' rights is still needed.

NOTES

1 According to national statistics, the exceptionally high sex ratio at birth started to appear in the 1980s and continued to increase in the 1990s. In 1990, the Fourth Population Census reported the sex ratio at

birth as 111.3 boys for every 100 girls (normally the sex ratio is about 106; that is, for every 100 girls 106 boys are born). The figure rose to 116.86 in 2000 according to the Fifth Census (119.92 in long sheet*).

2 Chinese modern fairytale by Zheng Yuanjie.

3 Chinese children's novel by Qin Wenjun.

4 The mainstream newspapers referred to in this research include *People's Daily*, *Guangming Daily*, *Worker's Daily*, *China Youth Newspaper*, and *China Women's News*. *People's Daily* is run by the Communist Party and is circulated nationwide. There were 212 reports related to girls' issues from 1 January 1996 to 31 March 2000 analyzed by key word search on the *People's Daily* online.

5 There were 117 news reports on high sex ratio from 1 January 2003 to 20 June 2004 selected for analysis through a key word 'sex ratio at birth'/'single male' in google.com.

6 The study is a content analysis on all reports, news, articles, comments, and pictures regarding issues of child protection (1509 items) from seven media sources (*Xinwen Lianbo* from CCTV, the *People's Daily*, *Beijing Youth Daily*, *Wenhui Daily*, *Yangcheng Daily*, *China Women's News* and *Legal Daily*), published from 1 January 2001 to 31 December 2002.

7 *Shenzhen Economy Daily*, 15 March 2004.

8 Originally in *Outlook Weekly*, 24 September 2002, and was adapted and quoted many times in 2004.

9 Qianlong.com, 17 May 2004.

10 *Tianjin Daily*, 7 March 2004.

11 Heilongjiang Channel, Xinhua Net, 29 March 2004.

12 Care for our Future Guanggun, *Shenzhen Economic Daily*, 15 March 2004.

13 Edited by Bu Wei, National Working Community on Children and Women (NWCCW) and UNICEF China, 2006, Beijing, China.

REFERENCES

Benedict, H. (1992) *Virgin and Vamp: How the Press Covers Sex Crime.* New York: Oxford University Press.

Byerly, C.M. and Ross, K. (2006) *Women & Media: A Critical Introduction.* Blackwell.

Carter, C. and Steiner, L. (2004a) 'Introduction to Critical Readings: Media and Gender'. In C. Carter and L. Steiner (eds) *Critical Readings: Media and Gender.* Maidenhead: Open University Press; 1–10.

Carter, C. and Steiner, L. (2004b) 'Mapping the contested terrain of media and gender research'. In C. Carter and L. Steiner (eds) *Critical Readings: Media and Gender.* Maidenhead: Open University Press; 12–35.

Cheng, S. (2004) '15 Years' Love – "Spring Bud Project"'. China Children and Teenager Fund website, http://www.cctf.org.cn [September 2007].

Croll, E. (2000) 'The current situation and main issues of girl child in Asia and China, UNICEF and ACWF'. In All-China Women Federation (ed.) *From Discrimination to a New Vision and Priority for Girls' Development: A Report of the National Symposium on the Girl Child.* UNICEF (China); 8–18.

Fenton, N. (2000) 'Feminism and popular culture'. In S. Gamble (ed.) *Critical Dictionary of Feminism and Postfeminism.* New York: Routledge.

Gamble, S. (2000) 'Stereotypes'. In S. Gamble (ed.) *Critical Dictionary of Feminism and Postfeminism.* New York: Routledge.

Hom S.K. and Xin, C. (1995) *English–Chinese Lexicon of Women and Law.* China Translation Publishing Company and UNESCO.

Judd, E. (2000a) 'Ensuring equal opportunities for girls' development'. In All-China Women Federation (ed.) *From Discrimination to a New Vision and Priority for Girls' Development: A Report of the National Symposium on the Girl Child.* UNICEF (China); 7–8.

Judd, E. (2000b) 'Statement at the opening of the media workshop on the girl child'. In *Collection of Papers From the Workshop on Media and Girls in China, sponsored by UNICEF and ACWF*, September, 2000, Beijing, China; 6.

Robinson, G.J. (2005) *Gender, Journalism and Equity: Canadian, U.S., and European Experiences.* Cresskill, NJ: Hampton Press.

Shoemaker, P.J. and Reese, S.D. (1996) *Mediating the Message: Theories of Influences on Mass Media Content*, second edition. New York: Longman.

UNICEF (2000) 'Activities Organized by UNICEF'. In Women Media Monitoring Network (ed.) *Five Years' Journey: From Beijing World Women Conference to New York Special United Nations Conference.* China Women Publishing House; 94–95.

Wei, B. (2003) 'The image of girls as reported by mainstream Chinese newspapers'. In H. Wang (ed.) *China Women Culture.* China Wenlian Publishing House; 91–102.

Wei, B. (2004a) 'Review report on Media Studies 1996–2000'. In *Almanac of Chinese Women's Studies 1996–2000*, compiled by Women's Studies Institute of China. China Women's Publishing House; 168–179.

Wei, B. (2004b) 'Single male issue or the girls' rights issue – gender analysis on the sex ratio at birth reported by the Chinese media'. In *Expert Workshop*

*In that census, two methods were used to collect data: the short sheet (a very simple, short questionnaire) and the long sheet (which had more questions).

on Ethical, Legal and Social Issues of Birth Sex Ratio (0–4) Imbalance in Mainland China, 27–28 June, Beijing, China (unpublished).

Wei, B. (2006a) 'Media study on child protection issues in China'. In U. Carlsson (ed.) *Regulation, Awareness, Empowerment: Young People and Harmful Media Content in the Digital Age*. Gothenberg: Nordicom/Goteborg University; 67–82.

Wei, B. (2006b) 'Women and the media (1995–2005)'. In J. Wang (ed.) *Blue Book of Women Development: Report on Women Development in China ('95+10)*. Social Sciences Academic Press (China); 291–333.

Wei, B. (2006c) 'Girls issues (1995–2005)'. In J. Wang (ed.) *Blue Book of Women Development: Report on Women Development in China ('95+10)*. Social Sciences Academic Press (China); 358–396.

Wei, B. and Milwertz, C. (2004) 'The interaction between the popular women's organization and mass media: a process of domestic violence from private to public issue in China'. In Research Center for Asian Studies of the China Communication University (ed.) *Asian Communication & Media Studies*. China Communication University Press; 61–71.

19

Contextualizing Media Competencies among Young People in Indian Culture: Interface with Globalization

Usha S. Nayar and Amita Bhide

INTRODUCTION

It is widely believed that India will soon enjoy the advantage of a 'demographic dividend'. According to one estimate, India will have the highest number of people in the younger age group: 700 million people out of 1.1 billion people are young. Around 555 million Indians are aged less than 25, and teenagers among them number about 160 million; it is estimated that by 2015 that Indians under 20 will make up 55% of the population.

The young people in India are growing up in a multicultural, heterogeneous social and political system in which diversity is placed along the lines of language, region, religion, caste, gender and class. A socio-psychological understanding of the young people in India and their interaction with political and social institutions, new media and technology and emerging communication processes in the period of globalization is the central theme of this chapter. An attempt has been made to examine the socio-cultural particulars of the young people's lives in India in the context of globalization and the communication 'revolution'. The geographical and cultural variations across different parts of India along the intersecting axes of region, caste, gender, and religion mediate the competencies of youth in interfacing with media and the culture industry as active consumers. Such an examination is essential to understand the existence, nature and texture of the 'digital divide', which is presumed to be abstract. In a diverse country like India where the press alone expresses itself in over 100 languages, such an examination is a challenge in itself. The rapid changes in media technologies and landscapes make this challenge even more onerous. It seems a huge cultural change, almost a paradigm shift, is clearly on the anvil in India in terms of change in the cultural and social orientation of the youth. The chapter argues that such contextualization is a must for a nuanced understanding of impacts and contours of this paradigm shift.

MEDIA LANDSCAPES IN INDIA

The media landscapes in India are characterized by one theme in the past decade, i.e. rapid change. From a largely static, development-oriented, state-controlled and operated, monochromous media, the scene has given way to a booming, vibrant entertainment and culture industry expected to bring in revenues of Rs 30,000 crore by 2010 (*Business Today*, October 2006). The advent of convergent, digitalized technology with a strong personalized interface has made the term 'mass media' redundant, though the outreach of these technologies is ever expanding. The media industry is replete with 'stories' of companies which were very small or nonexistent 10 years ago but are now amongst the 'Most Valued Companies' in the country (illustrations include Sun TV, New Delhi TV, etc.).

The patterns of media use and penetration as reflective of general population give some insights into the emerging trajectories of state of media in the country. The recent National Readership Survey (2006) indicates the following:

- The press continues to be a large force with an overall readership of 222 million. Dailies and the regional papers register a growth, whereas magazine readership has steadily declined in the last few years.
- Television, too, continues to grow, with current audience strength estimated at 230 million households, of which 61% are connected to cable and satellite.
- Radio audience, particularly through FM, has increased marginally to encompass 27% of people.
- Cinema viewing has declined steadily for the past 5–6 years with a current viewership of 9 million. On the other hand, revenues in foreign countries have become a major source of support to film. The other recent discovery is the multiplex.
- The internet user base in the country is small, i.e. 1.2%, but is steadily increasing.
- The mobile phone is rapidly acquiring the stature of a medium with 22 million individuals (9%) using value-added services at least once a week.

One of the most interesting dimensions of the emerging media landscape is its youthfulness, both in terms of its use and its propellants. Some of the new media are largely youth led. The 'call-centres' which have become icons of information technology-(IT-) enabled services are emerging as focal points of youth culture. The conventional media, such as the press and television, are not far behind in initiating special programmes and supplements to capture a proportion of this youth interest. Professionals in this field, too, are largely young.

Emerging theoretical perspectives

The interconnectedness between the youth in India and the new media and IT cannot be explained in simplistic narratives. The issues in this intersection are far too complex to be understood in terms of relationships between dependent and independent variables.

One of the key problematics here is to unravel the nature of media impacts without getting entangled in a simplistic notion of effects whilst subscribing to the idea of a 'free, unaffected' consumer. Another challenge is to unpack the seemingly contradictory but connected trends of globalization and localization and to unravel the disjunctures and differences in the global cultural economy (Appadurai, 1997), earlier believed to be homogenizing (Lee, 1980; Levitt, 1982). The ideology of new media and IT is displayed not through 'content' and its congruence in production processes and control, but through subtle grammar and setting up of the rules of the game. The unerring passage of societies into post-modernity, which Turner (1994) defines as an extension of processes of commoditification of everyday life, is to be noted. Patterns of social exclusion existing in society are changed in complex ways, including forms of expression. In a society like India, which is diverse and characterized by several intersecting layers of exclusion, this becomes an important dimension of study.

Thus, the purpose of this chapter is to set some of the markers for further study and explorations of the subject through a review of literature, facts and observations.

CONTEXTUALIZING MEDIA COMPETENCIES

Geographical setting and global culture interface

India's geographical particulars make linkages with the lifestyle and culture of the people, especially, the new consumption patterns, urbanization and modernization. India has a unique geographical setting; it imbibes a variety of subtropical climatic conditions. social groups to settle in different parts of the country according to their lifestyle and traditions. The contemporary distribution of rural and urban population and the regional disparities in terms of language, class, caste and religion have also been impacted by historic events and geographical particulars or what is called 'ecological differentiation'.

Differentiation among the urban and the rural is significant with a reduced penetration of the 'modern' media in rural areas. These differences are less pronounced in case of press and television with roughly equivalent audiences in absolute numerical terms; they are distinctly pronounced in case of Internet and computers (over 67% of users in urban areas) and mobiles (44% use of value-added services in 42 metros).

The ecological difference between a high press-reading north India and high television and cinema-viewing south India is striking. In fact, the triumph of the South in localizing Indian Broadcasting is notable (Kumar, 2006).

It is important to note, however, that such ecological differentiation is not a new phenomenon but, rather, an extension of earlier encounters with modernity. Thus, there is a resonance between Appadurai's (1996) reflections of his youth in 1960s Mumbai and the discussions that Monteiro and Jayasankar (2001) have with young males in the 1990s.

Appadurai (1997) reminisces:

> In my own early life in Bombay, the experience of modernity was notably synaesthesic and largely pretheoretical. I saw and smelled modernity reading 'Life' and American college catalogues at the United States Information Service library, seeing B-grade films from Hollywood at the Eros theatre. I begged my brother to bring me back Blue Jeans and smelled America in him when he returned.

The youth say:

> K: Earlier there was a limit … to lead a good life … One needs so much … not any more … now one needs everything … many many things.
> S: Yes, we have become more western.
> R: I think it is because of Western culture … it has come through TV, through the media.

The media-savvy, English-conversant image of Indian youth is largely an urban image and is closely connected to Internet cafés, shopping malls, multiplexes, pizza huts, Valentine's Day and several other such icons of the Mcdonaldized world (Appadurai, 1997). However, the penetration of these into smaller towns is quite rapid and deep.

Shikha Trivedi (2006) laments that none of these changes touches the 'heartland' of rural India and that the anguish of this 'Bharat' is largely invisible to the media. On the other hand, Maidul Islam (2006) points out that the advent of parallel economic and cultural processes has resulted in a shrinking of the autonomous space for rural cultural forms. Thus, rural youth, too, have imbibed aspirations for urban lifestyles and media use. This explains why there is a great demand for 'town' and local city news through online journalism that the *Deccan Herald* has experimented with in Karnataka and Tamil Nadu.

Caste, religion and new media

Historically speaking, when a hierarchical society revolving around caste and religion undergoes changes, it challenges old notions of privilege and also creates new layers of dominance and hegemony. In other words, systemic exclusion continues unabated. Even before the arrival of globalization and its technological aftermath, the notion of technology was closely tied to the traditional notion of hierarchical eminence. This was reflected in the high demand for a degree in the areas of science and technology and the domination of these sectors and administration by the superior castes. Neo-Brahmanical hegemony in the country was thus sustained through domination in education and occupations. The 1980s in India were characterized by increasing demands for a stronger policy for affirmative actions and reservations for the scheduled castes, tribes and, more recently, the religious minorities. A stagnant bureaucracy and private sector in terms of the employment generation potential meant a fierce contest for opportunities.

Liberalization, however, has come to the rescue of these 'middle' classes who, through their knowledge domination and English competencies, have an advantageous position to secure opportunities in the IT sector. Today, youth are motivated by higher salaries, and a faster short cut to the so-called goodies and freebies of the good life. It has often been noted that in the 'initial public offering' sector, where call-centres boom, and in software, young men and women come from socially privileged backgrounds. For them, call-centre jobs have opened up possibilities for consumption and earning that were previously unimaginable to middle-class young men, women and their families. It has its own secular, symbolic and psychological effects on the youth in India.

The all too frequent introduction of class as an element for reservation policies and the recent agitation of medical students against extension of reservations are illustrative of these changes.

Gender and new media technologies

At the heart of modern mass technology is the absence of the notion of other; it invariably revolves around the ideas of sameness and universality. The rights of women appear as fictional narratives. In the software industry, too, the gender divide is reducing by providing more space to women. However, this does not mean an unambiguous acceptance of women in these sectors. In some sectors of the IT and software industries, women's services are restricted because of their sex.

Women's continued discomfort remains at the centre of social construct of gender and technology. The boundaries between science and social reality are a optical illusion. Judith Butler (1990) says that gender is 'never fixed, always fluid'; working from the same premise, we would argue that technology is never the same, it is always fluid. In other words, technology leads to social construction of gender in many ways: manifest and latent. Sherry Turkle (1984), in her fascinating study of the cultural and psychological world of computers and computer science, attempts to redefine what constitutes the category of 'woman'. Based on a thick ethnography of women using computers, she contends that contradictory attitudes of women towards computers are not necessarily an inextricable part of biological sex, but rather of gendered construction. On the one hand, she describes the tendency for science and scientific activity to be described, in what she calls masculine terms, as a 'place for the abstract, the domain for microcosm of the male genderization of science' (Turkle, 1984: 118). On the other hand, she argues that the different methods brought to bear on computer science by girls and women reform our ideas of what constitutes science. In short, on an optimistic note, she argues that the computer has 'a special role', in this process, because it 'provides an entry to formal systems that is more accessible to women. It can be negotiated with, it can be responded to, it can be psychologized' (Turkle, 1984: 118).

These male technologies also create what cultural theorist Bharucha (2001) calls 'imaginary utopias' in which men continue to perceive women as primarily a creature of fun and pleasures. The virtual world has reinforced stereotypical gender characteristics: witness the incidence of mobile pornography. Zimmerman (1986: 355) informs us that, without political and financial control over new technologies, 'women will find themselves replaying a familiar scenario in which new technologies serve to reinforce old values'.

In the period of globalization, there are spaces available for women in the emerging domains of corporate institutions, visual media and software industries. However, the stigma attached to the traditional norms and values that prevented women occupying such spaces is not diminished to a large extent. The socially constructed lessons of treating women's capabilities, as homemakers, subjects of 'soft disciplines' and professions are still dominant in many of the contemporary texts of social relations and socialization norms practised in institutions like the family and schools.

The social construction that distanced women from the vicinities of technological discourse has to be analysed critically as part of a democratic political paradigm. Though changes are taking place in the configuration and practices within the family and school, there is a need to accept democratic values in such practices. In the dominant visual media, like television and popular cinema, the images of young Indian women have changed from the traditional settings. They are represented as symbols of modernity, possessing technological skills, managerial competencies and political capability. However, there are also an equal number which portray them as soft subjects and inferior citizens; in certain contexts, they have been represented as sexual objects. There is a correlation of these dual representational models with the contemporary society in India. The actual patterns of women's lives in India are a complex process of negotiation with tradition and modernity according to contexts.

Nowhere are these negotiations more evident than in the lives of young women who find themselves at the crossroads in making their own independent choices for life. In terms of accessing higher education, professions in technological fields and heavy industries and in those areas which have earlier been considered as male domains, young women confront enormous pressures, both internal and external, to take decisions. As bearers of traditions and values, young women in India find themselves bearing the brunt of these conflicts of aspirations and opportunities and of the dilemmatic societal attitudes towards these. More and more young girls scale new heights of achievement, while there is also an increase in the violence inflicted in the name of community and ethnicity. A provocative insight into these trends is offered by Mankekar's (1997) analysis of media representation of Ameena's case – the story of a young Muslim girl married to an old Arab.

Further, young women, too, imbibe and express many of these dilemmas. To recount the narrative of Monteiro and Jayasankar's (2001) discussions with young girls:

> A: I think overall attitudes have changed ... like more youngsters are working now ... even young girls ... even the look is changing. I mean now girls are more concerned about how they present themselves when they are going out, even to work.

A further challenge in understanding the gender interface with new media is its confluence with other axes of exclusion. Women's interface with the global is thus one that is full of contradictions and intersections between the private and the public, the notional and the real, the aspirational and the possible, and the representation and the actual.

ENGLISH COMPETENCY AS A KEY ELEMENT OF INTERFACE WITH NEW MEDIA

Competence in the English language has become a substantial part of Indian education and it constitutes the elitist version of acquiring power and dominance. Along with acquiring English as a medium of communication and a tool for social transformation, the upwardly mobile Indian youth from privileged backgrounds also began to aspire for certain Western lifestyles and practices that give a Western outlook. The dominance of Western epistemology in India's educational systems resulted in a neglect of the possibilities of exploring local knowledge systems. However, as Partha Chatterjee (1993) suggests, though Indians accepted the supremacy of the English language in the secular Western domain, they continued to valorize vernacular in the inner domain that is the cultural domain. In other words, the West triumphed in the political sense, but got defeated in the cultural realm. In this sense, India remained independent in its inner self. This explains why most Indian nationalists accepted, grudgingly, the introduction of Western institutions and values, but continued to remain anchored in what is called 'Indianness'. Chatterjee (1993) further points to the resurgence of regional languages and cultural aspirations as part of the making of Indian nationalism. So the discourse on the power of the English language is not hegemonic. Following Gramsci's Marxism, it could be argued that the English language led to domination, but without hegemony (Guha, 1997).

A discussion on the proliferation of the English language in Indian society makes sense in the analysis of the impact of new media and communication process on the life and culture of youth in India. The question of access to these radically shifting media and mediums of communication is largely dependent on the access to and competence in English.

Theoretically speaking, the public sphere of consumption of every product and entertainment package is open to all. But this openness does not make for equal access to knowledge systems of communication and information to the entire strata of the society. Cultural and economic barriers make a huge difference among people whose demographic and socio-economic profiles do not match with the demands that the new markets produce along with their new modes of consumption. In the Indian context, one of the powerful factors determining access to the changing technological domain is competence in the English language, since most of the scripts and methods are to be followed through English. English is not only a superior cultural marker, but it also leads to social exclusion of both active and passive kinds.

Several dimensions of media use and penetration reinforce this fact. The wide penetration of cell phones to even the remotest parts of the country have made the underprivileged class a part of the communication revolution. However, mobile phones are not getting connected to the global community compared with the use of the internet and other global communication technologies. Also, mobile phones require minimum skills of English language, compared with other digital technologies. This is one of the reasons for the widespread use of mobile phones among the urban working-class youth in India. In some of the coastal areas of western India, the fisher-folk use mobile phones for conducting business transactions. In most of these instances, the mobile phones are used more for verbal transactions.

Ecology and geography, caste, religion and gender are some of the key factors that cause differential access and exposure to new media among youth in India. These schisms have been further expanded because of the text and contents of the new technologies and media, which are shaped by the colonial language. The digital divide gets worsened because of the dominance of the English language. In the case of the internet, the access has been largely constrained to a small population who are conversant with English, though some inroads have been made into vernacular-based communication. English has thus emerged as a major marker of the discourse on media access.

Impacts of new media on the youth

There is a palpable difference in the awareness, attitudes and lifestyles of Indian youth in the post-independence era and those representing India's generation next. This first generation of Indian youth came of age during hard times: three wars, several famines and rigid protectionism. Pandit Jawaharlal Nehru (the first Prime Minister of independent India) and other nationalist leaders exhorted youth to emulate a Spartan kind of life style that severely restricted the 'cultural menu card' available to many among youth. Consumer choice was hardly available: one state-run TV channel, three brands of bath soap and car models that changed little through the decades. Even the political system did not escape the scarcity. One political party: Congress was voted into office again and again (which prompted political scientist Rajni Kothari (1970) to describe India as the'Congress System').

In contrast, in the current era the rhetoric of progress associated with ideas of the 'knowledge society' has taken on particular strength in India. The new hero of the middle class is no longer the builder of dams and steel plants of the Nehru era, but the highly paid, mobile IT professional. Yet there are significant continuities in these seemingly divergent pictures.

The young people, particularly those under the age of 25, have got increased interaction with the knowledge discourse, especially the emerging technologies of information and communication. The production and reception of the media texts and narratives have close associations with the social and cultural practices of the young people in contemporary India.

Information technology has emerged as an important agent of socialization for the youth and poses tremendous challenges to the mentors and pedagogists of the contemporary educational institutions. This process is not only confined to educational institutions, but spans over other institutions like the family, religion and communities. Presumably, the expansion of the knowledge gap and skills to use technologies between generations has added to this complex developmental phase of socialization in the present times, which was understood as 'a process in which an individual is trained socially and culturally to acquire the norms and values from the elder members of the society in order to fit into the normal domain of that particular society' (Brint, 1998). As mentioned earlier, the process of socialization in India has a definite linkage to geographical contrasts, multicultural lifestyles, ethnicity, and linguistic and gender differences. However, the sheer pace of change is one that lends uncertainty to this process of 'training' and generates turbulence.

The media, as used and shaped by the youth, reflect this turbulence in emphatic terms. The popularity of competitive, promotional shows such as *Nach Baliye* (couple dance), *Indian Idol* (Solo Singing), the frenetic participation in voting for these shows and the equally vigorous participation in Astha channel programmes (mostly spiritual in character); the reopening of the Jessica Lal murder case through an active media campaign, and the equivalent inability to comprehend the nature and scale of Dalit anger following the bestial killings in Khairlanji in Maharashtra and desecration of the Ambedkar statue in Kanpur are all pictures relativized to each other in the emerging global culture.

Sunil Khilnani (1998) points out that, 'in a fundamental sense, politics is at the heart of India's passage to and experience of modernity'. In other words, it is argued that modern India is an outcome of politics. Further, Rajni Kothari (1970) says that politics drives India and culture shapes politics in India. Therefore, the emerging relationship between the youth and the new knowledge economy in India may not be decided by the wish of the universal history, but by indeterminate, messy and raw adventures of democracy in India. The next generation in India is short of stable hierarchies, certitudes and comforts, yet continues to plunder new opportunities, skills and values unabashedly. And this certainly leads to a turbulent and intricate process of cultural regeneration and reinvention where the eternal India meets ephemeral India unapologetically.

CONCLUDING REMARKS

If India's encounters with modernity are marked by the 'politics of anxiety', to borrow Salman Rushdie's (1981) terms, then its passage to post-modernity is characterized by a politics of turbulence. A hierarchical and diverse society with wide schisms in opportunity and entitlement levels experiences globalization and global culture as 'contrary space'. It offers to youth new spaces of growth and excludes several others from choices in deciding life destinies. The media as vehicles of this global space reflect this turbulence, giving testament to the fact that culture is a site of contestation and struggle for the present young people.

REFERENCES

Appadurai, A. (1997) *Modernity at Large: Cultural Dimensions of Globalization.* Delhi: Oxford University Press.

Bharucha, R. (2001) *Politics of Cultural Practice.* New Delhi: Oxford University Press.

Butler, J. (1990) *Gender Trouble: Feminism and the Subversion of Identity.* New York: Routledge.

Chatterjee, P. (1993) *The Nation and its Fragments.* Cambridge: Cambridge University Press.

Guha, R. (1997) *Dominance Without Hegemony: History and Power in Colonial India, XV.* Cambridge, MA: Harvard University Press.

Islam, M. (2006) 'Postmodernized cultural globalization'. *Social Scientist,* 34(9–10).

Khilnani, S. (1998) *The Idea of India.* New Delhi: Penguin Books India; 9.

Kothari, R. (1970) *Politics in India.* New Delhi: Orient Longman.

Kumar, S. (2006) 'Localisation of Indian broadcasting'. *Seminar,* No. 561, May.

Lee, C.C. (1980) *Media Imperialism Reconsidered – the Homogenizing of TV Culture.* Beverly Hills, CA: Sage.

Levitt, T. (1983) 'The globalization of markets'. *Harvard Business Review* 61(May–June): 92–102.

Mankekar, P. (1999) *Screening Culture, Viewing Politics: An Ethnography of Television, Womanhood, and Nation in Postcolonial India.* Durham, NC: Duke University Press.

Salman, R. (1981) *Midnight's Children.* New York: Knopf.

Trivedi, S. (2006) 'Forays into the heartland'. *Seminar,* No. 561, May.

Turkle, S. (1984) *The Second Self: Computers and the Human Spirit.* New York: Simon & Schuster.

Zimmerman, J. (1986) *Once Upon the Future: A Woman's Guide to Tomorrow's Technology.* New York: Pandora.

20

Youth, Media and Culture in the Arab World

Marwan M. Kraidy and Joe F. Khalil

INTRODUCTION

'Traditionally, Arab society dealt with youth in a superficial and slightly condescending manner', an Arab columnist wrote recently, 'offering the occasional sports club and scout troop, a usually underfunded and dysfunctional government ministry or organization for youth issues, and a correspondingly noncredible occasional speech by a high-ranking official stressing that youths are the promise of the future' (Khouri, 2005). In light of this somber diagnosis with which many analysts of the Arab world would concur, it appears paradoxical that, today, Arab youth is at the center of some of the most important and controversial debates, from the impact of Western modernity on gender roles and social relations to consumerism and radical political violence. The scope of these debates transcends the borders of the 22 states making up the Arab world in a post-September 11, 2001, environment where Arab youth has become a site that is contested both internally and externally. Young Arab women and men are simultaneously subjected to competing and oftentimes conflicting messages from their parents, educational and religious institutions, the vibrant Arab satellite television industry, 'public diplomacy' from the USA, Iran and others, and the interlocking economic, technological and cultural forces of globalization.[1]

The central role the media play in the life of young people is widely acknowledged by scholars and policy-makers. Media and information technologies are instrumental in both youth cultural consumption and production; as such, they shape the dynamics of youth culture. In acknowledgement of this context, the exhaustive United Nations Youth Report 2005, states that '... *it is impossible to undertake an effective examination of youth cultures without exploring young people's relationship with the media*' (Department of Economic and Social Affairs, 2005: 82, emphasis added). Like youth in other parts of the world, young Arabs are avid users of mobile telephones and text-messaging, the internet, satellite television and popular music.

Aggressive advertising campaigns and synergies between telecommunications and media companies promote these media consumption activities. The explosion of commercial television genres has contributed to the creation of a 'hypermedia space' (Kraidy, 2006a) by activating interactive multimedia uses for television, the internet and mobile telephony. As the development of this commercial hypermedia space has intensified debates about the socialization of youth and children, these communication possibilities have empowered youth expression in new ways. The multifaceted and complex relationship between Arab youth and media may, therefore, be difficult to comprehend through traditional research approaches that focus on one type of media (television, internet, etc.) or one issue (violence, sexuality, etc.).

This chapter attempts to provide a comprehensive view of Arab youth and media that is multidisciplinary, historically informed, and conceptually based. It follows a top-down approach based on both secondary sources and on fieldwork at Arab media organizations. To meet this objective, we have organized the chapter into three main sections: The first focuses on socio-cultural de-traditionalization, treating issues of changing cultural values and social norms. The chapter's second section narrows down on the consumerist imperatives of the commercial Arab media environment, and discusses topics such as advertising, multimedia synergies and product placements. The third section discusses the political implications of media directed at Arab youth, ranging from local FM radio stations to US propaganda in the context of the so-called 'war on terrorism'. Our analysis will focus on established and emerging trends in the relationship between Arab youth and the media, dwelling on key case studies while referring to a diverse range of examples (institutions, genres, medium). By analytically linking old and new media in the lives of children and young people, we hope this chapter provides a comparative perspective on an area of research that suffers, according to at least one authoritative account, from 'fragmentation, small sample groups, non-comparability and a Western cultural focus' (Department of Economic and Social Affairs, 2005: 84). Because of this chapter's broad scope which covers numerous countries, several media, and a variety of social and political issues, some degree of generalization is inevitable. We hope that readers will make use of our references to access scholarship about specific Arab media issues.

The existence of tensions between global media-oriented youth culture and local traditions is beyond dispute. However, Arabs experience this clash in particularly acute form, for several reasons. First is the generational gap between contemporary Arab youth and their parents. According to the United Nations Population Fund, around 34% of the population of Arab countries is under the age of 15, and the median age for the Arab region is 22.[2] There is variation between states, but young people make up between one-third and one-half of national populations. While intergenerational differences are a universal phenomenon, in the Arab world these differences ride a wave of fundamental and far-reaching changes that have occurred over the last 30 years in the political, economic, cultural and educational structures of most Arab countries. These include the opening up since the 1960s of higher education to most Arabs, the transition from traditional desert culture to hyper-modern, oil-fuelled, media-saturated economies in the Gulf countries, the rise of political Islamism, and the major political and military upheavals experienced by Arabs in the last few decades. Especially important in shaping social and political developments in the Arab world is what Eickelman (1998) called the combination of 'mass education and mass communication'. Chances are that a 40-year old Arab father today grew up in a world where there was only one state television channel, which did not air advertisements, was the first in his family to obtain a university degree, and has had a decently paid job with a government agency. His 10-year-old son, however, was born amidst the Arab information revolution, can choose between more than 200 satellite television channels saturated with commercial messages, surf the internet and use his mobile telephone to vote for his favorite reality television contestant or to request his favorite music video. According to World Bank figures, the number of television sets per 1000 people in the Arab world is around 200, double that of low-income countries (for example in sub-Saharan Africa), but much smaller than the number in high-income countries, which is above 600 (UNDP, 2004). Internet penetration in the Arab region ranges from 30% of the population in the United Arab Emirates to close to 0% in Sudan, with Lebanon at 10% and Saudi Arabia below 3% (UNDP, 2004). Experiences of this generational gap are different from one Arab country to another, but the emerging regional youth culture, much of it revolving around hypermedia space, creates a sense of shared community among those who partake in it. The intergenerational gap is widened not only by the newly available technologies, but by the behaviors and vocabularies that youth culture develops around rituals of consumption and technology use, which tend to be exclusive of adults.

The global youth culture, to which some young Arabs gravitate with various degrees of belonging determined by language ability, socio-economic class and geographical location, navigates contemporary hypermedia space through rituals of consumption, like wearing the same clothing brands, listening to the same pop artists, eating the same fast-food and watching the same movies. Thus, the global, media-driven, consumption-centered youth culture reproduces itself through the ritualized consumption it promotes. This process does not necessarily lead to cultural homogenization. It mostly results in various forms of cultural hybridity embodied in so-called 'world music' or in branded mix-and-match clothing styles which indicates that global youth culture is a hodge-podge of international cultural influences.[3]

In the Arab world, this hybridity exacerbates intergenerational conflict because it hinders value transmission according to the postfigurative (hierarchical and strict) model by introducing horizontal value transmission between young people worldwide and within the Arab region.[4] This accelerates socio-cultural change to the extent that it reduces parents' influence on their children in favor of increasing their exposure to peer and foreign cultural influences, and increases the appeal of religiously couched, anti-popular culture arguments espoused by many Arab Islamist groups and political parties.

At the same time, global culture is locally appropriated by the Islamists, creating a different hybrid where local themes are grafted onto global forms: examples include Sami Yusuf, a British-born Muslim with Azeri origins, who has emerged as a creator of 'Islamic music videos', or, more generally, the advent of Islamic television. In the past, the notion of Islamic 'programs' on Arab state television were limited to short (few minutes) segments that reminded Muslims of prayer time five times a day. An exception to this trend was state television in Gulf countries, which routinely featured live broadcasts of sermons, religious talk shows and scripture readings. The advent of satellite television paved the way for fully dedicated religious channels, mostly based in Saudi Arabia with studios in Egypt and Dubai. For example, in 1998 the Saudi-owned Arab Radio and Television (ART) established 'Iqraa' (Read) as an Islamic channel appealing to women and youth worldwide. Until then, Saudi Channel One was the main religious channel, with 50% religious-oriented programming. Iqraa's appeal rests in its 100% religious programming emulating entertainment television with several male and female 'born-again' preachers, and live interaction with audiences. The trend set forth by 'Iqraa' was soon followed by Al Majd (the Glory) and Al Risala (the Message). The first grew in 2002 out of a Saudi-owned Islamic publishing house to include seven television and radio satellite channels Al-Majd channel, a Kor'an channel, a science channel, a historical channel, a news channel and two children's channels. The second, Al-Risala, was established in 2006 as part of the Rotana network with a youth focus. It has a slick screen appearance and features a mix of prayer, talk shows and music.

These channels helped create two types of religious star: the *tele-muftis* and *tele-dai'a* (or preachers). Starring in his Al Jazeera show titled *Al Sharia wal Hayat* (*Islamic law and life*), the Egyptian mufti Yusuf al-Qaradawi issues religious opinions known as *fatwas* and discusses general social and political issues. Traditionally, the dai'a is a born-again Muslim who dedicates his life to religious preaching. Satellite television gave dai'as like the Egyptian Amr Khaled superstar status. Khaled's charisma, trendy clothing, and 'modernist' Islamic discourse focusing on youth has led to over-the-air skirmishes between him and more established religious leaders, like al-Qaradawi. In addition to filling a market niche, mainstream Islamic media are seen as an antidote to the radical and sometimes violent media underground, largely restricted to the internet. Also, by adopting 'modern' media technologies and styles to spread their message, Islamic media indicate that as 'the cultural logic of globalization' (Kraidy, 2005), hybridity can sometimes operate as counter-logic. In other words, hybridity can reflect intercultural relations with various distributions of power.

Unlike the family-focused, living-room based, fixed-time radio listening or television viewing of the past, the new hypermedia space is based on personalized, interactive and mobile communication devices and practices. Therefore, it weakens the bonds of collective social life on Arab children and young people, contributing to the transformation of their cultural identities by changing the sources they use for 'identity work' (Ziehe, 1992). Although selecting foreign, regional (Arab) and local elements for identity construction existed before the advent of hypermedia space (e.g. see Havens (2001) and Kraidy (1999)), the environment permits a proliferation of cultural sources of identity. Also, the interactivity of text-messaging and internet chatting, for example, challenges the traditional, top-down model of socialization by making young Arabs active cultural producers. These developments reflect an intergenerational leap, since the media world of previous generations of Arabs consisted mostly of daily newspapers and state television channels. These were culturally policed in order to promote national identity and unity, and technically limited to the one-way, non-interactive, transmission of information. The combination of an ever-increasing number of cultural sources of identity with the interactive possibilities of hypermedia presents two challenges.

First, although the media provide some of the most significant components for building youth identity, the construction of Arab youth identity is complicated by the paucity of indigenous cultural production, including books, cinema and, to a lesser extent, television. While the hypermedia space involves numerous media and information technologies, television remains the dominant medium, and television, even when in the Arabic language, is permeated by Western ideas and values. In other words, sources from which young, especially middle-class, English-speaking, Arabs draw on when defining their identity tend to be influenced by Western, mostly US, popular culture and its focus on individual identity and consumerism (Khalil, 2005). This is a reflection of the crisis of Arab cultural production at large, detailed in the *Arab Human Development Report 2003*, which was written by Arab intellectuals and researchers under the aegis of the United Nations Development Programme and the Arab Fund for Economic and Social Development. Chapter 3, 'Knowledge production in arab countries', gives a view of the crisis: Arab countries, with 5% of the world's population, produce 1.1% of the world's books, a figure that falls below 1% if we only consider literary books. With a potential audience of 270 million Arab speakers in 22 countries, only 1000 to 3000 copies of a novel are usually published (UNDP, 2004: 77–78). Theatrical and cinematic production, in spite of the famed Egyptian cinema and the emergence of high-quality Syrian television drama, mirrors this situation. Battered by censorship, undermined by widespread illiteracy and hindered by the lack of funding, Arab literary and dramatic creative talent is unable to thrive.

Profiting from state-private cooperation, television drama has raised the profile and the income of writers in countries like Egypt and Syria and to a lesser extent Lebanon and the Gulf countries. But this trend has been thwarted, since television officials prefer the low-risk, high-yield strategy of format adaptation. Hence, the wave of reality television, game-shows, music videos and other formats imported from North America or Europe dominates Arab entertainment television, most starkly transnational satellite television. These shows present 'Western' formats that are adapted and reproduced in Arabic by Arab directors, actors and participants, and are often embedded in synergistic strategies including advertising or sponsorship deals, in addition to audio music and music video deals. As we explain later in this chapter, this mixing of worldviews has frequently triggered controversy for promoting commercialism and Western-style social relations between females and males, and for sapping putative Arab or Islamic identities.

Differential access to the new Arab hypermedia space is the second problem. The advent of a commercial media environment tends to exclude those Arabs who are not desirable targets of advertisers. It is well known that the focus of the overwhelming majority of Arab media products are the countries of the Gulf Cooperation Council, which includes Saudi Arabia, Oman, Qatar, Bahrain, the United Arab Emirates and Kuwait. Television programmers and other 'content providers' focus mostly on Saudi Arabia, by far the largest and wealthiest Arab market. Program previews and promotions on most satellite television channels, for example, give the time of a particular program in 'Saudi Arabia Time' in addition to GMT or the time of the location of the channel. With the growing financial importance of mobile phone toll calls or text messages in the context of voting in reality television programs, requesting music videos or sending love messages on music channels, the Arab media industry's focus on the oil-rich Gulf countries is increasing and reshaping production and programming decisions.

The rising importance of the markets of Saudi Arabia, Kuwait and the United Arab Emirates exacerbates the socio-economic gap between poor and rich Arab countries as the Arab public sphere becomes increasingly dominated by the desires, interests and voices of the wealthy. Poor young Arabs with bleak employment prospects and restricted social conditions are reduced to watching advertisers cater to a select golden Arab youth as they flaunt designer clothes, hip mobile phones and extravagant lifestyles. While this is to some extent true of commercial media worldwide, the large income differences and the speed with which the Arab media shifted from state-controlled monopolies to companies motivated by a mixture of commercial and political interests further complicate the situation. Highly popular reality television programs, which include participants from many Arab countries, mirror the inter-Arab cleavage with the Gulf countries on one side and everyone else on the other. Both alliances between contestants on these shows and audience voting patterns fall into this pattern in which differences in social class and sub-regional identities overlap.

The paucity of indigenous cultural production and differential access to the media, the two problems discussed above, indicate that the commercial media environment contributes significantly, both vertically and horizontally, to segregation of the Arab population. Vertically, it isolates young people from their parents. In addition to a communicative universe replete with logos, words, symbols and icons that are Western inspired and unpalatable to their parents, privileged young Arabs are increasingly spending leisure time surfing the internet, chatting on mobile phones, playing video games or watching youth-specific programs on television. These relatively solitary activities are transforming Arab social relations and older media consumption habits that had been based on communal listening or viewing followed by group or family conversations (this follows a similar trend towards individual usage in the West; for example, see Livingstone and Bovill (1999)). Horizontally, the new commercial media environment discriminates between young people on the basis of social economic status. The focus on the wealthy Gulf countries and the upper middle class in major cities like Cairo, Damascus or Beirut risks exacerbating class divisions both within and between Arab countries. The media's exclusion of large segments of the Arab population who are not relevant to advertisers raises a set of important questions about political participation in Arab societies, to be discussed later in this chapter.

ARAB YOUTH BETWEEN GLOBAL CULTURE AND LOCAL AUTHENTICITY

In the new communication environment that significantly overlaps with a global, media-driven youth culture, young Arabs have found a new space of socialization that is deeply permeated by 'foreign' cultural and social values, a process that started several centuries earlier with missionaries in the Levant but that is more recent in the Gulf region. The Arab world is similar in this respect to other parts of the world where youth media culture now competes with traditional family-based social structures in the socialization of children and young people. This process, which is embedded in a larger trend of 'detraditionalization' (Heelas *et al.*, 1996), is accelerating the creation of hybrid cultural forms and identities (for example in Lebanon; see Kraidy (1999)) in processes where youth cobble together social identities from a reservoir of resources in which youth media culture looms large. What makes the Arab countries distinct is that it is a region in which public discourse is consumed by concerns for identity and authenticity, within a field defined at one end by Islamic piety and religious identification (and that includes Christians such as Egyptian Copts and Lebanese Maronites) and at the other end by Arab nationalism and political identification. The current geo-political upheavals rocking the Arab region, such as the invasion of Iraq and the protracted conflict between Israelis and Palestinians, have intensified concerns about identity at a time when the USA has made it a policy to change the political, economic and culture structures of Arab countries. At the same time, the issue of political reform is a permanent fixture in Arab public discourse and is perhaps the only area where secular liberals agree with Islamist activists.

In this context, Arab media targeting young people play a balancing act, on the one hand respecting established traditions, but at the same time introducing new ideas both for commercial reasons and also as a social and political imperative. Commercially, Arab media entrepreneurs are cognizant that the consumerism and sexualized semiotics of global youth culture offer tremendous profit opportunities. They also know that young Arabs are alienated by the often poorly produced programs that state channels offer them, preferring an informal and interactive style, a situation in which they are similar to Western youth (e.g. Buckingham, 2000). Socially and politically, there is a general sense that the status quo is untenable, and some reform-minded media owners infuse the new communication environment with their ideas about reforming Arab societies. Nowhere is this search for a balanced recipe mixing tradition and modernity, entertainment with a social message, more visible than in the case of the Rotana media conglomerate.

The history of Rotana mirrors that of its owner, Saudi Prince Al Waleed Bin Talal, a 'forward-thinking' member of the Saudi royal family and a Lebanese citizen by virtue of his Lebanese mother. Bin Talal is a successful global investor whose media holdings have included the satellite channel of LBC and Murr Television, a now-defunct Lebanese station, in addition to Rupert Murdoch's News Corporation, CNBC and Star TV. In 1995, Bin Talal acquired 25% of Saudi-based Rotana Audio Visual Company, which specializes in the production and distribution of Arab music. Bin Talal's interest in music production increased over the years and so did his shares in Rotana, from 48% in 2002 to 100% in 2003.[5]

Bin Talal's plan to build a media empire that integrated music production and distribution led him in 2003 to acquire the music channel of the Arab Radio and Television (ART) bouquet. Rebranded Rotana, it expanded into a network of four music channels, one movie channel and a religious channel called al-Risala. Valued at over US$1 billion, Rotana has more than 2500 music videos and 5000 recorded live performances. Bin Talal is now capable of producing, distributing and marketing any singer in-house. While Kingdom Holding (Bin Talal's major company) and Rotana music are based in Saudi Arabia, Rotana television is based in Beirut. Rotana's four music channels do not follow MTV's tradition of using video jockeys (VJs) in the programs; instead the VJs are charged with tying different programs or sequences together. For instance, on the Rotana Khaleejiyyah, specializing in Arabian Gulf music, the VJs recite poetry as interludes between sets of music videos. Except for Rotana Clip, which caries audience requests, the three channels have regular programming that is primarily youth oriented. By 'translating' the MTV VJ tradition for an Arab audience and inserting poetry (a highly popular literary form in the Arab world) between songs, Rotana effectively localizes elements of the global youth culture.

Another localization strategy is visible in one show that addresses youth culture directly, *Rotana Café*. Following a wave of youth-oriented magazine shows that started in 2001, *Rotana Café* showcases the latest Rotana music videos and reviews international movies, gossip and fashion trends. Presented by Lebanese, Egyptian, Saudi and Kuwaiti teenagers, this daily one-hour show is set in a relatively large studio resembling a café. It is characterized by a relaxed attitude where presenters casually interact with a handheld camera while answering inquiries from callers about the most recent celebrity rumors. The framing of the program as a coffeehouse with free-wheeling and informal dialogue echoes the traditional role of the coffeehouse as a micro-public sphere in Arab and Ottoman culture.[6] However, unlike the male-only coffeehouses that still exist in Arab cities, the program features both genders as presenters and guests, illustrating a subtle process of localization, which entails grafting local themes and traditions onto the global music television genre, a process resulting in the partial transformation of these local themes and traditions.

Rotana's business strategy illustrates how Arab corporations profit from hypermedia space. Rotana's commercial viability rests to a large extent on what industry insiders call value-added services (VAS). These are available in the form of web downloads, short message services (SMS) displayed on a lower third ticker, multi-media services (MMS), ring tone and web downloads. In addition to being profitable, these services stimulate demand for programming and increase the prospects of synergy with other services. The Rotana Clip channel is a VAS flagship, since it features a number of interactive activities: chatting, MMS and SMS. Rotana Khaleejiyyah received as many as 50,000 SMS messages during its first 3 days on the air.[7] Through promotional clips, Rotana contributes to cultivating text messaging as a way of life for young Arabs who use Rotana's on-screen ticker to send messages to each other, including love messages or simply to inform friends that the sender will be late to an appointment.

Rotana's mantra of maintaining a conservative identity compatible with Saudi traditions but also introducing Bin Talal's relatively liberal views makes this channel a hybrid space in which traditions overlap with modern technologies. The choice of Lebanon, the Arab world's most culturally liberal country, as its major site of operation, reflects this policy. While Rotana's VAS indicate that the channel is cognizant of and cultivates hip trends among Arab youth, Rotana's commitment to Islamic religious practices is a clear indication of its commitment to tradition. During the holy month of Ramadan, presenters dress more conservatively and music videos are carefully selected. Throughout the year, programming is interrupted for prayer five times a day for 5 minutes as slick graphics overlaid with video footage of pilgrims praying in Mecca calls viewers to prayer. When the Saudi King Fahd died in 2005, Rotana paid tribute to its Saudi ownership by broadcasting mourning music for several days. At the same time, Rotana programs reflect relatively progressive views on women's rights, the Israeli–Palestinian conflict and terrorism.

Rotana reflects a wider trend across the industry, staying within the socio-political bounds of the Saudi mainstream while introducing new elements from both the global media industry and global youth culture to luring audiences. In the following section we analyze several youth media 'sites' to explain how commercial and socio-political concerns overlap and shape Arab youth media to various degrees. Located on a continuum of most to least commercialized, we analyze one Lebanese television program, *Mini Studio*, followed by a discussion of MBC 3 and Space Toons, a satellite channel dedicated to youth entertainment, and Al-Jazeera Children Channel, a recent venture launched under the mantra of 'edutainment'.

ARAB YOUTH BETWEEN CONSUMERISM AND EDUCATION

Arab media have become increasingly commercial in the past decade. Lebanese media were the early Arab pioneers in producing commercially viable television programs. The mushrooming of private television stations in the 1990s in the absence of an adequate regulatory framework revived Lebanon as the most dynamic Arab media market for some time, a role Lebanese television held in the 1970s when it exported drama series to the emerging Gulf government television channels.[8] It is in this context that *Mini Studio,* following a French tradition of children programs, was launched by Murr Television in 1992, first in Lebanon only, and later in the Arab world when MTV began satellite broadcasting in the late 1990s. The program moved to LBC in 2002. This daily half-hour show follows a magazine format featuring a regular group of performers and guest characters, with various parts, such as storytelling, songs, cartoons and games.

The show went through several stages. First, it focused on a simple magazine format with various segments, such as storytelling, gadgets and birthdays. It featured children as a studio audience. It emphasized a European 'feel', both in terms of the way the characters were dressed and the song lyrics in French and English. In the second stage, it maintained the previous elements with a focus on younger performers, as well as including children as actual talent. A main change was the inclusion of product placement as well as segment sponsors. The performers/hosts plug products either by using or distributing them to the studio audience. In addition, the show expanded into ancillary productions: plays, video cassettes and CD song compilations. As a result of this commercial success, the television and advertising industries dubbed the show as 'Mini Market'. After being launched on a pan-Arab scale first through MTV in 2000 and currently through LBC, *Mini Studio* adapted to this new demographic by including English as a second language for songs and dialogue. Producers of the show selected, supported and promoted an all-singing-and-dancing children band under the name Kids' Power.[9]

Mini Studio was a pioneering Arab television program for children. Culturally, it blurred the language barriers, as its performers crossed between Arabic, English and French, reflecting the Arabs' colonial past and the current multilingual landscape where English has become a global language, permeating youth media culture. Economically, this show revolutionized the ways the advertising industry targeted children; it introduced systematic product placement, with members of the audience shown on camera using products placed in the show and advertised during commercial breaks. This helped spread the notion that children's television in the Arab world can be a profitable business, a lesson that was not lost on the Middle East Broadcasting Center as it was expanding operations by essentially becoming a network. A key element in that expansion is MBC 3, a channel exclusively dedicated to children and young people.

Almost 15 years after its launch, the Middle East Broadcasting Center moved to create a multicasting platform for the Arab family. Moving from a traditional, one-channel, general audience approach, MBC now has two channels targeting young people: MBC 2 offers Western movies that attract both youth and their parents, and has been particularly successful in Saudi Arabia, where movie theaters are banned. MBC 3, launched from Dubai in 2005 to preempt the launch of the Al-Jazeera Children Channel, focuses exclusively on children and youth. During the afternoon, MBC 3 features young VJs who introduce the shows, comment on them and interact with the audience via telephone. Program offerings are primarily from the USA and the UK, broadcast in English, but also include Arabic-dubbed shows licensed from Space Toons, another Arab channel.

Taking advantage of the facilities provided by Dubai Media City, Space Toons was launched with a large library of children's programs in Arabic. Its Syrian owner, Fayez Sabbagh, has a long history of dubbing and distributing various Asian and European cartoons in Arabic. Space Toons broadcasts cartoons back to back in Arabic with commercial breaks in-between, eschewing program presenters common on Arab television. Space Toons soon grew into a media hub for children's programming. In addition to supplying MBC 3 with programs, Space Toons is carried by the Orbit pay-television 'bouquet', which brings in additional income as well as access to pay-for-television audiences. It also branched into Space Toons English, broadcasting original versions of its dubbed Arabic programs. Finally, and most interestingly, Space Toons ventured into producing its own Arabic cartoons in the forms of vignettes dealing with religious themes, such as 'Rihlat El Hajj', about the Muslim pilgrimage, and Ramadan issues. This is another example of 'localization', where local themes are grafted onto global formats to create culturally hybrid programs.

A venture of this scope is viable because it is integrated in a media conglomerate with three types of ancillary business: a magazine targeting parents and children, commercial representation and advertising of toys, and a website which ties in all these activities by offering online games and downloads. Following the logic of integration, the magazine carries television program schedules, the toys are featured in the programs, and the website functions as a gateway to the Space Toons brand. While this company is a case study of the commercialization of children and youth media culture in the Arab world, some of its rivals propound a radically different vision of the role of the media in the socialization of children and young people.

Reflecting a long-term media rivalry between Saudi Arabia and Qatar, the Saudi-owned MBC 3 was rushed into being to 'scoop' the imminent launch of the Qatari-owned Al-Jazeera Children Channel. While the two channels compete primarily for the Gulf Cooperation Council countries' audience, they reflect two different philosophies of youth media, with the former being a commercial station and the latter proclaiming a public service mission. For that reason, the Al-Jazeera Children Channel, launched on September 9, 2005, jointly by Al-Jazeera and the Qatar Foundation for Education, Science and Community Development, is worthy of a detailed examination. The Qatar Foundation, publicly financed by the Qatari state and headed by Sheikha Moza Bint Nasser Al-Missned, wife of Qatar's ruler, owns 90% of the venture, which broadcasts from Education City in Qatar.[10] The channel came on the heels of the flagship Al-Jazeera, Al-Jazeera Sports, Al-Jazeera live (public affairs) and the impending launch of the English-language Al-Jazeera English.[11]

Most distinctive about the new channel is the fact that it is 'a private company but with a public service mission and is publicly funded', in the words of Jean Rouilly, CEO of

Lagardere International Images, a subdivision of the French conglomerate Lagardere, which was instrumental in setting up the channel technically.[10] Thus, Al-Jazeera Children Channel is not a commercial channel, but, as Sheikh Hamad bin Thamer al-Thani, chair of the board of Al-Jazeera, explains, a 'bright alternative to the current trends in television broadcasting where children are exposed to violent and inappropriate material on a daily basis' (Ohrstrom, 2005). However, the new channel eschewed the didactic style of Arab educational or development television programs, aiming to provide what executives called 'educational fun'[10] while inculcating values such as tolerance, open-mindedness and freedom of expression. In press statements, the new channel espouses the concept of 'edutainment', through which it 'opens up avenues for the Arab children to … learn about different … cultures … [and] help them develop positive self-esteem, respect their traditions and values, and appreciate people around them and develop a passion for learning'.[12]

The declared commitment to local production expressed in statements by Al-Jazeera Children Channel executives makes the channel distinctive, at least until actual programming grids prove otherwise. The channel's programming grid comprises around 40% of original programming, amounting to 6 or 7 hours a day out of the 18 to 19 hours of transmission (Ohrstrom, 2005). According to channel director Mahnoud Bouneb, the channel will broadcast 18 hours per day, out of which 6 hours are live, 3 hours are commissioned abroad and 4 hours are produced in the channel's studios.[13] The locally made programs did not shy away from controversy. Within 1 month after launch, *Sehha wa Salama* (*Health and Safety*) broached the issue of female genital circumcision, and other programs featured children opining on relatively sensitive social and political issues (Ohrstrom, 2005). This is within Al-Jazeera's overall spirit to broach taboo issues.

An article published on the Aljazeera.net website provides a rationale for the channel. Titled 'Al-Jazeera Children Channel … A reading of the notion and a critique of the vision', the article argues that the new channel fills an important gap in Arab media because 'there were ambitious projects aiming to care for children, but they did not show children a real interest and dedicated themselves to talking about hobbies and movies …' and carries a stinging indictment of Arab media as 'media that jump at the peels in the absence of an essence … are … in all their forms sterile' (Bouqanoun, 2005). In contrast, Al-Jazeera Children Channel would advocate that Arab children should have a voice and be productive members of their societies: 'We must address Arab children in an interactive manner', the writer says, 'so as to transform them into instruments of knowledge and give them a productive capacity so that they express their opinions on issues that interest them and contribute to the foundation of a better future' (Bouqanoun, 2005). The new channel would thus contribute to educational reform throughout the Arab world by empowering children and young people and focusing on self-criticism and engagement in intercultural dialogues. The author also underlines the fact that the channel was created out of 'a strong political will', widely assumed to be that of Qatar's influential first lady, and that because of this support it was going to be viable.

For all these promises, the Al-Jazeera Children Channel still faced numerous problems. First, setting it up was a long affair that exceeded its budget. Plans called for a fully digitized, completely 'tape-less' operation from production to transmission. However, software and budgeting problems, along with varying visions of several key actors, undermined this aim.[14] Second, from the very first days of broadcasting, the new channel attracted criticism for delivering less than what its launchers promised. Because of the Al-Jazeera legacy, the channel faced skepticism even before its launch. In a column titled 'The children of Al-Jazeera', Ibrahim al-Ariss (2005), editor for television and cinema at the pan-Arab daily *Al-Hayat*, hoped that the channel will not promote extremism, and that 'language lessons not be to learn how to write *takfiri* statements ... and that program guests not be from outside of the era'.[15] Six weeks later, a columnist in the same newspaper poignantly criticized the station for 'putting amateurs in charge' and for having young adult talk-show hosts who knew less than their children guests about the topics under discussion (Amin, 2005). While these critiques are at least partially valid, more time is needed before a systematic appraisal of the channel's performance can be conducted. It is also important to note that the channel's avowed public service mission makes it a unique children-oriented media institution in the Arab world.[16]

The sudden interest of leading transnational Arab broadcasters to youth channels needs careful assessment. Arguably, the need for specific demographics to attract advertisers is important, but it cannot solely explain the surge of interest. MBC 3 can be understood as an attempt to prepare loyal adult audiences for its flagship channel as the MBC network reinvents itself as the one-stop channel for the Arab family. In addition, MBC 3 is free to air, with no costs incurred by the viewers. Furthermore, MBC 3 has been seriously attempting to present itself as a Gulf-based channel. Unlike Al-Jazeera Children Channel, its road shows have focused on the Arabian Gulf. While the use of English programs is attributed to a scarcity of Arab children's productions, it also reflects a multilingual audience. The choice of 'Space Toons' as a name for another children's channel reflects the growing pervasiveness and acceptance of English by Arab audiences, itself a symptom of media globalization. But if these channels' programs are revealing about the social and commercial dimensions of Arab youth, other media take on a more political dimension, whether directly as in the case of the US-funded 'public diplomacy' stations Radio Sawa and Al-Hurra television, or in the case of reality television shows that were politicized by viewers and appropriated in street demonstrations, most notably in Beirut. The following section of this chapter examines how Arab youth popular culture intersects with Arab political life.

POLITICS, YOUNG PEOPLE AND THE MEDIA IN THE ARAB WORLD

Because of the current geo-political juncture, myriad issues related to Arab mass media have been politicized between the Arab world and the West, especially the USA, but even more significantly, within the Arab world itself. Since the invasions of Afghanistan and Iraq by the USA and some allied forces, the Arab satellite news channels have been the sources of anxiety among Western, mainly American, politicians and military leaders. Most of this anxiety and anger have focused on Al-Jazeera, with some accusing the channel of cooperating with Al-Qaeda and the Iraqi insurgency. While a detailed discussion of these important issues falls beyond the scope of this chapter, American perceptions that Arab media are hostile to the USA has triggered major initiatives under the public diplomacy umbrella, including Al-Hurra television, Radio Sawa, and *Hi Magazine*. Unlike Al-Hurra, a news and public affairs television channel for Arabs of all ages, Radio Sawa was consciously conceived as a blend of news and entertainment targeted at Arab youth, hence its relevance to this chapter.

Radio Sawa is the brainchild of the Broadcasting Board of Governors, the body responsible for American international broadcasts referred to as 'public diplomacy' by their proponents and 'propaganda' by critics. This station offers a format that appeals to youth by focusing mostly on music, a sharp departure from Voice of America's Arabic service's blend of news, current affairs, documentaries and music. The station was officially launched in March 2002, and by late summer 2002 it was reaching more Arab listeners than had the Voice of America (Boyd, 2002). Indeed, Sawa is the only (relative) success story in the US public diplomacy initiative towards the Arab world, considering that *Hi Magazine* was shutdown in December 2005 and the status of Al-Hurra television is in question as of this writing, with the channel facing high-level staff departures in the wake of several surveys showing it with less than 1% of the Arab television news audience. Radio Sawa's success is partly due to the recognition by its overseers of the power of popular culture to reach young Arabs.

Sawa's great innovation was a station format that mixed Arabic and English-language pop music with short newscasts every hour. How this radio station was received is perhaps best described in the numerous stories of taxi drivers in Arab capitals listening to Sawa music and switching to another channel when the newscast began only to move the dial back when the new hour of music came in. Arabs liked the music and listened to it, but the newscasts were not credible because listeners knew it was a US government service. However, the innovative format was soon emulated by other stations, including Marina FM in Kuwait, the first private FM station in that country and one that is rapidly gaining listeners. Although innovative, this format is not unprecedented in the region, as some of the music video satellite television channels mixed Arabic and Western pop several years before the advent of Radio Sawa.

If Radio Sawa showed Washington policymakers that young Arabs can be reached by mixing politics with popular culture, the emerging hypermedia space gave young Arabs new opportunities for self-expression and participation in public life. The wave of reality television and music video programs and channels is evidence of the rampant commercialization of Arab hypermedia space. But these programs also provide Arab youth with the tools to participate in public debates. Nowhere is this more evident than in the way the rituals of reality television were 'recruited' in what Western observers called the 'Cedar Revolution' in Lebanon.[17]

The series of street demonstrations that occurred in Beirut in the wake of the assassination of Lebanon's previous Prime Minister Rafiq al-Hariri were perhaps the first major Arab political event in which the emerging hypermedia space played a visible role. Demonstrators used mobile phones and text-messaging to mobilize and organize supporters, exchange crucial tactical information, and take pictures that could be easily transmitted out of the area of the demonstrations. Young people played a pivotal part in the demonstrations, with university student organizations as the leading organizational force. There was clear media savvy among the young demonstrators, who used color-coordinated clothing and painted Lebanese flags on their faces like football fans worldwide. More importantly, several media friendly 'spectacles' were organized, including a gigantic human Lebanese flag made by 10,000 people holding green, red and white cardboard squares, the Lebanese colors. Most interesting were the signs that demonstrators carried, which included words, phrases and slogans from reality television, such as 'Addoum, Nominee', which called for the sacking of Lebanon's pro-Syrian prosecutor general.

On March 14, 2005, when approximately 1 million demonstrators filled Beirut's central Martyrs Square to protest at Hariri's assassination and to demand the withdrawal of Syrian troops from Lebanon, many signs featured pictures of despised politicians and security officers with 'nominations' to be voted out of the 'show', a clear appropriation of reality television for political activism. One sign in particular illustrated this appropriation. It featured a photograph of Lebanese president Emile Lahoud, a major ally of Syria whose mandate was unconstitutionally extended by Syrian fiat, with the word 'nominee' above the picture and the words 'Vote 1559' underneath it. *Star Academy*, the Arabic-language adaptation of a format owned by the Dutch format house Endemol and known in the UK as *Fame Academy*, has been the Arab world's most popular and controversial reality television show. Every week, audience members call dedicated four-digit mobile phone numbers to vote for one of two nominees they wish to save from expulsion from the show. In the demonstrator's sign, '1559' is an ironic appropriation in that it refers to United Nations Security Council Resolution 1559, which called among other things for the withdrawal of Syrian troops from Lebanon.

This overlap of politics and popular culture is indicative of a larger trend in the Arab world where political activists increasingly appropriate elements of youth media culture. This can be seen on several levels. First of all, the use of mobile phones and text-messaging to mobilize support for a reality television contestant and to forge alliances with like-minded viewers has been transferred to the organization of political demonstrations. Second, the hip sartorial style of reality television and music videos is employed by demonstrators to attract the attention of television cameras, something that young Lebanese excelled at in the Beirut demonstrations. Third, as the sign we analyzed indicates, the vocabulary of reality television is widely understood in the Arab world, and is thus an effective tool to express a political agenda. Finally, activists who protested against the authoritarianism of the Mubarak regime in Egypt, against Syrian control of Lebanon, or supported women's political rights in Kuwait have become adept at adopting short, memorable and media-friendly slogans like the ones that permeate youth popular culture.

CONCLUSION

The relationship that Arab youth have with media and information technologies is highly complex. In addition to the economic, social and cultural challenges faced by youth in developing countries, Arab youth and children have to contend with the radical politicization of their relationship with media and culture. Whereas children and youth worldwide are at the center of debates about education, consumerism and socialization, in the Arab world the youth and childhood are also a political site of struggle where hot-button issues such as terrorism, Arab–Western relations, and Arab governance play out. The corporations and governments that compete to win over this demographic are not only Arab, but include transnational corporations and the American government.

This media environment (what we referred to as hypermedia space) provided this chapter with several revealing case studies. First, the Al-Jazeera Children Channel is a promising venture because it has a self-declared public service mission and at the same time it enjoys a secure financial basis. As an initiative of Qatar's Sheikha Moza, probably the Arab world's most powerful and influential first lady, and ample funds from Qatar's vast natural gas reserves at a time when gas is at a record high price, the Al-Jazeera Children Channel transcends two difficulties that have often preempted successful children's programs in the Arab world and elsewhere: political backing and financial resources. These two issues are most important because they determine how much support goes to local production. Also, final judgment will have to await the channel's actual performance and the degree to which it fulfills plans that for the most part are still on paper. There are two other challenges that the channel will have to overcome: attracting an audience and having competent management. Success in those areas may stimulate competitors and increase the quality and quantity of children programming.

Second, it is clear that, in spite of the commercialization of social life, the new Arab commercial media environment enhances young people's ability for self-expression and participation in public life. The appropriation of reality television rituals and vocabulary during the 2005 Beirut demonstrations is perhaps the most notable example of how youth media culture contributes to social and political empowerment, but examples elsewhere (Egypt and Kuwait) suggest that this trend can be found throughout the Arab world. The ultimate challenge for Arab youth is translating the pluralism of public life into inclusive governance, taking into account the needs of children and young people in policy formulation and implementation.

Third, religion is important in the study of Arab youth and media as, on the one hand a social, cultural and political force, and, on the other hand, as a field of analysis. Having said this, we should eschew making Islam an independent variable sitting at the center of political, socio-cultural and communication processes in the Arab world. Rather, as the development of Islamic media and Islamic popular culture indicate, Islam is a differentiated, complex, and unstable category. Increasingly, the Arab media are becoming an arena of competition between various forms of Islam, as in the example mentioned before of Khaled challenging al-Qaradawi's interpretations, or of the variations that are set to emerge between relatively traditionalist Islamic channel, such as al-Majd and Iqraa on the one hand, and, on the other hand, those explicitly 'modernizing' Islamic channels, such as al-Risala. Many analysts of Arab societies, us included, believe that mainstream Islamic media provide an important space for the emergence of modern, i.e. self-reflexive, adaptive, and forward-thinking Islamic values and identities.

In this chapter we have attempted to provide a broad survey of the complex relationship between young people and the media in the Arab world. Socio-economic class, geographical location, religion and linguistic ability are some of the most important differences that shape how young Arabs relate to the media. We adopted a top-down, deductive and mostly theoretical approach in order to accommodate the large variety of issues to be discussed in order to understand Arab youth and media issues. This was partly due to the paucity of actual audience studies in the Arab world, hindered by a variety of factors, including the lack of systematic indigenous research activity and social and religious restrictions on field research. While the advantage of this approach is to account for the breadth of the topic, we point the readers to a variety of readings on Arab media that provide more location- and culture-specific sources.[18]

NOTES

1 We use 'Arab youth' broadly to include children. We use 'children' only when there are issues where children, and not older young people, are the explicit focus of discussion, such as our discussion of Al-Jazeera Children Channel.

2 The United Nations Population Fund. *Overview: The Arab States*. http://www.unfpa.org/profile/arab_overview.htm [August 2007].

3 For a detailed analysis and critique of this phenomenon, see Kraidy (2005).

4 Here we are using Mead's typology of postfigurative, cofigurative, and prefigurative cultures, which in descending order give more importance to hierarchy and vertical learning. See Mead (1970).

5 See Richard Agnew (2005) and Riz Khan (2005).

6 For a history of some urban coffeehouses in the Middle East, see Kirli (2004).

7 Second author interview with Fouad Tarabay, founding Managing Director of Rotana Khaleejiah, August 2005.

8 For a discussion of a crucial period in the development of Lebanon's television market, see Kraidy (1998).

9 The second author of this chapter was an MTV executive at the time. The show was renamed 'The Kids Power Show' for intellectual property purposes.

10 Al-Jazeera launches children's channel to teach tolerance (2005, September 10). *Daily Star* [Agence France Presse].

11 In fact, Al-Jazeera officially declared itself a 'network', as opposed to a 'channel', in early September 2005. See 'Before launching its children's channel next Friday: Al-Jazeera becomes a network … for privatization?' (2005, September 6). *Assafir*.

12 Al Jazeera launches kids channel (2005, September 11). Company Press Release.

13 'Before launching its children's channel next Friday: Al-Jazeera becomes a network … for privatization?' (2005, September 6). *Assafir*.

14 Personal interviews conducted by first author with members of the launching team, November 2005, Paris, France.

15 The word *takfiri* refers to the practice by some radical Islamists to declare Muslims who do not agree with their views non-Muslims, and thus indirectly promote violence against these 'fake' Muslims.

16 There could be an 'edutainment' trend developing in youth media, with Yemen recently announcing a new television service for young people in association with the national university there.

17 See Kraidy (2006b); for a discussion of how reality television entered the fray of politics in Kuwait and Lebanon, see Kraidy (2007).

18 For general references on Arab media, see Boyd (1999) and Sakr (2001). The volume by Eickelman and Anderson (1999) has a broader, Muslim world scope. For analysis of the Arab internet, see Gonzalez-Quijano (2003/2004). For Al-Jazeera, see El-Nawawy and Iskandar (2002) Lamloum (2004). For television and national identity in Egypt, see Abu-Lughod (2005) and Armbrust (1996). For a feminist, Islam-focused analysis, see Mernissi (1992).

REFERENCES

Abu-Lughod, L. 2005. *Dramas of Nationhood*. University of Chicago Press.

Agnew, R. (2005) 'The Arabian kings of cash'. *Arabian Business*, 21 August.

Al-Ariss, I. (2005) 'The children of Al-Jazeera'. *Al-Hayat*, 31 August.

Amin, A. (2005) 'Al-Jazeera kids: when we put amateurs in charge and we address the child "below his level"'. *Al-Hayat*, 10 October.

Armbrust, W. 1996. *Mass Culture and Modernism in Egypt*. Cambridge University Press.

Bouqanoun, I. (2005) 'Al-Jazeera Kids … A reading of the notion and a critique of the vision'. *Aljazeera.net*, 20 October.

Boyd, D. (1999) *Broadcasting In the Arab World*. Iowa State University Press.

Boyd, D. (2002) 'Radio Sawa: the creation of a new U.S. government Arabic service'. In *Annual Meeting of the Arab–US Association for Communication Educators*, Beirut, Lebanon, November.

Buckingham, D. (2000) *The Making of Citizens: Young People, News and Politics*. London: University College London Press.

Department of Economic and Social Affairs (2005) *World Youth Report 2005: Young People Today, and in 2015*. New York: United Nations.

Eickelman, D. (1998) 'Inside the Islamic reformation'. *The Wilson Quarterly*, 22(1): 80–89.

Eickelman, D. and Anderson, J. (eds) (1999) *New Media In The Muslim World: The Emerging Public Sphere*. Indiana University Press.

El-Nawawy, M. and Iskandar, A. (2002) *Al-Jazeera*. Westview.

Gonzalez-Quijano, Y. (ed.) (2003–2004) L'internet arabe. *Maghreb Machrek*, 178.

Havens, T. (2001) Subtitling rap: appropriating The Fresh Prince of Bel-Air for youthful identity formation in Kuwait. *Gazette*, 63(1): 57–72.

Heelas, P. Lash, S. and Morris, P. (eds) (1996) *Detraditionalization*. London: Blackwell.

Khalil, J.F. (2005) 'Blending in: Arab television and the search for programming ideas'. *Transnational Broadcasting Journal*, 13. www.tbsjournal.com/archives/Winter2004.htm.

Khan, R. (2005) *AlWaleed: Businessman, Billionaire, Prince*. London: Harper Collins.

Khouri, RG. (2005) 'Beyond sports and scouting: Arab youth imperatives'. *Daily Star*, 1 June.

Kirli, C. (2004) 'Coffeehouses: public opinion in the nineteenth-century Ottoman Empire'. In A. Salavatore and D. Eickelman (eds) *Public Islam and the Common Good*. Leiden: Brill; 75–97.

Kraidy, M.M. (1998) 'Broadcasting regulation and civil society in postwar Lebanon'. *Journal of Broadcasting and Electronic Media*, 42(3): 387–400.

Kraidy, M.M. (1999) 'The global, the local, and the hybrid: a native ethnography of glocalization'. *Critical Studies in Mass Communication*, 16(4): 458–478.

Kraidy, M.M. (2005) *Hybridity, or the Cultural Logic of Globalization*. Philadelphia: Temple University Press.

Kraidy, M.M. (2006a) 'Governance and hypermedia in Saudi Arabia'. *First Monday*, 11(9). http://firstmonday.org/issues/special11_9/kraidy/index.html.

Kraidy, M.M. (2006b) 'Reality television and politics in the Arab world (preliminary observations)'. *Transnational Broadcasting Studies*, 2: 7–28.

Kraidy, M.M. (2007) 'Idioms of contention: Star Academy in Lebanon and Kuwait'. In N. Sakr (ed.) *Arab Media and Political Renewal: Community, Legitimacy and Public Life*. London, UK: I.B. Tauris; 44–55.

Lamloum, O. (2004) *Al-Jazira: Miroir Rebelle et Ambigu du Monde Arabe*. La Découverte.

Livingstone, S. and M. Bovill (1999) 'Young people, new media'. Report of the research project Canadian Young People and the Changing Media Environment. London: London School of Economics and Political Science.

Mead, M. (1970) *Culture and Commitment: A Study of the Generation Gap*. New York: Doubleday.

Mernissi, F. (1992) *Islam and Democracy*. Addison-Wesley.

Ohrstrom, L. (2005) 'New kids' channel navigates "edutainment"'. *The Daily Star*, 7 December.

Sakr, N. (2001) *Satellite Realms: Transnational Television, Globalization and the Middle East*. I.B. Tauris.

UNDP (2004) *Arab Human Development Report 2003: Building a Knowledge Society*. New York: United Nations Development Program.

Ziehe, T. (1992) 'Cultural modernity and individualization'. In J. Fornas and G. Bollin (eds) *Moves in Modernity*. Stockholm: Almqvist and Wiksell International.

FURTHER READING

Kraidy, M.M. and Khalil, J.F. (2007) 'The Middle East: transnational Arab television'. In L. Artz and Y. Kamalipour (eds) *The Media Globe: Trends in International Mass Media*. Lanham, MD: Rowman and Littlefield; 79–98.

21

Constrained Appropriations: Practices of Media Consumption and Imagination amongst Brazilian Teens

Norbert Wildermuth

INTRODUCTION

This chapter develops a conceptually based analysis of the transformations in young people's media culture in Brazil. Recognizing the profound rootedness of media consumption and reception in everyday life, the chapter examines ways in which the media operate in young people's identity constructions in a rapidly changing society where adult norms and life trajectories lose legitimacy for the young. The aim of this chapter is to contribute to a contextualized understanding of the relationship between media texts and young people, as exemplified by a few individuals situated within the context of their urban lower-class life worlds, as active but also constrained media users. Thus, instead of attempting to provide the reader with as broad an overview as possible over the media practices of all kinds of young Brazilians, in all parts of the country, I will develop a conceptually based, detailed analysis of a few individual cases and discuss in conclusion the question of how and to what extent the interpretative results can be generalized. Moreover, I will seek to spell out some of the key methodological constraints and possibilities when studying media globalization across national boundaries.

MEDIA, LIFESTYLE AND CONSUMER CULTURE

In its totality the dynamic relationship between young people and media is a space of interaction too broad and multifaceted to be explored in a single study and presented in a single chapter. In the following, therefore,

I will focus on what I consider as a central, though far from exhaustive, dimension of young people's interpretative and consumptive activities associated with the 'mutually defining' (Livingstone, 2005: 346) symbolic and material uses of media as texts and objects.

Specifically, I will explore the modes of connection, relationship and communication which are enabled by young people's appropriation and 'working through' of the glocalized cultural imaginaries of lifestyle-centred youth cultures and consumption-based identity projects. With Drotner I perceive the media as enabling resources for experience-based forms of knowledge, which allow young people to explore the identity drafts and projects in which they are engaged (Drotner and Sørensen, 1996: 20). That is, the practices of media consumption and reception by which young people engage the media are understood as a form of cultural and aesthetic practice through which they seek to comprehend, define and create themselves. In the words of Steven Miles: using global and local media as part of their ongoing attempts to make sense of their lives, young people, in Brazil as elsewhere, use media to work through and 'construct opinions about what lifestyles might be *deemed* to be appropriate' (Miles, 2000: 69).

While the active production and attribution of meaning is a fundamental and unquestionable quality of young people's media appropriation, the textual and social determinations of media use, structuring the conditions under which this interpretative agency has to be realized, deserve equal attention. Thus, the relationship between young people and media cultures, which increasingly pervade (and are invited into) their everyday lives, is understood as a mutual exploitative one. Young people appropriate, transform and recontextualize the meanings of media texts, though always within the boundaries set by other people's interests; that is, by society at large. Hence, a holistic understanding of the communicative relations created by the dialectic processes of media production and reception demands a conceptualization in terms of both their agentic and structural dimensions (Holland *et al*., 1998: 5; Livingstone, 1998: 248).

A study of the mediated imaginaries of consumer-based lifestyles and youth cultures, their consumption, interpretation and appropriation provides us with an opportunity to explore the permeative processes of 'structuration' involved in the interaction between viewer and text. As I will argue, on the basis of my empirical findings, the particular imaginaries that are realized within this communicative space give rise to contrary forces of 'determination' and 'empowerment'. In fact, for the most part, the practices of media engagement[1] involved constitute spaces of communicative relation which occupy the textual–contextual spectrum in between. To conceptualize this pragmatic space of communicative practices 'located' in the space between hegemonic subordination and symbolic resistance I have adapted Appadurai's concept of the social imagination (though with modifications regarding Appadurai's individual/collective distinction[2]). Through this I will seek to live up to Livingstone's call for a broader framework for audience research, extending 'beyond the issue of the politics of representation, of making visible and validating marginalized and resistant voices' (Livingstone, 1998: 250).

The theory of media-enabled social imagination pays attention to the non-spectacular, everyday practices of media appropriation of ordinary (young) people. Conceptually, it expands the 'problematic practice' of active meaning production, which Cultural Studies have focused upon. Avoiding a narrow conceptualization of young people's interpretative agency as either subordination or resistance, it is sensitive to those forms of active viewing and consumption which are located in between. It allows us to understand and explore the textual and (psycho)social facets of the media–audience relationship as the outcome of both determinations *and* spaces for openness on a textual and social level.[3]

Understood as an interpretative practice which is directed towards the realization of increasingly diversified and individualized identity constructions, the media-enabled practices of imagination constitute more or less individualized lifestyles and identity drafts through cultural expression and consumption. At the same time, constrained by the de facto situated character of young people's agency as realized in their everyday lives, the media-enabled practices of imagination re-inscribe the collective in lifestyles and identity constructions, thus constituting a ground for collective social action and submission. In Appadurai's phrasing:

> ... the idea of fantasy carries with it the inescapable connotation of thought divorced from projects and actions, and it also has a private, even individualistic sound about it. The imagination on the other hand, has a projective sense about it, the sense of being a prelude to some sort of expression, whether aesthetic or otherwise. Fantasy can dissipate ... but the imagination, especially when collective, can become the fuel for action. It is the imagination, in its collective forms, that creates ideas of neighbourhood and nationhood, of moral economies and unjust rule, of higher wages and foreign labour prospects. The imagination today is a staging ground for action, not only for escape (Appadurai, 1996: 7).

The concept of mediated imagination, as I will use it, seeks to be attentive to both dimensions, that is, to the work of imagination as a collective and individual agency. Thereby, the duality of mediated imagination as individual escape (prone to ideological subordination) and collective empowerment (signifying symbolic resistance), which is questioned but not fully discarded within Appadurai's conceptualization, is challenged. Empowerment can be realized as an individual, introspective 'effect' of media engagement, while escape can be the outcome of collective acts of interpretation.

Finally, mine is an attempt to develop a perspective that seeks to compare the practices of media engagement of specific groups of young people, based on recognition of the fluidity and open-ended character of individual, culturally expressed identities in present-day society. However, I will do so without overstating their decentred and fragmented nature and without losing sight of their continued structuration along national, ethnic, gendered, class-based, etc. lines. In short, I put forward a perspective which acknowledges that the forming and reforming of identities in a 'process of continuous self-fashioning' (Holland *et al.*, 1998: 4) goes hand in hand with young people's effort to achieve stabilized identities and conceptions of self, based on their immediate experiences of life.

While the shifting interpretation and reinterpretation of primary and secondary experiences, articulated through practices of mediated imagination, indicates the dis-embedding and dislocating forces of late modernity (Hall, 1987, cited in Osgerby, 2004: 181), a desire for re-embedding and collective association continues to infuse young people's processes of identification. Under the conditions of consumer culture, their longing for belonging is increasingly sought to be satisfied through individualized, but comparable, practices of consumption.[4] However, young people's 'experimentation' with fluid and constantly reimagined identity drafts is severely constrained by the structural circumstances of life that underprivileged young people around the world face. Brazil is a dramatic example for such an unequal opportunity structure, as I will show.

BRAZILIAN 'LATE' MODERNITY AND THE PREDICAMENTS OF BEING YOUNG AND POOR

Present-day Brazil is a rapidly changing society in which the legitimacy of adult norms and life trajectories for the young has come under increasing pressure, due to the structural consequences of Brazil's uneven, globalized 'development'. As de Castro (2006: 180f) has it, in her lucid study on present identity constructions among poor Brazilian youth:

> ... 'periphery countries', Latin American and, especially, Brazil, ... are caught in contradictory demands that, on the one hand, push the country's investments towards ever more sophisticated development ..., whereas, on the other hand, very basic needs of the majority of the population such as housing, health and education remain

> unattended and are not prioritized. These contradictions produce and reproduce long established social inequalities, radicalized in the context of overall transformations accelerated by globalization processes. Brazil, at present, is a 'modern' country in its own sense. It is a de-traditionalized society where old values related to an agriculturally-based rural society were replaced by values of a post-modern world, a liberal free-market economy, though only partially modernized with respect to other values of the Enlightenment rationality: universal rights, individual freedom and equality ... In this sense, Brazilian culture lags behind modernization in the cultural and normative sense.

In a most appropriate expression coined by Oliveira (1984), urban Brazil is the space of 'unfinished social classes'. Urbanization in Brazil has not produced the expected swelling of the lower classes positioned in the industrial sector, but, rather, a bulging contingent of unemployed and sub-employed people who have migrated from rural areas to live in the periphery of the big cities. Especially in the urban areas, differences concerning access to material and symbolic goods between lower and upper classes are most visible and disparate.

Recife, the capital of the state of Pernambuco in Brazil's 'impoverished' north-east, though the site of a less spectacular display of wealth and though 'provincial' in comparison with the urban centres of Brazil's south, is no exception. Economic and social disparities have produced a scenario of glaring contradictions: post-modern skyscrapers are surrounded by shacks where thousands live without running water or drainage facilities.[5] From the point of view of educational and cultural rights, the situation is no better. 'Persistent educational inequalities prevail ... severely limiting the possibilities for the majority of young people to expand their self-construction projects through education' (de Castro, 2006: 181). Cultural inequalities, as observable and articulated, for instance, around the practices of mediated cultural consumption, signify some of the dramatic ramifications of this thoroughly stratified situation in that they constrain young, poor Brazilian's identity work. Thus, the examination of young people's media cultures, if contextualized within this scenario of gross social inequalities, introduces particular issues regarding how youth of different socio-economic backgrounds engage the media as part of their intentional and self-reflective practices of identification.

According to de Castro's rather bleak vision of the consequences of consumer culture, as realized in Brazil, the identity construction of poor young people is 'constrained by the demands of a post-modern consumer culture that is not ... modernized in relation to equality of opportunities, universal education and rights' (de Castro, 2006: 182). While global demands of 'inclusion' in the culture of commodities and enjoyment have become an overall determinant of youth identities, 'a differential impact on Brazilian youth can be noted, considering the large number who are debarred from commonplace consumption practices, such as going to the cinema, having digital and computer experience, or, simply, riding a car. As consumption and its external indicators become landmarks of "inclusion" and citizenship (Canclini, 2001), for poor Brazilian youth the construction of the "inclusive self" (Falk, 1994) becomes problematic' (de Castro, 2006: 183). For this reason, to direct attention towards young Brazilians' constrained engagement of the media-as-objects and the media-as-texts implies recognizing the contradictory socio-psychological forces at work in their ubiquitous everyday efforts to explore and render meaningful the mediated representations of consumption-based lifestyles.

In my media reception and consumption study of youth in Recife, I have approached the processes of circulation, appropriation and reiteration of meaning taking place between media texts and young people as basically characterized by a corresponding ambivalence of reading and viewing positions. That is, I have sought to keep in mind some of the outlined tensions and contradictions that exist within contemporary Brazil when exploring my informants' receptive experiences 'as part of their everyday practices that, together with a range of other activities, come to shape and constitute their positions as subjects within

Brazilian society' (Machado-Borges 2006: 4). In theoretical terms, paying attention to the situated, often contradictory, interpretative acts of media engagement observable and articulated by Recife youth acknowledges the fact that they cannot easily be characterized as either resistant or uncritical and duped. Basically, my conceptual understanding thus correlates with a position as outlined by a majority of media-ethnographic and (British) Cultural Studies-inspired, qualitative reception studies.[6]

Before I proceed to present and discuss some of the empirical and analytical results of my study let me, first, expand my contextual understanding of the structural conditions under which disadvantaged young people in Brazil engage with the media and, second, outline the methodological challenges of my approach.

Stressing the global transformations and the particularities of contemporary Brazilian society de Castro (2006: 182) argues, and it is difficult to disagree:

> ... that, for many poor urban Brazilian youngsters, demands to consume, and thereby to become part of society through the adequate markers of distinction, embed identity in a process of 'psychological survival'. This means that, as consumption establishes 'modes of inclusion' in present capitalist societies, urban poor youngsters are positioned in a liminal location subjectively experienced as not being able to come up to society's demands.

The resulting 'logic of survival' (in the midst of adverse material and existential conditions) encourages short-sighted evaluations of oneself and of one's life-chances, embracing what appears to be most advantageous in the short term and relinquishing prospective visions of the self. What is more, a systematic erosion of work values seems to take place under the impact of consumerism, radically changing the nature of the relationship between poor urban youth and work. In consequence, identification strategies tend to be established around rigid and 'encapsulated identities', de Castro concludes, before she moves on to describe, in detail, some of the potential 'responses' of young, disadvantaged Brazilians to their impoverished living conditions.

These are, on the one hand, short (and illusory) circuits 'to be included', exemplified by the drug dealer. Juxtaposing these criminal careers with the self-sacrificing, anti-pleasurable and -consumerist identifications of extreme religiousness, de Castro delineates, on the other hand, an opposite point of self-identification, 'resistant' in a very different way than the drug dealer, but enacted within the same shared social space of Brazil's urban barrios and favelas. Finally, she points out a third normative draft of identification, located between the drug dealer and the religious fanatic; that is, the modern, 'unwilling' labourer:

The majority of poor Brazilian youngsters manage to stay away from illicit activities – as a 'career' – despite the enormous appeals these might have. A career as a worker seems to await them in the long run, despite the severe difficulties in entering the formal market and the great frustrations related to income expectations (de Castro, 2006: 190). However, though seemingly in accordance with and a continuity of the norms and life trajectories of their parents' generation, the meaning of work as an identification possibility for poor youngsters has changed, it seems, upon closer inspection. Rather than a legitimate source of collective identity or a means of self-realization, work is nowadays primarily seen to constitute 'a necessary, pragmatic and instrumental device to go on living by making possible the necessary protection against police abuse or the purchase of necessary items' (de Castro 2006: 192).

Seemingly, the construction of a social identity centred around work, as a normative reference, is the most probable option for poor Brazilians, who, by virtue of their disadvantaged social situation, cannot take their time 'experimenting' with life-styles and a multiplicity of positions characteristic of an adolescent situation (de Castro, 2006: 190). Thus, 'the "logic of survival" retains its restrictive impact, pushing lower class youngsters into subaltern occupational positions as soon as possible, or making them wish for a job position as the means to cope with the adverse present' (de Castro, 2006: 190).

What role does the media and the possible identifications that they enable play in this context? The results of a large research project, run at 20 poor areas in Rio de Janeiro and involving 1,700 youths, suggests that although primary identification with the parental figure of the labourer (and especially with the hard-working mother) provides resistance to the overwhelming power of identity drafts related to drug dealing, secondary identifications related to the world of entertainment play a central role in poor urban youngsters' mediated imagination. That is, media and sports figures are the people most admired outside the family circle (de Castro and Correa, 2005).

In contrast to merit-based identifications of labour and higher education, being a media or sports star are projected and offered as ready-made identities which do not demand effort and need not be cultivated. Thus, the preferred readings of the mainstream media flow, as for example articulated in the entertainment-oriented programming of Brazilian television, seems to provide young disadvantaged people with strong incentives 'to put their expectations and chances on already-given talents to be "discovered" and shown in the media, in contradiction with normative appeals of labour and personal effort which stand as underpinnings for self-construction' (Castro, 2006: 191).

THE METHODOLOGICAL AND EPISTEMOLOGICAL CHALLENGE OF STUDYING YOUNG PEOPLE'S MEDIA APPROPRIATIONS IN BRAZIL

How can these rather generalized findings, which are the outcome of a broad and holistic survey of the lifeworld of poor urban youngsters in Rio de Janeiro, be substantiated and made more specific? How can we contrast the situated practices of media engagement outlined by de Castro and Correa (2005) evocatively with those of youth living under more privileged conditions or in another Brazilian city? Finally, how can we identify alternative projects of identification, enabled by the work of mediated imagination, which are neither subsumed under the normative framework of labour and merit, nor by its 'criminal' negation?

Obviously, such an endeavour demands a qualitative approach situated within the theoretical framework of both reception studies and media ethnography. Methodologically approached through the participant observation of young people's media-related practices of consumption and through the discursive (re)construction of the meaning-making practices as expressed in informal talk and interview, the epistemological aim of my study of youth in Recife was to investigate the role of mediated communication in the cultural practices of their everyday lives.

The interviews were recorded, with few exceptions, on mini disc. In all, more than 40 interviews, with about 50 participants, were realized in February–March 2003 and in December 2005. Amongst the respondents were young people from half a dozen low-income and two middle- to upper-middle-class residential areas, aged between 14 and 27 years.[7] Participatory observations took place at more than a dozen locations where young people spent time together, either to hang out or to participate in more organized (leisure) activities. Also, they took place at and around the homes of several youths and at media and cultural institutions providing for Recife's youth and involving them in their cultural production.

Some of the major non-residential sites of our research were:

1 Two internet cafés (in Boa Viagem and Olinda), which were the regular meeting points for several Counter Strike clans.
2 The 'Barraca de Meninas' (Boa Viagem), a beach stall run by a group of female youths.
3 'Aucuba', a non-governmental organization (NGO) media initiative, which runs among other activities a video training course for a group of young people from lower-class areas.

4 'Majê Molê', an Afro-Brazilian ballet including about 25 female dancers and 4 male drummers.
5 'Movimento Cultural Boca de Lixo', an autonomous youth group, which has started a cultural centre in the compounds of a former slaughterhouse ('Matadouro de Peixinhos').
6 A social awareness course and library ('Nascedouro') run at the same premises, involving 20-plus local youth of both sexes.
7 'Torceda Jovem', the youth fan club of Sporto, one of the major football clubs in town.
8 A Maracatou-dance ensemble, based at the 'Teatro Maurício de Nassau', a cultural centre and theatre in Recife Antigo.
9 The Recife studio of TV Guararapes, where the daily live entertainment show *Pedro Paulo na TV* is produced.
10 The community radio 'Alto Falante' in Alto José do Pinho.
11 The autonomous youth centre 'Casa de Jovens' in downtown Recife.
12 The Student Unions Centre at a public secondary school in Bomba de Hemetério.

Participatory observations included attention to the flow of conversation our informants were engaged in, as a way to obtain access to the moments when media intercepted with their everyday lives. These conversations were in part 'documented' on video, amounting to 15 hours of footage shot in December 2005. The use of a small and unobtrusive digital video camera allowed us to 'capture' some of the conversations and interactions through which youth spontaneously incorporated media practices and media-enabled imaginations in their mundane, everyday activities of living.

Admittedly, this 'capturing' constituted in itself an interpretative dimension, in that we selected what to film and how to frame this 'documentation'. No doubt, our informants adjusted to the altered interactional relation that was established through our filming. Recurring comments and suggestions on what to film and specific performances initiated for the sake of our shooting bear witness to its influence on the reality we sought to represent. Even so, upon analysis, some of the resulting reactions provided us with a deeper understanding of how our informants implicitly defined the interaction between us and them. That is, their examination provided us with insights into both our respondents' understanding of the purposes and the power of audiovisual media in general, signified by our use of the camera, and into key nodes of the identity projects they were engaged in. For that reason, I consider our interactional impact less as an empirical distortion and more as an analytically productive catalyst that has made the processes of media engagement and identification visible.

On a more general level, this experience demands acknowledging that our informants' conversations and interactions with friends, siblings, elders, me and my research assistant were inevitably influenced by our presence. In that we both arranged for some of the social situations we participated in and introduced topics into informal conversation, asking questions and providing answers to the many questions they asked us, we were truly participants rather than unnoticed flies-on-the-wall. A high degree of self-reflectivity, regarding the influence of our presence and social interaction, was the way we responded methodologically. In practical terms, this meant recurring conversations in which we sought to identify the social dynamics at play in the meetings and interviews with our informants.[8] What we sought to keep in mind and to determine as precisely as possible during these methodological exercises was the basic cultural differences between us and our informants[9] and their likely impact upon our empirical findings. Needless to say, these kinds of situational reflection are, per definition, tentative and hard to verify.

The analysis of observations and of articulations made in qualitative interviews or informal conversations is in itself a challenging task.[10] The additional challenge of conducting field-work in a culture not of one's own has been debated, most thoroughly, in the methodological and epistemological discussions raised by anthropology. As suggested by the latter, we are generally better qualified to detect and look through instances of self-conscious glossing over and omission if performed by a member of our own society. Therefore, my assistant's judgement, based on a greater social and cultural familiarity with our informants, had to function as a counterweight to my (at times) 'Western' naivety and lack of understanding. Even so, this recognition implied not buying into his interpretations unconditionally.[11]

This brings me to the final methodological issue I want to raise: the possible consequences of my limited, initial proficiency of Portuguese. In February 2003, when I started my actual field research,[12] the need of a translator and research assistant was obvious. Though he and I arrived rapidly at a profound personal and professional understanding, the disadvantages of the working procedure that we developed cannot be denied. Translating my questions and summing up the answers, every now and then, provided me with a rough idea about the interviews we conducted and the conversations while they unfolded. However, some of the argumentative details and more nuanced verbal utterances were inevitably lost.

The recording and subsequent detailed translation of our interviews sought to diminish the inherent limitations of our approach, but made me at the same time acutely aware of the challenge the issue of language posed. As for the non-recorded conversations unfolding during our presence, my assistant sought either to translate them and point out their significance immediately, or to make a notice in writing, based on his growing theoretical and analytical understanding of the objectives of my research. In December 2005, upon my third stay in Recife, the situation was rather different. Owing to the continued cooperation between me and my assistant, which included a discussion of analytical topics and of the resulting conference papers and publications, I had gained a deeper understanding of Brazilian culture and society in general and the local context of Recife in particular. Bringing our particular studies together in a joint publication with my anthropologist colleague on the project (Wildermuth and Dalsgaard, 2006) likewise furthered my 'contextual' understanding of the lives of young people in Recife.

Also, I started to learn Portuguese while in Brazil for 2 months in 2003 and continued upon my return to Denmark. This meant that I was able to follow, while not necessarily fully participate, in conversation during my field research in 2005. No less important was that, by then, I had become able to read secondary sources in Portuguese, though with considerable effort. This development of my capacity to participate more actively in conversations went hand in hand with a shift from a more interview-based approach in 2003 to a more participatory observation-based approach in 2005, a change of focus from a greater to a reduced number of core informants and a change in emphasis from public to private spaces of interaction as prime sites of research.

RECIFE'S URBAN MEDIA CULTURE

Media are a pervasive feature of everyday life in Recife. Such is the immediate impression, when visiting the capital of Pernambuco. A considerable variety of newspapers and magazines are on sale from newsstands, especially in downtown Recife and the better-off neighbourhoods. The occasional internet café and cinema contribute to this picture of a media-saturated urban environment. In the air-conditioned malls and shopping centres, which are the preferred sites of strolling, purchasing and public entertainment for those 'who can afford', the latest in home entertainment products is on display. In contrast, the bulk of less fashionable retailers, for example in the downtown shopping area of Boa Vista, have a choice of ordinary TV, video and audio equipment, both new and second hand. Street vendors, who sell music and movies of Brazilian and Western origin, are another common feature illustrating the desire of young and old to consume a broad variety of media products. They are seen with their pushcarts all over town, including Recife's poorer neighbourhoods. Like the hawkers, who find their customers along the beaches, they deal almost exclusively in pirate-copied audio-tapes, CDs, videos and DVDs. While domestic and foreign movies are also available from the established video chains, the majority of less stylish DVD and video rentals are located in the poorer neighbourhoods. Likewise, small, unpretentious video- and computer-game parlours, found in Recife's *barrios* and *favelas*, constitute low-budget counterparts to the upmarket city game centres frequented by middle- and upper-class youth. Bars and restaurants equipped with TV screens are a final example for the pervasiveness of media in Recife. Music videos and soccer games are the programming they most often show.

A visit to local homes demonstrates this impression of the ubiquity of the media in Recife. All the homes I visited in 2003 and 2005 had at least one television set. Access to television compares with patterns in the developed world, though households with a single TV still dominate the scene.[13] In the poorer parts of Recife, homes consisting of one or two small rooms are commonplace. Though poor, these homes usually have a TV, if only a small black-and-white one. These are usually placed so as to be watched from the central bed, which doubles as a daytime place to sit. The living room in slightly better off households is often organized around the consumer electronics, which satisfy both practical demands and an ambition to display the family's symbols of wealth and objects of pride. The widespread decoration of these assets with plastic flowers and family pictures underlines the affection with which they are invested.

While the mix of media available to young people in Recife and the patterns of use associated with different media 'styles' cannot be generalized, most of the young people we spoke to acknowledged to watch TV regularly. Listening to music, not only in public, but also in the realm of the private home, was another essential of their everyday practices of media use. Listening to music-centred radio broadcasts typically complements other activities, like doing school homework, chatting with friends, doing a job or housework. In the words of Paula (21):

> Sometimes when I am at home with my friends, I turn off TV and listen to radio. When TV is on you cannot pay attention on conversation. Sometimes you are near television and far from your friends. Then I turn off TV, turn on the radio, and we can talk.

While a substantial part of the young people we interviewed claimed to listen to music-centred radio formats frequently, talk-radio was rather low on their agenda.[14] This suggests that youth in Recife prefer, in tendency, television over radio when spending leisure time on forms of exclusive and attentive media consumption, while music and music-centred radio seem their prime choice to accompany other activities. Explains Luciana, a 15-year-old single young mother from the low-income residential area of Peixinhos:

> When I'm not listening to radio I watch TV. When I'm not watching I turn on the radio. It all depends on what I do.

Other forms of mediated communication, like print media, computer media, cinema, DVD and video films, if available, compete with television and radio for the undivided attention of young people. For the majority of lower-class youth, the availability of these commercially distributed media and communication technologies is meanwhile a limited one, a fact which puts into perspective the initial impression of a media-saturated environment. Only middle- and upper-class youth occupy a media environment characterized by broad choice and plentitude, comparable to the life-world of young people in the Global North.

'TEXTUAL' STRUCTURES AND APPROPRIATIONS OF POPULAR TELEVISION PROGRAMMING

A substantial part of the flow of terrestrial television in Recife is directed towards a young audience, though few programmes address youth exclusively. In recent years, the Brazilian telenovela has become much more attuned to the national reality, discussing current affairs and the social and political structure of the nation (Hamburger, 1999; La Pastina *et al.*, 2003). Nonetheless, the observed, pervasive popularity of television, not least among youth from the poorer sections, goes hand in hand with a supply of programmes that are highly commercialized and entertainment oriented, rather than educational and public service oriented.

Young people's engagement with television is realized against the totality of programmes they have access to. As their TV-enabled imagination is circumscribed by and, in its realization, dependent on the 'offers' that the medium provides, some detailed textual analyses have been a part of my media ethnographic approach. Availability, familiarity and popularity were the prime criteria by which I selected some for closer inspection. Meanwhile, being far from proficient at Portuguese, and hence in need of an assistant to 'watch' television, set a firm limit to respective efforts.

Amongst the plentitude of TV genres and programmes shown on the national and regional channels and transmitted terrestrially in Recife, the following were most commonly named, by my informants.

1 Talent and game shows: *Muito Mais,*[15] *Tribuna Show, Pedro Paulo na TV*, and *Caldeirão.*[16]
2 Popular entertainment and talk shows: *Luciana Gimenes,*[17] *Faustão, Gugu,*[18] *Programa do Gordo, Jô Soares.*
3 Reality TV shows: *Big Brother Brasil.*
4 Telenovelas and serial fiction: *O Beijo do Vampiro* (*The Kiss of the Vampire*), *Mulheres apaixonadas* (*Women in Love*), *Malhação,*[19] *Turma do Gueto.*[20]
5 Feature films: Brazilian and international.
6 Sitcoms and humour: *Casseta & Planeta.*
7 Sports programmes: *Esporte Total, Domingo Esporte, Globo Esporte.*
8 News and current affairs: Jornal da Globo, Bom Dia Pernambuco, Jornal Nacional.
9 Documentaries and cultural programmes as primarily shown on the non-commercial TV Cultura;.
10 Music and celebrity shows: *MTV Brazil, Video Show.*[21]
11 Cartoons: *Simpsons, Southpark, Dexter's Laboratory, Powerpuff Girls.*
12 Crime shows: *Cidade Alerta, Cardinot.*

None of these programmes was popular with all the youths we talked to, though each of them were, meanwhile, with some. Most often despised were the sensationalist crime shows, which report in drastic pictures about incidents of crime and violence committed in Recife (regional channels) and Brazil (national channels). Not a single one of our interview partners claimed to enjoy them, though everybody seemed to know them well and though several youths 'admitted' to viewing them on occasion, 'due to other household members' preference'. The youths were most split in their evaluation about Denny Oliveira's and Pedro Paulo's talent shows. While not many young people declared being ardent fans of these programmes, others distanced themselves vehemently from what they considered as commercial, vulgar and sexist formats, based on the exploitation of young people's dream of stardom and fame. So, for example, 20-year-old Ana Paula, who lives with her parents, a teen brother, a sister and a cousin in Bomba do Hemetério, one of Recife's poorer barrios. Asked:

> What do you think about TV programs like *Pedro Paulo na TV*, and *Muito Mais*? Have you seen them, before?

she replied:

> No. I don't watch, this kind of programmes ... they are brega.[22] I don't like this kind of music. At home, my brother Júnior watches television a lot. He likes this kind of programmes.

On a social, interactional level the media contribute to the processes of identity formation through the very act of stating and explaining one's preferences and dislikes in contrast to a comparably 'close', but nonetheless significantly 'different' other. For Ana Paula, therefore, it makes no sense to compare herself with young people her age who have a socio-economic and educational background radically different from hers. Those youths she mainly seeks to negotiate and define her identity in the making against are her siblings, friends and neighbours, who share her social conditions of living and possibilities of personal development. Typical for this kind of negotiation of an identity (in the making) is Ana Paula's emphatic statement of a very sharp divide between those who are into brega and pagode on the one hand, and into rock music on the other:

> I like rock. I listen to Bon Jovi, Guns 'n' Roses ... Linkin Park, music like that, you know? ... But things like brega, pagode, I *hate* [with emphasis] brega and pagode.
>
> I hate. I really don't like. When I'm at a party and it is played, I can listen to it, I can dance to it, normally ... I dance pagode sometimes, but brega I really don't like. – Those people who really like brega and pagode, they love also to dress indecorous. It's terrible, I just hate it.

At first view, Ana Paula's rejection of these rather commercialized forms of Brazilian dance music seems exaggerated, the emphatic statement of a young girl who tells us what she loves and hates. Moreover, given the fact that she admits to dance to pagode music on occasions, her claim seems somehow inconsistent. However, if we pay close attention to what she says, it becomes clear that it is not so much the music itself, Ana Paula 'hates', but the lascivious and hedonistic behaviour which is often associated with the popular youth and media cultures that are associated with these forms of dance. In Recife, pagode and brega is the music of the (lower income) masses, of the public dance halls, where the beer is cheap, the dresses short and the dance floor an arena for close physical contact. Like other popular forms of dance in Brazil, brega is saturated with explicit sexual overtones, the lyrics focused on love and romance. Not surprisingly, this local 'club culture' is widely associated with some of the perils and evils of a dangerous culture of youth and leisure. As we were told by Rosina, another female respondent,[23] brega shows are the places where men get into fights and young girls into trouble:

> I think girls who dance brega, they show their bodies all the time, with short clothes. I dislike. I know it's their job. But I'm still saying that rock and brega are completely different in terms of a way of living – you don't see this kind of attitude with people who enjoy rock. Sometimes there are brega shows – These girls dance on a stage wearing only small underwear. They wear a kind of transparent skirt. But in my opinion they're wearing only underwear.
>
> I can watch this kind of program, but I don't enjoy. When some brega songs are played on the radio, no problem, I like. ...
>
> The majority of brega fans are teenage girls, 12 or 14 years old. They go to places where brega bands play all night. From my home we can see these people passing, girls younger than those in Majê Molê ... as if they found a way to be a prostitute, you know? All of them wear very short clothes. Men come and go and say something indecent, obscene to them. My goodness! They're children. But the men say: 'You see that one? She is good to do it with.' ...
>
> I think that people who go to brega shows have no self-respect.
>
> I do not see people fighting in a rock concert, as they do at brega shows.
>
> ... at brega shows sometimes people pick a quarrel with someone else without a reason ... at brega shows a lot of men betray their girlfriends. This kind of attitude doesn't happen with people from rock.

What Ana Paula's and Rosina's vehement reserve against *brega* and their declared preference for rock music implies is, thus, a moral statement about their gendered self-identification as sexually attractive, but self-respecting local girls. Interpreting it as a mere statement about their cultural 'tastes' in regard to music and TV entertainment does not fully acknowledge the extent to which their aesthetic choice and media preference can be understood as attempts of self-reflective distinction. Part of the attraction of global media for local audiences is that their consumption often provides meanings which enable the imagination and enactment of identity drafts, delineated through 'the accentuation of symbolic distancing from the spatial-temporal contexts of everyday life' (Thompson, 1995: 175).

For Ana Paula and Rosina, *pagode* and *brega* signify the sexual availability of lower class girls, of female 'cheapness', as we were told. Stating their cultural 'preferences' in conversation with us, they implicitly declare that they want not to be confused with those younger females, who neither have a clear purpose with their lives as yet, nor the necessary experience to steer clear of some of those pitfalls which are common amongst female teenagers in their neighbourhood, namely unplanned pregnancies, sexual diseases, drug addiction and careers as full- or part-time prostitutes. What I find remarkable about this signification is that it challenges the common connotations of 'sex and drugs and rock and roll' by redefining the situated meanings of rock as a countercultural lifestyle. A trans-global form of cultural expression thus becomes appropriated and interpreted in the context of Ana Paula's and Rosina's everyday lives, means made significant through a process of localization.

Evidently, these elaborate acts of re-signification, though described as individuals' self-reflective accomplishment of identification, cultural preference and principled orientation, get articulated by reference to particular public discourses on rock music prevalent amongst young people in Recife. As became clear from subsequent talks, Ana Paula and Rosina deployed, above all, shared imageries concerning both local music groups, such as Chico Science & Nação Zumbi, Fred 04 and Mundo Livre SA, and Brazilian rock bands from the south when phrasing the above-outlined collocation between rock and 'following the right way'.[24] Thus, Ana Paula's and Rosina's cultural positioning, outlined in conversation with us, should be understood in relation to broader processes of cultural expression and collective identification, such as Recife's prolific *Mangue* movement.[25]

Not just in terms of class, gender and ethnicity, but also in terms of centre–periphery relations, the consumption of mediated forms of cultural expression provides youth with opportunities of 'empowered' local identifications. While the *Mangue* movement has sought to configure new forms for conceiving identities in Recife, this discursive redefinition and overcoming of the incomplete modernity of the peripheral metropolis described by Prysthon (2002, 2005) stands in contrast to the mainstream media images of a colourful but impoverished, underdeveloped and dissolute north-east. Strong judgments made by local youth regarding their cultural tastes and preferences in media thus signify their struggle with competing drafts of local identification and cultural recognition.

Consider, for example, the statement made by 19-year-old Carlos, who despises a locally produced game and talent shows (listed above). Asked:

> Do you like this [Pedro Paulo-like] kind of programs?

he responded:

> No. I find them too vulgar … Because, of the kind of songs, which I don't like … I find it too vulgar, made only to attract an audience … this gross behaviour, this shouting and vulgar stuff. Everybody is naked … They do it and think it's the best, because the people watch it, it has a huge audience … and then they say this is Culture. I think they don't even know the meaning of the word Culture … I keep imagining people in São Paulo and other states watching a crap like this …

How can we interpret this quote? To start with, it is mandatory to interpret this statement in relation to the totality of formal and informal conversations had with Carlos. This enlarged frame of signification provides us with a far from complete, but perhaps sufficiently (regarding the aims of our analysis) 'broad' understanding of the person involved. A thorough contextualization and recognition of the situated character of Carlo's interpretative agency, realized as practices of media engagement, is an ambition which by definition will always be partial, but not necessarily insufficient in its scope. Thus, the incorporation of other sources of knowledge about the subject of our enquiry may contribute to our analytical understanding, while the generation and integration of ever-wider circles of contextualization cannot be an end in itself. In fact, it may not even lead to more clear and differentiated research findings. In consequence, I have sought to determine the scope and incorporate a sufficient, rather than all-encompassing contextualization.

Meanwhile, seeking to identify the person we talk to and his/her deeper structure of psychological and social motivation to engage a particular media text in the way he/she does also raises the question of why this experience is communicated to us, in this particular way, as an act of discursive articulation. In other words, it points towards the specific communicative relation between researcher and the researched, questioned, observed subject (the informant in classical anthropological parlance) and the mutual motivations involved.[26]

To come back to our concrete case: Carlos lives with his mother in a lower-class neighbourhood some 15 km from the centre of Recife. Neither he nor his mother have full employment, though judging by their housing situation they have sufficient income to afford some basic amenities. Their small but well-kept house is clean, neat and witness to Donna Severina's industriousness. Obviously, Carlos, though finished with secondary school and without a regular occupation, does not spend his time hanging out with local youth his age.

His social distancing from male and female peers may function as a barrier against involvement in transgressing behaviours and a life of public pleasures, which characterizes the temptations and potentials dangers of young people's leisure culture in areas like his neighbourhood. Like comparable low-class residential areas, everyday life for young people in Camaragibe is influenced by a culture of violence and drug abuse surrounding them. Keeping away from youth in the neighbourhood (and probably being kept at a distance), Carlos seems to stay clear of trouble. However, he does so less in the sense of the anti-hedonistic struggles of religious converts, who, according to de Castro's (2006: 189) typification, construct identity positions 'within discourses of self-sacrifice and rejection of consumerist pleasures'. While in fact an evangelic, he is not very active in church or especially religious, judging by his own comments. Hence, his 'reluctance' to hang out with local peers is misunderstood, if seen either as moral rejection or as 'a defensive manoeuvre against a state of helplessness in face of extreme danger' (de Castro, 2006: 189).

His withdrawal from the streets and staying at home, watching TV for hours on end, is a pattern more common among girls. Judging by Carlos's media uses, preferences and appropriations the mediated imaginaries of consumption, pleasure and fashion do play a central role in the identity constructions in which he is involved. Dressing properly and appropriate to the respective situation was, for example, a central theme in Carlos's interpretative reflection and evaluation of the offers of Brazilian television, articulated in conversation with us. His preference for Brazilian telenovelas and for daytime shows like *Mais Você* underscores this observation.[27]

As Carlos explained to us, he usually starts to watch TV from eight o'clock in the morning, sometimes all day. Most of his evenings he spends either at home or at Avani's, his female friend's nearby house, where they watch TV and DVDs together. Avani, who is in her late 20s, is fully employed as representative for a food wholesale and catering company, located near Recife's airport. As we realize, upon meeting her, she lives in one of the most fancy and well-furnished houses of the neighbourhood, owns her own car and cultivates a glamorous appearance (in hairstyle, clothes, makeup, etc.), which altogether sets her clearly apart from her lower-class neighbours. Carlos's and Avani's unusual friendship has existed for several years.

For about a year, at the time of our meeting, Carlos had finished secondary school and commenced with an informal, though far from regular occupation. That is, he was selling Avon cosmetic products to women in the neighbourhood. This job involves visiting his neighbourhood clients at home, showing them samples of the products he provides on order. In conversation with us, Carlos strongly expressed his conviction that watching daytime and evening TV programmes, directed specifically at female viewers, helps him to sell. As he explained, socializing with his clients demands referring to the ads and product placements of cosmetics in telenovelas and daytime shows. Thus, he inscribes himself through his practices of TV viewing in an interpretative community of local women, several years his senior. No doubt, Carlos therewith transgresses perceived gender norms amongst Brazilian males, which demand an expressive distancing in relation to telenovelas and other 'female' TV programmes (La Pastina, 2005: 9). Engaging in practices of media reception, associated with the female sphere, provides him indeed with a specific cultural capital, positioning him, at the same time, as not typically male. Possibly, this social position as 'gayish' and not aggressively male, is in itself a prerequisite for Carlos to be able to visit women in private, at their homes, though their husbands or other family members may not be around.

While this identification in the making provides Carlos with a momentary sense of self, his identity seems far from stabilized. The tensions and contradictions, which became visible in the self-reflective description of his present life, underline the, in general, fluid and unconsolidated character of young Brazilians' (prolonged) transition to adulthood. On the level of the media-enabled work of imagination, this continuous process of challenged and redefined, contrasted and merged identifications can be empirically recognized and conceptually grasped as a contradiction of discourses mobilized. Carlos's 'critique' of *Pedro Paulo na TV*, a programme primarily directed at Brazilian teenagers, understood in such a relational perspective, is different from the critical distancing of Harlan. The latter, a 19-year-old male living nearby, rejects above all the 'girlish' character of the programme and the female dream of becoming a star that it projects. At the same time he acknowledges the attractive physique of one of the competing samba dancers shown on screen, thereby underlining his male point of view.

So, can we reduce Carlos's disgust over the vulgar, semi-nude performance of teenage girls in the programme to be the expressive aversion of a 'gayish' male? Or can we reduce it to be the condemnation of an interpretative community of grown-up women, who are critical of the exploitive, physical objectification of those girls, a discourse reproduced by Carlos in conversation with us? The answer is no. In my view, we also have to consider in which ways Carlos's ambitions and imaginary drafts for a future personal and social identity exceed the realities of his present life.

In conversation he put across a strong wish to work within the cultural industries, preferably radio or television. Though it didn't seem to us that he was taking concrete and promising steps to realize this ambition, we have to acknowledge the impact of this imagined future identity on the routines around which Carlos organizes his present everyday live. Likewise, we have to take his attempts to make use of television – together with radio, the only medium that he has an almost unrestricted access to – serious, no matter how misconceived and questionable a strategy these hopeful appropriations might appear in our eyes. Hence, a social analysis-oriented scepticism, informed by recognition of the almost insurmountable structural constraints a young person with Carlos's background will necessarily face in pursuing this kind of ambition, seems more appropriate than a personalized scepticism, which puts the blame on Carlos, a 'victim' of Brazil's extremely unequal opportunity structure.

As is important to recognize, Carlos's ambition points towards some of his motivations to spend time with us, a foreign researcher and his local assistant, who demand his attention without the promise of immediate material returns. In the process we promised and did get him in contact with a local media NGO, which occasionally trains youths like him as part of their video school. This motivational structure most certainly has had a formative influence on the way Carlos presented himself in conversation with us, namely as a knowledgeable viewer, not in opposition to the totality of terrestrial TV programmes, but selective, scrutinizing and 'in control'.

This is not to suggest that he merely occupied a temporary posture for the sake of possible future contacts through us. As became clear, for example, from the worn notebooks on TV programmes that Carlos kept and updated in our presence and from his detailed knowledge of who has been presenter on which show over the last few years, he had developed his own systematic style of TV viewing. Some of this meticulous knowledge he mobilized as cultural capital, such as, for example, when providing Avani with all the latest details of missed episodes, actors, etc. as a gratification for her company and hospitality.

In essence, Carlos's viewing strategy was thus to achieve, on the one hand, an exhaustive though somehow one-dimensional knowledge of television's programme flow. On the other hand, he sought to cultivate his discriminatory competence as a viewer familiar with the latest gossip, media personalities, formats and production trends. Both dimensions he sought to express in a language and by arguments different from the common TV talk found amongst lower-class youth of a comparable educational background and age. A final joint interview with him and Avani provided clear evidence for Carlos's adoption of Avani's parlance and TV-related discursive stance. With de Castro we can understand Carlos's attempt to develop his skills of media-related, 'critical' verbalization as a strategy of imitative impression management. In contrast to the young people dressing up in the hope of not being socially discriminated against, described by de Castro (2006), his strategy of social inclusion goes beyond issues off outer appearance and material consumption. Carlo's self-presentation and personalized struggle for social inclusion is thus directed at the appropriation of rhetoric skills; that is, skills that in his view might, at least partially, replace a perceived lack of higher education.

Comparable strategies of self-identification characterize Ana Paula's and Rosina's and media-savvy and self-reflective critique of the television programmes they encounter and engage with. While Ana Paula and Rosina echo some of the arguments, understandings and attitudes which are prevalent among the NGOs they are involved with, Carlo's parlance and discursive stance is a less politicized and pedagogic one in comparison. That is, Carlos's strong rejection of *Pedro Paulo na TV* emphasizes neither the consumerist, subaltern-social-positions-re-inscribing and deeply consumerist character of the programme, which constructs its female, lower-class teenage participants exclusively in terms of their physical attractiveness, nor the behavioural patterns that result from an overrating of physical attractiveness as markers of female value and self-respect. Instead, Carlos's critique is primarily phrased in terms of aesthetic judgements, cultural tastes and lifestyle-centred distinctions, such as the vulgar versus the decent, the gross versus the pleasant, and the gauche versus the sophisticated. This discursive self-positioning we may understand as an attempt of symbolic distancing from his class base, inspired by the successful social and cultural mobility of his mentor and friend Avani.

In sum, Carlos's media-enabled work of imagination is informed by elements of fantasy and wishful thinking, but also by concrete strategic attempts to increase his social and cultural capital. Other Brazilian youth which we have met, shared time with, observed and talked to have identified their own particular optimistic and pragmatic identity projects. All of them have sought to make use of the media cultures they had access to, to further their strategic attempts of survival and ideal achievement. Harlan, who focused on his talent for football, approached and explored the imaginaries of television along a football-centred perspective. His was the hope to 'learn' something about becoming a professional player by watching the daily early afternoon football shows on television. Others were inspired by other dreams and more or less concrete ambitions.

While lower-class Brazilian youth, in general, seek to maximize the uses of television, the middle and upper classes have a broader potential choice. That means, in practice, a greater opportunity to use other media, print and digital, to cultivate social relations and to develop a specific forms of knowledge, skills and cultural capital. Poor young people in Brazil are thus disadvantaged, deepening existing disparities that are, for example, created in parallel by unequal educational opportunities.

What discerns disadvantaged young Brazilians from their more privileged counterparts is not lack of will and strategic agency to improve their lives, but a widespread discrepancy between ambitious identity projects embraced and the paths imagined as leading to their achievement. One of the reasons for this discrepancy is an almost uncontested prevalence of popular narratives projecting spectacular cases of social mobility, not through hard work and/or education, but based on good looks, talent and other inborn qualities. Brazilian television offers utopian rather than realistic tales of successful trajectories, contrasted by bleak tales of young people straying from the right path and being, in consequence, killed.

While disadvantaged young people are well aware of the improbability of becoming a lucky 'winner' themselves and do know that their chances to end as one of the 'losers' portrayed in the daily crime shows are comparably high, the hopeful identifications which tales of success invite them to share are not discarded with ease. In the face of material deprivation and exclusion from educational and cultural networks, their consumption allows at least for the pleasure of hopeful identification and temporary relief from having to acknowledge the disparate and enormous gap between rich and poor in Brazil. As de Castro (2006: 191) states:

> Secondary identifications related to the world of entertainment are offered as ready-made identities, which do not demand effort and need not be cultivated. They [youth] put their expectations and chances on already-given talents to be 'discovered' and shown in the media, in contradiction with normative appeals of labour and personal effort which stand as underpinnings for self-construction.

In correspondence with this observation, Carlos, when asked whether he already had taken concrete steps to further his declared goal, told us:

> No ... there are some radios here, two evangelical and another ... I always arrange to go, but I actually never went to see how they are inside ... I'm much curious ... but ...I keep saying it all the time: I'm going to call Globo, to go there ... I will even set it up with Avani, for us to go there together ... And that's all ... Once in a while they come here to do some report. Then I go, talk to the journalist, and ask for an autograph.

Ellis's (2000) dictum of the TV viewer as 'able to over-look but under-act' attains, thus, its own meaning in the context of young Brazilians' engagements with the offers of local and national TV through practices of mediated imagination.

CONCLUDING REMARKS

With reference to the abundant, diversified and saturated media environments encountered in the late-modern societies of the Global North, the empirically observed diversification of media-centred lifestyles among 'Western' youth have been understood as the result of acts of playful, highly individualized and selective identification. Contemporary youth and media studies, which (increasingly) subscribe to this perspective, stress that these kinds of outlined identifications go hand in hand with youth's intentional and self-reflective diversification of cultural expression and consumption, and thus to identifications enabled by an ever-growing possibility for active, cultural choice.

As I have tried to show by presenting and discussing a few quotes in detail, the diverse 'critical' positions by which underprivileged young people in Brazil approach the dominant mass medium of television point to the dedicated, but often frustrated and ill-conceived, attempts of disadvantaged youth to take control and improve their conditions of existence. They signify individual strategies and pleasurable, media-facilitated fantasies of solving conflicts posed by social inequalities, rather than individual acts of symbolic resistance or even mobilizations towards collective social and political action. However, forms of media engagement and cultural expression which challenge the impoverished repertoires for identification and self-construction have also been encountered amongst young people in Recife, occasionally. Based on a claim for a new social contract, recognition and justice, the attitude of this latter, much smaller group of disadvantaged youth, regarding mainstream media and in specific television, was characterized by a more radical politicized, critical position. In a few cases their attitude towards the dominant media was one of total rejection.

Young Brazilians watching television and consuming other mainstream media confront images of youth and contemporary lifestyles which signify late-modern, globalized identities. Projected mainly as a phenomenon of life in the urban centres of São Paulo and Rio de Janeiro, the discursive practices of Brazilian television reproduce a stereotyped dichotomy between the white, prosperous, modern and rational south, and the black, impoverished, archaic but colourful north-east of Brazil. Optimistic perspectives on a globalized mediated consumer culture – which claim that it in principle enhances multiple identifications, thus providing young people with the means to explore and negotiate the 'local–global contradictions' of a rapidly changing society in a creative way – need to be qualified. In urban Brazil, where adult norms and life trajectories indeed lose legitimacy for the young, the impoverished living conditions of a large majority of Brazilian youth continue to constrain the multiplied possibility (and obligation) for making choices in the field of material consumption, leisure-time activities and more or less individualized lifestyles. That is, young people's everyday lives and practices of media engagement remain in many ways circumscribed by long-standing social inequalities.

NOTES

1 Admittedly, no single term can fully encompass the complex, multidimensional and multilayered interaction between text and reader/viewer. With La Pastina (2005) I use the term 'engagement' to imply the totality of experience the processes of media use and reception involve.

2 In *Modernity at Large* Appadurai (1996: 4) proposes that 'the core of the link between globalization and the modern' is defined by the global movement of media technologies into every aspect of individual lives and the unprecedented mass migration of peoples across the world. Mass media and migration are the 'building blocks,' he suggests, of contemporary imagined worlds. For Appadurai, the social imagination in the late twentieth century possesses historically unprecedented characteristics. To this end, he makes three claims.

First, the imagination, rather than being curtailed in a limited space, has become part of everyday life in many societies: discourses about politics, religion or art, for instance, are not confined to expert spheres but are part of the fabric of everyday life in a global society. Hence, the imagination, crafted across national boundaries, is deeply connected not just to modern science and rationality, but to religion, politics and ethnicity. Second, the social imagination has become distinct from fantasy: instead of being an avenue for escape into impossibilities, it has become an expression of possibilities. And inasmuch as people consume, on a global scale, the ideas articulated by the media, the financial world, political systems and local cultures, the imagination has become a platform for social action. Third, the imagination is not an individual faculty, but a collective property: the act of consuming and producing ideas is not an isolated act, but a cultural phenomenon; moreover, this culture is now inescapably global. Diasporic public spheres (such as those created by electronic message boards, chat rooms, and web pages) construct a subjectivity powered by our collective ability to imagine an identity that not only crosses old borders, but frees us of them.

3 A variety of concepts may beused to understand the forces at work in the resulting text–reader relation. Textual closure, preferred readings, generic conventions, naturalizing discourses and subject positioning, sociodemographic position, cultural capital, interpretive community, contextual discourses, sociocognitive resources, national identity and psychodynamic forces are pointed out by Livingstone (1998: 248) with regard to conceptualization as subordination, contradiction, agency, polysemy and ambiguity with regard to a conceptualization as resistance.

4 According to Miles *et al.* (1998), young people use their practices of consumption to develop a lifestyle in which they feel they 'fit in' with a wider peer group, whilst simultaneously giving them a sense of unique individuality in a world characterized by instability, flux and change (Osgerby, 2004: 143). Youth, Miles *et al.* argue, face a world in which their life experiences (in terms of family structure, educational opportunities and routes to employment) seem to become increasingly tenuous. In response,

young people seek a sense of stability through constructing an identity based on the symbolic values of the products they consume. 'Consumer goods', Miles *et al.* (1998: 93) conclude, 'appear to provide the only viable resource by which constructive and arguably creative, conceptions of self can be established'. With Wilk (1995) we may characterize the resulting global–local patterns of consumption as a 'structure of common difference'.

5 In her qualitative study of the social meanings of Shopping Boa Vista and Shopping Centre Recife, Bezerra (2005) has explored a field of urban culture where these disparities in economic, social and cultural capital are played out most visible.

6 Beltrão (1993), Fachel-Leal and Oliven (1987), Tufte (1993, 2000) and Vink (1988) are just a few examples of respective Brazilian studies in this area. In the Anglo-American context, Buckingham (1993) might be mentioned, exemplarily for the many researchers who have contributed to this neither completely determined, nor free-floating perspective on readers'/viewers' appropriation and reiteration of media flows.

7 The residential areas within Greater Recife that most of our informants came from were: Peixinhos, Alto José do Pinho, Morro da Conceição, Bomba de Hemetério, Camaragibe, Alto Santa Terezinha, Jaboatão dos Guararapes, Boa Viagem and Casa Forte.

8 Our daily, prolonged rides with Recife's city bus system provided ample occasion for immediate reflections, still fresh with impressions. Sharing a flat and downloading our latest digital audio and video recordings on my notebook was another occasion to discuss the motivation for particular interactions and statements made by our informants.

9 These are differences in terms of age, class, education, gender, etc., and in my case also differences of nationality and familiarity with Brazilian culture.

10 Alasuutari (1995), among others, has specified this endeavour's demands with respect to the overlapping field of media and cultural studies.

11 While my assistant's point of view has been informed by a different and probably 'lesser' cultural bias, his is, of course, still a subjective perspective. Then again, observing his unprejudiced, engaged and respectful attitude in dealing with the youth that we met, accepting them on their premises rather than judging them from 'above', has contributed to my growing trust and confidence in the validity and significance of his presumptions and judgements.

12 That is, almost a year after my first visit to Recife, participation in a joint workshop and meetings with our counterparts at the Federal University of Pernambuco in March 2002. On occasion we were introduced to some of the neighbourhoods we came to work in by Line Dalsgaard, a social anthropologist who has worked extensively in Recife and who has been one of the six principal researchers of 'Youth and the City', our joint, interdisciplinary research project.

13 The overall number of TV sets in Brazil was estimated at 39 million in 2003. Machado-Borges (2003: 6) reports 87% of Brazilian households to be TV-homes.

14 The major exceptions were sports reports and radio programmes on football by Rádio Clube, Jovem Cap and Rádio Jornal, which were popular with several of the male youths we interviewed.

15 At the time Denny Oliveira was a popular TV presenter. In his live studio programme (on SBT), many amateur brega bands are presented and compete for popularity with the audience. However, in January 2007 the 40-year-old Oliveira was charged for the rape of two 12-year-old girls and for the attempted rape/sexual abuse of three 11- to 13-year-old girls by the Court of Justice of Pernambuco, thereby bringing his career as a TV presenter to an abrupt end. Pedro Paulo (on the Tribuna channel), is another popular presenter in his late 30s. His programme is similar to Denny Oliveira's, with a live audience, performing singers, dancers and brega bands. Both have integrated commercial presentations of cosmetics, clothes, etc. as part of their shows.

16 A programme addressing teenagers with a mix of consumer goods promotion, games, dance and singing contests.

17 A national late-night entertainment programme, based on a mix of interviews, fashion shows and musical performances.

18 Faustão (on Globo) and Gugu (on SBT) are two other popular TV presenters who have their own show (named after them). Their Sunday afternoon programmes show dancers, singers and performing artists in general, complemented by interviews.

19 A teenage soap opera depicting student lives.

20 A series of films produced for TV in which the majority of actors and actresses are black. The main narratives are about people who live in the suburbs and favelas, prostitution, drugs, violence, etc.

21 A TV programme pointed at regular viewers of Brazilian soaps, interviewing actors, showing behind the scenes and telenovela sequences which were cut out.

22 Brega: very popular style of music with infidelity as the main theme of lyrics. From an Anglo-American perspective, we may characterize brega as the north-east Brazilian version of pop music meeting the hip gyrating culture of show and disco dance (admittedly a very crude description). Brega is originally a word for whorehouses in the countryside. Then it started to be used to refer to the kinds of song played in these places. It is also an adjective for kitsch, out of fashion.

23 We met 19-year-old Rosina when we interviewed several members of Majê Molê, an Afro-Brazilian dance company, founded in 1998, which recruits its members in the notorious lower-class barrio of Peixinhos. Rosina is a passionate dancer, the most senior in this group of 30-plus teenagers, who are organized by a male social activist and dance instructor. The intention of Majê Molê is both

to create a successful performing troupe and to be social–educational in the sense of keeping the girls engaged in something purposeful, given an environment where choices of leisure are few and tales of 'girls getting into trouble' all too common. Even so, several of the teenage dancers dropped out along the way, as we were told, to join the Recife sex tourism industry.

24 For a detailed anthropological study on this discursive collocation, articulated commonly amongst underprivileged youth in Recife, see Molde (2002).

25 The *Mangue Bit* is a cultural movement that has had a tremendous influence on youth from all classes since the early 1990s. Created in reaction to the cultural and economical stagnation of Recife, the *Mangue* (Mangrove) movement largely focused on music, with the result being a synthesis of local traditional music styles (such as maracatu and ciranda) with Anglo-American styles. As pointed out by de Castro (2006: 194), the *Mangue Bit* 'has opened up new possibilities to urban poor youth for new identifications affirming a positive self-concept in the identity of poor youth as well as denouncing the oppression and the social injustice of their social condition'. Thus, a collective image of who 'we are' was brought forward and affirmed, 'built upon feelings of pride, self-respect and demands for a fairer society ... creating new moral expectations in face of the frustrations and lack of meaning of poor urban youngsters oppressed life' (de Castro, 2006: 194). If at the beginning the *Mangue Bit* were urban bands led by middle-class children, to gain national recognition, in the late 1990s, artists of 'unquestionably popular' and proletarian origin, such as Selma do Côco, the cirandeira Lia de Itamaracá or the hardcore bands in the suburb Alto José do Pinho, were marketed under this label, all of them conquering space in the local and national media (Prysthon, 2005: 12).

26 I shall not dwell in detail on the prolonged debate within anthropology centring on issues surrounding the politics of ethnography, which is a questioning of the power relations between researcher and informants and a propagation of self-reflective and deconstructivist research practices in consequence. I do, however, acknowledge the epistemological significance of the issues raised by the poststructuralist critique of anthropology's *Writing Culture* and colonial, objectifying legacy, as I agree, in principal, with the suggested attempts to overcome these deficits. However, given the ensuing disciplinary paralysis of anthropology in recent years, I support calls for the development of a highly reflective, but pragmatic, approach that actually allows us to make analytical statements about 'external' realities observed. For a summary discussion of the consequences of this debate for media reception studies, see Murphy (1999).

27 For a detailed content, genre and discourse analysis of *Mais Você*, Ana Maria Braga's popular daytime show on Rede Globo, see Temer (2005).

REFERENCES

Alasuutari, P. (1995) *Researching Culture: Qualitative Method and Cultural Studies.* London: Sage.

Appadurai, A. (1996) *Modernity at Large.* Delhi: Oxford University Press.

Beltrão, M.S. (1993) 'Interpreting Brazilian telenovelas'. In A. Fadul (ed.) *Serial Fiction in TV. The Latin-American Telenovelas.* São Paulo: ECA-USP.

Bezerra, A.C.D.M. (2005) 'Entre lojas e teorias pós-modernas: um passeio pelo Shopping Boa Vista, O Shopping da Cidade'. *Congresso Brasileiro de Ciências da Comincação, 28, Rio de Janeiro.* São Paulo: Intercom.

Buckingham, D. (ed.) (1993) *Reading Audiences. Young People and the Media.* Manchester: Manchester University Press.

Canclini, G.N. (2001) *Consumers and Citizens: Globalization and Multicultural Conflicts.* Minneapolis: University of Minnesota Press.

De Castro, L.R. (2006) 'What is new in the "south"? Consumer culture and the vicissitudes of poor youth's identity construction in urban Brazil'. *Young,* 14(3): 179–201.

De Castro, L.R. and Correa, J. (eds) (2005) *'Mostrando a Real': Um Retrato da Juventude Pobre no Rio de Janeiro.* Rio de Janeiro: Faperj/NAU.

Drotner, K. and Sørensen, A.S. (1996) *Øjenåbnere. Unge, Medier, Modernitet.* Viborg: Dansklærerforeningen.

Ellis, J. (2000) *Seeing Things: Television in the Age of Uncertainty.* London: I.B.Tauris.

Fachel-Leal, O. and Oliven, R.G. (1987) 'A televisão e outras falas: como se reconta uma novela'. *Ciências Sociais Hoje,* 80–93.

Falk, P. (1994) *The Consuming Body.* London: Routledge.

Hall, S. (1987) 'Minimal selves'. In L. Appignanesi (ed.) *Identity: The Real Me.* ICA Documents 6. London: Institute of Contemporary Arts.

Hamburger, E.I. (1999) 'Politics and intimacy in Brazilian telenovelas'. Ph.D. dissertation, Department of Anthropology, University of Chicago.

Holland, D., Lachicotte Jr, W., Skinner, D. and Cain, C. (1998) *Identity and Agency in Cultural Worlds.* Cambridge, MA: Harvard University Press.

La Pastina, C.A. (2005) 'Audience ethnographies: a media engagement approach'. *Global Media Journal,* http://lass.calumet.purdue.edu/cca/gmj/sp05/gmj-sp05-lapastina.htm.

La Pastina, A.C., Rego, C.M. and Straubhaar, J.D. (2003) 'The centrality of telenovelas in Latin America's everyday life: past tendencies, current knowledge, and future research'. *Global Media Journal,* http://lass.calumet.purdue.edu/cca/gmj/sp03/gmj-sp03-lapastina-rego-straubhaar.htm.

Livingstone, S. (1998) 'Relations between media and audiences: prospects for the future'. In T. Liebes and J. Curran (eds) *Media, Ritual, Identity*. London: Routledge; 237–255.

Livingstone, S. (2005) 'The changing nature of audiences: from the mass audience to the interactive media user'. In A. Valdivia (ed.) *Blackwell Companion to Media Studies* (second edition). Oxford: Blackwell.

Machado-Borges, T. (2003) *Only for You! Brazilians and the Telenovela Flow*. Stockholm: Almqvist & Wiksell International.

Machado-Borges, T. (2006) 'Going with the flow: ethnography & dialogism in the reception of Brazilian telenovelas'. *Particip@tions*, 3(2) special edition (November).

Miles, S. (2000) *Youth Lifestyles in a Changing World*. Buckingham: Open University Press.

Miles, S., Cliff, D. and Burr, V. (1998) 'Fitting in and sticking out: consumption consumer meanings and the construction of young people's identities'. *Journal of Youth Studies*, 1(1): 81–96.

Molde, M. (2002) 'At følge den gode vej' ('To follow the right way'). MA thesis, Institute of Anthropology, Copenhagen University.

Murphy, P.D. (1999) 'Media Cultural Studies' uncomfortable embrace of ethnography'. *Journal of Communication*, 23(3): 205–221.

Oliveira, F. (1984) *A Economia da Dependência Imperfeita*. Rio de Janeiro: Graal.

Osgerby, B. (2004) *Youth Media*. London: Routledge.

Prysthon, Â.F. (2002) 'Negociações na periferia: mídia e jovens no Recife'. *Congresso Brasileiro de Ciências da Comincação, 25. Bahia de Salvador*. São Paulo: Intercom.

Prysthon, Â.F. (2005) 'A cidade e o mangue: a constituição da cultura pop recifense nos anos 90'. *Congresso Brasileiro de Ciências da Comincação, 28. Rio de Janeiro*. São Paulo: Intercom.

Temer, A.C.R.P. (2005) 'Mais Você: uma análise da Revista Feminina na Televisão'. *Congresso Brasileiro de Ciências da Comincação, 28. Rio de Janeiro*. São Paulo: Intercom.

Thompson, J.B. (1995) *The Media and Modernity*. Cambridge: Polity Press.

Tufte, T. (1993) 'Everyday life, women and telenovelas in Brasil'. In A. Fadul (ed.) *Serial Fiction in TV. The Latin American Telenovela*. São Paulo: ECA-USP.

Tufte, T. (2000) *Living with the Rubbish Queen: Telenovelas, Culture and Modernity in Brazil*. Luton: University of Luton Press.

Vink, N. (1988) *The Telenovela and Emancipation – a Study on TV and Social Change in Brazil*. Amsterdam: Royal Tropical Institute.

Wildermuth, N. and Dalsgaard, A.L. 2006. 'Imagined futures, present lives: youth, media and modernity in the changing economy of northeast Brazil'. *Young*, 14(1): 9–31.

Wilk, R. (1995) 'Learning to be local in Belize: global system of common difference'. In D. Miller (ed.) *Worlds Apart*. New York: Routledge.

22

Television Culture and Media Socialization across Countries: Theoretical Issues and Methodological Approaches

Letizia Caronia and André H. Caron

INTRODUCTION

This chapter illustrates the relevance of a socio-cultural approach in children and media studies and the challenges of adopting such an approach when comparing different cultures in order to identify their commonalities. Traditionally, universalistic approaches aim to identify recurrent patterns of action and meaning and are often characterized by a programmatic bracketing of any culturally grounded variable. Investigating what is recurrent despite cultural differences, universalistic approaches mostly lead to large-scale quantitative surveys on who consumes what and where; for example, experimental studies on relationships between semiotic features of television content and developmental characteristics of the child's 'pure' cognitive mind. Conversely, when culture is seen as the main matrix of media experience and sense making, a relativistic perspective is often required. A strong conceptual link between culture and relativism may explain why, historically, cultural approaches have mostly led to national-specific studies, the results of which are often hard to compare.

The growing globalization of cultural products of information and communication technologies explains the contemporary resurgence in interest in international studies. Nonetheless, comparable research projects are still rare. While some studies basically describe similarities and differences between different countries (Groebel, 1999, 2001), others provide a cultural interpretation of comparative data. Even though national cultures frame children's media experience, this localization also incorporates patterns of globalization. Comparing children and adolescents of three very different countries (Denmark, France and Israel), Lemish *et al.* (1998) show the coexistence of different cultures in children's lives and the ways children link local cultural references and international media contents. Adopting both a quantitative and a qualitative approach, Livingstone and Bovill (2001) compared children's access, use and attitudes towards media across 12 European countries. A common cultural and historical background, as well as a certain degree of similarity in socio-economic structures and media access, guaranteed the comparability of media practices and educed national differences. The main hypothesis of these comparative studies is that local cultural references are not in an aut–aut relationship with respect to the trans-national common world made up of media and contents. On the contrary, children are able to move in and out of these worlds, to cross the boundaries of the 'local' and 'global' in their everyday life and create situated lines of consistency. Their results aside, the value of this new generation of studies lies primarily in their attempt to identify the multiple and connected levels of media experience, to take into account both its local and global nature, and to explore how these levels interact.

After presenting a brief history of the changing paradigms in children and media studies, the chapter will focus on two main contemporary theoretical frameworks in studies of children's media experience: the socio-cultural approach and the phenomenological perspective. A critical examination of the main methodological approaches in investigating children's sense of television is followed by a report on a pertinent cross-national study. The general aim of the study involving seven countries (Argentina, Canada, Chile, Greece, Italy, South Africa, and Uruguay), was to examine different cultures in order to identify trans-national recurrent patterns of thinking about and experiencing television (if any). Particularly, we analysed:

1 The ways children perceive television as a member of their social world.
2 How they experience television as a routine activity of their everyday life.

As we will see in the conclusions, the relevance of this study is both substantive and methodological. The empirical results show how and to what extent children's television culture is grounded in their everyday world of interactions and situated discourses while also functioning as a connecting world of shared references. The methodological design is an attempt to cope with the challenges of adopting a socio-cultural perspective in cross-cultural studies.

MEDIA SOCIALIZATION AND TELEVISION CULTURE: FROM A COGNITIVE TO A SOCIO-CULTURAL DEFINITION

At least until the end of the 1970s, one of the main focuses of scientific research on children and media was the influence of television on children's attitudes, social competences and moral development. This behaviouristic model of children's development oriented both public discourse and social research. Inside this historical epistemic framework, the hypothetical relationship between television violence and aggressive behaviour in children was central to social interests, public debate and empirical research. The impact of Olson's cognitive theory on the development of media-specific knowledge and skills (Olson, 1970; Olson and Bruner, 1974) produced a first major change in children's and media studies. Since this 'cognitive turn' an increasing amount of studies have focused on the influence of media on children's cognitive development and processes. Relying mostly on content, exposure and children's developmental levels, research in this field put forth a number of significant hypotheses on the effects of television and yielded an enormous amount of knowledge on the processes underlying the encounter between the child and the media (Collins *et al.*, 1978; Meringoff, 1980; Beagles-Roos and Gat, 1983; Collins, 1983; Meringoff *et al.*, 1983; Caronia and Gherardi, 1991)

One of the more relevant contributions of these studies is what can be considered a cognitive definition of 'television culture'. This approach defines television culture as a system of ideas, representations, values and knowledge about the world, derived mostly from exposure to television content. Beyond these content-oriented dimensions, television culture also consists of a set of media-specific skills and competences needed to decode and recode content (Noble, 1975; Fitch *et al.*, 1993; Chandler, 1997). This conceptualization of 'television culture' is extremely articulated and strongly underlines that the child is an active producer of meaning rather than a passive consumer of media products. Nevertheless, the notion of 'activity' is limited to cognitive processing involved in the understanding of television content, which is considered the primary or only input. Far from being passive, children are viewed as cognitive processors, and television culture is perceived as the output of information processing. The cognitive definition of children's television culture notably stresses the importance of the relationship between the child's developmental levels and the semiotic characteristics of television content.

In the 1980s, two major paradigmatic changes in social sciences radically transformed contemporary studies on children and media: the 'active audience' approach in media studies (Lull, 1980; Morley, 1986, 1989, 1992; Lindlof, 1987; Silverstone and Hirsch 1992; Moores, 1993; Barker, 1997) and the neo-Vygotskian turn in developmental theories and educational research (Cole, 1985; Wertsch, 1985; Lave and Wenger 1991; Wenger, 1998; Wells, 2000) The first defined and legitimized a new focus in media research: the multiple ways audiences create meanings and functions of media according to their specific cultural frames of reference, 'moral economies' (Silverstone *et al.*, 1992) and social worlds. The neo-Vygotskian turn in developmental theories strongly stressed the shaping role of language, social interaction and culture in mediating the child's experience of the world and even in the construction of their cognitive mind. According to this framework, the mind–television text relationship is seen as deeply rooted in and strongly connected to the social and cultural dimensions of children's developmental contexts.

According to a socio-cultural perspective, children's television culture is embedded in everyday activities and social practices, and results from the social interactions and discourse that surround and accompany the use of television itself. The encounter between the child and the media is not solely a cognitive process, but rather a social activity mediated by socially shared knowledge and culture. Empirical studies and theoretical claims in children and media research increasingly adopt this definition of television culture, and consistently underscore that it needs to be conceived beyond content, exposure and cognitive developmental levels (Buckingham, 1993; Barker, 1997). Indeed, television culture is a system of shared ideas, knowledge, folk theories about the medium, and ways to cope with it in everyday life, rooted in the media socialization process (Caronia, 2002).

The everyday language through which people talk to children about the media in the social situations of their developmental environment is one of the most powerful ways through which children acquire the meanings and functions attributed to the media by the specific culture of their community. In the family and at school, children are introduced to culturally situated ways of thinking of and coping with the media environment through the everyday verbal exchanges concerning the media and their uses. By talking to children about media, adults convey ways of speaking about media that are concurrently ways of thinking what media are, what they are not and what they should or should not be and why. When children give their younger siblings instructions on how to use a medium, when parents formulate rules for media consumption and give their children the rationales behind restrictions and permissions, when children hear decontextualized comments on and references to television at dinnertime, when they are involved in family interactions about who uses what and when, children are introduced to culture-specific ways of interpreting media (Caron and Caronia, 2000a,b).

To summarize, the notion of media socialization refers to the specific process through which children become acquainted with the media through their participation in a social world that has developed specific cultural conceptualizations of the media, their uses and contents.

INVESTIGATING CHILDREN'S SENSE OF TELEVISION: A PHENOMENOLOGICAL PERSPECTIVE

Contemporary research strongly advocates adopting the audience's perspective when investigating social uses and effects of the media. Recently, most researchers have recognized the importance of understanding the child's perspective when analysing the role of television in children's lives. The relevance of this issue is grounded in the phenomenological approach to social life and in its emphasis on the role of social actor in making sense of reality (Schutz, 1967). Rooted in what phenomenology calls the 'life-world', constructed through everyday social interactions, the frames through which children make sense of the media and of media-related activities are ultimately the aspect of television culture that makes them experience media as a culturally active audience.

The dramatic relevance of children's point of view in making sense of television is underlined not only by the phenomenological approach in media studies, but also by research on child development. Both perspectives assume, however, that 'television', 'television viewing' and 'television contents' are defined. What shapes children's social and cognitive development the most is 'meaning'; that is how children interpret television content and viewing, not only with respect to their cognitive developmental level, but also to their cultural frames of reference and everyday social interactions.

Once we accept the importance of accounting for the phenomenological relevance of television for children, the question arises of how to gain access to the children's point of view and to investigate children's cultural ways of integrating television into their life-world. According to the neo-Vygotskian perspective, language and communication are not only the social and cultural matrix of the frames for interpreting reality, they are also tools for expressing and (re)constructing these ways of representing reality. As Bruner (1986: 131) pointed out, language has a 'two-faced' nature 'being both a mode of communication and a medium for representing the world about which it is communicating'. This theoretical perspective on the main functions of language (constructing and expressing ways of thinking) states that children's ways of communicating are sources for understanding the relevant phenomenological dimensions of what they are communicating about. Children's verbal communication, iconic symbols and drawings about television may then be considered as reliable first-hand material through which access to their world of meaning and to their television culture can be gained.

The question then is how to gather these communicative occurrences in a way that allows for cross-cultural comparison and understanding.

MAKING SENSE OF TELEVISION: THE METHODOLOGICAL CHALLENGES OF COMPARATIVE RESEARCH

In the early 1980s, a major epistemological change strongly affected the methodological reflection in social research: the 'interpretive turn' in social sciences (Rabinow and Sullivan, 1979, 1987; Lincon and Guba, 1985). This stream definitively confirmed the value of naturalistic inquiries and qualitative research as means of gaining access to people's worlds of meaning. Legitimized by this paradigmatic change, many researchers turned to qualitative research and ethnographic inquiry in media studies (Lemish and Rice, 1986; Palmer, 1986; Lemish, 1987; Messaris, 1987; Frenette and Caron, 1995; Pasquier, 1996, 1999). Epistemologically oriented towards the actor's point of view and the ecological validity of data, qualitative research seems to be an appropriate way to take into account the natural context of everyday media practices and discourses, along with children's phenomenological perspective on their television world. Such studies also yielded an extraordinary amount of 'thick descriptions' (Geertz, 1973) of single idiosyncratic worlds.

As always in social research, the strength of a methodological approach also sets its limits. When a research paradigm dictates a local understanding of local meanings and practices, it is difficult to look beyond the juxtaposition of collected papers reporting single idiosyncratic worlds. How can these different universes disclosed by ethnographies and naturalistic inquiries be compared? How does one search for commonalities and differences in the ways in which children belonging to different communities make sense of television? Moreover, how can this be done in a way that guarantees the ecological validity of data and their cross-cultural comparability? Although the phenomenological relevance of television in children's lives has been acknowledged, this issue remains underexplored on a comparative international level, partly owing to the methodological challenges of cross-cultural analysis.

The next sections present data from our cross-national study and discuss the methodological challenges of collecting comparable and ecologically valid data as a means of gaining access to these worlds of meaning.

GATHERING ECOLOGICALLY VALID DATA: THEORETICAL CONSIDERATIONS AND THE METHODOLOGICAL DESIGN OF THE STUDY

Most contemporary cross-cultural studies rely on surveys for quantitative analysis and on in-depth interviews for qualitative analysis of children's practices and points of view. The construction of representative samples and the use of these methodological tools maximize data reliability, internal validity and comparability. Discursive research tools, such as questionnaires and open-ended interviews, do not produce 'performance-like' behaviours as in experimental laboratory studies. Nevertheless, the ecological validity of the discourse gathered is problematic. Responding to standardized items and interacting with a professional interviewer are specific linguistic events strictly related to the research interaction itself and to the context in which they occur (Briggs, 1986; Mishler, 1986; Kvale, 1996; Caronia, 1997).

This issue is even more relevant when the objective is to gain access to children's worlds of meaning. Children are very sensitive to the social context and the social participation structure of the communicative event in which they are involved (Fine and Sandstrom, 1988; Buckingham, 1991). Most researchers that have done interviews with children have sensed that they recorded ad hoc constructed discourse and know quite well how children shape their answers according to the social features of the ongoing interaction. The context-dependent nature of children's discourse is unavoidable, as it is inherent in the social and interactive matrix of their ways of acting, talking and thinking. From a methodological point of view, the core issue is not how to eliminate this context-dependent dimension to gain a supposed unbiased discourse, but rather which context and verbal scaffolding create which discourse and how do they shape it.

The more the context and devices of the research are consistent with children's life-world, routines, media uses and related communication practices, the more the data gathered may be considered valid from an ecological standpoint. As stated above, these theoretical considerations generally lead to ethnographies. In those cases the context of the research coincides mostly with people's everyday life contexts and the intimate relationship between participants and researcher corresponds somewhat to ordinary communicative events. Even though these naturalistic enquiries gather ecologically valid data, they rarely provide comparable data and do not allow for cross-cultural comparison.

In our study we chose to adopt a methodological design that would maximize both the ecological validity and the comparability of our data. Inspired by a pilot project led by an Italian research team,[1] we adopted a qualitative approach and an original non-intrusive methodology: we used television and a television-specific genre, the Public Service Announcement (PSA), to elicit communication to and about the media. A television PSA spot entitled 'TV, this is how I'd like you to be...' was professionally produced and broadcast in Italy in 2000 on the initiative and on behalf of an Italian broadcaster.[2] The audio track of the PSA directly addressed children under 13 as the intended audience and basically gave them two semantic scaffoldings. It prompted them to think about 'their' TV and to imagine how it could be. It also provided pragmatic scaffolding by inviting children to communicate these ideas directly to the television through letters, drawings, e-mail or however they wished. The visuals consisted of an animated drawing of a stylized television whose features changed throughout the audio track.

The enormous success of this initiative in terms of children's responses warranted the transformation of this local media project into a major international study involving seven countries: Argentina, Canada, Chile, Greece, Italy, South Africa and Uruguay.[3] For cross-cultural purposes, the visuals remained invariant while the Italian audio was adapted and translated into the main languages spoken in the other countries: English, French, Spanish and Greek. The translation faithfully reproduced the semantic and pragmatic levels of the PSA. To ensure both the ecology of reception and broadcasting, each country determined the times of day and how many times a day the PSA was to be broadcast. On average, the 30-second PSA ran daily over a 2-month period.

CHILDREN'S REPLIES

More than 8000 responses were collected, including letters, drawings and e-mails. Nonetheless, these entries do not constitute a representative sample of children's opinions in any given country. The PSA addressed the potential universe of the under-13 audience and called for auto-selection by the respondents. This database thus represents an extraordinarily rich corpus of naturally occurring communications. 'Naturally' implies that messages were elicited in a way and in contexts that were both consistent with children's everyday life and media practices. For the most part, children sent letters that included a drawing. A majority of the entries came from girls, and the average age of children replying to the PSA was 10 years old.[4]

The analysis of children's replies: theoretical considerations and methodological devices

First, children's texts were segmented in units of analysis, defined as 'a statement conveying a single information'. It may be a single word or a graphic trait as well as a longer statement or a more detailed drawing. A statement such as 'you are my best friend' was considered one unit of analysis equivalent to a word such as 'PRETTY!' written in capital letters somewhere at the bottom of a drawing. A sentence could include more than one unit of analysis. For instance, a sentence such as 'I always watch you/with my parents/and I feel so fine' was coded as three units of analysis. The units of analysis were coded according to a grid analysis, which was jointly constructed by the national teams and based on a double theoretical approach.

According to a neo-Vygotskian theoretical framework, children's ways of speaking, acting and thinking are always and inevitably constructed in and through contingent social interactions and local semiotic mediations. This approach to situated ordinary action has relevant consequences on the epistemology of (at least) qualitative research: it strongly suggests connecting the communicative practices of the research process to the communicative occurrences that constitute the research products. Following these assumptions, we avoided subscribing to the commonsense fallacy of searching for something as children's 'original', 'spontaneous' or 'unbiased' words and thoughts about television. The replies to a text running on the domestic small screen needed to be conceived as situated constructions strongly related to the PSA-specific pragmatic and semantic scaffolding. In order to reflect such an assumption on our coding scheme, we took into account the communicative dimensions of the PSA. On the basis of its semantic and pragmatic scaffolding, we identified two main semantic areas of meaning and one pragmatic area:

1 Children's representation of television 'as it is'.
2 Children's representation of how television should be.
3 Pragmatic and interpersonal cues.

The second theoretical framework referred to is 'grounded theory' (Glaser and Strauss, 1967). Basically, this approach argues for a bottom-up perspective in creating not only the research hypothesis, but also the interpretive analytical categories. Researchers interested in standardizing results for comparison often apply a set of predefined 'etic'[5] categories on data. Commonalities are seldom the results of such a top-down work of selecting and forcing data into previously defined researcher-oriented categories. For researchers interested in how people interpret and make sense of their life-world, their analytical categories should be 'emic'; that is, oriented toward the participant's point of view. However, what may sound obvious in ethnographies is almost a challenge in cross-cultural studies. Adopting such a framework, we deliberately tried to create a shared interpretive schema oriented to children's own words and ways of communicating to and about television.

Of course data-driven categories are never pure; the researchers' inductive or grounded approach is invariably a theoretically oriented activity. The final interpretive scheme results from a back-and-forth process where the researchers' theoretical frameworks orient their interpretation of ecological data and data reorient his or her theoretical frames of references. A previous exploratory examination of 10% of randomly selected entries from all countries led us jointly to identify a set of clusters of meaning (macro and micro categories) for each of the three main areas. In addition, we defined the indicators for determining what counted as a token for each category of the grid.

After some pre-tests to gain an intersubjective agreement on codes, each national research team selected a representative sample of 20% or more of all the entries of their country, which they analysed according to the grid for a quantitative content analysis. Each country also selected a sub-corpus of paradigmatic examples, for each cluster of meaning, for qualitative in-depth textual analysis.

The code scheme for drawings

Consistent with the pragmatic scaffolding of the PSA and for the purpose of our study, we considered drawings as acts of meaning; that is, they were ways to express something about and to the television. To determine the messages children conveyed through pictures and icons, we analyse drawings from a communicational point of view. Based on our previous exploratory analysis of a sample of iconic texts, we defined 12 categories that cover the range of meaningful dimensions encoded in children's drawings:

- positive representation;
- negative representation;

- iconographic and typographic traits referring to broadcasters;
- iconographic and typographic traits referring to programmes;
- logos of international products;
- television as a multimedia device;
- television as an object of design;
- personification;
- everyday settings;
- cultural symbols;
- graphical quotations of PSA;
- other.

We jointly defined a range of graphic indicators for each category of meaning and coded it as present or absent in each drawing.

CROSS-CULTURAL RECURRENT PATTERNS OF MAKING SENSE OF TELEVISION

Although we analysed our data in approximately 60 categories, for the purposes of this chapter we will focus on the five most significant cross-cultural recurrent patterns of meaning:

- the positive representation of the media;
- the mythical and affective stances toward television;
- critical thinking and negative evaluation of the media;
- media awareness and competences;
- commonsense ideas and social discourse in children's interpretive repertoire.

By analysing commonalities in children's way of thinking of television, we will elucidate the main dimensions of the interpretive repertoire through which children make sense of this medium and show how and to what extent contemporary children may be considered members of a community of viewers sharing a common culture.

A positive representation of television: drawings and letters

One of our most relevant findings is that children in all the countries involved have a basic positive representation of television. The PSA's main message was:

> Hey! You're my TV, you know, you're pretty cool, but sometimes I'd like you to be different. If I could re-invent you, I would make you... I'd make you....

Even if the message offered a semantic scaffolding focused on positive traits, it allowed alternatives and encouraged children to adopt other stances, possibly critical. Given this interactive preface, children mostly replied with positive portrayals of television.

The most impressive evidence of children's positive representations comes from their drawings. Drawings containing one or more cues indicating a positive representation of television are significantly more frequent than drawings also or exclusively containing icons depicting a negative perception of television (Table 22.1).

Some examples of how children visually represented TV in a positive way, but also how, in a few cases, negative icons are used to represent television, are shown in Figure 22.1.

With a few and sometimes graphically sophisticated exceptions, children's pictorial narratives in all the countries exhibit their strong personal commitment to television and the extent to which they integrate this medium as a 'good' part of their world. This pattern is confirmed by data obtained from the analysis of letters and written messages (Table 22.2), although here the children's representations of television appear to be more

Table 22.1 Drawings: positive versus negative representations[a]

Representation	Argentina	Canada	Chile	Greece	Italy	Uruguay	South Africa
Positive (%)	88	92	91	72	94	96	30
Negative (%)	9	6	3	0	10	0	4

[a] Percentages indicate drawings containing at least one indicator for the category of meaning. Percentages are not mutually exclusive: one drawing may contain indicators of both or neither category of meaning.

Figure 1: Positive representation, South Africa

Figure 1: Positive representation, Greece

Figure 2: Negative representation, Argentina

Figure 4: Positive representation, Canada

Figure 5: Positive *and* negative iconic traits, Argentina

Figure 6: Positive *and* negative iconic traits, Italy

Figure 22.1 Drawings from the various countries

Table 22.2 Letters and written messages: positive versus negative references[a]

Reference	Argentina $N = 725$	Canada $N = 56$	Chile $N = 1087$	Greece $N = 252$	Italy $N = 516$	Uruguay $N = 87$	South Africa $N = 73$
Positive (%)	56	63	52	66	37	46	79
Negative (%)	39	21	40	19	33	44	16
Neutral and other (%)	5	16	8	15	30	10	5
Total (%)	100	100	100	100	100	100	100

[a] Percentages are calculated on the basis of total units of meaning referring to the semantic area no. 1

critical: their basic positive representation of television is tempered, in some instances, by critical views. Indeed, verbal accounts of television appear to be more nuanced than pictorial representations. By matching positive references with negative ones, adding critical stances to their basic positive view of television in their life, children exhibit a complex and internally articulated repertoire of ways of thinking about this medium. Data concerning the *kind* of references used by children when describing television, as they see it, provide a general insight into their perception of the medium.

Some examples of positive, negative or neutral references are as follows: 'you're good', 'super cool', 'I like your cartoons', 'I always watch you with my parents and *I feel so fine*' (positive); 'you're violent', 'nasty', 'ugly', 'you frighten me', 'you make me have nightmares in the night' (negative); 'you're big and square', 'you have buttons', 'you are in my bedroom', 'I watch you with my sister', 'I watch you always after school' (neutral).

Even if the quantitative divide between positive and negative references differs for each country (smaller for Italy and Uruguay, bigger for the other countries), positive references to television are always more frequent than negative ones. Nonetheless, this quantitative result provides only a general understanding of the significance of children's positive frames of thinking about television. To understand the phenomenological relevance of television better, we must perform a more qualitative analysis and take into account *how* children portray television in a positive way.

Good, powerful and faithful: mythical and affective stances toward television

Children's positive references to television are often sophisticated rhetorical constructions. Through 'personification', children portray television as a social actor that interacts positively with them and with others. At this level, children integrate television in their universe. They depict it as a member of their social world, strongly defined by positive characteristics and imbued with positive values. To understand the nature of children's positive representation of television better, we refer to data based on micro-categories used in the analysis of letters and written messages, in particular mythical references and social and affective references.

When children describe television as 'it is', and more significantly when they imagine how they would like television to be, they often move toward an unrealistic register that reveals the nature of their ties with the media. These links appear to be social, affective and strongly characterized by a mythical and magical representation of the media. Mythical representation of television refers to one of the most prominent and cross-cultural recurrent positive ways children think about television. Television is perceived as or wished to be a hero.[6] Here are a few prototypical examples:

> Television, I dream about the day when I switch you on and I see a country where everybody has water and where every child goes to school and not to work (Argentina, girl, age 12).

> Television, you who can make everything, please stop the war in the world and make all children be happy (Italy, boy, age 7).

> I wish you were magic (Canada, girl, age 8).

> Television you're at home and belongs to the family and I'm sure you can make us happy (Argentina, girl, age 9).

Personified as a mythical hero, television becomes a peace maker, a *deus ex machina* able to resolve famine and local dramatic social problems, a magical tool that allows people to attain their goal, someone children can trust to help humanity. This way of thinking about television is consistent with one of the children's cognitive approaches to reality: mythical and magical thought. Using the 'possible worlds' logic, children construct a universe where conditions of reality are different and they legitimate an unrealistic perception of people and things that inhabit their environment. Absorbed in and transformed by this logic, the medium becomes an omnipotent magical actor endowed with endless possibilities. As in the last example, the process of personifying television and providing it with power may rid it of mythical traits in favour of more 'realistic' ones. Television is then perceived as a family member, perhaps a less mythical actor, but still able to produce a warm and happy daily environment. Affective representation of television refers to this second cross-cultural recurrent positive way of thinking about television.

> I wish you were my great confidant, so I could reveal to you my private secrets, joys and sorrows, and you will not judge me and I could trust you (Canada, girl, age 8).

> You are my favorite teacher; you make me know so much and you never, never hurt me (Italy, girl, age 10).

> I'm writing to you as friend since I share a lot of moments with you. Sometimes you become indispensable, filling the emptiness there is at home since I don't have a sister and my mother is absent and I have to accept this because she needs to go out to work (Argentina, girl, age 13).

> Dear Television, I'd like you to be like flowers so I could smell your fragrance. I'd like you to sing to me in the morning so I could wake up in peace. I'd like you to have skin so I could caress you all day long (Chile, girl, age 10).

Television is perceived as an actor playing the role of the confidant or the caregiver, a good, available teacher or as the 'imaginary friend' when the child is alone. In short, television is ascribed affective and social traits, and thus becomes a personified member of the child's social world. Besides the quantitative frequency of such units of significance, these data are very significant from a qualitative standpoint. Notably, they illustrate how children represent television and some significant dimensions of the interpretive repertoire through which they make sense of this medium. With few exceptions, children view television as an emotionally and socially significant member of their social world. These data are consistent with the results of the qualitative analysis of the pragmatic level of children's texts[7] (area of meaning no. 3).

The cues of critical thinking: negative representations of television

As mentioned above, children's discourse related to television sometimes contains critical remarks. Following the semantic scaffolding of the PSA, and picking up on the adversative marker 'but', in some cases children add a negative dimension to an initially positive description of television. A typical example of such a construction is: 'I love you, I always watch the cartoons, they are my favorite programs, but sometimes you're violent, sad and not educational at all (Italy, boy, age 10). Other interesting instances of negative references were also noted in the way children imagine 'how they would like television to be' (average one in three of the evaluative references in this semantic area were negative). For example, they ask television to have less violence or none at all, or for television to have less bad news or programmes that frighten them (Figure 22.2).

Even if these negative stances are quantitatively less frequent than the positive views, they are nonetheless very significant from a qualitative standpoint. They show that children's representation of television is a complex and articulated construction consistent with the internal complexity and multifaceted nature of this medium. Without falling into a stereotyped one-dimensional vision of television, children's way of thinking and coping with this medium is profoundly dialectical and critical. Children systematically activate a complex frame of reference and articulate what they perceive as positive (even mythical) aspects and values of television, together with some negative judgments. While more present in some countries (Argentina, Chile, Italy and Uruguay) and less so in others (South Africa had the fewest negative references), the expression of

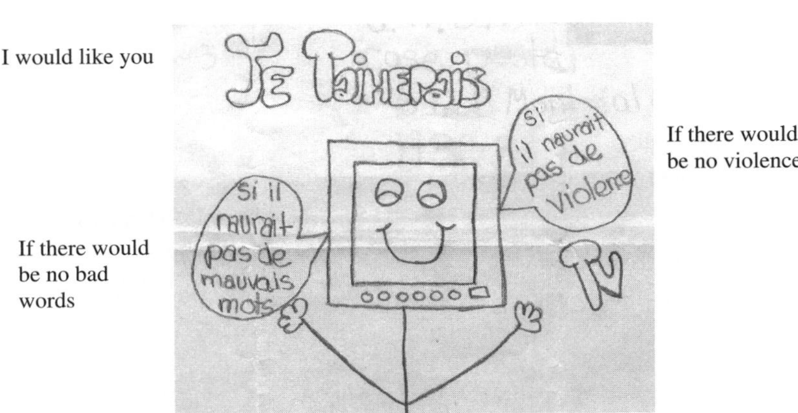

Figure 22.2 Positive iconic representation *and* written critical stances

a critical attitude is cross-cultural recurrent. This suggests that, nowadays, many children appear to grow up as *competent viewers* of television and as critical analysts of its characteristics and functioning.

In the next two sections we will investigate this cross-cultural recurrent pattern in greater detail, along with the cultural matrix of children's sense of television.

Media-specific culture and competence: children as competent viewers

In replying to the PSA, children showed a considerable and astonishing amount of knowledge about the specific culture and internal organization of the television industry. Generally, their descriptions, evaluations (appreciation and critical remarks), requests and other linguistic actions are rooted in and sustained by a specific knowledge of the media. Notions about television genres, their features and intended viewers, programming grids, audience constraints, economic matters concerning advertising and the competition between broadcasters are all present in children's discourses. Radically embedded in a pre-existing, shared web of cultural discourse about television, this set of knowledge is used in various ways by children to reflect, discuss and argue about the medium.

In our quantitative content analysis, we defined a specific macro-category to identify and measure this aspect of children's discourse: *Industry and Media Familiarity*. This macro-category was divided into three subcategories ('References to broadcasters', 'References to hours and programming grid', and 'Media awareness and competence') defining the nature and degree of children's knowledge of these areas.

Aside from the quantitative frequency of this pattern of meaning (the average of units coded totalled 22% for 'Industry and media familiarity' in six of the seven countries involved[8]), children's discourse about television reveals a true richness when submitted to a qualitative textual analysis. This more qualitative approach enables us to appreciate the level of sophistication of their knowledge and reasoning about the media, and their understanding of the logics underlying broadcasting and programme scheduling. Here are some paradigmatic examples of children's media awareness and competence.

> I'd like you to have no violence. *I know it is hard for you to take it out*, but... (Canada, boy, age 9).

> Dear TV,
> (...) May I ask you something? I wish *there were less advertising, but I Know, they are necessary unless there is no money for broadcasting the programs* I love, so please could you at least put them just in the night or *in Prime time*?(...) (Italy, girl, age 9).

With the exception of South Africa,[9] we found significant examples of this pattern of meaning and a relatively unexpected high degree of media competency in all the other countries. European and North and South American children seem to be able to make well thought-out judgements about television that they can support with arguments. At least through their written texts on television, many children appear to be sophisticated connoisseurs, skilled and empowered viewers of television. Their television culture entails more than knowing content and programmes; it also implies possessing media-specific competences and frames for critical reasoning. If children share this medium and its contents on a global level, then they also seem to share sophisticated ways of thinking about it.[10] As we will see, this cognitive aspect of children's television culture is strongly connected with the social and cultural dimensions of their everyday life.

Children as cultural viewers: the echoes of social discourse in children's words

If the occurrence of a critical form of reasoning about television indicates that, nowadays, children possess media competence and awareness, the negative statements (i.e. 'there is too much violence') educe another relevant trans-national recurrent phenomenon.

Children are not only competent viewers, they are also cultural viewers. Their discourse on television (especially the negative comments) is strongly related to the larger social discourse and commonsense frames of thinking on what television should or should not be, what it does and should not do to children. To get a better grasp of the social and cultural matrix of children's ways of thinking, we analysed data through two other macro-categories: 'References to television influence' and 'Cultural and social references'. The first category indicates what children perceived as effects of television, while the second encompasses items where children referred to the common encyclopaedic culture or used pieces of social discourse, commonsense ideas and stereotyped formulas of talking about television. The score for these categories was quite high (approximately 14% on all the coded units). The frequency analysis of these clusters of meaning shows that, aside from significant differences among the countries, the social and cultural matrix of children's discourses on television is clearly a recurrent cross-cultural pattern.

However, it is through a detailed qualitative textual analysis that we can appreciate and better understand how children construct their ways of thinking about television building on a background of commonsense discourse and everyday talk. Below we will analyse a few prototypical examples chosen from among those that represent how and to what extent children's discourse on television is rooted in and dependent on the larger discursive community to which they belong. In particular, we will focus on the use of reported speech, the most significant indicator of this widespread phenomenon.

Example 1

Dear 'Tv as I'd like you to be',
I'm an eleven-year-old girl [...] I spend hours and hours viewing television, I'm in a daze I can't move away, mum always scolds me because of that, and *she'd rather I dedicated one hour to reading a book which is much more educational*. She scolds me not so much because I spend so many hours watching television, but because instead of watching documentaries I watch cartoons. *Some of them may be educational* like Lady Oscar, or that one of gnomes and the environment, or those like Heidi. Sometimes you broadcast cartoons made in the '70s, with faded images and a soundtrack out of tune. You make beautiful cartoons and a lot of beautiful program things but sometimes you show things from 20 years ago [...] (Italy, girl, age 11).

Example 2

My name is Luca and I'm almost ten years old, I live in a very nice little town in the region of Varese. *I'm not a 'television dependent', as you the adults say*, but that's true I like to watch it, mostly funny films and cartoons. I wish you could show some cartoons just before dinnertime, like you made once with Game Boat. But cartoons without all that violence, there is enough of it in the News that mum and dad watch. I think that we, the children, we have the right to relax and have some moments of fun after school.
And if I see violent cartoons, *my mother will turn it off otherwise I will have nightmares in the night*. The same is for the films, even though sometimes they let me view them. You know, what's fun? Sometimes broadcasters make mistakes they too, sometimes there is the green marker, but they have made a mistake because there are some frightening scenes [...] Please, don't let me see sufferings, hospitals, killings and wars. At least in that little hour dedicated to children. Just let us imagine a little, as in fairy tales, just to do as if - at least in this little hour - the true world where we live was not as it is. Goodbye to all of you (Italy, boy, age 10).

Example 3

Dear TV,
I'm a ten year, three months and six day old girl. I write to you because you are changing but you are not becoming better but worse: *you broadcast too much violent films, and pornographic, too much advertising, too much scandalous programs. Dear TV, you are becoming a 'dark face', that is you are nasty, pornographic and scandalous. I beg you to moderate your language in the future, so that my children and those of everybody else may live in a better and more educational society and language.* Now I wish to talk to you about another thing: the stupid films. *This is my mummy's request that is to make films that are educational, serious and interesting.* One last thing concerning cartoons: *could you make cartoons with a happy ending, educational and not pornographic*? Please, remember, these are only requests and they are not obligatory (Italy, girl, age 10).

The examples show how children's discourse on television is radically polyphonic. Talking about television, children use various forms of reported speech: from the introduction of a new character and his point of view (example 1) to the free indirect quotation of a character whose words become the child's (see example 2); from the introduction of an adult's statement and the child's taking a distance from it (example 2) to the case where children use lexical occurrences belonging to an adults' linguistic register and formula based on stereotypes or conversational routines (see examples 1 and 3). Using different voices in constructing their own discourse on television, children echo adults' discourse and ways of speaking about television. If we assume that children became members of a community of ideas and practices to a large extent through the use of language, then it is clear that, by using somebody else's words, children adopt and actively use the cultural dimensions to interpret the world, reflected in the ways people speak about it. By repeating, formulating or quoting adults' discourse in various ways, children exhibit that they are part of a social world inhabited by people that talk to children about television. Second, they show how this social world has produced culture-specific perspectives on television, its content and its uses. Third, they demonstrate how they see themselves with respect to this social environment, its cultural beliefs and folk theories about the media. In short, they manifest their belonging to a community of discourse.

Children's use of adult words and ways of speaking about television does not necessarily mean that they are *passively* repeating and assuming somebody else's words and points of view, nor that they are strategically attempting to meet adults' expectations. As literature in developmental pragmatics has demonstrated, children's appropriation and use of other people's words and statements is one of the main ways through which children learn to talk and think in a culturally appropriated manner. Far from being a bias in children's responses, adult rhetoric in children's discourse strongly indicates that commonsense and everyday talk nurtures children's views of television, offers them cultural frames, and structures the repertoire of interpretive resources through which children manage the media in their everyday life. As cultural bricks, these ready-made pieces of discourse and socially shared interpretations are used to construct a personal point of view and individual interpretations.

Even though what counted as 'reported speech' or 'commonsense ideas' varies across the countries involved in the study, we found interesting similarities. The desire for a 'more educational television', for a 'television without violence', the idea of a television having some (generally negative) direct effects on children were the items most often coded by each national research team as 'commonsense references'. Through children's words echoing adults' discourse, we can reconstruct the features of a recurrent 'folk model' of thinking about television whose core is primarily a defensive, unidirectional causal model of the role of television in children's lives. This cross-cultural set of commonsense ideas and lay theories about television is one of the two phenomena that emerged from the analysis of reported speech in children's discourse. The second phenomenon consists of a developmental process. Across the countries studied, children's ways of thinking and speaking about television appear to be deeply rooted in everyday knowledge and discourse. These representations are also strongly linked to the everyday verbal interactions with the people that are relevant members of children's social world. The recurrence of references to 'Everyday setting', and the representation of television viewing as a situated activity embedded in the domestic routines are also consistent with these data.

TELEVISION AS A CONNECTING CULTURE: SOME CONCLUSIONS

Our study putatively supports (at a cross-cultural level) contemporary theoretical claims about the socio-cultural nature of children's television culture. Children's interpretations, perceptions and thoughts about television appear to be deeply rooted in the larger discursive culture and the media socialization practices in which children participate (Buckingham, 1993; Caronia, 2002). Television culture consists of much more than shared images and words, behavioural models and moral values provided by television texts and processed by a cognitive mind. At the core of television culture are the cultural frames, the meanings and the sense of 'watching television' that children learn while participating in their social world. Everyday conversations and discourse about television, along with verbal exchanges around the television set, condition the children's interpretation of television content and of the media itself. As we have seen, individual interpretations and collective interpretations are always interconnected and reciprocally constructed. Trying to distinguish what is individual and what is social, what depends on television, on children's cognitive development or on socially shared discourse, is then irrelevant if not misleading (Buckingham, 1993). Our research demonstrates that the shaping role of everyday language, interaction and culture is a trans-national recurrent phenomenon and that making sense of television is part of the larger media socialization process and a culturally mediated experience.

Although we might have expected that the local matrix of children's views on television would lead to the construction of different, non-sharable universes of meaning, this did not appear to be the case. While television culture is invariably shaped by local ways of interpreting the media, children all over the world appear to share a set of common contents, programmes, characters and stories. The study found abundant cross-cultural references to the same television programmes, series and characters. We also noted similar opinions and preferences for some television contents and a widespread use of symbols, icons and logos belonging to what is commonly defined the 'global market of cultural products'. These findings were not surprising given that most mass communication media, such as television, effectively present their audience with at least a subset of common products. In contrast, the more significant commonalities in children's television culture concern the ways children perceive and make sense of the media. Examining different 'television cultures' in order to identify their commonalities, we found empirical evidence that contemporary young viewers share some patterns of *thinking about television,* a significant amount of media-specific knowledge and competences and some common ways of perceiving the medium as a member of their social world. Children perceived television as a lively and friendly presence in their world, as an activity embedded in their everyday routines and as a practice related to their relationships with parents and peers. Sometimes eliciting criticism, television also putatively fulfils similar symbolic functions and roles for children in different countries.

This leads us to consider the hypothesis that this common world of shared meanings, practices and media-specific competences constitutes the core of a specific genre of community: *the community of viewers.* Of course, the boundaries of such a community are not necessarily defined by face-to-face interactions. Rather, they are defined by similar actions, social practices and meanings that are, or may become, common symbolic resources, sharable experiences and a possible universe of common references for children belonging to different communities.

Television culture across countries: directions for future research

Researchers experienced in cross-cultural studies acknowledge that the more they look for comparable data the more their methodological tools need to be consistent across different fields. Methodological consistency implies controllable and controlled eliciting tools that should attain the highest possible level of standardization. Always difficult to attain, a high level of standardization is nevertheless attainable in *product-oriented* research. Issues such as 'how many TV sets are in the household', 'what do children watch on television, at which time of the day, how many hours per week, etc.' may be easily explored through answers elicited by standardized questions. In *process-oriented* research, which issues concern people's making sense and in the social–interpersonal nature of the sense-making process, the 'answers' to researcher's questions need to be found more in people's everyday actions and practices than in the ad hoc (re)constructed world of interviews. Obviously, people's after-the-fact verbal accounts of their own practices are also meaningful discursive data, and may generate insights into the phenomena. Nevertheless, they should be considered nothing more (and nothing less) then what they are: artificially elicited reconstructions for the purposes at hand. Answers to predefined questions about media practices are by-products of a specific sense-(re)making activity (answering the items of a questionnaire) that occurs in a particular social event (participation in a research interview). These discourses do not belong to the realm of ordinary everyday actions, practices and discourses where the original game unfolds. In cross-cultural studies, the more the methodological tools satisfy the conditions of reliability, the less likely they are to grasp naturally occurring phenomena and processes. The more they are constructed ad hoc and controlled for internal validity, the less likely they are to be consistent with people's everyday culture and ordinary communicative events. Between this methodological Scylla and Charybdis, researchers seem to have to make a choice: either they strive for comparability, reliability and inner validity, or they seek ecological validity (Cicourel, 1964, 1982).

Is there a way to overcome this double bind? Is it possible to have access to everyday situated action and ordinary communicative practices in an ecological way and obtain comparable data? In our study we entered children's worlds through a media practice that was part of children's everyday life (an animated PSA running on a daily basis) and we used the media to freely elicit communicative practices that were part of the children's specific culture (writing and sending drawings to television). In so doing we by-passed the researcher's presence bias and the issues related to the sense remaking process occurring during field interviews. As we stated above, we are not asserting that the discourses we gathered were context-free occurrences of behaviour. We rather support the idea that what most conditions the ecological validity of data is *the kind* of context the research creates or identifies as relevant. The counter-example of South Africa dramatically sheds light on this issue. It showed by contrast how and to what extent watching television at home, writing and sending letters to this social interlocutor were common practices integrated in at least European, North and South American children's everyday life. Even if not necessarily occurring on a daily regular basis, they were emic performances; that is, they were meaningful actions from the standpoint of children's specific culture. Our study supports the methodological advice that, behind the issue of the intersubjective agreement among researchers on how to gather and interpret data, the crucial point of a comparative research on children's media practices and development is the people's local interpretation and perception of the research tools. That is, the ecology of the research itself.

Ecological data are never clean data. Because they belong to the realm of ordinary situated action, they share all the characteristics of naturally occurring social phenomena: fuzziness, incompleteness, implicitness and indexicality. Some occurrences in our corpus of written texts were unreadable, some authors did not declare their age, some texts were clearly created by more then one child (friends, siblings, etc.), some were signed by a parent and the child, others came from school and were a joint class project. We have little idea why and how that happened, but it was extremely interesting that it happened. Who saw the PSA and transformed it into a focus for joint peer activity or into a parent–child shared practice? Who spoke about it in the classroom and transformed it into a classroom activity? A pupil? The teacher? Of course it is always possible to separate this kind of data from the main corpus, to consider them as missing cases or biased data and not to analyse them subsequently.

However, these 'dirty data' are more than missing cases or biased and unreliable data. They are meaningful communicative events deeply rooted in local interpretations, local meaning-making processes, situated activities and contingent social interactions. Once considered as pieces of a living world, these data allow the researcher to formulate new unexpected grounded hypotheses. Some of our 'dirty data' were actually empirical evidence that television is a mediator in a peer relationship that generates joint action and jointly constructed discourse. Beyond children's and parents' verbal reports on television as a shared activity, the data showed that this shared activity in action is a naturally occurring phenomenon. Texts coming from the classroom showed that television culture indeed connects home and school and works as a bridge linking school-oriented culture and literacy with domestic cultures and leisure. Disregarding any worries about their quantitative representativeness, these naturally occurring cross-cultural phenomena are qualitatively representative of what actually occurs in the everyday life of children of different countries. They single out types of events and types of ordinary ways in which television culture nurtures and is nurtured by the everyday world of shared practices and interpersonal relationships. Simply put, ecological data are evidence of what meaning-oriented comparative research looks for: naturally occurring cultural ways of living with media.

NOTES

1 The pilot research was directed by Dr Piero Bertolini (Department of Education, University of Bologna, Italy).

2 The original PSA was produced and broadcast by the Italian broadcaster Mediaset.

3 Research teams were directed by: Italy – Dr Piero Bertolini, Dr Letizia Caronia and Dr Lucia Balduzzi (University of Bologna, Italy); Greece – Dr Tessa-Anastasia Doulkeri (Aristotle University of Thessaloniki) and Dr Chryssa Païdoussi (Hellenic Audiovisual Institute); South Africa – Firdoze Bulbulia and Nadia Bulbulia (Children and Broadcasting Foundation); South America (Argentina, Chile and Uruguay) – Dr Tatiana Merlo Flores (University of Buenos Aires, Argentina); Canada – Dr André H. Caron (University of Montreal). Dr Caron directed the international project and coordinated the comparative statistical analysis. Dr Caronia was responsible for the content analysis and coordinated the qualitative approach of the study. Dr Flores directed and coordinated the South American team. We wish to thank all our colleagues who participated in this study and made this international comparative analysis of children's ways of thinking about television possible, and we also express our gratitude to the European Children's Television Centre, UNICEF, MEDIASET, Instituto de Investigacion en Medios, HISTORICA Foundation and all the participating television stations in each country for their valuable support.

4 In the cross-national research the PSA addressed 7- to 12-year-old children. However, we also gathered replies from both younger and older children. Children's age-related competencies clearly affected the formal features of their written texts and drawings (syntax, orthography, graphic quality); also, the complexity of their messages increased with age.

5 The distinction between 'etic and emic' was introduced by the linguistic anthropologist Kenneth Pike (1954) as an analogy with linguistic distinction between phonetic and phonemic analysis. An etic perspective or category relies upon and refers to the researcher's frames of relevance. Extrinsic with respect to the informant's point of view, etic dimensions make meaningful distinctions *for* the analyst. Emic categories are intrinsic cultural distinctions that are meaningful for the informants themselves. Adopting an emic analytical perspective thus implies using categories that are oriented on and matched upon those used by people to account and interpret their own practices.

6 'Hero' refers to the corresponding narratological category intended to grasp the narrative role attributed to a character by providing him with powers to resolve incidents, disruptions and problematic situations.

7 The kinds of greeting, opening, closing and postscriptum reveal how much children care for television and how strong their attachment can be to this member of their social world. For similar results, see Pasquier (1996, 1999).

8 In South Africa we do not find any items clearly referring to this cluster of meanings. Even if this chapter does not interpret differences among countries, we wish to mention at least one factor that could explain this difference. As stated above, the PSA solicited *written* communication. In all the countries, children expressed detailed and nuanced descriptions, accurate accounts and reflective thinking about television much more through their written messages than through their drawings. In a mainly oral culture like South Africa, these literate practices appeared to be inconsistent with children's everyday ways

of communicating. This context-specific relation to literacy may explain why, in South Africa, we gathered fewer written texts than drawings and, consequently, fewer instances of critical reasoning. The lack of specific cues referring to *media competence and awareness* in South Africa thus needs to be interpreted according to a complex perspective that integrates multiple factors, including the local perception of the scaffolding offered by the PSA.

9 See note 8.

10 These data suggest that media awareness initiatives might have contributed to the development of this type of competence; they thus remain appropriate.

REFERENCES

Barker, C. (1997) *Global Television: An Introduction.* Oxford: Blackwell.

Beagles-Roos, J. and Gat, J. (1983) 'Specific impact of radio and television on children's story comprehension'. *Journal of Educational Psychology,* 75(1): 128–137.

Briggs, C. (1986) *Learning How to Ask. A Sociolinguistic Appraisal of the Role of Interview in Social Science Research.* Cambridge, MA: Cambridge University Press.

Bruner, J. (1986) *Actual Minds, Possible Worlds.* Cambridge, MA: Harvard University Press.

Buckingham, D. (1991) 'What are words worth? Interpreting children's words about television'. *Cultural Studies,* 5(2): 228–245.

Buckingham, D. (1993) *Children Talking Television: The Making of Television Literacy.* London: The Falmer Press.

Caron, A.H. and Caronia, L. (2000a) 'Contents in contexts: a study on Canadian family discourse about media practices at home'. In C. von Feiltzen and U. Carlsson (eds) *Children in the Media Landscape.* Goteborg: The UNESCO International Clearing House on Children and Violence on the Screen at Nordicom; 313–330.

Caron, A.H. and Caronia, L. (2000b) 'Parler de télévision, parler de soi. Une étude sur la mise en discours des pratiques médiatique au foyer'. *Communication,* 2(1): 123–154.

Caronia, L. (1997) *Costruire la Conoscenza. Interazione e Interpretazione nella Ricerca in Campo Educativo.* Firenze: La Nuova Italia.

Caronia, L. (2002) *La Socializzazione ai Media. Contesti, Interazioni e Pratiche Educative.* Milano: Guerini.

Caronia, L. and Gherardi, V. (1991) *La Pagina e lo Schermo. Libro e Tv: Antagonisti o Alleati?.* Firenze: La Nuova Italia.

Chandler, D. (1997) 'Children's understanding of what is 'real' on television. A review of the literature'. *Journal of Educational Media,* 23(1): 67–82.

Cicourel, A. (1964) *Method and Measurement in Sociology.* New York: Free Press.

Cicourel, A. (1982) 'Interviews, surveys, and the problem of ecological validity'. *American Sociologist,* 17: 11–20.

Cole, M. (1985) 'The zone of proximal development: where culture and cognition create each other'. In J.V. Wertsch (ed.) *Culture, Communication, and Cognition: Vygotskian Perspectives.* Cambridge: Cambridge University Press; 146–161.

Collins, W.A. (1983) 'Interpretation and inference in children's television viewing'. In J. Bryant and D.R. Anderson (eds) *Children's Understanding of Television: Research on Attention and Comprehension.* New York: Academic Press; 125–149.

Collins, W.A., Wellman, H., Keniston, A.H. and Westby, S.D. (1978) 'Age-related aspects of comprehension and inference from a televised dramatic narrative'. *Child Development,* 49: 389–399.

Fine, G.A. and Sandstrom, K.L. (1988) *Knowing Children. Participant Observation with Minors.* London: Sage.

Fitch, M., Houston, A.C. and Writh, J.C. (1993) 'From television forms to genre schemata: children's perceptions of television reality'. In G.L. Berry and J.K. Asamen (eds) *Children and Television: Images in a Changing Sociocultural World.* Newbury Park: Sage; 38–52.

Frenette, M. and Caron, A.H. (1995) 'Children and interactive television. Research and design issues'. *Convergence. The Journal of Research into New Media Technologies,* 1(1): 33–60.

Geertz, C. (1973) *The Interpretation of Cultures.* New York: Basic Books.

Glaser, B.G. and Strauss, A.L. (1967) *The Discovery of Grounded Theory.* Chicago: Aldine Publishing Company.

Groebel, J. (1999) 'Media access and media use among 12-year-olds in the world'. In C. von Feilitzen and U. Carlsson (eds) *Children and Media, Image, Education, Participation. Children and Media Violence, YearBook 1999.* Goteborg: The UNESCO International Clearinghouse on Children and Violence on the Screen at Nordicom; 61–68.

Groebel, J. (2001) 'Media violence in cross-cultural perspective: a global study on children's media behaviour and some educational implications'. In D.G. Singer and J.L. Singer (eds) *Handbook of Children and Media.* Thousand Oaks, CA: Sage; 255–268.

Kvale, S. (1996) *InterViews. An Introduction to Qualitative Research Interviewing.* London: Sage.

Lave, J. and Wenger, E. (1991) *Situated Learning. Legitimate Peripheral Participation*. Cambridge, UK: Cambridge University Press.

Lemish, D. (1987) 'Viewers in diapers: the early development of television viewing'. In T.R. Lindlof (ed.) *Natural Audiences. Qualitative Research of Media Uses and Effects*. Norwood: Ablex; 33–57.

Lemish, D. and Rice, M. (1986) 'Television as a talking picture book: a prop for language acquisition'. *Journal of Child Language*, 13: 251–274.

Lemish, D., Liebes, T., Maigret, E. and Stadl, G. (1998) 'Global culture in practice. A look at children and adolescents in Denmark, France and Israel'. *European Journal of Communication*, 13(4): 539–553.

Lincoln, Y. and Guba, E.G. (1985) *Naturalistic Inquiry*. Newberry Park, CA: Sage.

Lindlof, T. R (ed.) (1987) *Natural Audiences. Qualitative Research of Media Uses and Effects*. Norwood: Ablex.

Livingstone, S. and Bovill, M. (eds) (2001) *Children and Their Changing Media Environment. A European Comparative Study*. New York: Erlbaum.

Lull, J. (1980) 'The social uses of television'. *Human Communication Research*, 6(3): 197–209.

Meringoff, L.K. (1980) 'Influence of the medium on children's story apprehension'. *Journal of Educational Psychology*, 72(2): 240–249.

Meringoff, L.K., Vibbert, M.M., Char, C.A., Fernie, D.E., Banker, G.S. and Gardner, H. (1983) 'How is children's learning from television distinctive? Exploiting the medium methodologically'. In J. Bryant and D.R. Anderson (eds) *Children's Understanding of Television: Research on Attention and Comprehension*. New York: Academic Press; 151–179.

Messaris, P. (1987) 'Mothers' comments to their children about the relationship between television and reality'. In T.R. Lindlof (ed.) *Natural Audiences. Qualitative Research of Media Uses and Effects*. Norwood: Ablex; 95–108.

Mishler, E. (1986) *Research Interviewing. Context and Narrative*. Cambridge, MA: Cambridge University Press.

Moores, S. (1993) *Interpreting Audiences. The Ethnography of Media Consumption*. London: Sage.

Morley, D. (1986) *Family Television: Cultural Power and Domestic Leisure*. London: Comoedia-Routledge.

Morley, D. (1989) 'Changing paradigms in audience studies'. In E. Seiter, H. Borchers, G. Kreutzner and E. Warth (eds) *Remote Control: Television Audience and Cultural Power*. London: Routledge.

Morley, D. (1992) *Television, Audience, and Cultural Studies*. London: Routledge.

Noble, G. (1975) *Children in Front of the Small Screen*. London: Constable.

Olson, D.R. (1970) *Cognitive Development. The Child's Acquisition of Diagonality*. New York: Academic Press.

Olson, D.R. and Bruner, J.S. (1974) 'Learning through experience and learning through media'. In D.R. Olson (ed.) *Media and Symbols. The Form of Expression, Communication, Education*. Chicago, IL: Chicago University Press.

Palmer, P. (1986) *The Lively Audience. A Study of Children around the TV Set*. Sydney: Allen & Unwin.

Pasquier, D. (1996) 'Chère Héléne. Les usages sociaux des séries collège'. *Reseaux*, 70: 11–39.

Pasquier, D. (1999) *La Culture des Sentiments. L'Expérience Télévisuelle des Adolescents*. Paris: Éditions de la Maison des Sciences de l'Homme.

Pike, K.L. (1954) *Language in Relation to a Unified Theory of the Structure of Human Behavior*. Glendale, CA: Summer Institute of Linguistics.

Schutz, A. (1967) *The Phenomenology of Social World*. Evanston, IL: Northwestern University Press (1st edn, 1932).

Silverstone, R. and Hirsch, E. (eds) (1992) *Consuming Technologies. Media and Information in the Domestic Space*. London: Routledge.

Silverstone, R., Hirsch, E. and Morley, D. (1992) 'Information and communication technologies and the moral economy of the household'. In R. Silverstone and E. Hirsch (eds) *Consuming Technologies. Media and Information in the Domestic Space*. London: Routledge; 15–31.

Rabinow, P. and Sullivan, W.M. (eds) (1979) *Interpretive Social Science. A Reader*. Berkeley, CA: University of California Press.

Rabinow, P. and Sullivan, W.M. (eds) (1987) *Interpretive Social Science. A Second Look*. Berkeley, CA: University of California Press.

Wells, G. (2000) 'Dialogic inquiry in the classroom: building on the legacy of Vygotsky'. In C.D. Lee and O. Smagorinsky (eds) *Vygotskian Perspectives on Literacy Research*. New York: Cambridge University Press; 51–85.

Wenger, E. (1998) *Communities of Practice: Learning, Meaning, and Identity*. Cambridge: Cambridge University Press.

Wertsch, J.V. (ed.) (1985) *Culture, Communication, and Cognition: Vygotskian Perspectives*. Cambridge: Cambridge University Press.

PART 4

Perspectives

Notwithstanding the commonsense view that society is at a pivot point, overlooking the precipice even, of social change, this *Handbook* began by exploring the continuities threaded through the history of children, media and culture. We then undertook a critical examination of the problematics – the public anxieties, the moral concerns and the optimistic ambitious – that have motivated research on children's media culture, especially in the second half of the twentieth century. As mediated and cultural flows become increasingly transnational, along with the political movements and commercial organizations that underpin and intersect with them, we expanded our vision horizontally to encompass the geographic and cultural range of experiences that shape children's engagement with media. Now, we look ahead. For children, for the media, and for researchers interested in either and both, what are the pressing issues? What are the priorities for the future research agenda? Are there some broad perspectives to guide our thinking?

For some of our *Handbook* contributors, the starting point is a specialist focus on children and childhood in order, here, to examine the place of media in childhood. For others, the analysis of media, communications and culture comes first, this being adapted and developed in relation to children and young people in particular. Both approaches are valuable, for the strength of this field (or this intersection of fields) depends on a rich understanding of the specificities of children's life contexts combined with more general perspectives from the analysis media, culture and society. But these approaches have played rather different roles in each part of the volume. In Part 1, Prout and Holland sought continuities and change by telling the story of childhood, while Fleming and Reid-Walsh traced the history of particular media. In Part 2, we saw how the history of moral panics has led both research traditions to be wary of the intersection of children and media, though, today, the hype surrounding the newest technological developments also attracts the interest of both fields. A simple view of globalization would suggest that it is the media that move as part of transnational and global flows, while children stay where they have always been, in local settings defined largely by local traditions and cultures. While matters are undoubtedly more complex, much of Part 3 was concerned with children and young people's responses to and appropriations of mediated global culture.

And so to Part 4, where, from the foregoing, we draw out the themes of media mixing, new literacies, the de-Westernizing of research, media in the changing family, the pressures of commodification, the demands of media regulation, the potential of interactive media to revitalize civic and political participation and, last but not least, the potential for including communication rights within the growing movement to assert children's rights. The evident interest and importance of these themes will surely convince those generalists for whom children represent a small and marginal specialism in the field and those experts on childhood for whom mediated culture seems an optional afterthought, merely a means by which children fill their time not occupied by more important activities – education, work, family life, that questions of children, media and culture matter. This is not simply because children comprise a quarter of the population in developed countries, while in developing countries as much as half of the population may be under the age of 15 years old (see Nayar & Bhide and Kraidy & Khalil in this volume). Nor is it because they are, as popular wisdom pronounces blandly, 'the future'. But also because, in the here and now, children and young people represent a vast economic market, a focus of both political despair and hope, a test bed for innovators in technology and design and, last but certainly not least, a creative, emotional and ethical force shaping continuities and change in values for societies everywhere. Children and young people are not to be contained in the domestic sphere (not that this is in itself unimportant), and they should not be rendered invisible by any a wider or more abstract lens.

Several contributors in this part of the *Handbook* seem to be seeking a research direction that mixes (we might say, remixes) and takes forward the traditions developed for researching television audiences in a new media age, integrating reception studies and consumption studies so as to analyse both the interpretative practices associated with media as goods (the television, computer, mobile) and those associated with media as texts (programmes, websites, songs) (Press and Livingstone, 2006). Each tradition conceives of the agency/structure relation somewhat differently: in terms of the critical analysis of ideology or normative values (in reception studies, articulated most clearly in Hall's (1980) theory of encoding and decoding) or in terms of the relation between political economy and cultural/consumption studies (Murdock, 1996); however conceived, this relation must be central to research on children and media.

We begin with Ito's account of the emerging lineaments of the interactive, participatory digital environment, apparently so welcoming to today's youth, though often less so for today's researchers. Blurring the online/offline, mediated/face-to-face boundaries on which the analysis of media and communication has traditionally relied, the contemporary conceptual toolkit centers on the prefix 're-': remixing, reconfiguring, remediating, reappropriating, recombining (Bolter and Grusin, 1999; Dutton and Shepherd, 2004; Lievrouw and Livingstone, 2006). The familiar and the new are thus integrated, innovation being both continuous with and distinct from that which has gone before, simultaneously remediating the familiar with a shake of the kaleidoscope. The result is a convergent media culture – epitomized by the Japanese phenomena of Pokemon, Yugioh and Hamtaro – and broadly characterized by personalization, hypersociality, networking and ubiquity. This offers new 'genres of participation', engaging the collective imagination, indeed positively requiring creativity on the part of its typically youthful users, and raising many questions in the process (Jenkins, 2006).

The implications of such an engagement for people's life chances have yet to be traced. Takahashi looks beyond Japanese media to the anthropological analysis of Japanese society and its modernity. A de-Westernized media studies cannot simply reject Western theory, asserting the uniqueness of Japan (or anywhere else). Rather, she argues, it should identify concepts from diverse intellectual traditions and consider, question and apply them in particular contexts, thereby enriching the conceptual toolkit for the analysis of society as well as for new media. For example, the public/private distinction central to Western thinking provokes questions about visibility, sharedness and the public sphere. In Japan, a key distinction is that between *uchi* (an intimate interpersonal realm – e.g. within couples, friendships, work place camaraderie – now extended by the advent of peer-to-peer networking) and *soto* (a notion of 'outside' closely aligned with 'them' and so distinct from the Western 'public sphere'). Learning from the concepts and frameworks developed within the academy, and the society, of different countries poses an as yet little reflected-upon challenge for many of us, for though we are willing to consider empirical findings internationally, we remain implicitly reliant on familiar theories and concepts with which to analyse them.

Literacy is just such a concept, commonly used in the English-speaking world, that only imperfectly matches concepts from other linguistic traditions. Understood in a context of empowerment and human rights – for media literacy enables civic participation, cultural expression and employability[1] – it is certain that most cultures hope children will be critical media consumers, though not all provide, or can provide, the educational resources to enable this. However, the need for vigilance remains. In Europe, for example, media literacy is being repositioned as a strategic counterbalance to deregulatory moves to liberalize a converging market. Put simply, if children can discern good content from bad, use media to express themselves, and protect themselves from mediated harm, then the burden of regulation can be lessened (Livingstone, 2004).[2] Though debates over the purposes of media literacy are not new (Luke, 1989; Hobbs, 1998), what is new is the importance accorded to 'new media literacies' beyond the domains of entertainment, values and personal expression to encompass also educational success, competitive workplace skills and civic participation (see Hobbs in this volume). Consequently, we can also see the academic reframing of what was once a rather specialized area for media practitioners and educators as a central issue for all concerned with people's (and especially children's) interpretative and critical engagement with media and communication. Media literacy will surely occupy a central place on the future agenda for children, media and culture. However, arguably too, (media) literacy is one form of cultural capital, as theorized by Bourdieu (1984). Thus, it is one way of conceptualizing not only children's potential, but also the means of their exclusion, for literacy relies on cultural and economic resources, and these serve to divide or coerce as much (perhaps more) than they enable (see Pasquier in this volume).

While several contributors stress the importance of the family in mediating children's relation with the media (e.g. Hoover and Clark, Heller, Lemish), Pasquier is interested in the way that the family itself is changing in late modernity: is this a story of growing individualism, as families become less hierarchical, more democratic, enabling the plurality of individual tastes rather than inculcating traditional values (as argued in Livingstone (2002)) or, on the contrary, do the media open the door to an increasing tyranny of the peer group, as teenagers fear the social stigma of failing to follow the latest fad or fashion? Perhaps these arguments are compatible, just as the multiplicity of (especially personal, mobile) media permits some escape from parental supervision only to become subject to the scrutiny of one's peers (as suggested by Beck and Beck-Gernsheim (2002)). However, the fact that these arguments remain unresolved illustrates exactly the point this *Handbook* seeks to stress: that we need simultaneously to analyse trends in media and trends in childhood and the family if we are to explain, and evaluate, social change in a meaningful fashion, avoiding the reductionisms of both technological and social determinism.

Political economists are keen to point out that the market benefits considerably from teenagers' constant desire to have the latest product, to try the newest service, to seek out the niche media that make them both 'individual' and 'cool'. For those contemplating any celebration of youthful creativity or active media engagement, Wasko's chapter offers a salutary check (see also Kenway and Bullen, this volume). Children are not only bombarded with advertising and marketing for the latest commodity, but, arguably, as a new and profitable market, they have themselves been commodified, sold to advertisers as 'tweenies', 'kids' and 'teens' (Smythe, 1981; Seiter, 1993). Wasko's analysis of Disney and Neopets, to take two among many prominent cases of kids' brands, develops the cultural circuit argued for by Buckingham and others in Part 3, integrating audience, text, production and market analyses. Yet here again, and notwithstanding Wasko's depressing conclusions, the debate remains open. For Jenkins (2003), and perhaps Ito, Buckingham and others, the circuit is not closed; to be sure, the market capitalizes on children's creative appropriations, but then children reappropriate, the market watches and responds, and children again get their turn. Perhaps the next stage of research is not to analyse the popular brands or their reappropriation by children, but rather to scope the (possibly narrowing) range of available choices, thus developing a critique of choice itself.

Advertising to children has long been one among several priorities for those responsible for regulating children's media; though, as Oswell shows, in an age of media abundance in many parts of the world, with technological convergence across platforms providing new headaches for regulators, it is the moral issues regarding content appropriate for children that is occasioning the greatest concern. Oswell's critical reflections highlight the risk that current regulatory developments may by-pass democratic scrutiny, tending to devolve the burden of regulation from states or public institutions either to commercial bodies (i.e. self-regulation) or parents (i.e. media literacy and domestic regulation). However, for academic researchers of children, media and culture, the interface with regulatory and policy debates is fraught with pitfalls, partly because these deliberations (though increasingly public) are often highly specialized in terms of both legal and technological matters, as well as fast moving; moreover, the translation from evidence to policy, notwithstanding the stress on 'evidence-based policy', is far from straightforward.

Nonetheless, as 'experts' on questions of children's play, learning, participation and literacy, it is arguably incumbent on us, first, to ensure that good research reaches those stakeholders who might act on it and, second, and perhaps more contentiously, to ensure that certain outcomes, namely those in children's interests, are supported. Our last two chapters address highly topical domains in which the academy has been actively involved in policy engagement: Dahlgren and Olsson review attempts to use interactive media to facilitate political participation among a supposedly apathetic and disconnected youth, while Hamelink considers the justification for a communications rights agenda for children, in the context of the UN Convention on the Rights of the Child. Extending the circuit of culture into the civic domain, Dahlgren and Olsson propose a circuit of civic culture driven by the dynamic interrelations among knowledge, values, trust, spaces, practices and identities. They conclude that we must see beyond the formal political system if we are to recognize youthful civic engagement, for a traditional lens brands youth as passively distanced from politics. However, less optimistically, it seems to be the already active for whom the combination of new media and alternative politics seems especially potent, possibly because so many are socialized – by media and other means – not into a culture of activism, but rather into one of inefficacy and distrust. Partly for these reasons, but more because of the fundamental relation between mediation and cultural/individual rights, Hamelink advocates children's rights to express themselves, to be listened to, to privacy, to good quality information, to the avoidance of mediated harm, and to see their culture reflected and valued by others. How this agenda can and is being taken forward is a vital task for the coming years.

NOTES

1 On the tenth anniversary of the UN Convention on the Rights of the Child, UNICEF issued the Oslo Challenge: 'the child/media relationship is an entry point into the wide and multifaceted world of children and their rights – to education, freedom of expression, play, identity, health, dignity and self-respect,

protection – and that in every aspect of child rights, in every element of the life of a child, the relationship between children and the media plays a role'. See http://www.unicef.org/magic/briefing/oslo.html, accessed 28/3/07.

2 See http://ec.europa.eu/comm/avpolicy/media_literacy/expert_group/index_en.htm [28 March 2007].

REFERENCES

Beck, U. and Beck-Gernsheim, E. (2002) *Individualization.* London: Sage.

Bolter, J.D. and Grusin, R. (1999) *Remediation: Understanding New Media.* Cambridge, MA: MIT Press.

Bourdieu, P. (1984) *Distinction: A Social Critique of the Judgement of Taste.* London: Routledge and Kegan Paul.

Dutton, W.H. and Shepherd, A. (2004) *Confidence and Risk on the Internet.* Oxford: Oxford Internet Institute.

Hall, S. (1980) 'Encoding/decoding'. In S. Hall, D. Hobson, A. Lowe and P. Willis (eds) *Culture, Media, Language.* London: Hutchinson; 128–138.

Hobbs, R. (1998) 'The seven great debates in the media literacy movement'. *Journal of Communication,* 48(1), 6–32.

Jenkins, H. (2003) 'Quentin Tarantino's Star Wars? Digital cinema, media convergence, and participatory culture'. In D. Thorburn and H. Jenkins (eds) *Rethinking Media Change: The Aesthetics of Transition.* Cambridge, MA: MIT Press; 281–312.

Jenkins, H. (2006) *Convergence Culture: Where Old and New Media Collide.* New York: New York University Press.

Lievrouw, L. and Livingstone, S. (2006) 'Introduction'. In L. Lievrouw and S. Livingstone (eds) *Handbook of New Media: Social Shaping and Social Consequences* (updated student edition edition).London: Sage; 1–14.

Livingstone, S. (2002) *Young People and New Media: Childhood and the Changing Media Environment.* London: Sage.

Livingstone, S. (2004) 'Media literacy and the challenge of new information and communication technologies'. *Communication Review,* 7: 3–14.

Luke, C. (1989) *Pedagogy, Printing and Protestantism: The Discourse of Childhood.* Albany, NY: State University of New York Press.

Murdock, G. (1996) 'Culture, communications and political economy'. In J. Curran and M. Gurevitch (eds) *Mass Media and Society,* 3rd edition. London: Arnold.

Press, A. and Livingstone, S. (2006) 'Taking audience research into the age of new media: old problems and new challenges'. In M. White and J. Schwoch (eds) *The Question of Method in Cultural Studies.* Oxford: Blackwell; 175–200.

Seiter, E. (1993) *Sold Separately: Children and Parents in Consumer Culture.* New Brunswick: Rutgers University Press.

Smythe, D. (1981) *Dependency Road: Communications, Capitalism, Consciousness, and Canada.* Norwood, NJ: Ablex.

23

Mobilizing the Imagination in Everyday Play: The Case of Japanese Media Mixes

Mizuko Ito

INTRODUCTION

The spread of digital media and communications in the lives of children and youth have raised new questions about the role of media in learning, development and cultural participation. In post-industrial societies, young people are growing up in what Henry Jenkins (2006) has dubbed 'convergence culture': an increasingly interactive and participatory media ecology where internet communication ties together both old and new media forms. A growing recognition of this role of digital media in everyday life has been accompanied by debate as to the outcomes of participation in convergence culture. Many parents and educators worry about immersion in video gaming worlds or their children's social lives unfolding on the internet and through mobile communication. More optimistic voices suggest that new media enable young people to participate more actively in interpreting, personalizing, reshaping and creating media content. Although concerns about representation are persistent, particularly of video game violence, many of the current hopes and fears of new media relate to new forms of social networking and participation. As young people's online activity changes the scope of their social agency and styles of media engagement, they also encounter new challenges in cultural worlds separated from traditional structures of adult oversight and guidance. Issues of representation will continue to be salient in media old and new, but issues of participation are undergoing a fundamental set of shifts that are still only partially understood and recognized. My focus in this chapter is on outlining the contours of these shifts. How do young people mobilize the media and the imagination in everyday life? And how do new media change this dynamic?

A growing body of literature at the intersection of media studies and technology studies examines the ways in which new media provide a reconfigured social and interactive toolkit for young people to mobilize media and a collective imagination. After reviewing this body of work and the debates about new media and the childhood imagination, I will outline a conceptual framework for understanding new genres of children's media and media engagement that are emerging from convergence culture. The body of the paper applies this framework to ethnographic material on two Japanese media series, *Yugioh* and *Hamtaro*. Both of these cases are examples of post-*Pokemon* 'media mixes', forms of child-oriented convergence culture that bring together television animation, comic books, electronic gaming, card games and a wide variety of merchandise. *Yugioh* is an example of a boy-centered series centered on narratives of card game play, and *Hamtaro* is a more girl-centered series featuring cute hamsters and friendship narratives. I suggest that these contemporary media mixes in children's content exemplify three key characteristics that distinguish them from prior media ecologies: *convergence* of old and new media forms; authoring through *personalization and remix* and *hypersociality* as a genre of social participation. My central argument is that these tendencies define a new media ecology keyed to a more activist mobilization of the imagination in the everyday life of young people.

THE IMAGINATION IN EVERYDAY LIFE

Longstanding debates over the role of media, particularly visual media, in the lives of children provide context for current issues in new media and childhood. At least since television came to dominate children's popular cultures, parents, educators and scholars have debated the role of commercial media in children's creativity, agency and imagination. One thread of these debates has been concerned with the content of the imagination, examining issues such as representations of gender or violence. Another strand of the debate, which I will examine here, focuses on the form, structure and practice of the imagination. What is the nature of childhood imagination when it takes as source material the narratives and characters of commercial culture? What are the modes of social and cultural participation that are enabled or attenuated with the rise of popular children's media? Does engagement with particular media types relate to differences in childhood agency or creativity? Behind these questions is the theoretical problematic of how to understand the relation between the text produced by the media producer and the local contexts of uptake by young people. Framed differently, this is the question of how the imagination as produced by commercial media articulates with the imagination, agency and creativity of diverse children going about their everyday lives. In this section, I review how this question has been taken up and suggest that theories of participation and collective imagination are ways of resolving some of the conceptual problematics in a way amenable to an analysis of new interactive and networked media.

Before I outline my own conceptual framework for understanding media engagement and the imagination, I would like to review certain culturally dominant assumptions that I believe need to be challenged. Contemporary assumptions about media and the childhood imagination are framed by a set of cultural distinctions between an active/creative or a passive/derivative mode of engaging with imagination and fantasy. Generally, practices that involve local 'production', namely creative writing, drawing and performance, are considered more creative, agentive and imaginative than practices that involve 'consumption' of professionally or mass-produced media, namely watching television, playing video games or even reading a book. In addition, we also tend to make a distinction between 'active' and 'passive' media forms. One familiar argument is that visual media, in contrast to oral and print media, stifle creativity because they do not require imaginative and intellectual work. Until recently, young people almost exclusively 'consumed' dynamic visual media (i.e. television and film), unlike in the case of textual or aural media, where they also are expected to produce work. This may be one reason why we often do not think of reading and listening to music as 'passive' or 'mindless' in the same way that we view television, though all of these are modes of 'media consumption'. Visual media, particularly television, has been doubly marked as a consumptive and passive media form. These arguments for the superiority of 'original' authorship and textual media track along familiar lines that demarcate high and low culture, learning and amusement. For example, Ellen Seiter (1999) analyses the differences between a more working-class and an upper middle-class preschool, and sees the distinctions between 'good' and 'bad' forms of media engagement as strongly inflected by class identity. The middle-class setting works to shut out television-based media and media references, and values working on a computer, reading and writing text, and play that does not mobilize content derived from popular commercial culture. By contrast, the working-class setting embraces a more active and informed attitude towards children's media cultures.

Scholars in media studies have challenged the cultural distinctions between active and passive media, arguing that television and popular media do provide opportunities for creative uptake and agency in local contexts of reception. Writing in the early years of digital media for children, Marsha Kinder (1991) suggested that video games and postmodern television genres provide opportunities for kids to 'play with power' by piecing together narrative elements and genres rather than absorbing narratives holistically. Arguing against the view that commercial media stimulates imitation but not originality in children's imaginings, Kinder points out the historical specificity of contemporary notions of creativity and originality. She suggests that children take up popular media in ways that were recognized as creative in other historical eras. 'A child's reworking of material from mass media can be seen as a form of parody (in the eighteenth-century sense), as a postmodernist form of pastiche, or as a form of Bakhtinian reenvoicement mediating between imitation and creativity' (Kinder, 1991: 60). In a similar vein, Anne Haas Dyson (1997) examines how elementary school children mobilize mass media characters within creative writing exercises. Like Seiter (1999), Dyson argues that commercial media provide the 'common story material' for contemporary childhood, and that educators should acknowledge the mobilization of these materials as a form of literacy. 'To fail to do so is to risk reinforcing societal divisions of gender and of socioeconomic class' (Dyson, 1997: 7).

These critiques of culturally dominant views of the 'passivity' of children's visual culture are increasingly well established, at least in the cultural studies literature (for reviews, see Jenkins (1998), Kinder (1999), and Buckingham (2000)). Here, I build on these critiques and propose frameworks for understanding the relation between media, the imagination and everyday activity. Engagement with new media formats, such as with what we now find on the internet, with post-*Pokemon* media mixes, and with video games suggests alternative ways of understanding the relation between children and media that do not rely on a dichotomization of media production and consumption or between active and passive media forms. These binarisms were already being corroded by reception studies in the TV-centric era, and they are increasingly on shaky ground in the contemporary period. As digital and networked media have entered the mix, research has foregrounded active and participatory dimensions of media engagement, fundamentally undermining longstanding distinctions about children's relation to media.

In their analysis of *Pokemon*, David Buckingham and Julian Sefton-Green (2004) suggest that it has continuities with early media forms and trends in children's popular culture. But they also suggest some important new dimensions. Their analysis is worth reproducing, as it prefigures my arguments in the remainder of this essay:

> We take it for granted that audiences are 'active' (although we would agree that there is room for

> much more rigorous discussion about what that actually means). The key point for us is that the texts of *Pokemon* – or the other *Pokemon* 'phenomenon' – positively *require* 'activity'. Activity of various kinds is not just essential for the production of meaning and pleasure; it is also the primary mechanism through which the phenomenon is sustained, *and* through which commercial profit is generated. It is in this sense that the notion of 'audience' seems quite inadequate.

In other words, new convergent media such as *Pokemon* require a reconfigured conceptual apparatus that takes productive and creative activity at the 'consumer' level as a given rather than as an addendum or an exception. One way of reconfiguring this conceptual terrain is through theories of participation that I derive primarily from two sources. The first is situated learning theory as put forth by Jean Lave and Etienne Wenger (1991). They suggest that learning be considered an act of participation in culture and social life rather than as a process of reception or internalization. My second source of theoretical capital is Jenkins' idea of 'participatory media cultures' which he originally used to describe fan communities in the 1970s and 1980s, and has recently revisited in relation to current trends in convergence culture (Jenkins, 1992, 2006). Jenkins traces how fan practices established in the TV-dominated era have become increasingly mainstream due to the convergence between traditional and digital media. Fans not only consume professionally produced media, but also produce their own meanings and media products, continuing to disrupt the culturally dominant distinctions between production and consumption. More recently, Natalie Jeremijenko (2002) and Joe Karaganis (2007) have proposed a concept of 'structures of participation' to analyse different modes of relating to digital and interactive technologies. As a nod to cultural context and normative structures of practice, I have suggested a complementary notion of 'genres of participation' to suggest different modes or conventions for engaging with technology and the imagination. A notion of participation genre addresses similar problematics as concepts such as habitus (Bourdieu, 1972) or structuration (Giddens, 1986), linking activity to social and cultural structure. More closely allied with humanistic analysis, a notion of genre, however, foregrounds the interpretive dimensions of human orderliness. How we identify with, orient to, and engage with media and the imagination is probably better described as a process of interpretive recognition than a process of habituation or structuring. We recognize certain patterns of representation (textual genres), and in turn engage with them in routinized ways (participation genres).

A notion of participation, as an alternative to 'consumption', has the advantage in not assuming that the child is passive or a mere 'audience' to media content. It is agnostic as to the mode of engagement, and does not invoke one end of a binary between structure and agency, text and audience. It forces attention to the more ethnographic and practice-based dimensions of media engagement (genres of participation), as well as querying the broader social and cultural contexts in which these activities are conducted (structures of participation). Jenkins (2006, 4) writes:

> Rather than talking about media producers and consumers occupying separate roles, we might now see them as both participants who interact with each other according to a new set of rules that none of us fully understands.

Putting participation at the core of the conceptual apparatus asserts that *all* media engagement is fundamentally social and active, though the specificities of activity and structure are highly variable. A critically informed notion of participation can also keep in view issues of power and stratification that are central to the classical distinctions between production and consumption. The structure of participation can be one that includes the relation between a large corporation and child, as well as the relation between different children as they mobilize media content within their peer networks. Notice that in this framing, the site of interest is not only the relation between child and text – the production/consumption and encoding/decoding relations (Hall, 1993) that have guided much work in reception studies – but also the social relations between different people who are connected laterally, hierarchically, and in other ways. The research question has been recast from the more individualized, 'How does a child interpret or localize a text?' to the collective question of 'How do people organize around and with media texts?'

Let me return this to creativity and the imagination. A notion of participation leads to a conceptualization of the imagination as collectively rather than individually experienced and produced. Following Arjun Appadurai, I treat the imagination as a 'collective social fact', built on the spread of certain media technologies at particular historical junctures (Appadurai, 1996: 5). In my framing, imagination is not an individualized cognitive property, but rather is the shared store of cultural referents, common cultural source material that exceeds individual experience. This collective imagination requires not only ongoing interpretation, performance and expression, but also media technologies for representing and circulating products of the imagination. Benedict Anderson (1991), writing about an earlier era, argues that the printing press and standardized vernaculars were instrumental to the 'imagined community' of the nation state. With the circulation of mass electronic media, Appadurai suggests that people have an even broader range of access to different shared imageries and narratives, whether in the form of popular music, television dramas or cinema. Media images now pervade our everyday lives, and form much of the material through with we imagine our world, relate to others, and engage in collective action, often in ways that depart from the relations and identities produced locally. More specifically, in children's toys, Gary Cross (1997) has traced a shift in the past century from toys that mimicked real-world adult activities, such as cooking, childcare and construction, to the current dominance of toys that are based in fantasy environments, such as outer space, magical lands and cities visited by the supernatural. The current move towards convergent and digital media is one step along a much longer trajectory in the development of technologies and media that support a collective imaginative apparatus. At the same time, Appadurai (1996: 6–8) posits that people are increasingly engaging with these imaginings in more agentive, mobilized and selective ways as part of the creation of 'communities of sentiment'. The rise of global communication and media networks is tied to an imagination that is more commercially driven, fantasy based, widely shared and central to our everyday lives *at the same time* as the imagination is becoming more amenable to local refashioning and mobilization in highly differentiated ways.

Taking this longer view enables us to specify much of the current debate on children and media as defined by historically specific structures of participation in media culture. Until recently these structures of participation were clearly polarized between commercial production and everyday consumption. Yochai Benkler (2006) argues that computers and the internet are enabling a change in modes of cultural production and distribution that disrupts the dynamics of commercial media production. He lays out a wide range of cases, such as Wikipedia, open-source software development, and citizen science, to argue that cultural production is becoming more widely distributed and coordinated in internet-enabled societies. While people have always produced local folk and amateur cultures, with the advent of low-cost PCs and peer-to-peer global distribution over the internet, high-end tools for producing and sharing knowledge and culture are more widely accessible. My argument about children's culture parallels Benkler's arguments. 'Reception' is not only active and negotiated, but is a *productive* act of creating a shared imagination and participating in a social world. The important question is not whether the everyday practices of children in media culture are 'original' or 'derivative', 'active' or 'passive', but rather the structure of the social world, the patterns of participation, and the content of the imagination that is produced through the active involvement of kids, media producers and other social actors. This is a conceptual and attentional shift motivated by the emergent change in modes of cultural production.

UNDERSTANDING NEW MEDIA

Drawing from theoretical frameworks of participation and collective imagination, I would like to outline in more detail my conceptual toolkit for understanding emergent changes in children's media ecologies, and introduce the Japanese media mixes that are my topic of study. Digital or new media have entered the conversation about childhood culture holding out the enlightened promise of transforming 'passive media consumption' into 'active media engagement' and learning (Ito, 2003). Ever since the early 1980s, when educators began experimenting with multimedia software for children, digital media were seen as a vehicle for more engaged and child-centered forms of learning (e.g. Papert, 1980; Ambron, 1989). Although multimedia did not deliver on its promise to shake the foundations of educational practice, it is hard to ignore the steady spread of interactive media forms into children's recreational lives. Electronic gaming has taken its seat as one of the dominant entertainment forms of the twenty-first century, and even television and film have become more user driven in the era of cable, DVDs, digital download and Tivo. In addition to interactive media formats, where users control characters and narrative, now the internet supports a layer of social communication to the digital media ecology. Young people can reshape and customize commercial media, as well as exchange and discuss media in peer-to-peer networks through blogs, filesharing, social networking systems and various messaging services. While there is generally shared recognition that new media of various kinds are resulting in a substantially altered media ecology, there is little consensus as to the broader social ramifications for the everyday lives of young people.

In addressing these issues it is crucial to avoid the pitfalls of both hype and mistrust, or as Holloway and Valentine (2001) have described it, between the 'boosters' and the 'debunkers'. New technologies tend to be accompanied by a set of heightened expectations, followed by a precipitous fall from grace after failing to deliver on an unrealistic billing. In the case of technologies identified with youth subcultures, the fall is often tied to what Stanley Cohen (1972) has famously called a 'moral panic', the script of fear and crackdown that accompanies youth experimentation with new cultural forms and technologies. While the boosters, debunkers and the panicked may seem to be operating under completely different frames of reference, what they share is the tendency to fetishize technology as a force with its own internal logic standing outside of history, society and culture. The problem with all of these stances is that they fail to recognize that technologies are in fact embodiments, stabilizations, and concretizations of existing social structure and cultural meanings, growing out of an unfolding history as part of a necessarily altered and contested future. The promises and the pitfalls of certain technological forms are realized only through active and ongoing struggle over their creation, uptake and revision. I consider this recognition one of the core theoretical axioms of contemporary technology studies, and is foundational to the theoretical approach taken in this chapter. In this I draw from social studies of the technology that see technology as growing out of existing social contexts as much as it is productive of new ones (e.g. Edwards, 1995; Lessig, 1999; Hine, 2000; Miller and Slater, 2000).

New media produced for and engaged with by young people is a site of contestation and construction of our technological futures and imaginaries. The cases described in this chapter are examples of practices that grow out of existing media cultures and practices of play, but represent a trend towards digital, portable, and networked media forms becoming more accessible and pervasive in young people's lives. I propose three conceptual constructs that define trends in new media *form, production* and *genres of participation: convergence* of old and new media forms, authoring through *personalization and remix* and *hypersociality* as a genre of participation. These constructs are efforts to locate the ethnographic present of my cases within a set of unfolding historical trajectories of sociotechnical change. These characteristics have been historically present in engagement with earlier media forms, but now synergy between new media and the energies of young people has made these dimensions a more salient and pervasive dimension of the everyday lives of a rising generation. Let me sketch the outlines of these three constructs in turn before fleshing them out in my ethnographic cases.

Contrary to what is suggested by the moniker of 'new media', contemporary media need to be understood not as an entirely new set of media forms but rather as a *convergence* between more traditional media, such as television, books, and film, and digital and networked media and communications. By bringing together interactive and networked media with traditional media, convergent media enable consumers to select and engage with content in more mobilized ways, as well as create lateral networks of communication and exchange at the consumer level. Today, the internet and digital media are no longer ghettoized as marginal geek phenomena: they are becoming central to the ways in which all media are distributed and engaged with. Jenkins (2006: 2) writes that convergence culture is 'where old and new media intersect, where grassroots and corporate media collide, where the power of the media producer and the power of the media consumer interact in unpredictable ways'. In a related vein, I have used the term in popular currency in Japan, 'media mix', to describe how Japanese children's media relies on a synergistic relationship between multiple media formats, particularly animation, comics, video games and trading-card games. The Japanese media mix in children's culture highlights particular elements of convergence culture. Unlike with US-origin media, which tends to be dominated by home-based media such as the home entertainment center and the PC internet, Japanese media mixes tend to have a stronger presence in portable media formats such as Game Boys, mobile phones, trading cards and character merchandise that make the imagination manifest in diverse contexts and locations outside of the home. Although the emphases are different, both Euro-American and Japanese children's media are exhibiting the trend towards synergy between different media types and formats.

Digital and networked media provide a mechanism not to wholly supplant the structures of traditional narrative media, but rather to provide alternative ways of engaging with these produced imaginaries. In children's media cultures, the Japanese media mix has been central to a shift towards stronger connections between new interactive and traditional narrative forms. Children engaging with a media format like *Pokemon* can look to the television anime for character and backstory, create their own trajectories through the content through video games and trading-card play, and go to the internet to exchange information in what Sefton-Green (2004: 151) has described as a 'knowledge industry'. Convergent media also have a transnational dimension, as media can circulate between like-minded groups that cross national borders. The case of Japanese animation and media mixes is particularly intriguing in this respect, though the transnational dimension is not something that I will have space to address in this essay.

These changing media forms are tied to the growing trend towards *personalization and remix* as genres of media engagement and production. Gaming, interactive media, digital authoring, internet distribution and networked communications enable a more customized relationship to collective imaginings as kids mobilize and remix media content to fit their local contexts of meaning. These kinds of activities certainly predate the digital age, as kids pretend to be superheroes with their friends or doodle pictures of their favorite characters on school notebooks. The difference is not the emergence of a new category of practice, but rather the augmentation of these existing practices by media formats more explicitly designed to allow for user-level reshuffling and reenactment. This mode of engagement is related to what Sonia Livingstone (2002: 108–116) describes as the trend towards 'individualized lifestyles' tied to a diversification of media and forms of lifestyle expression among young people. At the same time, it is important to stress that this move towards personalized and niche media is not necessarily a mode of cultural fragmentation. Rather, these modes of engagement are predicated on a robust body of shared cultural referents, a collective imagination that provides the source material for individualized articulations.

Although all media genres are amenable to some forms of user-level recontextualization, particular genres and titles more actively invite personalization and remix. Jenkins (2006) has described the Matrix as a transmedia enterprise that invites deep fan engagement because of the multiple layers of allusion, the depth of backstory played out in multiple media formats and lack of referential closure. In a similar vein, Steven Johnson (2005) has suggested that contemporary television is characterized by increasingly complex and multiple narrative arcs, hidden and esoteric knowledge, and subtle referencing of elements of narrative significance. In my study of genres in children's software, I concluded that certain titles such as SimCity or exploratory sequences in narrative adventures more explicitly invited localized and unconventional player engagements (Ito, 2003). Media mixes like *Pokemon* and *Yugioh* are examples of media designed with player-level personalization and remix as a precondition rather than a side-effect of engagement. When gaming formats are tied into the imaginary of narrative media such as television and comics, they become vehicles for manifesting these characters and narratives with greater fidelity and effect in everyday life. While the role of the collective imagination in children's culture probably remains as strongly rooted in commercial culture as ever, the ability to personalize, remix and mobilize this imaginative material is substantially augmented by the inclusion of digital media and the growth of content genres that cater to more activist audiences.

At the level of everyday practice and social exchange, the tendency towards remix and personalization of media is also tied to the growth of deep and esoteric knowledge communities around media content. I've described the kind of social exchange that accompanies the traffic in information about new media mixes like *Pokemon* and *Yugioh* as *hypersocial*, social exchange augmented by the mobilization of elements of the collective imagination (Ito, 2007). Hypersociality is about peer-to-peer ecologies of cultural production and exchange (of information, objects and money) pursued among geographically local peer groups, among dispersed populations mediated by the internet, and through organized gatherings such as conventions and tournaments. Popular cultural referents become a shared language for young people's conversations, activity and social capital. This is a genre of participation in media culture that has historically strong roots in cultures of fandom or, in Japan, the media geekdoms of 'otaku' (Greenfeld, 1993; Okada, 1996; Kinsella, 1998; Eng, 2001; Tobin, 2004). While otaku cultures are still considered subcultural among youth and adults, children have been at the forefront of the mainstreaming of these genres of participation. It is unremarkable for children to be deeply immersed in intense otaku-like communities of interest surrounding media such as *Pokemon*, *Digimon* or *Teenage Mutant Ninja Turtles*, though there is still a social stigma attached to adult fans of science fiction or anime.

JAPAN'S MEDIA MIX

Like otaku culture, the Japanese media mix is both culturally distinctive and increasingly global in its reach. A certain amount of convergence between different media types, such as television, books, games and film, has been a relatively longstanding dimension of modern children's media cultures in Japan, as elsewhere. Japan-origin manga (comics), anime (animation) and game content are heterogeneous, spanning multiple media types and genres, yet still recognized as a cluster of linked cultural forms. Manga are generally (but not always) the primary texts of these media forms. They were the first component of the contemporary mix to emerge from the postwar period in the 1960s and 1970s, eventually providing the characters and narratives that go on to populate games, anime and merchandise. While electronic gaming was in a somewhat separate domain through the 1980s, by the 1990s it was well integrated in to the overall media mix of manga and anime characters, aided by the popularity of game-origin characters such as Mario and Pikachu. These media mixes are not limited to children's media (and includes a wide range of adult-oriented material), but children's media does dominate.

Pokemon pushed the media mix equation into new directions. Rather than being pursued serially, as in the case of manga being converted into anime, the media mix of *Pokemon* involved a more integrated and synergistic strategy where the same set of characters and narratives was manifest concurrently in multiple media types. *Pokemon* also set the precedent of locating the portable media formats of trading cards and handheld networked game play at the center rather than at the periphery of the media ecology. This had the effect of channeling media engagement into collective social settings both within and outside the home as kids looked for opportunities to link up their game devices and play with and trade their *Pokemon* cards. Trading cards, Game Boys and character merchandise create what Anne Allison (2004: 42) has called 'pocket fantasies', 'digitized icons … that children carry with them wherever they go', and 'that straddle the border between phantasm and everyday life'. This formula was groundbreaking and a global success; *Pokemon* became a cultural ambassador for Japanese popular culture and related genres of participation in media culture. Many other media mixes followed in the wake of *Pokemon*, reproducing and refining the formulas that Nintendo had established.

In the wake of the *Pokemon* phenomenon, I conducted fieldwork from 1998 to 2002 in the Greater Tokyo area among children, parents, and media industrialists at the height of *Yugioh's* popularity. My research focused on *Yugioh* as a case study, as it was the most popular series in currency at the time. My description is drawn from interviews with these various parties implicated in *Yugioh*, my own engagements with the various media forms, and participant observation at sites of player activity, including weekly tournaments at card shops, trade shows, homes and an afterschool center for elementary-aged children. Among girls, *Hamtaro* was the most popular children's series at the time, so it became a secondary focus for my research. I also conducted research that was not content specific, interviewing parents, participant observing a wide range of activities at the afterschool center and reviewing diverse children's media. I formally interviewed 30 parents, educators, and adult game-players, and spoke to many times that number of children during the course of participant observations at the afterschool center, at events, and in card duel spaces. I turn now to descriptions of *Yugioh* and *Hamtaro* at the levels of media form, authorship and genres of participation to illustrate how Japanese children mobilized these media mixes in their everyday lives.

YUGIOH

Like other media mixes, *Yugioh* relies on cross-referencing between serialized manga, a TV anime series, a card game, video games, occasional move releases and a plethora of character merchandise. The manga ran for 343 installments between 1996 and 2004 in the weekly magazine *Shonen Jump* and is still continuing as an animated series. In 2001, the anime and card game was released in the USA, and soon after in the UK and other parts of the world. The series centers on a boy, Mutoh Yugi, who is a game master and gets involved in various adventures with a small cohort of friends and rivals. The narrative focuses on long sequences of card-game duels, stitched together by an adventure narrative. Yugi and his friends engage in a card game derivative of the US-origin game *Magic the Gathering*, and the series is devoted to fantastic duels that function to explicate the detailed esoterica of the games, such as strategies and rules of game play, properties of the cards, and the fine points of card collecting and trading. The height of *Yugioh's* popularity in Japan was between 1999 and 2001. A 2000 survey of 300 students in a Kyoto elementary school indicated that, by the third grade, *every* student owned some *Yugioh* cards (*Asahi Shinbun*, 2001).

Compared with *Pokemon*, where games are only loosely tied to the narrative media by character identification, with *Yugioh* the gaming comprises the central content of the narrative itself. In media mixes such as *Pokemon* and *Digimon*, the trading cards are a surrogate for 'actual' monsters in the fantasy world: *Pokemon* trainers collect monsters, not cards. In *Yugioh*, Yugi and his friends collect and traffic in trading cards, just like the kids in 'our world'. The activities of children in our world thus closely mimic the activities and materialities of children in Yugi's world. They collect and trade the same cards and engage in play with the same strategies, rules and material objects. Scenes in the anime depict Yugi frequenting card shops and buying card packs, enjoying the thrill of getting a rare card, dramatizing everyday moments of media consumption in addition to the highly stylized and fantastic dramas of the duels themselves. The convergent media form, as well as the narrative that focuses on esoteric game knowledge, channels engagement into otaku-like participation in genres of remix and personalization. This is similar to *Beyblade* that followed *Yugioh*, which involves kids collecting and battling with customized battle tops. The objects collected by the fantasy characters are the same as those collected by kids in real life. When I was conducting fieldwork, *Yugioh* cards were a pervasive fact of life, a fantasy world made manifest in the pockets and backpacks of millions of kids across the country.

Personal authorship through collection and remix is at the center of participation with *Yugioh*. While many children, and most girls, orient primarily to the manga or anime series, game play and collection is the focus of both the narrative and the more high-status forms of *Yugioh* engagement. Players can buy a 'starter pack' or 'structure deck' of cards that is ready to play, but none of the children I met in my fieldwork dueled with a preconfigured deck. Players will purchase 'booster packs' which are released in different series that roughly correspond to different points in the narrative trajectory of *Yugioh*. The booster packs cost ¥150 (a little over $1US) for five randomly packaged cards from the series, making it a relatively lightweight purchase that is integrated into the everyday routines of kids stopping at local mom-and-pop shops on their way home from school, or accompanying their parents to a convenience store or a bookstore. The purchase of booster packs supports a collection and trading economy between players, because they quickly accumulate duplicate cards or cards that they do not want to keep or use. In duel spaces, players will buy, sell and trade cards to one another in order to build their collections and design their own playing decks of 40 or more cards. Since there are several thousand different cards on the market now, the combinations are endless.

Players I spoke to had a wide range of strategies that guided their collection and deck combinations. Some players orient toward the narrative content, creating decks and collections that mimic particular manga characters or based on themes, such as dragon cards, insect cards or occult cards. Serious duelists focus on building the most competitive deck, reading up on the deck combinations that won in the national and international tournaments, and pitting their deck against local peers. Others with more of a collector or entrepreneurial bent prioritize cards with a high degree of rarity. All cards have a rarity index that is closely tracked by internet sites and hobby shops that buy and sell post-market single cards. While most children I played with or spoke to did not have easy access to internet sites, which are the clearinghouses for most esoteric collection knowledge (card lists, price lists and rarity indexes), they were able to acquire knowledge by visiting hobby shops or through a network of peers, which might include older children or young adults. Even young children would proudly show me their collections and discuss which were their favorite cards that reflected their personal taste and style. When I would walk into the afterschool center with a stack of cards I was quickly surrounded by groups of boys who riffled through my deck, asking questions about which cards were my own favorites and engaging in ongoing commentary about the coolness and desirability of particular cards. While there is a great deal of re-enactment and mimicking of existing narrative content in the practices of card collection and play, the game enables subject positions that are highly differentiated and variable. The series sports thousands of cards and dozens of duelist characters that Yugi has encountered in his many years on the air. The relation between the subjectivities of players and the commercially produced narrative apparatus of *Yugioh* is indicative of the mode of authorship of remix and personalization that I have been working to describe in this chapter. Players draw from a massive collectively shared imagination as source material for producing local identities and performances. The practices of talking about and exchanging cards are an example of hypersociality as a genre of participation: the merging of local social negotiations with the exchange of media-based knowledge and signifiers.

The practices of card collection and deck construction are closely tied to the modes of participation and sociability of *Yugioh* play. The structure of the media mix is built on the premise that play and exchange will happen in a group social setting rather than as an isolated instance of a child reading, watching or playing with a game machine. It is nearly impossible to learn how to play the card game rules and strategy without the coaching of more experienced players. My research assistants and I spent several weeks with the *Yugioh* starter pack, poring through the rule book and the instructional videotape and trying to figure out how to play. It was only after several game sessions with a group of fourth graders, followed by some coaching by some of the more patient adults at the card shops, that we slowly began to understand the basic game play as well as some of the fine points of collection, how cards are acquired, valued and traded. Among children, this learning process is part of their everyday peer relations, as they congregate after school in homes and parks, showing off their cards, hooking up their Game Boys to play against one another, trading cards and information. We found that kids generally develop certain conventions of play among their local peer group, negotiating rules locally, often on a duel-by-duel basis. They will collectively monitor the weekly manga release in *Shonen Jump* magazine, often sharing copies between friends. In addition to the weekly manga, the magazine also featured information about upcoming card releases, tournaments and tournament results. The issues featuring the winning decks of tournament duelists are often the most avidly studied. When kids get together with their collections of *Yugioh* cards, there is a constant buzz of information exchange and deal-cutting, as kids debate the merits of different cards and seek to augment both their play deck and their broader card collection. This buzz of hypersocial exchange is the lifeblood of the *Yugioh* status economy, and fuels the social jockeying for knowledge, position, and standing within the local peer network of play.

In many ways, this kind of collection and hypersociality is reminiscent of stamp or sports card collection or play with marbles and may not seem so different from the play of an earlier generation. What distinguishes contemporary media mixes such as *Pokemon* or *Yugioh*, however, is the depth of the imaginary world and referents, the multiplicity of media formats and distribution mechanisms involved, and their translocal reach into everyday practice. *Yugioh* is an imaginary universe that is global in material reach as well as imaginary referents, drawing from medieval fantasy, science fiction, martial arts and gaming culture to build a narrative and referential cultural universe that is stunningly complex. Add to that the ability for kids to traffic locally in the manifestations of these imaginary worlds, as well as to connect to expert sources of knowledge on the internet, specialty shops or tournaments, and we have a media ecology that makes otaku-like engagement more accessible to the mainstream. Although every generation has had hardcore geeks, fans and connoisseurs who meticulously study baseball stats and cards, or collect train sets based on imaginary and real-life referents, *Pokemon* and *Yugioh* mark a moment when these genres of participation became popular and accessible to the mainstream of kids. Although we may decry the commercialism of these media mixes, television and popular global mega hits in children's media have the side effect of democratizing access to knowledge and the imagination and creating a globally shared store of rich cultural source material with high production value. The pleasures of what has been a relatively elite mode of collection, hypersociality and expert connoisseurship have become part of the everyday and widespread recreational practices of children.

HAMTARO

When we turn to media mix content oriented to girls, this shift toward otaku-like genres of participation has not been as pronounced, but is still visible. With girls, in contrast to boys, the status economy of skill in competitive play is less central to their social lives. They tend to engage in a wide range of media and play that differs depending on their particular playmate. The girls I spoke to preferred the more subtly competitive exchange of stickers to develop their connoisseurship and cement their friendship circles and did not participate as avidly in the hypersocial buzz of card trading. When *Yugioh* tournaments were held at the afterschool center I observed at, a handful of girls might participate, but they tended to watch from the sidelines even though they likely had their own stash of cards. None of this is news to people who have looked at the gendered dimensions of play. Although *Pokemon* crosses gender lines because of its cute characters, the same is not true for most Japanese media mixes. Overall, boys' content is culturally dominant. It sets the trends in media mixing that girls' content follows. But girls' content *is* following. The trend is slower, but as of the late 1990s most popular girls' content will find its way to Game Boy, though not to platforms like Nintendo consoles or Playstation. Otaku-like forms of character development and multiyear and multiply threaded narrative arcs are also becoming more common in series oriented towards girls. There is yet to be a popular trading-card game based on girls' content, but there are many collectible cards with content oriented to girls. The gender dynamics of the media mix is a complex topic that deserves more careful treatment than I can provide here. To give one example of how the dynamics of new media mixes is making its way in to girls' content, I will describe the case of *Tottoko Hamutarou* (or *Hamtaro*, as it is known in English), the series that was most popular among girls during the period of my fieldwork.

Hamtaro is an intrepid hamster owned by a little girl. The story originated in picture book form in the late 1990s and became an animated series in 2000. In 2006, the anime series passed the 300 episode mark. After being released as a television anime, *Hamtaro* attracted a wide following, quickly becoming the most popular licensed character for girls. It was released in the USA, UK and other parts of the world in 2002. *Hamtaro* is an interesting case because it is clearly coded as girls' content and the human protaganist is a girl. But the central character, *Hamtaro*, is a boy. It has attracted a fairly wide following among boys as well as girls, though it was dwarfed by *Yugioh* in the boys' market during the time that I was conducting my fieldwork. The story makes use of a formula that was developed by *Pokemon*, which is of a proliferating set of characters that create esoteric knowledge and domains of expertise. While not nearly as extensive as the *Pokemon* pantheon or *Yugioh* cards, *Hamtaro* is part of a group of about 20 hamster friends, each of which has a distinct personality and life situation. To date the series has introduced over 50 different quirky hamster characters, and complex narratives of different relationships, compatibilities, antagonisms and rivalries. The formula is quite different from the classic one for girls' manga or anime that has tended to have shorter runs and is tightly focused on a small band of characters including the heroine, friend, love interest and rival. Instead, *Hamtaro* is a curious blend of multi-year soap opera and media mix esoterica, blending the girly focus on friendship and romance with otaku-like attention to details and a character-based knowledge industry.

In addition to the narrative and character development that follows some of the formulas established by *Pokemon*, the series also exhibits the convergent characteristics of the contemporary media mix. *Hamtaro's* commercial success hinges on an incredibly wide array of licensed products that make him an intimate presence in girls' lives even when he is not on the screen. These products include board games, clothing, curry packages and corn soup, in addition to the usual battery of pencils, stationary, stickers, toys and stuffed animals. Another important element of the *Hamtaro* media mix is Game Boy games. Five have been released so far. The first (never released overseas), *Tomodachi Daisakusen Dechu* (*The Great Friendship Plan*), was heavily promoted on television. Unlike most game commercials that focus on the content of the game, the spot featured two girls sitting on their bed with their Game Boys, discussing the game. The content of the game blends the traditionally girly content of relationships and fortune telling with certain formulas around collection and exchange developed in the boys media mix. Girls collect data on their friends and input their birthdays. The game then generates a match with a particular hamster character, and then predicts certain personality traits from that. Players can get a prediction of whether different people will get along as friends or as couples. Girls can also exchange data between Game Boy cartridges. The game builds on a model of collection and exchange that was established in the industry since *Pokemon*, but applied to a less overtly competitive girl-oriented exchange system. In Japan, *Hamtaro* even has a trading-card game associated with it, though it pales in scope and complexity compared with those of *Yugioh* and *Pokemon*.

When I spoke to girls about *Hamtaro* they delighted in telling me about the different characters, which was the cutest or sweetest, and which was their favorite. At the afterschool center, I often asked girls to draw pictures for me of media characters, one of many activities that the girls favored. *Hamtaro* characters were by far the most popular, followed by *Pokemon*. In each case, girls developed special drawing expertise and would proudly tell me how they were particularly good at drawing a particular hamster or *Pokemon*. The authorship involved in these creations does not involve the same investments of card players and collectors, yet there are still dimensions of personalization and remix. The large stable of characters and the complex relational dynamics of the series encourage girls to form personalized identifications with particular hamsters, manifest in a sense of taste and connoisseurship of which drawing is just one manifestation. Girls develop investments in certain characters and relational combinations. If they mature into a more otaku-like form of media engagement, then these same girls will bring this sensibility to bear on series that feature human characters and more adult narratives of romance, betrayal, and friendship. The *doujinshi* (amateur comic) scene in Japan was popularized by young women depicting alternative relational scenarios and backstories to popular manga. Elsewhere, I have discussed in more detail the role of doujinshi in popular youth cultures (Ito, 2006). I simply note here that *Hamtaro* engagements include an echo of the more hypersocial participation genres of remix, personalization and connoisseurship that are more clearly manifest in boys' popular cultures and practices.

CONCLUSIONS

The cases of *Yugioh* and *Hamtaro* are examples of how broader trends in children and new media are manifest in Japanese-origin media and media cultures that are becoming more and more global in their reach. Part of the international spread of Japanese media mixes is tied to the growth of more participatory forms of children's media cultures around the world. At the same time, different national contexts have certain areas of specialization. For example, where Japan has led in the particular media mix formula I have described, the US media ecology continues to remain dominant in cinema and internet-based publication and communication. The conceptual categories – convergence in media form, personalization and remix in authorship, and hypersociality as a genre of engagement – were developed based on my ethnographic work with Japanese media mixes, but I believe also apply to the media and practices of young people in other parts of the post-industrial world (e.g. Livingstone, 2002; Jenkins, 2006). While a comparative look at these forms of participation is beyond the scope of this chapter, there are certainly indications of growing transnational linkages and resonances.

If, as I have suggested, young people's media cultures are moving towards more mobilized and differentiated modes of participation with an increasingly global collective imagination, then we need to revisit our frameworks for understanding the role of the imagination in everyday life. Assessed by more well-established standards of creativity, the forms of authorship and performance I have described would be deemed derivative and appropriative rather than truly original. It is also crucial that we keep in view the political and economic implications of having young people's personal identities and social lives so attuned and dependent on a commercial apparatus of imaginative production. At the same time, we need to take seriously the fact that cultural forms like *Yugioh* and *Hamtaro* have become the coin of the realm for the childhood imagination, and recognize them as important sources of knowledge, connoisseurship and cultural capital. Even as we look for ways of guiding these activities towards more broadly generative forms of authorship, we need to acknowledge *Yugioh* play as a source of creativity, joy and self-actualization that often crosses traditional divides of status and class. Further, we need to reevaluate what authorship means in an era increasingly characterized by remix and recombination as a mode of cultural production. Elsewhere, I have written about the activities of older fans who compete in official tournaments and engage in the craftwork of producing amateur comics, costumes and fiction based on anime narratives (Ito, 2006). While I don't have space to discuss these activities here, it is important to note that remix and alternative production extends into higher-end production practices well beyond card collection, doodling and everyday game play.

Now, as ever, individuals produce new cultural material with shared cultural referents. The difference is the centrality of commercially produced source material and, more recently, the ability to easily recombine and exchange these materials locally and through peer-to-peer networks. For better and for worse, popular media mixes have become an integral part of our common culture, and visual media referents are a central part of the language with which young people communicate and express themselves. It may seem ironic to suggest that these practices in convergence culture have resulted in a higher overall 'production value' in what young people can say and produce on their own. Our usual lenses would insist that engagements with *Yugioh* or *Hamtaro* not only rely on cheap and debased cultural forms, but that they are highly derivative and unoriginal. What I have suggested in this chapter, however, is that we broaden the lens through which we view these activities to one that keeps in view the social and collective outcomes of participation. While I am not suggesting that content is irrelevant to how we assess these emergent practices, I do believe that it is just one of many rubrics through which we can evaluate the role of new media in children's lives.

Acknowledging these participatory media cultures as creative and imaginative does not mean foreclosing critical intervention in these practices or abdicating our role as adult guides and mentors. The dominance of commercial interests in this space means that it is crucial for adults with other kinds of agendas to engage actively rather than to write off these practices as trivial and purely consumptive. Many efforts in media literacy and youth media are exemplary in this respect, but I believe there is much more work to be done to make these recognitions take hold more broadly. Unless parents and educators share a basic understanding of the energies and motivations that young people are bringing to their recreational and social lives, these new media forms will produce an unfortunate generational gap. Resisting the temptation to fall into moral panic, technical determinism, and easy distinctions between good and bad media is one step. Gaining an understanding of practice and participation from the point of view of young people is another step. From this foundation of respectful understanding we might be able to produce a collective imagination that ties young people's practices into intergenerational structures and genres of participation in convergence culture.

ACKNOWLEDGEMENTS

The research and writing for this chapter was funded by a postdoctoral fellowship from the Japan Society for the Promotion of Science, the Abe Fellowship, the Annenberg Center for Communication at The University of Southern California, and a grant from the MacArthur Foundation. My research assistants in Japan were Tomoko Kawamura and Kyoko Sekizuka. This chapter has benefited from comments from Andre H. Caron, Michael Carter, Henry Jenkins and Dan Perkel.

REFERENCES

Allison, A. (2004) 'Cuteness and Japan's Millenial Product'. In J. Tobin (ed.) *Pikachu's Global Adventure: The Rise and Fall of Pokémon*. Durham, NC: Duke University Press; 34–52.

Ambron, S. (1989) 'Introduction'. In S. Ambron and K. Hooper (eds) *Interactive Multimedia: Visions of Multimedia for Developers, Educators, & Information Providers, Learning Tomorrow*. Redmond, WA: Microsoft Press.

Anderson, B. (1991) *Imagined Communities*. New York: Verso.

Appadurai, A. (1996) *Modernity at Large: Cultural Dimensions of Globalization*. Minneapolis, MN: University of Minnesota Press.

Asahi Shinbun (2001) 'Otousan datte Hamaru'. *Asahi Shinbun*, Tokyo, 7 January; 24.

Benkler, Y. (2006) *The Wealth of Networks: How Social Production Transforms Markets and Freedom*. New Haven, CT: Yale University Press.

Bourdieu, P. (1972) *Outline of a Theory of Practice*, J. Goody (ed.), R. Nice (transl.). New York: Cambridge University Press.

Buckingham, D. (2000) *After the Death of Childhood: Growing up in the Age of Electronic Media*. Cambridge: Polity.

Buckingham, D. and Sefton-Green, J. (2004) 'Structure, agency, and pedagogy in children's media culture'. In J. Tobin (ed.) *Pikachu's Global Adventure: The Rise and Fall of Pokémon*. Durham: Duke University Press; 12–33.

Cohen, S. (1972) *Folk Devils and Moral Panics*. London: MacGibbon and Kee.

Cross, G. (1997) *Kids' Stuff: Toys and the Changing World of American Childhood*. Cambridge, MA: Harvard University Press.

Dyson, A.H. (1997) *Writing Superheroes: Contemporary Childhood, Popular Culture, and Classroom Literacy*. New York: Teachers College Press.

Edwards, P. (1995) 'From "impact" to social process: computers in society and culture'. In S. Jasanoff, G.E. Markle, J.C. Petersen and T. Pinch (eds) *Handbook of Science and Technology Studies*. Thousand Oaks: Sage; 257–285.

Eng, L. (2001) 'The politics of otaku'. http://www.cjas.org/~leng/otaku-p.htm [15 May 2006].

Giddens, A. (1986) *The Constitution of Society: Outline of the Theory of Structuration*. Berkeley, CA: University of California Press.

Greenfeld, K.T. (1993) 'The incredibly strange mutant creatures who rule the universe of alienated Japanese zombie computer nerds'. *Wired* (1).

Hall, S. (1993) 'Encoding, decoding'. In S. Durin (ed.) *The Cultural Studies Reader*. New York: Routledge; 90–103.

Hine, C. (2000) *Virtual Ethnography*. London: Sage.

Holloway, S. and Valentine, G. (2001) *Cyberkids: Children in the Information Age*. New York: Routledge.

Ito, M. (2003) 'Engineering play: children's software and the productions of everyday life'. Anthropology, Stanford University, Stanford.

Ito, M. (2006) 'Japanese media mixes and amateur cultural exchange'. In D. Buckingham and R. Willett (eds) *Digital Generations: Children, Young People, and the New Media*. London: Lawrence Erlbaum; 49–66.

Ito, M. (2007) 'Technologies of the childhood imagination: *Yugioh*, media mixes, and everyday cultural production'. In J. Karaganis (ed.) *Structures of Digital Participation*. New York: SSRC Books; in press.

Jenkins, H. (1992) *Textual Poachers: Television Fans and Participatory Culture*. New York: Routledge.

Jenkins, H. (1998) 'Introduction: childhood innocence and other modern myths'. In H. Jenkins (ed.) *The Children's Culture Reader*. New York: New York University Press; 1–37.

Jenkins, H. (2006) *Convergence Culture: Where Old and New Media Collide*. New York: New York University Press.

Jeremijenko, N. (2002) 'What's new in new media'. *Mute Beta: Culture and Politics After the Net*. http://www.metamute.org/en/node/5779/print [September 2007].

Johnson, S. (2005) *Everything Bad Is Good for You*. New York: Riverhead Books.

Karaganis, J. (2007) 'Introduction'. In J. Karaganis (ed.) *Structures of Digital Participation*. Durham, NC: Duke University Press.

Kinder, M. (1991) *Playing with Power in Movies, Television, and Video Games*. Berkeley, CA: University of California Press.

Kinder, M. (1999) 'Kids' media culture: an introduction'. In M. Kinder (ed.) *Kids' Media Culture*. Durham: Duke University Press; 1–12.

Kinsella, S. (1998) 'Japanese subculture in the 1980s: otaku and the amateur manga movement'. *Journal of Japanese Studies*, 24: 289–316.

Lave, J. and Wenger, E. (1991) *Situated Learning: Legitimate Peripheral Participation*. New York: Cambridge University Press.

Lessig, L. (1999) *Code and Other Laws of Cyberspace*. New York: Basic Books.

Livingstone, S. (2002) *Young People and New Media*. London: Sage Publications.

Miller, D. and Slater, D. (2000) *The Internet: An Ethnographic Approach*. New York: Berg.

Okada, T. (1996) *Otakugaku Nyuumon* (*Introduction to Otakuology*). Tokyo: Ota Shuppan.

Papert, S. (1980) *Mindstorms: Children, Computers, and Powerful Ideas*. New York: Basic Books.

Sefton-Green, J. (2004) 'Initiation rites: a small boy in a Poké-world'. In J. Tobin (ed.) *Pikachu's Global Adventures: The Rise and Falll of Pokémon*. Durham: Duke University Press; 141–164.

Seiter, E. (1999) 'Power Rangers at preschool: negotiating media in child care settings'. In M. Kinder (ed.) *Kids' Media Culture*. Durham: Duke University Press; 239–262.

Tobin, S. (2004) 'Masculinity, maturity, and the end of Pokémon'. In J. Tobin (ed.) *Pikachu's Global Adventure: The Rise and Fall of Pokémon*. Durham: Duke University Press; 241–256.

Japanese Young People, Media and Everyday Life: Towards the Internationalizing of Media Studies

Toshie Takahashi

INTRODUCTION

Researcher: 'Why do you have this long Disney string attached to your mobile phone?'

Yuka: 'Because I don't want to lose my mobile, so I hang it from my neck. I can live no longer if I lose it'.

Yuka is a 15-year-old junior high-school girl from Shibuya, Tokyo. This is the place, according to Howard Rheingold, with the highest mobile phone density in the world.

For today's children and young people, media and information and communication technologies (ICTs), such as mobile phones, game consoles, television, video/DVD and personal computers, play increasingly important roles in their everyday lives. In my fieldwork, they described these media devices as 'necessaries', 'a part of the body', 'my partner' or 'something indispensable, like air'. This chapter considers how Japanese youths engage with media and ICT amidst the current social and cultural changes in Japanese society in the face of globalization. The primary aim of this chapter is to analyze the complex and diverse ways in which Japanese youths engage with media and ICT, understanding and bringing together audience activities under the concept of 'audience engagement'. Further, the analysis of the Japanese audience can serve as a modest step towards the internationalization of media studies. In the process, some Japanese emic concepts are employed, adapting them in ways that reject as myth the homogeneity of the Japanese, in order to highlight culturally specific ways of constructing self and other. Methodologically, the qualitative approach adopted is intended to complement the quantitative emphasis to audience research within Japanese academia. Specifically, the present study is conducted as an ethnography of audiences, among the so-called 'modern' Japanese families living in the media-rich Tokyo Metropolitan Area.[1]

After introducing the concept of 'audience engagement', which is the key concept of my research, I will address the issue of internationalization of media studies. The discussion is first set in the issues existing in the body of social science methodology: that is, the dichotomy between the 'universalism of the West' and 'the peculiarity of the Rest'. Further, it is set in the historical context of postwar Japan, its responses to its techno-orientalism as projected by the West, and the formation of a Japanese identity out of this imagining of itself as a high-tech society. Recent Japanese children and youths have grown up accustomed to an extremely media-rich environment. I will briefly introduce the current research on children and media in Japanese society before discussing diverse ways in which Japanese young people engage with the media – using key Japanese emic concepts. Drawing on my ethnographic research on 'audience engagement' in Japan, the chapter addresses the cultural specificities and commonalities between Japanese and Western childhood media, while offering insights from a non-Western perspective. This is a move which I hope will contribute towards an internationalizing of media studies.

THE CONCEPT OF 'AUDIENCE ENGAGEMENT'

The primary aim of this chapter is to understand and bring together audience activities under the concept of 'audience engagement', as this term (a) encompasses the multiple dimensions of audience activities and thereby (b) moves beyond simplified or dichotomized visions of audiences. The concept of audience engagement encompasses some of the ideas developed within active audience theories in both Western and Japanese media audience studies. I have borrowed the following types of audience engagement from uses and gratifications studies within American communication studies, audience reception studies of British cultural studies and European reception theory, and *Joho Kodo* (information behavior) studies of Japanese audience studies: information and communication behavior (Hashimoto, 1986; Mikami, 1991); selectivity (Klapper, 1960; Levy, 1983); involvement (Rubin and Perse, 1987); utility (personal use (McQuail *et al*., 1972); social use (Lull, 1990)) and interpretation (Hall, 1980; Fiske, 1987). *Joho Kodo* studies of Japanese information society theory (Umesao, 1963; Hayashi, 1969)[2] began to emerge in response to the penetration of new communication technologies into Japanese society in the 1970s. Scholars within this body of research make assumptions similar to those employed in the uses and gratifications studies, but employ a broader understanding of the concept of use. Studies within *Joho Kodo* have considered a remarkable range of media and information technologies, from one of the favorite Japanese pastimes, taking photographs, to the use of mobile phones, in a bid to understand the impact of such technologies in the lives of Japanese people. I also borrow from the following varieties of engagement from alternative traditions, namely diffusion (DeFleur, 1988) and participation (Livingstone and Lunt, 1994). I have identified seven dimensions of audience engagement (information and communication behavior, selectivity, involvement, utility, interpretation, diffusion, and participation) from my previous research on audience activity, both theoretically (Takahashi, 1998c) and empirically (Takahashi, 1998a,b).[3] In addition to these forms of engagement I hope to discover, from my research, new dimensions via which Japanese young people engage with not only television, but also other media, such as mobile phones and the internet. I will look at this engagement in its social context and, thus, view it in terms of different dimensions of social interaction. That is, I hope to discover a variety of ways in which Japanese young people engage socially (or even antisocially) with the rich media environments of their everyday lives.

In the following sections I will address the issue of 'internationalizing' media studies and its methodologies.

TOWARDS THE INTERNATIONALIZING OF MEDIA STUDIES

Western social science has produced a plethora of theories concerning, and concepts pertaining to, people and societies, derived both from theoretical and empirical studies. The concepts this research has produced have been taken by many scholars and researchers to be etic concepts; that is, they are universally applicable to any and all people and societies. Japanese scholars have themselves used these etic concepts in their studies of Japanese society and, thereby, as some critics claim, have erroneously analyzed Japan through 'West-colored' spectacles. *Nihonjinron* (Japanese culture studies) has criticized such an application of Western concepts and theories to Japan, claiming that, because Japan is unique, such an application is not only unenlightening, but is also distorting of the reality of Japan. Nakane (1967) argued that Japan has had its unique process of modernization and that, in order to understand Japanese society, our own unique measure is required: a pair of spectacles 'Made in Japan'. Such an analysis would produce Japanese emic concepts; that is, concepts uniquely applicable to Japan, giving the 'real' picture of the society and possibly (depending on the scholar) capable of being usefully applied to understanding other societies.[4]

In this chapter, I wish to avoid fitting exclusively into either of these approaches; that is, I hope neither to use exclusively Western etic concepts nor exclusively Japanese emic concepts. Instead, I aim to appropriate concepts from any tradition that will be relevant to and enlightening of Japanese audiences. Thus, I take the following two steps towards 'internationalizing' media studies. First, the appropriation and adaptation of Japanese emic concepts will introduce new concepts into audience research, concepts that may be relevant not only to Japanese audiences, but also to non-Japanese audiences as well. Second, the appropriation of Western concepts and their use in a Japanese context will show their relevance to audiences outside of the West, thus providing further evidence of the cross-cultural validity (and strength) of such concepts. Evidence of cross-cultural validity also constitutes an internationalizing of concepts.

The concept of uchi

In searching for the most enduring, unchanging and essential or definitive feature of Japanese society, Nakane (1967) looked towards relations, which she argued are the one phenomenon of Japanese society and culture that have not changed since Japan's modernization. *Uchi* (inside, us) is opposed to *soto* (outside, them) and it exists in the belonging of people to social groups linked by close interpersonal relationships. Nakane argued in the 1960s and 1970s that a person can belong to only one such *uchi*, due to its membership requiring exclusive loyalty and commitment of time and energy. She claimed that a woman's *uchi* is her family, a man's is his company and a child's is his or her classmates. I accept that the *uchi* is a fundamental aspect of Japanese social relationships and want to see if contemporary Japanese people having multiple *uchis* is in fact made possible by ICT.[5]

HIGH-TECH JAPAN: JAPAN'S SELF-IDENTITY AND TECHNO-NATIONALISM

The defeat at the hands of the Allied forces in the Pacific War challenged the Japanese pride and sense of nationalism and brought about tremendous change in its values and institutions. With the American

BOX 24.1 The Media Environment in Japan

Japanese broadcasting consists of three systems: terrestrial, satellite and cable; each of these offers both national and international programs. The public broadcasting service channels are NHK1 and NHK3, the commercial channels are NTV, TBS, Fuji Television and TV Asahi, and Tokyo's regional channels are TV Tokyo and Tokyo Metropolitan Television. Digital service was started 2003 in a few metropolitan areas, and will cover all parts of Japan by 2011. Satellite television offers over 100 channels, both national and international. It is divided into BS and CS (both digital). There are countless cable television suppliers, and 38.2% of households subscribe to one company or another. In addition, 3.41 million households also take advantage of cable internet (Soumushou (Ministry of Internal Affairs and Communications), 2006). The average time each person spends watching television is 4 hours and 6 minutes a day (8 hours and 2 minutes per household) (Video Research, 2006).

Some 68.5% of the population have access to or use the internet, in the form of using email and accessing the World Wide Web, via personal computers, mobile phones, games machines, television sets (WebTV) or other gadgets. There are 101.7 million mobile phones (out of a total population of 127.8 million people) used in Japan (Soumushou (Ministry of Internal Affairs and Communications), 2007). According to a Cabinet Office of the Government of Japan (2007) research report ('Information Society and Youth'), 31.3% of children in elementary school have their own mobile phones, 57.6% in junior high school and 96% of high school students have mobile phones. These days figures for i-mode use (allowing access to the internet via mobile phone for the purposes of sending email, getting news and information and banking) show increasing popularity. This results in a general figure of 94.1% of mobile phones in Japan having access to the internet, placing it first in the world, with the second being Korea (89.0%) and the third the USA (33.5%) (Yuseisho (Ministry of Posts and Telecommunications), 2005).

occupation, Japanese leaders were forced to adopt Western-styled political, economic and educational institutions and even created a new constitution. Japanese leaders have tried to create a national identity based on an image of a 'high-tech Japan', in place of its strong militaristic nationalism before the war. Techno-orientalism (Morley and Robins, 1995) describes the stereotypical image of Japan as a 'strange high-tech other' to the West, as exemplified in many Hollywood movies which portray Japan. Instead of rejecting the image, the Japanese have come to adopt and appropriate this as part of their self-image (Abe, 2004). In January 2001, the Japanese government drew up an 'e-Japan strategy', to make Japan the most advanced ICT nation in the world within 5 years. Japan's techno-nationalism helped spur a media-rich environment in which succeeding generations of Japanese children have grown up; see Box 24.1. How will these Japanese children and young persons relate to the media and ICT from now on?

CHILDREN AND YOUNG PEOPLE AND MEDIA STUDIES IN JAPAN

With the rapid development of digital technology and penetration of ICT come fears being expressed about its undesirable consequences, especially for children. Periodically there have been outcries from worried parents blaming television and the internet for social ills from pornography and cult behavior to violent crimes and suicides. Some are worried that using the internet and mobile phone may impair their children's ability to communicate or interact in face-to-face situations.

Broadly, the research in Japan on ICT concerns has come from four main groups. The first consists of the Parent–Teacher Association, police department and lawyers. They focus on dating sites and ICT-related crimes. They are concerned about media regulation and problems of prostitution facilitated by dating sites.

The second group is the educators, media scholars and engineers who see the potential of using ICT for education. They work towards media literacy among Japanese children, organizing forums like the Forum for Citizens' Television and Media, NPO Child and Media, the 'BEAT' project and the 'MELL' project.

The third group consists of medical doctors, psychiatrists, psychologists and public administrators whose research focuses on how playing video games, exchanging emails and using mobile phones influence children. They focus on damage on the brain and eyes and also on relationships between media exposure and children's crime. Mori (2002) published a sensational book, *Geimu Nou no Kyohu* (*Terror of the Video Game Brain*) and people have become more and more worried about the serious harmful effects on children of video games. Sakamoto (2005) conducted several panel studies on the effects of video games on children's aggression, social adaptation, cognitive abilities and academic achievement, comparing his Japanese data with previous research findings in the USA. Sakamoto suggested the necessity of cross-cultural research in future Japanese video game research because Japan can provide non-Western findings.

The final group is made up of the social psychologists and administrative researchers, whose work has been described as *Joho Kodo* (information behavior) research. While *Joho Kodo* research surveys Japanese people in general, many scholars tend to focus on young people (mainly because of the availability of college students as a sample) and their use of the mobile phone. For example, Hashimoto (2005) examined the correlations between ICT use and Japanese young people's communication behavior in terms of friendships, sense of solitude and family relationships, by using the results of some quantitative research.

In the following sections I will look at how children and young people engage with media, based on my ethnographic research on the Japanese family in the current rich media environment, in connection with the findings from current research on children and media in Japan.

JAPANESE YOUTH'S ENGAGEMENT WITH MEDIA AND INFORMATION AND COMMUNICATION TECHNOLOGY

This chapter looks at the various ways in which Japanese young people engage with the media and ICT. Some of these may be universal categories, while others are more specific to the Japanese audience. The seven modes of engagement I will consider are: information-seeking activity, connectivity, 'world-creation', parasocial interaction, utility, interpretation and, finally, participation.

Information-seeking activity and selectivity

Both *Joho Kodo* and the uses and gratifications studies have identified information-seeking behavior and selectivity as being significant aspects of audience activity. My research revealed some of the factors involved in creating the various needs people have for the information they seek.

The first factor concerns the role of the primary *uchi* of the informant in creating a need for particular information. I allude here to people's embeddedness of the local life that other theorists (Giddens, 1990) have also identified as a factor in people's behavior in general. Informants (usually housewives) who primarily identified with the domestic *uchi* tended to use the internet and television to seek information relating to the family. Similarly, business people (usually men), spending most of their waking time at the office or with colleagues and belonging, therefore, primarily to a business *uchi*, tended to seek information related to their business or to money. Finally, children and young people embedded in a classmate *uchi* tended to seek information related to schoolwork or to entertainment, in order to maintain and reinforce their friend *uchi* membership. According to Kayama and Mori (2004), elementary school boys tended to browse the game, football and television programs' websites on the internet, while girls tended to use the internet for chatting or for writing their blogs. Thus, boys tend to use the internet for gaining information to sustain interpersonal relationships, while girls tend to use new media for the purpose of communication (Livingstone and Bovill, 1999; Buckingham, 2002). In this way, social context and *uchi* roles (which may turn out to correspond to gender roles) seem to have a great influence on the kinds of information people need.

The second factor involved in selectivity was the current rich media environment. People have expressed fear of the destruction of the family resulting from the increased private or isolated use of new media technology. In an environment of limited television choice, family members share time, space, conversation and ideas as they watch television together. However, it is likely that family members will increasingly become isolated from each other as they each indulge privately in their personally selected form of media entertainment. While for some television has in the past served as a 'hearth' bringing families together, it is now increasingly considered as serving to drive families apart. Haruko (mother, age 46) recalled that her family used to watch television together, in a cozy pile on the floor, but that has all changed. Now, each member prefers to engage in his or her favorite type of media entertainment in a separate room. Somehow, none of the family members' favorite television programs coincide: Haruko likes 2-hour suspense dramas and news, Haruo (father, 50) watches *samurai* dramas and historical documentaries, Harumi (daughter, 20) prefers *torendiidoramas* ('trendy dramas') and music shows, while Haru (son, 14) watches variety shows and sports shows on the second television set and plays video games. Thus, after dinner, the children usually go to their own rooms while Haruko either cleans up or watches television alone. She is aware of the role that televisions and so forth play in keeping her family apart. Her children have asked for their own television sets and a computer for their rooms, but she refused, explaining to me, 'I said no because otherwise I will never see them'.

Researcher: 'So, you can't watch television together, because everybody is busy?'

Haruko: 'Oh, is television a thing that families watch together?'

Haruko had not even conceived of television being a tool for bringing families together, merely adapting family television viewing time to become a time for her to observe her children quietly.

In the current rich media environment, people have become more selective. While a cross-cultural survey across European countries has suggested that 'having a media-rich bedroom is associated with greater use of the bedroom' (Livingstone, 2002: 143), in Japan, ICT contributes to a fragmentation of the family *uchi* in ways I will discuss in the following section.

Connectivity

This dimension of engagement with media revealed itself to me in my fieldwork as I became more aware of the variety of motivations my informants had in using ICT. They seemed to be exploiting it as a means of connecting to a variety of phenomena for a variety of reasons. Tomlinson (1999) talked of increasing global-spatial proximity in the world today and the media and ICT naturally play a significant part in this process of 'making the world a smaller place'. The ICT my informants regularly use enables them to disembed themselves from their local life (be it home or the office) and embed themselves into 'other worlds'. The embedding into these non-spatial localities and subsequent re-embedding back into spatial localities or local lives changes the nature of those local lives in the sense that the home, for example, becomes open to the world. People increasingly exist and operate in non-spatial locations as this process of 'deterritorialization' (Appadurai, 1990; Morley and Robins, 1995; Lull, 2000), driven largely by ICT, is taken advantage of by people who benefit from a sense of transnational connectivity.

One evening, I was invited to dinner at an informant's place and had hoped to join in their family viewing. But it was not what I had expected. Dinner had just finished and I made my way to sit comfortably at the sofa facing the television set. My host, Youichi (father, 51), stayed at the dining table with a laptop computer in front of him because he wanted to access the internet. From where he was sitting, he said, 'I can watch TV from here'. With me on the sofa were his wife (Yoshie, mother, 48) and 13-year old daughter Yoshiko. Yone (grandmother, 73) had already gone to bed, while Yoshiki (Youichi's oldest son, 21) had not come home yet. The younger son, Yoshikazu (19) had gone to his room, where apparently he was watching the same program. Youichi explained that his younger son does not usually join in the 'family viewing'.

On television was a local drama, *Antique*, which starred Taki, a member of the pop group Johnnys, over which Yoshiko was crazy. We were watching and talking about the show when Yoshiko suddenly received an email on her mobile, after which we practically 'lost' her, as she continued to exchange emails on her mobile with her friend, another fan of Taki: 'Yeah, he looks so cute tonight!!'. She typed away her messages without looking at the mobile phone; she was a member of the new generation subculture, *oyayubibunka* (thumb culture, referring to those so skillful at operating their mobile phones that they can do so merely by swift manipulations of their thumbs and without looking). Suddenly, Yoshie stood up, declaring that she had to do some housework and she went off to the kitchen. With my host lost in cyberspace, his children embedded in their respective personal spaces created by personal media and his wife retreating into her domestic space, I was left pretty much alone (but for the family dog, Yon) in this so-called situation of 'family viewing'.

Even though some of the family members, at least periodically, share time-space in front of the television set in the living room, they are connecting with other *uchis*, such as their friends, colleagues, fan *uchi* and so forth. Because of the personalization of television and ICT, the domestic space, or 'home', is opened up to the outside, thereby contributing to a fragmentation of the family 'hearth'.

The mobile phone allows children and young people to connect with their friends beyond time-space and they use it to maintain and reinforce their friend *uchi*. According to a Cabinet Office of the Government of Japan (2002) research report ('Information Society and Youth'), 'the average number of telephone numbers registered in the mobile phones of females between the ages of 15 and 22 is over 80. Over 40% of them register over 100 phone numbers in their mobile phones'. Teenagers I interviewed in Shibuya, Tokyo, in 2005 told me that the number of people in their mobile phone address books is an indication of the width and richness of the social interaction they have.

However, even though they register over 100 people in their mobile phone, the number with whom they frequently exchange emails and call is usually limited. According to World Internet Project Japan (2002), the number of emails sent by teenagers via mobile phone per week is 62.6, but the number of people with whom they frequently exchange emails is 7.8. The research concluded 'young people send emails to the same person via mobile phone very frequently' (World Internet Project Japan, 2002: 153–154). Nakajima *et al.* (1999) conducted surveys on the use of mobile phones by the youth and concluded that mobile phone promotes the creation of a 'full-time intimate community' with their close friends.

According to an NTT DoCoMo survey (2005), 55% of elementary school students, 77% of junior high-school students and 82.2% high-school students had more frequent contact with friends after getting a mobile phone. About 60% of children and young people 'immediately respond if they receive an email'.[6] Yoshiko, a typical *oyayubibunka*, is an example of this case. In the 1960s and 1970s, Nakane (1967, 1970) argued that the internal structure of the *uchi* emerges through its 'tangibility', the constant sharing of the locale and constant face-to-face interaction. At the beginning of the twenty-first century, the structure of the *uchi* has emerged, not just through face-to-face interaction in spatial localities, but also through constant mediated interaction via the internet in non-spatial localities.

Mobile phones connect people not only with their friends, but also with family members. In my next example, a case in which ICT benefits the extended family, the family is what is known as a *tanshinfunin* family, a living arrangement in which the father lives apart, to be close to his workplace, while the rest of the family lives close to the children's schools. Shingo (father, 36) is one such father, living away from home on weekdays. To stay in touch, he makes it a point to email his daughter, Shiori (daughter, 8), on her mobile phone daily. Their mobile phones can also be used to send and receive digital pictures, which is what they do often. Shingo's wife also works during the daytime. Because of this, Shiori has to stay home to look after her younger brother Shinji (son, 6) after school, until about seven o'clock, when their mother comes home, after picking up baby Shoko (daughter, 1) from the nursery. A few times a day, her mother calls Shiori to make sure they are all right.

This situation has been described as the modern nuclear family in Japan. The children are called *Kagikko* (or latch-key kids). A common feature among these children is that, despite their young age, they hold the key to the family's apartment and let themselves in and out unsupervised. Babysitters are expensive and hard to come by in Japan. This arrangement is not well favored, but many such families will tell you they have no choice. Such children carry their mobile phones as if they were parts of their bodies. This case shows separated family members recreating their interpersonal relationships via ICT beyond time-space, trying to keep their connectivity and reinforce their social intimacy by the exchange of messages and pictures via mobile phone while at the same time enabling them to take on more 'modern' economic roles within the family.

Another example I found of transnational connectivity by using media and ICT was that of Yoshiki and Yoshikazu, who stayed up until midnight to watch a live football match. Their participation in this international media event gave them a sense of connectivity to fellow football fans around the world as they disembedded, via satellite, from their home locality to embed in a global-communal time-space.

These informants, whether physically at home or not, all use television and other forms of ICT to, in some sense, transport themselves to non-spatial locations in which a sense of connectivity with a sense of belonging to other communities can be achieved. It may be a case either of wanting to disembed *from* or embed *in* the home, but what is significant in this mode of engagement is a desire to achieve connectivity with something which is not physically in the immediate spatial location of the person.

World-creation

Another mode of engagement, both revealed from the field and stemming originally from uses and gratifications studies' concept of 'involvement', was the use of ICT in the process of creating informants' own 'worlds' within their lives. This type of engagement is based around the idea of appropriation and borrows from concepts such as bricolage (Levi-Strauss, 1966), poaching (de Certeau, 1984) and the 'cultural supermarket' (e.g. Hall, 1992). De Certeau (1984) talks of 'productive consumption', and I want to use this idea to understand the ways in which my informants appropriated images, styles, values, relationships and ideas in a process of producing the respective natures of their identities or 'worlds'.

Yoshiko is a fan of Johnnys, and this is strongly evidenced by the overbearing presence of posters and paraphernalia of its members stuck all over her room, their appearance on the wallpaper and ring tone of her mobile phone, and on stickers on her notebooks and other stationery. She spends most of her free time talking to or emailing friends about Johnnys, browsing their website, watching their weekly television show, and attending fan-club events. Yoshiko has created in her life her 'Johnnys world', using non-mediated, mediated and mediated quasi-interaction. Most of her engagement with television and ICT has the aim of creating and recreating her 'Johnnys world'.

Kenta (7) and Jin (7) collect Poke-mon products. They almost always play Poke-mon cards and Playstation games, talk about Poke-mon stories and remember all about names and information about Poke-mon characters. They create their 'poke-mon world'. Aki (13) creates a 'Disney world' by downloading the wallpaper and ring tone for her mobile phone, and attaching it with a Mickey Mouse strap, a little Dambo doll and seals.

Contemporary childhood culture has been constructed by 'transmedia intertexuality', such as video games, films, television series, card games, books, comics, toys and so on (Kinder, 1991; Buckingham, 2002). Children and young people consume cultural products that are neither Japanese nor American, but shop from the 'youth cultural supermarket' internationally, buying, for example, Japanese Poke-mon and Hello Kitty games, American Disney products and English Harry Potter DVDs. They create a bricolage of international consumer products to create their own world.

Para-social interaction

This dimension of engagement with media and ICT was first identified from within uses and gratifications studies (Horton and Wohl, 1956; Levy, 1979), when it was observed that many people watch television in order to have some kind of (quasi) interaction with its characters. Reception studies have developed this idea and used it extensively in attempts to explain women's fascination with soap operas (Modleski, 1982; Radway, 1984; Ang, 1985). I observed the same phenomenon occurring among several of my informants, comprised of housewives, children and young people who fantasized about pop or sports stars as if they really were intimate friends or lovers. Yoshiko provides the most extreme example among my informants of para-social interaction, through her involvement with Taki, her favorite member of the boy band Johnnys.

When we listened to children's conversations with their friends, we could realize how much the media world revolving around figures such as Poke-mon or Johnnys is embedded into their everyday life. They create their own worlds by using media and ICT and they para-socialize with television characters and images even when they are not in front of a television.

Parents and researchers worry such children might no longer be able to distinguish between the real and media world, as they have increasingly encountered children who engage so entirely with media and embed themselves so fully into their own media world. The *Otaku* (stay-at-home tribe) has become a serious social phenomenon among young people in Japan, which is such a media-saturated country. In Japan, as well as in Britain, the number of NEETs (Not in Employment, Education or Training) has been rapidly increasing recently. The more young people engage with television, video, *manga*, video games and mobile phones and fanatically para-socialize with their characters at home instead of going to school or work, the more people have become concerned about the apparent correlation between the accelerated development of new media technology and the increasing number of NEETs. However, in Japanese media studies to date there has been no clear evidence of such a correlation, for example as between playing video games and social inadaptability.

Utility

Uses and gratifications studies have identified various dimensions of the personal use of media, and Lull (1990) has investigated the social uses of television. I have already discussed a variety of uses of television and ICT that were revealed to me in the field, such as information seeking, world-creation and connectivity. I also observed other ways of utilizing television and ICT that have been identified by previous studies. The most prevalent one I came across was that of filling in time and relaxation. This finding corroborates the quantitative research (Dentsu Souken, 2000).

NTT DoCoMo (2005) conducted a survey on children and young people's access to information sites. The highest use of mobile phone internet sites comes from ring tone downloads (60% of elementary school student users, 80.2% of junior high-school student users, and 90.5% of high-school student users). The second most popular is taking photographs (82.5%, 72.2%, and 84% respectively). The third is wallpaper downloads (30%, 49.2%, and 68% respectively).

Aside from these personal uses, my informants also put media and ICT to a variety of social uses. The fourth highest use of mobile phones is for emailing photographs which they have taken on their mobile phones (40%, 43.7% and 60.9% respectively). Children and young people take photographs of what they find on the street, what they eat at lunch, their cat or dog or anything else in their everyday life and send the photographs to their *uchi* members via mobile phone at any time and any place. They share their feelings, experiences, thoughts and images with their friends and reinforce the friend *uchi*, more visually through constant mediated interaction.

While parents have been giving mobile phones to their children to help protect them in case of emergencies,[7] Shimoda (2004: 116) suggests that 'what is the most attractive of mobile phone for children is perhaps "its power of escape from parents" control'. When the home telephone was situated at the entrance hall or living room at home, before mobile phones became popular, parents could control the people who tried to enter into their domestic *uchi* from outside. However, now that they have their own PCs and mobile phones, the home has been opened to the outside world. They can easily access any information from outside and communicate with friends and strangers whom parents have never met or known beyond domestic time-space, as I discussed in regard to the dimension of connectivity.

Parents use television to maintain and reinforce the domestic *uchi*. Mothers use television as a babysitter for their children and to direct their attention to various activities (for example, the news makes them focus on their dinner, cartoons take their attention from their mother and so forth). Some parents hand over control of the remote control device to their children in order to create a shared family space. Fathers who embed into business *uchi* and usually do not stay at home use watching television to facilitate familial relationships. On weekends they pass the remote control device to their children and watch television cartoons all day as this enables them to spend time with their children, sharing their favorite activities with them and thus making up for time lost during the week by rebuilding their relationship. They use television to maintain intimacy with their children.

Although Japan has been forced to open up to the rest of the world since World War II, sometimes the processes involved and the routes taken have been quite tortuous. In the example of one of my informants' family, comprised of Kazuo (father, 45), Kazue (mother, 41) and their two children, Kaito (son, 14) and Kayo (daughter, 11), living in the USA for 3 years had meant that there was quite a bit of readjustment to be made on returning to Japan. Kaito and Kayo, in particular, had difficulty in reassimilating into the *uchi* to which they had belonged before going abroad. For Kaito, his newly acquired 'American characteristics' made it difficult for him to fit in with his old classmates. All was not lost, however, as Kaito told me how the 'subversive' playing of video games helped him overcome the initial difficulties and provided opportunities for cultural exchange and integration. One of Kaito's friends had wanted to go over to his house to play Playstation, but he was forbidden by his mother. This friend, however, found a way around her objection by claiming that he was learning English at Kaito's house, knowing that his mother thought this was worthwhile. The boys rekindled their friendship in front of the Playstation, helped by the excitement of the 'underground tactics' used to defy the friend's parents. The *uchi* had thus been recreated, but now with elements of cultural hybridization, borrowing from Kaito's experiences of living in America.

Playing video games together often gives children and young people a chance to share the time and space for constructing, sustaining and reinforcing their friend *uchi*. As Buckingham (2002: 80) has discussed, 'The culture of games playing involves an ongoing construction of an "interpretive community" (Radway, 1984)'. Gillespie (1995: 208) also stated from her ethnography among British Asian youth in London, 'Media are not only being used by productive consumers to maintain and strengthen boundaries, but also to create new, shared spaces in which syncretic cultural forms such as "new ethnicities", can emerge'. Gillespie's focus was on television talk; but, equally, ICT and other media can also provide similar opportunities for their participants (or 'productive consumers').

I found numerous cases of media being utilized for their ability to relieve stress and offer an escape from local life and the pressures created by the obligations, loyalties and commitment membership to its *uchis*. All of my informants, to greater or lesser degrees, used television or ICT as a means of disembedding from their immediate locale and embedding in a non-spatial location in which they could simply forget and relax. The other most significant use of media and ICT was its utilization for the purposes of facilitating both communication and social relationships. My informants used ICT and other media to maintain and strengthen the bonds that held together the various *uchis* to which they belong.

Interpretation

Audience reception studies have investigated the diversity of interpretations amongst audiences and tried to understand these in terms of the various social contexts of audience members. Fiske's (1987) model of semiotic democracy and Hall's (1980) encoding–decoding model made use of aspects of social context in understanding differing interpretations of media content. In considering people's interpretation of media messages, I want to focus on the extent to which viewers or readers view or read critically.

Haruko was not at all critical of or reflective on the information that television reports. This phenomenon perhaps has special significance in Japan, as it relates to compliance to authority, something Japanese culture scholars often have pointed to as being important in understanding 'Japanese culture'. When I asked Haruko, who welcomes a sense of responsibility in regularly reporting information she gets from television to her family, whether she usually agrees or disagrees with experts on television, she replied unhesitatingly, 'Oh no, I trust everything they say. I'm *sunao*. If someone on TV gets something wrong, then I will too'. *Sunao* means without doubting, questioning or being cynical and is a quality indisputably understood as being desirable. It reflects dependence on and trust in the judgment of one's senior, mother and so forth, over independence and faith in one's own judgment. Here, we can see evidence of the primacy of the Japanese 'hierarchical system' of social relationships and Hamaguchi's (1998) model of 'the contextual' gives us insight into why Haruko may readily accept the 'preferred reading' (Hall, 1980). Through quasi-mediated interaction with 'television others', governed by the relational concept of interpersonal relating

(Hamaguchi, 1998), Haruko creates herself into a virtuous and *sunao* person, a good traditional Japanese housewife. Here, we see the undesirable side of 'the contextual', as it can lead to unquestioning acceptance of media messages.

I also found instances of 'negotiated' and 'oppositional' readings amongst my informants. Chika (daughter, 20) studies and is interested in politics and believes there is a 'backstage' to political behavior and television news stories of which the public is not generally made aware. Her skepticism of television news daily brings her into conflict with her mother, who watches it *sunao*ly:

> My parents are just ordinary people, if someone on TV says, 'Koizumi [the Japanese PM] is good', Mum goes, 'yeah, he's good.' But if someone else says that he is no good, she says, 'Oh, he's no good after all'. I said to Mum, 'People believe whatever they see on TV is true' and she said, 'Everything on TV *is* true.

Noritaro (father, 51), who was involved in the student protests of the 1970s and is still very cynical of the government and media, believes very little he sees on the news. When watching television with his wife and daughter he frequently explains to them what he thinks is going on behind the political scenes, but his daughter, Norika (20), is mostly unappreciative and says of this habit, 'He goes on too much!'. She feels, however, that she does not have enough alternative information or independent knowledge to disagree with or criticize what she sees on television, 'so, all I can do is believe it'.

Chika and Noritaro each interpret media messages in a more resistant way, while other members in their families (Chika's mothers and Noritaro's daughter, Norika) give the more preferred reading, led by the tendency to be *sunao* in their approach to particularly television news. The informants having resistant readings each seemed to have a particular 'lived experience' or knowledge which had resulted in them becoming more skeptical, even cynical in some cases, of what is reported.

While Norika was generally *sunao* in her interpretations, she did have one lived experience that gave her some skepticism, at least of television interviewers and hence interviews.

> Norika: 'Actually I was interviewed on the street and the interviewer led my response. She asked me a question which she hoped would give her the answer she wanted to hear from me... In the end, the producers just pick up what they want to broadcast so it's not wise to take it from face value.'
>
> Researcher: 'Tell me more about the interview.'
>
> Norika: 'Oh, it was about some girl band... *Morning Girls*, I think. The interviewer asked me to ask a question but I there wasn't anything I wanted to ask! She said, 'What about this...?' 'What about this...?', suggesting different questions she wanted me to ask and then she told me to just repeat a question she gave me. So I did...'

After this experience, Norika watches television a little more critically.

The informants I have discussed represent the diversity I found of interpretations of television. They ranged from Hall's 'preferred readings', what I called, contextualizing to Japan, 'compliant viewing', to 'resistant readings' or 'critical viewing'. Compliant viewing, dominated by a tendency to respond to authority in a *sunao* manner, was predominantly found amongst housewives and children and young people, or anyone embedded in the domestic time-space and for whom television is the primary window to the world. For these informants, a preferred reading of television is perhaps not surprising, especially with the value attributed by the Japanese to being *sunao*. Critical viewing tended to be the predominant way of responding for those who had had particular lived experiences, giving them alternative perspectives or particular knowledge which had, in turn, given rise to a healthy skepticism of authority, particularly in the media. What also enabled many of my informants to form such readings was their access to ICT and a variety of alternative news sources.

Participation

Habermas's (1989) idea of the 'public sphere' has often been used by scholars in an attempt to understand people's participation in the media (Scannell, 1991; Livingstone and Lunt, 1994). While it is not true that there is no public sphere in Japan, I found no instances amongst my informants of any kind of political participation in the media. I found, instead, a lot of evidence of my informants being not only fearful of doing so, but of believing that such participation is pointless due to its inefficacy.

Children and young people participate in the on-line communities for their relaxation, filling in time and escaping from the locales which give them pressure in their everyday lives, as I discussed in the dimension of utility.

When I visited Yoshiko's home one day, I found she had escaped from her mother's control and was participating in a virtual community based on the *Johnnys* fan sites.

Researcher: '(In front of PC) Do you participate in chat rooms?'

Yoshiko: 'I do. I like to chat with other *Johnnys* fans. (Her eyes are on *Johnnys* websites and clicked on *Johnnys'* news and comments one after another, very quickly.) But sometimes strange guys enter the chat room'.

Researcher: 'Can you recognize when this happens?'

Yoshiko: 'I can. 'Cause they ask a lot of questions about me, rather than about *Johnnys*'.

Mother: '(She was listening to our conversation, behind us, but suddenly she interrupted in surprise on hearing her daughter's comment.) You never write anything by yourself or chat with strangers in such a place, do you?'

Yoshiko: '(Her face changed color.) No! I don't! (She obviously was telling a lie to her mother.)'

In recent years, children have increasingly created their own websites and blogs to communicate with their school *uchi* members or to create some kind of a virtual community in which they can share their 'tastes' and feelings. They use media and ICT in order to escape from pressure within local *uchi,* such as family and school *uchis*, disembed from the locale and embed into a virtual community by the Internet. They participate in 'taste communities', where they can express themselves freely, rather than in political ones.

CONCLUSION

Japanese youth's audience engagement

In this chapter I have investigated the multiple dimensions of 'audience engagement' with media and ICT in terms of children and young people within the social context in Japan. I identified and described the dimensions of youth's engagement with media; see Table 24.1.

In the postwar period in Japan, the media environment has expanded rapidly. Children and young people have been available to

Table 24.1 Japanese youth's audience engagement

Audience engagement	*Examples of audience activities*
1. Information-seeking activity and selectivity	Seeking information relevant to school life or general interests
2. Connectivity	Forming a connection to people or groups, disembedding from immediate locale
3. World-creation	Appropriation from the 'cultural supermarket', creation of one's 'own world'
4. Para-social interaction	Fantasizing about television characters or real people on television
5. Utility	Relaxation and stress relief, facilitation of communication and social intimacy, *uchi*-creation and recreation
6. Interpretation	Compliant and resistant viewing
7. Participation	Lack of political participation through fear and disbelief in efficacy, and participation in taste community for self-expression

interact with a great variety of media messages and cultural resources since they were born. Their information needs stem from their social contexts and, thus, they use media and ICT selectively. I described how my informants use media and ICT to disembed from their immediate spatial locations to achieve cultural and social connectivity. Through appropriation from 'cultural supermarkets', my informants created and recreated their own worlds, re-embedding global phenomena in their local lives. For some of my informants, television offered opportunities for para-social interaction in their own worlds.

The preceding findings are possibly fairly universal, but there were other findings which perhaps showed the Japanese to be significantly different in some respects, particularly from Western audiences. The prevalence of compliant viewing, or 'preferred readings', amongst my informants, stemming from a tendency to interpret messages from authorities in a non-questioning manner (the concept of *sunao* and 'the contextual') and the relative lack of interest in participating in the media, are significant if we are interested in differences between Japanese and other audiences. While using media and ICT to relax is not exclusive to Japanese audiences, I want to emphasize this aspect of engagement, as I feel it reflects another significant aspect of the way the Japanese tend to be. The lack of both questioning and participation found amongst my informants is, I believe, part of a wider tendency to avoid self-expression, which can result in an increased need for the creation of a personal space in which one can relax and express themselves comfortably. Thus, media and ICT play a particularly important role for the youth's creation and recreation of both their *uchis* and self-identity.

Towards the internationalizing of media studies

In order to address the issue of the internationalization of media studies, where I have used Western etic concepts, I have attempted to situate them in Japanese contextuals. In appropriating and applying Western etic concepts useful for understanding Japanese audiences (for example, selectivity, para-social interaction, fantasizing and personal use), I have provided further support for the claim that these concepts are indeed etic. There are various similarities in the psychological and personal levels of audience engagement with media and ICT in between Japan and the West, although some social and cultural contexts in which people use the media are different. Therefore, these findings from my ethnographic research in Japan may show the universalism of media audiences in terms of those dimensions of audience engagement.

However, I recognize the fact that other concepts of audience engagement must be negotiated within the Japanese social and cultural context because of the peculiarities in both the West and Japan. For example, in the dimension of utility, Lull's (1980) notion of social use must be expanded because of the differences in social relationships between the USA and Japan. In everyday life, Japanese people reflexively and socially use media and ICT in order to organize and reorganize the *uchis* to which they belong. Thus, the most significant aspect of the social use of media and ICT in Japan is that of *uchi*-creation and recreation.

Hall's (1980) encoding–decoding model must be remodeled in terms of *sunao*, which means 'compliant viewings' or, in Hall's terms, 'preferred reading' in a Japanese context. However, I do not want to give a stereotyped and simplistic picture of either Japanese or Western audiences by using the dichotomy between 'the West' and 'the Rest', for which *Nihonjinron* has been highly criticized. I also discovered critical viewing amongst my informants in Japan, just as Morley (1980) found a diversity of decoding in terms of social contexts in the UK. Recently, by introducing the Western notion of media literacy into Japan, this *sunao* attitude increasingly has been criticized, particularly by feminists, as being naïve. If the authorities (broadcasters, in this case) are misleading viewers, which feminist critics claim to be the case regarding the propagation of patriarchal ideologies, then a *sunao*, or compliant, attitude towards television images is surely a naïve one. Such discourse, and the recent public discovery that television producers do not always report the truth, has led to the demand for media literacy classes in elementary schools. The debate as to whether or not such classes should be included in the curriculum is still continuing. It is another issue as to whether or not such classes would indeed create a critical reception of media without stimulating corresponding changes in social values; for example, without encouraging school children to develop and express individual opinions.

This argument is related to the dimension of participation from the Habermasian notion of 'public sphere' (Habermas, 1989), as interpreted in a Japanese context. This 'etic' concept may have to be reconsidered with regard to its cross-cultural validity because of, on the one hand, the political and social differences between Japan which was modernized by the West, and the West which was in contrast, modernized by its own people. On the other hand, it may relate to the role of contemporary information and communication technology in general, as well as to the culturally mediated influence of personal communication technology. In many Japanese households, I saw 'postmodern audiences' who were fragmented by their multiple engagings with media and ICT. Family members engage not only with multiple television sets, channels and programs by using the multiple remote control devices of new communication technologies with connect with television, but also engage with ICT, and they do this simultaneously. Such multiple engagements with media and ICT in Japanese people's everyday life may make it more difficult to create a 'public sphere'. The mobile telephone which is equipped with internet access and a digital camera has become a 'part of the body' for the Japanese youth and their so-called 'thumb' culture. While we can see a significant tendency towards fragmentation and individualization of audiences, people may *re*connect with each other as *uchi* members rather than as 'public' and may create social intimacy while maintaining their *uchi* rather than 'public sphere' by means of their constant engagement with personalized media and ICT in Japan.

Japan has been portrayed as unique not only by observers in the West, who find 'techno-orientalism', but also by the Japanese themselves, who point to their growing 'techno-nationalism' since the end of World War II. However, it might be useful for media scholars to gain a better understanding of Japanese young people's engagement with media and ICT because it shows not only the case of the most advanced ICT users, but it also provides non-Western findings, shedding light on the role of media in the social context of the ICT revolution and globalization. Addressing the issue of the cultural specificities and commonalities between Western and non-Western childhood media culture, I believe this reflexive approach will give us a significant conception of the role of the media and ICT, and will lead us to a better mutual understanding and interconnectivity in the global age. Children and young people create and recreate their self-identity, community and culture by using media and ICT in the expanded social interaction beyond time-space. Both Western and non-Western media scholars should create a global communicative time-space which can encompass the role of media in the context of globalization, reaching beyond the dichotomy between 'the West' and 'the Rest'. I believe this 'dialogic time-space' which exists beyond our cultural, geographical and national boundaries may provide a modest step towards the 'internationalizing' of media studies.

NOTES

1 In my research, I have worked with 30 families. My informants all have rich media environments in their homes or accessible in their offices or schools. Informants were recruited through snowball sampling, a method deemed appropriate for overcoming two problems: the difficulty of identifying families with a rich media environment and that of gaining

access to their homes. In order to understand the social relationships of my informants I employed a multi-sited approach (Marcus, 1998). Not only did I interview and observe my informants in their homes, I tried to 'follow the *uchi*' to take me to other sites of media engagement, e.g. the office and school. I used Glaser and Strauss's (1968) method of grounded theory to arrive at my analysis from my data (Takahashi, 2003). In order to update the data, I am doing additional fieldwork on children's and young people's engagement with media and ICT. I wish to express my gratitude for supporting my research on children and young people and media to the Okawa Foundation in 2005, Takahashi Shinzo kinen hoso-bunka Foundation in 2006 and the Telecommunications Advancement Foundation in 2007.

2 The Japanese cultural anthropologist Tadao Umesao (1963) named the coming age the 'information industry age', in accordance with the development of the mass media industry, while Daniel Bell talked about his ideas of a postindustrial society in the late 1960s in the USA. Ideas of an information society theory emerged separately in both Japan and the USA in the 1960s. The English term 'information society' was also first created by Masuda (1970), who translated the Japanese term *Joho shakai* into English; his conception of the information society has greatly influenced not only Japanese, but also Western academia and the wider society (Ito, 1990; Dordick and Wang, 1993). Information society theory has been developing since the 1960s in Japan, as well as in the USA; however, the conception of the information society has been challenged because of its imprecise use of the term 'information' and other problems (Webster, 2002).

3 I have conducted both quantitative research – on cable television audiences and their internet use in Tokyo (Takahashi, 1998b) – and qualitative research – on Princess Diana's death in London (Takahashi, 1998a).

4 *Nihonjinron* has been criticized for emphasizing the uniqueness of Japanese people and culture because this 'uniqueness' has been politically used to foster nationalism (Befu, 1997).

5 The question may come up as to why I have used the Japanese emic concepts of *uchi* and *soto* rather than the Western etic concepts of 'private' and 'public'. The reason is that these pairs of terms are not equivalent (see Takahashi (2007)). Perhaps the pair of English terms closest in meaning to *uchi* and *soto* are 'us' and 'them', but the antagonistic connotations of the latter are in many cases, but not all, inappropriate to those captured by *uchi* and *soto*. Also unsatisfactory are attempts to translate *uchi* and *soto* into the terms 'inside' and 'outside', as they fail to imbue any notion of group or family.

6 Hakuhodo Institute of Life and Living (2005) found that the mobile phone can be a source of stress for teenage girls. Some 60% of teenage girls report they sometimes feel stress because of mobile phones.

7 According to a Survey Research Center survey (2005), 56.7% of parents who gave their children mobile phones support this finding.

REFERENCES

Abe, K. (2004) 'Tekuno-nashionalizumu' ('Techno-nationalism'). In S. Yoshimi and T. Hanada (eds) *Shakaijoho Handobukku* (*A Handbook of Socio-information and Communication Studies*). Tokyo: Tokyo University Press.

Ang, I. (1985) *Watching Dallas*. London: Methuen.

Appadurai, A. (1990) 'Disjuncture and difference in the global cultural economy'. In M. Featherstone (ed.) *Global Culture*. London: Sage.

Befu, H. (1997) *Ideorogii toshiteno Nihonbunkaron* (*Japanese Cultural Theory as an Ideology*). Tokyo: Shisou no Kagakusha.

Buckingham, D. (2002) 'The electronic generation? Children and new media'. In L. Lievrouw and S. Livingstone (eds) *The Handbook of New Media*. London: Sage.

Cabinet Office of Government of Japan (2002) *Johoka Shakai to Seishonen nikansuru Chousa* (*Survey on Information Society and Youth*). http://www8.cao.go.jp/youth/kenkyu/jouhou4/pdf_z/0-1.html [October 2007]

Cabinet Office of Government of Japan (2007) *Johoka Shakai to Seishonen nikansuru Isikichousa* (*Survey on Information Society and Youth*). http://www8.cao.go.jp/youth/kenkyu/jouhou5/g.pdf [October 2007]

De Certeau, M. (1984) *The Practice of Everyday Life*. Berkeley, CA: California University Press.

DeFleur, M. L. (1988) 'Diffusing information'. *Society*, 225(2): 72–81.

Dentsu Souken (2000) *Jouhou Medya Hakusho* (*Survey of Information Media*). Tokyo: Dentsu.

Dordick, H.S. and Wang, G. (1993) *The Information Society: A Retrospective View*. Newbury Park, CA: Sage.

Fiske, J. (1987) *Television Culture*. London: Methuen.

Giddens, A. (1990) *The Consequences of Modernity*. Cambridge: Polity Press.

Gillespie, M. (1995) *Television, Ethnicity and Cultural Change*. London: Routledge.

Glaser, B.G. and Strauss, A.L. (1968) *The Discovery of Grounded Theory: Strategies for Qualitative Research*. London: Weidenfeld & Nicolson.

Habermas, J. (1989) *The Structural Transformation of the Public Sphere*, T. Burger (transl.). Cambridge: Polity Press.

Hakuhodo Institute of Life and Living (2005) *Juudai no Zenbu* (*All about Teenagers*). Tokyo: Popurasha.

Hall, S. (1980) 'Encoding/decoding'. In S. Hall, D. Hobson and P. Lowe (eds) *Culture, Media, Language*. London: Hutchinson.

Hall, S. (1992) 'The question of cultural identity'. In S. Hall, D. Held and A. McGrew (eds) *Modernity and its Futures*. Cambridge: Polity Press.

Hamaguchi, E. (ed.) (1998) *Nihon Shakai toha Nainika <Fukuzatsukei no Shiten kara>* (*What is Japanese Society? From the Paradigm of <Complex Systems>*). Tokyo: NHK Books.

Hashimoto, Y. (1986) 'Joho Kodo Sensasu no tameno Pairotto Sutadei' ('A pilot study on "Joho Kodo Census"'). *Joho Tsushin Gakkai-shi*, 12: 81–86.

Hashimoto, Y. (2005) 'Paasonaru medya no fukyuu to komyunikeishon kodo' ('Diffusion of personal communication and communication behavior'). *Medya Komyunikeishon Ron II*. Tokyo: Hokuju shuppan.

Hayashi, Y. (1969) *Johoka Shakai* (*Information Society*). Tokyo: Kodansha.

Horton, D. and Wohl, R.R. (1956) Mass communication and para-social interaction: observations on intimacy at a distance. *Psychiatry*, 19: 215–229.

Ito, Y. (1990) 'Joho shakai ron' ('Information Society Theory'). In H. Ariyoshi (ed.) *Komyunikeishon to Shakai*. Tokyo: Ashishobo.

Kayama, R. and Mori, K. (2004) *Netto Ouji to Keitai Hime* (*King Net and Queen Mobile*). Tokyo: Chuokoran-shinsha.

Kinder, M. (1991) *Playing with Power in Movies, Television and Video Games*. Berkley, CA: University of California Press.

Klapper, J.T. (1960) *The Effects of Mass Communication*. New York: Free Press.

Levi-Strauss, C. (1966) *The Savage Mind*. London: Weidenfeld and Nicolson.

Levy, M.R. (1979) 'Watching TV news as para-social interaction'. *Journal of Broadcasting*, 23: 69–80.

Levy, M.R. (1983) 'Conceptualizing and measuring aspects of audience "activity"'. *Journalism Quarterly*, 60: 109–114.

Livingstone, S. (2002) *Young People and New Media: Childhood and the Changing Media Environment*. London: Sage.

Livingstone, S. and Bovill, M. (1999) *Young people, new media*. Report of the Research Project 'Children, Young People and the Changing Media Environment'. London: London School of Economics and Political Science.

Livingstone, S. and Lunt, P. (1994) *Talk on Television: Audience Participation and Public Debate*. London: Routledge.

Lull, J. (1980) 'The social uses of television'. *Human Communication Research*, 6(3): 197–209.

Lull, J. (1990) *Inside Family Viewing*. London: Routledge.

Lull, J. (2000) *Media, Communication, Culture*. Cambridge: Polity Press.

Marcus, G. (1998) *Ethnography through Thick & Thin*. New Jersey: Princeton University Press.

Masuda, Y. (1970) Social impact of computerization: an application of the pattern model for industrial society. *Challenges from the Future*, 2: 13–24.

McQuail, D., Blumler, J.G. and Brown, J.R. (1972) 'The television audience: a revised perspective'. In D. McQuail (ed.) *Sociology of Mass Communications*. London: Penguin Books.

Mikami, T. (1991) *Jouhou Kankyou to Nyumedia* (*Information Environment and New Media*). Tokyo: Gakubunsha.

Modleski, T. (1982) *Loving with a Vengeance: Mass-Produced Fantasies for Women*. London: Routledge.

Mori, A. (2002) *Geimu Nou no Kyouhu* (*Terror of the Video Game Brain*). Tokyo: Japan Broadcast Publishing.

Morley, D. (1980) 'The "nationwide" audience: structure and decoding'. *Television Monographs* 11. London: British Film Institute.

Morley, D. and Robins, K. (1995) *Spaces of Identity: Global Media, Electronic Landscapes and Cultural Boundaries*. London: Routledge.

Nakajima, I., Himeno, K. and Yoshii, H. (1999) 'Ido-denwa riyono fukyu to sono shakaiteki-imi' ('Diffusion of cellular phones and PHS and its social meanings'). *Joho Tsuushin Gakkai-shi*, 16(3): 79–92.

Nakane, C. (1967) *TateShakai no Ningenkankei -Tanitsu Shakai no Riron-* (*Interpersonal Relationships in a Vertically Structured Society*). Tokyo: Koudansha Gendaishinsho.

Nakane, C. (1970) *Japanese Society*. London: Weidenfeld & Nicolson.

NTT DoCoMo (2005) *Mobairu Shakai Hakusho* (*White Paper on Mobile Society*). Tokyo: NTT Shuppan.

Radway, J. (1984) *Reading the Romance: Women, Patriarchy and Popular Literature*. Chapel Hill, NC: University of North Carolina Press.

Rubin, A.M. and Perse, E.M. (1987) 'Audience activity and television news gratifications'. *Communication Research*, 14: 58–84.

Sakamoto, A. (2005) 'Video games and the psychological development of Japanese children'. In I. Sigel (Series Ed.), D.W. Shwalb, J. Nakazawa and B.J. Shwalb (Vol. Eds.) *Advances in Applied Developmental Psychology: Theory, Practice, and Research from Japan*. Greenwich, CT: Information Age Publishing.

Scannell, P. (ed.) (1991) *Broadcast Talk*. London: Sage.

Shimoda, H. (2004) *Keitai Literashi* (*Mobile Literacy*). Tokyo: NTT Shuppan.

Soumushou (Ministry of Internal Affairs and Communications) (2006) *Keiburu Telebi no Genjou to Kadai* (*Current Status and Task of Cable Television*). Soumushou Johotsusinseisakukyoku.

Soumushou (Ministry of Internal Affairs and Communications) (2007) http://www.johotsusintokei.soumu.go.jp/index.html [August 2007].

Survey Research Center (2005) http://k-tai.impress.co.jp/cda/article/news_toppage/23429.html [August 2007].

Takahashi, T. (1998a) 'Telebishichou niokeru noudousei' ('Audience activity in TV viewing'). In I. Takeuchi, K. Kojima, T. Takeshita, Y. Furukawa, M. Obi and T. Takahashi (eds) *Medya kankyo no henyo to Shichoushazou* (*Changes of Media Environment and Conceptions of the Viewer*). NHK Housou Bunka Foundation; 55–65.

Takahashi, T. (1998b) 'Ohdiensu akutibiti no tagensei ni kansuru teiseiteki bunseki' ('A qualitative study on diversity of audience activity – a case study on media coverage of Princess Diana's death'). *The Research Bulletin of the Institute of Socio-Information and Communication Studies*, 10: 207–226.

Takahashi, T. (1998c) 'Ohdiensu kenkyuu ni okeru akutibu–passibu ronsou wokoete' (Beyond the active–passive dichotomy in the media audience studies – limit of dichotomy). *Mass Communication Kenkyu*, 53: 137–152.

Takahashi, T. (2003) Media, audience activity and everyday life – the case of Japanese Engagement with media and ICT. Doctoral dissertation, The London School of Economics and Political Science, University of London.

Takahashi, T. (2007) 'Internationalizing media studies from a Japanese perspective'. *Global Media and Communication*, 3(3): in press.

Tomlinson, J. (1999) *Globalization and Culture.* Cambridge: Polity Press.

Umesao, T. (1963) 'Joho sangoron' ('Information industrial theory'). *Hoso Asahi* 104: 4–17.

Video Research (2006) http://www.videor.co.jp/ [August 2007].

Webster, F. (2002) The Information Society Revisited. In L. Lievrouw and S. Livingstone (eds.) *The Handbook of New Media.* London: Sage.

World Internet Project Japan (2002) *Sekai Intaneto Riyo Hakusho* (*Internet Usage Trends in the World: White Paper 2002*). Tokyo: NTT Shuppan.

Yuseisho (Ministry of Posts and Telecommunications) (2005) *Tsuushin Hakusho* (*Survey of Telecommunications*). Tokyo: Gyousei.

25

Debates and Challenges Facing New Literacies in the 21st Century

Renee Hobbs

INTRODUCTION

When the Educational Testing Service launched a new online test to measure students' critical thinking and technology proficiencies in the spring of 2006, many scholars and educators from the fields of education, communication and library and information sciences realized that the concept of 'new literacies' had reached a new phase. More and more educators have begun to recognize that, despite their students' familiarity with the internet and other technology, young people may or may not have skills necessary to access, analyze, and evaluate the abundance of information and entertainment available online. For example, some students may know how to upload videos and construct websites but they may be unable to identify reliable, authoritative resources from the web. Many students do not know how best to interpret, analyze, and communicate a website's content via a well-supported argument. In justifying the need for such a test, one expert pointed out, 'Today's undergraduates are generally far less prepared to do research than were students of earlier generations, despite their familiarity with powerful new information-gathering tools' (Breivik, 2005: 22). Some wonder whether, by making information accessible and convenient, the rise of the Internet has contributed to a *decrease* in young people's critical thinking skills.

Educators are attempting to respond to the emerging but significant changes in literacy, technology and culture that are now underway in contemporary society. But in many ways, schools have made only the most superficial accommodation to the changing nature of knowledge that is resulting from the digital multimedia revolution. The lecture and the textbook are still the dominant modes of instruction at both the secondary and university levels. Students still demonstrate their mastery over printed knowledge either through oral or written presentation. According to Henry Jenkins (2006c), emergent forms of knowledge production or communication are seen as peripheral to the core mission of education, and are usually the first item to be cut in each new budget crisis.

Among some educators, the use of media, technology and popular culture is regarded as a part of remedial practice, so that it is considered acceptable for students to watch and discuss the film adaptation of *Hamlet* because teachers may believe that the drama alone will not hold students' attention. The practice of critically analyzing films, advertising, news media or popular culture is still not offered for its own inherent value in promoting reasoning and analysis skills (Marsh, 2006). In many schools in the USA, computer use is limited to isolated sessions in the library or computer lab, where students are likely to be drilling math problems, checking sports scores, or listening to music instead of gathering information or creating digital texts (Oppenheimer, 2003). In general, there continues to be a substantial disconnect between the visionary language of education and communication professionals, scholars and industry leaders and the actual practices of elementary and secondary educators in both school and non-school settings.

The rise of the internet has created a sense of urgency concerning the need to redefine literacy to incorporate technology, mass media and popular culture. There are a number of diverse conceptualizations of literacy (or 'new literacies') which have been proposed in the USA, the UK and many Western nations over the past 15 years or more. In 1998, when I first identified the 'great debates' among stakeholders in media literacy, it was the perspectives of K-12 educators, activists and scholars whose voices proliferated, arguing about whether media literacy should be conducted in school or after-school programs, whether it should be integrated within existing curricular areas or stand alone as a separate subject, and whether or not media companies should contribute to the media literacy movement (Hobbs, 1998). Today, various perspectives on new forms of literacy are now being articulated by education practitioners in elementary and secondary schools as well as scholars in the fields of education, library and information science, and communication/media studies. Other important voices include ideas from technology leaders, heads of government agencies and political leaders, medical and public health professionals, leaders of non-profit youth-serving organizations, multimedia artists and activists, and members of the business community. All these stakeholders are invested in shaping the future of new literacies.

Most people agree on the importance of both helping children and young people use and create messages using technology. In the process, students can enter into the process of critically analyzing digital media, popular culture and the array of technology-infused social practices that are part of contemporary life. This chapter shows some of the key disagreements and arguments that are developing among stakeholders as new debates have begun to emerge about why and how this work should occur. There are a multiplicity of aims and goals associated with the process of accessing, analyzing, evaluating and using media and technologies. Some seek to expand the concept of literacy so that it will reinforce existing cultural and personal values, while others seek to challenge and transform society. In this chapter, I discuss four distinct approaches to these new literacies that have emerged in the past 15 years, outlining the major themes of each and describing some of the argument and criticism that has circulated. Then I examine some of the ongoing challenges for practitioners in the youth media field, which has experienced significant growth in recent years and where new literacies are being explored with children and teens in after-school programs, technology centers and other non-school environments. Next, I articulate the tensions between 'old' media literacy and 'new' media literacy, a debate which results from the intersection of two phenomena: the inevitable standardization of topics and instructional approaches resulting from more widespread local implementation in schools and the rapidly changing digital landscape, which has led to an explosion of new forms of online social interaction and cultural participation. Then, I address the longstanding debate concerning the appropriate role of media and technology companies in their efforts to support media literacy and information and communication technology (ICT) literacy financially. Finally, I examine a newly emerging political view which positions media literacy as an approach that minimizes the need for government regulation of the mass media, a perspective now emerging in Great Britain, the USA and other nations.

DISCIPLINARY APPROACHES EXPAND AND DIVIDE

Four distinct approaches have been termed *media literacy*, *information or ICT literacy*, *critical literacy*, and *media management*. While all approaches conceptualize literacy as the ability to use digital tools effectively and to apply critical thinking skills to media and popular culture texts, they differ in their focus in several ways, emphasizing digital technologies and workplace skills, genres of mass media and popular culture, the identification of sociopolitical contexts and resistance to inequitable power relationships, and media consumption in the context of the home and family. There are a number of differing terms used to refer to the processes involved in critically analyzing and creating media and technology messages. The term *critical viewing skills* had been used as a synonym until the mid-1980s, but it has gradually faded from general use. Other terms now in use include *media education*, *visual literacy*, *technology literacy*, *critical literacy*, *critical media literacy*, *youth media*, *media competence*, *cyberliteracy*, *media management*, *multimodal literacy* and others.

Over the past 10 years there has been a dramatic expansion of this work through practical program development and implementation, theoretical and empirical research, and advocacy (Schwartz and Brown, 2005). There are important differences among these conceptualizations of literacy in their relative emphasis on the author, reader or the text, in the emphasis on the socio-historical and political contexts in which production and reception takes place, in the pedagogical issues concerning the power/authority relationship between teacher and learner, in specific positions on particular social, political and regulatory issues, and on questions concerning the media's impact on child health and behavior. There are also key differences in their orientation towards particular media forms, with differential emphasis on the internet, print media, popular culture and visual media (Meyrowitz, 1998; DiSessa, 2000). Tyner's (1998) distinction between these different visions of literacy as 'tool literacies' or 'literacies of representation' still characterizes an essential distinction among the different approaches. Sonia Livingstone (2003) has pointed out that the new literacies differ in their aims and goals: some approaches reinforce existing institutional practices and values and others aim to challenge and transform them. Four of the new literacies are highlighted below in order to illustrate some of the ongoing tensions, contradictions and differences between them.

Information literacy/ICT literacy. Educators who adopt the term *information literacy* or *ICT literacy* center upon non-fiction texts and position technology-centered research skills as a key component of literacy. These skills are emerging within a world economy based increasingly on the effective use of information and communication. These scholars and educators emphasize the idea that new literacies build upon (and do not replace) reading, writing, speaking and listening skills; the focus instead is on an examination of how these practices take new forms when texts are combined with images, graphics, sound and linked within complex social and information networks. While during the 1970s and 1980s information literacy was promulgated primarily by librarians and the business community (Kapitzke, 2003), a number of scholars specializing in the use of technology in English-language arts have added their voices to this perspective (Hagood *et al.*, 2003; Kinzer and Leander, 2003). As a result, ICT literacy is conceptualized with a focus on both tool literacies and literacies of representation.

Table 25.1 shows a list of skills measured in the ICT literacy assessment developed by the Educational Testing Service (2004), and the strategic blending of technical skills and critical thinking skills is evident. But although the language of scholars emphasizes critical thinking, technical proficiency takes center stage at the school level (Andrews, 2004). Why? Because different forms of technology contain different contexts and resources for constructing meaning; people need the practical knowledge gained from using technology tools in order to make effective use of the information resources available (Goodwyn, 2000). Practitioners and observers in elementary and secondary schools often see students in English or Social Studies classes learning to use I-movie software for video editing, or mastering the finer dimensions of PowerPoint to create elaborate, often animated visual materials to support oral presentations. ICT literacy advocates see this as the ideal way to integrate technology into the classroom. Critics of this approach fear that the emphasis on mastering the software encourages students to emphasize superficial qualities like image and appearance over content and ideas; others argue that a focus on technical skills is essentially supplanting humanistic education with an industrial skills orientation as a means to cultivate technologically sophisticated workers (Oppenheimer, 2003). According to critics, involvement of the business community will risk appropriation by its focus on 'workplace productivity and the absence of a social justice agenda' (Kellner and Share, 2005: 381).

Table 25.1 Cognitive and technical skills measured by the ICT literacy assessment (Educational Testing Service, 2004)

Define:	the ability to use ICT tools to identify and represent an information need (asking questions, completing a concept map)
Access:	the ability to collect and identify likely digital information sources and get information from those sources (browsing linked websites, searching through databases)
Manage:	the ability to organize and classify digital information (sorting information using specific criteria, re-ordering information from a table)
Integrate:	the ability to interpret and represent information (comparing and contrasting information from IMs and web pages)
Evaluate:	the ability to judge the authority, point of view/bias and accuracy of digital information (determining relevance, ranking web pages in terms of specific criteria)
Create:	the ability to generate information by adapting, applying, designing or inventing information using ICT tools (creating a graph that supports a point of view)
Communicate:	the ability to express ideas by gearing information to a particular audience and medium (adapting presentation slides, formatting a document, preparing a text message for a cell phone)

Media literacy. Those who use the term *media literacy* or *media education* emphasize an understanding of mass media and popular culture, particularly news, advertising, entertainment and popular culture. Media literacy is defined as the ability to access, analyze, evaluate and communicate messages in a wide variety of forms. This definition arose in the early 1990s as media literacy educators from across the USA gathered at the Aspen Institute for a leadership conference on media literacy (Aufderheide and Firestone, 1993). The term *access* generally means the ability to locate information or find messages and to be able to comprehend and interpret a message's meaning. *Analysis* refers to the process of recognizing and examining the author's purpose, target audience, construction techniques, symbol systems and technologies used to construct the message. The concept of analysis also includes the ability to appreciate the political, economic, social and historical context in which media messages are produced and circulated as part of a cultural system. *Evaluation* refers to the process of assessing the veracity, authenticity, creativity or other qualities of a media message, making judgments about a message's worth or value. Finally, the definition of media literacy includes the ability to *communicate* messages in a wide variety of forms (using language, photography, video, online media, etc.). Media literacy emphasizes the ability to use production processes to compose and create messages using various symbol systems and technology tools.

Media literacy is primarily conceptualized as a learning outcome within an educational framework that aims to give children and young people opportunities to learn about mass media, popular culture, and communication technologies, although the term is sometimes used in relation to larger theories about the relationship between literacy, visual media, and technology (Kress, 2003). *Media literacy education* (or *media education*) is a term used to refer to the pedagogical processes used to develop media literacy (Buckingham, 2003).

Unlike ICT literacy, media literacy educators distinctively focus on mass media and popular culture. There is a focus on the processes involved in analyzing, evaluating and constructing news, advertising and entertainment media, with explicit examination of the stance of the persons producing the message. Similarly, the audience is conceived of as a construction that exists within a particular economic, political and cultural framework. Media literacy educators see collaborative student-centered media production activities as a key dimension of pedagogy and emphasize how the practice of critical analysis of popular culture alters the power dynamic in the student–teacher relationship (Alvermann, 2002; Buckingham, 2003; Hagood *et al*., 2003; Hobbs, 2004).

However, teachers' longstanding antipathy towards the use of popular culture texts in the classroom limits implementation of media literacy in educational settings in the USA, Britain and in many other nations, as teachers fear, for example, that children will prefer acting out dramatic scenes featuring Jennifer Lopez and the Spice Girls instead of characters from *Little Women*, resulting in a loss of focus on literary works (Pailliotet, 2003; Felini, 2004; Marsh, 2006). Justin Lewis and Sut Jhally (1998) criticize media literacy for being too focused on textual analysis to the detriment of explorations of sociopolitical dimensions of media's social functions in maintaining hegemony.

Critical literacy. Scholars who conceptualize their work through the lens of *critical literacy* (or *critical media literacy*) distinguish between operational, cultural and critical literacies. The operational dimension of literacy emphasizes the medium of the language system; the cultural dimension focuses on the production and circulation of meaning; and the critical dimension is concerned with the socially constructed cultural system which privileges some perspectives and marginalizes others (Lankshear and Knobel, 1998). Advocates of critical literacy use the perspectives of critical and cultural studies as a means to strengthen young people's commitment to radical democratic social transformation. Because literacy is embedded within social and political contexts, literacy practices inevitably embody power relationships within society. When we interpret media messages, our interpretation is partly individual, but it also reflects our positions as readers: our age, race, gender, social class and family backgrounds. 'Multimedia literacy … will always be a social process with repercussions for the transformation of society itself' (Martin and Hottmann, 2003: 75). Through both reading and writing of multimodal texts, critical literacy encourages students to recognize and resist the ideological framing embedded in texts that position readers as subjects and construct social reality through inclusions and exclusions. As Lankshear and Knobel (1998: 1) point out, 'Critical readings of texts aim to unveil the representational and other material effects of texts, and critical rewritings of texts are "moves" to redress these effects by encoding alternative possibilities'.

Critical media literacy involves analyzing media culture as products of social production and teaching students to be critical of media representations, but it also stresses 'the importance of learning to use the media as modes of self-expression and social activism' (Kellner and Share, 2005: 369). For example, some critical media literacy educators in the USA have been active in the media reform movement, which is an international interest-group coalition seeking to decrease the centralization of corporate ownership of media outlets and increase support for public broadcasting, independent/alternative media and cable access (Johnson, 2003). Rather than merely indulging in textualist readings or audience studies of how people use and enjoy popular culture, scholars who emphasize critical literacy target the corporations who circulate messages that reinforce capitalism's status quo. These educators see media culture as a dangerous form of pedagogy in itself and encourage educators to see themselves as responsible for helping nurture a kind of cultural criticism that will enable young people to recognize and resist the political functions of popular culture which stimulate and manufacture desires (Giroux, 2003).

Critics of critical literacy point out its highly theoretical dimensions and its problematic pedagogy (Buckingham, 1998). They point out that critical literacy educators tend to situate the teacher as hero, the 'only individual in the classroom who has achieved critical consciousness and whose job it now is to enlighten his or her students so that they can be transformed and emancipated' (Guerra, 2004: 21). Even when teachers are self-conscious and reflective, 'it does not take long for "empowered" students to become disempowered when they begin their quest for employment in a world where "marketable skills" are both preferred and financially rewarded over "critical skills"' (Frechette, 2002: 111).

Media management. Scholars and researchers with interests in youth, media and public health sometimes resist the conceptualization of media literacy as a new type of literacy or a particular approach to pedagogy, preferring to conceptualize media literacy as a *treatment* or *intervention* to counteract negative media effects. Such work can promote critical thinking about the dominance of media consumption as a lifestyle and the role of media messages in glamorizing unhealthy behaviors, including violence, substance abuse, adolescent sexuality or the consumption of high-fat foods. During the 1990s in the USA, Great Britain, Italy and other nations, this approach focused on informing parents and the general public about issues related to the uses of television and the internet in the family, encouraging parents to develop responsible viewing habits by using the TV, videogame, and film ratings systems and establishing limitations on time and type of programming (Steyer, 2002). Sometimes termed *media management*, this perspective emphasizes the importance of transforming passive, habitual media use into intentional, active and strategic use as a response to the negative dimensions of mass media and popular culture.

Pediatricians and other child health advocates almost universally believe that children's media use negatively affects children's aggressive behavior, eating habits, physical activity levels, risk for obesity, high-risk behaviors, and school performance (Gentile *et al.*, 2004). As a result, a 2001 policy statement by the American Academy of Pediatrics provided specific recommendations for pediatricians to incorporate media education and advocacy into their anticipatory guidance and parental education. Recommendations advise parents (1) to limit children's media time, (2) to discourage television viewing among children under age two, and (3) to encourage alternative entertainment for children. A survey of pediatricians in one state showed that pediatricians perceive a lack of parental motivation or support for the recommendations, with approximately one-third of pediatricians also citing a lack of time and a sense of futility in affecting patients' media habits (Gentile *et al.*, 2004).

Critics of media management fear that it positions children and youth as victims of an oppressive media culture without an appropriate level of attention to the pleasures of media consumption (Hobbs, 1998). Others object to the practice of medical professionals who position themselves as arbiters of appropriate media content for children and youth. Many dispute the use of social science research methods to investigate the complexities of people's relationship with media messages, as researchers must inevitably use oversimplified measurement tools and theoretical models (Barker and Petley, 1997; Buckingham, 2003). According to this view, researchers abuse the public's trust in science when they claim that children's media consumption is associated with public health problems like attention-deficit disorder, obesity, and aggression.

It is important to note that these four approaches to new literacies frame up very different 'problems' that can be 'solved' through the application of critical analysis and media production skills training for children and youth. Conceptualized as a tool, different stakeholders can use new literacies for building workplace productivity, responding to mass media and popular culture, resisting media hegemony, or minimizing the negative effects of media influence. Each of these goals resonates with (or alienates) specific individuals and groups in society. Fortunately, there are some points of consensus evident in reviewing the four different approaches to new literacies. Despite their differences, to some extent these approaches all acknowledge three broad themes:

1 The constructed nature both of authorship and of audiences within an economic, political and sociocultural context.
2 The circulation of messages and meanings, and the relative contribution of audience interpretation and specific features of message design, format and content.
3 An exploration of questions about how texts represent social realities, reflect ideologies, and influence perception, attitudes and behaviors about the social world and one's place in it (Hobbs, 2006).

Some effort is underway among policymakers to unify these different approaches both in Europe and the USA. Many politicians are using elements of all four discourses simultaneously to appeal to diverse stakeholders. For example, a recent declaration from the Council of Europe was issued supporting the needs of children in the new information and communications environment. It uses arguments representing all four of the conceptualizations of new literacy outlined above (Council of Europe Committee of Ministers, 2006). In the USA, the Partnership for 21st Century Skills, an advocacy organization supported by the federal government, educational leaders, and technology corporations, has focused on providing resources to educational leaders to help integrate the various conceptualizations of new literacies into K-12 education, even while privileging the perspective of ICT literacy (Partnership for 21st Century Skills, 2002).

Whether these four discourses will continue to thrive, merge or compete for limited resources over the next 10 years is unclear. Whereas in 1998 the 'great debates' in media literacy centered on the tensions between *protectionist* educators whose concerns about the toxicity of media's cultural environment and others who emphasized student *empowerment*, the current situation is made more complex because of the four perspectives just described, each with its own proponents, scholarly literature, conferences, and practitioner base. It is difficult for academic specialists to keep up with the increasingly vast literature emerging from even one of these four approaches. There is some evidence that disciplines are encouraging cross-fertilization, as in the USA, where public health researchers oriented towards media management make use of theoretical models of media literacy (Primack *et al.*, 2006). During the 1990s, I imagined that the media literacy movement was a 'big tent' where people with a wide range of different approaches could share ideas (Hobbs, 1998). Today, there are a number of different tents, each offering more or less the same set of tools, but making different claims about the values and benefits of their use. Paradoxically, the disciplinary specialization and competing visions about the aims and goals for new literacies may serve both to broaden the scope of public support and potentially to decrease the coherence and clarity of its aims and goals.

DESIGN AND EVALUATION OF YOUTH MEDIA PRODUCTION PROGRAMS

In the USA, Great Britain and many other nations, there has been an explosion of initiatives that involve young people in creating media and technology programs. Within this community of practitioners, there is tension concerning the aims, goals and practices of this work. In many Western nations, *youth media* programs are widespread. In the USA, Listen Up! (2006) lists 118 organizational members consisting of diverse groups with a wide range of aims, goals, target participants and audiences, and instructional philosophies. Some examples from the USA illustrate the diversity of programs. Swept Away TV is a public access television program in the state of Florida that is written, edited, filmed and directed by college and high-school students, where productions feature performances by local bands and where media career training and mentoring is available for young people. The Media Lab at Mountain Lake PBS, located in rural New York State, is a community outreach program of a local public broadcasting affiliate which offers media training to at-risk teens in collaboration with the local housing authority. There is comparable diversity of such youth media programs now emerging in Austria, Germany, England, Australia and other nations (Buckingham and Domaille, 2002; European Charter for Media Literacy, 2006). Such programs may be sponsored by nonprofit youth-serving organizations, federal, state and local agencies, media and technology professionals, artists, activists, public, cable or commercial broadcasters, and business entrepreneurs.

As with the various approaches to new literacies in the context of school-based programs, the primary challenge of youth media programs relates to our still-limited understanding of the benefits of these programs in the lives of children and youth. As a result of its confusing theory base, which includes elements from developmental psychology, social work, and education (Tyner, 1999), some have claimed that the lack of research has limited the momentum in the field.

A significant reason for the lack of research is the field's straddling and marginal position within the fields of both media studies and education (Hobbs, 1994; Hagood *et al.*, 2003; Mihailidis, 2006). However, the most experienced practitioners have made important contributions to our knowledge of youth media programs through qualitative, ethnographic reports of practice (Sefton-Green and Sinker, 2000; Goodman, 2003; Jeffers and Streit, 2003). While program evaluation is embraced by researchers, policy-makers and funders as a means to strengthen the knowledge base of the field, there has been some resistance among youth media nonprofits to complete evaluations, which are at times treated as an arduous chore. Among small grassroots organizations with few staff, evaluation is sometimes viewed as something to add on at the end of a proposal to justify the funding. The impetus for evaluation is often external, since youth media practitioners are 'true believers,' already convinced of the value of media production for young people and not feeling that evaluation enhances their work (Campbell *et al.*, 2001; Jeffers and Streit, 2003). Some funders have complained that youth media programs use a bean-counting approach, specifying the number of young people who attended and the number of after-school sessions offered with little identification of outcomes or goals.

In addition, there is some tension regarding the relative emphasis of *product and process* among youth media educators and their funders. Some educators value the educational process of learning to compose using media tools and technologies over the ultimate quality of the video or multimedia product actually produced, while funders tend to value the distribution of a quality production as an important benchmark. According to Robert Sherman of the Surdna Foundation:

> To produce media that is not seen, read, heard or experienced doesn't get at the great benefit of what youth media has to offer – which is young people communicating about issues that are important in

their lives. The goal of making media and finding voice is to be heard (Hahn, 2002: 1).

But when product is valued over process, then adults take greater responsibility for youth media productions, shifting the balance between youth and adults and raising questions about authorship and student learning. When there is pressure to create media products suitable for community audiences, the responsibility for quality control is placed more firmly in the hands of the staff. Rather than use digital media as a tool for discovery, experimentation and inquiry, some programs use an 'artist-in-residence' model, where an experienced multimedia professional guides young people in apprenticeship fashion. In these programs, artists or teachers may orchestrate much of the content and tone of the production. Students get to brainstorm ideas, perform in front of the camera, learn to conduct an interview, or use the lighting and camera equipment, but adults do most of the concept planning and production logistics. In many programs, adults take responsibility for the editing process as well. At youth media festivals and screenings, one can often overhear suspicious muttering about a production that looks too professional to have been done by youths themselves. These sources of tension will be resolved as research is better able to contribute to our understanding of how different approaches to youth media production best support and enhance the development of young people intellectually, socially and emotionally.

Internationally, the youth media field has begun to recognize the need to articulate a shared set of aims and goals and devote increased attention to the process of evaluation (Sefton-Green *et al.*, 1995; Buckingham and Domaille, 2002). In the United States, Tony Streit and his colleagues at the Education Development Center and the leaders of 14 youth media programs developed four broad categories that represent a kind of 'fluency' in youth media. Using a consensus-based process with an expert base of youth media practitioners, they identified four primary learning outcomes for youth media programs, as shown on Table 25.2.

These include: (1) positive youth development; (2) technical and creative skills; (3) critical media analysis; and (4) civic engagement and activism (Jeffers and Streit, 2003). It is not clear whether the systematic measurement

Table 25.2 Primary outcomes for youth media programs (Education Development Center, 2006)

Positive youth development	Technical and creative skills	Critical media analysis	Civic engagement and activism
Life skills, personal responsibility, confidence, assertiveness, open-mindedness	Hard skills with various media-making tools and formats	Awareness of media landscape, what kind of media is out there, how they are put together, how one consumes it	Finding your voice, representing oneself, being honest and authentic
Collaboration, teamwork, interpersonal skills	Awareness of how media works are put together	Look at media with a critical eye, sifting and analyzing messages	Work mirrors social issues and issues of personal significance
Risk-taking, being curious/curiosity	Writing skills, organizing ideas, interactive/virtual communication skills	How they consume media, not just how much-scale, content, how often	
Working in a diverse setting, learning to talk about differences	Comfort in interviewing and being interviewed	Finding one's place as a media maker	Developing perspective and taking actions based on one's opinion/interests
Effective communication, confidence to express ideas in a group setting, able to give and receive feedback	Prioritizing tasks, operating on timeline, following through, self-direction	Exploring the impact of their own media on others	Aware of community needs and issues, relevant/contextual content, cultural literacy

of these outcomes will continue to develop as youth media programs develop; typically, leaders of youth media programs match program aims to the specific needs of the target population; as such, there may continue to be enormous variation in the design, implementation and assessment of these programs.

OLD MEDIA LITERACY VERSUS NEW MEDIA LITERACY

In the USA, Canada, Australia, Great Britain and other nations, media literacy has become established enough that there exists a set of now-conventional content, themes, materials and instructional methods that are becoming normative. For example, in New Zealand, high-school students are offered a Media Studies course where they investigate how news stories are selected and packaged, explore how ethical issues affect the media, and strengthen writing skills by producing messages in print, radio and video formats (New Zealand Qualifications Authority, 2007). Educational standards in most US states now call for students to be able to, for example, 'analyze media as sources of information, entertainment, persuasion, interpretation of events and transmission of culture' (California Department of Education, 2005). The vast majority of media literacy practitioners (particularly in school settings) include a focus on news, advertising (particularly tobacco and alcohol marketing) and popular film and television. Certain instructional practices are also typical: (1) reflection on the process of home media management; (2) message analysis or deconstruction of media texts; (3) media composition/production activities; and (4) the exploration of media and society issues, including topics such as propaganda in war coverage; advertising and materialism; stereotyping and issues of representation; alcohol and tobacco advertising; media ownership; media violence; media's impact on body image, sexuality and self-esteem; and the role of the First Amendment in contemporary society (Hobbs, 2004; Thoman and Jolls, 2005). At the primary level, media literacy tends to focus on home media management, where students compile 'media diaries' and have 'TV turn-off weeks'. At the high-school level, English, Social Studies, Communication or Health teachers (many of whom face upwards of 120 students per day) manage the demands of the job by employing a set of standard lessons, videotapes, and activities that can be used year after year, sometimes even after these materials have lost their relevance to students' lived experience (Hobbs, 2007).

But some scholars claim that these now-standard practices of creating media diaries, analyzing news and advertising, and creating video documentaries no longer map onto the rapidly changing technological environment of the 21st century. The prevalence of broadband internet access has increased the scope of ordinary users' online activity; many are actively involved in creating diverse new sorts of texts using creative remixing and editing techniques. Educators are just beginning to explore what it means to build critical thinking and communication skills around these new online genres and digital media forms, like instant messaging, social networking software, blogs, podcasts and user-modified videogames, where user-generated content and participation are central (Lewis and Fabos, 2005; Shaffer *et al.*, 2005).

Remixing is now becoming a dominant form of self-expression and communication, and some argue that media literacy must position itself in relation to these new production practices. For example, commercial advertisers have invited viewers to create TV ads for their products and post them online (Pfanner, 2006). Iraqi teenagers are creating blogs that capture the trials of daily life in Baghdad as they live with an ongoing war all around them, using clips from television, images, the sounds of local news, and their own writing and artwork (HNK, 2006). Educators are modifying videogames to add educational content to formerly shoot-em-up scenarios to teach science or social studies (Squire and Jenkins, 2004). Rather than continuing to focus on the top-down model that positions 'authors' as those in corporate profit-centered media institutions who create messages for mass audiences, educators are beginning to celebrate the increasing convergence between authors and audiences, where meanings emerge collaboratively as people sample, appropriate and repurpose media texts within and among knowledge-sharing communities (Hagood *et al.*, 2003; Jenkins, 2006b).

For example, the scholarship on fan fiction suggests that young people who write stories, scripts or create videos featuring their favorite media characters may be developing important media literacy skills in the process. Henry Jenkins argues that students' appropriation of existing media content in their own creative work may be understood as a process which involves both analysis and commentary:

> Sampling intelligently from the existing cultural reservoir requires a close analysis of existing structures and uses of this material; remixing requires an appreciation of emerging structures and latent potential meanings. Often, remixing involves the creative juxtaposition of materials which otherwise occupy very different cultural niches (Jenkins, 2006a: xx).

It may be that remixing production activities provide a kind of intellectual scaffolding for the development of students' imagination that reduces anxiety about the writing process. For example, children can use a drag-and-drop editing tool to explore how a palette of existing images can be manipulated and recombined to communicate new and different meanings. This activity has key parallels to the sequential processes involved in learning to write a well-developed paragraph. The tool can support students' learning about the role of sequence in the construction of meaning.

But skeptics wonder whether such new teaching approaches are reasonable, given teachers' longstanding antipathy to popular culture and new technology; current approaches to staff development and an aging work force are also complicating factors. In the USA, education schools on college and university campuses are among the least technologically sophisticated among departments (George Lucas Educational Foundation, 2001). Few teachers are evaluated on their ability to use technology in the classroom, despite the fact that large amounts of financial resources are dedicated to placing technology in schools. A recent study found that only one in five districts include technology skills as a criterion for evaluating K-12 teacher performance (Whale, 2006). For most teachers, videogames, instant messaging and social networking websites are viewed with suspicion; word processing, email, and the use of search engines represent the extent of their experience with computer technology.

Thus, educators and other stakeholders wonder whether K-12 schools are up to the challenge of implementing new media literacy. This remains just as vital and significant a debate in 2006 as it was in 1998, continuing the tension between the positions of scholars who point out the active way teachers resist media and technology (Cuban, 2001; Demetriadis *et al.*, 2003; Oppenheimer, 2003) and those who showcase the rich array of potential learning opportunities that new media literacy can provide (Brunner and Tally, 1999; Martin and Hottmann, 2003; Lewis and Fabos, 2005). But a vision of the entrenched, conservative nature of schools and schooling vastly overgeneralizes the more complex and dynamic reality of education, both in the USA and in many European nations. Each year, more and more teachers are becoming comfortable with the internet and making more active use of it in the classroom. Blogs, digital cameras and video editing tools are not as intimidating to the newest generation of teachers just beginning their careers. Many public and private schools are now using a number of innovative instructional practices involving multimedia production that are contributing to the intellectual, social and cognitive skills required for 21st century participatory culture. These include collaborative learning, project-based multimedia production, critical reading of digital texts, and writing for authentic audiences. A new generation of teachers is experimenting with new forms and genres to discover the opportunities and challenges of implementing a new vision of literacy.

THE ROLE OF MEDIA CORPORATIONS IN MEDIA LITERACY

The debate about the appropriate role of media companies in supporting the media literacy movement was a major conflict of the 1990s, leading to the creation of two competing national membership organizations in the USA (Heins and Cho, 2003). Although it remains a vociferous argument among American educators, it is unclear how this argument resonates internationally, where K-12 education is more institutionally centralized and uniformly funded and public broadcasters have more actively embraced their responsibilities to promote their educational mission.

While some American educators view media companies as having a social responsibility to contribute to people's ability to understand, analyze and create media messages, others feel that such involvement is destined to co-opt the movement and eliminate critical perspectives (Hobbs, 1998). The Alliance for a Media Literate America (AMLA) believes that effective media education requires broad support. Its founding sponsors included both the nonprofit educational television company Sesame Workshop and the corporate media entities AOL Time Warner, Fox Family Channel, and the Discovery Channel. The backers of its founding conference in 2001 included the New York Times Foundation, the educational publishing house Holt, Rinehart and Winston, a government agency (the National Endowment for the Arts), a non-profit company (Media Education Foundation) and an educational institution (the College of Communication at the University of Texas). Its website states:

> We believe that corporations, especially media corporations, have a social responsibility to support media literacy. If we deny them the opportunity to do so and then criticize them for not doing so, we create a no-win situation, both for them and for the potential beneficiaries of their efforts.

Educators and scholars who were opposed to this vision created the Action Coalition for Media Education (ACME) in reaction to the AMLA founding conference in 2001, which was the fifth US meeting organized nationally during the significant growth experienced in the media literacy community during the 1990s. ACME's explicit purpose is to use media education to deal with corporate censorship, racism, commercialism in the schools, news monopolies and the misrepresentation of women and minorities. As reported in *The Nation* magazine, 'leading media scholars and educators are forming a new progressive media literacy organization, one that will remain independent of media conglomerates that bankroll existing groups' (McChesney and Nichols, 2002: 17). Since its founding conference in October 2002, ACME has participated in a number of grassroots campaigns, including the massive national effort to urge the Federal Communications Commission not to eliminate its limitations on media ownership. Its mission statement emphasizes: (1) teaching media literacy skills to children and adults so they can become more critical media consumers and active citizens; (2) championing a wide array of independent media voices; and (3) democratizing our media system through political reform.

It doesn't appear that questions about corporate funding resonate in other nations with the same vitriol evident in the USA. In Great Britain, a media literacy curriculum for elementary educators entitled Media Smart was funded by a consortium of corporate funders including the British Toy and Hobby Association, Lego, Proctor & Gamble, Kellogg's, and Cadbury (Media Smart, 2006). Media Smart included three curriculum packages for elementary teachers in England, Scotland and Wales with accompanying print, video and internet support materials designed to teach children ages 6–11 about advertising. This effort largely escaped criticism, perhaps because of the involvement of key academics and support from government agencies.

In the USA, the public nature of debates about sources of funding may have contributed to perceptions among the philanthropic community that media literacy educators were not ready for prime time. Corporate philanthropies like AOL Time

Warner and the George Lucas Educational Foundation have supported specific youth media programs but preferred to focus on the development of ICT literacy. Only recently have major philanthropies begun to invest in new literacies, as demonstrated by the John D. and Catherine T. MacArthur Foundation's recent grants of more than US$4 million to universities and non-profit organizations in 2005.

More broadly, questions of profit have affected the creation and distribution of media literacy resource materials. In the USA, media professionals and educators are concerned about whether the use of copyrighted materials, used as part of media literacy education, is legal within current US copyright regulations. Such regulations evaluate the 'fair use' of copyrighted materials based on four criteria, including the commercial or noncommercial nature and usage (Center for Social Media, 2006). It is not known whether or how concerns about copyright violation have affected creation and distribution of media literacy curriculum materials. However, a few educational publishers have created textbooks, videos and ancillary materials for integrating media literacy into the primary and secondary English curriculum and some large textbook publishers have avoided the use of copyrighted materials.

Ironically, in 2006 it was the *lack* of media literacy in a particular set of curriculum materials published by a media corporation that contributed to a controversy, when the US television network ABC aired *The Path to 9/11*, a 5-hour docudrama written by Cyrus Nowrasteh, dramatizing the 1993 and 2001 attacks on the World Trade Center and the US government's response. An educational publishing company, Scholastic, joined with ABC to co-release a teaching guide, which was delivered to more than 25,000 high-school teachers with activities and lessons on using the docudrama in the classroom. Concerns were raised about the misinformation and inaccuracy in the docudrama; former 9/11 Commissioners, former administration officials, prominent historians, and even conservative pundits called the show an undisguised form of conservative propaganda. The educational materials also came under heavy criticism for its assumptions about the Iraq War, drawing fire from bloggers by including a suggested question asking students to debate whether 'the media help or hinder our national security'. When Scholastic pulled the discussion guide from its website, it released a statement introducing new materials to accompany the miniseries. These materials focused specifically on media literacy and critical thinking. Said Dick Robinson, Chairman, President and CEO of Scholastic:

> We believe that developing critical thinking and media literacy skills is crucial for students in today's society in order to participate fully in our democracy and that a program such as *The Path to 9/11* provides a very 'teachable moment' for developing these skills at the high school level. We encourage teachers not to shy away from the controversy surrounding the program, but rather to engage their students in meaningful, in-depth discussion (Rood, 2006: 1).

Media corporations may be becoming more adept at recognizing the value of being able to claim that they are promoting media literacy at times when their judgments fall under public scrutiny. It remains to be seen how financial support from media corporations will be perceived by educators and scholars from among the four emerging perspectives articulated earlier, but it is reasonable to anticipate that those with primary orientations towards critical literacy will continue to resist the efforts of media corporations, while those who favor ICT literacy will seek out opportunities to collaborate with media corporations and extend their influence.

MEDIA LITERACY AS AN ALTERNATIVE TO MEDIA REGULATION

In the UK, media literacy has recently been positioned as a means to transform relationship between the media industry, the public and the national government. When the British government decided to reorganize the regulatory bodies that relate to broadcast and electronic media (except for the BBC), they created a new authority, the Office of Communications (OFCOM). Despite their comparatively limited regulatory role, the Communications Act of 2003 gave OFCOM responsibility for media literacy. This was the first time that any statutory body in the world had been given explicit powers for anything to do with media education (Bazalgette, in press).

In the USA, media literacy has also been positioned by media industry leaders and government officials as an alternative to regulation. For example, the National Cable Television Association, the industry lobbying organization, developed a three-part video designed especially for children ages 5–7, 8–11 and 12–17, providing an introduction to media literacy. Members of Congress joined cable industry executives at a nationally televised press conference, the premier event for the first National Critical Viewing Day in 1998. (However, the US Federal Communications Commission has been utterly silent on the topic.) In 2006, a major public service promotional campaign was initiated by the Motion Picture Association of America (MPAA), the organization that rates Hollywood films, and the Ad Council, the leader producer of public service announcements in the USA. The campaign, entitled 'TV Boss', has a media management focus and is aimed to empower parents to take charge of what they and their children see on TV (Ad Council, 2006). According to Jack Valenti, former MPAA head:

> You don't want government stepping in to do this. I'm an implacable enemy of the government trying to tell parents how to raise their children, what they should read or where to go to school, or how they should conduct themselves. This is parental responsibility (KUHF Houston Public Radio, 2006: 1).

A newly emerging tension pits those who see media literacy as an 'alternative to the blunderbuss of media regulation' (Silverstone, 2004: 447) against those who object to that an educational effort is being positioned as replacing the need for media deregulation. Media literacy makes viewers and listeners responsible for informing themselves of television and radio content in order to avoid harmful or offensive content. The British media activist group MediaWatch-UK points out that, despite the high levels of interest in media literacy among members of Parliament, British media regulators don't emphasize the process of teaching viewers and listeners how to *respond* to harmful or offensive content (MediaWatch-UK, 2006). As Livingstone (2003: xx) puts it, media literacy 'may be promoted as individual empowerment but clearly it enables the state to roll back its own responsibilities'. Whether media literacy is actually expanded as a result of new approaches to government regulation of media, or whether it remains simply a bureaucratic cover for an emphasis on industry self-regulation and limiting government's role, is yet to be seen.

CONCLUSION

This chapter has provided a review and analysis of some of the conflicts and tensions now emerging as a result of changing conceptualization of literacy. New visions of literacy now include perspectives from education practitioners, scholars in communication, technology and education, government leaders, public health and medical professionals, and members of the business community. Some of the tensions and conflicts center on the purposes and aims of new literacies. As youth media programs expand around the globe, practitioners and scholars question the aims, goals and assessment methodologies used to evaluate these programs. The appropriate role of critical theory for the development of the field continues to be debated among practitioners, scholars and advocates. As media literacy becomes somewhat more established in the K-12 curriculum, there is concern about how the field will adapt to include the increasingly participatory culture of the internet in relation to social networking tools and online gaming. Tensions continue about the appropriate role of educational publishers and multimedia corporations in the media literacy movement. Finally, both international governments and global media corporations are reconceptualizing media literacy as an alternative to government regulation of media content, an approach that creates tensions between educators, activists and policymakers concerning the fundamental nature of media literacy and its purpose and function in society.

We face the new millennium with our websites, blogs, voice mail, email, I-Movies, IMs, I-Tunes, podcasts, webcasts, DVDs, online comics, electronic magazines, e-books, online multiplayer games and cellphones all offering more and more choices of entertainment and information, shifting old conceptualizations of author and audience, of mainstream and alternative media. These new choices take us beyond the already vast offerings of television, movies, newspapers, books, magazines and radio. Our knowledge of the role of these new genres, tools and technologies in shaping literacy practices will grow only as a result of some significant investment on behalf of scholars and educational practitioners from a wide variety of disciplines and specializations. By contributing our diverse voices to the next round of 'great debates' and continuing to respect the vitality of cross-disciplinary and interdisciplinary scholarship and reflective practice, we are beginning to develop an understanding of literacy's function in relation to new media and technologies. The implementation of new forms of literacy education in schools, at home, and after school are certain to affect the intellectual, social and emotional development of children and youth.

REFERENCES

Ad Council (2006) 'TV boss'. http://tvboss.org [22 August 2006].

Alvermann, D.E. (2002) *Adolescents and Literacies in a Digital World.* New York: P. Lang.

Andrews, R. (2004) *The Impact of ICT on Literacy Education.* London: Routledge.

Aufderheide, P. and Firestone, C. (1993) *Media Literacy: National Leadership Conference.* Washington, DC: Aspen Institute.

Barker, M. and Petley, J. (1997) *Ill Effects: The Media/Violence Debate.* London: Routledge.

Bazalgette, C. (in press) 'The development of media education in England: a personal view'. In J. Flood, S.B. Heath and D. Lapp (eds) *Handbook of Literacy Research: Visual, Communicative and Performative Arts.* Mahwah, NJ: Erlbaum Associates.

Breivik, P. (2005) 21st century learning and information literacy. *Change,* (March–April): 20–27.

Brunner, C. and Tally, W. (1999) *The New Media Literacy Handbook: An Educator's Guide to Bringing New Media into the Classroom.* New York: Anchor Books.

Buckingham, D. (1998) *Teaching Popular Culture: Beyond Radical Pedagogy.* London: UCL Press.

Buckingham, D. (2003) *Media Education: Literacy, Learning, and Contemporary Culture.* Cambridge, UK: Polity.

Buckingham, D. and Domaille, K. (2002) *Where Are We Going and How Can We Get There? General Findings from the UNESCO Youth Media Education Survey.* Southampton: Centre for Language in Education.

California Department of Education (2005) 'English-language arts content standards for California public schools'. Sacramento, CA: California Department of Education.

Campbell, P., Hoey, L. and Perlmann, L. (2001) *Sticking with my dreams: defining and refining youth media in the 21st century.* www.campbell-kibler.com/youth_media.html [20 January 2002].

Center for Social Media (2006) *Documentary filmmakers' statement of best practices on copyright and fair use.* Center for Social Media, American University, Washington, DC.

Council of Europe Committee of Ministers (2006) *Recommendation Rec(2006)12: On Empowering Children in the New Information and Communications Environment.* Adopted 27 September 2006. http://www.coe.int [11 November 2006].

Cuban, L. (2001) *Oversold and Underused: Computers in the Classroom.* Cambridge, MA: Harvard University Press.

Demetriadis, S., Barbas, A., Molohides, A., Palaigeorgiou, G., Psillos, D., Vlahavas, I. *et al.* (2003) ' "Cultures in negotiation": Teachers' acceptance/resistance attitudes considering the infusion of technology into schools'. *Computers and Education,* 41(1): 19–37.

DiSessa, A.A. (2000) *Changing Minds: Computers, Learning, and Literacy.* Cambridge, MA: MIT Press.

Educational Testing Service (2004) ICT literacy assessment: an issue paper from ETS. www.ets.org/ictliteracy/whitepaper1.html [6 November 2005].

Education Development Center (2006) *YouthLearn initiative.* http://youthlearn.org/youthmedia/evaluation/collaborative_research.asp [9 September 2006].

European Charter for Media Literacy (2006) *Euro media literacy* http://www.euromedialiteracy.eu/index.php?Pg=charter [4 September 2007].

Felini, D. (2004) *Pedagogia dei Media: Questioni, Percorsi e Sviluppi.* Brescia: La Scuola.

Frechette, J.D. (2002) *Developing Media Literacy in Cyberspace: Pedagogy and Critical Learning for the Twenty-First- Century Classroom.* Westport, CT: Praeger.

Gentile, D.A., Oberg, C., Sherwood, N.E., Story, M., Walsh, D.A. and Hogan, M. (2004) 'Well-child visits in the video age: pediatricians and the American Academy of Pediatrics' guidelines for children's media use'. *Pediatrics,* 114(5): 1235–1241.

George Lucas Educational Foundation (2001) 'Teacher preparation research. Edutopia'. *Edutopia* (September): 4.

Giroux, H.A. (2003) *The Abandoned Generation: Democracy Beyond the Culture of Fear.* New York: Palgrave Macmillan.

Goodman, S. (2003) *Teaching Youth Media: A Critical Guide to Literacy, Video Production & Social Change.* New York: Teachers College Press.

Goodwyn, A. (2000) *English in the Digital Age: Information and Communications Technology (ICT) and the Teaching of English.* London: Cassell.

Guerra, J.C. (2004) 'Putting literacy in its place: nomadic consciousness and the practice of transcultural repositioning'. Center for Chicano Studies. Rebellious reading: The Dynamics of Chicana/o Cultural Literacy. Paper guerra. http://repositories.cdlib.org/ccs_ucsb/rrc/guerra [16 April 2006].

Hagood, M.C., Leander, K., Luke, C., Mackey, M. and Nixon, H. (2003) Media and online literacy studies. *Reading Research Quarterly,* 38(3), 386–413.

Hahn, C. (2002) 'Valuing evaluation: youth media begins proving itself'. *Youth Media Reporter, Soros Foundation.* www.soros.org/initiatives/youth/articles_publications/articles/valuingevaluation [12 January 2005].

Heins, M. and Cho, C. (2003) *Media Literacy: An Alternative to Censorship.* New York: Free Expression Policy Project.

HNK (2006) 'HNK's blog'. http://iraqigirl.blogspot.com [11 August 2006].

Hobbs, R. (1994) 'Pedagogical issues in media education'. In S. Deetz (ed.) *Communication Yearbook,* Vol. 17. Newbury Park: Sage Publications; 453–466.

Hobbs, R. (1998) 'The seven great debates in the media literacy movement'. *Journal of Communication,* 48(2): 9–29.

Hobbs, R. (2004) 'A review of school-based initiatives in media literacy'. *American Behavioral Scientist,* 48(1): 48–59.

Hobbs, R. (2006) 'Multiple visions of multimedia literacy: emerging areas of synthesis'. In M. McKenna, L. Labbo, R. Kieffer and D. Reinking (eds) *Handbook of Literacy and* Technology. Mahwah, NJ: Erlbaum Associates; 15–28.

Hobbs, R. (2007) *Reading the Media: Media Literacy in High School English.* New York: Teachers College Press.

Jeffers, L. and Streit, T. (2003) *Self Evaluation in Youth Media and Technology Programs.* Newton, MA: Education Development Center.

Jenkins, H. (2006a) *Confronting the Challenges of Participatory Culture: Media Education for the 21st Century.* Chicago, IL: John D. and Catherine T. MacArthur Foundation.

Jenkins, H. (2006b) *Convergence Culture.* New York: New York University Press.

Jenkins, H. (2006c) 'Project New Media Literacy white paper'. Massachusetts Institute of Technology.

Johnson, N. (2003) 'The history of media reform: scanning the horizon'. History of Media Reform Panel. National Conference on Media Reform, Madison, WI, 7 November. www.nicholasjohnson.org/writing/masmedia/ncmr1107.html [15 August 2006].

Kapitzke, C. (2003) 'Information literacy: a positivist epistemology and a politics of information'. *Educational Theory,* 53(1): 37–53.

Kellner, D. and Share, J. (2005) 'Towards critical media literacy: core concepts, debates, organizations, and policy'. *Discourse: Studies in the Cultural Politics of Education,* 26(3): 369–386.

Kinzer, C. K. and Leander, K. (2003) 'Technology and the language arts: Implications of an expanded definition of literacy'. In J. Flood, D. Lapp, J.R. Squire and J.M. Jensen (eds) *Handbook of Research on Teaching the English Language Arts.* Mahwah, NJ: Lawrence Erlbaum Associates; 546–565.

Kress, G.R. (2003) *Literacy in the New Media Age.* London: Routledge.

KUHF Houston Public Radio (2006) 'TV boss campaign'. kuhf.convio.net/site/News2?JServSessionIdr005=73b7liu5t1.app5b&page=NewsArticle&id=17190&news [29 August 2006].

Lankshear, C. and Knobel, M. (1998) 'Critical literacy and new technologies'. Paper presented at the American Education Research Association, San Diego, CA.

Lewis, C. and Fabos, B. (2005) 'Instant messaging, literacies and social identities'. *Reading Research Quarterly,* 40(4): 470–501.

Lewis, J. and Jhally, S. (1998) 'The struggle over media literacy'. *Journal of Communication,* 48(1): 109–120.

Listen Up! (2006) 'Listen up'. http://listenup.org [30 January 2006].

Livingstone, S.M. (2003) 'The changing nature and uses of media literacy'. *Media Culture Online*, http://www.mediaculture-online.de/fileadmin/bibliothek/livingstone_changing_nature/livingstone_changing_nature.pdf [12 February 2006].

Marsh, J. (2006) 'Popular culture in the literacy curriculum: a Bourdieuan analysis'. *Reading Research Quarterly*, 41(2): 160–174.

Martin, A.G. and Hottmann, A. (2003) *Democracy, Multimedia Literacy, and Classroom Practice: A European Experience*. Berlin: Mondial Verlag.

McChesney, R. and Nichols, J. (2002) 'The making of a movement: getting serious about media reform'. *The Nation*, (January 7–14): 11, 17.

Media Smart (2006) 'Media smart: who is involved?' http://www.mediasmart.org.uk/media_smart/who_is_involved.html [5 August 2006].

MediaWatch-UK (2006) 'Annual general meeting, 2006'. http://mediawatchUK.org/aboutus.htm [1 September 2006].

Meyrowitz, J. (1998) 'Multiple media literacies'. *Journal of Communication*, 48(2): 96–108.

Mihailidis, P. (2006) 'Media literacy in journalism/mass communication: can the United States learn from Sweden?' *Journalism & Mass Communication Educator*, 60(4): 416–428.

New Zealand Qualifications Authority (2007) 'Domain, media studies'. http://www.name.org/nz [11 January 2007].

Oppenheimer, T. (2003) *The Flickering Mind: The False Promise of Technology in the Classroom and How Learning Can Be Saved.* New York: Random House.

Pailliotet, A.W. (2003) 'Integrating media and popular-culture literacy with content reading'. In J. Richards and M. McKenna (eds) *Integrating Multiple Literacies in K-8 Classrooms.* Mahwah, NJ: Erlbaum Associates; 172–233.

Partnership for 21st Century Skills (2002) *21st Century Skills*. Washington, DC: Partnership for 21st Century Skills.

Pfanner, E. (2006) 'Advertising: leave it to the professionals? Let consumers make their own ads'. *New York Times*, 4 August.

Primack, B., Gold, M., Switzer, G., Hobbs, R., Land, S. and Fine, M. (2006) 'Development and validation of a smoking media literacy scale'. *Archives of Pediatric and Adolescent Medicine*, 160: 369–374.

Rood, J. (2006) 'Scholastic veers from path to 9/11'. *TPM Muckraker.com.* www.tpmmuckraker.com/archives/001483.php [15 September 2006].

Schwartz, G. and Brown, P.U. (2005) *Media Literacy: Transforming Curriculum and Teaching.* Malden, MA: Blackwell.

Sefton-Green, J. and Sinker, R. (2000) *Evaluating Creativity: Making and Learning by Young People.* London: Routledge.

Sefton-Green, J., Grahame, J. and Buckingham, D. (1995) *Making Media: Practical Production in Media Education.* London: English and Media Centre.

Shaffer, D.W., Squire, K.D., Halverson, R. and Gee, J.P. (2005) 'Video games and the future of learning'. *Phi Delta Kappan*, 87(2): 104–111.

Silverstone, R. (2004) 'Regulation, media literacy and media civics'. *Media, Culture and Society*, 26(3): 440–449.

Squire, K.D. and Jenkins, H. (2004) 'Harnessing the power of games in education'. *Insight*, 3(1): 5–33.

Steyer, J.P. (2002) *The Other Parent: The Inside Story of the Media's Effect on our Children.* New York: Atria Books.

Thoman, E. and Jolls, T. (2005) 'Media literacy education: Lessons from the center for media literacy'. In G. Schwartz and P.U. Brown (eds) *Media Literacy: Transforming Curriculum and Teaching*, Vol. 104. Malden, MA: National Society for the Study of Education; 180–205.

Tyner, K. (1998) *Literacy in a Digital World: Teaching and Learning in the Age of Information.* Mahwah, NJ: Erlbaum Associates.

Tyner, K. (1999) 'New directions for media education in the United States. Media literacy: an online salon for educators. July 15–August 15, 1999'. http://www.namac.org/Forums/newdir.html [22 July 2001].

Whale, D. (2006) 'Technology skills as a criterion in teacher evaluation'. *Journal of Technology and Teacher Education*, 14(1): 61–74.

26

From Parental Control to Peer Pressure: Cultural Transmission and Conformism

Dominique Pasquier

INTRODUCTION

In the 1960s, Bourdieu and Passeron's (1964) *The Heirs: Students and Culture* became a best seller in France. The authors argue that cultural capital, measured by familiarity with such upper-class cultural practices as going to museums, concerts, art exhibitions or theatres, is a much more important factor than economic capital. It is the key to understanding success in school and, more globally, the social reproduction of elites. Alongside the formal curriculum of school programmes is a 'hidden curriculum', which requires a certain 'style, taste, spirit' that can only be acquired by a long familiarity with high culture. And only upper-class families can successfully manage such cultural transmission.

Forty years later, we can see that this social reproduction of high culture does not work as automatically as Bourdieu and Passeron suggested, even though today's younger generation has a much higher level of education than any before them. What happened? Sociologists of culture give a partial answer, by pointing to the rise of cultural eclectism among upper classes. Peterson and Kern (1996) evoke the 'omnivore' type, DiMaggio and Toqir (2004) the 'meltdown scenario', Donnat (1994) the 'diversification of cultural wallets', and Lahire (2004) the spread of 'cultural dissonance'. They are all referring to the same phenomenon: the last two decades of the 20th century have been marked by a decline of the 'pure legitimate' cultural profiles and a rise of new combinations of tastes associating 'low' cultural products (such as television series) with higher forms (such as visits to art museums). Moreover, they all note that younger cohorts' attendance rates have fallen for most high-culture performing arts, and that each cohort tends to develop a culture of its own; this is especially striking in the sector of music listening.

I would like to reconsider here, from the standpoint of media sociology, the question of cultural transmission, and the specific tension between vertical and horizontal transmission. Media research strengthens the hypothesis that the peculiar cultural profile of younger generations has much more to do with practices that involve mass media and new technologies of communication than with the general decline in high-art participation. Research also shows a strong decline of parental cultural guidance relative to peer group authority. In that sense, these results cast doubt on Bourdieu's scheme of vertical cultural hierarchies imposed by elites, and lead us to focus instead on two competing ways of constructing cultural legitimacy: at a micro level, peer groups; at a macro level, social representations transmitted by the media industries.

More radically, this question of transmission leads to the question of individualization. In *The Society of Individuals*, a text partly written in the 1940s, Norbert Elias argues that individualization is a characteristic of institutions in 'highly differentiated societies', which ask individuals to be autonomous subjects looking for self-realization. For Elias, the process of individualization is also a process of civilization:

> With the increasing differentiation of society and the resulting individualization of individuals, this differentness of one person to all others become something that is ranked especially highly on the social scale of values. In such societies it becomes a personal ideal of young people and adults to differ from others in one way or another, to distinguish oneself – in short, to be different (...) A person does not freely choose this ideal from a number of others, this being the one that appeals to him personally. It is the ideal of the individual person that is socially demanded and inculcated in the great majority of highly differentiated societies (Elias, 1991: 140–141).[1]

Several sociologists of the family and intimate relationships have recently revisited this thesis, defending the idea of increasingly contingent and tenuous social links, even among people related by kinship (Giddens, 1993; Bauman, 2001; Beck and Beck-Gernsheim, 2001). Giddens describes a democratization of the domestic sphere shown in the decline of links based on traditional arrangements and the generalization of a new model of links based on choice and affinities. Beck and Beck-Gernsheim have insisted on the risk biographies this individualization model leads to.

At first glance, research on family media uses clearly confirms the individualization thesis (Livingstone and Bovill, 2001; Livingstone, 2002). And it is surprising that sociologists of the family paid so little attention to the major role that media and communication practices have played in accompanying and consolidating the model of a contractual family, in which parental cultural guidance has become much less important. It is also surprising that most researches in the sociology of youth and sociology of education rarely study seriously the articulation between sociability and media practices, or the relation between popular culture and school culture.

But a closer look at the role that media products play in social relations between peers tells another story. The debate about conformism, so important in the 1950s (Parsons, 1942; Riesman *et al.*, 1953; Arendt, 1968) should not be dismissed as an outmoded lament from authors critical of mass media and their supposedly passive audiences. Media and communication practices open the way to an analysis of the increasing role of peer groups in the normative definition of codes in youth society, and show that their practices are as restrictive as those found in the intergenerational context. Individualization does not produce autonomous or 'free' individuals. Rather, in contrast to prevailing writing on this theme, such as Beck's or Bauman's, it paradoxically produces individuals who feel compelled to be like others in order to confirm their own identities.

OLD PROCESSES, NEW MODES: THREE STEPS TOWARDS YOUTH AUTONOMY

The second half of the 20th century has been marked by the conjunction of three phenomena, each of which, in their own way, allows children more independence from their elders at home: spatial, cultural, and relational autonomy. This resulted from long-term processes that accelerated during the 1980s and 1990s, involving a variety of changes in objects, technologies, family structures, cultural industries and social links.

Spatial autonomy results from the specialization of spaces inside the home. This is linked to transformations of modes of intimacy and increased distinctions by social status, generation and sex. Historians like Philippe Ariès have shown that the trend towards specialized rooms for the different members of a household began in the late 18th and early 19th centuries under the pressure of the bourgeois style of life (Ariès, 1960). Domestics began to be located in separate parts of the house (which was not the case in the late Middle Ages, when servants used to sleep in their masters' rooms); wives and husbands continued to occupy different rooms or suites, and children began to have their own private spaces. The invention of the corridor, the long empty space which distributed the different privatized spaces, formalized the process. In the long term, the urban upper-class home expanded to lower segments of the population, and to rural areas. During the 20th century, the spatial distribution changed again, with the new norm of parents' common rooms and a drastic decrease in the number of servants. It now stressed only one distinction, that between generations. As the ideal of large families moved towards the middle-class model of one or two children which largely predominated after the 1970s, children more often had a room of their own. The space for the 'bedroom culture' (Frith, 1978; Livingstone and Bovill, 2001) became standard, a late consequence of the several-centuries-old transformation of the notions of privacy and intimacy at home, which concretely influenced the social distribution of space. The bedroom territory – a personal universe expressed through specific cultural products and equipment – is highly relevant for children today. They increasingly restrict parental access to their space, less by such traditional symbolic signs as 'Do not enter', than by unofficially imposing a new rule of respecting privacy between generations. Paradoxically, children are now more welcome in their parents' rooms than parents are welcome in their children's rooms, a veritable irony of history.

Cultural autonomy marked a second step. The development of a cultural market specifically aimed at young people is not recent either – Kirsten Drotner (1988) shows that children's magazines were already very important in the late 19th century – but it has been clearly strengthened by changes in cultural production and consumption during the post World War II years. In the 1960s, Edgar Morin, studying the new social values promoted by mass culture, showed clear links between cinema or music and the birth of a youth culture that positioned itself against the background of generational conflicts (Morin, 1962). At the same time, the British School of Cultural Studies produced several seminal studies describing the transformations of youth subcultures in working-class settings (Cohen, 1972; Hebdidge, 1979).

Two other changes marked the end of the 20th century. The early 1980s saw diversification and segmentation in media industries: in France, for example, this is when radio stations aimed at a youth audience first appeared, and most of the television programmes dedicated to young people's musical preferences were launched. Recent data show that only 7% of those under 20 listen to 'generalist' radio stations. In other words, the segmentation of radio audiences by generation is almost complete (Glevarec, 2005). Specialized magazines aimed at youth have also become common since the end of the 1980s, with, in France, 105 different titles selling 108 million copies a year (Charon, 2002). Moreover, the movie industry now relies largely on young audiences for ticket sales, and a majority of players and buyers of video games are under 25. The list of cultural products specifically marketed to young people, or highly dependent on the youth market, is extensive, especially if we include clothes and accessories. None of this is new, even in France, but the scale of change has been dramatically different since 1980.

Relational autonomy is the most recent, and probably the most challenging, change. Adults' control of communication between children is a complex story. Adults have never been able to control communications inside peer society totally. In his classic essay on the 'problem of generations', Manheim (1952) argued that youth cultures originate in the concrete groups of young people he calls 'generational units', who create new perspectives and develop distinctive cultural patterns which are subsequently diffused to others. Sociologists interested in the knowledge young people share have studied intra-generational modes of communication: dirty jokes, pranks, and forms of teasing. They note the speed at which children's lore spreads to distant communities, which shows that peer society has specialized channels of communication that most adults are unaware of (Opie and Opie, 1959). Following Fine and Kleinman (1979), one could suppose that this 'cultural spread occurs through an interlocking group network characterized by multiple group membership'. Thus, informal forms of communication have always existed.

Still, adults have traditionally tried to control officially mediated communication channels. Control and censorship of correspondence is well known, and a major element in the plots of 19th century novels. For a long time, women were taught how to read, but not how to write, for just that reason (Chartier, 1993). Closer to us, historians of telephone use show that the persistence of party lines and other collective forms of use kept the instrument from becoming a private mode of communication for more than 50 years (Fischer, 1992). It took several decades for the idea of private conversations to become socially acceptable. When it did, parents still resisted their children's overuse of the phone, especially for sociable talking, and they could find out about their children's social networks simply by asking who was on the phone, or listening to bits of conversation.

The spread of cellular phones, and communications through the internet, especially in the last 10 years, marks a real change. These devices are not just two more items in a list of cultural products aimed at and loved by young people. They create a new map of domestic life, giving children the official right to develop social links with friends away from home and without parental regulation. It is too early to know what the consequences of this new phenomenon will be, but we can guess they will seriously affect the relational balance between parents, their children, and their children's peers. In France, 75% of people between 11 and 20 years of age have a mobile phone (the figures are over 90% for the 18–20 age group[2]); and, as every study shows, portables phones bought by parents in order to keep track of their children when they are away from home are mostly used by the latter to consolidate social links within their peer groups (Ling, 2005).

Interactive communication through the internet soon made anonymous contacts between people possible, and teens became very fond of such chats and, to a lesser degree, forums. This type of interaction has gone through an interesting change recently with the development of instant messaging and blogs. Those are not just two more technological modes of communication: they are based on a different conception of electronic interaction, both functioning as a kind of elective *sociability*. Instant messaging proposes a 'club' formula of links, either with people you have already met or with friends and acquaintances recommended by those people. Blogs, with their blog rolls giving links to other blogs and thus making it easy for bloggers to connect with each other, illustrate a theme I will take up in more detail later, i.e. the interlocking of cultural practices and social networks.

For the moment, one should just note that children are careful to keep parents out of these exchanges. Whether anonymous or with friends, parents no longer know who their children are interacting with. A field study about blogs even shows that most parents would consider it intrusive to take a look at their children's blogs, comparing it to opening their private letters or reading their diary (Delaunay, unpublished data). One anecdote illustrates the strange status youth give to these private expressions in the public sphere of the internet. Several pupils at a French high school put pictures of their teachers, taken with their mobile phones when in class, on their blogs with funny captions. These blogs were very popular with the other pupils. When they were caught and expelled, they argued that the blog was a personal thing, and that they never thought adults could or would look at them. In other words, they considered the blog as a private sphere and not a public access sphere. To be more precise, they consider it confined to their own generation, to which teachers and parents should not have access.

As I noted above, most parents apparently accept this sudden increase in the presence of horizontal links in the home, just as they had accepted that their children developed a culture of their own, having their own musical tastes and their own radio programmes, and enjoying these things in the privacy of their bedrooms. In this sense, it is a different kind of intergenerational relationship scheme than the one that prevailed in the 1960s and 1970s, when youth culture developed in opposition to adult culture. The counter culture model that stressed the conflict of generations has been replaced by a new model based on peaceful cohabitation inside the home (much more than inside the school system, where, in France at least, conflict between classical humanist culture and mediated popular culture is still very important). At home, different cultures and social circles live together with no special antagonism. As noted in several studies, there are still common practices between generations at home, such as mother–daughter watching TV series or father–son using the computer; but, as Sonia Livingstone notes, most children express the desire to be on their own when watching TV or playing video games (Livingstone, 2002). And most parents accept this cultural cohabitation.

Nor does this model resemble the one proposed by the discipline of cultural studies. The localized approach of fieldwork done in that tradition cannot take account of the major role now played by the increased circulation of social representations in the mass media. Furthermore, a central theme of cultural studies emphasizes the opposition between domination and resistance which clearly can no longer be formulated in the same terms. As Sarah Thornton (1996) argues, it is difficult to identify a dominant culture today: she contrasts the subcultures of the 1970s, opposed to a dominant mainstream middle-class culture, with the subcultures of the 1990s, which opposed a dominant culture defined as feminine and a popular culture marked by its commercial dimension.

THE PEERS' TRIBUNAL: REFERENCE GROUPS AS AFFILIATION AND CONSTRAINT

So today's youth world is more 'free' than they used to be, with parents promoting the individual realization of the self for their children to whom they give a lot of autonomy to realize that goal. Globally, sociologists of the family have been praising this new 'contractual' family. But they paid little attention to the transformations this evolution produced in youth society. Paradoxically, we may be helped by a book published over 50 years ago in the USA: David Riesman *et al.*'s *The Lonely Crowd*. When it appeared in 1950, the question of conformism had begun to be a major debate in sociology.[3] As Eugene Lunn (1990) suggests:

> Riesman's ostensibly well-known *Lonely Crowd* (…) has almost always been read as simply a jeremiad against social and cultural conformity. The inner-directed entrepreneurial character of the nineteenth century bourgeois variety has been generally taken as Riesman's ideal against which he judged the contemporary outer directed type – the malleable personality formed by the stress upon affability in bureaucratic organizations and the influence of peer pressures in leisure activities. What most readers have failed to note was that the gyroscopic directions of the older character were internalizations of external authority and thus at least as conformist as the radar sensitive new personality.

Riesman *et al.* do not hold mass media responsible for conformism, they simply evoke a shift from conformism through vertical cultural transmission to conformism through horizontal transmission. The visible and palpable barriers of family and authority that typically restricted people in the past, argue Riesman *et al.* do not coerce those seeking autonomy, but they are not necessarily freer than before.[4]

> Each peculiar peer group has its group fandoms and lingoes. Safety consists not in mastering a difficult craft but in mastering a battery of taste preferences and the mode of their expression. The preferences are for articles or heroes of consumption and for members of the group itself. The proper mode of expression requires feeling out with skill and sensitivity the probable tastes of the others and then swapping mutual likes and dislikes to manoeuvre intimacy (…) What matters, is an ability at continual testing out of others' tastes, often a far more intrusive process than the exchange of courtesies and pleasantries required by etiquette (Riesman *et al.*, 1953: 94–95).

Arendt's essay on the crisis in education, first published in 1954, makes a similar point (Arendt, 1968). She sharply criticizes progressive education for its eagerness to downplay the need for adult guidance. When they avoid adult authority, Arendt says, children are subject to the more terrifying tyranny of their peer group. This 'tyranny of the majority' pressures children to conform to the group and forces of normalization prevail. Her essay is part of a larger reflection about the crisis of culture; Riesman *et al.*'s specific observations about conformity in the leisure sphere among young people are based on fieldwork about musical tastes. They both assume that the replacement of authoritarian by democratic education increases the probability of conformity through peer groups. But neither pays much attention to the social organization of those groups, thus leaving several unanswered questions. Who are the conformity-producing agents? Is the process uniform? Is conformity more prominent in some cultural sectors than others? Can a non-conformist cultural form impose conformity codes? In fact, it is hard to answer those questions precisely because, as Shibutani pointed out, the concept of reference group is ambiguous. 'All kinds of groupings with great variations in size, composition and structure may become reference groups' (Shibutani, 1955). Reference groups, he argues, might be the groups that serve as a comparison point; they might be the groups to which someone aspires; or they might be the groups whose perspectives are assumed by the actor. But, 'of greatest importance for most people are those groups in which they participate directly – what have been called membership groups – especially those containing a number of persons with whom one stands in a primary relationship' (Shibutani, 1955). This is what Mead (1934) refers to as taking the role of the generalized other: shared perspectives with others in transactions that make it possible to anticipate the reactions of others, inhibit undesirable impulses, and guide one's conduct.

TV FANDOM AND REFERENCE GROUPS

I would like now to examine some of these issues more closely on the basis of two recent field studies: one about the reception of a sentimental television series by young viewers and one about the transformation of older adolescents' relation to culture. These two studies demonstrate young people's relations to complex and multiple reference groups and, moreover, they indicate that being a member of primary relation groups, often at school, is a starting point for formulating moral evaluations of groups which serve as comparison or aspiration references. I will take two concrete examples of memberships groups to examine this process.

The first one is fans of television series (Pasquier, 1996, 1999). I studied the fan letters sent to the actors of a popular French sentimental TV show, *Hélène et les Garçons*.[5] In these letters, young writers give a lot of details about their daily activities as fans, and we understand that this micro social world is organized very precisely, with rules, rituals, members and opponents. We could here use the interactionist concept of 'social world' to study the cooperative work done by fans to adjust their comportment to other members of the same world. Following Strauss (1978) and Becker (1982), a 'social world' is composed by social actors acting collectively, usually for a specific activity, and regulating their mutual comportments by the means of shared conventions, that may be implicit or explicit, and might move. This flexible model is very useful to give an account of the specific form of collective action of fans.

One does not become a fan by chance, by just watching television, even though that may be the way fandom begins. Fandom is a social activity. There are intermediaries: a sister, a friend at school, a cousin, a neighbour: 'Dear Hélène, I have a friend who is a fan of yours, she's the one who told me about you and made me love you. Before, I only knew you through television'. The cult is always collective. Most fans have a best friend who is also a fan and with whom they share and exchange objects and information. The letter writers talk about these friends in their fan letters, give her name and explain how this fandom friendship started. In addition, the fans participate in small communities organized, generally, at school, four or five girls who play role games together. The roles are fixed; each one plays a regular character, one she feels something in common with, either physically or psychologically: 'When playing, I am Laly, because I think we look alike, same hair cut, same nature'. Some competition might arise between different players, each child trying to prove she knows more things about the star, or has obtained special favours from her. Anna, 9 years, asks for a letter with a special word at the end 'to make some friends at school jealous'. Sabrina describes a contest at school to find out who will obtain more things from the producer.

Letters refer to all kinds of rumours: 'Emilie told me you let her come to see you backstage at your concert and that afterward you went to her house. Is that true?' 'One day I told a friend you were my little cousin, and she believed me. If only it could be true!' Allies, competitors, but also enemies. For young girls, the enemies at school are mainly boys. They accept this situation as natural: 'Boys make fun of us when we play *Hélène*, but you have to understand them, they are boys'. As the girls get older, things get more difficult because some of the other girls begin to make fun of them too, always with the same argument: *Hélène* is a series for younger kids.

> At college [11/14 years] everyone tells me that watching *Hélène* is childish. Me, I think it is a wonderful series for adolescents. When they criticize the program, I defend you, and I notice that all those girls who say it is for babies wouldn't miss an episode!

These examples show that being a member of this reference group, *Hélène's* fans, require constant work to adjust your comportment to that of the other members. You must have the same information (usually in the fanzines), buy the same objects linked to the series, wear the same kind of clothes and even have the same hairstyle. In that sense, conformity is a prerequisite for claiming fan status.

Nevertheless, beyond this membership reference group, there is also an aspiration reference group: the group of fans that would be recognized as 'good' fans by the star herself, who could then pretend to gain a much higher status, being the star's friend. Here, uniqueness is highly valued. Fans know perfectly well that there are many, many other fans who they don't personally know and will never meet, but who might also write to the star. This knowledge is both an incentive (it proves the choice was right since it is socially shared) and a great worry:

> I know that you receive letters every day and that you may throw them in the wastebasket. I know you can't answer every letter, but think of all these children who watch you, love you, think of you. They admire you and think you are full of talent. They think you might help them, giving advice. It is so hard to be fan of a star! You hope all the time that she thinks of you even just for a moment. My dream is that you would come to my home… I have 3 brothers, Richard 20, Antony 17, and Antonin 9. Maybe you would fall in love with one of my brothers?

This young writer, like many others, wants to differentiate herself from the multitude of other fans and explains how unique her love for the star is ('I write you this letter so that you'll know I exist, I am not a regular fan, just wanting to touch you, I consider you as a friend').

Examples like these show how tightly linked the two reference groups are: the membership group articulated around local micro practices and the elective aspiration group where membership is never taken for granted. It also illustrates the tension between conformity and authenticity, since, to be able to pretend to be recognized as a unique individual by the star, you first have to strictly respect the common routines shared with other fans.

MUSIC TASTE AND THE POWER OF PEERS

My second example deals with musical tastes (Pasquier, 2005). Music is central in the cultural universe of adolescents, not only because listening to music is their favourite cultural practice, but also because a large part of juvenile social life is organized around musical tastes: music is a strong support for the elaboration and exhibition of identities. It is not by chance that Riesman *et al.*'s analysis is partly based on fieldwork about teenagers' musical preferences which showed how anxious they were about having the 'right' preferences:

> The product approved by most of the others, or by a suitable testimonial from a peer consumer, becomes the *best*. The most popular products, by this formula are the products that happen to be used by the most popular. Compared with their inner directed predecessors, other directed children are extraordinary knowledgeable about popularity ratings (Riesman *et al.*, 1953: 103).

Music, being so central in adolescents' tastes and culture, is the major sector where we can observe concretely both stylization processes and the role of sociometric peers as a jury that delimits what it is possible to like and listen to without risking social marginalization. Specific musical cultures are the settings in which social groups develop normative prescriptions or proscriptions as well as common, accepted behaviours.

I carried out fieldwork in three suburban secondary schools in 2002, with adolescents 15 to 20 years old. At that age, music is much more important than television and, in contrast to video games, both sexes affirm a strong link to specific musical universes, with rap (for boys) and R&B (for girls) at the top of the list. Classical music and, to a lesser degree, jazz are largely rejected. When I asked Paul (17, upper class family) what kind of music he listened to, he first answered: 'Everything, I like many types of music, I listen to anything'. But when asked, 'Even classical music?' he quickly answered:

> Ah, no! Ah no. None of my pals listen to that, and I don't know, people who listen to classical music are very special, they have their own culture. Well, maybe I listened to two or three pieces that I liked, but mainly it was because I was looking for instrumental ideas. No, I am not a lover of classical music…

If classical music acts as a negative norm because it is associated with the cultural universe of older generations, rap is a strong referent for youth culture, especially among boys. A taste for rap is related to the homology system described by Hebdidge (1979): liking rap is associated with liking football, having a very short hair cut, wearing street wear with logos, using certain slang words, ritual ways of walking and greetings. It is also associated with a specific state of mind towards society: rejection of school values, strong solidarity with ethnic groups, and a systematic depreciation of feminine values or universes. At the end of the 1990s, when rap was a dominant musical genre, some adolescents felt it very difficult to develop alternative tastes:

> At school it is rap, rap and R&B, all that music everyone knows. Girls are more R&B and boys rap. Their look, well, if you are not dressed like them, you are wrong…Baskets, Nike. Only clothes with logos. And it is the same for girls, they all dress alike, showing the belly, high heels, large studded belts… Everyone dresses more or less alike and everyone listens to the same music. If you are not like them, they can't stand it (girl, 17, middle class).

We could make the same observations about such less popular genres as grunge rock. Anna (17, middle class) discovered the group Nirvana through a friend when she was 15.

Since then, this musical preference is at the centre of her social life:

> At school those who like Nirvana are like a clan! There are twenty of us, more boys than girls, only two girls, me and my best friend (Q: How did you meet them?) Well, first we saw them! By their schoolbags, they have Nirvana stuff on them. And they had noticed us also, because we dress gothic, trash, black. Hard. It is a special style. In my class, other girls hate me because of that; they say I look like a witch. Very nice. It's because they can't stand people who are different from them. They like R&B or rap; they dress according to the fashion, the fashion style. Here, it is: might is right. But I don't mind, when they attack me I fight, I kick them.

What is striking is that the different universes organized around musical preferences function as an exclusive choice, not of music (most adolescents listen to a large range of musical genres), but of social links; the tastes they declare publicly are usually more homogeneous than the ones they actually display when at home. They possibly have their backstage practices, in the Goffmanian sense, that might include listening to music linked to their parents' cultural universe, such as jazz or classical music.

Moreover, their declared tastes often differ from one public scene to another. These tastes should thus always be analysed in their specific social context. Sociologists of networks have established a useful distinction between *weak* and *strong* social links (Granovetter, 1983). Individuals, however dense their social network, are likely to develop acquaintance relationships outside the groups with which they have close relations. These outside contacts, or weak links, are crucial to understanding the dissemination of information and culture throughout adolescent social systems: 'Cultural content and identification change through direct or indirect contact with outsiders' (Fine and Kleinman, 1979).

The distinction is important for understanding the organization of reference groups in adolescence. Life at school is very specific, organized around regular association with a large number of people you know more or less well, and who are in the same places at the same time you are. Within this large population are smaller generational units of friends and acquaintances, which may include the friends and acquaintances of your friends, which increases the size of the group you associate with considerably. In this setting, teenagers can develop more intimate friendships. The 'pal' group is based on weak links, the friends' circle on strong links. Paradoxically, it is in the groups formed around weak links that conformist mechanisms are the most active: the individual is under scrutiny. To maintain a certain level of popularity and, thus, to be sure of being integrated, teens have to repress any signs of difference. Liking the wrong music, i.e. music others don't like, is socially dangerous, like wearing the wrong clothes. But teens may reveal more authentic parts of their selves when alone with close friends and, as we saw in the case of fans, a common cultural preference can transform weak links into strong links.

REASSERTING THE SIGNIFICANCE OF THE MEDIA

None of this sounds especially new. Most youth cultures elaborate their own codes by opposition and contrast to others. At the most, we might agree that there is only a reinforcement of peer authority related to the decline in parental guidance, as Riesman *et al.* or Arendt argued. But that would ignore the major role that media representations now play in socialization processes. As we saw earlier, it is more or less since the 1980s that the media industry developed massive cultural programming aimed at young people. The interlocking group networks analysed by Fine and Kleinman must now merge with other major sources of dissemination of information: radio and television programmes, articles in youth magazines, internet forums and chat groups. Youth culture is intertwined with the dynamics of commercial media in a way that contributes to the rapid diffusion of detailed cultural codes. Entrepreneurs understand the importance of these new modes of dissemination. TV clips not only advertise music and musicians, but also sportswear logos, hairstyles and, not least, modes of talking. In France, several young suburban sportswear designers, such as Dia or Bullrot, turned into large enterprises with contracts with big sports federations, such as with the NBA, just by having their rap artist friends wear their branded clothes on TV. Radio talk shows, as Glevarec (2005) pointed it, also act as a common reference. Peer identification and acceptance of specific cultural prescriptions are also much discussed on internet forums or chats. All these competing resources linked to the media industry are used to elaborate valid codes within locally situated peer groups, with a major result: popular culture products become more salient, become the ones teens are supposed to know and talk about, to adopt or reject. These constitute the shared reference points of the youth universe.

It is very difficult to distance oneself from this common grounded culture. Let us take an example from our fieldwork in secondary schools that shows how social marginalization is the price paid for living outside a cultural world defined by specific routines of communication, peculiar modes of social links, and the mastering of definite musical or television references. Sarah is 18 years old, she is an excellent student, and has cultural tastes which are rare for her generation (classical music, 19th century novels). Her younger brother, 15, on the contrary, is very typical of what she labels 'a normal young person':

> It is funny to have this 'real' young guy in the room next to mine, here he is, a normal young guy. When I see him, I say to myself: 'I could have been like him'. Even my father thinks that in fact I am bizarre, too far from real things, cut off from real life, he thinks I am like an older person. My brother, he goes out a lot... Me, at his age, I had never got drunk, things like that, silly things, he drinks, he smokes, he does things one should do at his age. He is cool, he has a lot of pals, a lot, a large group that have a classical kind of young person's life. Their communicate by mobile phone, mobile phone all the time, for jokes, silly things, I hear him on the phone, sometimes he talks nonsense, imitating animal noises, god, they have nothing to say to each other! They call to have a laugh together. He tells me 'All the young people do that, it's normal, you are not normal, all the normal young people like talking on the phone'. In his group, they care a lot about the media, all that, television series or *Loft Story* (the French Big Brother), programs for young, but it is more a pretext to talk together than anything else. Anyway, it is a social phenomenon to watch those series or programs, it is 'I am young, I do like the other young people do' In his group, they take nicknames from the series characters, they use those names to talk together, or pretend to dress like someone in *Loft Story*, well, I'm not into that, I never watch. My brother watches so he can talk with his friends afterward, that's all. Once there was a television show with singers, and I discovered that most of them I didn't know, I used to know some stars from when I was younger, but all the recent ones, I didn't know them, never even heard their names, and my brother told me 'Come on, you don't know that one? But her record is always on the radio! You don't know her! Everyone talks about her!' I felt like an extraterrestrial. But I don't miss it, I don't do it on purpose, I don't know... the problem is that my social life is with other people who are disconnected, like me, my social life is mainly dinners with friends, just that, talking together.

CONCLUSION

The decline in parental guidance, in the name of the autonomy of children and the culture of authenticity, has had the paradoxical effect of facilitating conformism in the society and strengthening the normative role of reference groups based on weak ties. Cultural preferences and practices are at the very heart of the organization of youth sociability, the base on which one elaborates individual and collective identities. New technologies of communication play an active role in contemporary youth cultures, acting as a way of reaffirming links: exchanges on mobile phones are often less important for what is talked about than for being a proof *per se* of integration in a social circle.

Still, face-to-face relations are the most valued mode of interaction. Teens are very clear about this. But in a context where the expression of self is continually scrutinized by reference groups, exchanges and discussions on the internet may be a sort of emotional safety valve, a place where interactions, which may have been constrained during the day, can develop more fluidly, often with the same interlocutors. In that sense, one might consider that the development of elective kinds of relationships on the internet (such as instant messaging) or network modes (such as blog rolls) promote new forms of 'relational self-production' (Cardon, and Delaunay, 2006). Electronic sociability sheds light on the dead ends or difficulties of teenagers' social lives. Boys, who are most often submitted to the scrutiny of people with whom they have weak ties, find in them a place to express self-reflexivity without fearing to be made fun of by other boys, for whom the expression of intimacy connotes feminine sentimentality. They might also discover the pleasure of intimate writing, a quite new phenomenon, since self-disclosure was traditionally something women did, both in correspondence and on the phone. In that sense, it is less interesting to study new technologies of communication as self-enclosed universes than as mirrors of the changes and transformations of social links in the daily life of young people.

NOTES

1 And 40 years before Beck, Elias was already insisting on the risk factor in those new biographies 'More freedom of choice and more risk go together (Elias, 1991: 129) (...) For the chances of achieving the fulfilment of such a striving in such a society are always slight in relation to the number of people seeking it (Elias, 1991: 142).

2 Data from Médiametrie, Youth barometer, 2005.

3 See also Parsons: 'The peer group may be regarded as a field for the exercise of independence from adult control ... But another very important function is to provide the child a source of non adult approval and acceptance ... On the one hand, the peer group is a field for acquiring and displaying various types of "prowess"; for boys this is especially the physical prowess which may later ripen into athletic achievement. On the other hand it is a matter of gaining acceptance from desirable peers as "belonging" in the group, which later ripens into the conception of the popular teenager, the "right guy"' (Parsons, 1942). For a review of works about the thematic of conformity see Thomson (1992).

4 For Riesman *et al.* this evolution is due to a change in education and parents' new concerns with their own children's popularity: 'the adults are anxious that the child succeed in the peer group and therefore are concerned with his adjustment. They tend to ignore and even suppress invisible differences between their child and other children. Such differences might cast doubt on their own adjustment, their own correct tuning to the signals concerning child rearing' (Riesman *et al.*, 1953: 92).

5 I have got access to this mail from April 1994 to January 1995, which means thousands and thousands of letters –500 to 1000 letters arrived every day. Besides the contents themselves, those letters give some indications about children's social profile: the age (first thing the child says usually), the sex (by first names), the geographical origins (by zip codes), and, in many cases, what is said in the letters about the family and the life of the child gives some kind of indication about the social background. To present briefly the main characteristics, a huge majority of the letters are written by little girls, aged 8 to 12, living in rural settings or lower class suburbs. Some of the letters also comes from foreign countries where the series was aired: Algeria, Greece, Turkey, and Norway. These foreign correspondents are, in general, older (14 to 18) and more often boys than the French ones are.

REFERENCES

Arendt, H. (1968) *Between Past and Future.* New York: Penguin Books.

Ariès, P. (1962) *Centuries of Childhood: A Social History of Family Life.* New York: Vintage Books.

Bauman, Z. (2001) *The Individualized Society.* Cambridge: Polity Press.

Beck, U. and Beck-Gernsheim, E. (2001) *Individualization.* London: Sage.

Becker, H. (1982) *Art Worlds.* Berkeley, CA: The University of California Press.

Bourdieu, P. and Passeron, J.C. (1964) *Les Héritiers. Les Etudiants Face à la Culture.* Paris: Editions de Minuit.

Charon, J.M. (2002), *La Presse des Jeunes.* Paris: La Découverte.

Chartier, R. (1993) *Pratiques de la Lecture.* Paris: Payot.

Cohen, S. (1972) *Folk Devils and Moral Panics. The Invention of the Mods and Rockers,* London: Blackwell.

Cardon, D. and Delaunay, H. (2006) 'La production de soi comme technique relationnelle. Un essai de typologie des blogs par leurs publics'. *Réseaux,* 24(138): 15–71.

DiMaggio, P. and Toqir, M. (2004) 'Art participation as cultural capital in the United States, 1982–2002: signs of decline?' *Poetics,* 32: 169–194.

Donnat, O. (1994) *Les Français Face à la Culture, De l'Exclusion à l'Eclectisme.* Paris: La Découverte.

Drotner, K. (1988) *English Children and their Magazines 1751–1945.* Yale University Press.

Elias, N. (1991) *The Society of Individuals*. Cambridge: Blackwell.

Fine, A.G. and Kleinman, S. (1979) 'Rethinking subcultures: an interactionist analysis'. *The American Journal of Sociology*, 85(1): 1–20.

Fischer, C. (1992) *America Calling, a Social History of the Telephone to 1940*. University of California Press.

Frith, S. (1978) *Sociology of Rock*. London: Constable.

Giddens, A. (1993) *The transformation of intimacy: sexuality, love and erotism in modern Societies*, Cambridge: Polity Press.

Glevarec, H. (2005). 'Youth radio as a social object: the social meaning of free radio shows for young people in France'. *Media, Culture and Society*, 27(3): 333–351.

Granovetter, M. (1983) 'The strength of weak ties: a network theory revisited'. *Sociological Theory*, 1: 201–233.

Hebdidge, D. (1979) *Subcultures. The Meaning of Style*. London: Methuen.

Lahire, B. (2004) *La Culture des Individus, Dissonances Culturelles et Distinction de Soi*. Paris: La Découverte.

Ling, R. (2005) 'Control, emancipation and status: the mobile phone in the teen's parental and peer group control relationships'. In R. Kraut (ed.) *Information Technology at Home*. Oxford University Press.

Livingstone, S. (2002) *Young People and New Media*. London: Sage.

Livingstone, S. and Bovill, M. (eds) (2001) *Children and Young People in a Changing Media Environment*. Los Angeles, CA: Erlbaum.

Lunn, E. (1990) 'Beyond "mass culture": the lonely crowd, the uses of literacy, and the post war era'. *Theory and Society*, 19(1): 63–86.

Manheim, K. (1952) 'The problem of generations'. In *Essays in the Sociology of Knowledge*. London: Routledge & Kegan Paul.

Mead, G.H. (1934) *Mind, Self and Society*, C.W. Morris (ed.). Chicago, IL: Chicago University Press.

Morin, E. (1962) *L'Esprit du Temps*. Paris: Grasset

Opie, P. and Opie, I. (1959) *The Lore and Language of Schoolchildren*. New York: Oxford University Press.

Parsons, T. (1942) 'Age and sex in the social structure of the United States'. *American Sociological Review*, 7(7): 604–616.

Pasquier, D. (1996) 'Teen series reception: television, adolescence and the culture of feelings'. *Childhood*, 3(3): 351–375.

Pasquier, D. (1999), *La Culture des Sentiments. L'Expérience Télévisuelle des Adolescents*, Paris: Ed de la Maison des Sciences de l'Homme.

Pasquier, D. (2005) *Cultures Lycéennes: La Tyrannie de la Majorité*. Paris: Autrement.

Peterson, R. and Kern, R. (1996) 'Changing highbrow taste: from snob to omnivore'. *American Sociological Review*, 61: 900–917.

Riesman, D., Glazer, N. and Denney, R. (1953) *The Lonely Crowd. A Study of the Changing American Character*. New York: Doubleday (second revised edition, original 1950, Yale University Press).

Shibutani, T. (1955) 'Reference groups as perspectives'. *American Journal of Sociology*, 60: 562–569.

Strauss, A. (1978) 'A social world perspective'. In N. Denzin (ed.) *Studies in Symbolic Interaction*, Volume 1. Greenwich, CT: JAI Press; 119–128.

Thomson, I.T. (1992) 'Individualism and conformity in the 1950s vs. the 1980s'. *Sociological Forum*, 7(3): 497–516.

Thornton, S. (1996) *Club Cultures: Music, Media and Subcultural Capital*. Hanover: Wesleyan University Press.

27

The Commodification of Youth Culture

Janet Wasko

> What is most troubling is that children's culture has become virtually indistinguishable from consumer culture over the course of the last century... Childhood makes capitalism hum over the long haul (Cook, 2001).

INTRODUCTION

In 1955, Disney put together three segments of one of its popular television series into one movie and released it as *Davy Crockett, King of the Wild Frontier*. The movie, starring Fess Parker as the famous frontiersman and Buddy Ebson as his sidekick, was an immediate box office hit and also created a nationwide phenomenon never witnessed before in the USA, featuring movie merchandising specifically targeting young children. Davy Crockett coonskin caps were everyday apparel for most young boys, while a wide array of other merchandise flooded the market, including flintlock pistols complete with powder horns, Davy Crockett trading cards and lunch pails, as well as Alamo playsets featuring Mexican soldiers and the Texan defenders. While not the first example of marketing to children, the phenomenon certainly drew much more attention to the process.

While several scholars have traced the evolution of marketing to children (Kline, 1993; Seiter, 1993; Cross, 2002; Cook, 2004; Jacobson, 2005), it is obvious that the commodification and commercialization of childhood and youth has accelerated dramatically since the 1950s. Not only are children and youth avid consumers of a growing array of media and other cultural products, but the process of targeting youth for consumption through the media and advertising has become increasingly more developed and sophisticated. New methods of advertising and marketing to children are developing with new forms of communication, while the control of media oriented to young people has been concentrated into a handful of transnational media conglomerates that typically dominate the rest of the media landscape, as well.

While much research has focused on the effects of media use and content on children, these political economic factors involved with youth and media are often underplayed or ignored, at least by many academic researchers.[1] This chapter will argue that it is necessary to understand this process more completely to be able to fully explicate the relationship between youth and media.

The approach used in this chapter might be referred to as the political economy of media or communications, which incorporates those characteristics that define political economy generally, as well as its application to the study of media and communications. In *The Political Economy of Communication*, Vincent Mosco has defined this version of political economy as 'the study of the social relations, particularly power relations, that mutually constitute the production, distribution and consumption of resources' (Mosco, 1996: 25). He explains that political economy is about survival and control, or how societies are organized to produce what is necessary to survive, and how order is maintained to meet societal goals.

Political economy is crucial to understanding youth culture, where there has been a proliferation of products and new media forms (commodification) and increased advertising of products in a variety of new ways (commercialization). A brief overview of these general tendencies as they have developed in the world of youth culture will be followed by case studies of the Walt Disney Company and Viacom's Neopets, which exemplify these trends in more detail. And, while there are broader issues such as identity, creativity, participation, etc. involved in assessing contemporary youth culture, this chapter will focus mostly on the processes of commodification and commercialization, providing the underpinning for considering these other important issues. While the commercialization of youth culture is generally growing in many parts of the world, the focus here is mostly on the situation in the USA, which certainly is the most accelerated example, as well as being dependent on resources from other parts of the world to maintain its hyper-consumer culture.

YOUTH MEDIA/CULTURE INDUSTRY

While, historically, products have been aimed at children and youth, the development of a youth market grew substantially during the last half of the twentieth century. But until the early 1980s, the marketing of youth products was more or less haphazard.

In the late 1980s, James McNeal (1987) pointed to the significance of the 'kids' consumption' (his term), identifying three focuses: kids as consumers, kids as future consumers, and kids as influences on consumption. Advertising and marketing experts began to get the picture, and the marketing of products for children and youth expanded considerably.

By the beginning of the 21st century, many analysts maintained that children and youth were at the heart of consumer culture (at least, in the USA, as well as many other consumption-oriented countries). Harvard economist Juliet Schor (2004: 9) concluded in her study of 'the commercialized child' that, 'Kids and teens are now the epicenter of American consumer culture'. (Also, see Bogart (2005)). It is not surprising, then, that the media and advertising industries have created more deliberate, elaborate and widespread efforts to tap this increasingly important market.

These days, most American youth have more money for consumption, are consuming more at an earlier age, and have an even stronger influence on family consumption. These roles have been increasingly recognized, as highlighted by one media analyst:

> With spending power of $78.5 billion annually, kids are an increasingly vital economic force. A growing number of non-traditional advertisers are moving into kids' television not only to reach them but to reach their parents in a relevant environment. According to Yankelovich Youth Monitor, 72 percent of kids say commercials influence their purchase decisions and a growing majority of adults admit they are significantly impacted by their children's requests and recommendations (Myers, 2005).

McNeal estimated that American children aged 4–12 directly influence US$330 billion of adult purchasing in 2004 and 'evoked' another US$340 billion. But this is not just an American phenomenon: global estimates for tween influence (roughly, from first grade to age 12) topped US$1 trillion in 2002 (Schor, 2004: 23).

More commodities, more consumption

With more money to spend, the number and range of commodities aimed at children and teens is considerable. The US market for young people's products has been estimated at over US$166 billion (Marketresearch.com, 2006). McNeal reports that children aged 4–12 made US$6.1 billion in purchases in 1989, compared with US$30 billion in 2002. Older youth, aged 12–19, spent US$170 billion in 2002.

To get a sense of the way that this market is developing, note this description of a marketing report published by marketresearch.com (and available for US$2,750):

> This report analyzes the $166-billion U.S. market for kids' products, which is being transformed by sweeping changes in kids' preferences, strong undercurrents of e-commerce and advanced marketing techniques. The report offers a detailed discussion of kid demographics, market size, growth and composition, kids' behavior as consumers, retail trends and the new fundamentals of marketing to kids. Market projections through 2004 are included. Purchasers can expect a thorough discussion of specific kid-targeted marketing strategies and campaigns that have succeeded in the following product segments: food and beverages, play items, video, apparel, and health and beauty care. Kid-oriented media is comprehensively analyzed, with a special new emphasis on electronic media.

Many observers have noted that this increased consumption of commodities by kids is occurring at the same time as changes in the nature of childhood itself, with earlier involvement by children in the adult world. Consequently, the role that children play in the consumption process has shifted, with children becoming the household experts on the latest products, especially new technologies. Children's familiarity with an increasing number of brands has also accelerated. One often-cited study found that the average 10 year old has memorized 300–400 brands (Del Vecchio, 1997).

Advertising and marketing strategies

And the reason that children are familiar with so many brands has a good deal to do with advertising, or the greatly enhanced commercialization of media. Since the 1990s, many would agree that there has been a virtual revolution in youth marketing. Young people with more money and influence, plus more exposure to more forms of media (television, especially) has prompted companies to greatly increase their advertising budgets and marketing efforts directed at this segment of the population.

No matter what ages are included, the advertising expenditures aimed at children are extensive and have grown significantly over the last few decades. McNeal (1987: 21) estimated that, by 2004, total advertising and marketing expenditures directed at US children would reach US$15 billion, compared with only US$100 million in 1983. However, other estimates are even higher, with one source claiming that kids' advertising represented nearly US$262 billion in 2004 (Weiskott, 2005).

Advertising and marketing companies also have employed armies of researchers, who have developed specialized expertise and produced 'a deluge of industry-generated research'. A wide range of research methods beyond surveys and polls are used to obtain information about young people, as well as in developing strategies to encourage them to consume. Some of these techniques involve children themselves providing and distributing (peer-to-peer) consumer information (see the Neopets case study later in this chapter).

An example of the glut of marketing expertise and research is the tendency to develop new categories for specific groups of consumers. For instance, 'tweens' have recently attracted attention as representing the focal point for consumer trends. Martin Lindstrom, one of the world's leading branding gurus, explains that '...80 percent of all global brands now requires a tween strategy' (Schor, 2004: 12). An industry trade magazine writer echoes this point:

> ...when this pre-teen, toy-abandoning, video-game loving, fashion forward, techno-savvy, fickle consumer demographic makes a move, we all watch while holding our collection breath. Never before has a group of youngsters – with an age span from 8- to 12-years old – wielded so much consumer clout (Weiskott, 2005).

Media exposure

The media obviously play key roles in the growing market of commodities to young people. The estimates of children's exposure to media are seemingly endless, produced by the media, marketers and advertisers, as well as public advocacy groups. No matter what the source, the exposure, at least for American youth, is substantial, as has been discussed elsewhere in this volume.

In one of the most comprehensive national public studies ever conducted of young people's media use, the Kaiser Family Foundation in 1999 found that an average youth in the USA, aged 2–18, spent around 5 hours and 29 minutes each day with a variety of media, or a total of 38 hours per week. The study was based on a nationally representative sample of more than 3,000 children aged 2–18, and examined how much time youth spent watching TV and movies, using computers, playing video games, listening to music, and reading (Kaiser Family Foundation, 1999). A later study by the Kaiser Family Foundation (2005), however, discovered that children between 8 and 18 spend about eight and a half hours a day with media, indicating increasing use of media as children grow older.

A more recent report from the same foundation reported that parents may use electronic media as babysitters for young children, with 80% of children under age 6 watching an average of 2 hours of TV each day, Also, 60% of babies 1 year old and younger watch TV at least some of the time. The Kaiser study found that 30% of children 6 and under live in homes where the TV is on during most or all meal times (Kaiser Family Foundation, 2006).

Another Kaiser report examined the media use of 3rd through 12th graders and found that they are spending an increasing amount of time using 'new media' like computers, the internet and video games, but without cutting back on 'old media' like television and music (Kaiser Family Foundation, 2005).

While there are new forms of media that offer commercialized content, there are also advertising messages that 'infiltrate everyday life', including product placements in television and movies, 'real life placement' (individuals paid to promote products in various everyday settings), in-school media (such as Channel One), 'advergaming' (as exemplified by the Neopets case study below), and a wide array of consumer news stories.

While many studies have focused on the effects of exposure to media violence and sexual content on young people, fewer researchers seem as interested in the effect of exposure to a massive quantity of commercial messages and the influence on a consumer or materialistic mentality. Of course, there has been an on-going debate about children (and older people, for that matter) and their ability to interpret cultural materials (including advertising) in their own way. While this has been discussed in other chapters in this volume and will not receive further discussion here, it might be appropriate to recall Dan Cook's comments:

> Granting children magical transformative powers of the imagination, however, only further romanticizes an already oversentimentalized view of childhood. Children are human. Imaginations can be colonized. ... And, as any marketer will tell you, exposure to target market is nine-tenths of the brand battle (Cook, 2001).

Youth media

Media aimed at children and teens have been important for the development and growth of the youth commodity markets in a number of ways. Children's media programs are commodities themselves that are bought and sold in an ever-expanding marketplace.

But these media are often commercialized, with advertising playing a key role in promoting other products, both through commercial breaks or product placements and with content itself serving as an advertisement for some products (see Pecora (2002) for a good discussion of this development in US television). As one trade paper writer points out: 'Children's programming has been quite simply the engine that drives young customers and their parents to the toy and video game and apparel markets' (Brennan, 2000: 1).

Television

In most countries, television has always attracted children, both through specifically targeted programming, but also as viewers of adult programming. As Norma Pecora (2002) illustrated in her study, *The Business of Children's Entertainment*, children's television in the USA must be analyzed in relation to manufacturers of children's products, especially the toy industry, which virtually subsidized children's television for decades. For quite awhile, this type of children's programming was scheduled at specific periods of time (afternoons and Saturday mornings) on television networks and channels that included a wide range of programs.

But since the introduction of MTV in 1981, there has been an explosion of electronic media outlets aimed specifically at children and teens (see Kunkel and Gantz (1991), McGrath (1996) and Banks (1996)). While MTV appealed directly to the teen market, Nickelodeon has developed into the leading children's channel in the USA, as well as becoming a significant franchise embracing a wide range of media and product lines (see Hendershot (2004)).

An extensive review of channels around the world that targeted children in 1999 reported 87 channels, with 50 having launched during the previous 3 years (*Screen Digest*, 1999: 105–111). While the growth in channels is explained by the expansion of multichannel television, the development of the youth market must also be a contributing factor in this rapid growth.

More recently, the introduction of BabyFirstTV in May 2006 has expanded the focus even beyond the children and teen market. As the channel's website boasts:

> Welcome to BabyFirstTV – the nation's first channel for babies! The channel offers 24/7 DVD-quality programs with a unique parent co-viewing experience for only $9.99 a month, less than a single baby DVD.

The cable and satellite channel is aimed at children ages 6 months through 3 years, offering a variety of programming, including shows meant to teach colors, counting and shapes. Shows, which vary from 2 to 7 minutes in length, are often accompanied by cheerful songs, classical music or soothing sounds meant to help babies relax. 'It's all about facing reality', explained BabyFirstTV co-founder Sharon Rechter, who referred to the Kaiser Family Foundation (2006) study when she quipped that 'four out of 10 babies under 2 are watching television anyway' (Churnin, 2006).

Video/computer games

In addition to broadcast/cable channels, additional media commodities are continuously introduced and aimed at the youth market. Video and computer games have developed into important and lucrative products that rely a good deal on children and youth.

In 2005, US$7.4 billion were spent on computer and video games in the USA for more than 228.5 million units. This does not include spending on hardware, books, and other merchandise (Entertainment Software Association, 2006). According to another source, roughly US$10.5 billion was spent on hardware in the USA (Sinclair and Feldman, 2006). Globally, the industry has grown dramatically as well, reporting US$32.6 billion in sales in 2005 (Gamustra.com, 2006). Meanwhile, the 2005 Kaiser report found that young people aged 8–18 spent almost an hour of each day (49 minutes on average) with video games.

The internet

Online activities are emerging as a significant influence on youth culture and attracting a good deal of attention from researchers and policy-makers. Much of the attention is directed at the online porn business, which is said to generate US$12 billion dollars in annual revenue – larger than the combined annual revenues of ABC, NBC and CBS (Family Safe Media, 2006). And, the largest group of viewers of internet porn is claimed to be children between ages 12 and 17 (Family Safe Media, 2005).

Meanwhile, other activities continue to attract children and teens. For instance, online gaming is an increasingly important part of the youth media marketplace, and includes a growing number of MMOGs, or 'massively multi-player online games', that are sometimes connected to other media outlets (for instance, Disney's Toontown). Not only is the internet attracting children and teens to a myriad of online sources and activities, it is developing into a unique marketing tool for the growing commodity market of children's products. Advertising expenditures for the internet continue to grow, as over US$8.3 billion was spent in 2005, compared with US$7.3 billion in 2004 (TNS Media Intelligence, 2006). While nowhere near the advertising spending for other media (for instance, local newspapers still attract over US$25 billion per year), the internet is evolving into a somewhat unique medium for marketing efforts. Kathryn Montgomery (2001) has identified several recent developments that point to new strategies used in online marketing as it relates to children:

- Integration of advertising and content (as exemplified in the case study to follow on Neopets).
- Viral marketing that takes full advantage of instant messaging and other peer-to-peer forms of digital communication popular with children and teens.
- Branded environments, where you can spend hours interacting with the product.
- Web-based cross promotions that are designed to 'drive' kids to advertising sites on the Web.
- Cell phone and text messaging advertising.

Interestingly, the last development on the list involves yet another commodity that has become a staple for many young people. The cell or mobile phone phenomenon is worldwide, as the global mobile phone market is expected to rise to 850 million units, roughly double 2002's level and up 5% from the 810 million shipped the previous year. This compares with a television set market of 200 million units a year, with handsets the single biggest consumer electronics category in the world (Sandoval, 2006).

By the end of 2005, one-third of youths aged 11 to 17 had their own cell phones, and it was expected that half would have them within the next 2 years (English, 2005). Cell phones are increasingly being linked to other media and advertising sources, thus becoming an important part of the commercialization of youth culture.

Corporate power

While the proliferation of young people's media is often emphasized in research, it is important to acknowledge and understand the power behind these media activities. Four major transnational companies (Disney, Viacom, News Corp, and Time Warner) are especially active in children's media and entertainment markets, as well as dominating many other media activities. In addition to these entertainment conglomerates, a handful of other large multinationals dominate the business of toys, video games, candy, soft drinks and food.

The Big Four in children's television have also spread their influence globally, drawing on their financial muscle and extensive program libraries (see *Screen Digest* (1999)). Certainly, there are also local competitors that are challenging these dominant global corporations, but they still hold a good deal of power over much of the media that children inhabit. In the next section, we will look more closely at one of the Big Four to understand more fully some of the corporate strategies for exploiting youth culture.

CASE STUDIES

Disney: the quintessential 'family' media corporation

The Disney Company has played a key role in the commodification and commercialization of youth culture for many years, not only in the USA, but also around the world. While the company no longer has a unique monopoly over certain areas of the children's market, Disney is still a powerful and significant force in the marketing and promotion of products to young people. Disney represents an example of the deliberate and ongoing efforts to introduce new commodities to the youth market and promote them systematically through various means. People don't often realize the scope of the Disney empire and its intensive contribution to the commercialization of youth culture. Thus, looking more closely at this one company provides an illustration of the character of the companies that dominate the youth market, plus some of the strategies that are used.

The Disney Company's Studio Entertainment division includes a wide range of entertainment products, including animated and live-action films under the Walt Disney label, as well as the Touchstone, Hollywood, Miramax and Merchant-Ivory labels that appeal to other than 'family' markets. The company has also recently taken over Pixar, the co-producer of some of the most successful children's or family films over the past decade. Disney's home video business and interactive products are distributed around the world; the company led the global sales of children's home video for many years.

Disney's television business is similarly diversified, with a variety of programming produced and distributed under the ABC, Buena Vista, Touchstone and Walt Disney labels. Disney also produces theatrical versions of successful animated films, as well as offering audio and musical products related to their films and television properties.

Disney's merchandising activities are legendary in terms of their historical precedence as well as more recent strategies. The company is still the foremost merchandising company in Hollywood and produces or licenses a seemingly endless array of products or commodities, many aimed directly at the children's or youth market. Disney Consumer Products is one of the largest licensors in the world. Indeed, the *Licensing Letter*, a key publication for the entertainment merchandising industry, has reported that 'Children are the dominant consuming audience of licensed entertainment/character properties' (*Youth Markets Alert*, 2002).

It is especially important to recognize Disney's dominance in the baby and toddler merchandise markets, where parents often find that the company's numerous products are difficult to avoid. Disney merchandise is marketed at retail outlets around the world, as well as through its own outlets at the theme parks, through online sites, by way of the Disney Catalogue and at Disney Stores around the world. The Disney brand is commonly recognized worldwide and often associated with youth (see Wasko *et al.* (2001)).

In addition, Disney Publishing is the world's number one children's publisher. At the end of 1998, the company claimed that their print products were published in 37 languages and distributed in more than 100 countries. The company claims to lead all other publishers in the world in the area of children's books and magazines.

Meanwhile, Disney OnLine creates and distributes content for online services, interactive software, interactive television and internet websites: www.disney.com is consistently rated as one of the Web's most popular sites.

The Disney empire includes six major theme parks: Disneyland, Walt Disney World Destination Resort, Tokyo Disneyland, Disneyland Paris and Hong Kong Disneyland. The role of these theme parks cannot be overstated in terms of reinforcing the impact of other Disney commodities, such as films and television programming, but also serving as the ultimate leisure activity for children and families around the world. Visits to the Disney theme parks have become cultural pilgrimages that are considered mandatory for many young people, who may consider themselves deprived if they haven't been to one of the sites.

Since 1995, Disney has firmly established its role as one of the dominant players in the US media industry. The ABC television network provides abundant opportunities to promote Disney-produced programming and other businesses, as well as exploiting ABC's more popular programs throughout the rest of the Disney empire.

In addition, Disney owns television and radio stations, including the Radio Disney network, which features special radio programming for children. A description of the network on their website indicates the aim and global reach:

> Created and produced by ABC Radio Networks, Radio Disney reaches millions of kids, tweens and families through great music, out-of-this-world prizing and brand extensions like the best selling Radio Disney Jams CDs, as well as the Radio Disney apparel line found in Kohl's Department Stores nationwide. Internationally, Radio Disney can be heard in Japan, the UK, Poland, Argentina, Paraguay, Guatemala, Uruguay and the Dominican Republic (http://radio.disney.go.com/media/generalinfo.html).

Other Disney's media activities aimed at young people include the Disney Channel (including international channels) and Toon Disney (with recycled Disney programming). Meanwhile, the ESPN franchise, an extensive global group of cable networks, radio, internet, retail, print and location-based dining and entertainment, is also popular with some of the youth market.

The Disney/ABC presence in television is significant. As explained by Tricia Wilbur, an executive for the Disney/ABC Cable Networks Group:

> ...the strength of the Disney/ABC kids' platforms is the ability to deliver targeted kids. If they're looking for targeted audiences we offer the most efficient ways to deliver them. ... Plus, the uncluttered environment of Disney Channel is a place where marketers are breaking through and making emotional connections with kids (quoted in Myers (2005)).

Disney and youth

It is clear that the Disney company today represents a dominant player in the media and entertainment business – a sector that, at least in the USA, has become increasingly more concentrated over the last few decades, as corporations have moved or converged across industry lines to form diversified, transnational conglomerates. Several of these media giants look very much like Disney: The News Corp., Time Warner Inc., and Viacom Inc.

But Disney still represents the entertainment brand that is associated most closely with young people and families, having built a strong and enduring reputation that is almost 'naturally' associated with children. The brand continues to be carefully developed, with an integration of commodities that are built and coordinated to maintain the Disney name. Disney's 'synergy' is legendary and is built on the exploitation of a franchise or characters across various businesses within the company discussed previously.

While the company's brand is most often associated with children, the company profile above indicates that many of Disney's businesses are not aimed purely at young people. While it seems clear that exposure to Disney-branded products has been found to be typically strongest during childhood, the company's products cut across age groups in assorted ways. Of course, targeting 'families' immediately means appealing to different age groups, not just children, and the company carefully constructs and coordinates such attractions. One example is Disney's *Winnie the Pooh* franchise, which the company acquired in the 1960s. As a Disney spokesman explained:

> ...Disney now has three distinct Pooh lines, each targeted at a different market. Each line is aimed at a distinct demographic and market, but even within a product line there's segmentation. Individuals and even groups tend to make a connection to particular characters. Eeyore, for example is most popular with teens, possibly because he is a little different from the others. But teens seem to be attracted to characters that are a little different (Hirsch, 1999).

With over 100 companies producing Pooh products, plus the promotion of Pooh across the company's other business sectors, the Pooh characters now apparently outsell Mickey, Minnie and friends. As an industry trade journal reported: 'Disney has done a magnificent job overall with Pooh, licensing and marketing products that appeal to a lot of different audiences and demographics' (Hirsch, 1999).

The important point here is to acknowledge the company's efforts in developing a wide range of markets that provide unique exposure to Disney products at different periods of people's lives. But while the generational attraction to Disney is legendary, the essential foundation of this strategy, however, is the appeal to consumers at the earliest age possible.

In addition, Disney has consistently adjusted its marketing strategies to produce and distribute commodities that appeal to global audiences. This sometimes involves adjusting product design and marketing techniques for specific markets (see Wasko (2001)). While this is a tricky business and sometimes does not succeed, Disney's brand is still highly valued in many parts of the world and often represents the ultimate producer of commodities aimed at youth (see Wasko *et al.* (2001)).

Neopets: a neophyte entertainment franchise

This section explores the Neopets site or franchise as another example of commodified and commercialized children's culture, as well as reinforcement of consumer ideology. The popular site is an example of the new ways that advertising appeals are developing, especially those directed at youth. It also represents an example of how the concept of consumption is taken for granted and even taught to young people.

Neopets grows: the birth of a franchise

Neopets.com is a 'virtual pet site' that can be described as a combination of Tamagotchi (the virtual pet craze of the mid-1990s), The Sims, and Pokeman, with a little bit of Disney thrown in.[2] It is a 'free site' supported by advertising – lots of advertising, which is also integrated into the site. Members are allowed to create or adopt up to four pets from a wide array of unique animal species. The pets must then be fed and entertained. Although this sounds simple enough, the site is quite complex and includes a wide range of activities.

There are 10 different themed lands around Neopia, such as Faerieland, Mystery Island, the Lost World, etc. These include a wide range of features, including stores and shops where you can buy food and other items (toys, books, clothes, weapons, etc.) for your pets using Neopoints. Neopia has its own post office, newspaper, hotel, concert hall, restaurants and bank. Pets can own their own pets, called PetPets.

Communication is possible through the neoboards and neomail, greetings and other forms of messaging. There are guilds (which are actually clubs with different themes). Other interactive features include members' art work, poetry, coloring pages, etc. In this sense, the site boasts that 'Neopet members are not merely passive visitors…'. Many of these features are organized as competitions, including beauty contests, caption contests, pet contests, Neohome competitions, etc. And then there are the games: over 160 different games revolving around manufacturing, competitive battles, puzzles, luck/chance or action activities. (More on these features of the site follows.)

Neopets is free, but includes advertising in various forms (to be discussed later). The emphasis is on 'safe and friendly' entertainment, with various safeguards in place for protecting young children. The company boasts that it adheres to government regulations of children's sites, and is proud of its monitoring of language use, etc.

The website was created in November 1999 by Adam Powell and Donna Williams, sometimes described as two 'bored' British college students.[3] Doug Dohring, described as 'a marketing executive', bought the site a few months later, and formed Neopets Inc. in February 2000. Only a few months later (April 2000), Neopets, Inc., a privately held corporation based in Glendale, California, began business operations as the owner and operator of Neopets.com. By July of the same year, the company was said to have 'reached profitability', with annual revenue of 'eight figures' from advertising (60%) and merchandising (40%).

Neopets includes sites translated into Japanese, Chinese (both traditional and simplified), Korean, Spanish, German, French, Italian, Portuguese and Dutch. Interestingly, they explain that these sites will 'increase cross-border communication and understanding by young people everywhere'. They also acknowledge that one of their 'core missions' is to be the largest online youth community in the world.

Neopets membership has continued to climb, with the site claiming over 70 million individual members at the end of 2006. The demographics of members around this time was reported as follows: under 13 years old, 39%; 13–17 years old, 40%; 18 and older, 21%. Around 57% of the members are female and 43% are male. Neopets is claimed to be 'the stickiest site in the world', enticing its members to remain at the site for long periods of time. According to one source, members spend an average of 6 hours 15 minutes per month at the site, and was ranked second on the entire internet.

Neopets matures: ownership and diversification

The Neopet company's goal is stated clearly in its press material: 'Continue development as the largest global youth entertainment network on the Internet, and further its revenue generation through opportunistic offline ventures'.

As NeoPets Chairman and CEO Doug Dohring explained:

> Since early 2000, when we founded the company, I felt that we could create a strong connection between the youth of the world and our NeoPets-created characters and storylines, which we would ultimately extend into television, movies, merchandise, publishing and other offline vehicles in a very significant way.

In March 2005, Neopets made a deal with Warner Bros. Pictures to develop Neopets characters and stories into several feature films. A few months later, in June 2005, Viacom purchased the Neopets company for US$160 million.

Viacom is a huge diversified conglomerate, with revenues of over US$9.6 billion and net earnings of US$1.3 billion in 2005. The company describes itself like this:

> Fueled by our world-class brands, including BET, Famous Music, MTV Networks – MTV, VH1, Nickelodeon, Nick at Nite, Comedy Central, CMT: Country Music Television, Spike TV, TV Land and more than 120 networks around the world – Paramount Pictures and Paramount Home Entertainment, we are among the world's leading creators of programming and content across all media platforms.

A month after the sale of Neopets, Nickelodeon launched TurboNick, a broadband video platform available on Nick.com that, for the first time, allows children to watch full-length shows online at any time. The company explained:

> As the first kid's network to provide full length video programming online, combined with the recent acquisition of Neopets,® a global online entertainment network … Nickelodeon now offers more multiplatform experiences than any other kid's entertainment company.

But Viacom is not the only company making moves into internet territory. Indeed, there is a growing trend by media owners to buy successful online companies. News Corporation recently bought videogame and movie website company IGN Entertainment (which owns GameSpy and Rotten Tomatoes) and Intermix Media (owner of myspace.com) as part of a US$2 billion internet spending spree. Viacom also recently bought the popular websites iFilm.com and gametrailers.com.

Neopets and commercialization

The Neopets company claims to have pioneered the idea of 'immersive advertising' – 'customized activities and scenarios', or 'creative programs that integrate the advertisers' commercial products, services, brands and names into existing or customized activities and scenarios within the site, thereby making the product an important part of the activity or game'. There are also sponsored locations and sponsored games. Not all games are sponsored, but a significant number are. For instance, McDonalds, Disney and General Mills sponsor a number of ongoing features (games and locations in Neopia), while other games appear periodically that are connected to current films or television programs, or other sponsors (examples: Limited Too Clothes, Universal Studios, Reebok, etc.). While the company admits that this is 'an evolution of the concept of traditional product placement', it is debatable whether or not Neopets invented the idea, as there are other examples known as 'advergames' or 'in-game marketing'.

The company typically downplays the effects of immersive advertising, but their company press material boasts that the process '…produces lasting awareness, retention and brand affinity, with impressions that effectively and repeatedly convey the advertiser's message to the intended consumer'. Advertisers seem to have responded positively to Neopets. For instance, Courtney Lane, Director of Mattel Girls Online, explains: 'It becomes addictive, … It has tremendous stickiness, and that helps us gain the exposure we need'. The 'immersive advertising' feature of the site seems to attract the most attention and criticism, as discussed by Seiter (2005) and Montgomery (2005). However, there are other features that might be considered worrisome, as well.

Neopets and commodification

The Neopets site has developed rather quickly as the base for an entertainment franchise. A franchise, in this sense, can be defined as copyrightable properties or concepts that can be repeated or continuously remade in multiple media platforms/outlets with merchandising and tie-in potentials.

The site promotes and sells a wide variety of merchandise and the franchise has indeed expanded into other outlets and commodities beyond the internet, including hand-held games, mobile phones, trading cards (and magazine) and video games. Tie-ins are frequent and include McDonald's, Disney, Limited Too, and others. Also recall the deal with Warner Bros. for Neopets films. With various global activities, including translation of the site into 10 different languages, the 'free' Neopets site has indeed expanded into other commodities and media outlets. Neopets has developed as an entertainment franchise that works especially well with Viacom's other franchises (MTV, Rugrats, etc.), and seems likely to continue to expand.

Neopets' ideology

The Neopets site is not just about adopting and caring for a pet – it easily can be interpreted as a training ground or 'grooming' for capitalist or consumer culture. Neopia is obviously organized as a capitalist society. There are some obvious signs: the bank and stock market, as well as the game 'Plushie Tycoon' where one can become a successful manufacturing tycoon.

And there are lots and lots of shops: 63 created by the site, plus members are encouraged to open their own shops, which become huge, and sometimes come together as malls and various forms of markets. Overall, there is an overt emphasis on materialism and consumption, as players are encouraged to acquire (buy) items and sell them for Neopoints. The company explains that 'through smart purchases and trades with others, members can turn a "virtual" profit, increase the size of their shops, and thereby increase their visibility on the site'.

A huge number of 'neoitems' are available (for a price), with over 17,300 items accounted for on one of the fan's sites that itemizes them. When pets do not 'own' anything, they are portrayed as desperately sad and dejected (often crying), and encourage their owners to purchase something. Even when one feeds or plays with pets, they may still request the owner to buy something else.

To participate in many of the activities on the site, one must pay. Players can own their own home (for a fee) and furnish it with items purchased with Neopoints, as well as paying to attend concerts, or visit restaurants and pubs. Even when a pet comes down with a disease, the hospital diagnoses the problem and sends the owner to the pharmacy where drugs and cures must be paid for with a significant amount of Neopoints. No socialized medicine here.

Games of luck and chance are prominently featured, including some overt gambling activities such as slot machines and games of chance. And lots of activities are organized around competitions, including those interactive features. The battledome is an attraction for many members, who purchase various kinds of weapons or strengths to wage battles with other members. There are also ongoing narratives that are featured on the site, often involving wars between different lands, complete with heroes and villains.

Overall, the company claims that '...the only limitation of the site is the member's own imagination'. However, the site appears quite a lot like the 'real world', with many boundaries set and numerous limits on imaginative activities. (This is also reminiscent of Disney and its theme parks, where imagination is promoted, but limited by a variety of control mechanisms (see Wasko (2001)).

Market research

There are numerous offers on the Neopets site for earning Neopoints by filling out surveys for Neopets, as well as for other companies. A 'Survey Shack' has recently been added to one of the marketplaces, featuring a 'youth panel' feature and games related to the panel.

While Neopets revenue has been mostly from advertising and merchandising, the company has recently reported that market research has become a source of revenues. Indeed, the Neopets company has become somewhat of an expert in market research through its relationship with OpinionSurveys.com, the online marketing research division of The Dohring Company, and other marketing research companies. Founded by Doug C. Dohring, Chair/CEO of Neopets, The Dohring Company has been listed recently as one of the top 100 market research firms in North America in *Advertising Age* magazine's list of the largest research companies in the USA. More specifically, Neopets' annual youth survey is now used by numerous companies and publications, including *Advertising Age* and other marketing publications.

Summary

This section has discussed the Neopets site/franchise as an example of commodified and commercialized children's culture, as well as reinforcement for consumer ideology. While this development may not be surprising to many, maybe that is the point. The popularity of Neopets, as well as its imitative sites (and there are many[4]), feed into the naturalization of commodification and commercialization that are at the core of advanced capitalism. Though the internet is currently still open for the development of commercial-free, open and truly interactive sites, the potential of yet another new technology is increasingly being harnessed for commercial purposes, as well as promoting and teaching consumption to young people. Sites like Neopets may provide 'safe' and 'free' entertainment that is embraced by parents and educators, but this type of entertainment comes with a price, and it's not payable in Neopoints.

Neopets represents an example of the new media that are attracting the attention of policy makers and media reformists in the USA. As Kathryn Montgomery (2005), founder of the Center for Media Education, explained during a recent policy gathering:

> The forms of advertising, marketing, and selling that are emerging as part of the new media depart in significant ways from the more familiar commercial advertising and promotion in children's television. The interactive media are ushering in an entirely new set of relationships, breaking down the traditional barriers between 'content and commerce', and creating unprecedented intimacies between children and marketers. Much of the new digital advertising takes place under the radar of parents and teachers. It is consciously designed to tap into the developmental needs of children, tweens, and teens, and to follow them everywhere in their journeys through the digital landscape.

As discussed in this section, Neopets represents an obvious example of these trends.

And, while it might be argued that Disney long ago broke down the barriers of content and commerce (through their theme parks, for instance), the Disney Company also has moved aggressively into new media where content and commerce increasingly mingle. Disney continues to use its sophisticated marketing techniques and products aimed at the youth market in a wide range of online activities and computer products, as discussed previously. Not only does Disney advertise on the Neopets site (as well as others), the company's own website (www.disney.com) integrates a wide range of products and interactive gaming activity. The popular Disney's Toontown Online might be seen as a kind of imitator of Neopets, although gamers pay a user's fee (thus, avoiding the criticism about 'immersive advertising').

Again, both of these case studies represent the increasingly commercial use of new media. Disney has been an ongoing and strong contributor to consumer culture generally, and the commodification and commercialization of youth culture in particular. Viacom's ownership of Neopets indicates that the successful site will continue to develop along these lines, as well. In addition, both Disney and Neopets represent examples of how media and marketing are influencing youth culture in many parts of the world. Both the Disney Company and Neopets/Viacom are global efforts that involve the commercialization of media aimed at youth, as well as the production of a myriad of commodities that are marketed to children and young people.

CONCLUSIONS

This chapter has presented a political economic analysis of some of the recent developments in youth culture, pointing to the increasing commodification and commercialization, particularly in the USA. The case studies of the Disney Corporation and the Neopets site represent the historic and ongoing development of these trends, with new technologies such as the internet often developing in similar ways as previous media technologies. While these cases may represent enjoyable and popular activities that appeal to young people (as well as adults), it is important to use political economic analysis to look behind the compelling pixels to identify these troubling trends.

Such analysis also reveals that companies such as Disney and Viacom currently control much of the media that comprises a good chunk of youth culture. And it is the marketing and consumption of commodities that have become primary aims of these media resources. While the internet may offer new, alluring and more interactive activities for youth, the Neopets example demonstrates how some of the most successful sites have relatively quickly become part of larger entertainment conglomerates, contributing to a concentrated, commercial media landscape.

Attempts to reduce the amount of advertising, to limit exposure of children to certain kinds of content and to moderate the concentrated power of the media conglomerates are ongoing, and sometimes these efforts succeed. However, the question of commercialized youth culture also is related to consumerism generally, and there seem to be few efforts to curb the excessive consumption that is rampant in many societies.

It is important to repeat that overconsumption affects different parts of the world in different ways, as might be indicated in a more careful political economic analysis of the distribution of global resources. As Anup Shah (2003) concludes on the Global Issues.org website:

> … the effects of things like mass consumption, the intense advertising, and targeting to children and its emphasis over so many aspects of daily lives is of concern. That is, the effects of constantly buying things, while discarding older but often functioning things, increasing demands on the world's resources for this consumption, managing more waste, exploiting other people to labor over this, and so on. And all this while many still go hungry and poor because their lands are being used to export away food and other resources for producing products to be consumed elsewhere. It is in this way that the pressure and drive for profits has led to an over-commercialized consumerism, which has wider effects around the world and on the unseen majority peoples of the world.…

Although this chapter has focused on the (perhaps) unique situation in the USA, it may provide an example of future overconsumption and commercialization that may come to pass in other cultures, especially if commercialized and commodified media are accepted as an inevitable and 'natural' development. More international research that contrasts different cultural settings would be helpful, especially focusing on the unequal production and distribution of resources related to youth culture. Nordicom's International Clearinghouse on Children, Youth & Media (http://www.nordicom.gu.se/clearinghouse.php) is an excellent example of this type of effort. It might also be helpful if international organizations, such as UNICEF or UNESCO, were to focus more attention on this issue through international research projects and, ultimately, global initiatives.

In addition, research related to youth culture would benefit from linking some of the political economic forces discussed in this chapter with studies of young people's media reception. The Global Disney Audience project (Wasko *et al.*, 2001) represented an attempt to connect the study of market forces and audience reception worldwide, although not necessarily limited to children or teens. While this type of research presents serious challenges related to resources and expertise, the situation described in this chapter would seem to demand this type of integrated research effort.

NOTES

1 Scholarly work on children and media that employed strong political economic analysis would include Kapur (2005), Pecora (2002), Schor (2004), and Steinberg and Kincheloe (1997), while many other researchers regularly incorporate such elements in their work, including, but not limited to, Seiter (1993), Buckingham (2000), Buckingham and Sefton-Green (2003) and Montgomery (2001). Also see Ward *et al.* (1976) and Wartella (1995).

2 This analysis draws on Grimes and Shade (2005) and Seiter (2005).

3 The information describing business aspects of Neopets is taken from the press kit, offered online at http://info.neopets.com/presskit/press01.html.

4 Towards the end of 2006, Top Web Games, one of the sites that lists online games, included 99 games for the pet game genre – everything from AlleyPets to Zetapets. See http://www.topwebgames.com/cat.asp?name=pet (accessed 26 November 2006).

REFERENCES

Banks, J. (1996) *Monopoly Television: MTV's Quest to Control the Music.* Cambridge, MA: Perseus Publishing.

Bogart, L. (2005) *Over the Edge: How the Pursuit of Youth by Marketers and the Media has Changed American Culture.* New York: Ivan R. Dee.

Brennan, S. (2000) 'New and improved'. *Hollywood Reporter*, 1 September; 1, 3.

Buckingham, D. (2000) *After the Death of Childhood: Growing Up in the Age of Electronic Media.* Cambridge: Polity Press.

Buckingham, D. and Sefton-Green, J. (2003) 'Gotta catch 'em all: structure, agency and pedagogy in children's media culture'. *Media, Culture & Society*, 25(3): 379–399.

Churnin, N. (2006) 'Is BabyTV a good thing?' *Dallas Morning News*, 6 July.

Cook, D. (2001) 'Lunchbox hegemony? Kids and the marketplace, then and now'. *LiP Magazine*, 20 August. http://www.lipmagazine.org/articles/featcook_124.shtml [20 May 2006].

Cook, D. (2004) *The Commodification of Childhood: The Children's Clothing Industry and the Rise of the Child Consumer.* Duke University Press.

Cross, G. (2002) 'Valves of desire: a historian's perspective on parents, children, and marketing'. *Journal of Consumer Research*, 29: 441–447.

Del Vecchio, G. (1997) *Creating Ever-Cool: A Marketer's Guide to a Kid's Heart.* Gretna, LA: Pelican.

English, B. (2005) 'The Secret life of boys: pornography is a mouse click away, and kids are being exposed to it in ever-increasing numbers'. *The Boston Globe*, 12 May. http://www.boston.com/ae/media/articles/2005/05/12/the_secret_life_of_boys/ [1 July 2006].

Entertainment Software Association (2006) 'Essential facts about the computer and video game industry'. http://www.theesa.com/archives/files/Essential%20Facts%202006.pdf [1 June 2006].

Family Safe Media (2005) 15 December. http://www.familysafemedia.com/pornography _statistics.html [2 July 2006].

Family Safe Media (2006) 10 January. http://www.familysafemedia.com/pornography _statistics.html [2 July 2006].

Gamasutra.com (2006) 16 February. 'Gaming industry revenues expected to double by 2011'. http://www.gamasutra.com/php-bin/news_index.php?story=8205 [1 July 2006].

Grimes, S. and Shade, L. (2005) 'Neopian economics of play: children's cyberpets and online communities as immersive advertising in NeoPets.com'. *International Journal of Media and Cultural Politics*, 1: 2.

Hendershot, H. (2004) *Nickelodeon Nation: The History, Politics and Economics of America's Only TV Channel for Kids.* New York: New York University Press.

Hirsch, J. (1999) 'Winnie the Pooh gains momentum across Disney product lines'. *Knight-Ridder/Tribune Business News*, 4 Jan.

Jacobson, L. (2005) *Raising Consumers: Children and the American Mass Market in the Early Twentieth Century.* New York: Columbia University Press.

Kaiser Family Foundation (1999) 'Kids & media @ the new millennium'. http://www.kff.org/entmedia/1535-index.cfm [1 June 2006].

Kaiser Family Foundation (2005) 'Generation M: media in the lives of 8–18 year-olds'. http://www.kff.org/entmedia/entmedia030905pkg.cfm [1 June 2006].

Kaiser Family Foundation (2006) 'The media family: electronic media in the lives of infants, toddlers, preschoolers and their parents'. http://www.kff.org/entmedia/7500.cfm [1 June 2006].

Kapur, J. (2005) *Coining for Capital: Movies, Marketing, and the Transformation of Childhood.* New Brunswick, NJ: Rutgers University Press.

Kline, S. (1993) *Out of the Garden: Toys and Children's Culture in the Age of TV Marketing.* London: Verso Press.

Kunkel, D. and Gantz, W. (1991) 'Children's television advertising in the multi-channel environment'. *Journal of Communication*, (Autumn): 134–152.

Marketresearch.com (2006) 'The kids' market'. http://www.marketresearch.com/product/display.asp?productid=143502&xs=r [1 June 2006].

McGrath, T. (1996) *MTV: The Making of a Revolution.* Philadelphia, PA: Running Press.

McNeal, J.U. (1987) *Children as Consumers: Insights and Implications.* Lexington, Mass.: Lexington Books.

Montgomery, K. (2001) 'Digital kids: the new on-line children's consumer culture'. In D.G. Singer and J.L. Singer (eds) *Handbook of Children and the Media.* Thousand Oaks, CA: Sage Publications; 640–643.

Montgomery, K. (2005) 14–15 July. 'Statement at Federal Trade Commission Workshop: perspectives on marketing, self-regulation, & childhood obesity'. http://www.soc.american.edu/main.cfm?pageid=1345 [1 June 2006].

Mosco, V. (1996) *The Political Economy of Communications.* London: Sage.

Myers, J. (2005) 30 March. 'Kids market buoyed by non-traditional categories'. *Upfront Chronicles Part 9. 'Jack Meyers Media Village'.* http://www.mediavillage.com/jmr/2005/03/30/jmr-03-30-05/ [1 July 2006].

Pecora, N.O. (2002) *The Business of Children's Entertainment.* New York: Guildford Publications.

Sandoval, G. (2006) 11 January. 'Falling revenue for cell phone makers'. *C/Net News.com*, http://news.com.com/Falling+revenue+for+cell+phone+makers/2100-1039_3-6026127.html [10 June 2006].

Schor, J.B. (2004) *Born to Buy: The Commercialized Child and the New Consumer Culture.* New York: Scribner.

Screen Digest (1999) 'Children's television: a globalised market'; 105–111.

Seiter, E. (1993) *Sold Separately: Parents and Children in Consumer Culture.* New Brunswick, NJ: Rutgers University Press.

Seiter, E. (2005) 'The internet playground'. In J. Goldstein, D. Buckingham and S. Brougere (eds) *Toys, Games and Media.* Mahwah, NJ: Lawrence Erlbaum.

Shah, A. (2003) 28 October. 'Children as consumers'. *Behind Consumption and Consumerism, Global Issues.org.* http://www.globalissues.org/TradeRelated/Consumption/Children.asp#Encouragingandincreasingchildhoodconsumerism [20 May 2006].

Sinclair, B. and Feldman, C. (2006) '2005 a record year for US gaming'. *Gamespot News*, 13 January. http://www.gamespot.com/news/6142407.html [1 July 2006].

Steinberg, S.R. and Kincheloe, J.L. (eds) (1997) *Kinderculture: The Corporate Construction of Childhood.* Boulder, CO: Westview Press.

TNS Media Intelligence (2006) 27 February. http://www.tns-mi.com/news/02282006.htm [15 June 2006].

Ward, S., Wackman, D. and Wartella, E. (1976) *How Children Learn to Buy.* Beverly Hills, CA: Sage Publications.

Wartella, E. (1995). 'The commercialization of youth'. *Phi Delta Kappan*, 76: 6.

Wasko, J. (2001) *Understanding Disney: The Manufacture of Fantasy.* Cambridge: Polity Press.

Wasko, J., Phillips, M. and Meehan, E. (eds) (2001) *Dazzled by Disney? The Global Disney Audience Project.* Leicester: Leicester University Press.

Weiskott, M. (2005) 'Tweens: a consuming army'. *Playthings*, (September): 42–50.

Youth Markets Alert (2002) '5–8-year-olds account for largest share of entertainment and character property sales'. December; 1.

28

Media and Communications Regulation and Child Protection: An Overview of the Field

David Oswell

INTRODUCTION

In an age when there is a plurality of content providers, in a system of media abundance, and with an increasing uncertainty to centralized regulatory monopolies, how are children to be protected from harm and illegalities, without chilling the creative heat of invention and new synergies? In this chapter, I look to the broader historical context and then to contemporary discussion about regulation. I provide an overview of some significant aspects of the current landscape concerning legislative discourse, regulatory agency and methodology. My discussion focuses on media and communications regulation and child protection in the USA and European Union, primarily the UK, and, by and large, I focus on the regulation of 'content', rather than on 'contact'.

SOME HISTORICAL ISSUES

Historically, media and communications (including newspaper, magazine and book publishing, theatre, radio, cinema, television, video, and telecommunications) have been regulated in the context of the nation state (namely, national jurisdiction concerning content, access, and competition and international treaties concerning trade and technological standards). Governments, regulatory agencies, industry bodies, academics, religious organizations, moral arbiters, and 'responsible' persons have made decisions concerning the role of media and communications in the lives of children inasmuch as the systems of distribution and the content distributed could be controlled and shaped in such ways to maintain and facilitate the well-being of the national population. By and large, concern focused on understandings of children as impressionable and easily influenced either by the type of media content or by the technology itself. Thus, in the nineteenth century, religious societies in England produced magazines initially aimed at the poor, encoding the moral values of the middle class, containing stories about zealous missionaries in foreign lands or pious and poverty stricken children in the heart of depraved London (Drotner, 1988). But equally in the mid- to late-nineteenth century, the penny dreadfuls – which drew from the gothic novel and grim tales of characters, such as Sweeny Todd and Varney the Vampire, and which were popular with a newly literate working-class juvenile population – gathered a mass readership and gave the established English middle class cause for concern (Pearson, 1983). In the 1940s and 1950s, concern about the dangerous influence of comic books on young people fed into US Senate hearings. Psychiatrists reported on the effect of some comic book stories on the mental stability of children (Wertham, 1954). In the UK, similar concerns were articulated, not simply around the problem of violence, youth and popular culture, but on the pathologization of 'horror comics' as a peculiarly US phenomenon. Thus, moral panic about comic books in the UK was explicitly anti-American and partly orchestrated by the Communist Party of Great Britain (Barker, 1984a). The campaign led to the Children and Young Persons (Harmful Publications) Act of 1955, which was applied to publications ('mainly of stories told in pictures') portraying 'the commission of crimes', 'acts of violence or cruelty', and 'incidents of a horrible or repulsive nature' that 'would tend to corrupt a child or young person' (quoted in Newburn (1992)). Sociologists have argued that public anxiety about the moral regulation of society tends to occur during times of social crisis at particular historical conjunctures. Demands for public order have been understood either as genuinely emerging from the people or as an 'authoritarian populism' orchestrated by elite political and social groups (Hall *et al.*, 1978; Goode and Ben-Yehuda, 1994).

Ideological standpoints and misconceptions have plagued debates about media and communications regulation across Europe and the USA. In the 1950s and early 1960s the television western became a focus of political and popular regulatory discussion. In the USA, the western and the ideology of the 'wild west frontier' were seen to parallel the scientific progress of the NASA space programme (Cross, 1997). But in the UK, *Gunsmoke*, *Maverick*, *Roy Rogers*, *Hopalong Cassidy* and others were seen as commercial, 'American' and a source of social violence and were the subject of lengthy discussion by the Pilkington Committee on broadcasting (Oswell, 2002). A fresh focus in the press and parliament on their imitative affect on young people committing suicide by hanging helped establish the conservative Christian pressure group, the National Viewers and Listeners Association (NVLA) led by Mary Whitehouse. The NVLA was particularly vocal in public regulatory discourse from the 1960s onward, calling for greater restrictions on the distribution of sexual, violent and non-Christian content on television, video, and cinema (Tracey and Morrison, 1979). With respect to broadcast television, much academic research, with the exception of a number of experimental and laboratory investigations, has from the late 1950s onward demonstrated largely that its influence is dependent on the nature of the programme, the psychological development, disposition and cognitive capacity of the child, the social and emotional economy of the family, interpersonal peer relations, and the broader discursive context (Luke, 1990). The US Surgeon General's Advisory Committee on the impact of television violence gathered evidence and deliberated on the matter in the 1970s. Caught up in the different political, industry and academic interests, the conclusions were inconclusive (Rowland, 1997).

Nevertheless, throughout much of the post-war period the issue of media violence dominated the discussion and framing of media regulation. Some critics have argued that moral panics and media regulation have been responses to the 'newness' of new media technologies (Drotner, 1992; Livingstone, 2002); others have argued that they are cyclical responses to generational difference (Pearson, 1983; Barker, 1984b). In the early 1980s there was a notable public concern with 'video nasties' in the UK. There were various calls from the press, child experts, religious organizations, and others for the regulation of the video rental and domestic purchasing market. The Video Recordings Act of 1984 introduced the statutory classification of video under the charge of the, then, British Board of Film Censors (BBFC). After the murder of a 2-year-old James Bulger in 1993, a similar collection of social actors called for further regulation of the video market. It would be correct to say that (despite moments of 'panic' and wide public discussion), far from being a response to 'new' media, anxiety about the adequacy of media regulation (whether framed in moral, religious, or psychological terms) has been an ongoing feature of modern media regulatory discourse and that much of that anxiety has been focused on the relations between imaging technology, violence, and young people.

In the early to mid-1980s, concern about commercial culture – that had been ongoing as a significant regulatory issue since the mid-1950s, if not before – had become focused on the problem of advertising and marketing to children. A particular issue was the relation between television programming and toy merchandising. From its beginning in the 1940s and 1950s, children's television in the USA (e.g. *Davy Crockett*) and UK (e.g. *Muffin the Mule*) had merchandising tie-ins (Cross, 1997; Oswell, 2002). Yet it was the distribution of the animation *He-Man and the Masters of the Universe* in 1983 that galvanized a huge debate in the USA and elsewhere. The toy manufacturer Mattel, which had produced a range of 'Masters of the Universe' dolls since 1974, licensed the concept to the animation company Filmation. Both toy range and television animation were hugely successful. Prior to that, in 1969, the Federal Communications Commission (FCC), the US media and communications regulator, had acted against a similar merchandising deal concerning Mattel's 'Hot Wheels' toy car range and a television animation of the same name and had referred to this as 'disturbing' inasmuch as it 'subordinates programming in the interest of the public to programming in the interest of its saleability' (FCC, 1969: 149). But during the period of the Reagan government, the head of the FCC, Mark Fowler, declared that broadcasters should not be held responsible for children's culture and that television should operate as a free market (Kunkel and Watkins, 1987; Herman and McChesney, 1997). In the 1980s, the best-selling toys in the USA were marketed through 'programme-length commercials', including *G.I. Joe*, *Thundercats* (Hasbro toys), *Care Bears*, and *Strawberry Shortcake* (Kenner) (Cross, 1997). In 1985 the FCC stated that 'the profit-sharing arrangement is an innovative technique to fund children's programming ... [and] we should have diversity in the method of financing that programming' (FCC, 1985: 713). This worrying trend was the object of much public criticism, most notably by the campaigning group Action for Children's Television in the USA, headed by Peggy Charren. By the late 1980s and early 1990s, FCC policy shifted away from the harsh deregulatory principles of the Fowler regime to more sanguine attempts to limit the perceived negative influences of advertising and marketing.

At the heart of the debate about television merchandising were concerns that children's media culture would become thoroughly commercialized, that the best interests of the child would not be served, and that children's media might itself disappear as a distinct market. In the USA, the Television Act of 1990 limited the amount of advertising per hour, stipulated that a condition of television station licence agreements should be that they serve the 'educational and informational needs of children', and stated that broadcasters needed to air a minimum of 3 hours of educational programmes to meet the needs of children under the age of 16 (Jordan, 1999). Similarly, in the UK, but also in other European countries, there was sustained debate from the mid-1980s to the 1990s about the quality and quantity of children's television. The traditions of public service broadcasting (of which children's broadcasting was seen to be a key aspect) were seen to be threatened by a deregulated commercial television market. Initially, there were demands made to government and regulators to protect the provision of children's television (Broadcasting Act of 1990 in the UK), but, as with the USA until quite recently, instead of seeing a drop in the quantity of children's television programming, a more competitive, liberalized, internationalized, multi-platform television market has produced an increase in provision. In this context, the concern about the quality of children's television programming has been defined in terms not simply of educational programming, but more broadly of a diversity of children's television output and its ability to meet the needs and interests of children (Davies and Corbett, 1997; Blumler and Biltereyst, 1998).

AFTER SOVEREIGNTY: FROM SCARCITY TO ABUNDANCE?

A major theme in current regulatory debate is that we are now living in an age of abundance, increasingly global, and with more horizontal relations between production and consumption. Much of this discourse has been simmering over the last 30 years (initially in relation to video, satellite and cable technology), but recent discourse (since the early 1990s) has been typified by a technological and paradigm shift from 'terrestrial broadcast television' to 'broadband digital internet connectivity'. Thus, John Perry Barlow, co-founder of the Electronic Frontier Foundation, heralds a new 'global and antisovereign' space that has the capacity to regain freedoms lost to broadcast media and its censorial 'standards of purity', 'undo all the authoritarian powers on earth' and is 'too widespread to be easily dominated by any single government' (Barlow, 1996a: 56). Even a cursory glance at some of the central regulatory issues concerning children over the last 200 years suggest that such a typification of the changing media and communications regulatory environment presents a severely limited and myopic vision.

A significant moment in European regulatory discourse and policy is the publication in 1994 by an expert group of the European Commission. The Bangemann report (High Level Group on the Information Society, 1994) considered, what was then called, the 'information society'. It made visible existing media and communications as a network of networks, not only within member states, but also across Europe as a networked region. In concert with other dominant policy discourses at the time, synergy across national boundaries and across industrial sectors was seen as central to the development of national and European information economies. There was seen to be a need for policy-makers to be aware that greater competitive advantage relied on a greater confluence between historically distinct industries, such as computing, broadcasting, and telecommunications. The technology that was seen to symbolize such confluence was the internet, but the platform, or model, upon which such communication across sector and national boundaries was materially based was that of telecommunications (Hills and Michalis, 1999; Melody, 2003: 9). Telecommunication networks provided the infrastructure for high-capacity data transfer between governments, businesses, organizations, and homes. Media industries historically with a high level of vertical integration (i.e. from transmission infrastructure to production to service and content provision), such as broadcasting, now faced increasing uncertainty with regard to that value chain. Moreover, the governance and regulation of the information society was predicated, not on a broadcasting model that foregrounded matters of content, but on a telecommunications model that was based on competition. The Bangemann report helped set the agenda for European regulatory policy for the ensuing years.

In conditions of convergence, standardized languages and terminologies are adopted in order to provide structures of intelligibility and translation across historically different media and communications industries. In the past, regulation of media and communications with regard to questions of the protection of children has been dependent on an understanding of the difference between different media technologies, delivery and distribution systems, and generally different industrial contexts. Thus, the regulation of cinema was different from that of television and required a different regulatory agency and a different set of skills and competencies. Even, if the regulation of different media was to be housed within the same regulatory agency (such as the FCC in the USA), the different media were treated as different regulatory objects. Today, though, although there is still an understanding of differences across media, the principle for their regulation is often stated in terms of uniformity and standardization (Melody, 2003). We should be wary, though, of assuming that (although there are moves toward regulatory convergence) contemporary media and communications are now simply governed according to a new set of principles and mechanisms completely different from those within older media and communications environments. Richard Collins, for example, has distinguished between three modes of governance for internet communications: hierarchical, market and network governance. Collins (2006: 20) argues that the phenomenal take-up of internet communications does not imply a simple shift in mode of governance, namely to one predicated on networked, or self-regulated, governance; rather there is 'a flexible and shifting articulation of different modes of governance, market, hierarchy and network'.

The shifting allegiances to historic industry-specific regulatory terminologies, paradigms and resources help to shape contemporary understandings of media and communications regulation with regard to children. Most notably, '[t]elecommunications operators are not normally held responsible for the content of messages or services that they carry across their networks', whereas, in contrast, 'broadcasting has … been traditionally highly regulated' (Campbell and Machet, 1999: 142). Telecommunications operators have been viewed as 'common carriers', whereas broadcasters have been construed as publishers of content. In the mid- to late-1990s the language of responsibility was central to the governance of internet service providers (ISPs): should they be liable for content accessible via their service provision or not? Whatever the veridicality of claims concerning technological neutrality and market convergence, regulatory agencies construct such convergence as a regulatory objective. Thus, for example, ex-head of content regulation at Ofcom, Richard Hooper (2005: 4) states that: '[t]he regulation of communications should aspire to be technology and platform neutral, as set out in the European Directives on telecommunications regulation. Yet in practice, achieving technology neutrality can be very difficult to do'. Instead of assuming asymmetries between technologies as obstacles to regulation, they provide the incentives for intended resolutions (whether in terms of convergence or harmonization or the marking of regulatory boundaries between different sectors and industries) and constitute the basis of ongoing problematization. Such an understanding of media and communications regulation does not presume the absolute decline of national sovereign institutions, nor of a simple abundance of capacity and content. As Brian Loader has argued, although new digital broadband networked technologies facilitate 'new forms and expressions of governance' ('a paradigmatic change in the constellation of power relations between individuals, governments and social institutions'), they do not give rise to 'an uncontested domain and the stakeholders in the politics of the modern nation-state are not so easily displaced' (Loader, 1997: 1–2). Any sociology of media and communications regulation needs to account not only for the rhetoric of change, but also for its mobilization and institutionalization by interested and embodied social actors.

REGULATORY OBJECTIVES AND STATUTORY LEGISLATION

Some commentators have been sceptical of claims about new communication technologies bringing about new forms of criminality and, hence, have been critical of calls for new regulatory codification and legislation. For some, the internet is simply a vehicle for existing criminal behaviours (Williams, 2004). David Wall has argued that the term 'cybercrime' 'has no specific referent in law', that it is a notion 'largely invented by the media' and that, 'despite the rather unsystematic attempts to define it, the term nevertheless invokes a knee-jerk response from the media, policymakers, politicians, academics and the public alike' (Wall, 2001: 2). Such an understanding serves itself to invoke earlier Luddite reactions to the perceived risks of new media and communication technology, in a manner similar to that of sociological accounts of media panics (Drotner, 1992). Although the rhetoric of 'cybercrime' may be unhelpful, it nevertheless signals the mobilization of social actors, the development of new regulatory terminologies, and the invention of new regulatory codification and legislation in the context of perceived new or developing forms of criminality. It is in this sense that new legislation and regulatory codification must be taken seriously and analysed as sociologically significant.

Regulatory and legislative responses to internet communications have been wide-ranging, but also noticeably tempered by national and regional differences. The European Commission from the start had an understanding that 'over-hasty legislation should be avoided' (Commission of the European Communities, 1996a) and that, in the first instance, greater cooperation was needed across different national governments, law enforcement agencies, and cultures of the European Union. Any move toward greater harmonization would need to surpass existing definitions of illegalities across the different jurisdictions of the different member states. Nevertheless, although the European Union already had in place existing commitments to cooperation regarding justice and home affairs, proposals were made for greater harmonization of new national legislation regarding the internet (Campbell and Machet, 1999). Rather than seeking, in the first instance, European-wide formal regulatory structures regarding illegal content, the European Commission recommended moves toward greater industry self-regulation and greater parental responsibility in the domestic regulation of their children (Commission of the European Communities, 1997: 30). The responsibility for formulating legal definitions of 'cybercrime' was thus left to decision-makers and law-makers in particular national contexts. Moreover, early in the discussion, the European Commission clearly differentiated between two concerns (illegal content, which 'may be banned for everyone, regardless of the age of the potential audience or the medium used' and harmful content, which 'might affect the physical and mental development of minors' and which should be 'allowed only for adults' (Commission of the European Communities, 1996b: 6)) and defined 'different legal and technological responses' (Commission of the European Communities, 1996c: 10). In doing so, they reduced the horizon of illegalities to that of images of child sexual abuse, race-hate material and extreme violent pornography, and thus radically realigned and rearticulated historic concerns and criteria (concerning harm, offence and obscenity) established with regard to older media, such as broadcast television, film and video (which had institutionalized responses to harm in the context of notions of the socially, emotionally, cognitively and physically developing child). Such a considered and strategic approach initially allowed a high degree of local interpretative flexibility. Needless to say, it was this strategy that was also pursued by other national governments (e.g. the Australian Broadcasting Authority's focus on 'contact and safety issues', 'illegal content', and 'unsuitable content' (Grainger, 1998: 18)).

In the UK there has been legislative reform. Thus, regarding the issue of child pornography and obscenity, the Criminal

Justice and Public Order Act of 1994 amended the Protection of Children Act of 1978 so as to include reference not only to photographs, but also 'pseudo-photographs' (see Oswell (2006)). The act refers not only to actual images, but also to 'data' that may be 'converted' into an image. It implicitly encodes a principle of technological symmetry or neutrality, inasmuch as a ' "[p]seudo-photograph" means an image, whether made by computer-graphics or otherwise howsoever, which appears to be a photograph'; and it constructs childhood not straightforwardly as defined by age (originally 16 years, but increased to under 18 years by the Sexual Offences Act of 2003), but as an 'impression', such that:

> [i]f the impression conveyed by a pseudo-photograph is that the person shown is a child, the pseudo-photograph shall be treated for all purposes of this Act as showing a child and so shall a pseudo-photograph where the predominant impression conveyed is that the person shown is a child notwithstanding that some of the physical characteristics shown are those of an adult.

Similar versions of this legal formulation are found in other jurisdictions (e.g. 163.1 (1) of the Criminal Code in Canada). Legislation concerning child pornography across member states of the European Union indicates greater standardization in recent years, compared with the significant differences (for example, regarding age of maturity and severity of punishments with respect to possession, distribution, or production) in past years.

Definitions of 'harmful content' are wide-ranging. Some commentators seem to have interpreted the European Commission policy regarding 'harmful content' as by definition referring to material that is not illegal (Akdeniz, 2001: 304). Such an understanding frames 'harm' within a definitional context different to that of prior legislation and regulation concerning radio, television, film, and video. Bad language, promotion of drugs and alcohol, and overly violent and sexually explicit content has been consistently prohibited from broadcast terrestrial and non-encrypted satellite and cable television in the UK, whether governed by the BBC Board of Governors or Ofcom (or its predecessors). Similarly, the British Board of Film and Video Classification (BBFC) has regulated video (in the context of the Video Recordings Act of 1984) according to the criterion of 'harm' and particularly with respect to children and other vulnerable people. The Williams Committee Report on Obscenity and Film Censorship (1979), although never translated into legislation, sought to restrict offensive material, but to prohibit material seen to cause harm. Williams stated that 'no conduct should be suppressed by law unless it can be shown to harm someone' (quoted in Newburn (1992: 182)). Historically the categorical differentiation between material likely to cause offence and that likely to cause harm has been significant in media and communications regulation. Despite persistent calls in the 1990s to reform obscenity legislation, the UK has not redefined legal understandings of obscenity in the context of internet communications, but only extended the notion of obscenity – as that whose tendency is to deprave and corrupt – to include computer-generated content. The Obscene Publications Acts of 1959 and 1964 criminalize the publication and distribution of obscene content, but they are inadequate to the task of regulating obscene content on the internet, not least because providers of such material may well be based outside the reach of UK jurisdiction. Moreover, although the downloading of internet child pornography constitutes a criminal offence, possession of obscene material has yet to be criminalized. Similarly, in contrast to policing and prosecutions relating to the downloading of child pornography, there have been very few cases with regard to obscene internet publications (Akdeniz, 2001). Discussion concerning the revised European Commission Television Without Frontiers Directive has sought to address the issue of 'harmful' content, but fails to tackle the problem of convergence properly (Commission of the European Communities, 2005).

Thinking in this area is fast changing and historic concerns about 'content' are increasingly constructed and contextualized with concerns about 'contact'. Looking to growing concerns in Japan and the USA, the realization that mobile telephony and internet technologies were being used by adults for inappropriate, sexualized, and abusive contact with children (Childnet International, 2004) has led to the questioning in the UK of existing legislation. The Indecency with Children Act of 1960 had made reference to 'incitement' to commit a sexual offence with a minor, but many professionals in the field (including government ministers, civil servants, judges, police and non-governmental organizations) argued that the use of the internet for 'grooming' and 'luring' young people was not adequately addressed (Childnet International, 2001; Gardener, 2003). The Sexual Offences Act of 2003 now criminalizes indecent text messaging and online and offline grooming of minors. Similar legislation can be found, for example, in Australia, Canada, New Zealand and the USA (Childnet International, 2001).

In contrast to European governance and legislation, US administrations have met with much resistance (from civil liberty groups, the sex entertainment industry, and others) over attempts to introduce legislation regarding obscenity and indecency on the internet. In early 1996, the Communications Decency Act (CDA) was introduced. The act had intended to criminalize whomever knowingly used a telecommunications device to make, create, solicit or initiate the transmission of material which is 'obscene, lewd, lascivious, filthy, or indecent, with intent to annoy, abuse, threaten, or harass another person', which is 'obscene or indecent, knowing that the recipient of the communication is under 18 years of age', and the use of an 'interactive computer service to display in a manner available to a person under 18 years of age, any comment, request, suggestion, proposal, image, or other communication that, in context, depicts or describes, in terms patently offensive as measured by contemporary community standards, sexual or excretory activities or organs' (Sections 223 (a)(1)(A) and (B), and (d)(1)(B)). The act was appealed by the American Civil Liberties Union (ACLU) in June 1996, taken to the Supreme Court in March 1997, and overturned in June 1997. The Supreme Court held that the CDA provisions of 'indecent transmission' and 'patently offensive display' abridged the freedom of speech protected by the First Amendment. Among other things, the Supreme Court stated that the CDA:

> fails to provide any definition of 'indecent' and omits any requirement that 'patently offensive' material lack socially redeeming value; neither limits its broad categorical prohibitions to particular times nor bases them on an evaluation by an agency familiar with the medium's unique characteristics; is punitive; applies to a medium that, unlike radio, receives full First Amendment protection; and cannot be properly analyzed as a form of time, place, and manner regulation because it is a content-based blanket restriction on speech (*Reno v ACLU*, June 26 1997, Syllabus (b)).

In the earlier appeal, it had been stated that, unlike the FCC's regulation of cable and dial-up programming with regard to indecency, the CDA had failed to provide consideration of context in terms of 'the particular medium from which the material originates and the particular community that receives the material' (*ACLU v Reno*, June 11 1996). It had stated that '[l]aws regulating speech for the protection of children have no limiting principle, and well-intentioned law restricting protected speech on the basis of its content is, nevertheless, state-sponsored censorship' (*ACLU v Reno*, June 11 1996). Unlike some other media, the internet was seen by both courts as a vast, open, global, geographically non-localized medium that was nevertheless seen to be non-invasive: 'the content on the Internet is as diverse as human thought' (929F Supp at 8422). The government had argued that its 'patently offensive' standard was not vague as it accorded with the decision of *Miller v California*. In that earlier case in 1973, it had been decided that the test for obscenity was as follows:

> (a) whether the average person applying contemporary community standards would find that the work taken as a whole, appeals to the prurient interest; (b) whether the work depicts or describes, in a patently offensive way, sexual conduct specifically defined by the applicable law; and (c) whether the work, taken as a whole, lacks serious literary,

artistic, political, or scientific value' (quoted in *Reno v ACLU*, June 26 1997).

The Supreme Court argued that reference to 'prurient interest' and 'serious literary, artistic, political, or scientific value' properly limited the breadth of that earlier decision. Moreover, and importantly, the Supreme Court argued that the second criterion 'absent in the CDA, allows appellate courts to impose some limitations and regularity on the definition by setting, as a matter of law, a national floor for socially redeeming value' (*Reno v ACLU*, June 26 1997). The Supreme Court held that the CDA would impact upon 'large amounts of nonpornographic material with serious educational or other value': 'the "community standards" criterion as applied to the Internet means that any communication available to a nation-wide audience will be judged by the standards of the community most likely to be offended by the message' (*Reno v ACLU*, June 26 1997). It gives the example of a parent sending their 17-year-old child at college in another state some birth control information and the parent being open to prosecution, not because either the parent, the child, or the home state would deem the material indecent or patently offensive, but because the college town community might do so.

The Child Online Protection Act (COPA) 1998, which sought to restrict the distribution of materials that are harmful to minors, was also appealed soon after its signing. The US Court of Appeals for the Third Circuit in June 2000 (*ACLU v Reno*, 99-1324, June 22 2000) held that – although the government had tried to learn the lessons of the Supreme Court declaration regarding the unconstitutionality of the CDA and Congress was 'cognizant of the fact that "the application of community standards in the context of the Web is controversial"' – there was not sufficient account that '[u]nlike a "brick and mortar outlet" with a specific geographic locale, and unlike the voluntary physical mailing of material from one geographic location to another, as in Miller, the uncontroverted facts indicate that the Web is not geographically constrained'. The Court of Appeals did not accept the argument that 'community standards' should be understood not as a 'geographic standard', but as an 'adult standard'. The Court of Appeals stated that with reference to existing case law 'community standards have always been interpreted as a geographic standard without uniformity' and that such a notion is to be understood in terms of 'a localized geographic content'. COPA would have made internet content subject to the most conservative community standard and to the most conservative interpretation of what is deemed harmful to minors. Such legislation would, the Court of Appeals argued, put an 'overreaching burden and restriction on constitutionally protected speech'. Whatever the final outcome of this legislation, there are considerable problems with regard to any definition of obscenity that relies on a notion of 'community standards' in the context of internet communications and of multi-cultural, multi-faith, multi-ethnic communities (howsoever formed) with different values and levels of tolerance.

Even attempts to legislate against images of child sexual abuse have been forlorn. The Child Pornography Prevention Act of 1996 (CPPA) was seen to be 'overbroad' and 'unconstitutional' in relation to two provisions. First, the act was seen to be inconsistent with *Miller v California* on the grounds that it failed to take account of the 'community standards' criterion and that it criminalized speech without regard to the specificity of time, place or manner. Thus, for example, an online filmic version of *Romeo and Juliet*, in which the two young lovers are played by adult actors, might be deemed illegal on the basis of the content alone, without due regard to the artistic value of the work. It was argued that the act would criminalize sexualized images of children even though no child might be involved in the production of those images and hence contrary to the decision of the *New York v Ferber* case, which only prohibited child pornography on the grounds that it records an actual abuse of a child. Thus, the CPPA, it was argued, would criminalize, for example, images of an adult having sexual conduct with another adult dressed up as a child. Moreover, if the image of sexual conduct with a child is not real, but fabricated or virtual, then it was argued that it should not be prohibited on the grounds that it cannot be deemed to have harmed a child in its production nor necessarily able to harm a child through its affect (i.e. as a method of enticement or as behaviour forming). It was argued that prohibition of content cannot be on the basis of a consequentialist argument (i.e. that certain things happen as a consequence of certain content). Second, the act was deemed overbroad and unconstitutional with respect to its criminalizing the advertising and marketing of content that 'conveys the impression' of 'a minor engaging in sexually explicit conduct' (US Court of Appeals for the Ninth Circuit, 16 April 2002).

The difficulties of enacting legislation in the USA and differences in legislation between the USA and the European Union indicate the subtle, but sometimes stark cultural and social contextualization not only of technology, but also of legal jurisdiction. Equally though, the apparent increasing harmonization of legal standards across the European Union indicates the force of increasing cooperation at sub-legal institutionalized levels.

REGULATORY AGENCIES

Monroe Price and Stephan Verhulst (2005: i) have claimed that '[t]he Internet challenges classic patterns of regulation for both the identity of the rule makers and the instruments used to establish the rules of regulation' (see also Reidenberg (1996) quoted in Akdeniz (1997)). In part, this is certainly correct. The movements and mobilizations surrounding the introduction of the internet have led to a sea change in thinking about media and communications regulation (Verhulst, 2002). Many have talked about this shift, often with reference to the failure of the CDA, in terms of a move away from legal mechanisms of regulation toward more flexible forms of industry self-regulation. But there are various forms of self-regulation across different national and regional contexts and there are different understandings of whether self-regulation is viewed as a purely private market-based method of regulation (i.e. involving no form of statutory intervention) (Stein and Sinha, 2002) or as a form of network governance (i.e. sidestepping traditional state and market mechanisms) (Thompson, 2003; Collins, 2006). Yet, as Price and Verhulst (2005: 3) argue, '[s]elf-regulation rarely exists without some relationship between the industry and the state', albeit 'a relationship that varies greatly': '[t]he actual meaning of self-regulation changes depending on the extent of government action, the history of the relationship between industry and government, and the nature of the public perceptions of the relationship between the private sector and the state'. As Tony Prosser has argued, 'in many cases self-regulatory techniques have been adopted to head off threats of government intervention' and there is a 'mixture of official regulation and self-regulation through public authorities specifying general standards or principles the implementation of which is delegated to firms themselves or trade associations' (Prosser, 2000: 103; Campbell, 2003). Historically the degree of independence of self-regulatory agencies is inversely related to their closeness (the degree of 'capture') to the sector that they regulate (Collins and Murroni, 1996: 176). Self-regulation is not separate from legal regulation, but rather operates in the context of statutory powers and law enforcement agencies. In the UK, for example, the Internet Watch Foundation (IWF) was formed in the context of the London Metropolitan Police threatening to arrest directors of ISPs and to confiscate property if they did not comply with demands for greater responsibility with regard to the circulation of child pornography on UK servers; and the IWF operates as a reporting and monitoring body only inasmuch as it is able both to call on ISPs to remove content suspected of being illegal and to pass on information regarding illegalities to law enforcement agencies (Akdeniz, 1997; Oswell, 1998b). In Australia, industry codes of practice and self-regulation sit in the context of Commonwealth, State and Territory legislation, and the Australian Communications and Media Authority (ACMA, formerly the Australian Broadcasting Authority (ABA) prior to July 2005) (Grainger, 1998; Electronic Frontiers Australia, 2006). Interdependencies exist across government control, industry self-regulation, and market governance (Verhulst, 2002; Price and Verhulst, 2005), not least to head off any 'generalized lack of public trust in the medium' (Programme in Comparative Media Law and Policy, 2005: 5), but also to frame 'trust' in the context of 'responsibility' and through historic issues concerning family welfare. In the absence of such interdependencies, it is possible, even likely, that industry would not be vigilant in policing itself nor know by what criteria it should do so (Campbell, 2003). Equally though, such semi-autonomy (between state and industry) can be seen to occlude the mechanisms of power from public and democratic accountability (Starr, 2003). Nevertheless, despite some recognition of the rights of adults, a major lack of accountability of self-regulatory bodies may concern their lack of representation for those audiences that they claim to speak for and protect, namely children.

The condition of communication abundance has led to shifts in regulatory authority. Equally, increased visibility of social being as multi-cultural, multi-ethnic, and multi-faith across and within national and regional territories has led to uncertainty about enforcement of any common values (encoded through regulation), a questioning of statutory regulatory agencies, and the decentralization of regulatory authority to families. Such delegation of responsibility, though, is double-edged. The policing of children's media consumption is such that, on the one hand, there is a recognition that statutory bodies are unable to police cultural taste and 'harmful' content in the manner that was possible in the past with cinema, radio, and television and that, as a consequence, responsibility falls into the hands of parents; on the other hand, the making of parents responsible is caught up in historically devolved mechanisms for making those persons aware of their responsibilities and the criteria through which their responsibility might be judged by others (i.e. notions of 'good' and 'bad' parenting, 'normal' and 'pathological' families, and so on) (Oswell, 2002; Livingstone and Bober, 2004). Thus, any devolution of authority (in the context of moral, religious, and cultural value) is matched by a continuation and accentuation of historic forms of normalization (mediated by scientific and professionalized expertise) (Walkerdine and Lucey, 1989). Of course, the responsibilization of parents is often tied to the making of children into critical media consumers, such that the endowing of children with agency with regard to their media and communication use is seen to be able to offset any harm that such media might carry. In this sense, media literacy campaigns (often involving non-governmental organizations) – addressed either to children or parents or both – have sought historically to readjust the balance between media and child (Lusted, 1985). Such strategies of responsibilization tend to displace the burden of risk downward and lead to a greater individualization of regulatory agency. Although not inevitable, there is a tendency for the reduction and management of risk to be left to individual parents or individual children (Programme in Comparative Media Law and Policy, 1999; Livingstone and Bober, 2004).

There is a strand of regulatory debate that has sought to make visible grass-roots communities (whether online or offline) as viable relays and resources for regulatory authority. Such an argument relies on viewing regulatory responsibility not simply as an individual or organisational duty, but as a social and collective act. For example, Adam Newey has argued that 'some notion of community is essential if we are to understand how to impose any effective regulation on the Internet'; Newey construes 'computer-mediated communities' as 'real social entities' in the 'real world' of 'local community': '[t]he network is rooted in a social context which, in the end, will determine the limits of acceptability' (Newey, 1999: 15, 30–31). An understanding of the power of communities to regulate themselves is found equally in more libertarian writers such as Barlow (1996b), who envisages forms of governance emerging from 'the commonweal', a community of 'lovers of freedom and self-determination', facing and resisting colonial and authoritarian power. Online community regulation may take the form of 'vigilante' groups – such as the Brazilian Anjos do Orkut or the US CyberAngels or the American Ethical Hackers against Pedophilia – attacking race-hate and child pornography sites, whether verbally, through 'flaming', through viral and other software attacks or through surveying chatrooms and websites and reporting illegal material to ISPs and the police. It may also take the form of a governance within particular communities by recognized community regulators or activists. Matthew Williams has documented how those recognized as causing offence in the Cyberworlds community may be castigated online and even expelled from the collective: '[e]ffective online deviance reduction then lies in the balanced integration of community-led and formal modes of regulation' (Williams, 2006: 16).

REGULATORY METHODOLOGIES

Across the different regulatory agencies (statutory, industry, parent, child, and community) different methodologies of regulation are pursued. Although different mechanisms may be used in relation to different media and communications in different contexts, there are certain methodologies (prohibition, boundary marking and wall making, labelling and rating, reporting and monitoring, and empowerment) that are reiterated over time. Much discussion of content regulation from the early to late 1990s turned, on the one hand, on the seeming inadequacy of formal methods of censorship in the face of communication abundance and, on the other hand, on the perception that new legislation and regulatory technologies were themselves censorial. In response, there has been a marked shift away from a problematic of prohibition to consideration of more nuanced mechanisms of regulation. Christina Murroni and Nick Irvine (1998: 78), for example, have argued that although it may be impossible to 'suppress' internet content, it is feasible to 'restrict' it to particular users. Nevertheless, as we have seen, many governments and regulatory agencies now consider the possibility of prohibiting production and distribution of, and access to, certain types of content (e.g. images of child sexual abuse and race-hate material) as a legitimate policy goal.

Murroni and Irvine (1998: 79) argue that ability to restrict access to particular content is dependent on the degree of privateness or publicness of a medium and whether access to content is likely to be accidental or voluntary. In this way a telephone conversation would constitute a private communication that can be restricted to voluntary users. In contrast, a billboard poster on a street corner is public and can be seen by anyone, whether they intend to see it or not. Some commentators have argued that because the internet is supposedly a public medium available to all (i.e. both adults and children), all the time, it should be heavily regulated in order to protect children and vulnerable persons (Wilson-Thomas, 1996). As discussed above, time, manner and place criteria have played a significant part in legislative discourse in the USA. They have also been a persistent feature of media and communications regulatory discourse, certainly, over the last 200 years. More recently, the placing of sexually explicit magazines on the 'top-shelf' of newsagent stalls, the establishment of 18R restricted video retail outlets for sexually explicit material in the UK, and the zoning of adult cinemas away from residential areas in the USA all demonstrate, in different ways, time, manner and place criteria. The zoning of internet content helps to construct a layering of architectures that ward off or encourage users; the ability to move across geography is dependent on the degree of access afforded to a user. As the degree of access hardens, boundary marking becomes less an issue of description of types of material (a relatively permeable membrane) than of thick walls that deny access to many (i.e. codified points of access, such as credit card restriction).

But zoning is as much to do with repelling that which certain types of content are seen to attract (e.g. crime, antisocial behaviour, and so on) as with restricting access of certain persons. Moreover, the zoning of content occurs not only within cyberspace, but also in the relations across online and offline. There has been extensive research on the placing of media and communication technologies in 'public' (e.g. the sitting room) or 'private' (e.g. the bedroom) spaces in the home and on the temporal regularities of domestic media scheduling and use (Spigel, 1992; Oswell, 1999, 2002; Livingstone and Bovill, 2001). The architectures and geographies of media and communications become visible as governmental possibilities. Time and space become intelligible as the means for boundary marking and wall building. Time and space are mobilized in order to zone the geographies of media and communications. Such governmental architectures are more than code (Lessig, 1999).

Labelling and classificatory systems have been longstanding regulatory mechanisms. The BBC in the 1940s and 1950s considered on-screen labels and prior verbal warnings for certain types of content (notably at this time concerning close-up shots of teeth, ghosts, witches and 'figures with ghoulish faces' (Oswell, 2002)) and terrestrial television broadcasters in the UK have continued that tradition of forewarning viewers of potentially unsuitable content. Equally, the BBFC has classified content (including 'bad' language, sexual explicitness, and violence) according to normative age groups and such classifications are enforced through statutory legislation with regard to video and through local government powers with regard to cinema (the Cinematograph Act of 1909). Classificatory guidelines act in many ways as interpretative tools for consumers (parents, children, and others) to choose filmic material suitable to their own tastes and concerns (Buckingham, 1996). From the mid-1990s, classificatory systems and technological means of enforcement have become a favoured regulatory mechanism with regard to communication abundance. The USA and Canada adopted the 'V-chip' system, whereby rating levels can be set on the television set in the home and inappropriate content blocked thereafter. Some commentators have viewed the technology as overly authoritarian and claimed that it constructs parents 'as their children's enemy or drill sergeant, who must carry out the orders of the experts in order to control children and protect them from television' (Kapur, 1999: 122). Others though have argued that the demand for simple parameter settings for parents has meant that the competency threshold is such that children themselves are able to change the settings (Programme in Comparative Media Law and Policy, 1999: 4–5). There is substantial research to suggest that 'the V-chip has had little impact because of the lack of public knowledge of the meaning of the ratings, the existence of the V-chip and how to use it' (Campbell, 2003: 8; Kaiser Foundation, 2004). Nevertheless, labelling, rating, filtering and blocking technologies (such as PICS and RDF or Net Nanny and Cyber Patrol) have been developed with regard to internet communications. Recent classification and filtration systems analytically and functionally compress notions of labelling and rating, differentiate between labelling and filtering, and facilitate decentralized mechanisms for rating and blocking content. It is claimed, for example, by the Internet Content Rating Association (ICRA) that such functional differentiation allows for value-neutral labelling (ICRA, 2005). One of the problems with an abundance of content and content providers is that the task of classification is indefinite (inasmuch as content is constantly being produced and revised). If content is to be labelled, then such a task needs to be delegated downward. There can be no longer any centralized and totalizing vision of the all-seeing censor. Censorship is now decentralized and localized. Labelling, though, is far from neutral; it makes possible the internet as 'regulable' (Negroponte, 1986; Lessig, 1998). Far from providing more nuanced mechanisms than the clumsy legislation of the CDA, filtering software may block access to content which is appropriate and legitimate and those providing such services are not democratically accountable (Lessig, 1998; Akdeniz, 2001).

The methodology of the hotline, similarly, delegates responsibility downward. It has been enthusiastically adopted, with regard to illegal internet content, in Europe (see INHOPE association of hotlines), the USA, and elsewhere since the mid-1990s (Williams, 1999). Hotlines (or 'tiplines'), such as Meldpunt Kinderporno in the Netherlands and the IWF in the UK, provide a means of allowing members of the public to report crime visible on the internet. Some hotlines are funded and run by government and some by industry or voluntary organizations; some cover only material hosted within their country, others material from across the globe; all are concerned with child pornography, and some also with race-hate and other material. In the past, statutory regulatory bodies (such as the Broadcasting Standards Commission in the UK) have been responsive to reports from the public as to particular issues around particular content (i.e. in the form of letters of complaint). But whereas the public in that respect was invited to complain about content they disliked or felt unsuitable, the public, with regard to internet hotlines, is constructed as a monitorial body that is able to survey the internet and report perceived illegalities accordingly. In this sense, members of the public are not invited to report in any personal capacity, but only in respect of their collective capacity as a form of modern policing. On the basis of reports from Australian citizens concerning perceived illegal content, ACMA, for example, is able to issue take-down notices to ISPs and to inform filtering and law enforcement agencies of prohibited content (Electronic Frontiers Australia, 2006: 5–7). In large part, the capacity of the public to report is dependent on the public visibility of such hotlines (i.e. media consumers need to know that there is a body to which to report issues), the communication of the types of content that come within its concern and of procedures for reporting by the public (i.e. the public need to know on what matters they might report and how to do so), and the public display of such a body in responding to and acting upon the views and reports of the public in ways appropriate and in keeping with that public (i.e. the public needs to view its reporting as an exercise of its power). But some have argued that 'illegality remains a matter to be decided by courts of law and not by private organizations or by quasi-regulatory bodies' (Akdeniz, 2001: 307).

Increasingly, regulatory agencies draw upon media education and media literacy campaigns as means to responsibilize and educate citizens as critical users (Grainger, 1998). The methodology of empowerment is defined not only with respect to providing parents and children with the capacity to prohibit or restrict access to certain content, but also to making users of internet content sufficiently robust as a means of defence against harm and to facilitate forms of sociality, bonding and mediation, that might mitigate against harm. Thus, although empowerment might mean that '[w]e will all become gatekeepers for content coming into our homes' (Ofcom, 2004; quoted in Livingstone and Bober, (2004: 7)), it also means that interpretative skills and greater talk about media use and content between different social actors (such as parents, children, non-governmental organizations and schools) become instituted as regulatory responses to communication abundance. Such a methodology can, in part, be seen as a response to greater visibility of children's rights, to changing understandings of the family as a democratic space (Livingstone, 2002), and to the historical development of children's critical media competencies (Oswell, 1998a, 2002).

CONCLUSIONS

Across the different regulatory agencies and methodologies, media and communications become visible to legal control and governance. We can, on the basis of existing evidence, offer some conclusions.

(a) For much of the nineteenth and twentieth centuries, although there were common themes and concerns (e.g. regarding violence, delinquency, national culture, and commercialism) across different media and communications, there were also clear asymmetries. The regulatory exigencies of radio were seen to be different from film or television or print. Where once different regulatory agencies and methodologies would have been spread over different industries and technologies and across different local, national and regional contexts, today we see an increasing demand for their standardization and location within centralized locales (such as the European Commission, ICRA, Ofcom). The imagined ease of translation across delivery systems and 'neutralization' of technological difference has led, in one sense at least, to a concentration of regulatory powers. The motor of regulatory convergence is not statutory legislation, but the sub-legal movements and assemblages of regulatory officials, non-governmental organizations, industry-hybrid associations, expert groups, and local, national, regional and transnational governmental bodies. Across the moments of social gathering of these actors, the regulatory languages and protocols, objectives and programmes, and legislative formalizations get problematized and articulated. These gatherings, statements, and actions constitute significant points of post-national governance.

(b) The internet has presaged not only a new age of complexity, but also a series of simplifications and centralizations of regulatory authority and power. Whereas once there was not a single table upon which all the regulatory problems and issues of all the different media and communications industries across all the different local, national and regional locales could be made visible, the 'internet' (as a discursive object) begins to provide such a totalizing space, a surface upon which all the cards can be laid and a new trans-media regulatory game is to be played. Regulatory convergence begins to constitute a single plane of understanding and problematization.

(c) Greater cognizance of national and cultural difference is a spur to greater harmonization and standardization of regulatory protocols, processes and forms of policing. The hotline and self-regulation are model responses to internet crime and child protection that have been spread and picked up rapidly since the mid-1990s (with regard to Malaysia and Lithuania, see Azmi (2004) and Kiškis and Petrauskas (2006)). They demonstrate a sharing of expertise across national jurisdictions. But they also constitute forms of interdependency. Regulation across national jurisdiction takes the form of serial linkage, of co-national organization, rather than overarching control.

(d) The convergence toward a singular plane of understanding is demonstrated in the shift from moral languages for regulation to scientific ones. This is not a new trend and has certainly been in evidence in other areas of social life since the nineteenth century. But in the field of child protection and media and communications, there has been (increasingly since the mid-twentieth century onward) expert explanation and public discussion of media 'panics' in scientific, rather than moral, terms. Regulatory bodies attempt to frame internet content in culturally neutral, normative terms.

(e) There is a greater reliance on 'black-boxed' regulatory technologies, such as filters and labelling standards. Regulatory models and protocols are encoded not simply in the human decision-making processes of organizations, but in computer software and hardware. Such encodings, as with the shift from moral to scientific languages, help to by-pass democratic debate and to seal regulation as an 'expert' field, out of reach from ordinary citizens.

(f) The devolution of regulatory authority downward is indicative of 'privatization' and 'responsibilization', rather than actual autonomy and control. Media-literate children, parental supervision, self-regulation, and legal mechanisms are not mutually exclusive techniques, but are co-extensive and interdependent.

(g) The black-boxing of regulatory technologies is not evidence of a 'super-panopticon' or more efficient and extensive surveillance and policing. Technologies of regulation are myopic. Regulatory agents only work with each other.

(h) Technological developments become incitements for the extension of regulatory knowledge and the submission of communications to a singular plane of understanding. Regulatory problematization becomes a key stage in the process of making new forms of communication regulable. Temporal and spatial technological architectures become regulable and change in response.

In the broad spread of history, the texture, incommensurability, and asymmetry of media and communications governance of the past has given way to a greater instrumentalization of debate and regulatory mechanisms, a reduced universe of regulatory discourse, a greater convergence of regulatory domains and agencies, and a shifting of the burden of regulatory responsibility downward. That said, the shortsighted supervision of the regulator is both a curse and saving grace.

REFERENCES

Akdeniz, Y. (1997) 'Governance of pornography and child pornography on the global internet: a multi-layered approach'. In L. Edwards and C. Waelde (eds) *Law and the Internet: Regulating Cyberspace*. Oxford: Hart Publishing; 223–241.

Akdeniz, Y. (2001) 'Internet content regulation: UK government and the control of internet content'. *Computer Law and Security Report*, 17(5).

Azmi, M.I. (2004) 'Content regulation in Malaysia: unleashing missiles on dangerous web sites'. *Journal of Information, Law and Technology*, (3). www2.warwick.ac.uk/fac/soc/law2/elj/jilt/2004_3/azmi/[February 2006].

Barker, M. (1984a) *A Haunt of Fears: The Strange History of the British Horror Comics Campaign*. London: Pluto Press.

Barker, M. (ed.) (1984b) *The Video Nasties: Freedom and Censorship in the Media*. London: Pluto Press.

Barlow, J.P. (1996a) 'Thinking locally, acting globally'. www.eff.org//Misc/Publications/John_Perry_Barlow/?f=think_local_act_global_011596.article.txt [November 2006]. (Originally published in *Time*, 15 January 1996.)

Barlow, J.P. (1996b) *A Declaration of the Independence of Cyberspace*. http://homes.eff.org/~barlow/Declaration-Final.html [August 2007].

Blumler, J. and Biltereyst, D. (1998) *The Integrity and Erosion of Public Television for Children: A Pan-European Study*. London: Broadcasting Standards Commission.

Buckingham, D. (1996) *Moving Images: Understanding Children's Emotional Reponses to Television*. Manchester: Manchester University Press.

Campbell, A. (2003) 'Self-regulation and the media: four years later'. Paper presented to the *Programme on Comparative Media Law and Policy*, Oxford University, 10 March.

Campbell, P. and Machet, E. (1999) 'European policy on regulation of content on the internet'. In J. Liberty (ed.) *Liberating Cyberspace: Civil Liberties, Human Rights and the Internet*. London: Pluto Press.

Childnet International (2001) *Online Grooming and UK Law: A Submission by Childnet International to the Home Office*. www.childnet-int.org/downloads/online-grooming.pdf [November 2005].

Childnet International (2004) *Children and Mobile Phones: An Agenda for Action*. www.childnet-int.org/downloads/CMPAAA_A4.pdf [October 2005].

Collins, R. (2006) 'Networks, markets and hierarchies. Governance and regulation of the UK internet'. *Parliamentary Affairs*, www.open.ac.uk/socialsciences/staff/rcollins/networks_markets_hierarchies.pdf [November 2005].

Collins, R. and Murroni, C. (1996) *New Media, New Policies: Media and Communications Strategies for the Future*. Cambridge: Polity Press.

Commission of the European Communities (1996a) *Communication on the Implications of the Information Society for European Union Policies – Preparing the Next Steps*. Brussels: COM(96) 395; 24 July.

Commission of the European Communities (1996b) *Green Paper on the Protection of Minors and Human Dignity in Audiovisual and Information Services*. Brussels: COM(96) 483; 16 October.

Commission of the European Communities (1996c) *Illegal and Harmful Content on the Internet*. Brussels: COM(96)487; 16 October.

Commission of the European Communities (1997) *Green Paper on the Convergence of the Telecommunications, Media and Information Technology Sectors and the Implications for Regulation: Towards and Information Society Approach*. Brussels: COM(97)623; 3 December.

Commission of the European Communities (2005) *Proposal for a Directive of the European Parliament and of the Council amending Council Directive 89/552/EEC*. Brussels, COM(2005) 646 final 2005/0260 (COD); 13 December.

Cross, G. (1997) *Kids' Stuff: Toys and the Changing World of American Childhood*. Cambridge, MA: Harvard University Press.

Davies, M.M. and Corbett, B. (1997) *The Provision of Children's Television in Britain: 1992–1996:*

An Enquiry for the Broadcasting Standards Commission. London: Broadcasting Standards Commission.

Drotner, K. (1988) *English Children and their Magazines, 1751–1945*. New Haven, CT: Yale University Press.

Drotner, K. (1992) 'Modernity and media panics' in Skovmand, Michael, and Schröder, Kim (eds.) *Media Cultures. Reappraising Transnational Media*. London: Routledge.

Electronic Frontiers Australia (2006) *Internet Censorship in Australia*. www.efa.org.au/Issues/Censor/Cens 1.html [February 2006].

Federal Communications Commission (1969) *Federal Communications Commission Reports*, 21(2d), 3 December.

Federal Communications Commission (1985) *Federal Communications Commission Reports*, 100(2d), 6 May.

Gardener, W. (2003) 'The Sexual Offences Bill: progress and the future'. In *Tackling Sexual Grooming Conference*, 29 September. www.childnet-int.org/downloads/online-grooming2.pdf [November 2005].

Goode, E. and Ben-Yehuda, N. (1994) *Moral Panics: The Social Construction of Deviance*. Oxford: Blackwell.

Grainger, G. (1998) 'Freedom of expression and regulation of information in cyberspace: issues concerning potential international cooperation principles for cyberspace'. Speech to UNESCO International Congress, 1 September. www.aba.gov.au/newspubs/speeches/documents/ggmon98.pdf [November 2005].

Hall, S., Crichter, C., Jefferson, T., Clarke, J. and Roberts, B. (1978) *Policing the Crisis: Mugging, the State and Law and Order*. London: Macmillan.

Herman, E. and McChesney, R. (1997) *The Global Media: The New Missionaries of Corporate Capitalism*. London: Cassell.

High Level Group on the Information Society (1994) (Martin Bangemann, Chair) *Europe and the Global Information Society: Recommendations to the European Council*. Brussels: European Commission; 26 May.

Hills, J. and Michalis, M. (1999) 'Is convergence a purely European obsession?' Paper presented to the *CCIS/Euricom Colloquium on The Political Economy of Convergence*. London: University of Westminster.

Hooper, R. (2005) 'Content regulation in the multiplatform multichannel digital age'. *Regulation in a Digital Environment Seminar*, Hong Kong, August. Ofcom: www.ofcom.org.uk/media/speeches/2005/08/hk [January 2006].

ICRA (2005) *ICRA Labelling System Specification*. Internet Content Rating Association. http://www.icra.org/systemspecification/ [February 2006].

Jordan, A. (1999) *The Three-Hour Rule: Insiders' Reactions*. Pennsylvania: Annenberg Public Policy Centre, University of Annenberg.

Kaiser Foundation (2004) *Parents, Media and Public Policy*. Washington: Kaiser Family Foundation.

Kapur, J. (1999) 'Out of control: television and the transformation of childhood in late capitalism'. In M. Kinder (ed.) *Kids Media Culture*. Durham, NC: Duke University Press.

Kiškis, M. and Petrauskas, R. (2006) 'Internet content regulation: implications for e-government'. *Journal of Information, Law and Technology*, (2–3). http://www2.warwick.ac.uk/fac/soc/law/elj/jilt/2005_2-3/kiskis-petrauskas/ [November 2005].

Kunkel, D. and Watkins, B. (1987) 'Evolution of children's television regulatory policy'. *Journal of Broadcasting and Electronic Media*, 31(4): 367–389.

Lessig, L. (1998) 'What things regulate speech: CDA 2.0 vs filtering'. *Jurimetrics*, 38: 629–670. (Draft available at www.cyber.harvard.edu/works/lessig/what_things.pdf).

Lessig, L. (1999) *Code and Other Laws of Cyberspace*. New York: Basic Books.

Livingstone, S. (2002) *Young People and New Media*. London: Sage.

Livingstone, S. and Bober, M. (2004) 'Regulating the internet at home: contrasting the perspectives of children and parents'. http://www.lse.ac.uk/collections/media@lse/pdf/SLstaff_page/Livingstone-Bober_Regulating_the_internet_at_home.pdf [November 2005].

Livingstone, S. and Bovill, M. (2001) 'Bedroom culture and the privatization of media use'. In S. Livingstone and M. Bovill (eds) *Children and their Changing Media Environment: A European Comparative Study*. Hillsdale, NJ: Lawrence Erlbaum Associates.

Loader, B. (1997) 'The governance of cyberspace'. In B. Loader (ed.) *The Governance of Cyberspace: Politics, Technology and Global Restructuring*. London: Routledge.

Luke, C. (1990) *Constructing the Child Viewer: A History of the American Discourse on Television and Children, 1950–1980*. New York: Praeger.

Lusted, D. (1985) 'A history of suspicion: educational attitudes to television'. In D. Lusted and P. Drummond (eds) *TV and Schooling*. London: British Film Institute.

Melody, W. (2003) 'Can the Internet economy be governed and if so, how?' *LSE Public Lecture*, 1 May. www.lse.ac.uk/collections/LSEPublicLectures AndEvents/pdf/20030501Melody.pdf [November 2006].

Murroni, C. and Irvine, N. (1998) *Access Matters*. London: IPPR.

Negroponte, N. (1986) *Being Digital.* London: Hodder and Stoughton.

Newburn, T. (1992) *Permission and Regulation: Law and Morals in Post- War Britain.* London: Routledge.

Newey, A. (1999) 'Freedom of expression: censorship in private hands'. In J. Liberty (ed.) *Liberating Cyberspace: Civil Liberties, Human Rights and the Internet.* London: Pluto Press.

Ofcom (2004) *Ofcom's Strategy and Priorities for the Promotion of Media Literacy: A Statement.* www.ofcom.org.uk [November 2005].

Oswell, D. (1998a) 'Early children's broadcasting in Britain, 1922–1964: programming for a liberal democracy'. *Historical Journal of Film, Radio and Television*, 18(3): 375–393.

Oswell, D. (1998b) 'The Place of "childhood" in internet content regulation: a case study of policy in the UK'. *International Journal of Cultural Studies*, 1(2): 271–291.

Oswell, D. (1999) 'The dark side of cyberspace: internet content regulation and child protection'. *Convergence*, 5(4): 42–62.

Oswell, D. (2002) *Television, Childhood and the Home: A History of the Making of the Child Television Audience in Britain.* Oxford: Oxford University Press.

Oswell, D. (2006) 'When images matter: internet child pornography, forms of observation and an ethics of the virtual'. *Information, Communication and Society*, 9(2): 244–265.

Pearson, G. (1983) *Hooligan: A History of Respectable Fears.* London: Macmillan.

Programme in Comparative Media Law and Policy (1999) *Final Report: Parental Control of Television Broadcasting.* http://ec.europa.eu/avpolicy/info_centre/library/studies/index_en.htm#finalised [September 2007].

Programme in Comparative Media Law and Policy (2005) *Internet Self-Regulation: An Overview.* www.selfregulation.info/iapcoda/030329-selfreg-global-report.htm [November 2005].

Prosser, T. (2000) 'International lessons on law and regulation'. In T. Lees, S. Ralph and J. Langham Brown (eds) *Is Regulation Still and Option in a Digital Universe?* Luton: University of Luton Press.

Price, M. and Verhulst, S. (2005) *Self-Regulation and the Internet.* The Hague, The Netherlands: Kluwer Law International.

Reidenberg, J. (1996) 'Governing networks and cyberspace rule-making'. *Emory Law Journal*, 45: 911.

Rowland, W. (1997) 'Television violence redux: the continuing mythology of effects'. In M. Barker, and J. Petley (eds) *Ill Effects: The Media/Violence Debate.* London: Routledge.

Spigel, L. (1992) *Make Room for TV.* Chicago, IL: University of Chicago Press.

Starr, S. (2003) 'Responsible regulation'. *Spiked*, 23 July. www.spiked-online.com/Printable/00000006DE74.htm [February 2006].

Stein, L. and Sinha, N. (2002) 'New global media and communication policy: the role of the state in the twenty-first century'. In L. Lievrouw and S. Livingstone (eds) *The Handbook of New Media.* London: Sage.

Thompson, G. (2003) *Between Hierarchies and Markets: The Logic and Limits of Network Forms of Organization.* Oxford: Oxford University Press.

Tracey, M. and Morrison, D. (1979) *Whitehouse.* London: Macmillan.

Verhulst, S. (2002) 'About scarcities and intermediaries: the regulatory paradigm shift of digital content reviewed'. In L. Lievrouw and S. Livingstone (eds) *The Handbook of New Media.* London: Sage.

Walkerdine, V. and Lucey, H. (1989) *Democracy in the Kitchen: Regulating Mothers and Socialising Daughters.* London: Virago.

Wall, D. (2001) 'Cybercrime and the internet'. In D. Wall (ed.) *Crime and the Internet.* London: Routledge.

Wertham, F. (1954) *Seduction of the Innocent.* New York, Rinehart.

Williams, M. (2004) 'Cybercrime'. In J. Mitchell Miller (ed.) *Encyclopaedia of Criminology.* London: Routledge.

Williams, M. (2006) 'Policing and cybersociety: the maturation of regulation within an online community'. *Policing and Society* 16(4). www.cybercrimeresearch.com/Williams,%20M%20(2006)%20Policing%20and%20Cybersociety.pdf [February 2006].

Williams, N. (1999) *The Contribution of Hotlines to Combating Child Pornography on the Internet.* www.childnet-int.org/downloads/combating-child-pornography.pdf [February 2006].

Wilson-Thomas, C. (1996) 'Report on legislation related to pornography and obscenity: the case for reform'. In Parliamentary All Party Family and Child Protection Group, *Violence, Pornography and the Media*, 25 June.

29

Facilitating Political Participation: Young Citizens, Internet and Civic Cultures

Peter Dahlgren and Tobias Olsson

INTRODUCTION

In the context of the dilemmas of Western liberal democracy, the apparent lack of civic engagement, especially among the young, has become a topic of growing concern. Further, the role of the internet and other newer forms of interactive communication technologies has been aired considerably over the past decade, with various positions being asserted in regard to the role of these media in positively enhancing the pubic sphere and political participation. At the same time, manifestations of newer forms of political participation, where younger citizens and new communication technologies are often central elements, are also drawing research attention. In the discussion that follows, we bring together these trajectories, integrating them into a unified research horizon.

Thus, in the first section of the presentation, we review and engage with some of the major conceptual issues about the political role of the internet among young people. We begin with the basic arguments about internet and democratic participation in the public sphere. From there we turn to the theme of youth and political engagement, highlighting socio-cultural perspectives and the role of the internet. In the second section, we summarize the civic cultures framework and its six dimensions that we have been developing in this regard, and illustrate it in the third section with some empirical examples. The concluding fourth section pulls together the main points, arguing for a multi-perspective approach, and indicates further research directions.

Our argument, in brief, is that the role of new media is qualified and filtered through frameworks of civic cultures, especially the dimension of civic identities. We conceptualize civic cultures as multidimensional cultural patterns that offer resources relevant for political engagement. Using examples from an ongoing research project on young activists aged 16 to 19, we suggest that people's identities as political agents are central for understanding the political use of the internet – and that this is particularly true among youth. Also, the civic cultures perspective can help us get a better understanding of the particular forms that such engagement takes. Further, we underscore that the net must be seen as an integrated element of a larger media milieu which has relevance for political participation – it cannot be understood in isolation. In this regard, the use of the net in relationship to mainstream media also takes on considerable importance.

We posit, moreover, that in using the internet as a tool to pursue their political activities, these young citizens are themselves impacting on civic cultures. Our study builds on interviews with young activists working, on the one hand, within the youth groups of the parliamentarian political parties and, on the other hand, in extra-parliamentarian settings. These include environmentalists, feminists and advocates of alter-globalization. These young activists, all of whom are very skilled in using new media technology, integrate and adapt their use of the net into their respective political horizons. They use the net in different ways and thereby contribute to shaping two basic modes of civic cultures, as well as two different versions of civic identities.

INTERNET, POLITICS, YOUTH: CONCEPTUAL HORIZONS

The internet and political participation

The internet's significance for the public sphere and the life of democracy has been a recurrent theme within research, as well as in popular debates, for about a decade now (Holmes, 1997; Poster, 1997; Hague and Loader, 1999; Hoff *et al.*, 2000; Margolis and Resnick, 2000; Meikle, 2002; Shane, 2004; Dahlgren, 2000, 2005). Some of this literature emphasizes traditional political parties (e.g. Nixon and Johansson, 1999; Anderson and Cornfield; 2003; Bimber and Davis, 2003; Gibson *et al.*, 2003). Other, more recent efforts have extra-parliamentarian settings as their focus (e.g., Castells, 1997; Caemmerts and van Audenhove, 2003; McCaughey and Ayers, 2003; Kahn and Kellner, 2004; van de Donk, 2004; de Jong *et al.*, 2005; Caemmerts and Carpentier, 2006; Dahlgren, 2007a). In addition, there have been contributions using statistical studies that have tried to present an overarching view of the internet's political significance through an analysis of the access to and the use of the internet among various groups of users (cf. Wilhelm, 2000; Quan-Haase *et al.*, 2002).

These discussions (especially in the early days of internet research) often had a certain theoretical bias. In simple terms, the net's political significance was estimated by merely looking at the technology itself, by analysing aspects of its form. It has, for example, been asserted that the net's interactivity, co-presence of vertical and horizontal communication, disintermediation, speed and its absence of boundaries would foreground a new, different public sphere (Bentivegna, 2002), one that would follow network logic (e.g. Barney, 2004; Hassan, 2004). Moreover, some of the relevant literature also suffers from a lack of a 'media perspective', not treating the internet as part of a larger, integrated media environment, as several have argued (e.g. Olsson, 2002; Livingstone, 2004). In addition, much of the research has taken a macro, overarching perspective of internet and democracy, and not paid much attention to the internet's significance in the context of the more concrete practices of political engagement in everyday life.

Two basic contending perspectives emerged in regard to the role of internet in democracy. One view posits that, while there have been some interesting changes for the way democracy works, on the whole, the import of the internet is modest; the net is not deemed to be a factor of transformation (e.g. Margolis and Resnick, 2000). This 'business as usual' view acknowledges that the major political actors may engage in online campaigning, lobbying, policy advocacy, organizing and so forth, but claims the overall political landscape remains basically the same. It is noted that even the consequences of modest experiments to incorporate the internet formally into the political system with 'e-democracy' have not been overwhelming (e.g. Malina, 2003). The alternative perspective, on the other hand, asserts that the internet is a significant resource for political change, contributing to the transformation of the institutions of democracy and the modes of participation. This 'catalyst' view argues that internet impacts particularly on the public sphere.

What should be emphasized is that the 'business as usual' perspective, strong within political communication, is anchored in sets of assumptions that largely do not see beyond the formal political system, and the traditional role of the media in that system. Indeed, much of the evidence is based on electoral politics in the USA (cf. Hill and Hughes, 1998). While the problems of democracy are acknowledged, this view is that the solutions lie in revitalizing the traditional models of political participation and patterns of political communication. The alternative, 'catalyst' view takes as its point of departure the understanding that we are moving into a new, transitional era in which the certitudes of the past in regard to how democracy works have become problematic – a view that we share. Democracy is seen to be, precariously, at a new historical juncture, and in this context, the impact of internet use becomes significant. While few observers would dismiss the central importance of electoral politics, the alternative view underscores the growth and importance of what we can call advocacy or issue politics, often in the form of ongoing campaigns or social movements outside parliamentarian party politics, representing versions of 'new' politics (called 'life politics' by Giddens (1991) and 'sub-politics' by Beck (1998)). Such politics can materialize all over the social terrain and manifest itself in many contexts, including popular culture.

When it comes to empirical research on the internet as an institution of the public sphere, studies focusing on what is happening online have been numerous. We can, for instance, note the early collection by Tsagarousianou *et al.* (1998), which presents and analyses different efforts in digitalizing municipal communication in various cities. Another frequent type of study is analyses of online forums. In a considerable way, they have looked into the dynamics of online discussions and to what extent the internet facilitates (or not) a Habermasian inclusive, rational and deliberating public sphere (Hill and Hughes, 1998; Wilhelm, 2000; Dahlberg, 2001a,b; Stromer-Galley, 2002). There is also a broader literature of relevance, addressing the internet and other newer communication technologies from broad socio-cultural perspectives (e.g. the collection by Lievrouw and Livingstone (2006)), as well as more specific studies on the uses of internet, not least focusing on everyday practices and perception of among various groups (Bakardijeva and Smith, 2001; Olsson, 2006. See also Wellman and Haythornthwaite (2002) and Warschauer (2003)).

Young citizens and 'new politics'

In looking at the young in Western democracies, we can say that, basically, they manifest the same tendencies towards disengagement from formal politics as do adults, though more strongly so. Young people today in the West tend to have a low trust in politics and politicians, though they still affirm their support for democracy (Amnå (1999) gathers a number of commissioned studies in Sweden on this theme). Bennett (2007), in synthesizing a number of international studies (among them, IDEA, 1999; Pirie and Worcester, 2000; Instito di Ricerci, Milan, 2001; Deutches Jugend Institut, 2003; Keeter *et al.*, 2002), concludes that young citizens often feel personally remote from the formal political system. They say that they have difficulty identifying with the political actors, who are usually much older and do not seem to have insight into the life situations of youth. European experience suggests such difficulties are so deep that they lie beyond what the schools can do in terms of civic education (Ferry and De Proost, 2003).

Moreover, the origins of these trends are to be found in the larger patterns that shape late modern society and the life courses of young people. Vinken (2007) summarizes research on this theme (e.g. Beck *et al.*, 1994; Bynner *et al.*, 1997; Howe and Strauss, 2000; Mayer, 2000; Chauvel, 2002; Heinz and Marshall, 2003; Thomson *et al.*, 2004). He notes that, for many young people, much time and energy is spent on what is termed 'identity work': they are engaged in formulating who they are, what life goals they want to strive for, what their vocational calling will be. This kind of 'reflexive biographization' emerges as the life courses of late modern society become increasingly 'de-standardized', forcing young people increasingly to develop newer, flexible personal strategies. The processes of individualization translate into resistance towards external control and collective solutions, scepticism towards traditional authority, loose institutional loyalties, and an avoidance of 'long marches' through organizational structures. Young people do value having influence and tend to demand participation and desire community if they are to become engaged in social issues. Party politics, however, increasingly tends not to fulfil these needs for them. Neither do they reflect much class identification.

Identities are shaped increasingly via consumption, leisure and popular culture, to the point that classic discussions about the transmission of cultural values from the older generation to the young have been renewed (Pasquier, 2005). In terms of political socialization, many young people say that their parents seldom talk about politics, thus further loosening the 'passing on of political tradition' within the family (Sörbom, 2002). Coleman (2006) has been studying how and why young people seemingly are more engaged in voting in *Big Brother* than in political elections, suggesting that, among other things, that such popular cultural phenomena should not *a priori* be defined as beyond the political. Many viewers see the issues arising in such programmes as central to their sense of 'life politics'. Also, they feel they are offered stronger experiences of being represented there than in the formal arena of politics, from which they feel estranged.

While young people have generally a good orientation about societal matters, they tend not to have detailed political information (Boggs, 2000). However, among those of middle-class background, many have a high capacity in handling information and the new media, giving them a sense of self-confidence and social competence. For those active in alternative politics, the boundary between the political and the personal, especially normative concerns about, for example, how we live, about gender, about our environment, about what we eat, is no longer so rigid. The private domain can become a springboard for political concerns and engagement, with issues of identity often intertwining with societal engagement. In reflecting on this theme, Buckingham (2000) comments that part of the problem is that modern society has tended to equate politics with the public arena. In other words, society operates on (and hands down to the young) a constricted notion of the political. Buckingham argues that a sense of the political actually emerges for children early in life – within the family, school, neighbourhood. Politics in this sense has not just to do with the traditional arena dominated by political parties; in principle, it can concern questions about rights, privileges, obligations, rules, power in any social circumstance (see Dahlgren (2007a)).

In the arena of new politics, the internet becomes not only relevant, but also central: it is especially the capacity for the 'horizontal communication' of civic interaction that is paramount, as well as the social learning that it facilitates (see Dahlgren (2007b)). Access to the net and to other new technologies, such as mobile phones, has helped facilitate the growth of large digital networks of activists. While the internet makes political participation easier, we would not argue that it actually recruits people to politics. The interviews in our own study suggest that engagement among the young activists was not prompted by the internet per se, but emerged as a result of various experiences in their lives. Certainly, the net has relevance here, but it would be misleading to claim that it was an independent factor in promoting engagement. We can, however, say that it at least serves as an incomparable tool for those who are politically active. Relative to the population as a whole, the numbers of young people who are actually politically involved are probably rather modest. However, the embryonic patterns taking shape within these new politics may, with historical hindsight in the future, prove to have been quite significant (Granjon, 2001; Graber *et al.*, 2002).

CIVIC CULTURES AS AN ANALYTIC FRAME

The research themes addressed here cluster within the broad field of media and communication studies, but have been shaped to a great extent by some particular traditions, chiefly political communication, public sphere theory and, to a lesser degree, cultural theory – or what we call the culturalist perspective. We see these three traditions as basically complementary. This is not the place for a comparative discussion (see Dahlgren (2004) for a more detailed exposition), but we just wish to suggest that, despite their disparate qualities and respective limitations, each has something to offer. We emphasize, however, the particular importance of the culturalist perspective, which accentuates, among other things, citizenship in terms of meaning, identity and social agency (e.g. Clarke, 1996; Preston, 1997; Isin and Wood, 1999). It can turn our attention to the subjective realities of citizenship, their processes of sense making in concrete settings, and how these may impact on participation and the modes of (dis)engagement.

The culturalist perspective provides the inspiration for our own research framework of civic cultures (Dahlgren, 2003, 2006). This framework seeks to conceptualize the factors that can promote or impede political participation. We use the plural form of civic cultures to underscore that there are many ways of enacting citizenship in late modern society. Taking the notion of political agency as a starting point, we see citizenship as a mode of individual and collective action, and try to probe the cultural conditions that can impinge on this identity, that strengthen (or weaken) people's perceptions of their civic selves. Cultures consist of patterns of communication, practices and meaning; they provide taken-for-granted orientations (factual and normative), as well as other resources for collective life. They are internalized, intersubjectively, guiding and informing action, speech and understanding. We can thus think of civic cultures as cultural patterns in which identities as citizens are an integrated part.

Civic cultures are resources, storehouses of assets which individuals and groups draw upon and make use of in their activities as citizens. Civic cultures are potentially both strong and fragile. They can shape citizens; they can serve to empower or disempower. At the same time, they are shaped by an array of factors: the nature of the legal system, factors of social structure, economics, education, organizational possibilities, infrastructure and spatiality can all have their impact. Class position, not to mention the specific histories of democracy (or its absence) impact strongly; for example, the experience of colonial oppression or authoritarian political systems will be visible in civic cultures. For our purposes here, however, we emphasize the media-related factors that impact on civic cultures, in particular the internet.

Conceptually, civic culture can be modelled as an integrated circuit of six dimensions of mutual reciprocity, underscoring their dynamic and contingent character. The first three are familiar from the tradition of political communication, the last three emerge from cultural theory: (1) knowledge, (2) values, (3) trust, (4) spaces, (5) practices and skills, and (6) identities. The circuit metaphor underlines their reciprocal interaction, but there is, of course, never anything mechanical or inevitable about how cultures operate. In terms of understanding civic agency, we suggest that identities and practices are the most compelling, though the interplay between all six should be kept in mind.

Knowledge: active appropriation

That citizens need knowledge in order to participate politically is obvious and basic. People must have access to reliable reports, portrayals, analyses, discussions, debates and so forth about current affairs and society in general. This can be accomplished in many ways; however, in the modern world the media play a key role in this regard. This role is problematic, as we know. Accessibility, for instance, has to do not just with technical and economic aspects, but also with linguistic and cultural proximity. The sources of knowledge must be comprehensible, cast in modes that communicate well with different collectivities, reiterating the need for multiple modes of journalism and political communication. Some degree of literacy is essential; people must be able to make sense of that which circulates in public spheres, to understand the world they live in. To speak of knowledge in this regard presupposes that it builds upon the raw material of 'information' and that information is in some way made meaningful to become knowledge. Also, precisely what kinds of knowledge are required for the vitality of civic cultures can never be established once and for all, but must always be open for discussion, especially given that forms of knowledge evolve, not least in the modern digital landscape.

Values: anchored in the everyday

Democracy will not function if such virtues as tolerance and willingness to follow democratic principles and procedures do not have a grounding in everyday life. Even support for the legal system (assuming it is legitimate) is an expression of such virtue: democracy will not survive a situation of widespread lawlessness. Reports from troubled zones around the world confirm this. Just which are the 'best' or 'real' democratic values, and how they are to be applied, can, of course, be the grounds for serious dispute – and should be. It is precisely in such situations that the procedural mechanisms take on extra importance, where fundamental views are wrestled with, yet there exists a framework of rules by which all parties abide. Resolution of conflict, striving for compromise in situations where consensus is impossible, is a key task for a democratic society and requires a commitment to the rules of the game. The conceptual necessity that these are integrated into the taken-for-granted sensibilities of daily life reminds us that, fundamentally, democracy is as much about a democratic society – how people live together and treat each other – as it is about a system of institutional frameworks.

Trust: optimal and focused

Trust has long been seen as an important component for democracy; it has been presented as a self-evident 'good thing' – the more trust, the better; and declines in trust signal trouble. The bearers of trust are usually seen as the citizens, and the objects of trust are the institutions or representatives of government. More recently, however, the theme of trust among or between groups of citizens has also been explored, and in the context of political participation and the collective action it requires, horizontal civic trust is clearly vital. While trust is usually accorded a positive role in democracy, there are some paradoxes at work (see Warren (1999)): minimal degrees of trust are necessary to make life bearable, but very high trust (i.e. a lack of scepticism and critical thinking) is also unsuitable. Such excessive trust can in fact suppress conflict and sustain oppressive relations. Trust must be balanced with a built-in antenna for scepticism.

Spaces: communicative contexts of action

There are still many situations where people can and do talk to each other face to face, and where the political can potentially still rear its head. With the media, of course, the conditions for civic encounter expand; possible civic communicative spaces multiply. Historically, the mass media contributed to the reconfiguration of private and public space; and, as we continue with the interactive electronic media, we see an intensification of the sense of being co-present with others who are physically removed, contributing to the growth of 'despatialized simultaneity' (Thompson, 1995), where the experience of a shared now is uncoupled from the imperatives of physical proximity. Moreover, the new telephony is contributing to mobile publicness, where cultures of civil society are increasingly in geographic transit, as citizens move about and yet communicate with each other (see Scheller and Urry (2003), Drotner (2005) and Stald (2007)). Thus, new communicative spaces are emerging in which civic cultures can develop and flourish, and in which the political can be developed, and where politics can be pursued (e.g. Barnett and Low, 2004; Couldry and McCarthy, 2004). For civic cultures, the availability and accessibility of suitable communicative space (physical and virtual) is crucial.

Practices: embodied agency and skills

A viable democracy must be embodied in concrete, recurring practices (individual, group, and collective) relevant for diverse situations. Such practices help generate personal and social meaning to the ideals of democracy, and they must have an element of the routine, of the taken for granted about them, if they are to be a part of civic cultures. Practices can be and are learned; they often require specific skills, especially communicative competencies. Thus, to be able to read, write, speak, work a computer and get around on the internet can all be seen as competencies important for modern democratic practices. Education will thus always play a key role in nurturing democracy, even if its contents and pedagogic approaches periodically need to be scrutinized and debated.

Participating in elections is usually seen as the paramount concrete practice for democracy's citizens. Talk, too, has a prominent position, and has been associated with democracy and opinion formation from the start. Yet, civic cultures require other practices as well, pertinent to various political projects and circumstances. For example, having the social competence to call and hold a meeting, identifying issues, managing a discussion, and organizing and administering collective activities, are all important practices involving skills. Lobbying, bargaining, negotiating, mobilizing, initiating legal action, networking, and other activities can also be a part of a repertoire of civic practices.

Today's democracy needs to be able to refer to a past, without being locked in it. New practices and traditions can and must evolve to ensure that democracy does not stagnate. We see today how the lack of civic practices, skills, and traditions is an obstacle for many citizens in many societies attempting to develop their democratic character. Skills can develop through practices, and in this process promote a sense of empowerment. Practices interplay forcefully with knowledge, trust and values; practices involve defining, using, or creating suitable spaces, and, most compellingly, practices help enhance civic identities.

Identities: recognition, empowerment, affinity

We return, thus, to identities, to the theme of people's subjective views of themselves as members and participants of democracy. As a foundation for agency, identities can be seen as the centerpiece of civic cultures, with the other dimensions contributing, reciprocally, to shaping the conditions of its existence. Today, identity is understood as plural: in our daily lives we operate in a multitude of different 'worlds' or realities; we carry within us different sets of knowledge, assumptions, rules and roles for different circumstances, we operate in different registers in different contexts.

There are many ways of being a citizen and of doing democracy; civic identities are protean and multivalent, and evolve via civic cultures in relation to social milieus and institutional mechanisms. Analytically, a robust civic identity implies an empowered political agent and achieved citizenship. Engagement in issues becomes meaningful, citizens feel that they, in concert with others, can in some way make a difference, that they can have some kind of impact on political life, or least make a contribution in a political struggle. Civic identities involve some sense of political community, or affinity, with other, like-minded people. The emergence of sets of 'we–they' polarities, with the corresponding degrees of trust and suspicion, becomes important. Such positions are always to some degree in transition, as political issues and even ideologies evolve. A big challenge to civic identities in late modern democracies is that they can be overpowered by identities relating to consumption, which get considerably more reinforcement from the dominant media culture.

INTERNET AND CIVIC CULTURES: SOME EMPIRICAL EXAMPLES

Our research project thus far (see Olsson (2004, 2005a,b)) focuses on two sets of young activists aged 16–19; they all belong to the generation of young Swedes for whom the internet has been a natural part of their school environment; all of them even have some kind of formal education in internet use. We see, though the interviews, how their political engagement relates to their civic identities and, more generally, how the internet facilitates their participation. In a sense, these youngsters can be seen as 'deviants', in that political engagement is far from the norm among their peers. Also, it is apparent that the two groups generate two different versions of civic culture, not just because they have different political views, but because they have different understandings of what constitutes politics. The internet does not impose a uniform mode of engagement upon the two groups; they use the internet in somewhat different ways.

The first example illustrates typically the position of the net in their everyday lives. Patrik is 16 years old and has been a member of one of the political parties' youth organization for a year:

Interviewer: Could you describe an ordinary week in your life?

Patrik: Hmmm... That's hard... But I usually get up early in the morning, around five o'clock. Then I take a shower and... I usually tap into my e-mail, then I go to school. That's one of the most important things; one never knows what one might have missed out on during the night. So I guess I answer to some e-mails in the morning. [...]

Interviewer: How much time to you spend with the internet everyday?

Patrik: About an hour or an hour and a half. But then you also... I do a lot of LAN [Local Area Network] too, at nights and stuff.

Just as almost all of the other respondents, Patrik is a quite extensive user of the internet. All the respondents most obviously have the *skills* to navigate and make use of the net as communicative *space*. These routine practices provide them not only with knowledge, but also serve to reinforce, on a daily basis, their *identities* as active civic agents. They are offered a form of confirmation. Also, the fact that the questions they feel strongly about are accorded importance by the traditional media confirms the mainstream character of these identities.

The fact that the internet is well integrated into the routines of everyday life becomes even more obvious if we turn to what seems to be one of the main internet practices among the young, active citizens: using the internet in order to stay up to date on current issues and to gain *knowledge* of relevance to their roles as active citizens. This is done in a couple of different but interrelated ways. To start with, the respondents spend a lot of time keeping up to date on the news through the internet (Olsson, 2004), a widespread practice among Swedish internet users (Bergström, 2005). But there are also other relevant dimensions here. First, their use of the internet to seek information from various primary sources and, second, their seeking of what we might call alternative information through the internet. An extract from the interview with Rita, a 17-year-old activist within the alter-globalization movement, illustrates the latter point quite well. To her – as to all other extra-parliamentarian activists in the study – the internet is an important resource when it comes to seek out alternative information connected to her political interests, i.e. information and perspectives not provided by the dominant mass media:

Interviewer: Mmmm... But I thought... When it comes to your ideas on important political issues... The media [traditional media, such as TV, radio and newspapers] covers that. Aren't you interested in that?

Rita: Yes, well of course... That's what I read in the papers and what I watch when I watch TV, of course. But... anyhow... There're a lot of internet sites where there're a lot of people who are interested in [for instance] environmental issues and... You know, you talk to people and get to know about forthcoming events. There you can read and also check up on things... That's an important way of reaching out and I guess that's [the kind of information] I try to seek out on the internet.

Rita carefully makes the point that she is not too impressed by the traditional media's way of presenting news about her areas of political interest. The themes that are of special interest to her (environmental issues and global equality) are not covered extensively by the traditional media, and when they are covered they are framed to reproduce the mainstream interpretation of the issues. Instead, for her, the internet makes up a much better source of information when it comes to issues of alter-globalization. On the internet Rita not only finds the information she needs, but also in various public spheres on the net she can also interact with people sharing her views and exchange experiences. All in all, this points to the fact that the internet has been shaped into a tool for alternative learning, a tool making it possible for the young, active citizens to bypass traditional media and their views of the world in their search for various kinds of knowledge.

Another dimension in civic cultures is loyalty to *democratic values* and procedures. The internet's role in this regard is not a directly observable phenomenon, it happens implicitly. As such, it is rather difficult to bring up empirical examples. However, it is possible at least to 'sense' this process from the concrete practices that the respondents present. Thus, it can be argued that as the young, active citizens use the internet, they inevitably become involved in discussions and debates. Even if this takes place largely on sites where they encounter like-minded participants, this suggests the existence of sets of assumptions about, for example, equality, reciprocity, discursive ethics and other aspects that pertain to democratic values and procedures. The participation in these debates – at least to the extent that they resemble the communicative ethos of a democratic discussion – would logically help fostering such loyalty.

Similarly, the *trust* dimension within the notion of civic cultures is not directly revealed through interview data. On the other hand, we have good reasons to claim that at least trust towards other citizens evolves out of the affinity manifested by the internet practices of the young, active citizens. In dealing with people of similar political persuasion, a degree of trust is likely to emerge. To what extent it carries over to people with differing views would need to be explored further. Also, at least some qualified trust in certain democratic institutions would seemingly also be implied by such participation, and would in all likelihood be enhanced by continued engagement.

A key *practice* that involves net use is that of the coordination of political activities.

For instance, Asta, who holds an important local-level position within her alternative political organization, describes in more detail in which way the internet is a resource for coordination:

Interviewer: [B]ut you also said Green Globalisation…

Asta: E-mail lists… We've got one for [the local group]. You subscribe to that list and then you can hand out… if you want to send something to all members in this [local area]. […] I use that quite a lot to hand out schedules and calls for meeting. […]

Interviewer: That's locally, but do you have one for the regional level?

Asta: Yes, one for the region as well as one for the whole nation. We also have a newspaper […] for all members. Then we also have […] There are networks too, like 'the network for the forests' and they also have e-mail lists. We also have a list for the people in the board, there we mostly… well… send protocols and discuss places to meet and when we've to set up the next meeting.

In the extract, Asta describes how she and her alter-globalization movement make use of the internet for organizational purposes. To start with they use e-mail lists on the local level. Through them she receives and delivers information on, for instance, new meetings and schedules. But she also mentions the regional lists from which she continuously gets information. Her organization, Green Globalisation, also makes use of e-mail lists on a national level, including all Swedish activists. Then the movement also has additional lists partially outside the movement's 'formal' organization, connecting activists with other movements that have similar interests. Asta's story is by no means unique; most of the respondents tell similar stories. Through this coordination, Asta and other active citizens learn about how political organizations work and how to coordinate political activities.

There are a variety of other practices that centre around net use. One interesting example comes from the interview with Sara, who is involved in the alter-globalization movement, but who also calls herself an antifascist and a feminist. In the interview she explains how she lately has started to make a particular use of the internet as a resource in her everyday activism:

Sara: [We're into] ad-busting, that's something new, where we… You know… unethical commercials… We collect information about the company in question in order to make sure that we're right to criticize them. Then we've – if it is perhaps sexist commercials – balloons that say: 'You can't buy me', that we put on the ads. Or: 'The ad has been taken away due to its unethical message'.

Interviewer: What's the name of the web site?

Sara: [Addestruction.org (in Swedish: reklamsabotage.org)]… But you have to be careful, you need to check on your facts before you move on to action. If you get it wrong it'll be destructive for the whole organization.

Interviewer: How does it work?

Sara: They've for instance… You can order and then print these balloons and they also have instructions about how you can go about. But we're careful not to destroy anything. We're only trying to make people open their eyes.

Basically, what Sara and her activist friends are up to is the destruction of what they perceive to be unethical, commercial messages, mainly by slightly changing their content by help of adding messages to them. In this practice the internet is an indispensable resource. On websites such as reklamsabotage.org – which is a kind of Swedish equivalence to the internationally famous adbusters.org – she and her friends find the necessary material for this destruction: stickers with pre-printed alternative messages, models for posters and also a gallery to inspire the creation of alternative messages.

In terms of the *identity* aspect of civic cultures, there are a lot of interesting issues to consider. In a way we have already seen elements of the internet's contribution to the civic identity among the young activists. Internet practices, such as organizational coordination and participation in internal and external debates, also have a qualitative, subjective side to them; as such, they also encourage and cultivate the perception of active citizen among these young people. But there are additional and more obvious examples of how the internet contributes to civic identity.

First, and perhaps paradoxically, when it comes to the respondents affiliated with the political parties' youth organization, the internet is used to participate in web-based nonsense discussions. Marcus, who is 18 years old and holds an important position within his youth party organization, presents a typical example. He is often involved in nonsense discussions within his political party on the internet. On a weekly basis, and in a humorous manner, the most hippie-like person in the party is elected. Not without a sense of pride, Marcus also reveals that he himself once had the honour of becoming 'hippie of the week'. Marcus's participation in the hippie elections, of course, encourages his identity as both a socially integrated member of his party and as politically active in general. The humour is no doubt an important element, expanding his sense of self to include a frivolous, fun dimension. Second, the internet's contribution to civic identity appears even more obvious among the respondents within the alternative political movements. For them, the internet is arguably the most important resource for the continuous cultivation of their civic identities. This is because they, to a great extent, consider themselves to be marginalized by traditional news media. Also, some of them are geographically remote from each other.

The interviews with the activists within the Animal Rights movement provide illustrative examples of their downgrading of traditional media and upgrading of the internet. For instance, Gina has rather clear ideas about what the problem is with traditional news media:

Interviewer: [Newspaper, what do you think of them?]

Gina: For reading about culture, they're good, but you can't really...

Interviewer: What's bad?

Gina: Perhaps that they get things wrong all the time, like in the case with the furrier's shop. It was this autumn, I think, and it got its thirtieth attack, I think, and the newspaper went: 'Militant vegetarians has destroyed the shop.' Then they just mention in passing that the attack in fact was conducted by a very specific organisation that's dealing with illegal actions. Thus, we [Gina's organization] end up [being blamed for things that we've not been involved in]. Cause we're legal! So I guess... how they put things... They could be more accurate.

It is rather obvious that Gina is not too impressed by how the newspapers present her Animal Rights movement. They are hardly represented in traditional news media, and her organization becomes heavily misrepresented when they occasionally do appear in the media – they are negatively angled and they quite often mistake her organization for another militant organization engaged in illegal activities.

CONCLUSIONS

The internet functions as an important tool for practices for both mainstream and alternative groups; yet, there is a difference. In the youth groups of the political parties, mail contact tends to follow, or at least recognize, the organizational structures. Within the alternative groups, which do not have such a clear organizational structure and a firm membership list, the internet becomes a kind of glue that actually helps hold the active participants together. While both groups meet face to face in various constellations and various extents, the particular net dependency in the case of the alternative groups underscores the centrality of this communication technology for not only identity, but also *trust* and *affinity*. It is thus apparent to the members of the respective camps that they belong to – and are nurtured in their engagement by – two different kinds of civic culture. Their respective practices contribute, in fact, to reproduce different forms of democratic engagement. There are, of course, similarities, yet these differences suggest that that the internet does not impose just one model of civic engagement or promote only one form of political participation. It is a rather open technology that can be adapted to a very wide variety of democratic purposes.

We have tried to demonstrate here the usefulness of a culturalist approach, as a complement to the more traditional horizons of political communication and the perspectives of public sphere theory, in understanding and researching the role of the internet in young people's democratic engagement. In particular, we feel that the framework of civic cultures, with its dimensions, helps us to focus our analytic attention, both theoretically and empirically, helping us to highlight, for example, how identity and practices/skills are operative dimensions of civic engagement. We find that, within distinctive versions of civic cultures, the internet is appropriated for particular strategies, even if it does shape in general terms the ways in which engagement is enacted. For alternative movements, given their stance of scepticism towards the mainstream mass media, the net becomes crucial.

Our study is a small-scale qualitative effort that still leaves important issues unanswered. For example, we would like to probe deeper into the question of how and why these particular young people became politically active: what factors were most decisive in their lives? What separates them from the large majority? For another thing, it would be useful to get a clearer quantitative picture of the numbers involved in political participation, but this is especially difficult with the alternative movements, given both the fluid character of much of such engagement, and even the contested notion of what constitutes the political. Which movements are 'genuinely political'? This, in turn, reminds us that we need to further problematize precisely the traditional distinction between politics and non-politics. While theorists of late modernity, such as Beck *et al.* (1994; Beck, 1998), and the media research of, for example, Coleman (2006) and Bennett (2007) open up this discussion, we need to further illuminate the issue both at the level of subjective experience and at the level of theoretical and conceptual development. Moreover, within the large area of media policy, it is clear that, in most contexts, there remains the dual problem of simply assuming that making the technology accessible will automatically enhance participation, and the overriding assumption that the market is the best way to ensure such distribution (e.g. see Olsson (2006) for an analysis of the Swedish situation).

While some may wish to argue that the alternative movements are still a small phenomenon and, thus, of minor importance, the decline in civic engagement is a problem of undeniable concern, and one that is clearly marked by a generational character: at present, nothing suggests that this will change in the future; in fact, an educated guess would be that disengagement among the young will grow and be carried forward as they get older. Here, we encounter a profoundly disturbing pattern in the established Western democracies, which is already making itself in the newer democracies. Research, allied on multidisciplinary fronts, has an enormous task here; the question is to what extent those holding power are willing to listen to uncomfortable results.

ACKNOWLEDGEMENTS

We wish to acknowledge a generous grant from the LearnIT Research School in Sweden that made the research and this text possible.

REFERENCES

Amnå, E. (ed.) (1999) *Det unga folkstyret.* SOU 1999:93. Stockholm: Fakta info direct.

Anderson, D.M. and Cornfield, M. (eds) (2003) *The Civic Web.* Lanham, MD: Rowman & Littlefield.

Bakardjieva, M. and Smith, R. (2001) 'The internet in everyday life: computer networking from the standpoint of the domestic user'. *New Media & Society*, 3(1): 67–84.

Barnett, C. and Low, M. (eds) (2004) *Spaces of Democracy.* London: Sage.

Barney, D. (2004) *The Network Society.* Cambridge: Polity Press.

Beck, U. (1998) *Democracy Without Enemies.* Cambridge: Polity Press.

Beck, U., Giddens, A. and Lash, S. (1994) *Reflexive Modernization.* Cambridge: Polity Press.

Bennett, W.L. (2007) 'Civic learning in changing democracies: challenges for citizenship and civic education'. In P. Dahlgren (ed.) *Young Citizens, New Media, and Learning for Democracy.* New York: Routledge.

Bentivegna, D. (2002) 'Politics and new media'. In L. Lievrouw and S. Livingstone (eds) *The Handbook of New Media.* London: Sage; 50–61.

Bergström, A. (2005) *Nyhetsvanpr.nu.* Gothenborg: Gothenborg University.

Bimber, B. and Davis, R. (2003) *Campaigning Online: The Internet in U.S. Elections.* Oxford University Press.

Boggs, C. (2000) *The End of Politics: Corporate Power and the Decline of the Public Sphere.* New York: Guilford Press.

Buckingham, D. (2000) *The Making of Citizens: Young People, News and Politics.* London: Routledge.

Bynner, J., Chisholm, L. and Furlong, A. (eds) (1997) *Youth, Citizenship and Social Change in a European Context.* Aldershot: Ashgate.

Caemmerts, B. and Carpentier, N. (eds) (2006) *Reclaiming the Media: Communication Rights and Democratic Media Roles.* Bristol: Intellect Books.

Caemmerts, B. and van Audenhove, L. (2003) *Transnational Social Movements, the Network Society and Unbounded Notions of Citizenship.* Amsterdam: ASCoR, University of Amsterdam.

Castells, M. (1997) *The Information Age: Economy, Society and Culture. Vol. 2: The Power of Identity.* Blackwell Publishers.

Chauvel, L. (2002) *Le Destin des Générations. Structure Sociale et Cohorts en France au XXe Siècle.* Paris: Presses universitaires de France.

Clarke, P. (1996) *Deep Citizenship.* London: Pluto.

Coleman, S. (2006) *How the Other Half Votes: Big Brother Viewers and the 2005 General Election.* London: Hansard Society.

Couldry, N. and McCarthy, A. (eds) (2004) *Mediaspace.* London: Routledge.

Dahlberg, L. (2001a) 'The internet and democratic discourse: exploring the prospects of online deliberative forums extending the public sphere'. *Information, Communication and Society*, 4(4): 615–633.

Dahlberg, L. (2001b) 'Democracy via cyberspace: examining the rhetoric and practises of three prominent camps'. *New Media & Society*, 3(2): 157–177.

Dahlgren, P. (2000) 'Media, citizenship and civic culture'. In J. Curran and M. Gurevitch (eds) *Mass Media and Society.* London: Arnold; 310–328.

Dahlgren, P. (2003) 'Reconfiguring civic culture in the new media milieu', in J. Curran and D. Pels (eds) *Media and the Restyling of Politics* . London: Sage, pp. 151–170.

Dahlgren, P. (2004) 'Theory, boundaries, and political communication: the uses of disparity'. *European Journal of Communication*, 19(1): 7–19.

Dahlgren, P. (2005) 'Internet, public spheres and political communication: dispersion and deliberation'. *Political Communication*, 22(2): 147–162.

Dahlgren, P. (2006) 'Doing citizenship: the cultural origins of civic agency in the public sphere'. *European Journal of Cultural Studies*, 9(3): 267–286.

Dahlgren, P. (2007a) 'Civic identity and net activism: the frame of radical democracy'. In L. Dahlberg and E. Siapera (eds) *Radical Democracy and the Internet.* London: Palgrave MacMillan.

Dahlgren, P. (ed.) (2007b) *Young Citizens and New Media: Learning for Democracy.* London: Routledge.

De Jong, W., Shaw, M. and Stammers, N. (eds) (2005) *Global Activism, Global Media.* London: Pluto Press.

Deutshes Jugend Institut (2003) 'Bulletin: On the state of young people and youth policy in Europe'. http://cgi.dji.de [21 July 2004].

Drotner, K. (2005) 'Media on the move: personalised media and the transformation of publicness'. In S. Livingstone (ed.) *Audiences and Publics: When Cultural Engagement Matters for the Public Sphere.* Bristol: Intellect.

Ferry, J.-M. and De Proost, S. (eds) (2003) *L'École au Défi de l'Europe.* Brussels: Éditions de l'Université de Bruxelles.

Gibson, R., Nixon, P. and Ward, S. (eds) (2003) *Political Parties and the Internet: Net Gain?.* Routledge.

Giddens, A. (1991) *Modernity and Self-Identity.* Cambridge: Polity Press.

Graber, D., Bimber, B., Bennett, L., Davis, R. and Norris, P. (2002) 'The internet and politics: emerging perspectives'. In M. Price and H. Nissenbaum (eds) *The Internet and the Academy.* London: Peter Lang; 1–16.

Granjon, F. (2001) *L'Internet Militant: Mouvement Social et Usage des Réseaux Télématiques*. Rennes: Èditions Apogée.

Hague, B. and Loader, B. (eds) (1999) *Digital Democracy: Discourse and Decision Making in the Information Age*. Routledge.

Hassan, R. (2004) *Media, Politics and the Network Society*. Open University Press.

Heinz, W.R. and Marshall, V.W. (eds) (2003) *Social Dynamics of the Life Course. Transitions, Institutions, and Interrelations*. New York: Aldine de Gruyter.

Hill, K. and Hughes, J. (1998) *Cyberpolitics: Citizen Activism in the Age of the Internet*. Lanham: Rowman & Littlefield Publishers.

Hoff, J., Horrocks, I. and Tops, P. (eds) (2000) *Democratic Governance and New Technology: Technologically Mediate Innovations in Political Practice in Western Europe*. Routledge.

Holmes, D. (ed.) (1997) *Virtual Politics: Identity & Community in Cyberspace*. Sage.

IDEA (1999) *Youth Voter Participation: Involving Young People in Tomorrow's Democracies*. Institute for Democracy and Electoral Assistance, Stockholm. www.idea.int/99df/daniela-int2.html [2 September 2007].

Isin, E. and Wood, P. (1999) *Citizenship and Identity*. London, Sage.

Howe, N. and Strauss, W. (2000) *Millennials Rising. The Next Great Generation*. New York: Vintage Books.

Istituto di Ricerca, Milan (2001) *Study on the State of Young People and Youth Policy in Europe*.

Kahn, R. and Kellner, D. (2004) 'New media and internet activism: from the "Battle of Seattle" to blogging'. *New Media and Society*, 6(1): 87–95.

Keeter, S., Zukin, C., Andoline, M. and Jenkins, K. (2002) 'The civic and political health of the nation: a generational portrait'. Center for Information and Research on Civic Learning and Engagement. www.civicyouth.org [2 September 2007].

Lievrouw, L.A. and Livingstone, S. (eds) (2006) *The Handbook of New Media*, 2nd edition. London: Sage.

Livingstone, S. (2004) 'The challenge of changing audiences: or, what is the audience researcher to do in the age of the internet'. *European Journal of Communication*, 19(1): 75–86.

Malina, A. (1999) 'Perspectives on citizen democratisation and alienation in the virtual public sphere'. In B. Hague and B. Loader (eds) *Digital Democracy and Decision Making in the Information Age*. Routledge.

Margolis, M. and Resnick, D. (2000) *Politics as Usual: The Cyberspace 'Revolution'*. Sage.

Mayer, K.U. (2000) 'Promises fulfilled? A review of 20 years of life course research'. *Archives Europeenes de Sociologie*, XLI(2): 259–282.

McCaughey, M. and Ayers, M. (eds) (2003) *Cyber-activism: Online Activism in Theory and Practice*. Routledge.

Meikle, G. (2002) *Future Active: Media Activism and the Internet*. Routledge/Pluto Press Australia.

Nixon, P. and Johansson, H. (1999) 'Transparency through technology: the internet and political participation'. In B. Hague and B. Loader (eds) *Digital Democracy: Discourse and Decision Making in the Information Age*. Routledge.

Olsson, T. (2002) *Mycket väsen om ingenting: hur datorn och internet undgår att formas till medborgarens tekniker* (*Much ado about nothing: How the computer and the Internet miss their plight as tools for the citizen*). PhD thesis, AUU, Uppsala Studies in Media and Communication.

Olsson, T. (2004) *Oundgängliga resurser: Om medier, IKT och lärande bland partipolitiskt aktiva ungdomar* (*Indispensable resources: on media, ICTs and learning among young, politically active people*). Lund: Department of Sociology, Lund University.

Olsson, T. (2005a) 'Young citizens ICT's and learning: a project description'. In *Nordicom Review* 1(2005). Nordicom.

Olsson, T. (2005b) *Alternativa resurser: Om medier, IKT och lärande bland ungdomar i alternativa rörelser* (*Alternative resources: on media, ICTs and learning among young people in alternative movements*). Lund: Lund Studies in Media and Communication.

Olsson, T. (2006) 'Appropriating civic information and communication technology: a critical study of Swedish ICT-policy visions'. *New Media & Society*, 8(4): 611–627.

Pasquier, D. (2005) *Cultures Lycéenes*. Paris: Autrement.

Pirie, M. and Worcester, R. (2000) *The Big Turnoff*. London: Adam Smith Institute/MORI. http://www.adamsmith.org/index.php/publications/details/the_big_turnoff/ [5 September 2002].

Poster, M. (1997) 'Cyberdemocracy: internet and the public sphere'. In D. Porter (ed.) *Internet Culture*. Routledge.

Preston, P.W. (1997) *Political/Cultural Identity*. London: Sage.

Quan-Haase, A., Wellman, B., Witte, J. and Hampton, K. (2002) 'Capitalizing on the net: social contact, civic engagement, and the sense of community'. In B. Wellman and C. Haythornthwaite (eds) *The Internet in Everyday Life*. Blackwell Publishing.

Scheller, M. and Urry, J. (2003) 'Mobile transformations of "public" and "private" life'. *Theory, Culture and Society*, 20(3): 107–125.

Shane, P. (ed.) (2004) *Democracy Online: The Prospects for Political Renewal Through the Internet*. Routledge.

Sörbom, A. (2002) *Vart tar Politiken Vägen?* Stockholm: Almqvisat & Wiksell International.

Stald, G. (2007) 'Mobile monitoring: questions of trust, risk and democratic perspectives in young Danes' use of mobile phones'. In P. Dahlgren (ed.) *Young Citizens, New Media, and Learning for Democracy.* New York: Routledge.

Stromer-Galley, J. (2002) 'New voices in the public sphere: a comparative analysis of interpersonal and online political talk'. *Javnost/The Public,* 9(2): 23–42.

Thompson, J.P. (1995) *The Media and Modernity.* Cambridge: Polity Press.

Thomson, R., Holland, J., McGrellis, S., Bell, R., Henderson, S. and Sharpe, S. (2004) 'Inventing adulthoods. A biographical approach to understanding youth citizenship'. *The Sociological Review,* 52(2): 218–239.

Tsagarousianou, R., Tambini, D. and Bryan, C. (eds) (1998) *Cyberdemocracy: Technology, Cities and Civic Networks.* Routledge.

Van de Donk, W. Loader, B.D., Nixon, P.G. and Rucht, D. (eds) (2004) *Cyberprotest: New Media, Citizens and Social Movements.* London: Routledge.

Vinken, H. (2007) 'Changing life courses, citizenship, and new media: the impact of reflexive biographization'. In P. Dahlgren (ed.) *Young Citizens, New Media, and Learning for Democracy.* New York: Routledge.

Warren, M.E. (ed.) (1999) *Democracy and Trust.* Cambridge, MA: MIT Press.

Warschauer, M. (2003) *Technology and Social Inclusion: Rethinking the Digital Divide.* Cambridge, MA: MIT Press.

Wellman, B. and Haythornthwaite, C. (eds) (2002) *The Internet in Everyday Life.* London: Macmillan.

Wilhelm, A. (2000) *Democracy in the Digital Age: Challenges to Political Life in Cyberspace.* Routledge.

30

Children's Communication Rights: Beyond Intentions

Cees J. Hamelink

INTRODUCTION

On 20 November 1989, the United Nations General Assembly (in resolution 44/25) adopted unanimously the Convention on the Rights of the Child. With this convention children became, in their own right, subjects of international law.

Although there had been declarations on the rights of the child by the League of Nations already in 1924 and by the United Nations in 1959, it was felt by some UN member states that these rights should be brought under the authority of binding international law. The convention has been ratified by all UN member states with the exceptions of the USA and Somalia.

The parties to the convention have accepted the obligation to undertake all appropriate legislative, administrative, and other measures for the implementation of the rights recognized in the convention. The almost unanimous ratification of the Convention on the Rights of the Child by the international community does represent a major advance in the promotion and protection of standards to guide society's treatment of those under the age of 18.

PUBLIC AND PRIVATE SPHERE

Through the adoption of this convention the legal obligations of international human rights law were extended to include children. In a strictly formal manner one could argue that this inclusion was unnecessary. The essential characteristic of human rights is their inclusive nature. Nobody is excluded, and this would seem to suggest that children are among the subjects of human rights provisions. However logical this may seem to be, in daily realities (around the world) distinctions are made between adults and children. Political systems around the globe treat adults and children in different ways. Article 21 of the Universal Declaration of Human Rights provides that 'Everyone has the right to take part in the government of his country, directly or through freely chosen representatives'. Even democratic societies do not extend this basic citizen's right to those under the age 18.

One can easily find robust arguments to rationally defend this differentiation between adults and children. Such arguments usually refer to 'what is good for children'. They often go back to the Greek philosopher Plato, who was strongly against the thought that children should engage in philosophical reflection. In Book VII of *The Republic* Plato proposes a differentiation between the adult world and the world of children. Engaging children in philosophy would, in his opinion, be both destructive for children and for philosophy. Since he believes children are incapable of philosophical thought, their engagement in it would lead to indifference and the future Republic would be crowded with people who cannot discuss and who are not interested in discussion. By the way, in Plato's thinking there also was no place in philosophy for women and slaves.

The exclusion of children from philosophical practice was intended for their 'good'. In reality, however, it was those defending this position who actually wanted the best for themselves and their future polity. This reflects the very common desire that children should develop in accordance with the expectations that adults have. Adults want to shape the children's world according to their desire to control and manipulate the world. In this line of thought children should not ask too many questions and should accept things as they are. In most parts of the world this has become the prevailing educational model!

Fortunately, there are those who disagree. For Lipman (1988: 14), for example, children's philosophy is the basis of a democratic society:

> If children are not given the opportunity to weigh and discuss both ends and means, and their interrelationship, they are likely to become cynical about everything except their own well-being, and adults will not be slow to condemn them as 'mindless little relativists'.

If one agrees with John Dewey (1888), that democracy is more than the rule of the many and represents primarily a way of living together whereby all voices matter, then the capacity for autonomous thinking and for asking questions is basic to a democratic society. Since philosophy is primarily the asking of questions, children should be encouraged to engage with philosophy since they can often ask questions on topics that are all too evident for adults. The convention opens up new avenues here, as it wants to facilitate children's participation in public communication. The convention's legal provisions combined with the new possibilities of advanced information and communication technologies suggest an immense creative potential for the future of democratic societies. Children can help adults to understand that intelligence is more that the ability of provide answers to questions and solutions to problems. This limited understanding is almost daily demonstrated in television's endless presentation of 'quiz' programmes. Even science and technology are today often presented in the format of testing how much people know. Children's programmes could further the understanding that much more important than knowing answers to questions is asking the right questions.

The convention makes the adult–child distinction problematic, since it provides children with a series of entitlements that are essential to democratic citizenship, such as the right to free speech and the right to freedom of association.

The convention allows children to establish their own political association (with its own beliefs and ideas), but the association would be excluded from the formal political arena.

Children's entitlements to fundamental rights pose new challenges to thinking about the public sphere. In the literature on public sphere one finds the conception of public sphere as a single space where society's public discourse is located. Against this position, others, like Nancy Fraser, argue that, since most societies are characterized by deep inequalities, a single public sphere will always be controlled by the privileged groups in society. They propose to think in terms of a plurality of competing publics. In this conception, subordinated groups organize their own subaltern counter-publics (Fraser, 1993, 14). If public sphere is seen as single entity, then children are certainly among the less-privileged participants. And indeed, children play no role of significance in the public sphere of most (if not all) societies.

Does this provide an argument for the multiplicity of public spheres so that children can organize their own public sphere as a location where they can express opinions, share experiences and develop protest actions? Would this, however, not lead towards the creation of separatist enclaves to whose interests overall society would be conveniently immune?

It would seem that children need to have their subaltern public sphere but should also be able to interact with other sub-publics and eventually contribute to the overall direction of society.

A further complication is that in case children's rights would be conceived of as citizen's rights, many children would be excluded. If human rights are conceived of as citizen's rights, then the common implication is that human rights standards are valid for national citizens only. However, in most countries there are large numbers of people who, for different reasons, cannot claim citizenship, such as asylum seekers or illegal aliens. Among those non-citizens are children who, because of this status, are denied the fundamental entitlements that the children's rights convention promises to them.

The recognition of children's rights gives extra urgency to the legal debate about the validity of human rights standards beyond the public sphere. Human rights are still primarily seen as legal mechanisms that protect and empower people in the public sphere. They provide a defence against acts of governments against individuals. It remains a bone of legal contention whether human rights provisions can equally be reinforced when they are violated by private parties in people's private spheres. Yet, when one thinks about provisions to protect children's physical and mental integrity, it would seem that such protection is particularly needed in the private sphere of family life. Exactly where children should confidently expect security and warmth they often experience harm done to them by parents or other guardians

GOOD VERSUS RIGHT

The awarding of fundamental rights means that a list of entitlements to forms of decent and humane treatment is provided. The complication is that the list contains rights that may in certain circumstances conflict with each other or that collide with other pressing interests, such as parental care and responsibility in the case of children's rights. International treaties do not provide keys for the solution of such conflicts and dilemmas. As a result – in actual daily practice – solutions will be sought in a casuistic way and often they have to be provided by courts of law. Since such solutions would ideally reflect the interests of all stakeholders involved, the casuistic approach needs a discursive method through which those affected try to find a consensual judgement on a given situation. This discursive approach is only meaningful once the rights as enlisted in the children's convention are put into the frame of a broader normative theory. To this end, it deserves exploring whether such a theory may be found in the political philosophy of John Rawls. Whatever the shortcomings of the Rawlsian argument may be, it certainly provides a crucial argument for the prioritizing of rights over conceptions of the common good. The essence of his argument is that 'Each person possesses an inviolability founded on justice that even the welfare of society as a whole cannot override' (Rawls, 1973: 3). And he concludes that 'justice denies that the loss of freedom for some is made right by a greater good shared by others' (Rawls, 1973: 4). There is a tendency among politicians to be guided by their visions of what constitutes the common good; and equally, many parents and other guardians tend to have compelling ideas about what is good for children. This prioritizing of good over right finds a fertile philosophical ground in post-modernist forms of normative relativism and in consequentialist approaches to ethical issues in which the ultimate 'good' goal sanctions the means deployed. In all fairness it cannot be ignored that there may be very sensible conceptions of the good in society, like the protection of children against pornographic or violent imagery. However, a Rawlsian normative theory would propose that right always has priority over good. This is particularly important with regard to children because of the understandable inclination of their guardians to propose that what they perceive as good for children's welfare takes precedence over children's rights. Often this really means that the parent's conception of the good for children equals the welfare of the parents.

The welfare of parents and other guardians might indeed seem better served by children who do not say things they do not want to hear, who do not want access to information deemed inappropriate for them, who would not have to be listened to and whose privacy does not constitute a serious concern. However, to be able to see one's own welfare as parent or guardian as secondary to children's rights, is the essential challenge of the effort to move children's communication rights beyond mere intentions.

COMMUNICATION RIGHTS

The Convention on the Rights of the Child offers several essential provisions that relate to information and communication (see Appendix I). Communication rights are important in the convention, because provisions related to information and communication were, from the beginning of the UN, seen as important. Already in 1946 the General Assembly stated that freedom of expression should be seen as the touchstone of all human rights.

More recently, the realization emerged that, in the lives of children, information and communication are ever more central with the availability of new communication media, such as the internet and the possibility of weblogs, email, chatting and the creation of individual homepages.

The relevant articles are reproduced here in the child-friendly version that was produced by the United Nations Children Fund (UNICEF), Canada:

Article 12: You have the right to give your opinion and for adults to listen and take it seriously.

Article 13: You have the right to find out things and share what you think with others, by talking, drawing, writing or in any other way unless it harms or offends other people.

Article 14: You have the right to choose your own religion and beliefs. Your parents should help you decide what is right and wrong, and what is best for you.

Article 16: You have the right to privacy.

Article 17: You have the right to get information that is important to your well-being, from radio, newspaper, books, computers and other sources; Adults should make sure that the information you are getting is not harmful, and help you find and understand the information you need.

Article 28: You have the right to a good quality education. You should be encouraged to go to school to the highest level you can.

Article 30: You have the right to practice your own culture, language and religion – or any you choose. Minority and indigenous groups need special protection of this right.

Article 42: You have the right to know your rights! Adults should know about these rights and help you learn about them, too.

All these provisions mean that some important children's communication rights are today codified as legal standards for the international community. The international community has made a binding commitment to respect these rights. On the 10th anniversary of the convention in 1999, the Norwegian government and UNICEF organized a meeting at which children, young people, media professionals and child rights experts discussed the development of children's rights in relation to media. From this meeting emerged the Oslo Challenge. The text of the Oslo Challenges is a call to action for governments, media professionals, media owners, children and parents to contribute to the realization of the rights as laid down in the convention. Thus, the intentions are clear and solid – at least on paper. As is the case with all other human rights, it needs to be questioned how the international community can move beyond laudable intentions towards equally laudable practices.

MOVING BEYOND INTENTIONS: THE OBSTACLES

General obstacles

The lack of enforcement

The weakest component of the international human rights regime is the lack of a solid and effective mechanism for the implementation of its provisions. People should be able to seek effective remedy when their human rights are violated. Unfortunately, such remedy does not exist today on the global level. The European region has a fairly effective system of human rights adjudication through its Court of Human Rights. The existing global arrangements, however, such as the UN Human Rights Commission and the committees that monitor the various human rights treaties do not constitute an independent world tribunal where complaints can be treated with supra-national jurisdiction.[1] The UN World Conference on Human Rights (Vienna, 1993) declared that 'the promotion and protection of all human rights is a legitimate concern of the international community'. In reality, however, the majority of UN member states have little interest in interference with their human rights record. In current world politics, states still maintain a large measure of sovereignty in the treatment of their citizens. This implies, among other things, that the committee that examines the implementation of the Convention on the Rights of the Child does not have the authority to receive individual complaints. This lack of detailed jurisdictional scrutiny on the international level implies most likely that provisions on children's rights will not be subject to such examination on the national level either.

Many countries have various enforcement arrangements that address legal situations in which children want to complain about maltreatment by their parents or when they are accused of criminal conduct. Such mechanisms (such as children's help telephone lines or children's law centres) do not presently exist on the international level.

Most critical in terms of enforcement is the extension of the protection of rights to include horizontal relations. Fundamental rights are often violated between private actors, such as children and parents, or children and private school boards. The communication rights of children are most often violated within the family. The enforcement within the private sphere is both most difficult and most needed. In order to achieve this extension of the application of fundamental rights, jurisdictional changes, but also a great deal of education for both parents and children, would be required.

Next to these procedural issues there are also complex conceptual issues that may put obstacles in the way of implementing the convention's legal standards.

Children as subjects of rights pose an especially difficult issue. There is already a good deal of divergent opinion about the interpretation and application of human rights standards for adults; the disagreements are even stronger when it comes to children. This is largely due to the different cultural settings within which human rights are to be implemented. There is a continuing international controversy about a Western, liberal bias in the prevailing conception of human rights and the need to recognize non-Western interpretations of rights. The widely diverging cultural conceptions of parental responsibility, for example, make worldwide consensus very difficult, if not impossible. Parental responsibility is across the world conceived in rather permissive versus more restrictive ways. A related problem arises because of different interpretations of Article 3 of the convention, which provides that 'the best interests of the child shall be a primary consideration'. The definitions of what the best interests of children are will vary greatly across cultural borders. An extra complication concerns the age of children. In different parts of the world, people have different conceptions about ages at which children come of age.

The core concept in the human rights regime is 'human autonomy'. Ideally, we conceive of rights holders as autonomous individuals. What does this mean in the case of children? Children are initially dependent upon parents or other guardians, but as they grow up they become, to greater or lesser degrees, independent beings. In the process of their growth, individual autonomy begins to emerge. Yet, as with adult human beings, there remains throughout life a level of dependence upon others. And the intriguing complexity of the recognition of human rights is to find the balance between dependence and autonomy. With regard to children's rights, this implies that parents and other guardians have the responsibility to facilitate the process of children becoming autonomous subjects. This often seems a thankless task. The facilitators need to make themselves redundant while not distancing themselves totally from the children. Facilitating requires presence but with limited options to express one's views, since the views of the children take precedence. It requires a fundamental change from a more common commanding mode of communicating to a more difficult listening mode. There is (like in the case of mentally incapacitated people) the inevitable tension between the right to autonomous decision-making and the capacity to take autonomous decisions. Too often, however, the claim to autonomy is easily overridden by the dependency argument. It needs to be realized, though, that the priority of autonomy over dependence-induced heteronomy is a fundamental normative standard in international human rights instruments. It follows that in case dependence is prioritized over autonomy a basic human entitlement is violated. The defence of this violation will need very strong, substantial arguments.

The rights that the international community grants children stem from the body of international law and specifically from the Convention on the Rights of the Child. However, identifying children's rights with the law may in several countries raises enormous obstacles, since children in impoverished environments tend to see the law more as a tool of oppression than as an instrument of protection. African kids may experience, for example, that the support they provide for their families by hawking and begging makes them, for purposes of law enforcement, criminals who perform illegal acts. For many children around the world the law represents what you cannot do, not what you are entitled to do, or even less what others (including law enforcement officials) are not allowed to do to you. The implementation of children's rights should, therefore, go beyond the application of legal rules. Children need to see their rights as their own constructions, as conditions of daily life that they identified themselves as necessary for a better life. A good illustration of this approach are the 12 rights that were proposed in 1994 by young street workers in Dakar and that meanwhile have become the common framework for action planning by working children in Africa.[2]

Most children in the world do not know they have fundamental rights. The child-friendly version of the convention that UNICEF Canada produced is not yet accessible to all the world's children, and children's rights are not yet common in school programmes around the world.

At the time the international human rights regime emerged, the prime concern was to provide protection of the rights of individuals against states. There was little attention for individual duties, as the common notion was that states did not need to be protected against individuals through the imposition of civic responsibilities. Over the past decades it became increasingly clear that human rights are not only violated by states but also by individual parties and that individual rights need to be protected against the conduct of other individuals. This made it imperative to recognize the duties of individuals *vis-à-vis* the rights of other individuals. The Universal Declaration of Human Rights provides the moral basis for such duties, particularly in its Articles 29 and 30. Article 29.1 states 'Everyone has duties to the community in which alone the free and full development of his personality is possible' and Article 30 imposes upon everyone the duty to refrain from 'any activity or act aimed at the destruction of the rights and freedoms' set forth in the declaration. Since individuals have both rights and duties under international law, the question of children's responsibilities in relation to their communication rights has to be addressed. Now that children are subjects of international law, they are entitled to the protection of fundamental rights; but they also have the obligation to respect and protect the rights and freedoms of others (Table 30.1).

What does this mean for communication rights?

One more general obstacle to the transformation of intentions into practices is the limited understanding about human rights violations. There is abundant evidence that the most universal feature of human rights is their universal violation. Incessantly, fundamental human entitlements are violently ignored by states, by corporations, and by individuals alike. In order to make any progress at all in the protection and implementation of human rights, the forces, interests and motives behind their violation need to be better understood. Therefore, it is essential to investigate the reasons that underlie the violations of children's communication rights. Can they be found in culture- or class-bound conceptions of parental care and responsibility? Can a factor be the convenience of children's exploitation for commercial, military or sexual purposes? Does the underestimation of the intellectual and emotional capabilities of children provide an explanation? Do artificial distinctions between childhood and adulthood play a role?

Specific obstacles

Regarding the freedom of speech

The free speech provision in Article 13 of the Convention on the Rights of the Child implies the right to say things that others (for example parents) do not want to hear. This is always problematic in situations of unequal power relations. Why would the more powerful allow this? Can it be expected that parents and other guardians possess the moral maturity to deal with this challenge to their authority?

Article 13 also provides for children's access to information. This usually raises the key issue of the protection of children against harmful content. However, adults and children will often have different assessments of what constitutes harm, and the question is who can legitimately be the final arbiter. Is it a legitimate part of parental responsibility to interfere with children's right of access?

The focus of much debate on the protection of minors against the abuse of free speech to disseminate pornography may distract public attention away from instances of censorship that limit children's access to information. An illustration was the action of the American Booksellers Foundation for Free Expression

Table 30.1 Children and communication

Rights	*Responsibilities*
To be heard and to be taken seriously	To listen to others
To free speech	Allowing other children to speak freely
To privacy	To respect the privacy of other children and of parents
To cultural identity	Not to discriminate
To be proud of their heritage and beliefs	To respect the origins and beliefs of others

against schools that imposed restrictions on children's access to the Harry Potter books. Obstacles against the use of these books included asking for parental permission or removing of the books from the open shelves in school libraries. The concerned censors will usually claim that their action is in the best interest of the children. However, one needs to realize that, throughout the ages, those who limited access to information always had (in their perception) benevolent reasons. Whatever the rationale may be, censorship always constitutes a human rights violation. Only in situations of imminent danger to the existence of the state does international law make an exception to this norm.

Article 13 also implies children's right of access to the media and, thus, suggests that here should be more children's voices in the media. If one puts this within the context of the essential human rights standard of human equality, it means that children around the world should have equal opportunity to access communication media. From this perspective the current global digital divide (between and within countries) has serious implications for children. The bridging of the divide is especially urgent in view of the future participation in knowledge societies by young people.

The Oslo Challenge (referred to above) proposes that children should learn as much as they can about the media 'so that they can make informed choices as media consumers and gain maximum benefit from the diversity the media offer'. The Oslo meeting also challenges children 'to grasp opportunities to participate in production of media output'. There are at present around the world a growing number of good practices that demonstrate how children can contribute to media production. Illustrative examples come from a wide range of projects, from the Young Reporters of Albania who are responsible for selecting stories and planning TV production, to 'Our Own Voice' in Haiti that empowers child journalists, to street-level youth media in Chicago that educates inner-city youth in media arts, to the Free News project in Bangladesh that trains young journalists and provides a model of opportunities for child participation in the media, or to the French Journalist for a Day event that provides young people with a chance to participate in a real in-house newspaper enterprise.[3]

The realization of children's participation in media production often confronts such obstacles as the child-unfriendly work culture in many media institutions, the absence of appropriate facilities, and inadequate safety measures.

In addition to the present provisions on freedom of speech, the question can be raised about the extension of the freedom of expression and access to information provisions towards a children's right to communicate. This new right suggests that the right to express views is meaningful only if those views are taken seriously. It questions how useful it is to speak freely if no one listens. This inevitably evokes the question of why children should be heard and why anyone would listen to children. The best answer refers to the use of children's experiential knowledge! They should speak on issues that affect their daily lives. On these issues they are the best advocates and their views can play an important role in finding solutions.

Regarding privacy

For children, all four dimensions of privacy are of eminent importance. These dimensions are the protection of the child's physical privacy; the protection of territorial privacy, i.e. one's own space; the protection of the confidentiality of private communications; and the protection of informational privacy, i.e. the control over person-related data.

With regard to the protection of privacy, the issue of the horizontal effect of fundamental rights is especially urgent. This is because not only do parents often neglect their children's privacy right, but also because private, corporate interests increasingly invade the children's online world.

Marketing to children has become a billion dollar industry. Studies at the Department of Nutrition and Food Studies, New York University, estimate that US$13 billion is annually spent on marketing to American children alone.[4] Several studies[5] also show that the amounts to which children influence their parents' purchases have been increasing rapidly in recent years. With the use of the internet by children, online marketing has taken on growing significance. Online marketers enter children's private domains through surveillance of their conduct on virtual playgrounds and by building the kind of trusted relations with them that facilitate the commercial manipulation of their desires and preferences. One problem is that free speech provisions create important legal barriers to protecting children's rights to privacy on the internet. Advertisers can claim that their approaches to the kids market are protected under freedom of information rules. Moreover, there is, today, no consistent international legal framework on content regulation.

Regarding the production of children's materials

Article 17 of the Convention on the Rights of the Child is important because there tends to be more concern for the protection of children against harmful materials than with the more constructive project of creating specially suited materials for children. The Children's Television Charter that was approved at the Prix Jeunesse Round Table at Munich, May 1995, states that 'Children's programmes should be wide-ranging in genre and content, but should not include gratuitous scenes of violence and sex'. It may be somewhat unfortunate that the production of children's materials in the media becomes law at a time when in many countries public service broadcasting is under threat. However, it cannot be excluded that commercial companies would be interested in such production, but this will inevitably only be the case when there is an interested and potentially profitable market. This cannot be guaranteed, and the pertinent article thus provides for a clear public responsibility. One of its implications is that adequate finances need to be allocated from public funds. The Children's Television Charter proposes on this issue that 'Sufficient funds must be made available to make these programmes to the highest possible standards'.

Article 17 would also seem to refer to the issue of media portrayal of children in the media. This raises the important question of how children's integrity can be protected in media reporting. The ethical guidelines for reporting on children, proposed by UNICEF,[6] provide several principles to assist journalists to cover children in an age-appropriate and sensitive manner.

Regarding the right for children to enjoy their own culture and to use their own language

Globalization processes and the concomitant cross-border movements of people (migration, labour, economic prospects, refugees, tourism) imply that more and more children grow up in multi-cultural, multi-ethnic, multi-religious and diaspora environments. This urgently requires the capacity for intercultural dialogue. This is a difficult form of communicating that needs to be learned. This learning should be part of the formal educational process.

It is important to observe that the dialogue only works if the participants refrain from verbal and non-verbal violence in the process. The implementation of Article 30 of the Convention on the Rights of the Child, therefore, requires training in non-violent communication. Even small children can be very violent in their communicative behaviour. They can be biased, judgmental, rejecting, and just plain nasty. All of this obstructs the dialogue. The international community should address this through the generous support for a global project in which children are educated to be partners in dialogical communication.

ACTIVE PARTNERS

Most of the thinking about children's rights in general and their communication rights in particular comes from adults. Even child-friendly versions of relevant texts are often produced by adults. There is an enormous risk in all these well-intended efforts that adults shape the children's world to serve adult interests. The crucial challenge that the Convention on the Rights of the Child poses to adults is to listen to children, to consult them, work with them and to make them active partners in shaping humanity's common communication future.

NOTES

1 For more analysis, see Hamelink (2004).

2 The African Movement of Working Children and Youth in 2004 is made up of 57 associations in 57 towns of 18 African countries; its 400 grassroots groups comprise 20,000 female housemaids, sellers in markets, independent working children and youths in streets and markets. The children organize themselves in their places of residence and work. The 12 children's rights as formulated by African working children are:

- the right to be taught a trade
- the right to stay in the village (not to emigrate)
- the right to work in a safe environment
- the right to light and limited work
- the right to rest when sick
- the right to be listened to
- the right to healthcare
- the right to learn to read and write
- the right to play
- the right to self-expression and to form organizations
- the right to equitable legal aid, in case of difficulty.

3 More illustrations can be found on the following websites: http://www.listenup.org – a youth media network that connects young video producers; http://pbskids.org/dontbuyit – a media literacy site for young people; http://www.kqed.org/topics/education/medialiteracy/youthmedia – a site that wants to add youth voices to mainstream media.

The Adobe Youth Voices initiative empowers youth worldwide to use multimedia and digital tools to communicate and share ideas; see youthvoices@adobe.com for more information.

The World Radio Forum aims to develop children's and youth radio. Among its goals is that children have the right to participate in radio production. The forum works with children and youth to publish and promote the Radio Manifesto: http://www.worldradioforum.org.

The Radio Manifesto (the result of 3 years of discussions with children and launched at the 4th World Summit on Media & Children, Rio de Janeiro, 2004) can be found at: http://.worldradioforum.org/icyrmanifesto.shtml.

4 The Food Institute Report (2002). Marion Nestle and Margo Wootan, New York University.

5 Among others, by Patty Valkenburg of the University of Amsterdam. See also, Kim Campbell and Kent Davis-Packard, 'How ads get kids to say I want it', in the *Christian Science Monitor*, 18 September 2000.

6 Source: www.unicef.org/media/media_tools_guidelines. Other sources for responsible reporting on children include: International Federation of Journalists (2002) 'Putting children in the right'; the International Federation of Journalists' Guidelines and Principles for Reporting on Issues Involving Children.

APPENDIX I

The relevant articles of the UN Convention on the Rights of the Child are as follows.

Article 12

States Parties shall assure to the child who is capable of forming his or her own views the right to express those views freely in all manners affecting the child…

Article 13

1 The child shall have the right to freedom of expression; this right shall include freedom to seek, receive and impart information and ideas of all kinds, regardless of frontiers, either orally, in writing or in print, in the form of art, or through any other media of the child's choice.

2 The exercise of this right may be subject to certain restrictions, but these shall only be such as are provided by law and are necessary:

(a) For respect of the rights or reputations of others;or

(b) For the protection of national security or of public order (ordre public), or of public health or morals.

Article 14

1 States Parties shall respect the right of the child to freedom of thought, conscience and religion.

2 States Parties shall respect the rights and duties of the parents and, when applicable, legal guardians, to provide direction to the child in the exercise of his or her right in a manner consistent with the evolving capacities of the child.
3 Freedom to manifest one's religion or beliefs may be subject only to such limitations as are prescribed by law and are necessary to protect public safety, order health or morals, or the fundamental rights and freedoms of others.

Article 16

1 No child shall be subjected to arbitrary or unlawful interference with his or her privacy, family, home or correspondence, nor to unlawful attacks on his or her honour and reputation.
2 The child has the right to the protection of the law against such interference or attacks.

Article 17

States Parties recognize the important function performed by the mass media and shall ensure that the child has access to information and material from a diversity of national and international sources, especially those aimed at the promotion of his or her social, spiritual and moral well-being and physical and mental health. To this end, States Parties shall:

(a) Encourage the mass media to disseminate information and material of social and cultural benefit to the child and in accordance with the spirit of article 29;
(b) Encourage international co-operation in the production, exchange and dissemination of such information and material from a diversity of cultural, national and international sources;
(c) Encourage the production and dissemination of children's books;
(d) Encourage the mass media to have particular regard to the linguistic needs of the child who belongs to a minority group or who is indigenous;
(e) Encourage the development of appropriate guidelines for the protection of the child from information and material injurious to his or her well-being, bearing in mind the provisions of articles 13 and 18.

Article 28

1 States Parties recognize the right of the child to education, and with a view to achieving this right progressively and on the basis of equal opportunity, they shall, in particular:
2 Promote and encourage international co-operation in matters relating to education, in particular with a view to contributing to the elimination of ignorance and illiteracy throughout the world and facilitating access to scientific and technical knowledge and modern teaching methods. In this regard, particular account shall be taken of the needs

Article 30

In those States in which ethnic, religious or linguistic minorities or persons of indigenous origin exist, a child belonging to such a minority or who is indigenous shall not be denied the right, in community with other members of his or her group, to enjoy his or her own culture, to profess and practise his or her own religion, or to use his or her own language.

Article 42

States Parties undertake to make the principles and provisions of the Convention widely known, by appropriate and active means, to adults and children alike.

APPENDIX II: ADDITIONAL SOURCES

Africa Charter on Children's Broadcasting, Africa Summit on Children and Broadcasting, Accra, Ghana, October 1997.

African Movement of Working Children and Youth (1999). *Voice of African Children.* AMWCY Book Commission.

Article 12: The UK children's rights organization (run by under 18-year-olds) that promotes the UN Convention on the Rights of the Child and that has petitioned the US government to sign the convention.

Privacy Rights Clearing House (2005), *Children's Privacy and Safety on the Internet: A Resource Guide for Parents.* San Diego, USA. www.privacyrights.org.

Samtani, A. (2003) 'Protecting children in cyberspace'. *Singapore Academy of Law Journal,* 15.

Terenzio, F. 'Why is child participation so important?' Youth Action Team of ENDA, Dakar, Senegal. www.gmfc.org/.

UNICEF (2005) *The Media and Children's Rights Manual.*

REFERENCES

Dewey, J. (1888) *The Ethics of Democracy.* Michigan: Andrews & Company Publishers.

Fraser, N. (1993) 'Rethinking the public sphere: a contribution to the critique of actually existing democracy'. In B. Robbins (ed.) *The Phantom Public Sphere.* Minneapolis, MN: University of Minnesota Press.

Hamelink, C.J. (2004) *Human Rights for Communicators.* Hampton Press; 7–18.

Lipman, M. (1998). *Philosophy Goes to School.* Philadelphia: Temple University Press.

Rawls, J. (1973) *A Theory of Justice.* Oxford: Oxford University Press.

FURTHER READING

Daes, E.-I.A. (1983) 'The individual's duties to the community and the limitations of human rights and freedoms under Article 29 of the Universal Declaration of Human Rights'. New York: United Nations.

Feilitzen, C. and von Bucht, C. (eds) (2001) *Outlooks on Children and Media.* Goteborg: Nordicom.

Hamelink, C.J. (2002) 'Media globalisation: consequences for the rights of children', in C. von Feilitzen and U. Carlsson (eds) *Children, Young people and Media Globalisation.* Goteborg: Nordicom, Goteborg University; 33–41.

Index